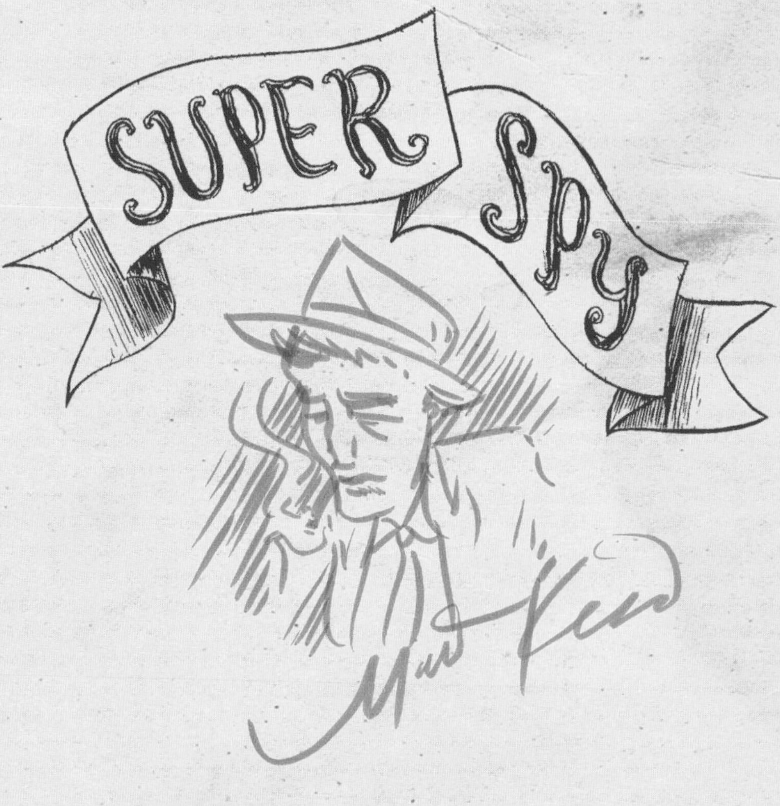
SUPER
Spy

To Ella,
the littlest super spy.
— M.K.

About the Author:
Matt Kindt is the author of 2 Sisters: A Super Spy Graphic Novel and the artist and co-creator of the Pistolwhip series of graphic novels with Jason Hall. He lives and works as an author and illustrator in St. Louis, Missouri with his wife and daughter. For more information go to: supersecretspy.com or email the author: mskindt@prodigy.net.

A Note on the Book:
The chapters are arranged in a nonlinear format in the order that the author intended that they be read. However, it is possible to read the chapters in the order that events actually took place by using the dossier numbers as your guide.

Special thanks to Chris Staros and Robert Venditti for going above and beyond during the editing of Super Spy.

Published by Top Shelf Productions, PO Box 1282, Marietta, GA 30061-1282 USA. Publishers: Brett Warnock & Chris Staros.

First Printing, August 2007. Printed in China.

ISBN 978-1-891830-96-9
1. Graphic Novels
2. Historical Fiction
3. Espionage

SUPER SPY

by

Matt Kindt

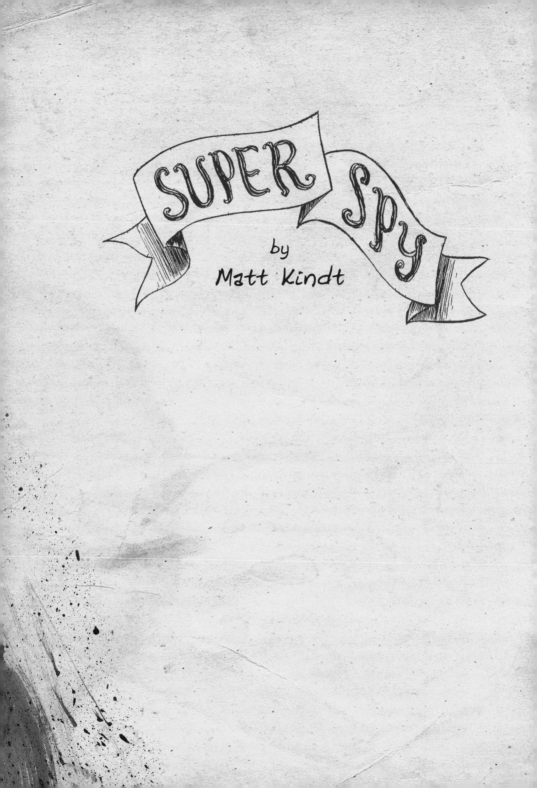

A .-
B -...
C -.-.
D -..
E .
F ..-.
G --.
H ....
I ..
J .---
K -.-
L .-..
M --
N -.
O ---
P .--.
Q --.-
R .-.
S ...
T -
U ..-
V ...-
W .--
X -..-
Y -.--
Z --..

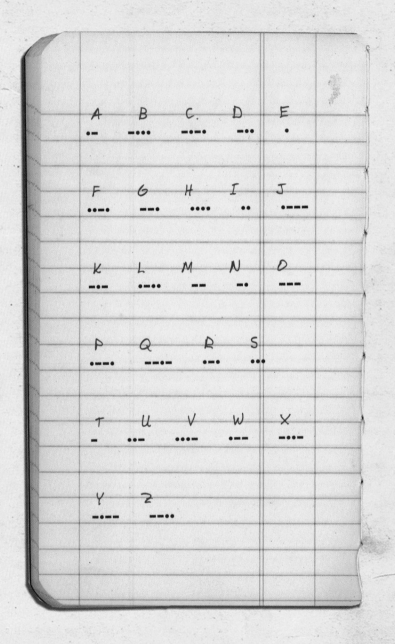

DSR. #	TABLE OF CONTENTS	

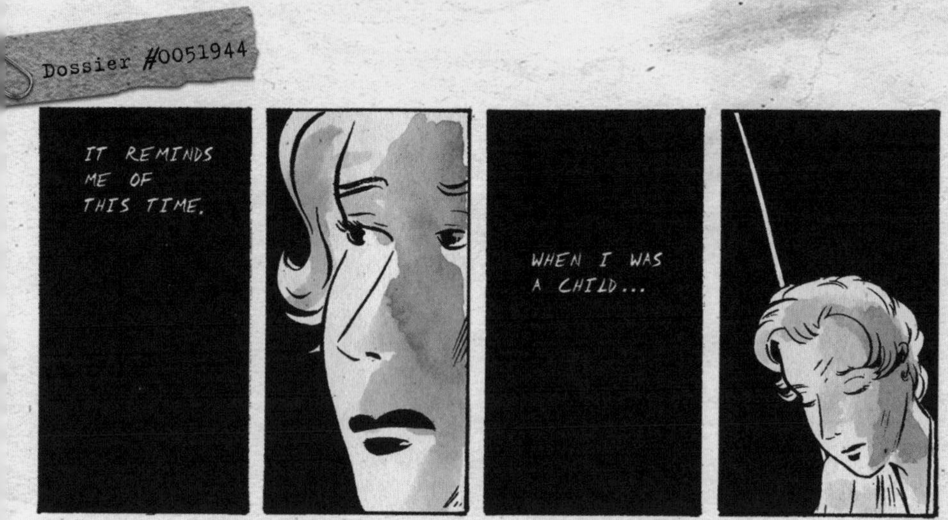
Dossier #0051944
IT REMINDS ME OF THIS TIME.
WHEN I WAS A CHILD...

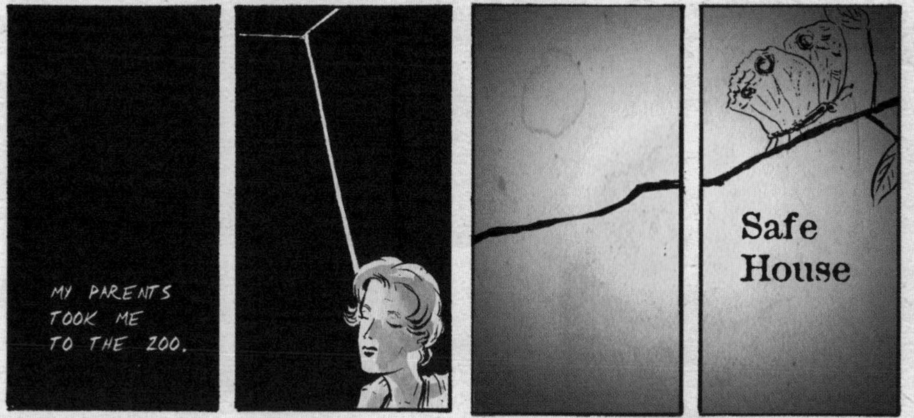
MY PARENTS
TOOK ME
TO THE ZOO.
Safe
House

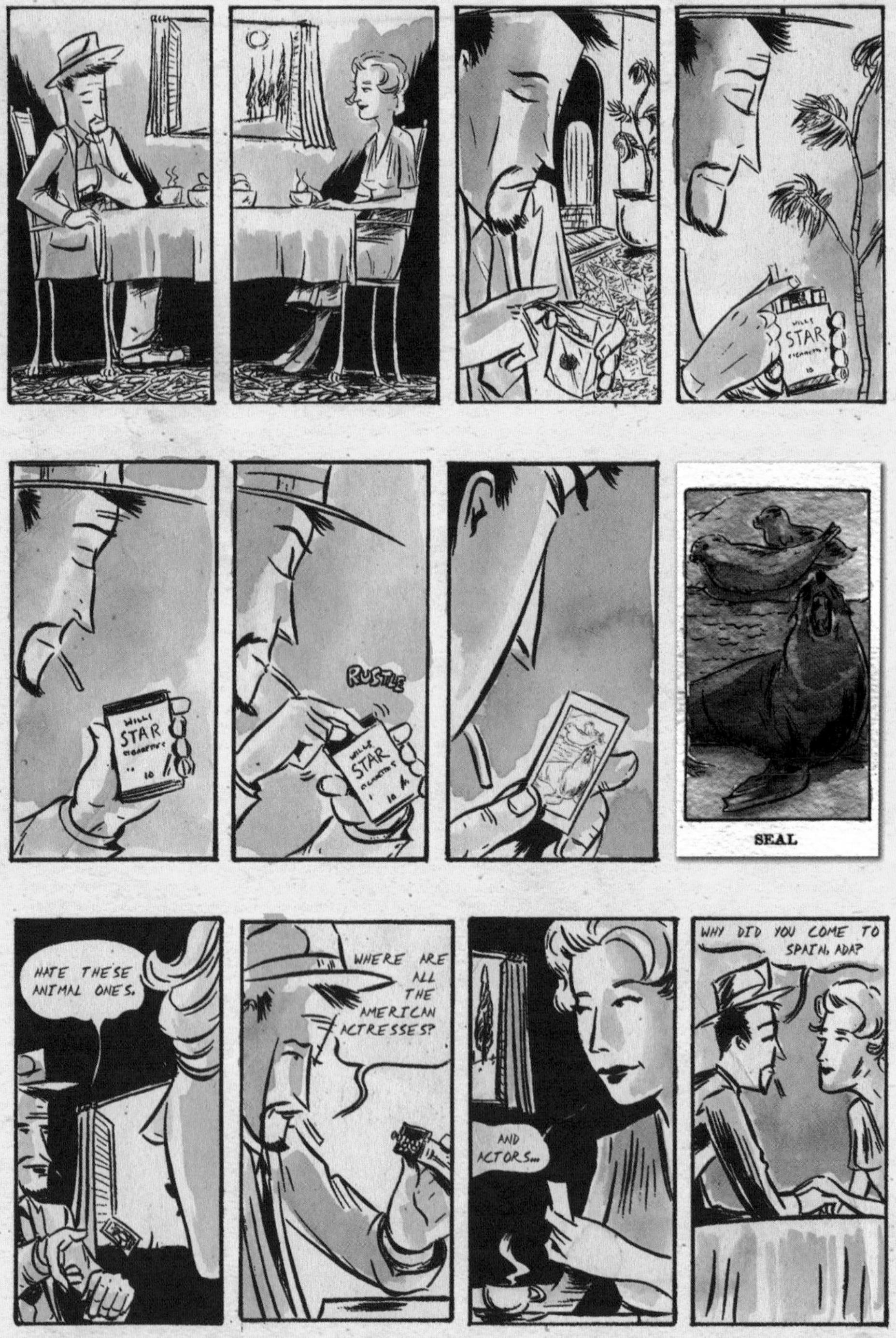
WILLS STAR CIGARETTES
RUSTLE
SEAL
HATE THESE ANIMAL ONES.
WHERE ARE ALL THE AMERICAN ACTRESSES?
AND ACTORS...
WHY DID YOU COME TO SPAIN, ADA?

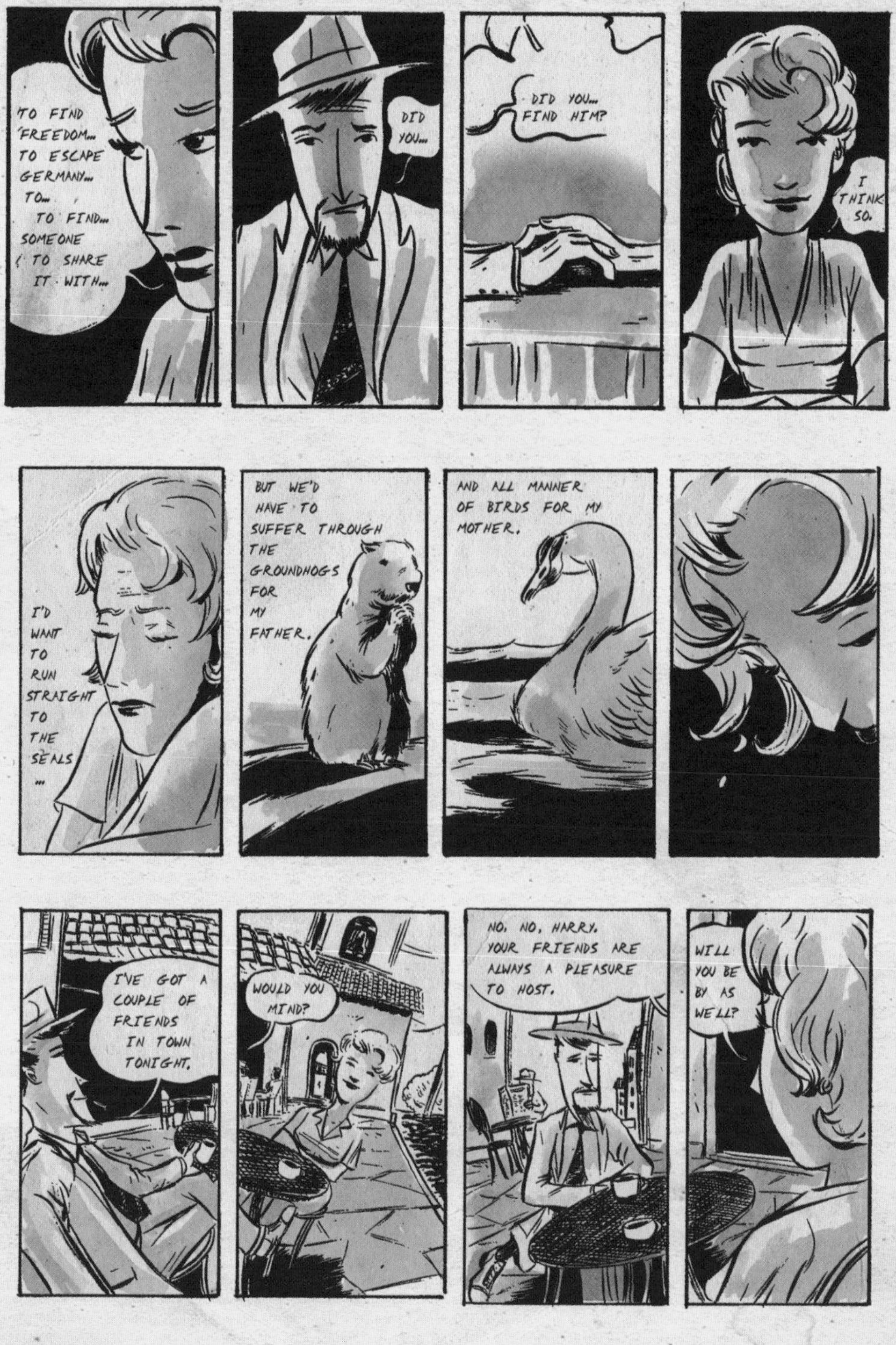
TO FIND FREEDOM... TO ESCAPE GERMANY... TO... TO FIND... SOMEONE TO SHARE IT WITH...
DID YOU...
DID YOU... FIND HIM?
I THINK SO.
I'D WANT TO RUN STRAIGHT TO THE SEALS ...
BUT WE'D HAVE TO SUFFER THROUGH THE GROUNDHOGS FOR MY FATHER.
AND ALL MANNER OF BIRDS FOR MY MOTHER.
I'VE GOT A COUPLE OF FRIENDS IN TOWN TONIGHT.
WOULD YOU MIND?
NO. NO, HARRY. YOUR FRIENDS ARE ALWAYS A PLEASURE TO HOST.
WILL YOU BE BY AS WELL?

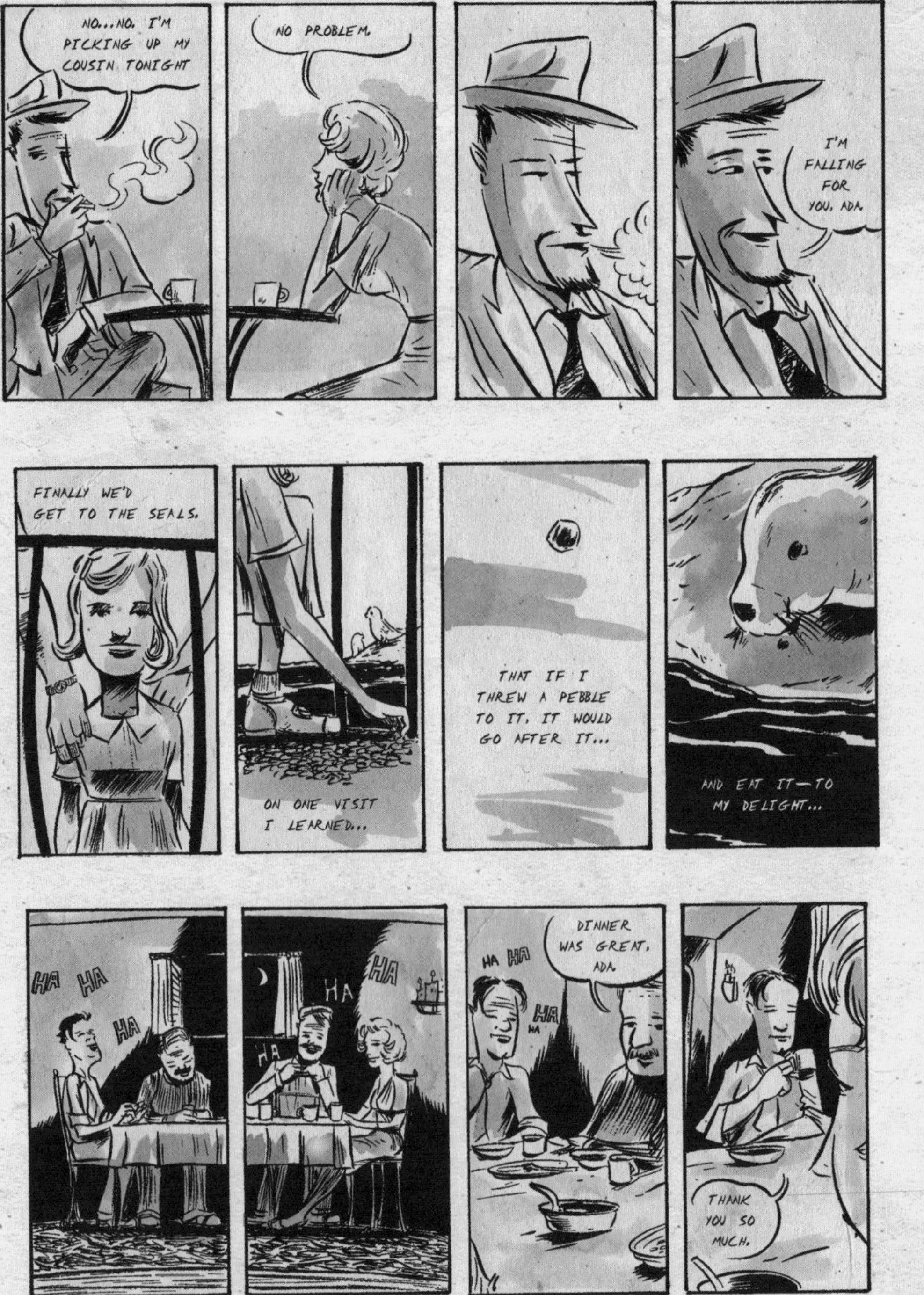
NO...NO. I'M PICKING UP MY COUSIN TONIGHT
NO PROBLEM.
I'M FALLING FOR YOU, ADA.
FINALLY WE'D GET TO THE SEALS.
ON ONE VISIT I LEARNED...
THAT IF I THREW A PEBBLE TO IT, IT WOULD GO AFTER IT...
AND EAT IT—TO MY DELIGHT...
HA HA
HA
HA
HA
HA
HA HA
DINNER WAS GREAT, ADA.
HA
HA
THANK YOU SO MUCH.

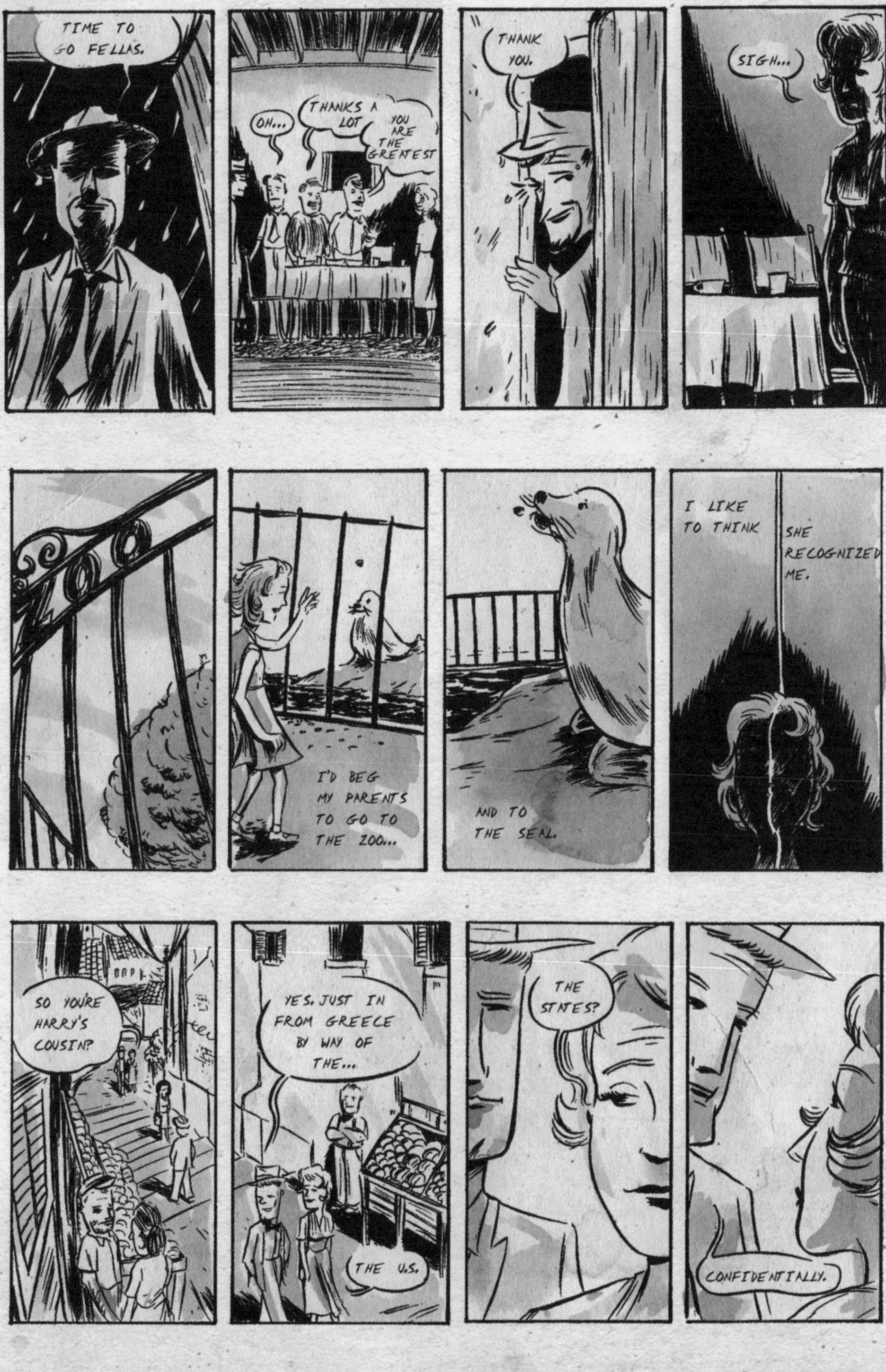
TIME TO GO FELLAS.
OH...
THANKS A LOT
YOU ARE THE GREATEST
THANK YOU.
SIGH...
I'D BEG MY PARENTS TO GO TO THE ZOO...
AND TO THE SEAL.
I LIKE TO THINK
SHE RECOGNIZED ME.
SO YOU'RE HARRY'S COUSIN?
YES. JUST IN FROM GREECE BY WAY OF THE...
THE U.S.
THE STATES?
CONFIDENTIALLY.

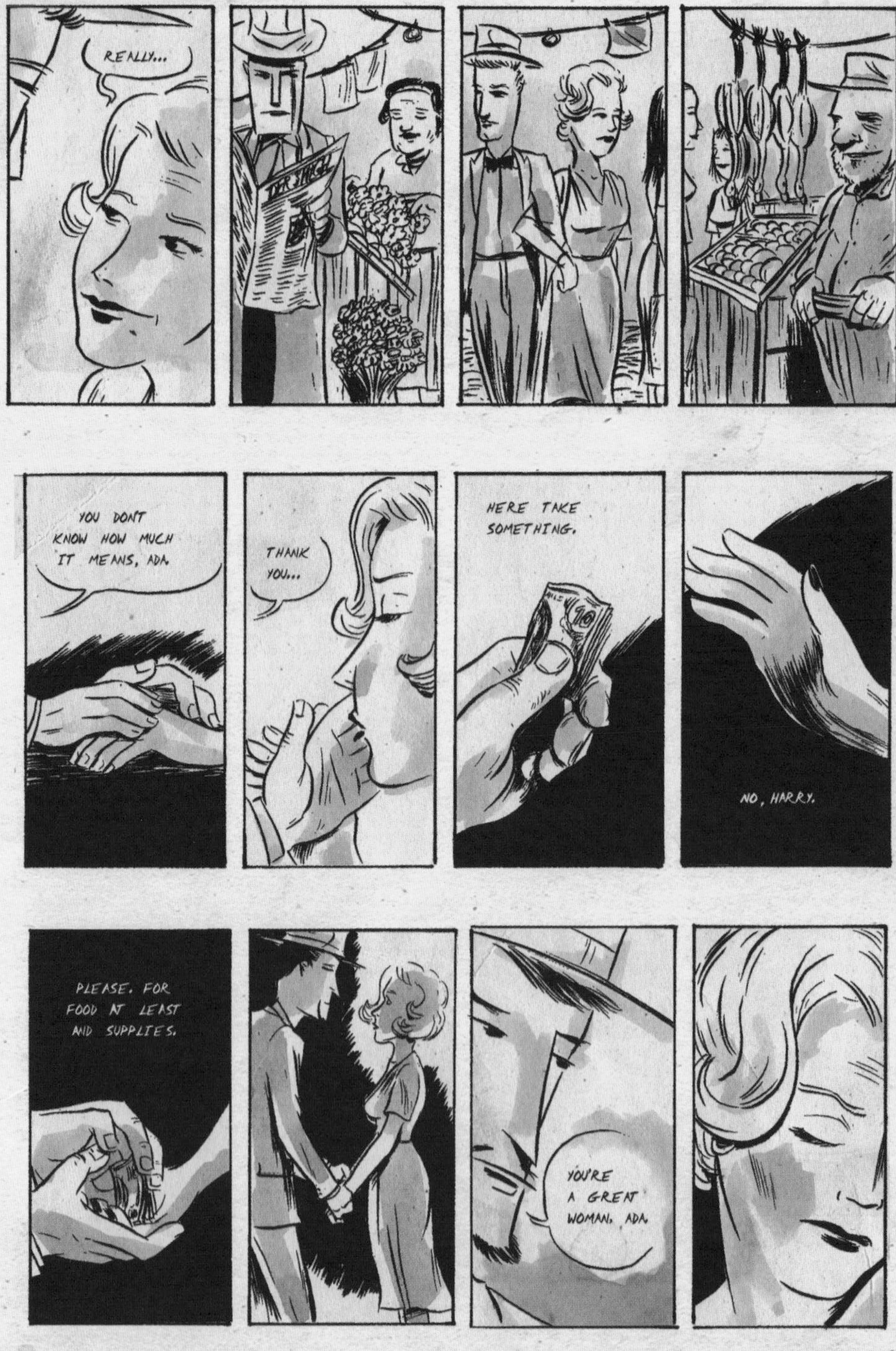
REALLY...
YOU DON'T KNOW HOW MUCH IT MEANS, ADA.
THANK YOU...
HERE TAKE SOMETHING.
NO, HARRY.
PLEASE. FOR FOOD AT LEAST AND SUPPLIES.
YOU'RE A GREAT WOMAN, ADA.

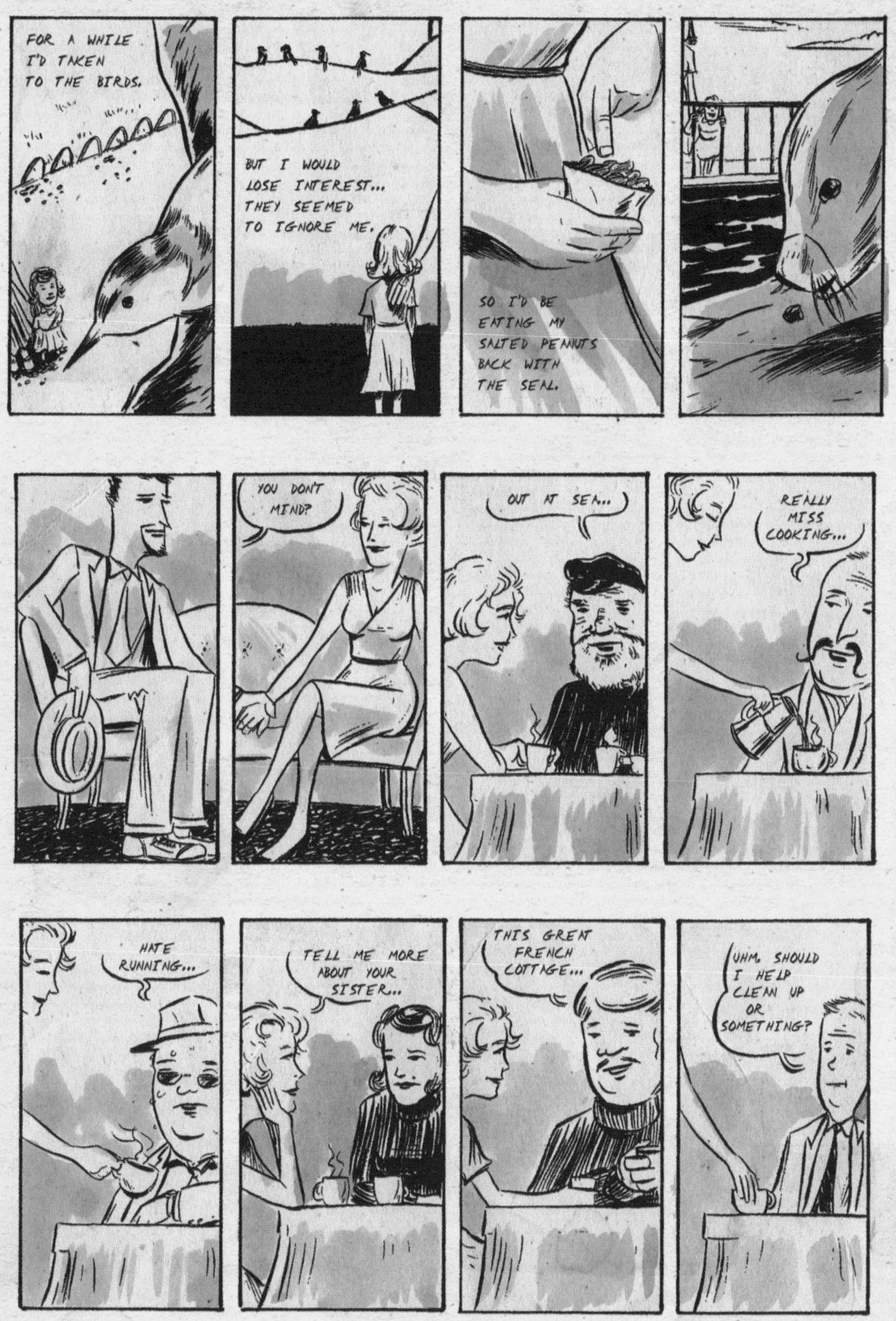
FOR A WHILE I'D TAKEN TO THE BIRDS.
BUT I WOULD LOSE INTEREST... THEY SEEMED TO IGNORE ME.
SO I'D BE EATING MY SALTED PEANUTS BACK WITH THE SEAL.
YOU DON'T MIND?
OUT AT SEA...
REALLY MISS COOKING...
HATE RUNNING...
TELL ME MORE ABOUT YOUR SISTER...
THIS GREAT FRENCH COTTAGE...
UHM, SHOULD I HELP CLEAN UP OR SOMETHING?

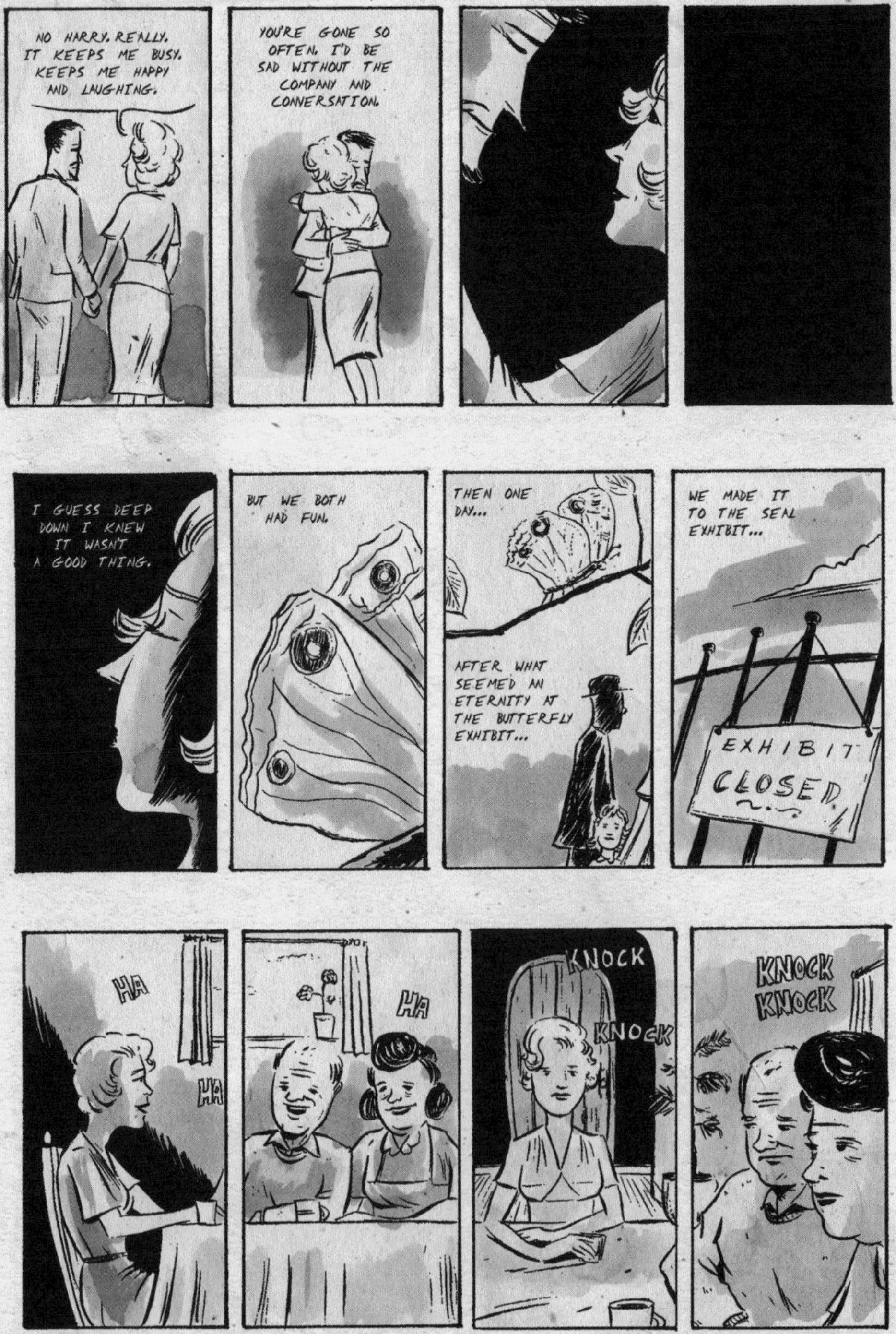

NO HARRY. REALLY. IT KEEPS ME BUSY. KEEPS ME HAPPY AND LAUGHING.
YOU'RE GONE SO OFTEN. I'D BE SAD WITHOUT THE COMPANY AND CONVERSATION.
I GUESS DEEP DOWN I KNEW IT WASN'T A GOOD THING.
BUT WE BOTH HAD FUN.
THEN ONE DAY...
AFTER WHAT SEEMED AN ETERNITY AT THE BUTTERFLY EXHIBIT...
WE MADE IT TO THE SEAL EXHIBIT...
EXHIBIT CLOSED
HA
HA
HA
KNOCK
KNOCK
KNOCK
KNOCK

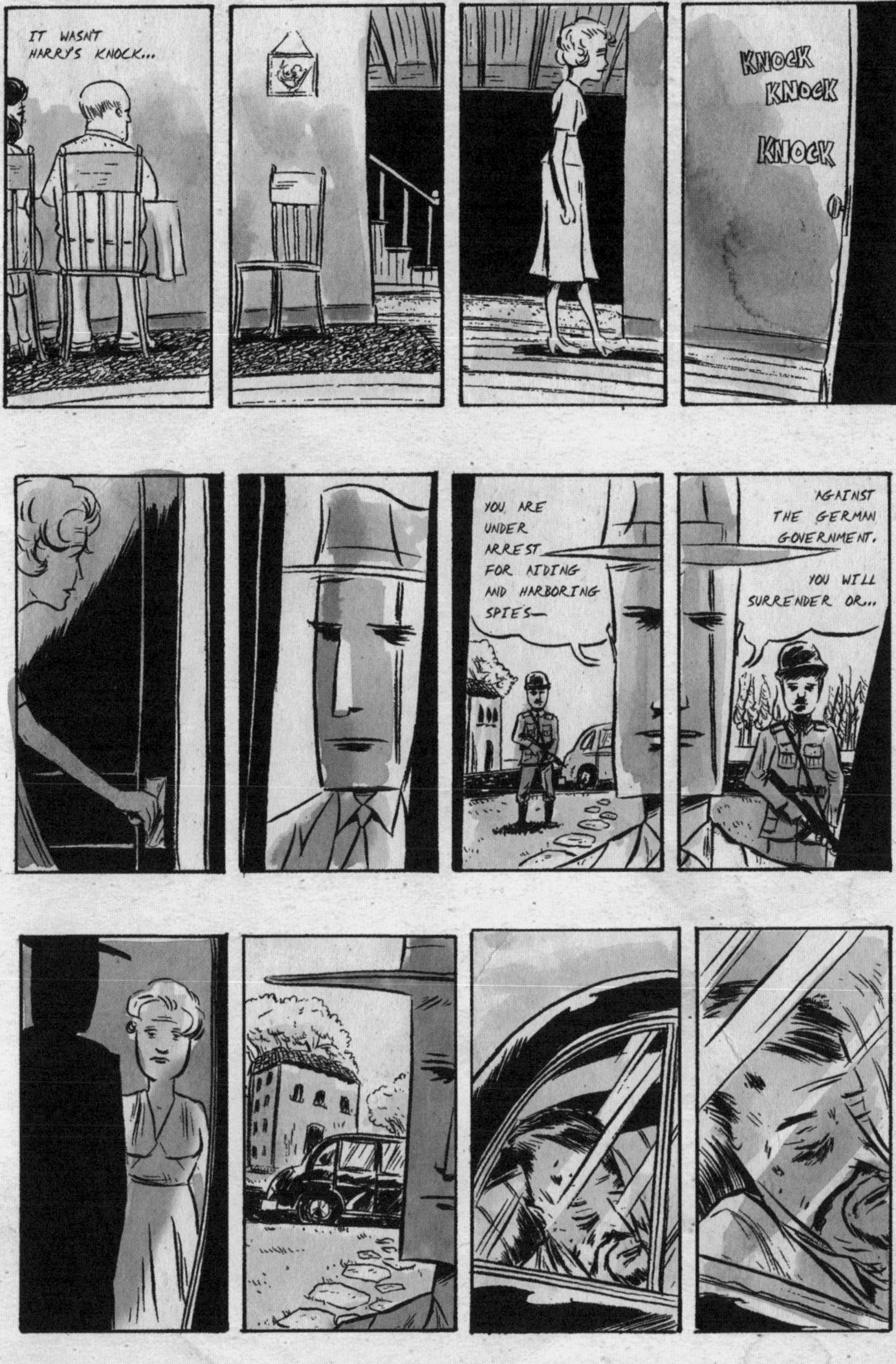
IT WASN'T HARRY'S KNOCK...
KNOCK KNOCK
KNOCK
YOU ARE UNDER ARREST FOR AIDING AND HARBORING SPIES—
AGAINST THE GERMAN GOVERNMENT.
YOU WILL SURRENDER OR...

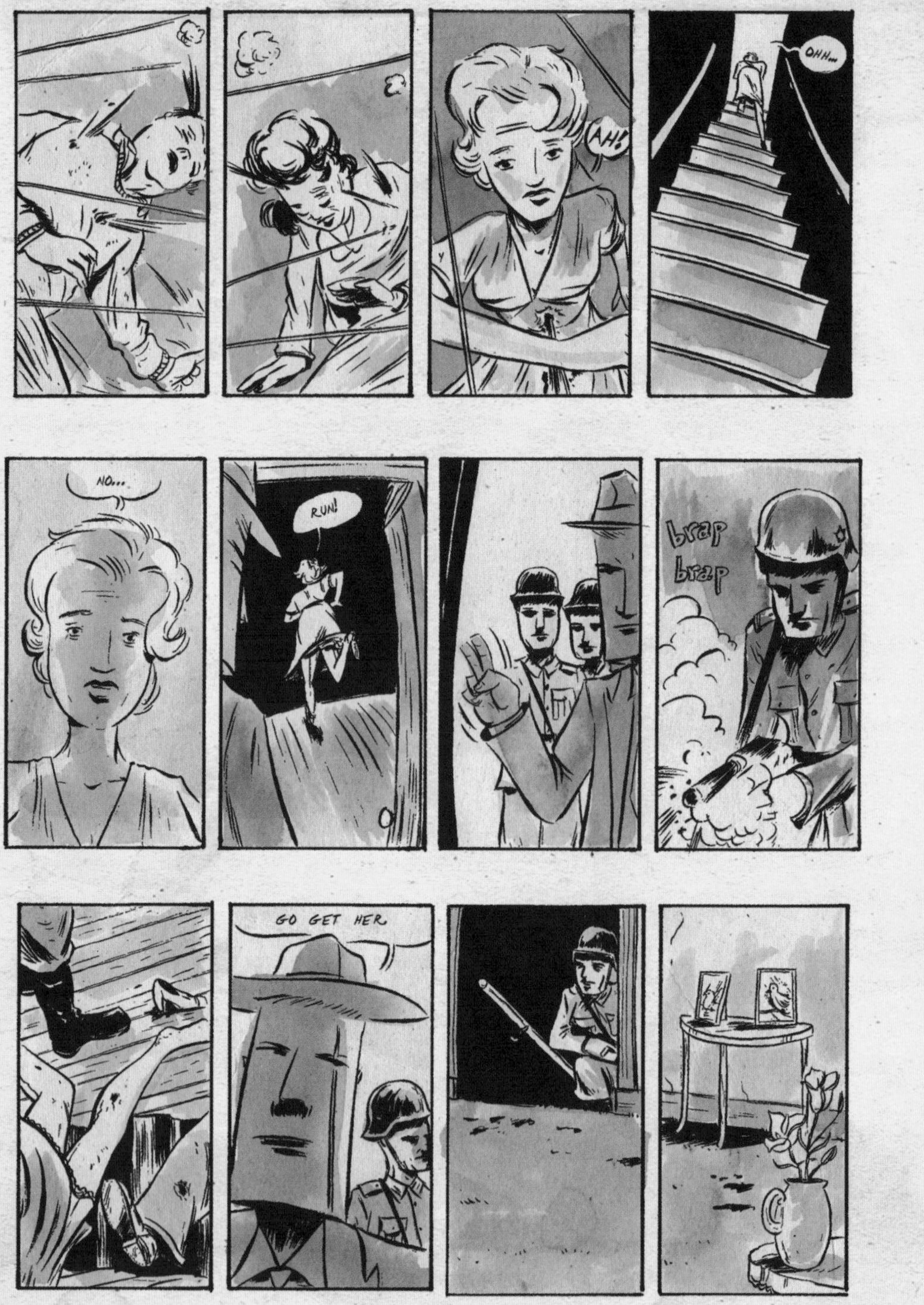
AH!
OHH...
NO...
RUN!
brap
brap
GO GET HER

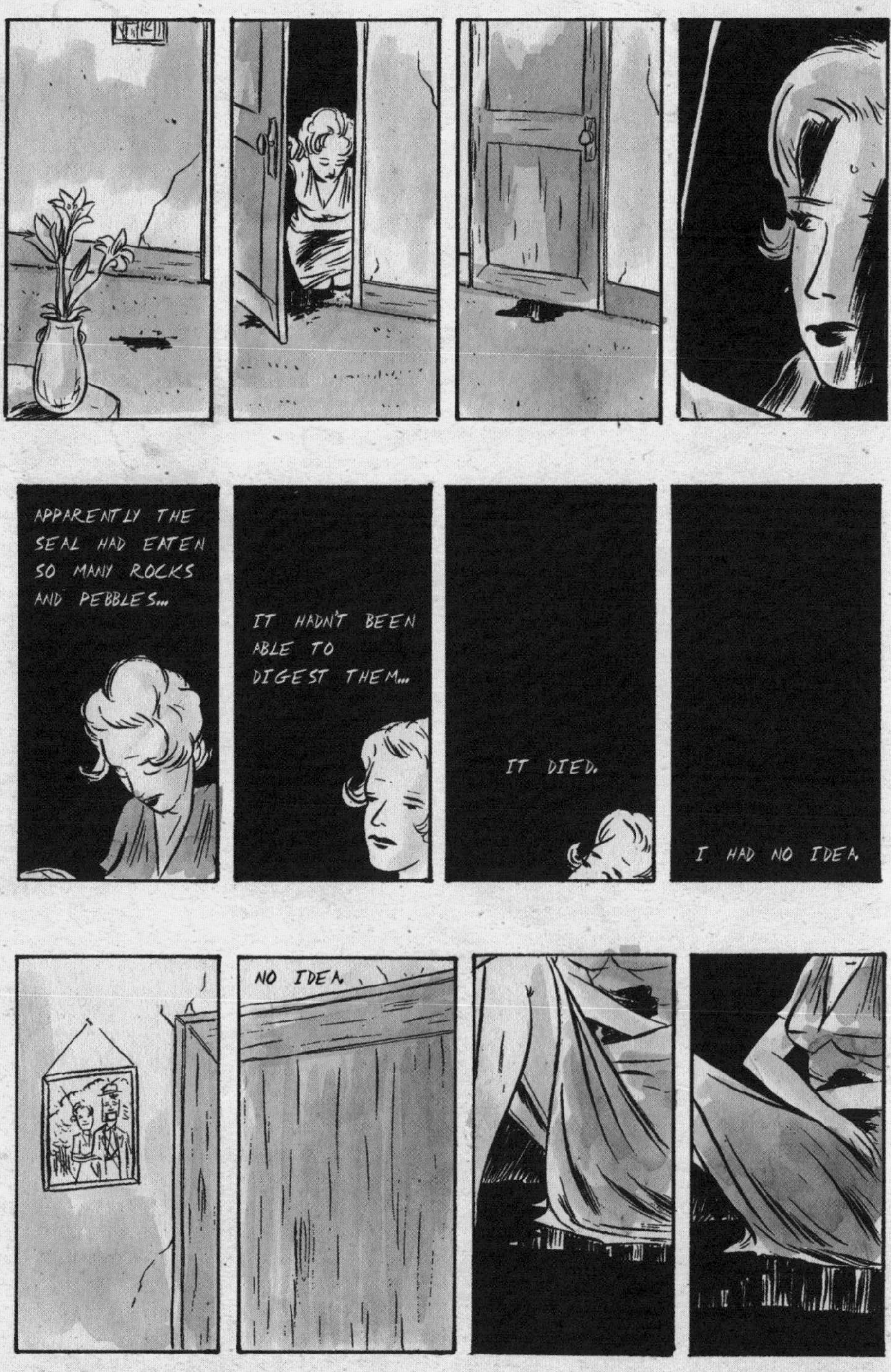
APPARENTLY THE SEAL HAD EATEN SO MANY ROCKS AND PEBBLES...
IT HADN'T BEEN ABLE TO DIGEST THEM...
IT DIED.
I HAD NO IDEA.
NO IDEA.

THE END

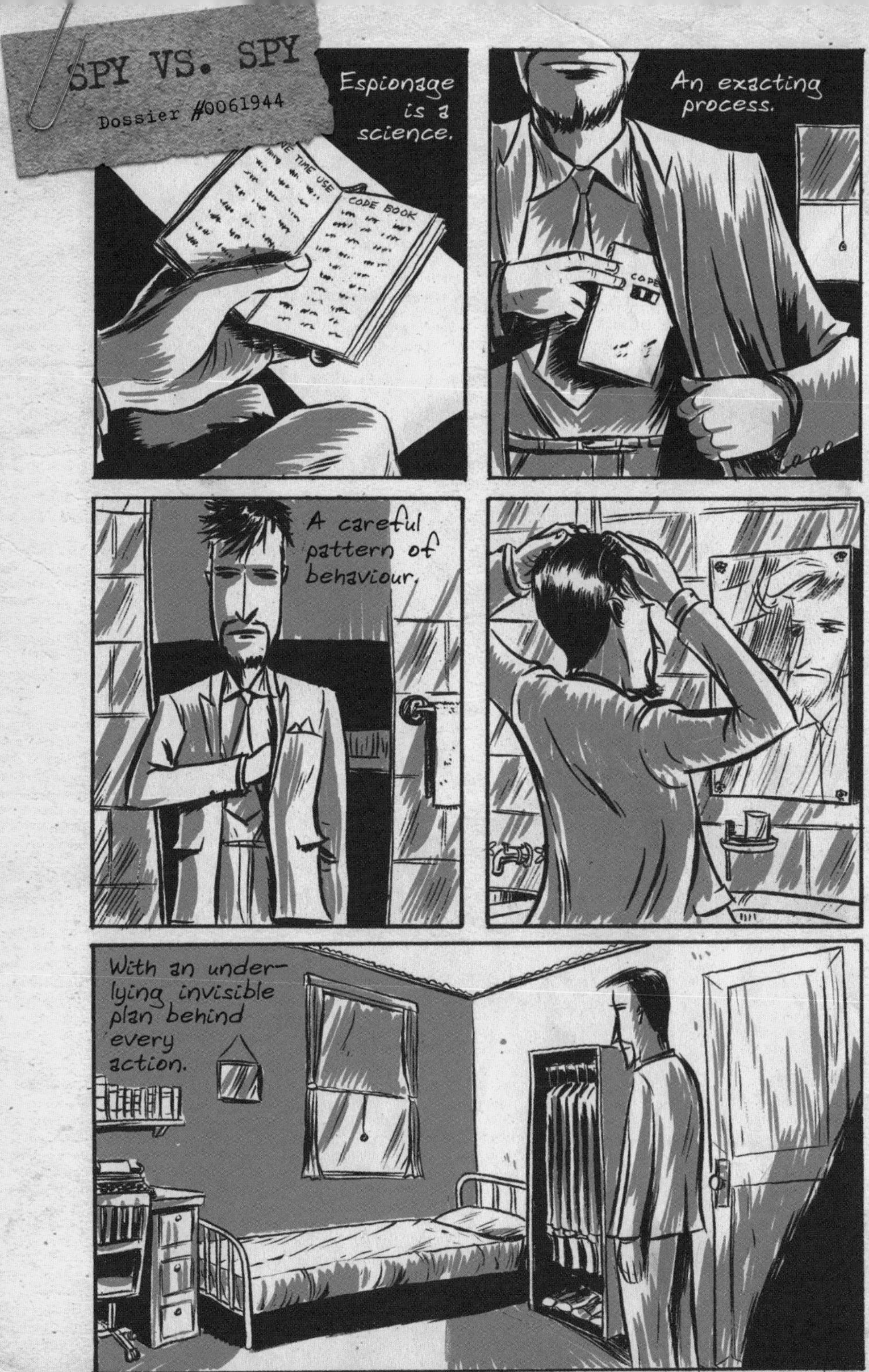
SPY VS. SPY
Dossier #0061944
Espionage is a science.
CODE BOOK
An exacting process.
A careful pattern of behaviour.
With an underlying invisible plan behind every action.

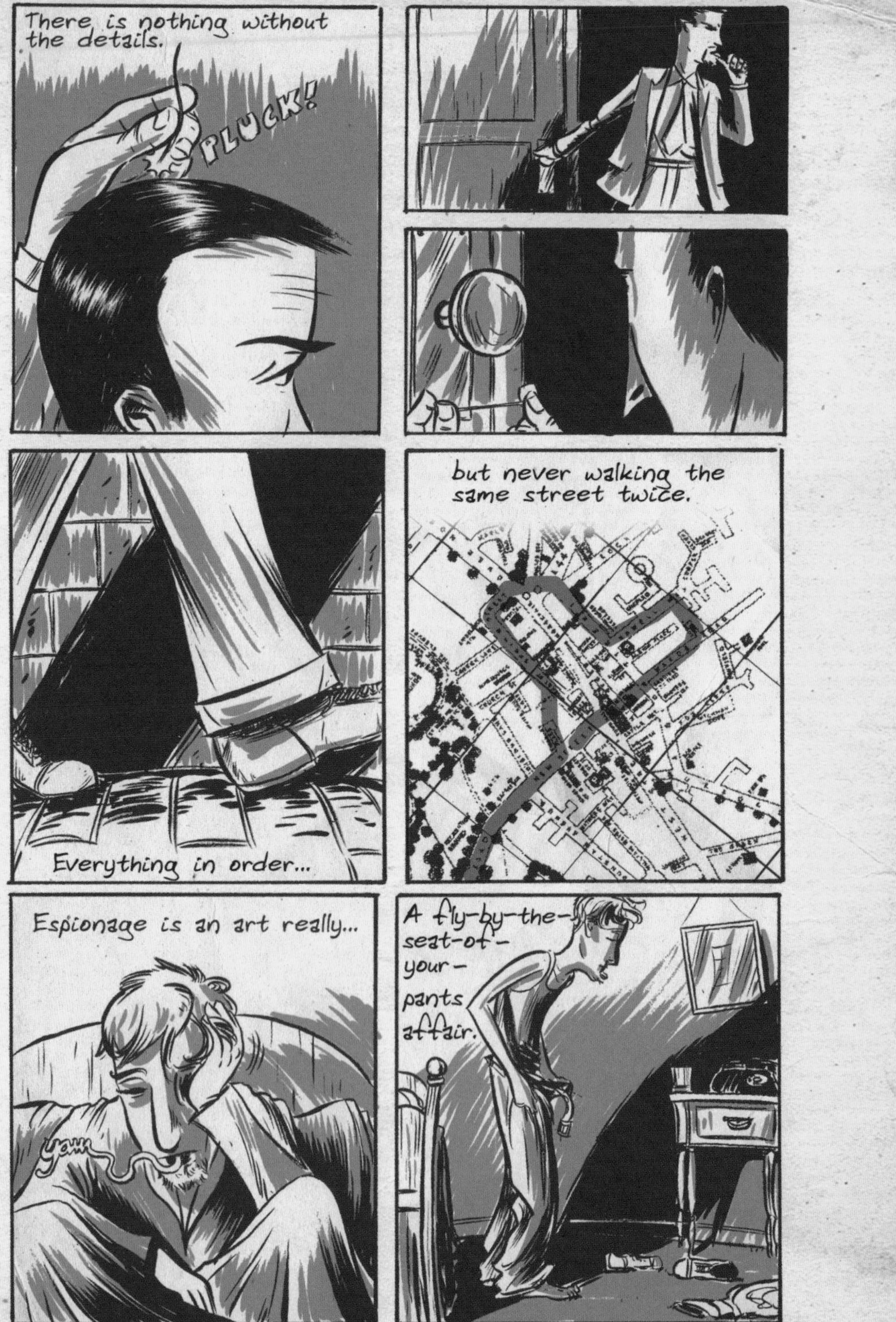
There is nothing without the details.
PLUCK!
Everything in order...
but never walking the same street twice.
Espionage is an art really...
yawn
A fly-by-the-seat-of-your-pants affair.

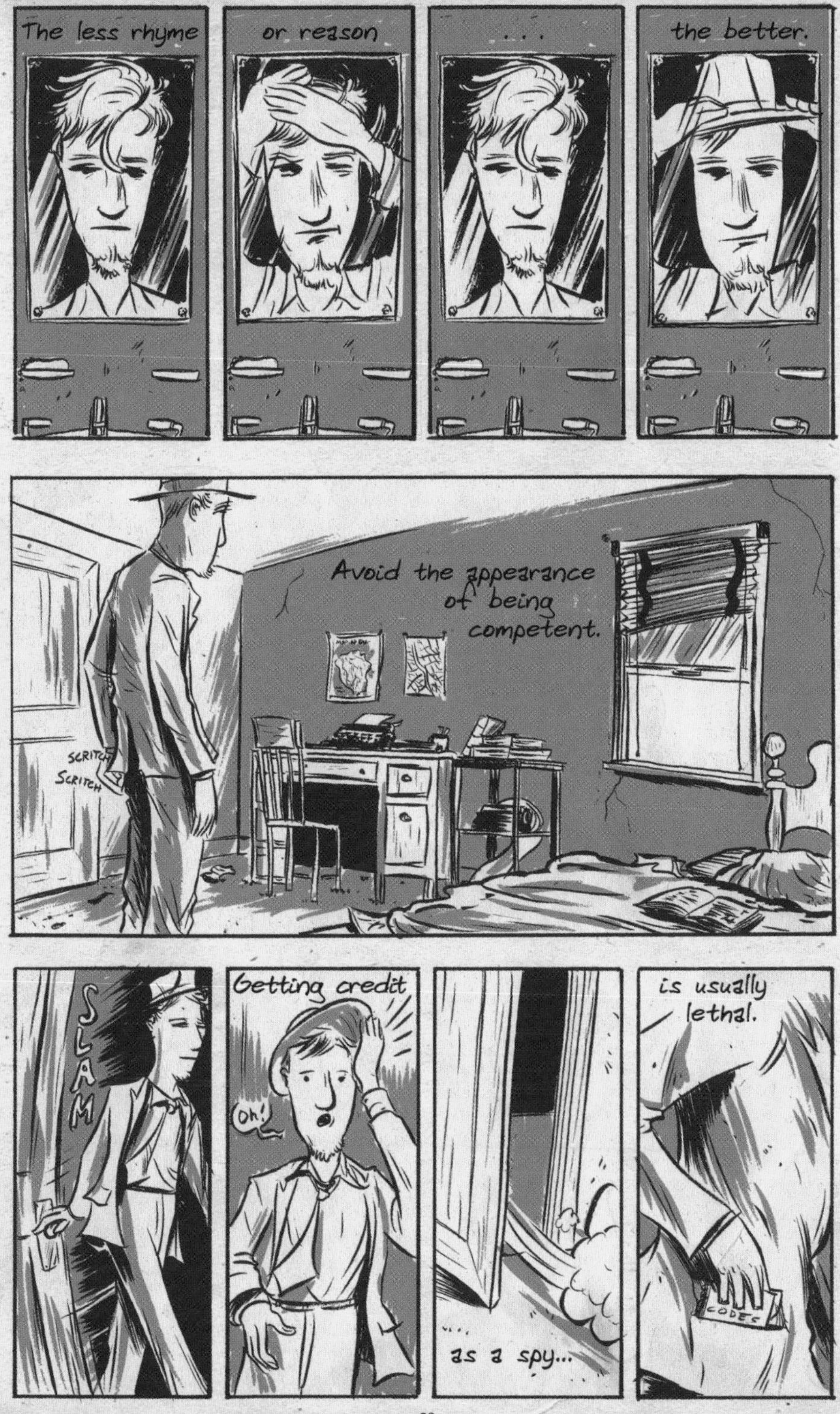
The less rhyme
or reason
. . .
the better.
Avoid the appearance of being competent.
SCRITCH
SCRITCH
SLAM
Getting credit
Oh!
...
as a spy...
is usually lethal.
CODES

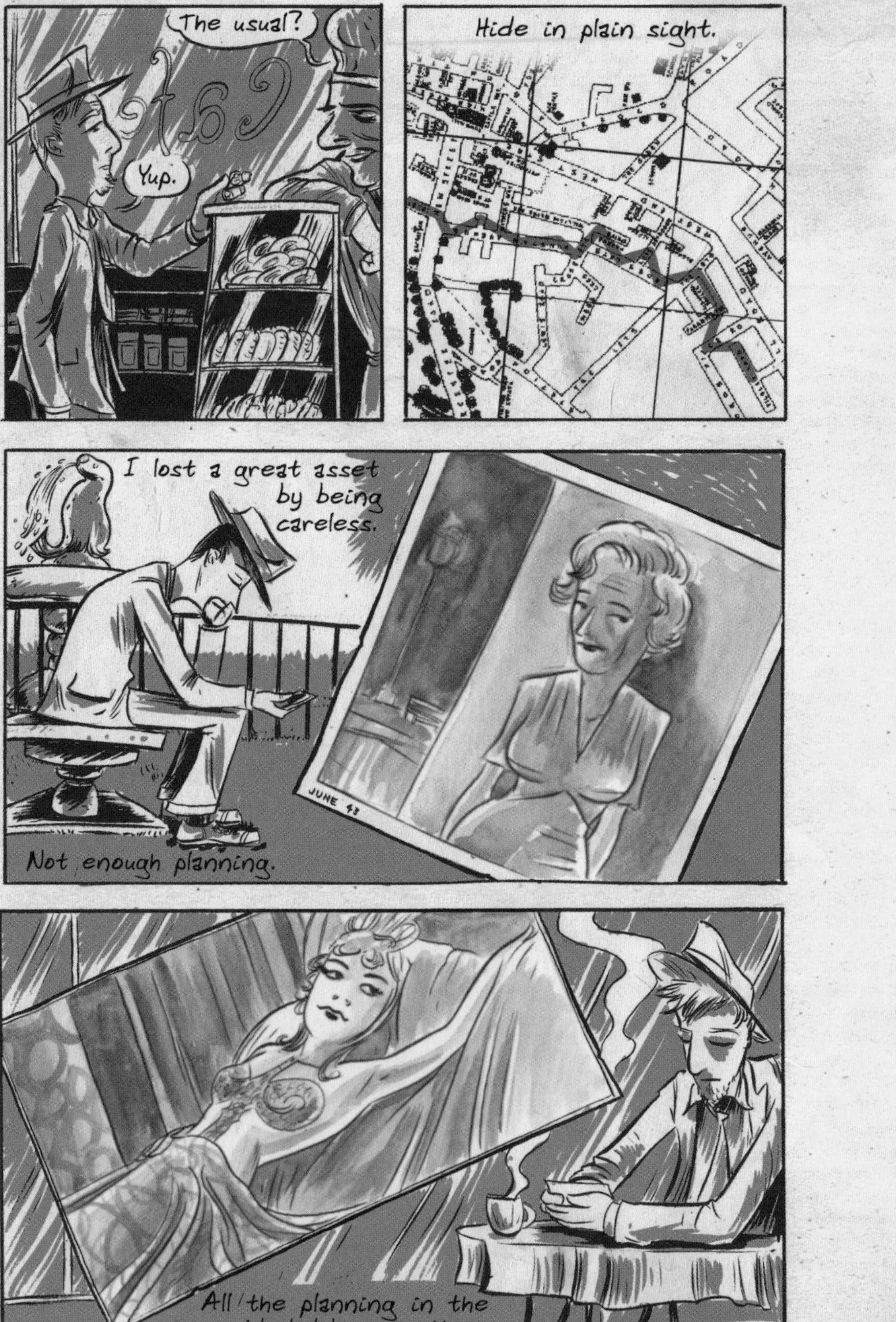
The usual?
Yup.
Hide in plain sight.
I lost a great asset by being careless.
JUNE 43
Not enough planning.
All the planning in the world didn't save Mattie.

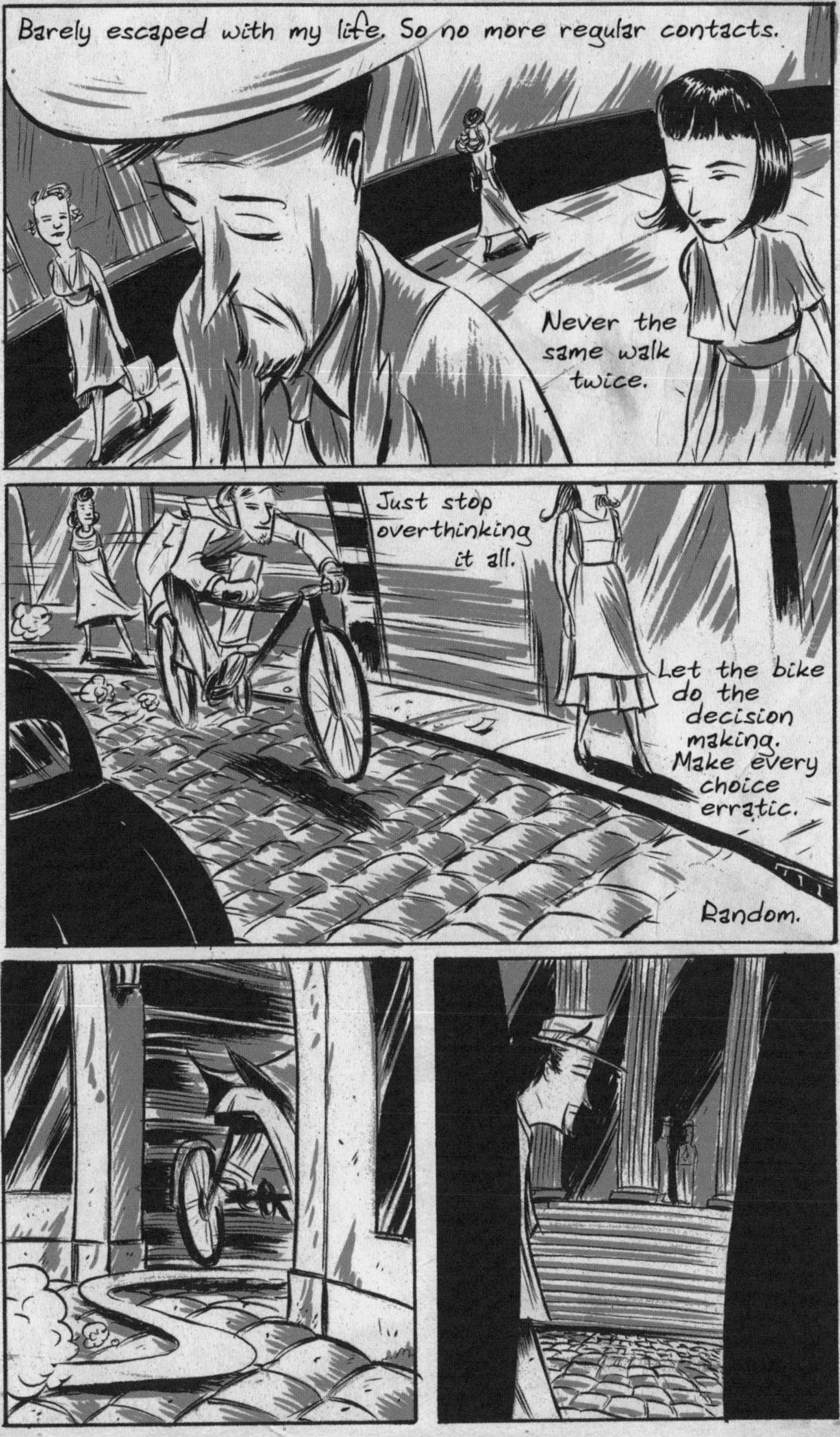
Barely escaped with my life. So no more regular contacts.
Never the same walk twice.
Just stop overthinking it all.
Let the bike do the decision making. Make every choice erratic.
Random.

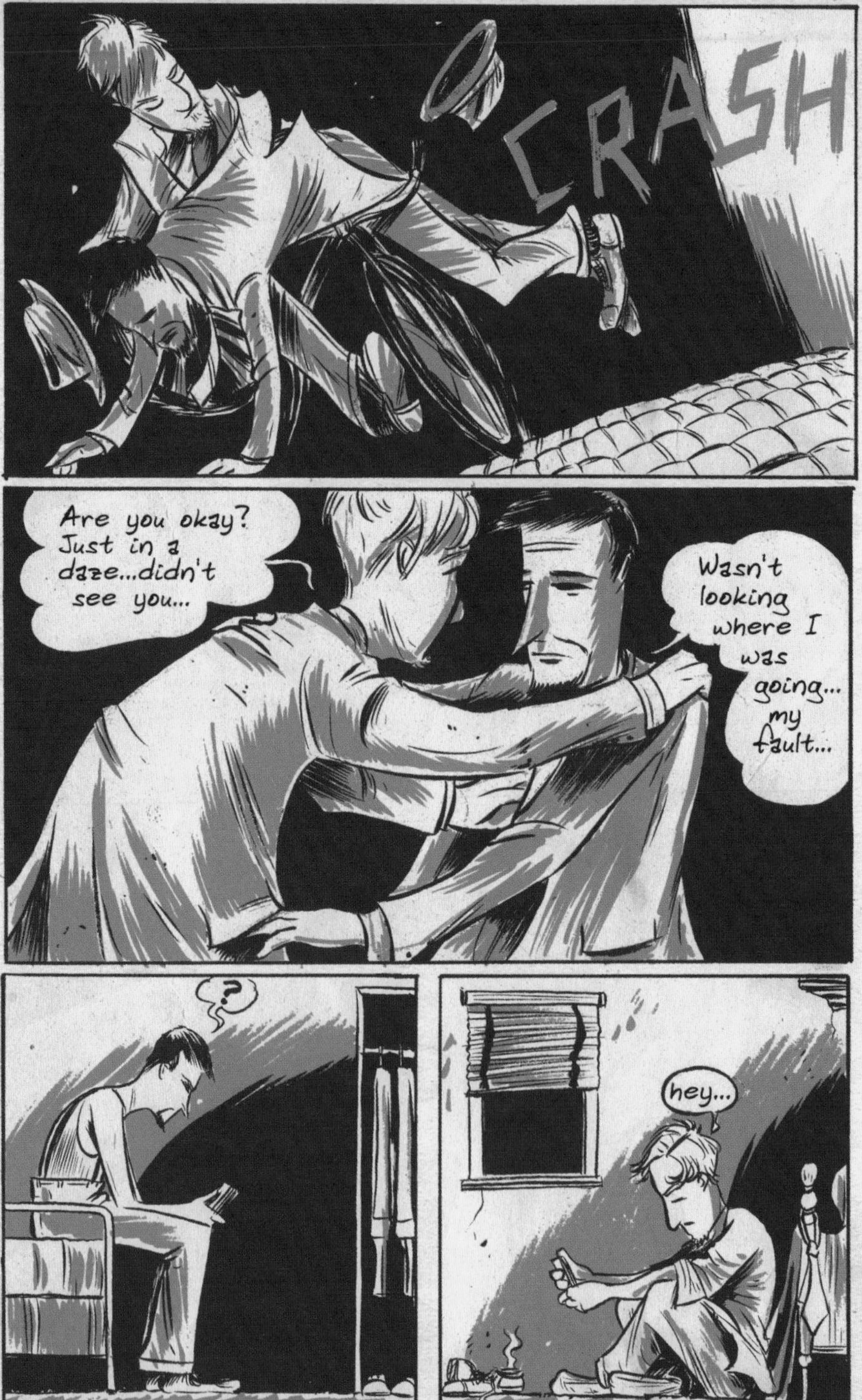
CRASH
Are you okay? Just in a daze...didn't see you...
Wasn't looking where I was going... my fault...
?
hey...

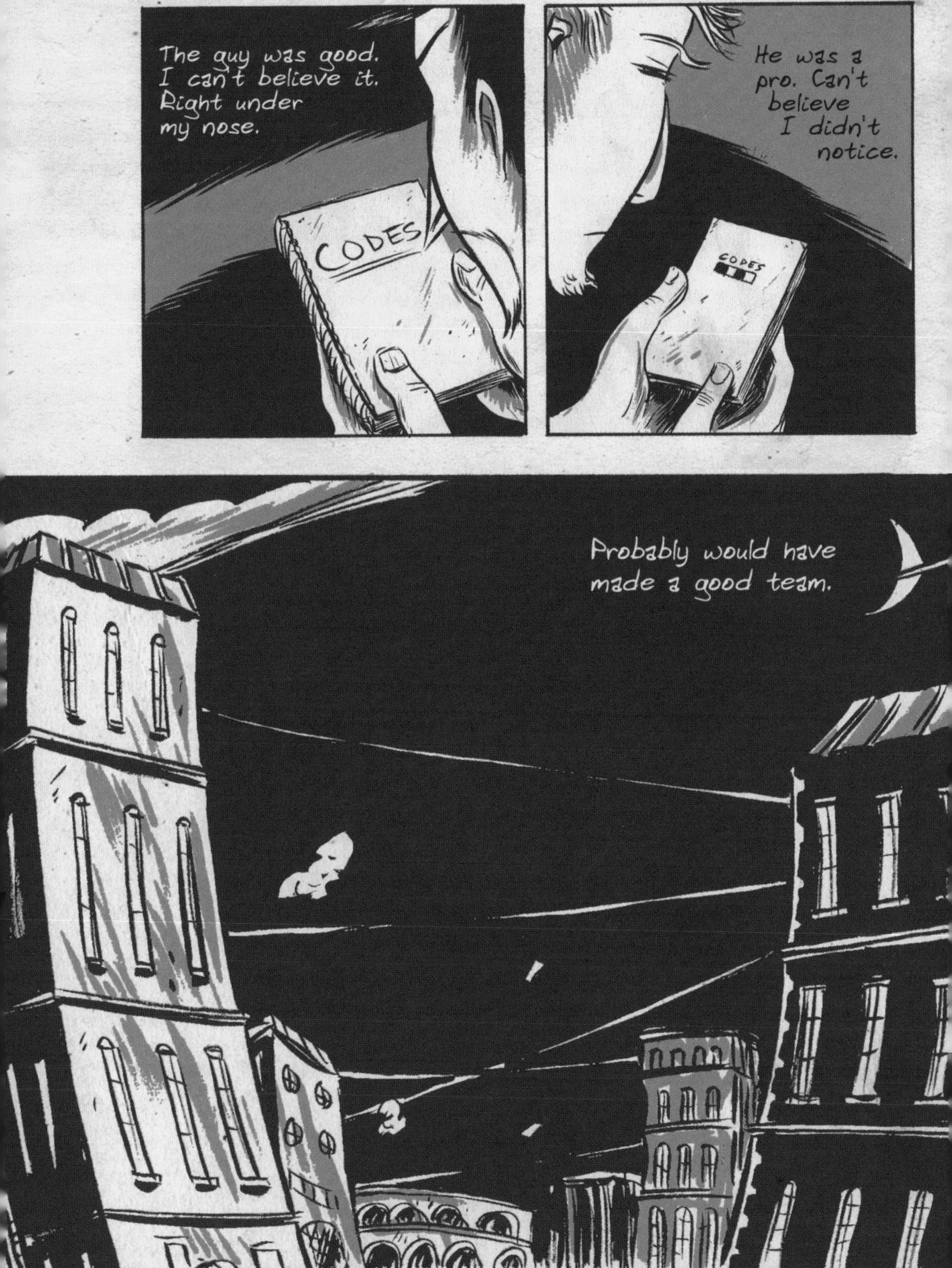
The guy was good. I can't believe it. Right under my nose.
CODES
He was a pro. Can't believe I didn't notice.
CODES
Probably would have made a good team.

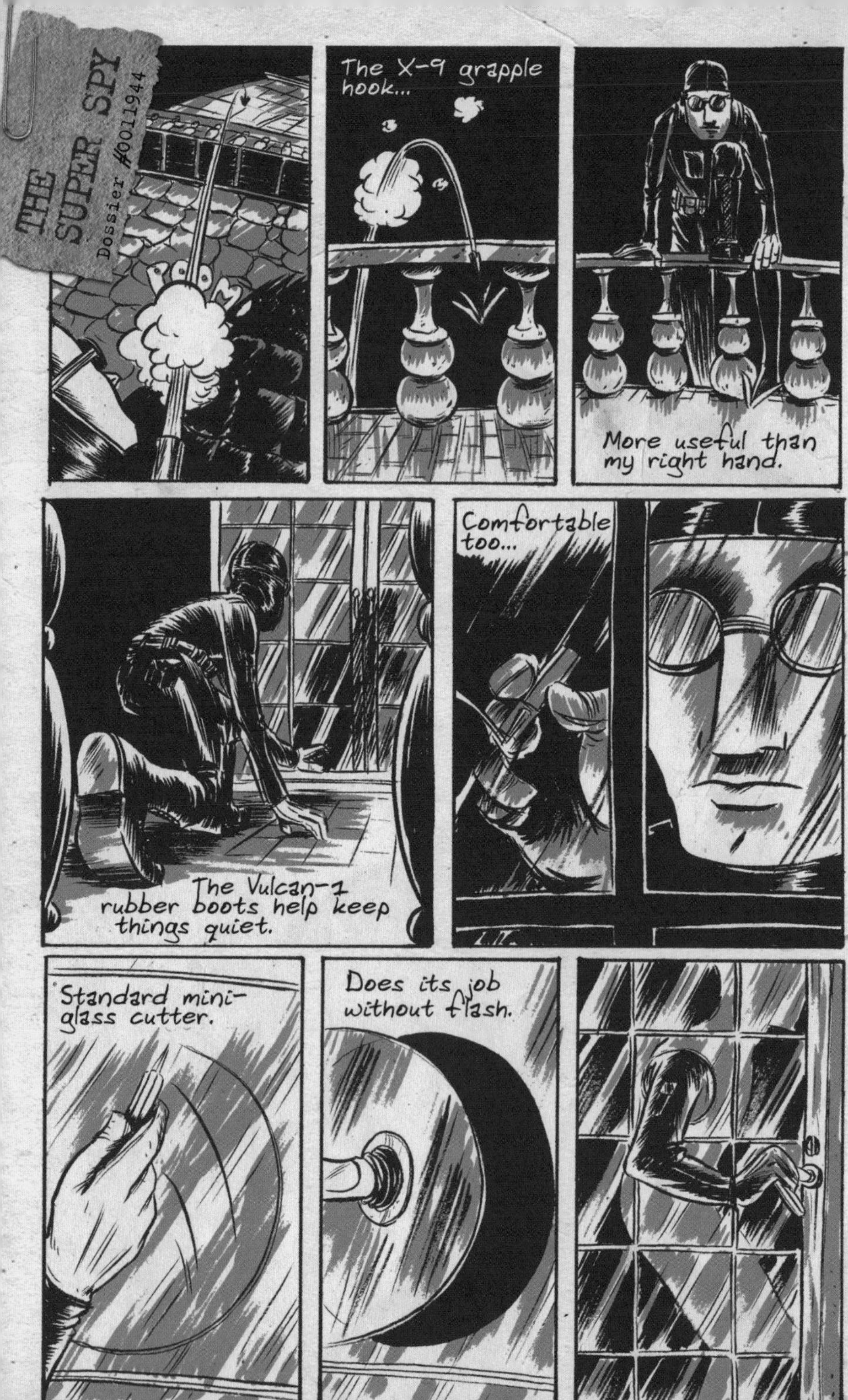
THE SUPER SPY
Dossier #0011944
BOOM
The X-9 grapple hook...
More useful than my right hand.
The Vulcan-7 rubber boots help keep things quiet.
Comfortable too...
Standard mini-glass cutter.
Does its job without flash.

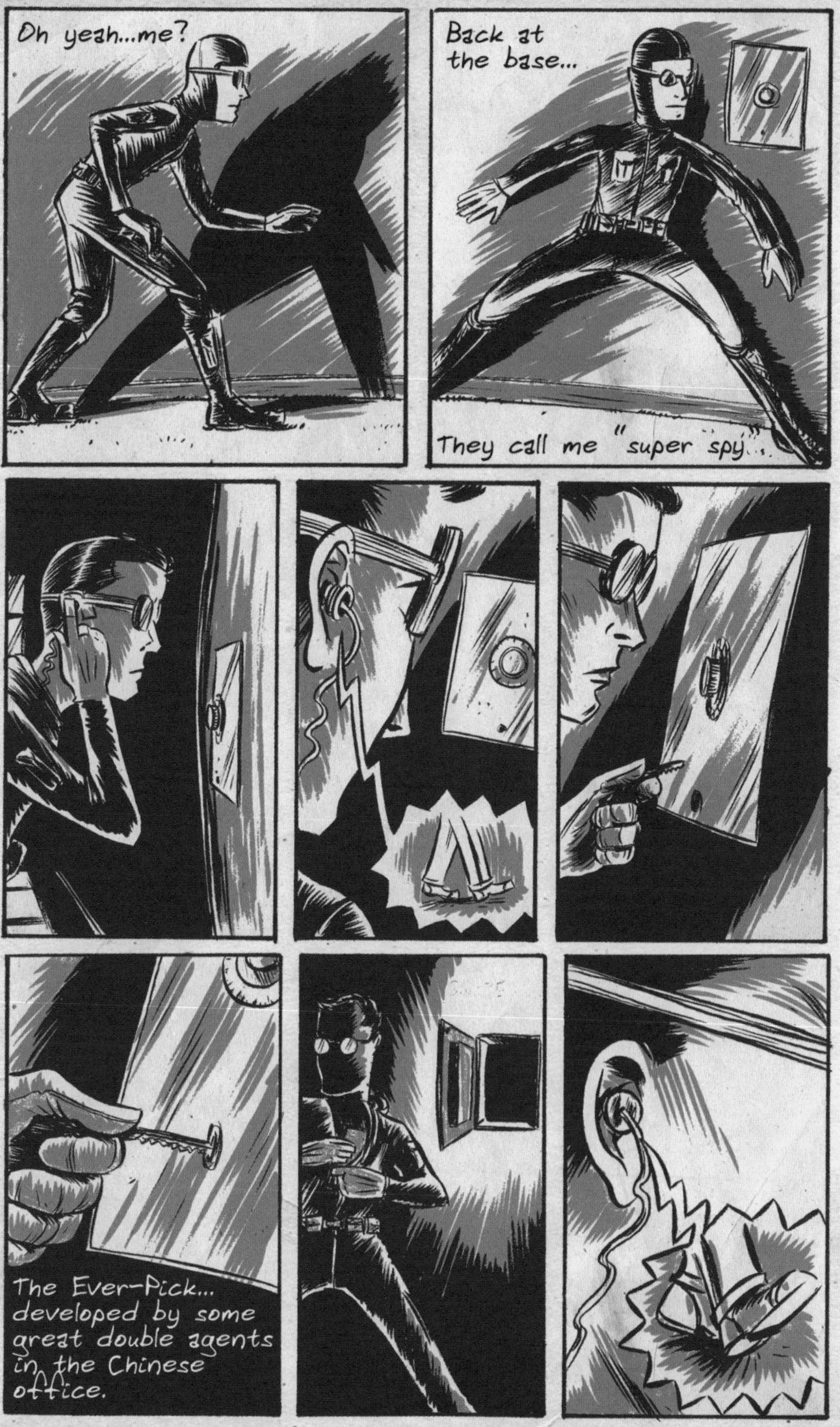
Oh yeah...me?
Back at the base...
They call me "super spy"...
The Ever-Pick... developed by some great double agents in the Chinese office.

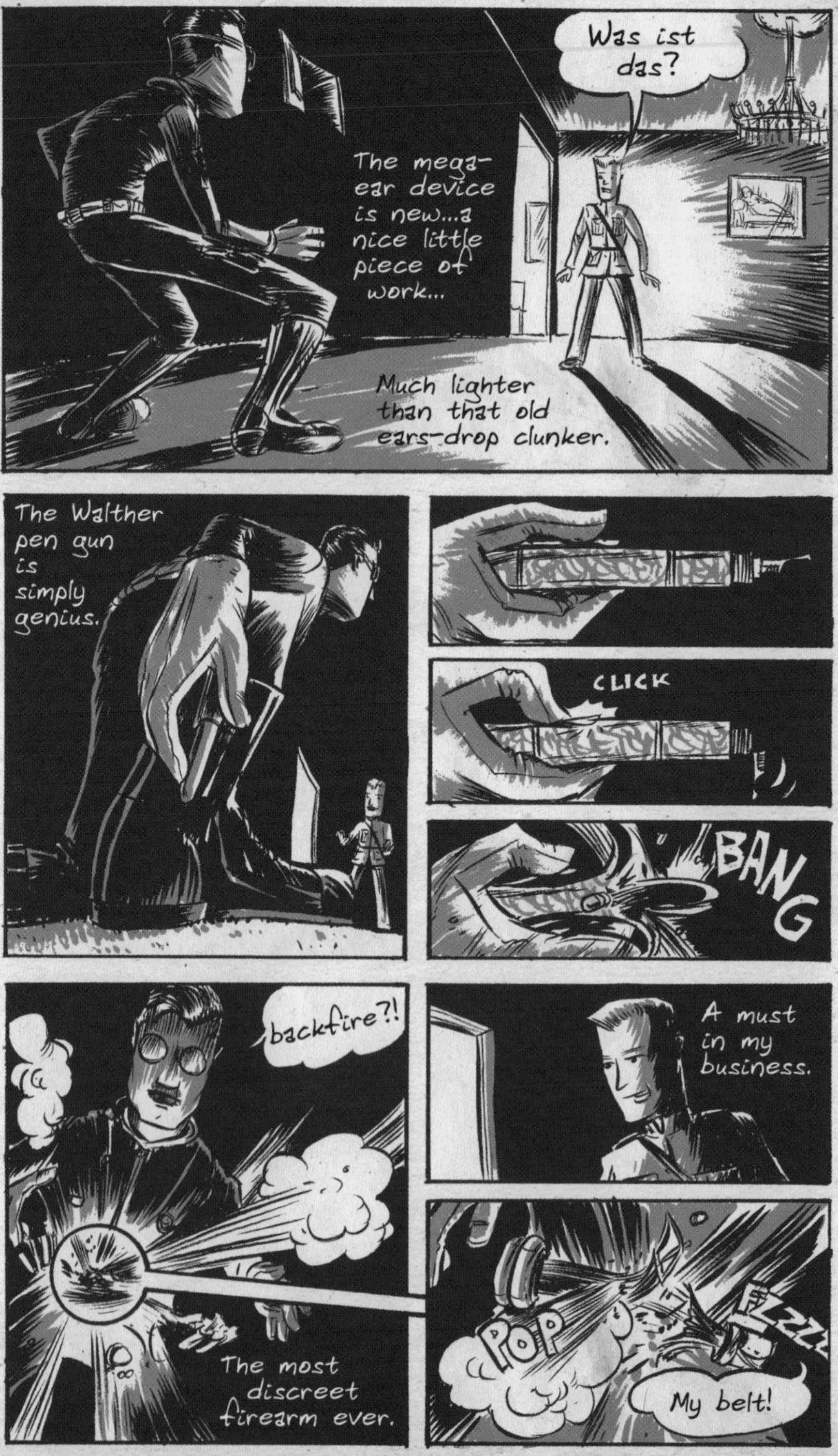
Was ist das?
The mega-ear device is new...a nice little piece of work...
Much lighter than that old ears-drop clunker.
The Walther pen gun is simply genius.
CLICK
BANG
backfire?!
The most discreet firearm ever.
A must in my business.
POP
FZZZ
My belt!

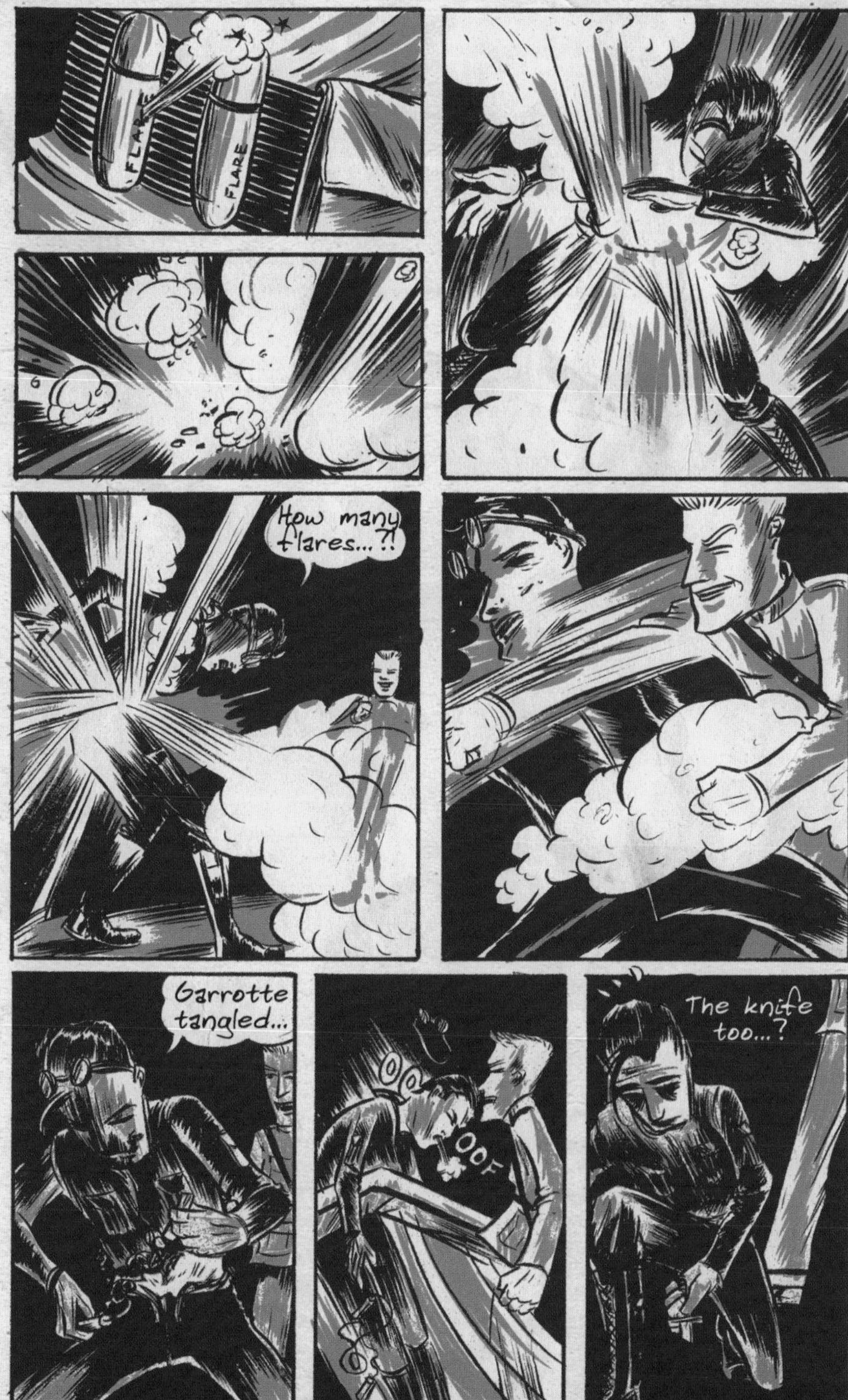
FLARE
FLARE
How many flares...?!
Garrotte tangled...
OOF
The knife too...?

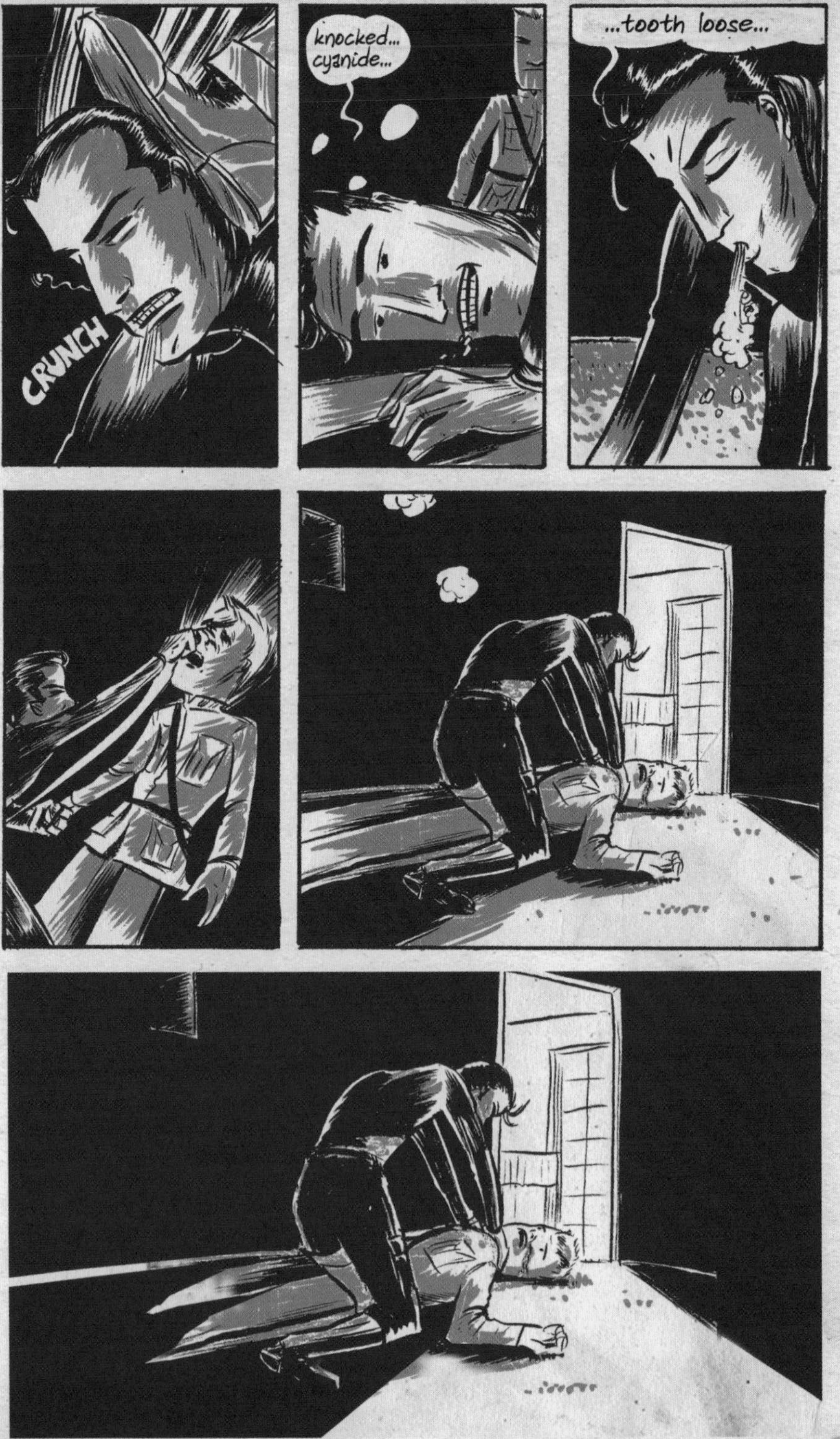
CRUNCH
knocked... cyanide...
...tooth loose...

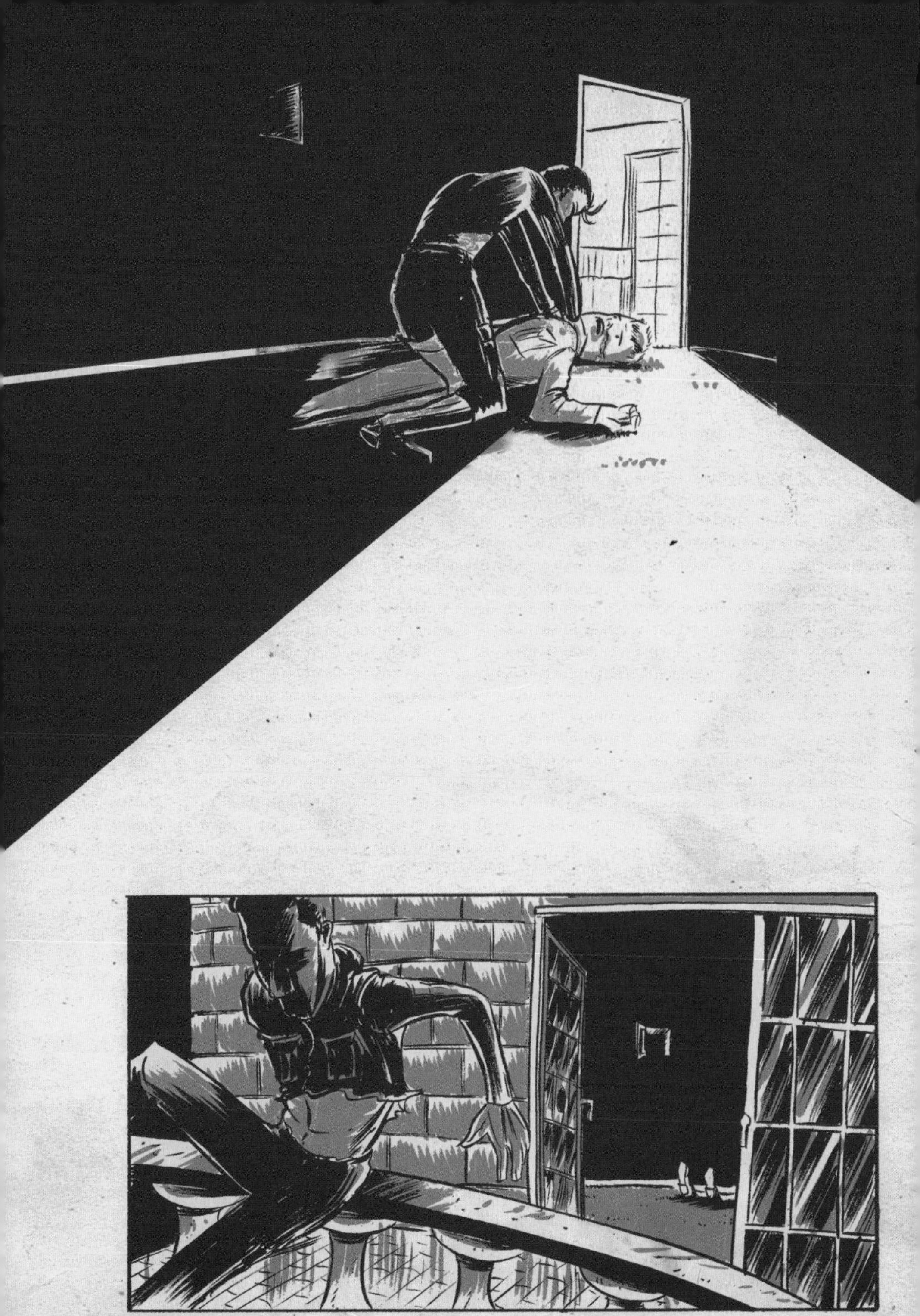

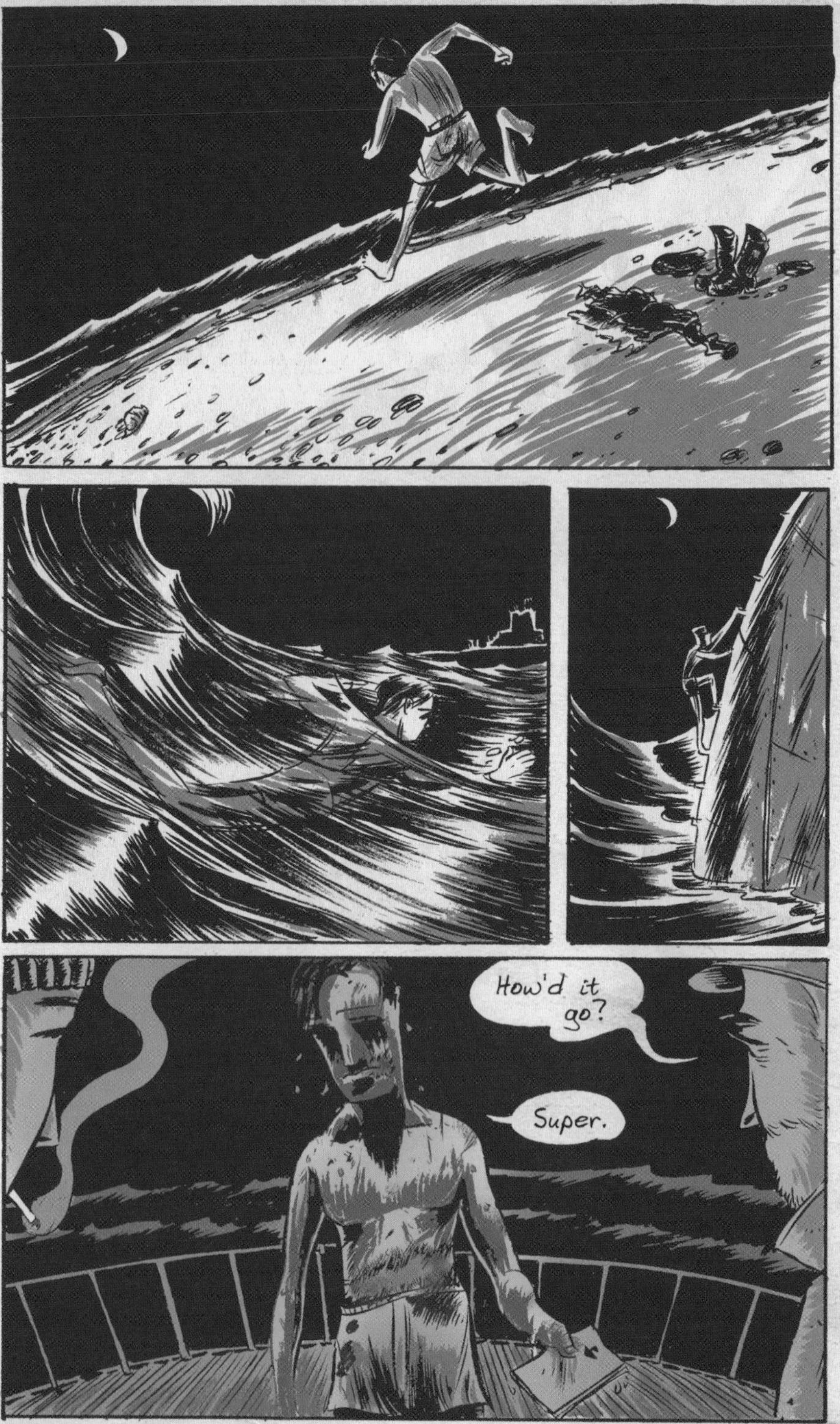
How'd it go?
Super.

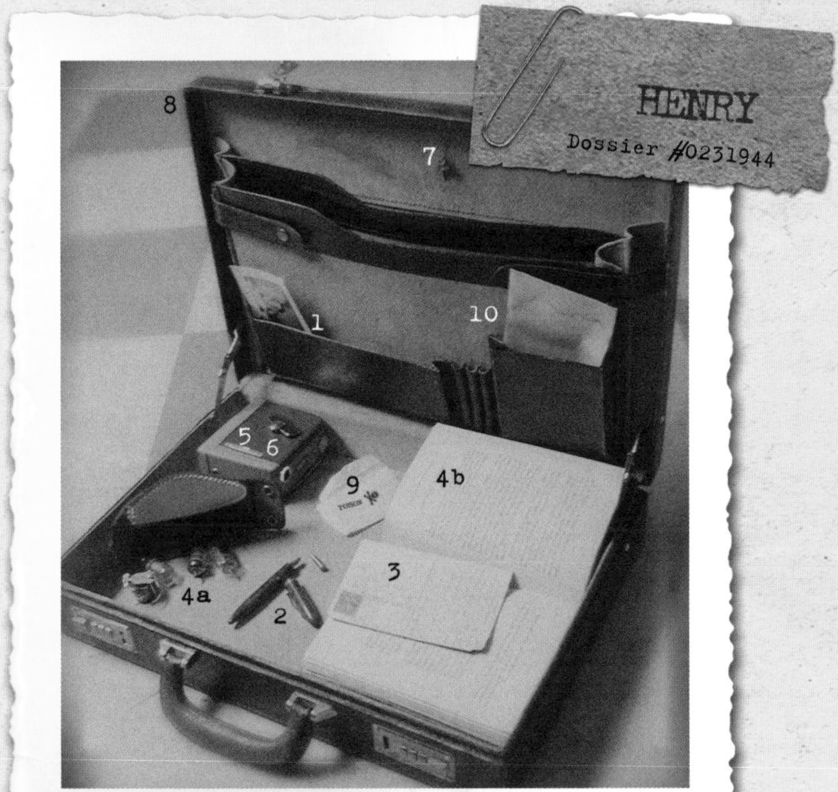
HENRY
Dossier #0231944
8
7
1
10
5
6
9
4b
3
4a
2

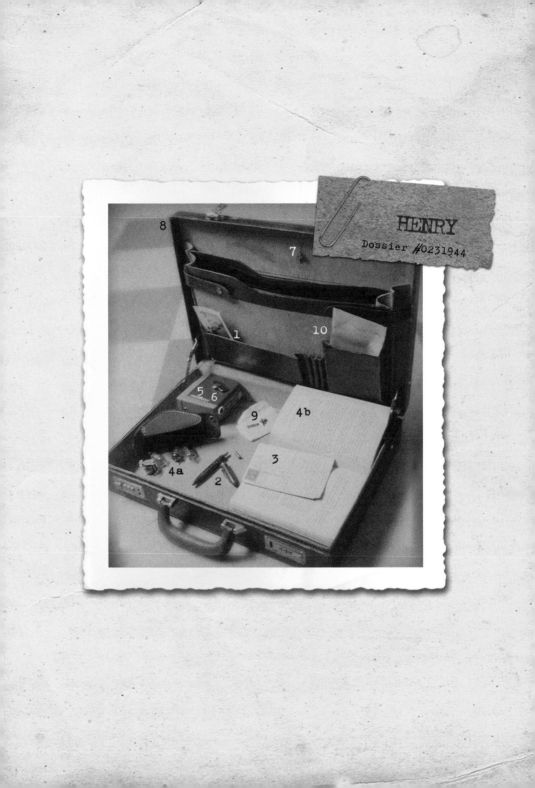

1. SUPER SPY by M. Kindt

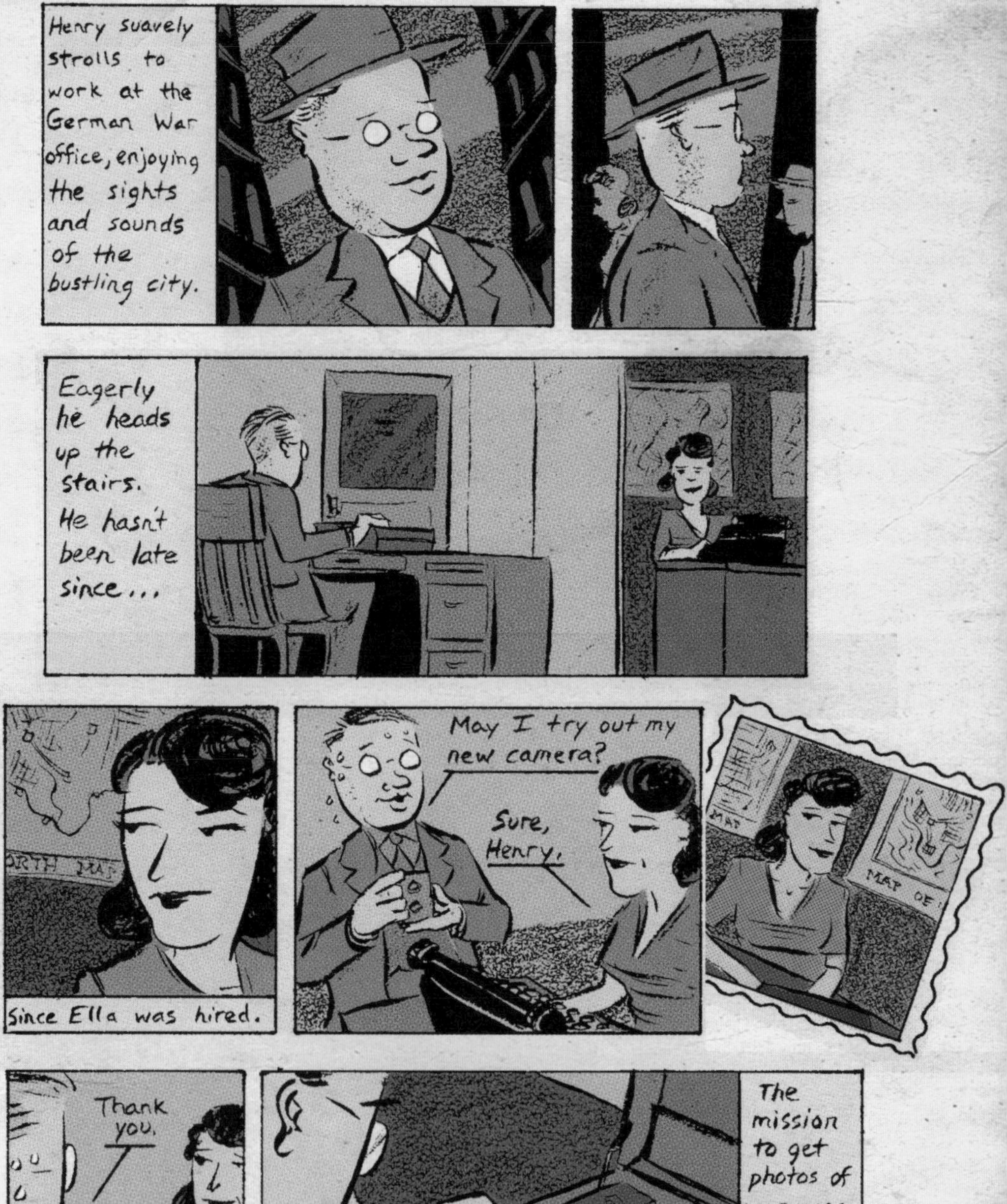

Henry suavely strolls to work at the German War office, enjoying the sights and sounds of the bustling city.
Eagerly he heads up the stairs.
He hasn't been late since...
Since Ella was hired.
May I try out my new camera?
Sure, Henry.
MAP
MAP OF
Thank you.
You're welcome.
The mission to get photos of war maps is another success for... Henry, English super spy.

2. SUPER SPY by M. Kindt

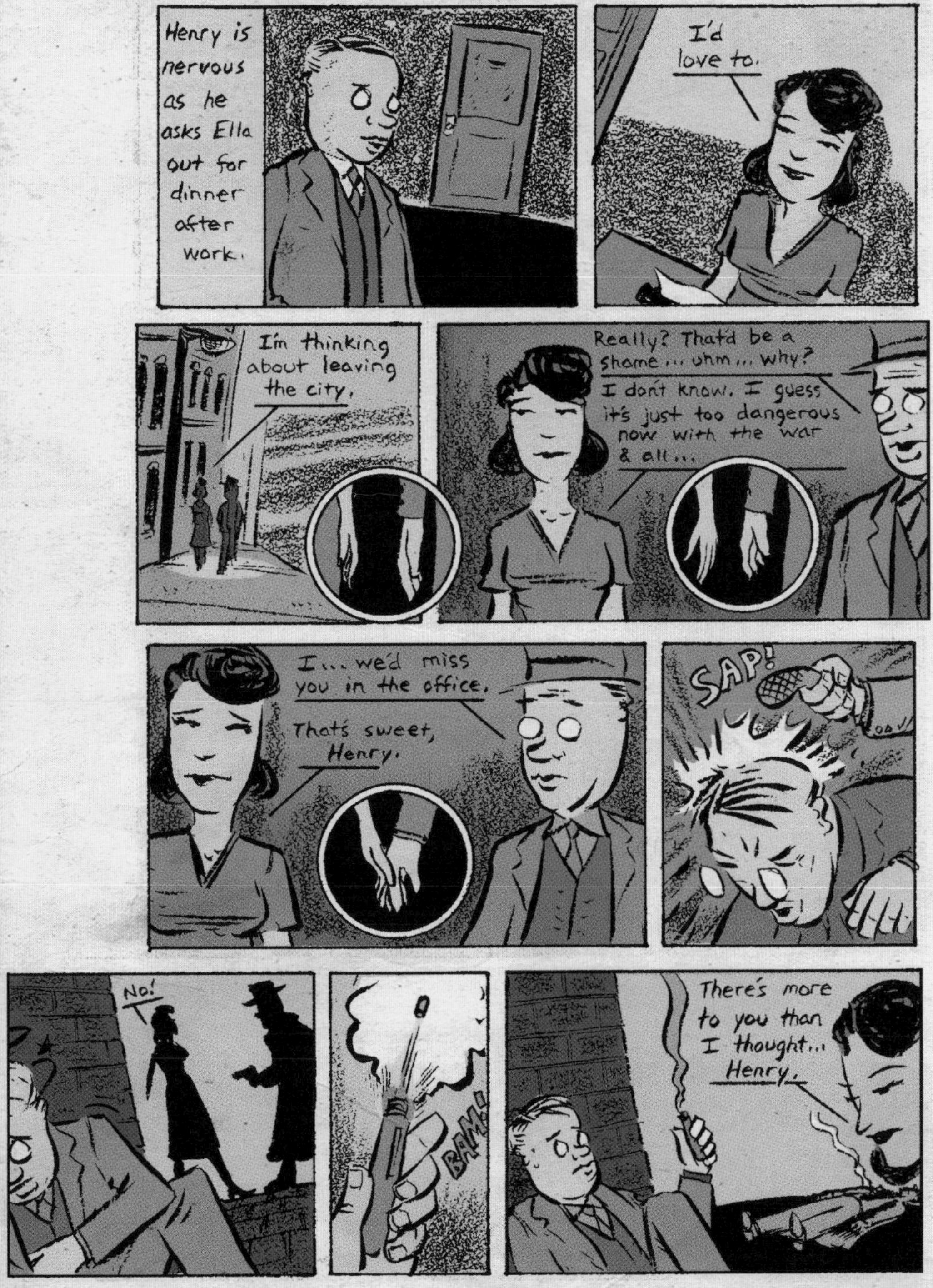

Henry is nervous as he asks Ella out for dinner after work.
I'd love to.
I'm thinking about leaving the city.
Really? That'd be a shame... uhm... why?
I don't know. I guess it's just too dangerous now with the war & all...
I... we'd miss you in the office.
That's sweet, Henry.
SAP!
No!
BAM!
There's more to you than I thought... Henry.

3. SUPER SPY by M. Kindt

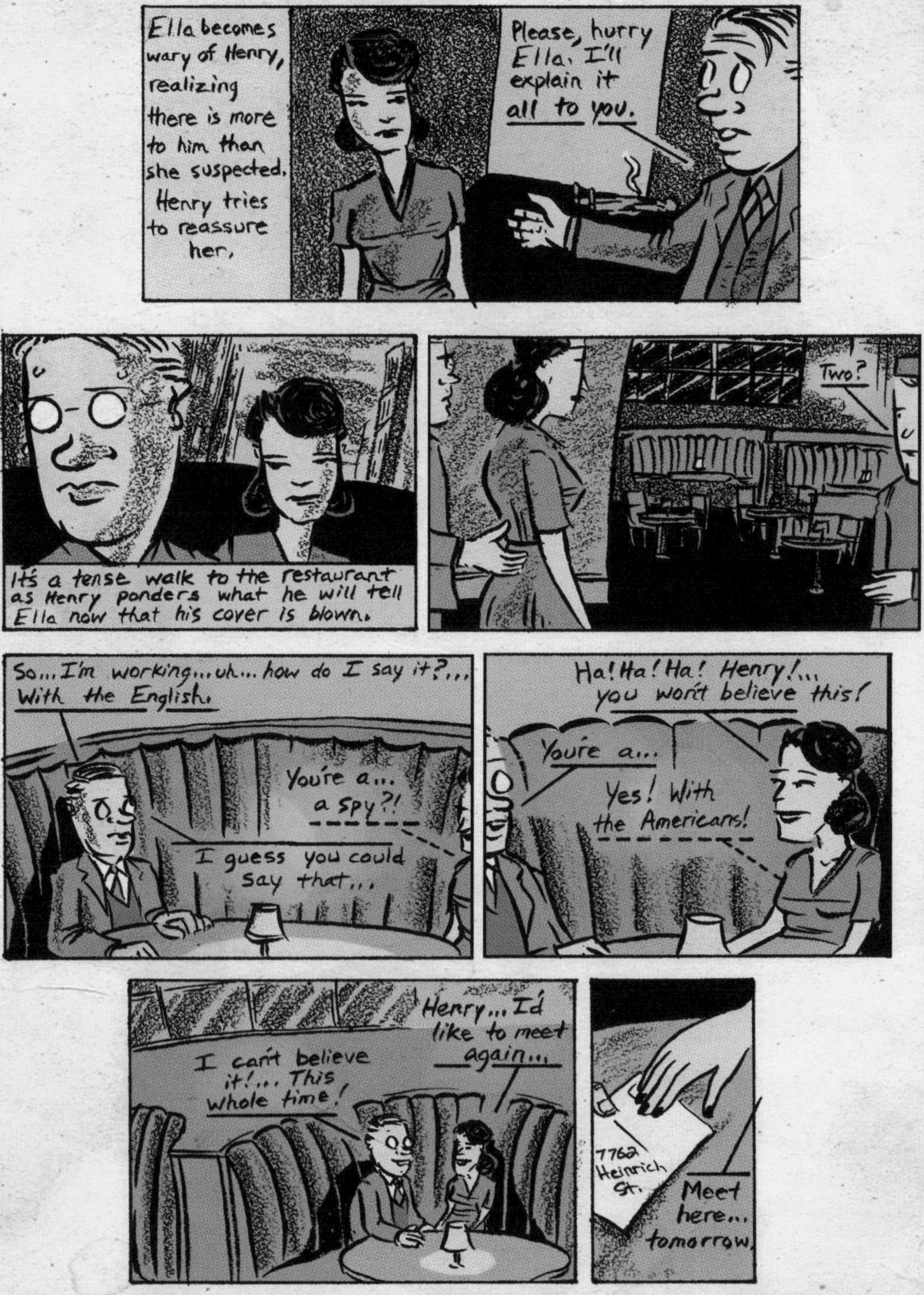

Ella becomes wary of Henry, realizing there is more to him than she suspected. Henry tries to reassure her.
Please, hurry Ella. I'll explain it all to you.
It's a tense walk to the restaurant as Henry ponders what he will tell Ella now that his cover is blown.
Two?
So... I'm working... uh... how do I say it?... With the English.
You're a... a spy?!
I guess you could say that...
Ha! Ha! Ha! Henry!... you won't believe this!
You're a...
Yes! With the Americans!
I can't believe it!... This whole time!
Henry... I'd like to meet again...
7762 Heinrich St.
Meet here... tomorrow.

4. SUPER SPY by M. Kindt

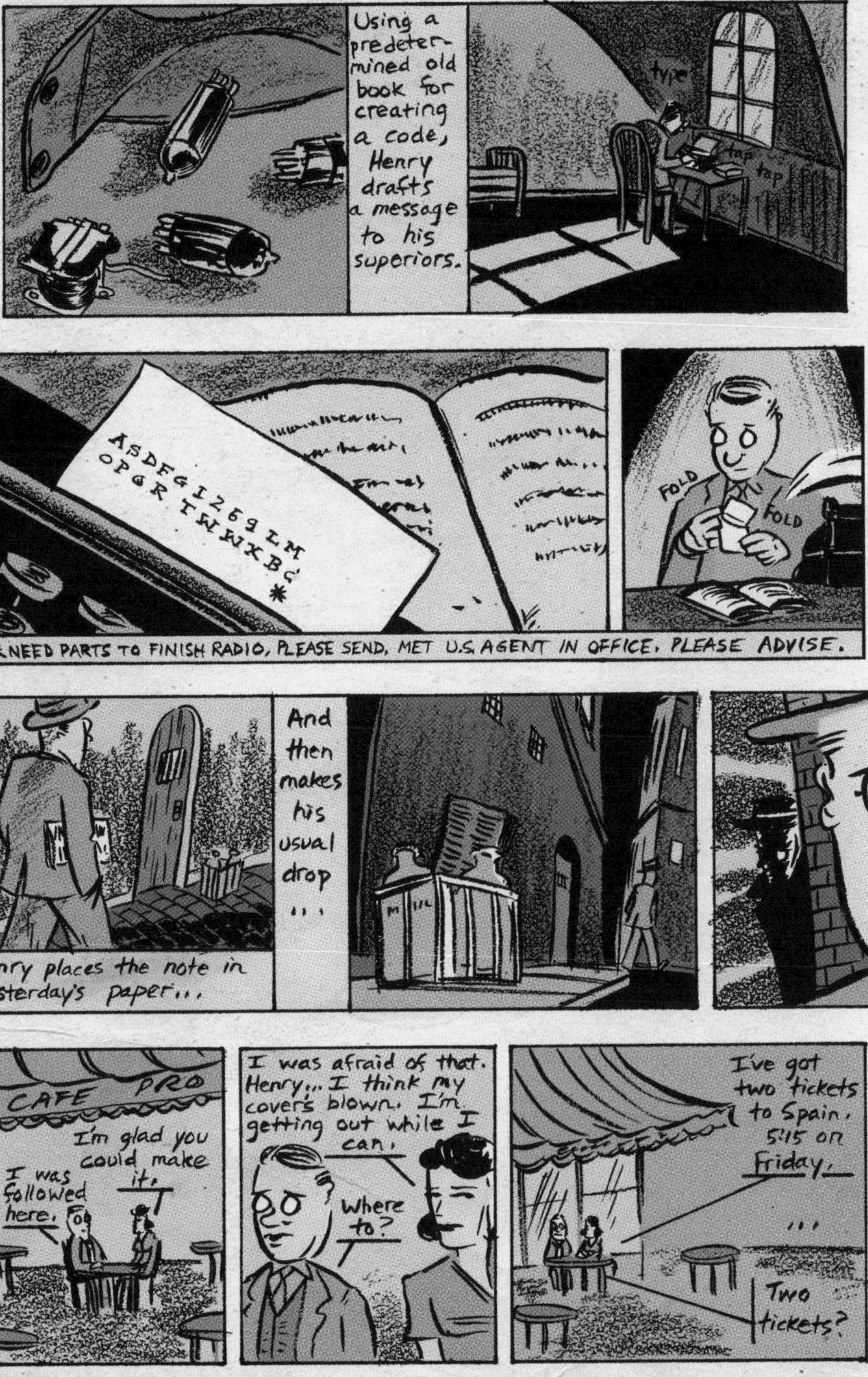

Using a predetermined old book for creating a code, Henry drafts a message to his superiors.
type
tap tap
FOLD FOLD
*NEED PARTS TO FINISH RADIO, PLEASE SEND. MET U.S. AGENT IN OFFICE. PLEASE ADVISE.
Henry places the note in yesterday's paper...
And then makes his usual drop...
CAFE PRO
I'm glad you could make it.
I was followed here.
I was afraid of that. Henry... I think my cover's blown. I'm getting out while I can.
Where to?
I've got two tickets to Spain. 5:15 on Friday.
...
Two tickets?

5. SUPER SPY by M. Kindt

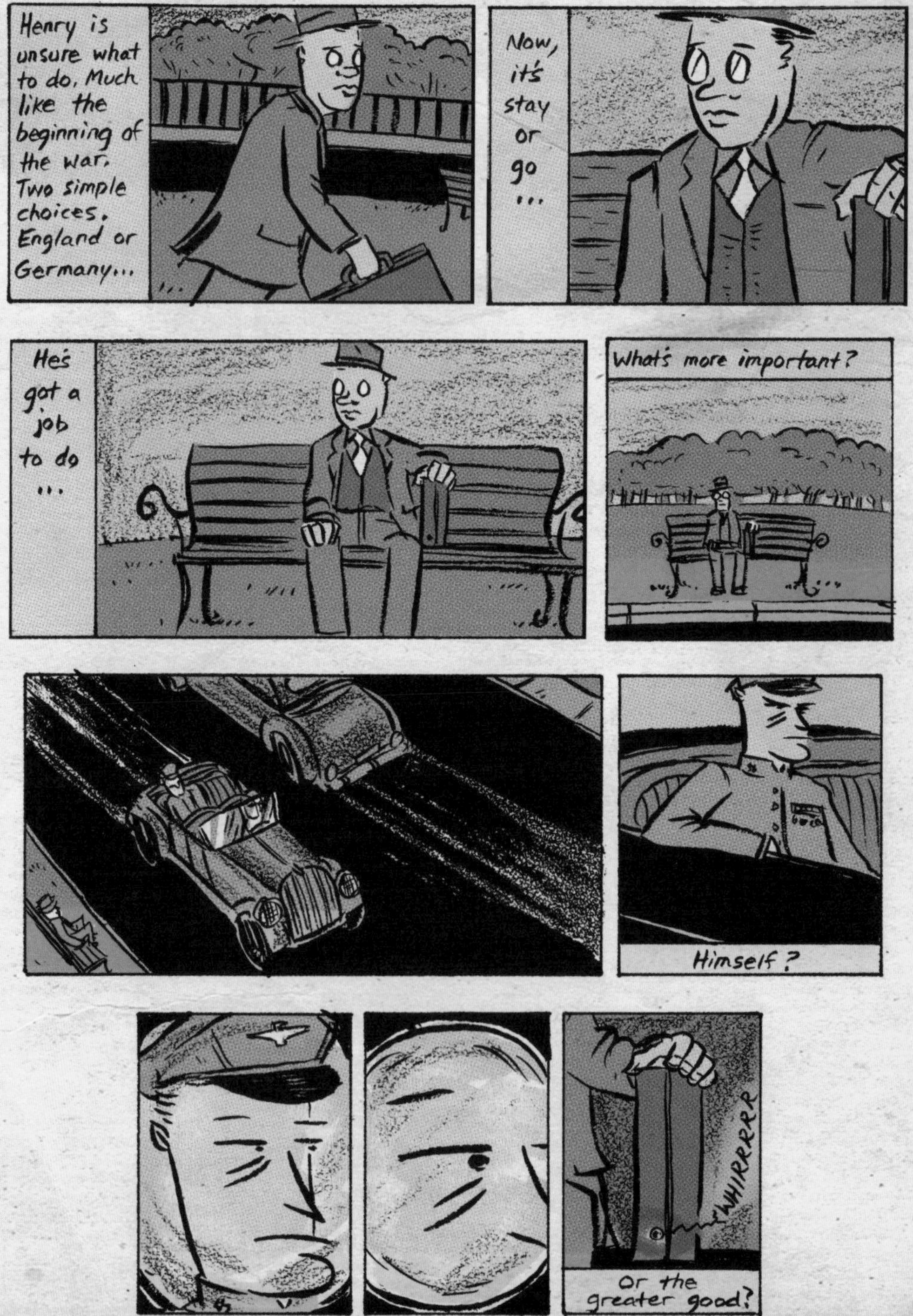

Henry is unsure what to do. Much like the beginning of the war. Two simple choices. England or Germany...
Now, it's stay or go...
He's got a job to do...
What's more important?
Himself?
WHIRRRRR
Or the greater good?

6. SUPER SPY by M. Kindt

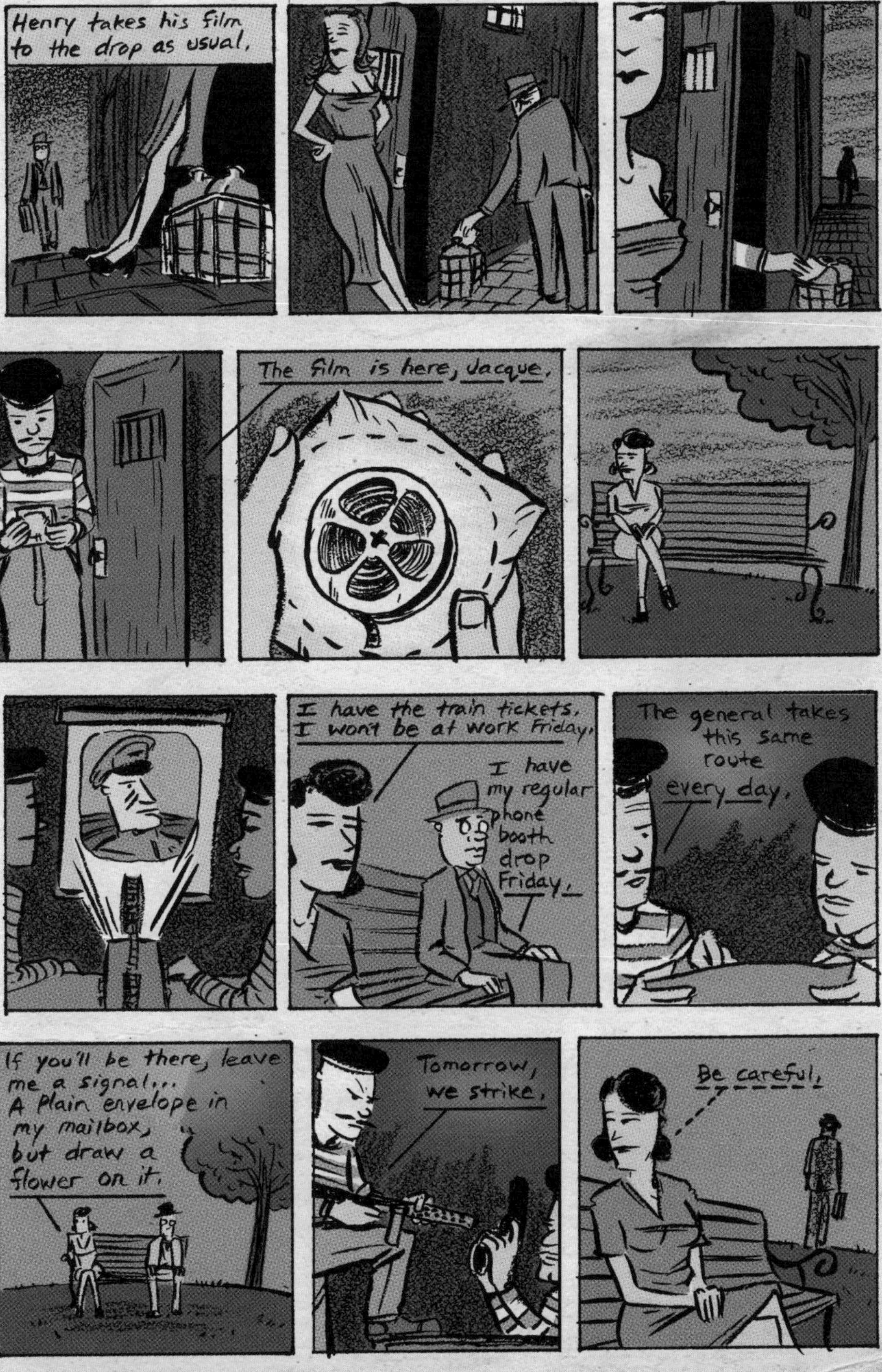

Henry takes his film to the drop as usual.
The film is here, Jacque.
I have the train tickets. I won't be at work Friday.
I have my regular phone booth drop Friday.
The general takes this same route every day.
If you'll be there, leave me a signal... A plain envelope in my mailbox, but draw a flower on it.
Tomorrow, we strike.
Be careful.

7. SUPER SPY by M. Kindt

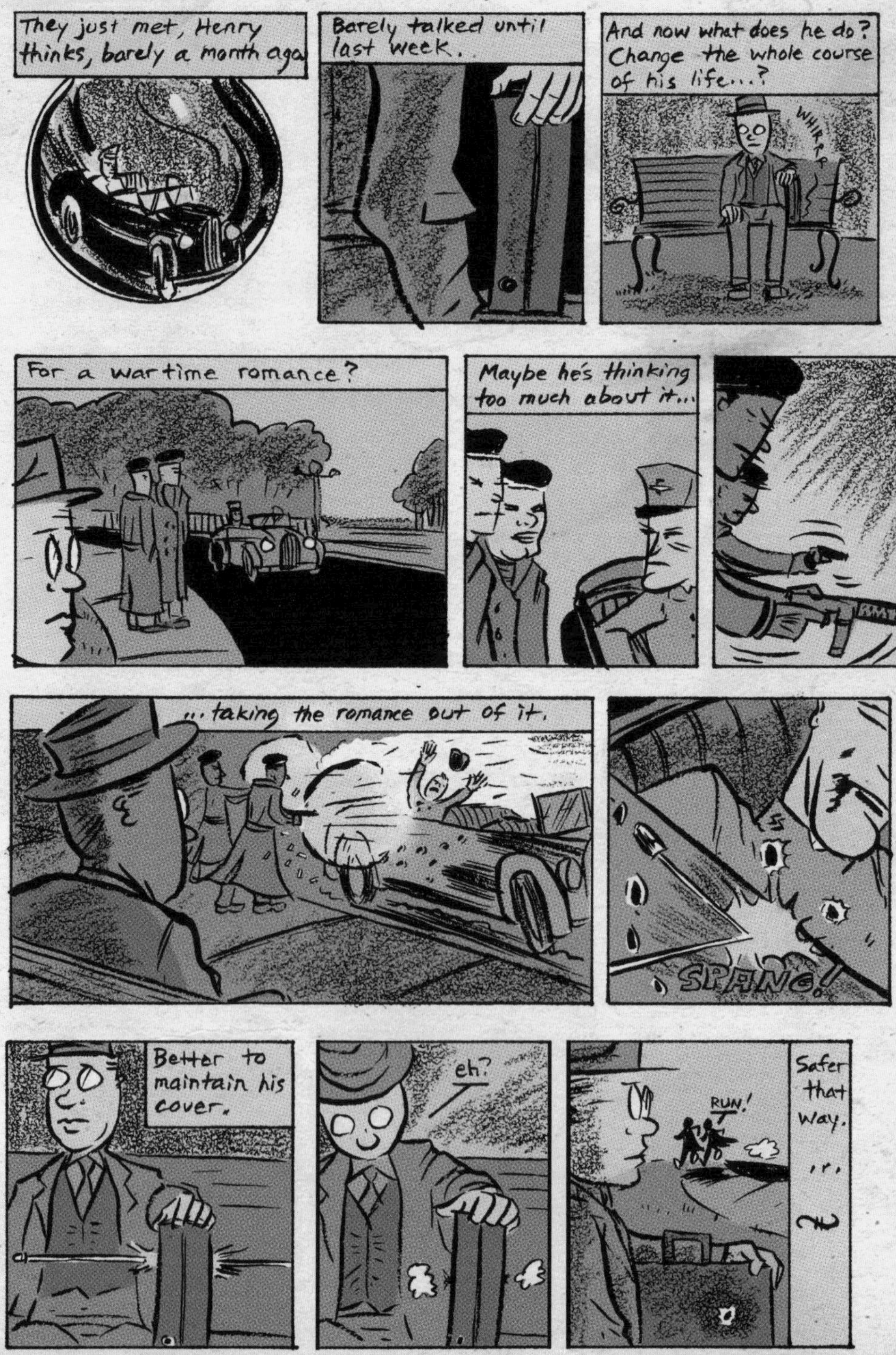
They just met, Henry thinks, barely a month ago
Barely talked until last week.
And now what does he do? Change the whole course of his life...?
WHIRRR
For a wartime romance?
Maybe he's thinking too much about it...
...taking the romance out of it.
SPANG!
Better to maintain his cover.
eh?
RUN!
Safer that way.

8. SUPER SPY by M. Kindt

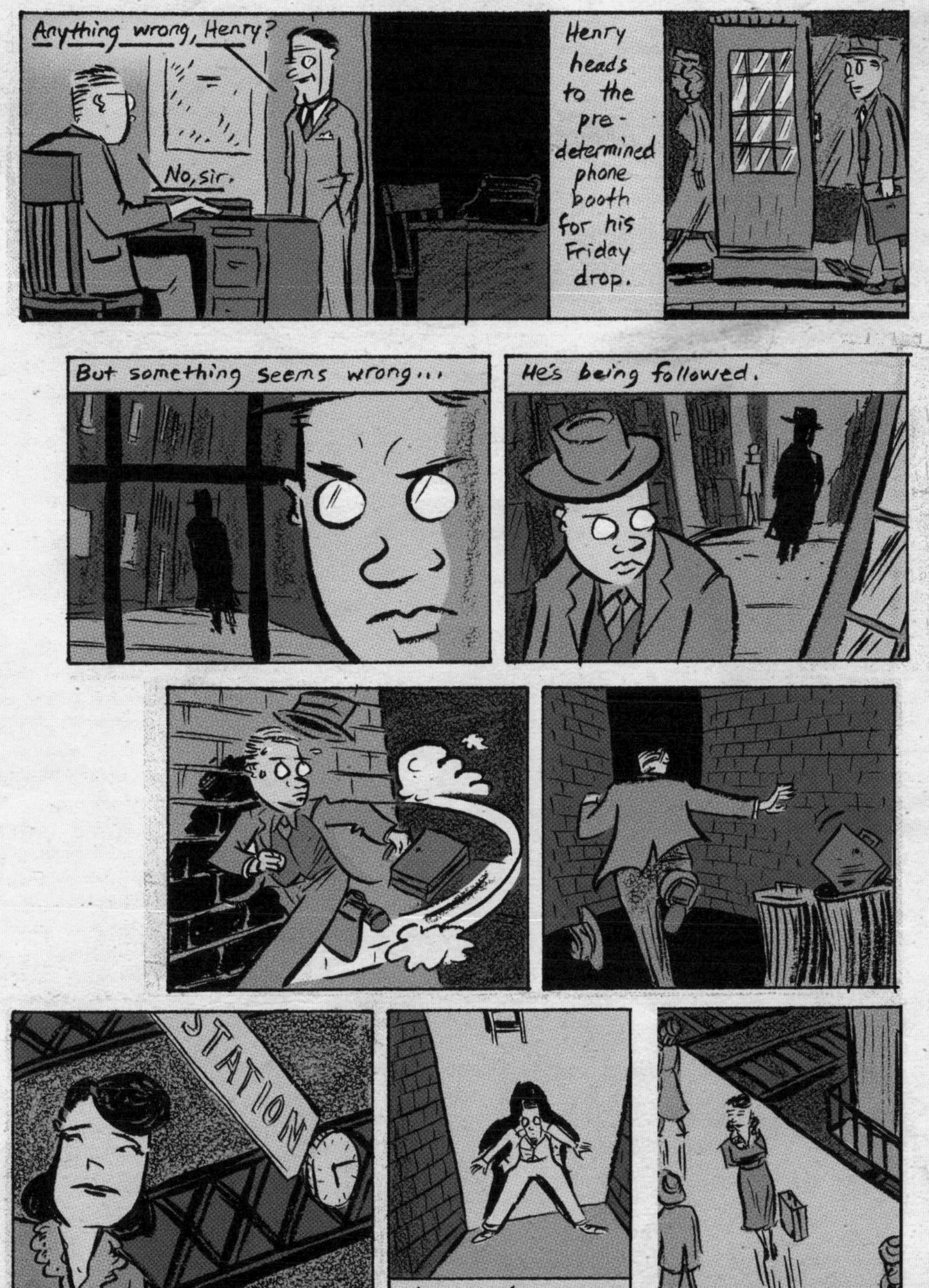

Anything wrong, Henry?
No, sir.
Henry heads to the pre-determined phone booth for his Friday drop.
But something seems wrong...
He's being followed.
STATION
A cul-de-sac..

9. SUPER SPY by M. Kindt

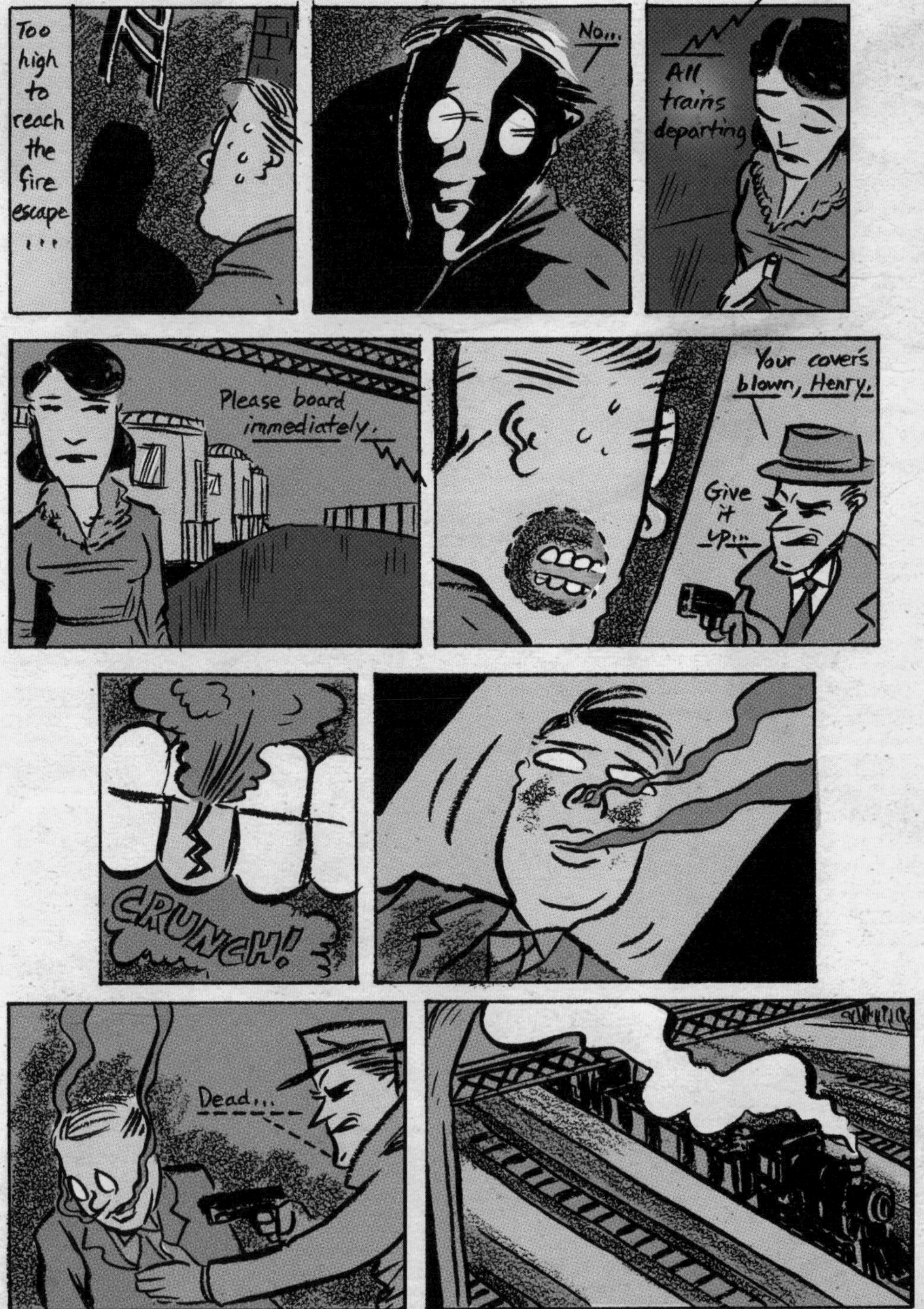

Too high to reach the fire escape...
No...
All trains departing
Please board immediately.
Your cover's blown, Henry.
Give it up...
CRUNCH!
Dead...

10. SUPER SPY by M. Kindt

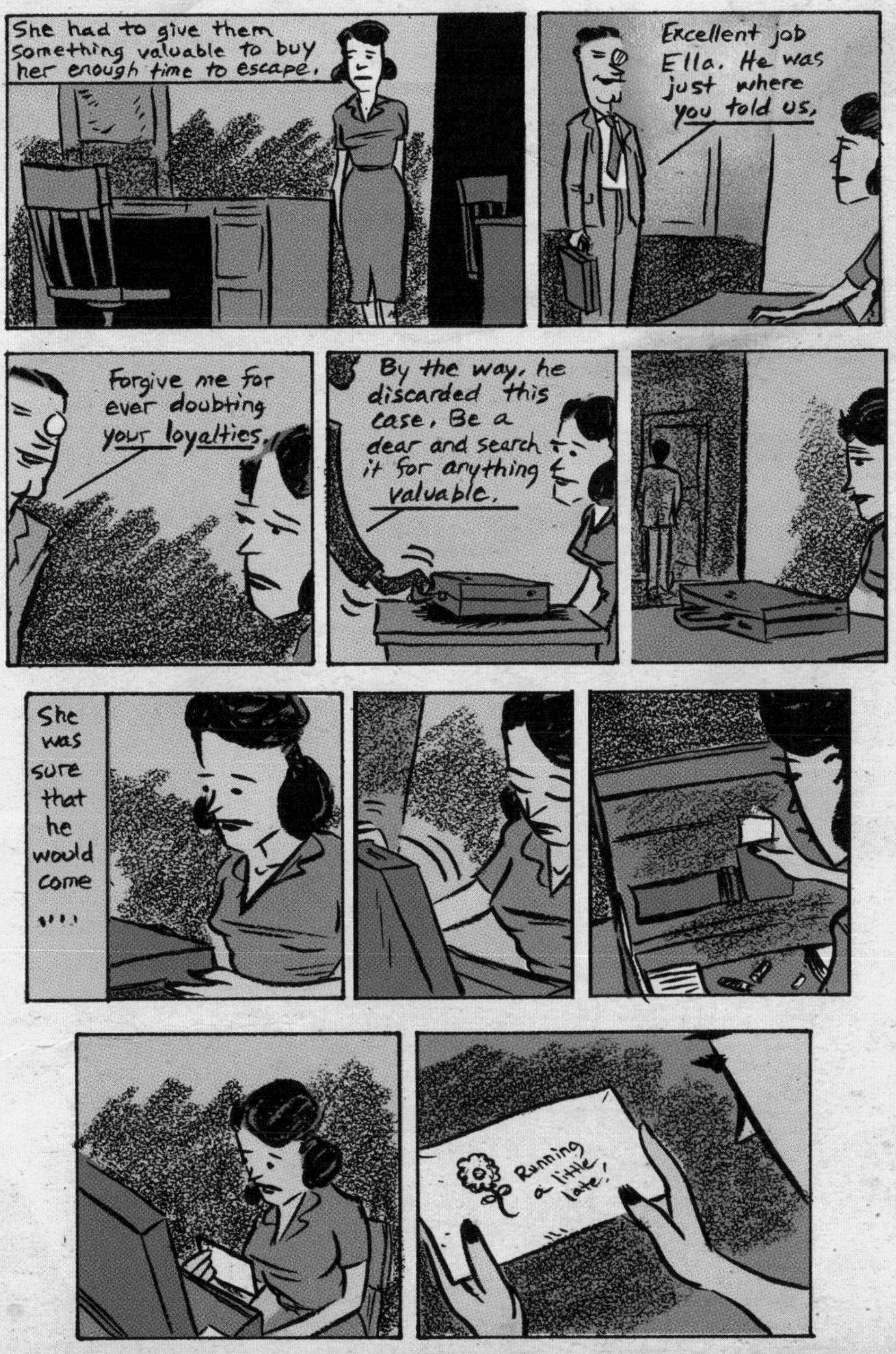
She had to give them something valuable to buy her enough time to escape.
Excellent job Ella. He was just where you told us.
Forgive me for ever doubting your loyalties.
By the way, he discarded this case. Be a dear and search it for anything valuable.
She was sure that he would come ....
Running a little late!

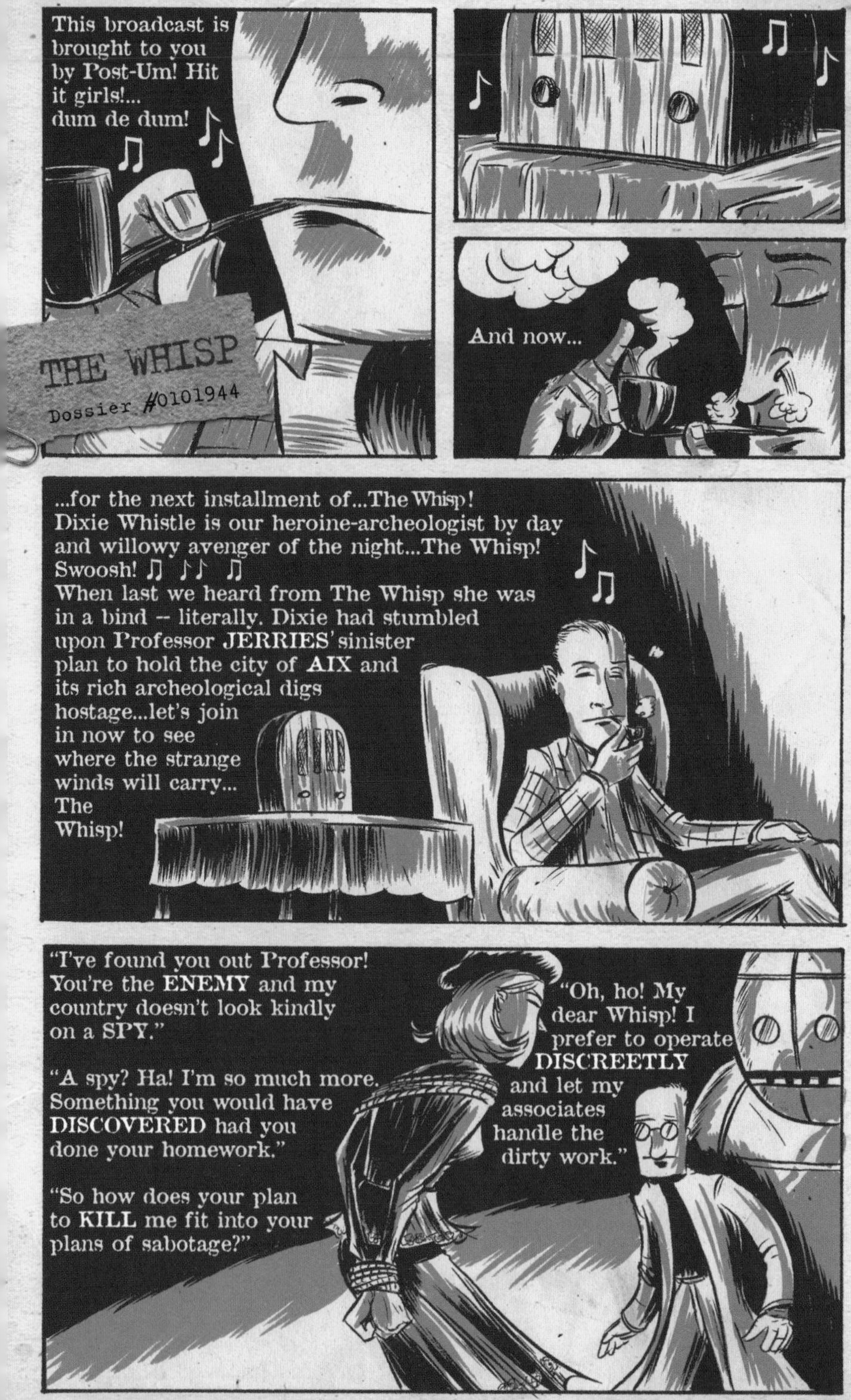
This broadcast is brought to you by Post-Um! Hit it girls!... dum de dum!
THE WHISP
Dossier #0101944
And now...
...for the next installment of...The Whisp! Dixie Whistle is our heroine-archeologist by day and willowy avenger of the night...The Whisp! Swoosh!
When last we heard from The Whisp she was in a bind -- literally. Dixie had stumbled upon Professor JERRIES' sinister plan to hold the city of AIX and its rich archeological digs hostage...let's join in now to see where the strange winds will carry... The Whisp!
"I've found you out Professor! You're the ENEMY and my country doesn't look kindly on a SPY."
"A spy? Ha! I'm so much more. Something you would have DISCOVERED had you done your homework."
"So how does your plan to KILL me fit into your plans of sabotage?"
"Oh, ho! My dear Whisp! I prefer to operate DISCREETLY and let my associates handle the dirty work."

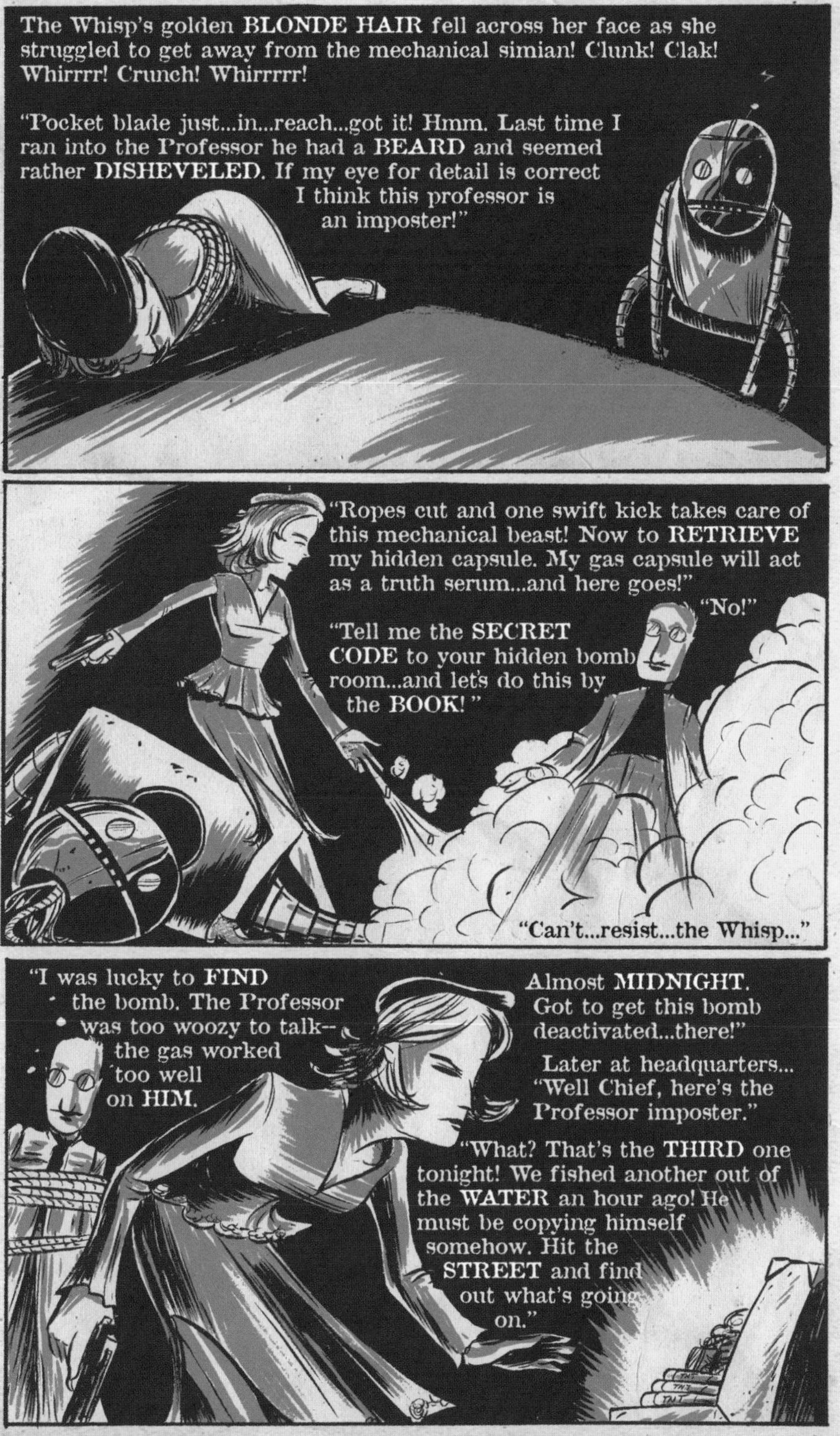

The Whisp's golden BLONDE HAIR fell across her face as she struggled to get away from the mechanical simian! Clunk! Clak! Whirrrr! Crunch! Whirrrrr!
"Pocket blade just...in...reach...got it! Hmm. Last time I ran into the Professor he had a BEARD and seemed rather DISHEVELED. If my eye for detail is correct I think this professor is an imposter!"
"Ropes cut and one swift kick takes care of this mechanical beast! Now to RETRIEVE my hidden capsule. My gas capsule will act as a truth serum...and here goes!"
"No!"
"Tell me the SECRET CODE to your hidden bomb room...and let's do this by the BOOK!"
"Can't...resist...the Whisp..."
"I was lucky to FIND the bomb. The Professor was too woozy to talk--the gas worked too well on HIM.
Almost MIDNIGHT. Got to get this bomb deactivated...there!"
Later at headquarters... "Well Chief, here's the Professor imposter."
"What? That's the THIRD one tonight! We fished another out of the WATER an hour ago! He must be copying himself somehow. Hit the STREET and find out what's going on."
TNT
TNT
TNT

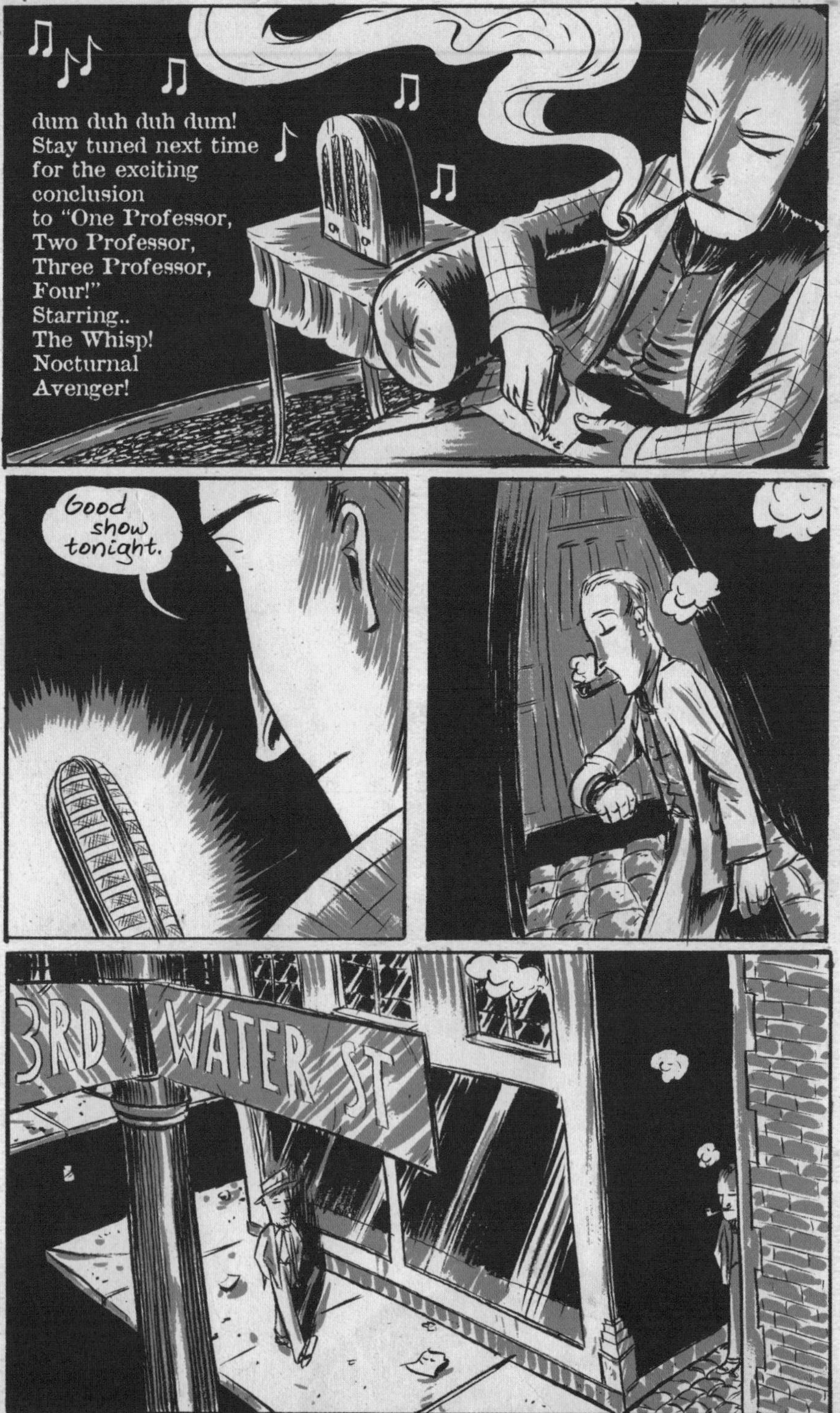
dum duh duh dum!
Stay tuned next time for the exciting conclusion to "One Professor, Two Professor, Three Professor, Four!" Starring.. The Whisp! Nocturnal Avenger!
Good show tonight.
3RD
WATER ST

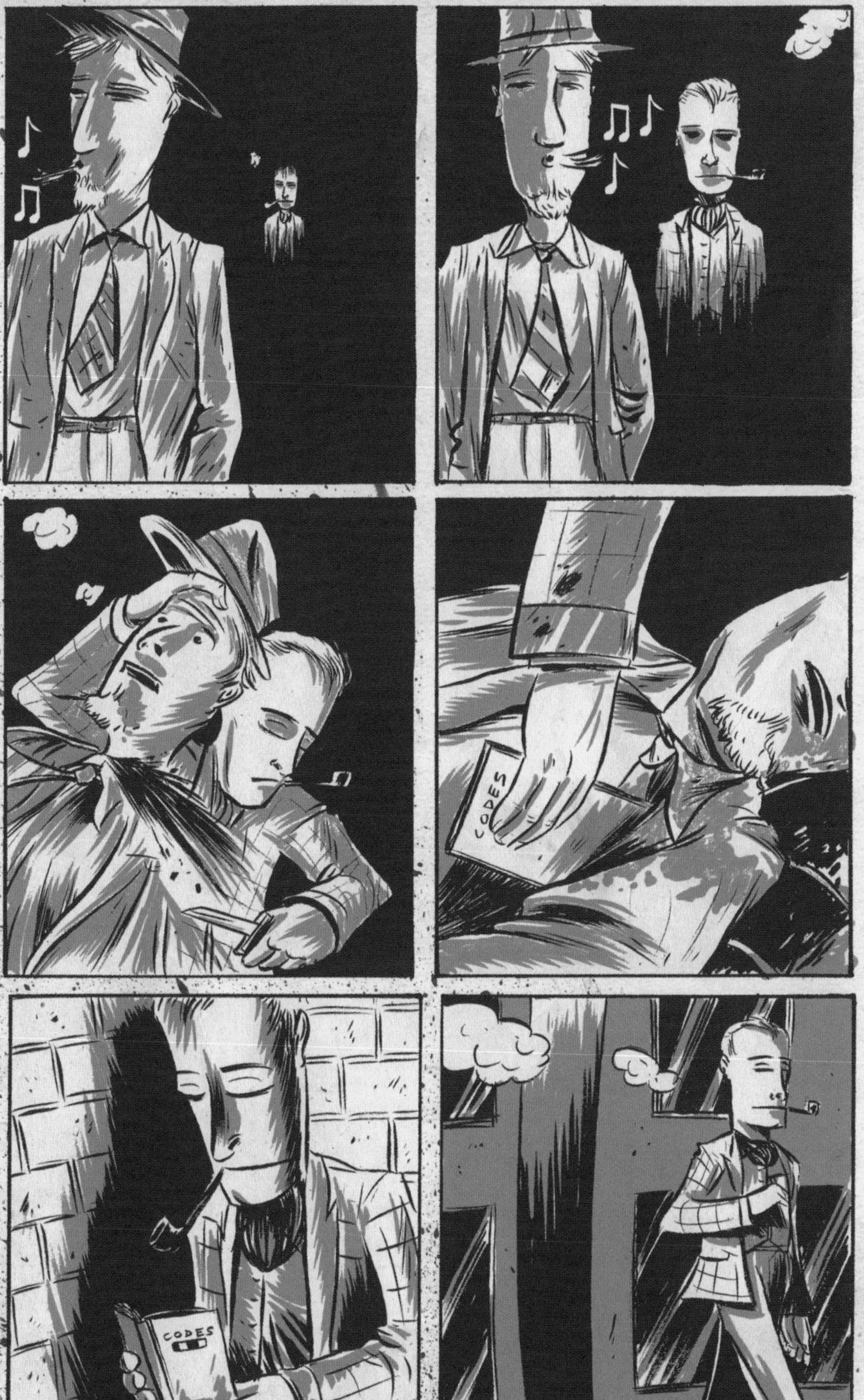
CODES
CODES

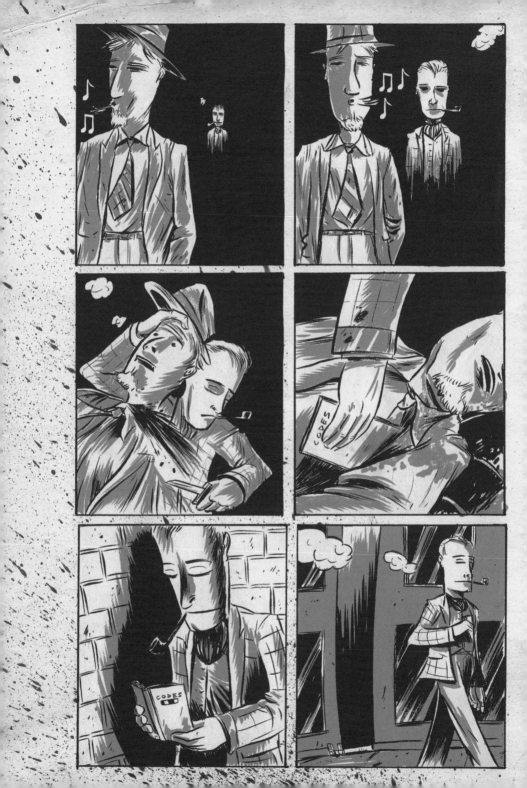

ALL IN THE GAME

Dossier #0181944

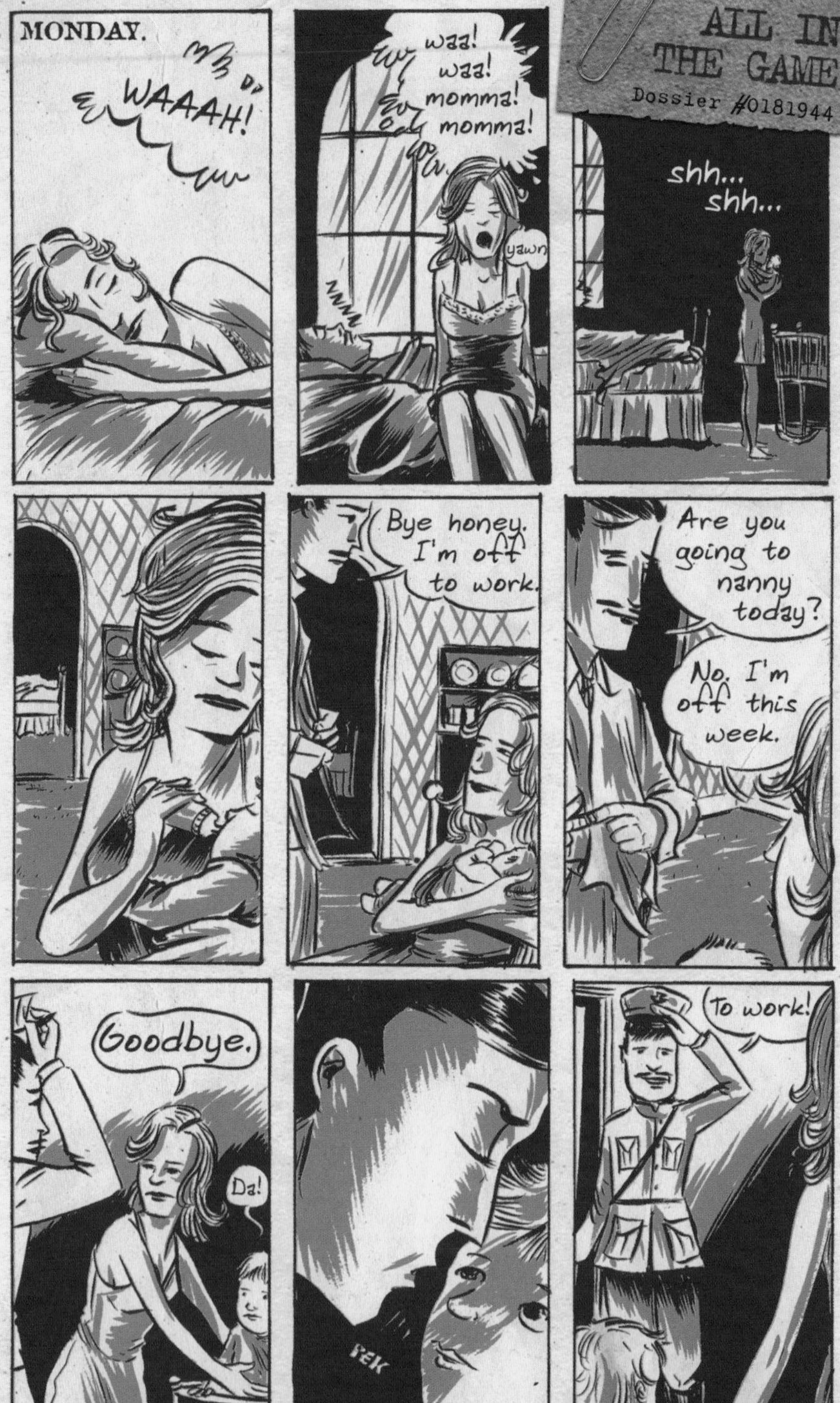
MONDAY.
WAAAH!
waa! waa! momma! momma!
yawn
NNN
shh... shh...
Bye honey. I'm off to work.
Are you going to nanny today?
No. I'm off this week.
Goodbye.
Da!
PEK
To work!

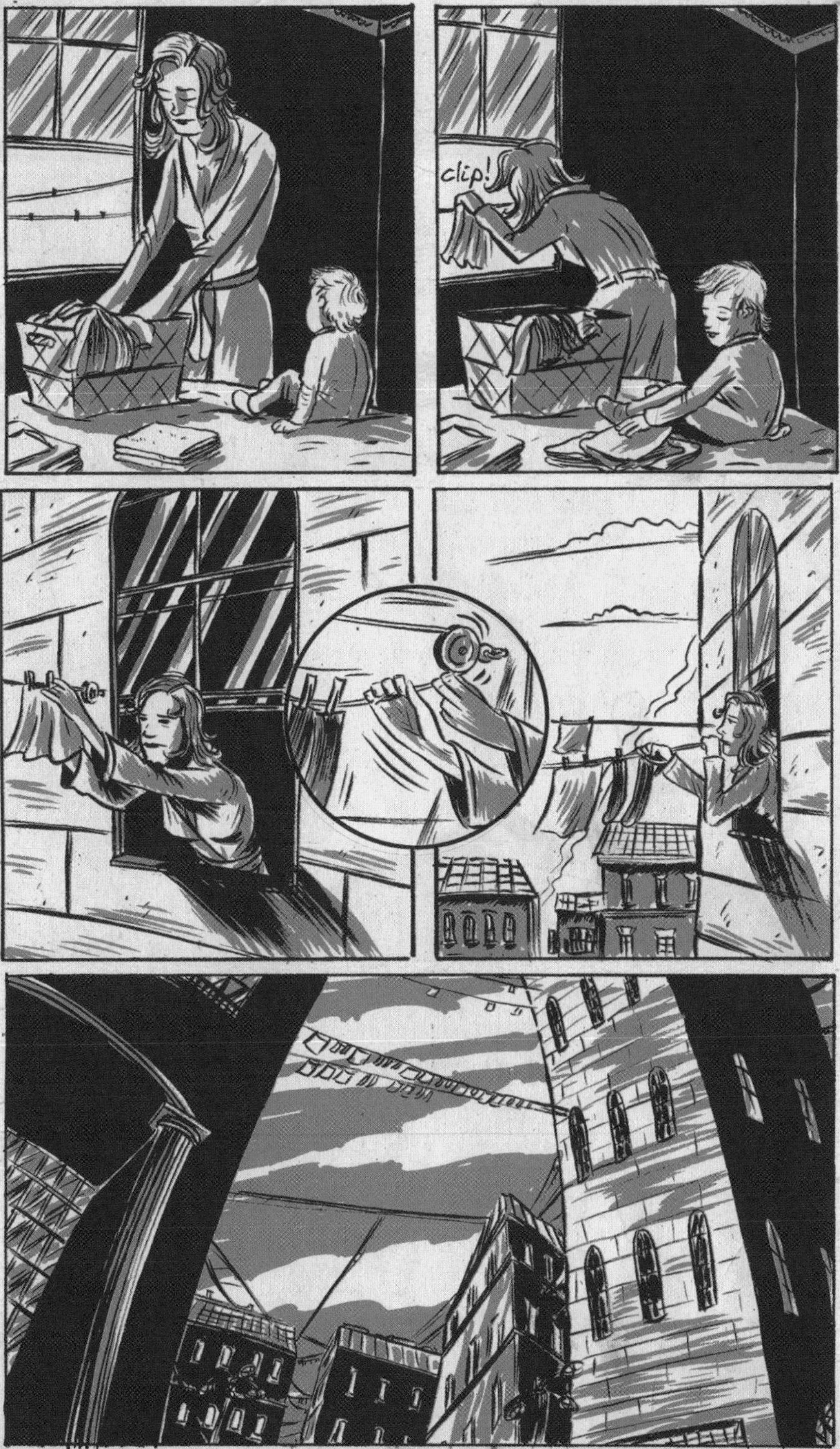
clip!

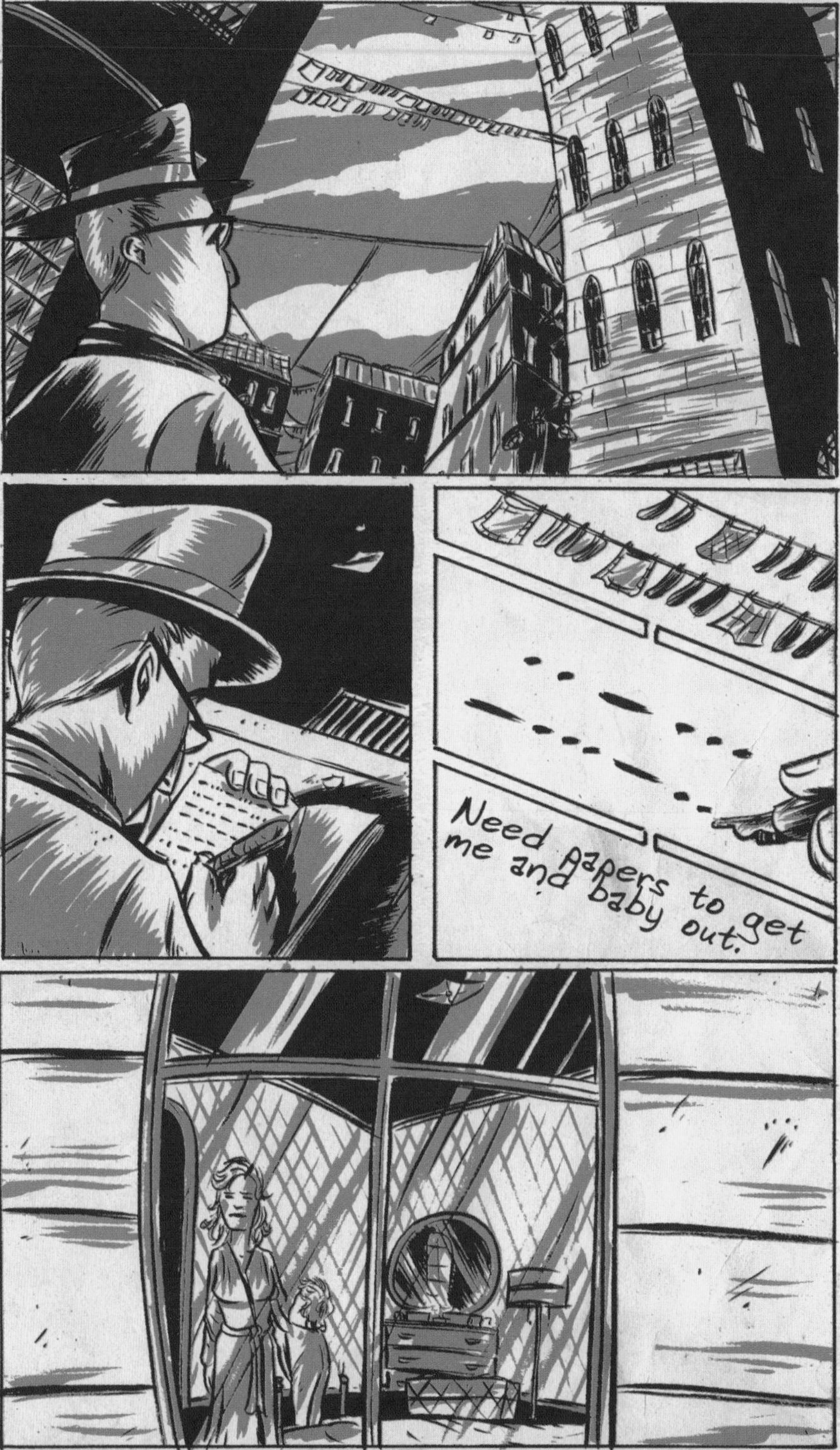
Need papers to get
me and baby out.

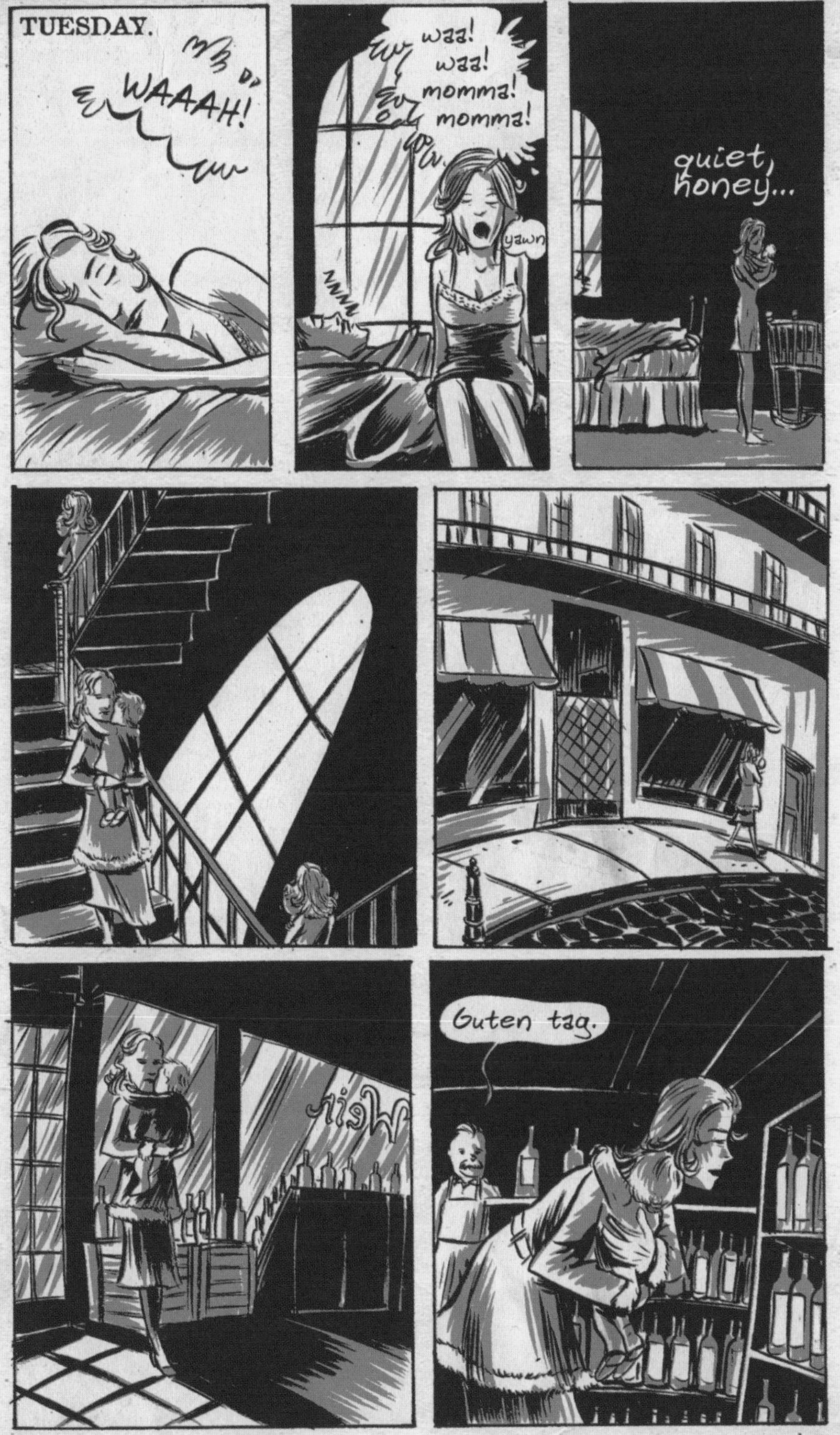

TUESDAY.
WAAAH!
waa! waa! momma! momma!
yawn
quiet, honey...
Guten tag.

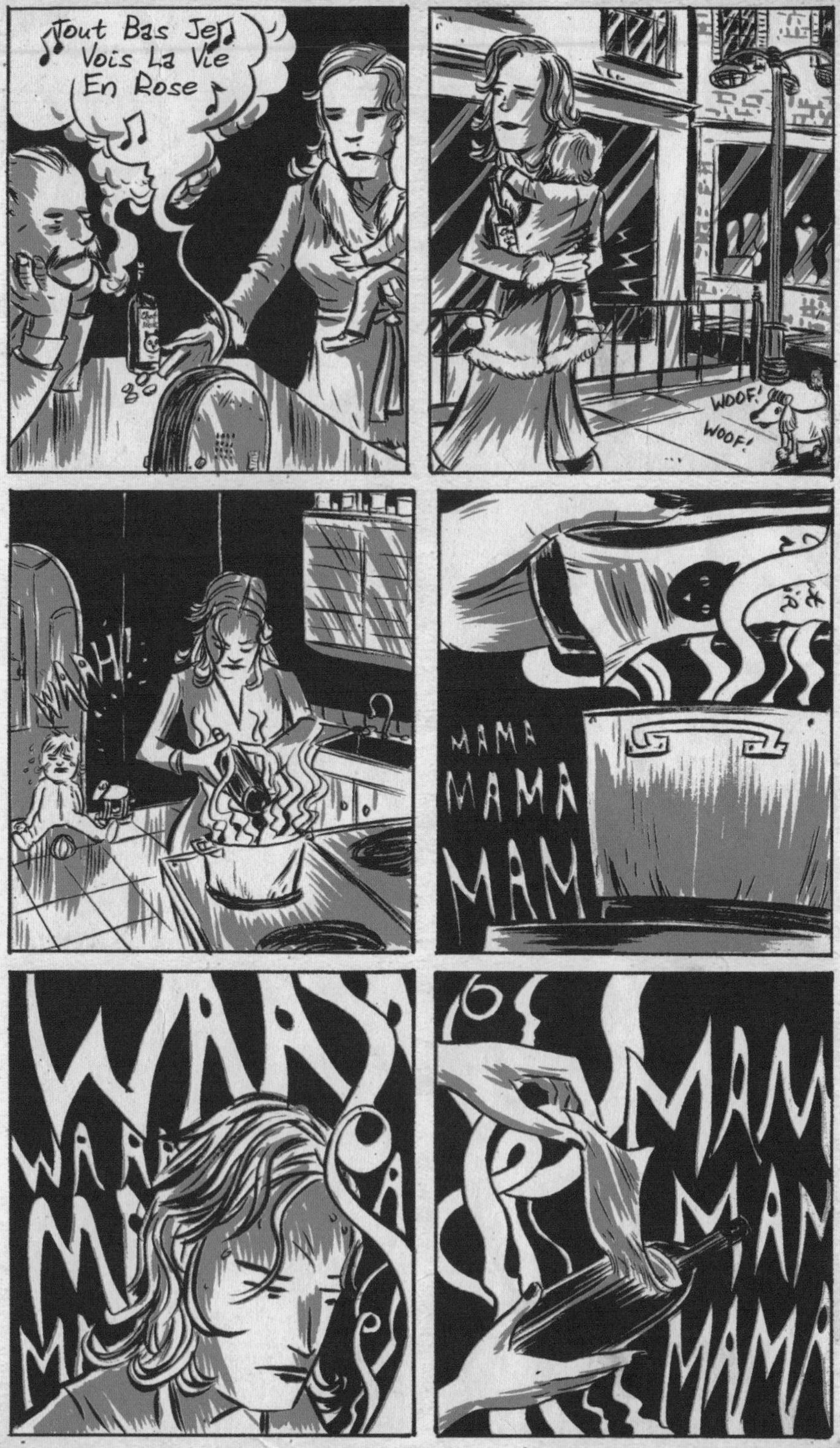
Tout Bas Je Vois La Vie En Rose
WOOF! WOOF!
WAAH!
MAMA MAMA MAM
MAM MAM MAMA

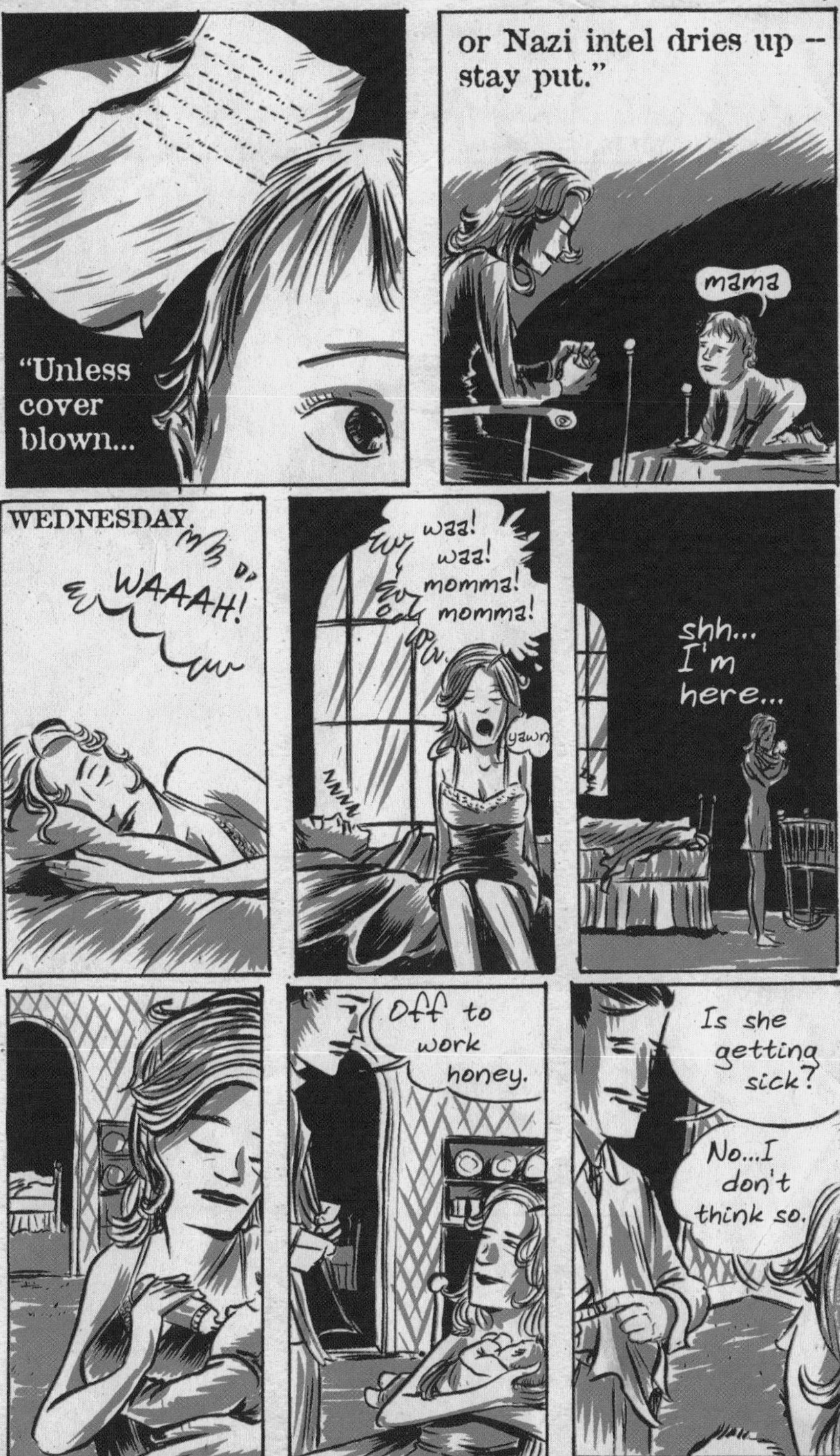
"Unless
cover
blown...
or Nazi intel dries up --
stay put."
mama
WEDNESDAY.
WAAAH!
waa!
waa!
momma!
momma!
yawn
shh...
I'm
here...
Off to
work
honey.
Is she
getting
sick?
No...I
don't
think so.

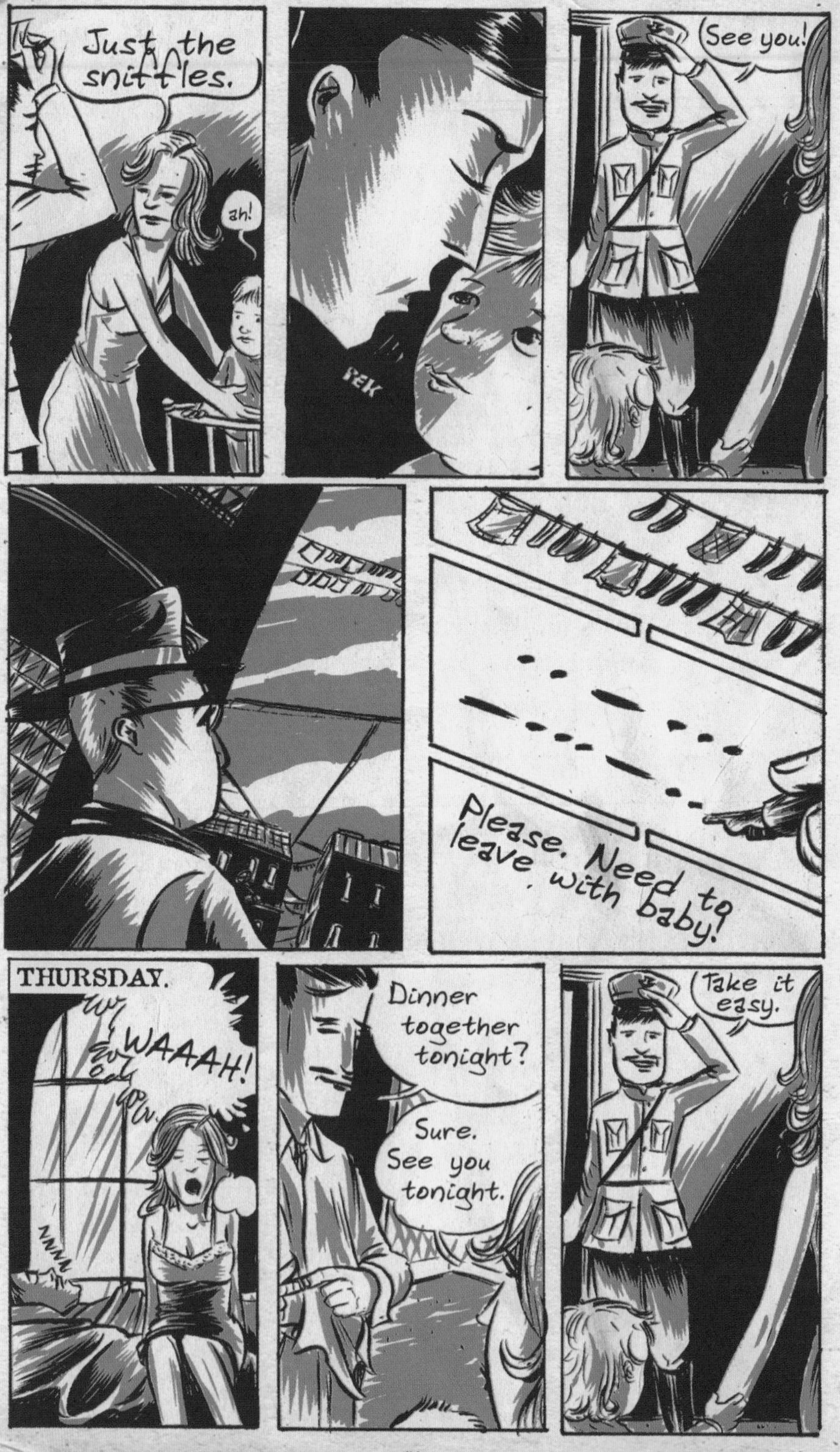
Just the sniffles.
ah!
PEK
See you!
Please. Need to leave with baby!
THURSDAY.
WAAAH!
Dinner together tonight?
Sure. See you tonight.
Take it easy.

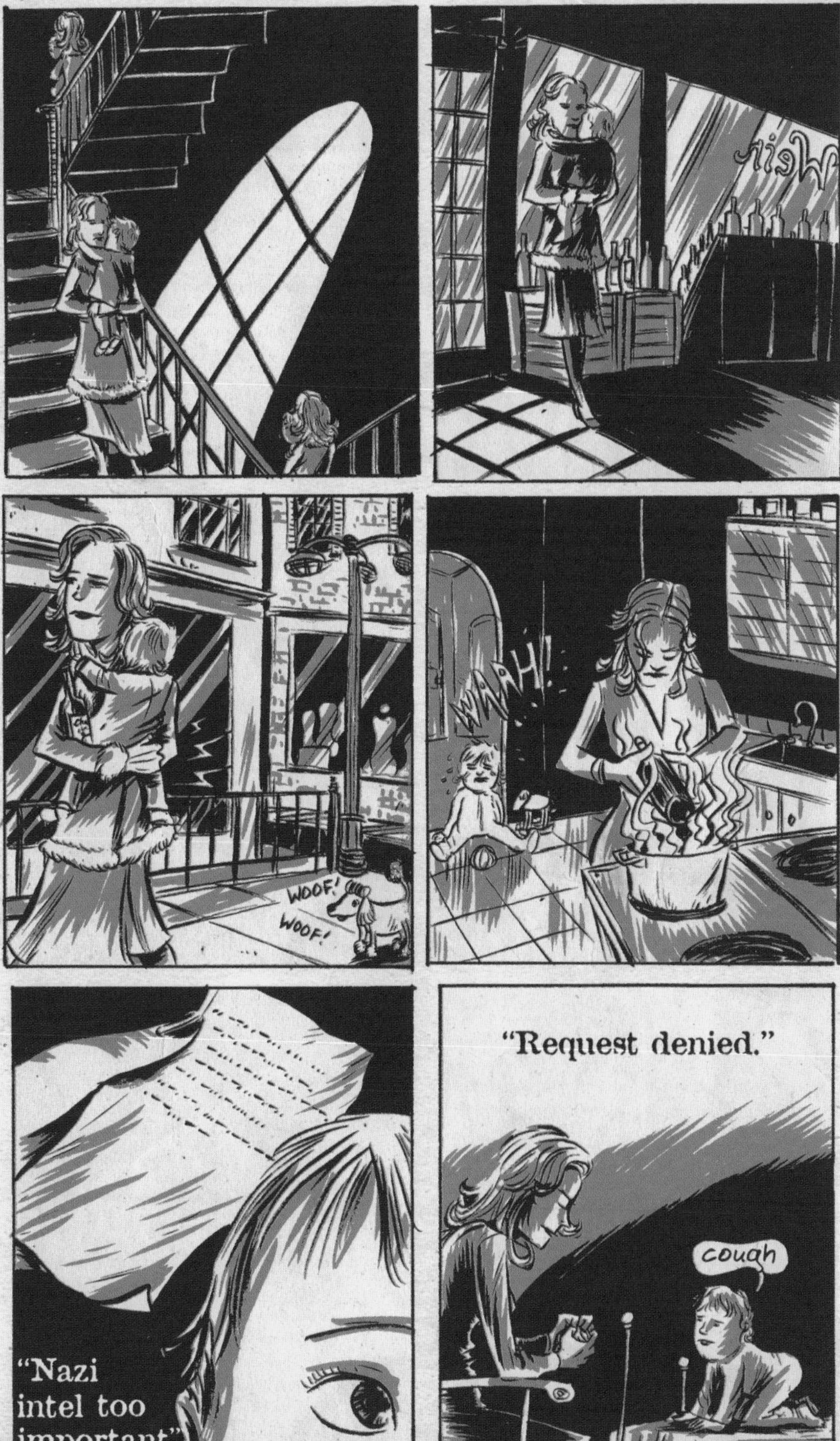
WOOF!
WOOF!
WAAH!
"Nazi intel too important."
"Request denied."
cough

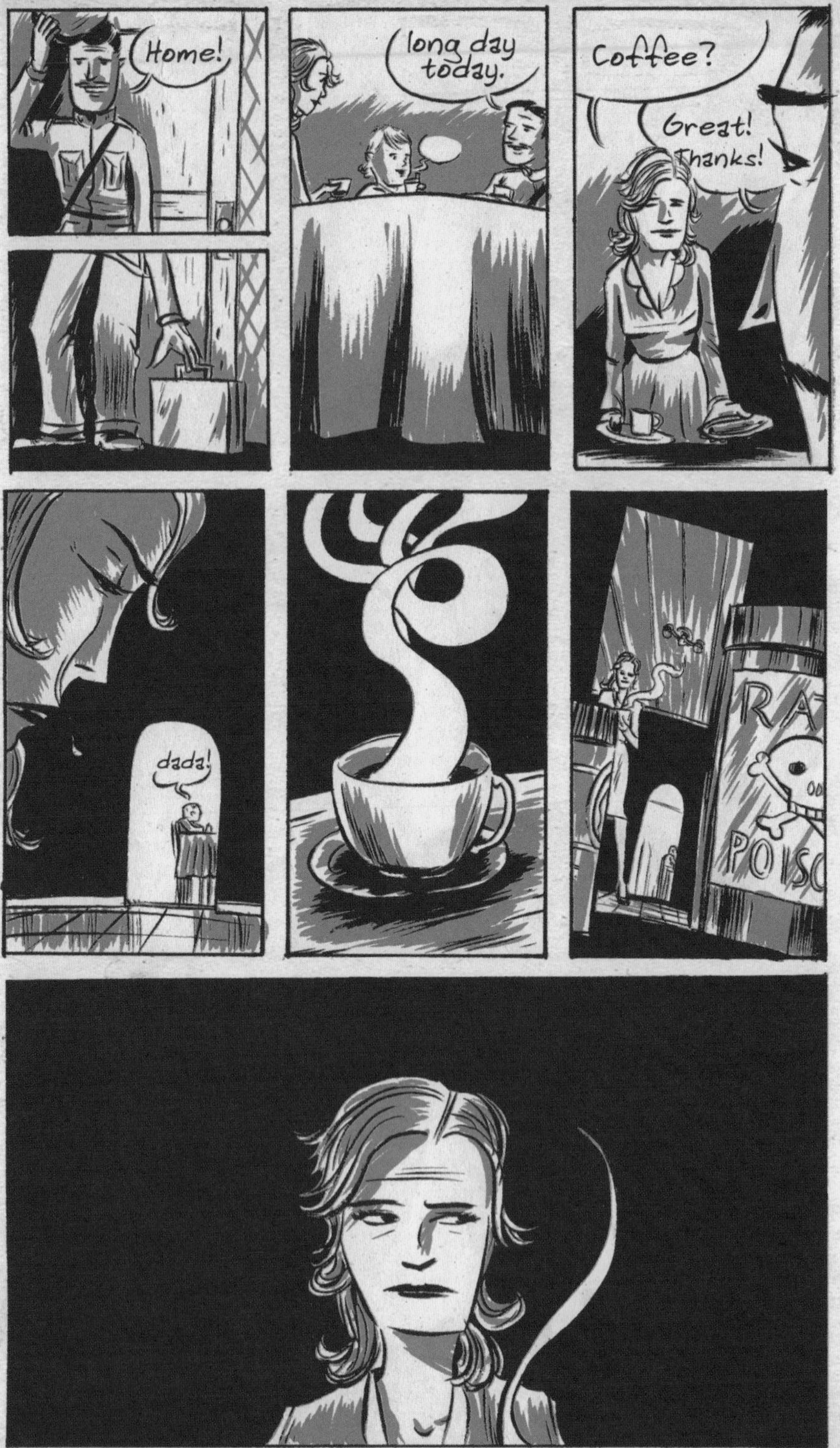
Home!
long day today.
Coffee?
Great! Thanks!
dada!

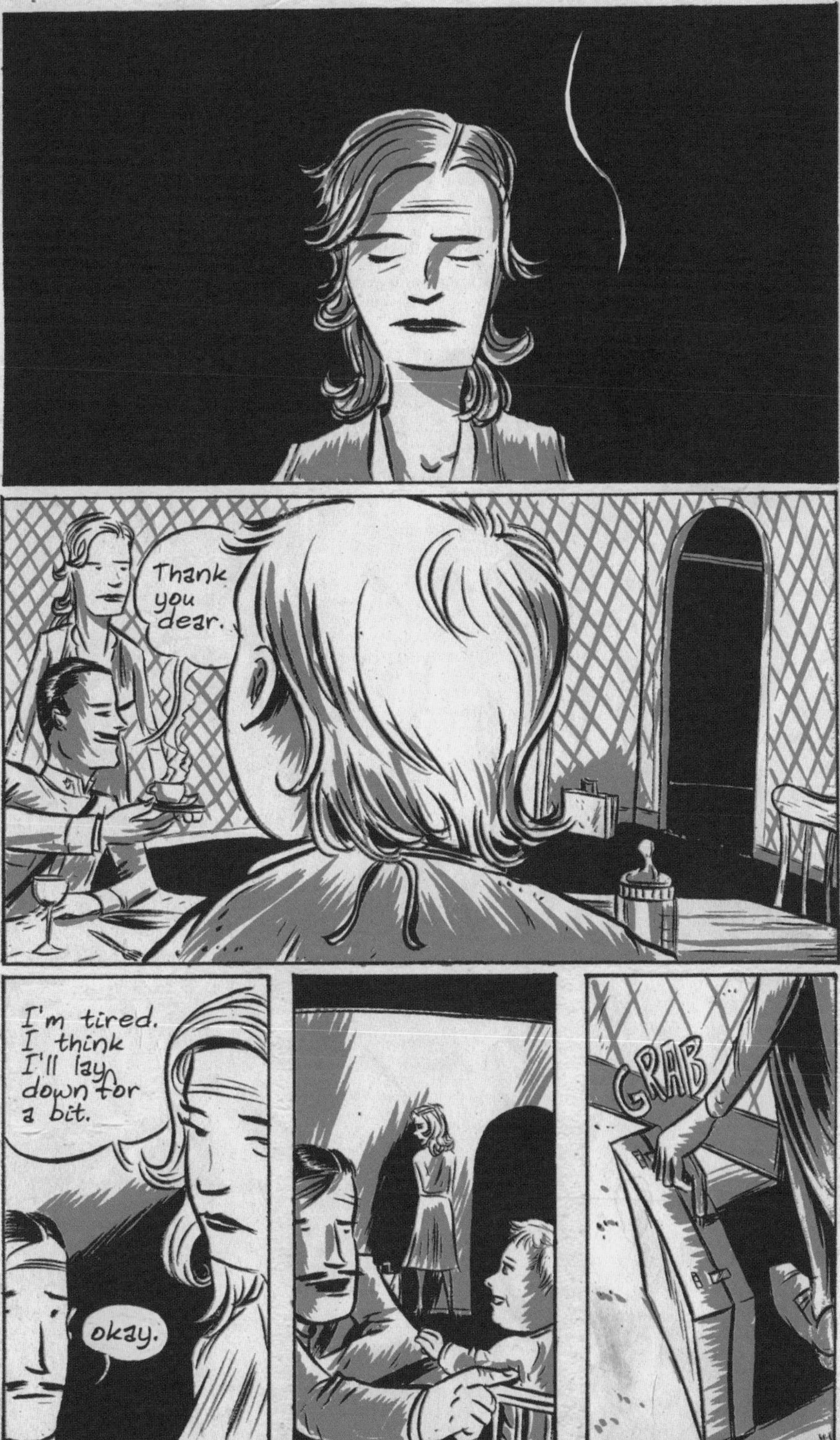
Thank you dear.
I'm tired. I think I'll lay down for a bit.
okay.
GRAB

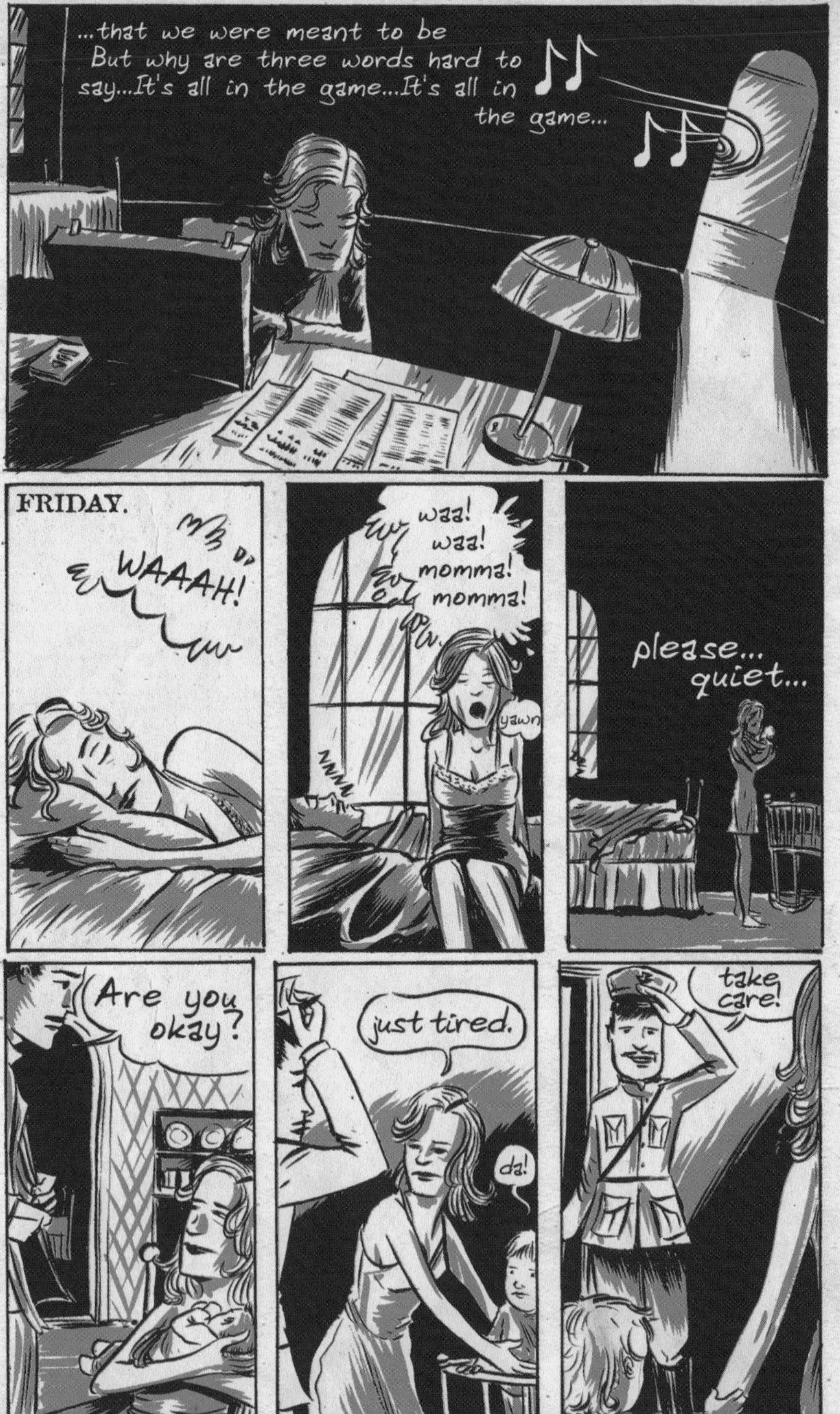
...that we were meant to be But why are three words hard to say...It's all in the game...It's all in the game...
FRIDAY.
WAAAH!
waa! waa! momma! momma!
yawn
please... quiet...
Are you okay?
just tired.
da!
take care!

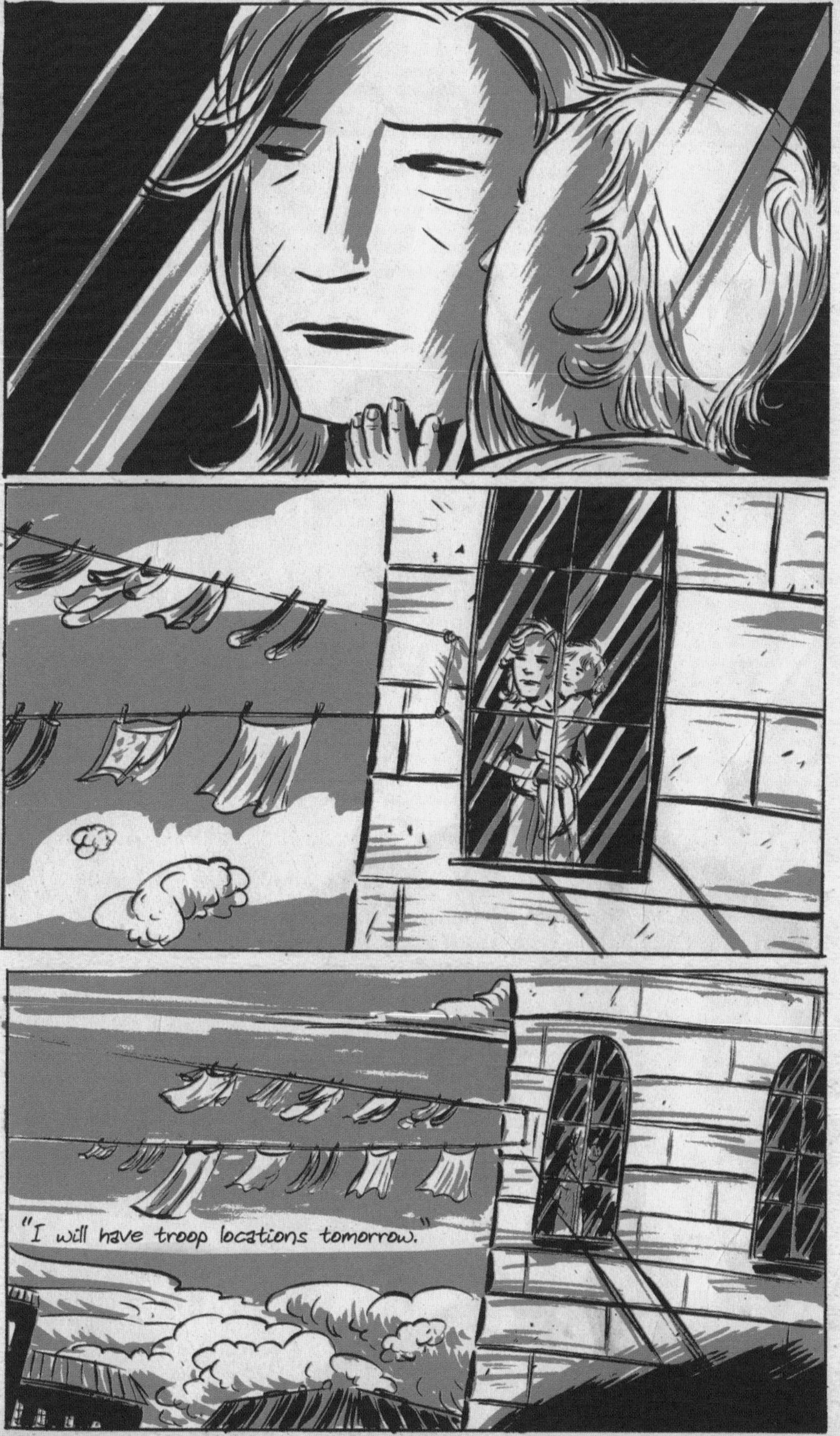
"I will have troop locations tomorrow."

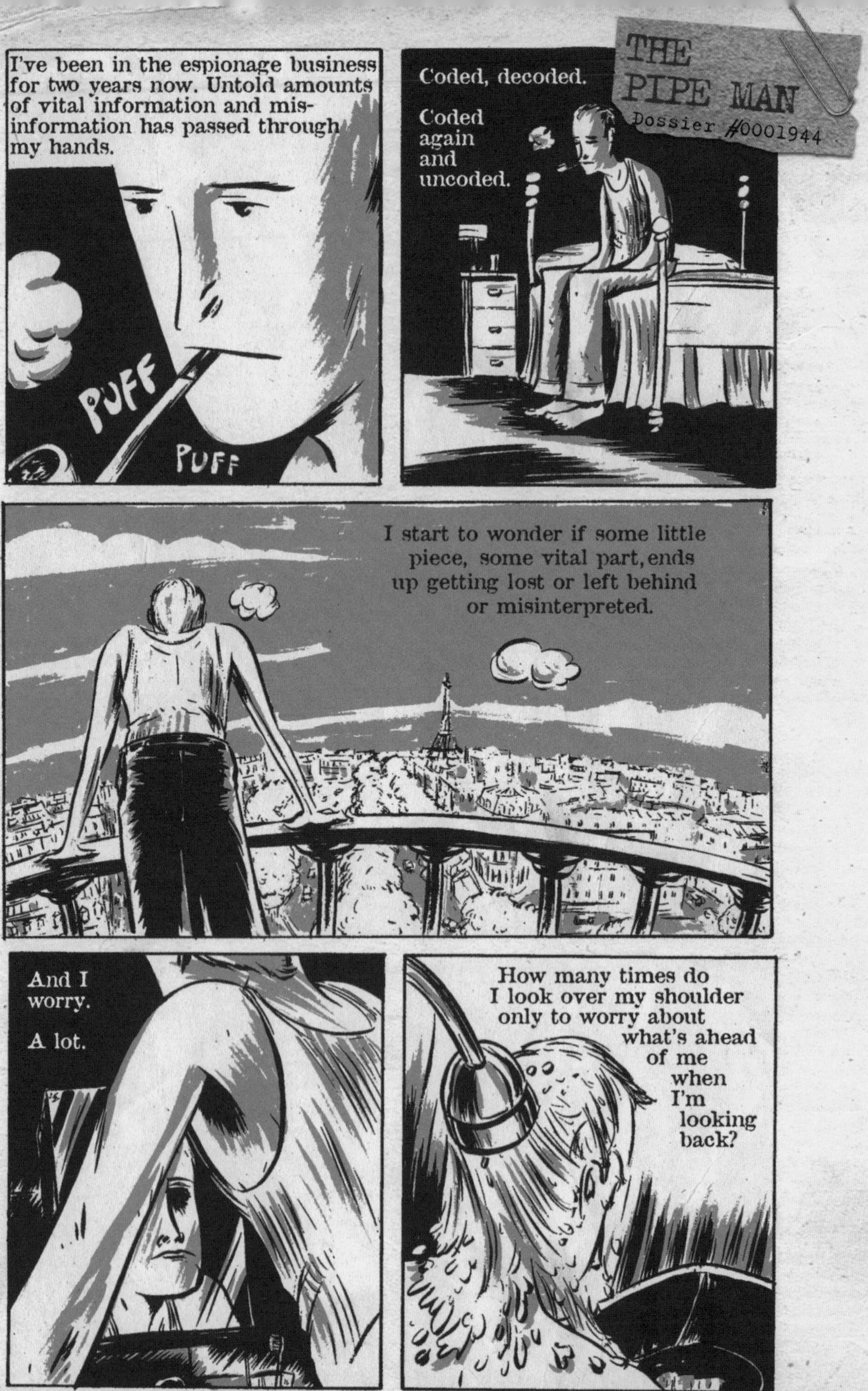
THE PIPE MAN
Dossier #0001944
I've been in the espionage business for two years now. Untold amounts of vital information and mis-information has passed through my hands.
PUFF
PUFF
Coded, decoded.
Coded again and uncoded.
I start to wonder if some little piece, some vital part, ends up getting lost or left behind or misinterpreted.
And I worry.
A lot.
How many times do I look over my shoulder only to worry about what's ahead of me when I'm looking back?

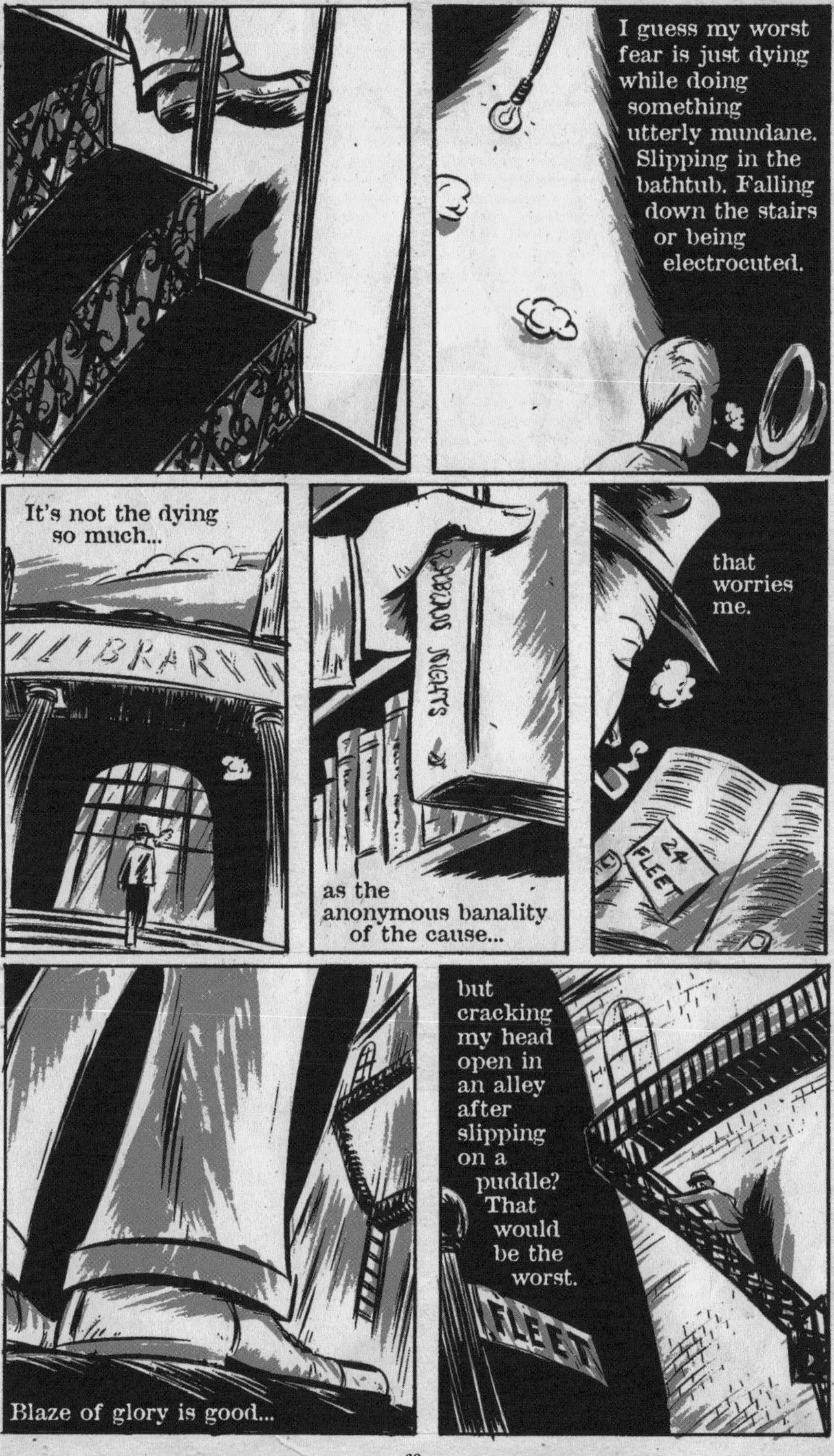

I guess my worst fear is just dying while doing something utterly mundane. Slipping in the bathtub. Falling down the stairs or being electrocuted.
It's not the dying so much...
LIBRARY
as the anonymous banality of the cause...
that worries me.
24 FLEET
Blaze of glory is good...
but cracking my head open in an alley after slipping on a puddle? That would be the worst.
FLEET

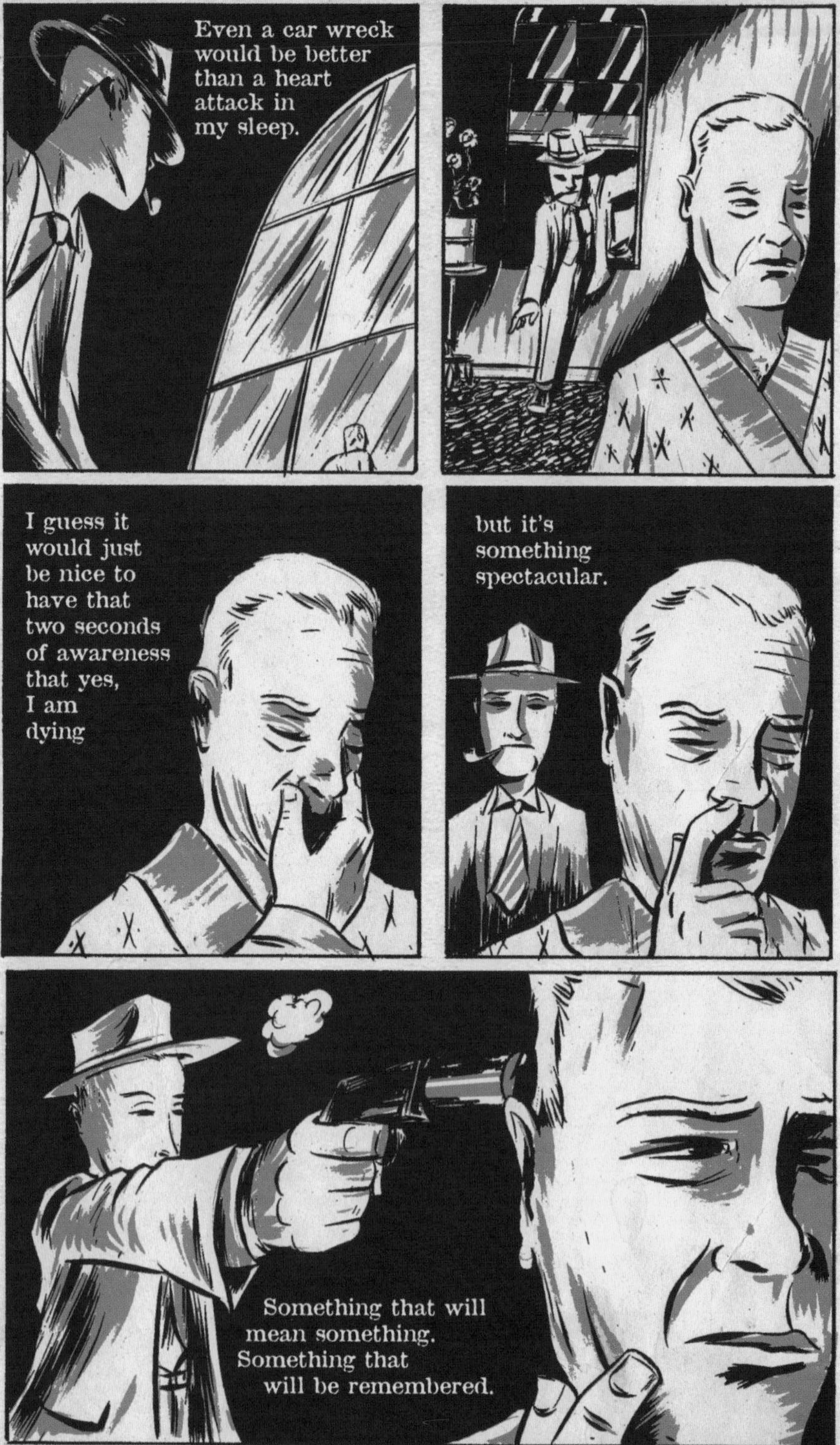
Even a car wreck would be better than a heart attack in my sleep.
I guess it would just be nice to have that two seconds of awareness that yes, I am dying
but it's something spectacular.
Something that will mean something. Something that will be remembered.

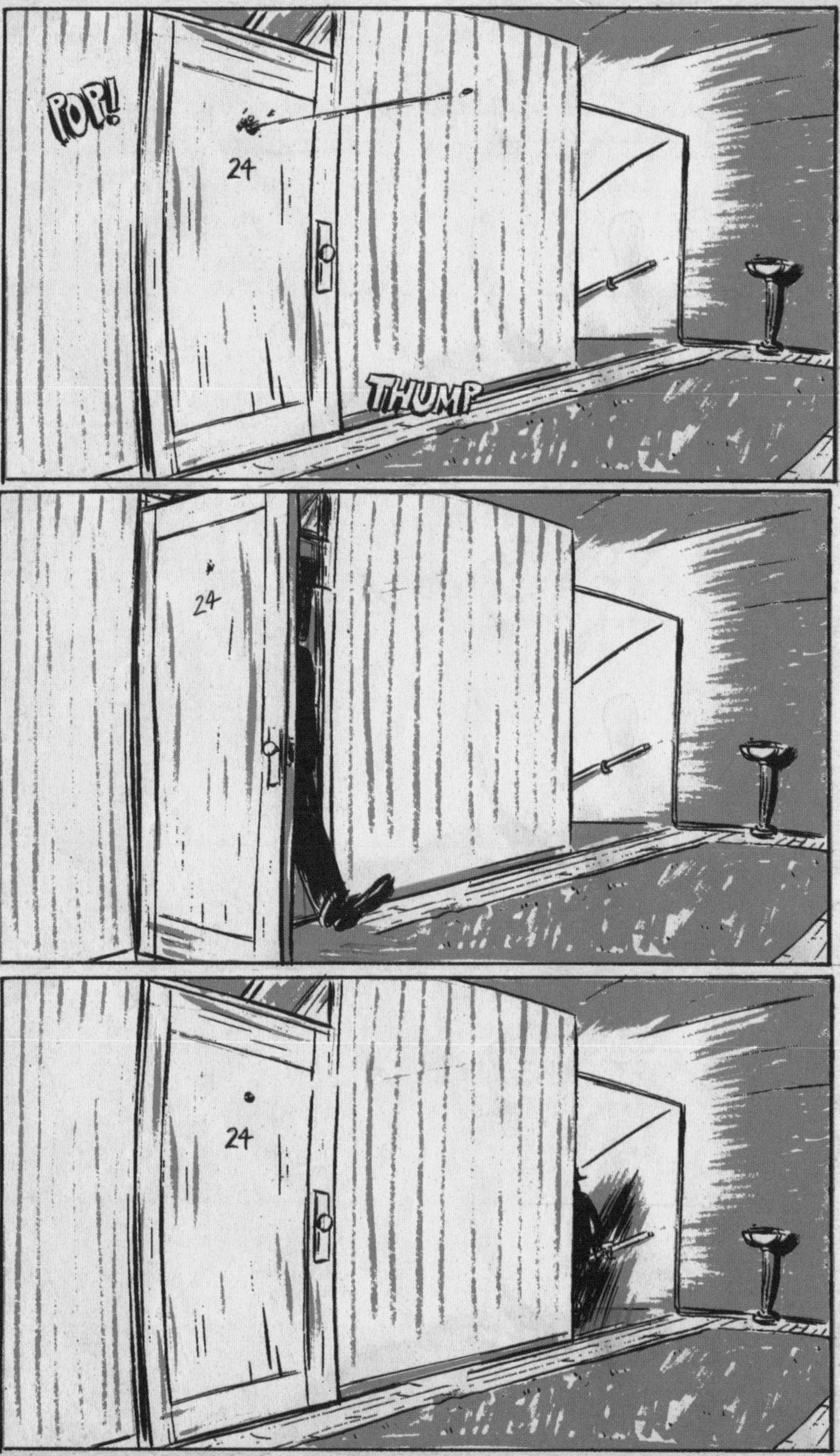
POP!
24
THUMP
24
24

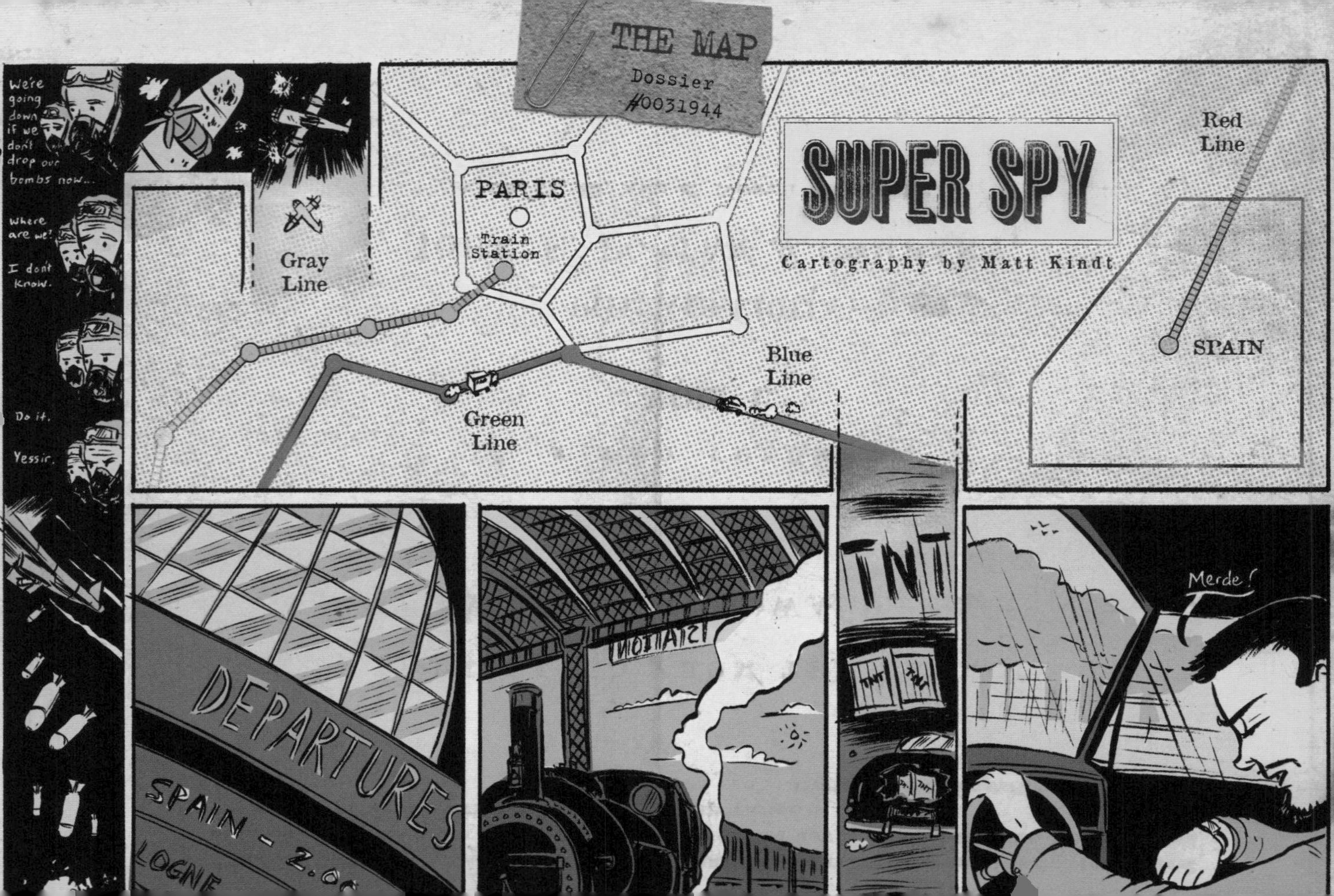
THE MAP
Dossier
#0031944
SUPER SPY
Cartography by Matt Kindt
We're going down if we don't drop our bombs now...
Where are we?
I don't know.
Do it.
Yessir.
PARIS
Train Station
Gray Line
Green Line
Blue Line
Red Line
SPAIN
DEPARTURES
SPAIN - 2.00
LOGNE
TNT
Merde!

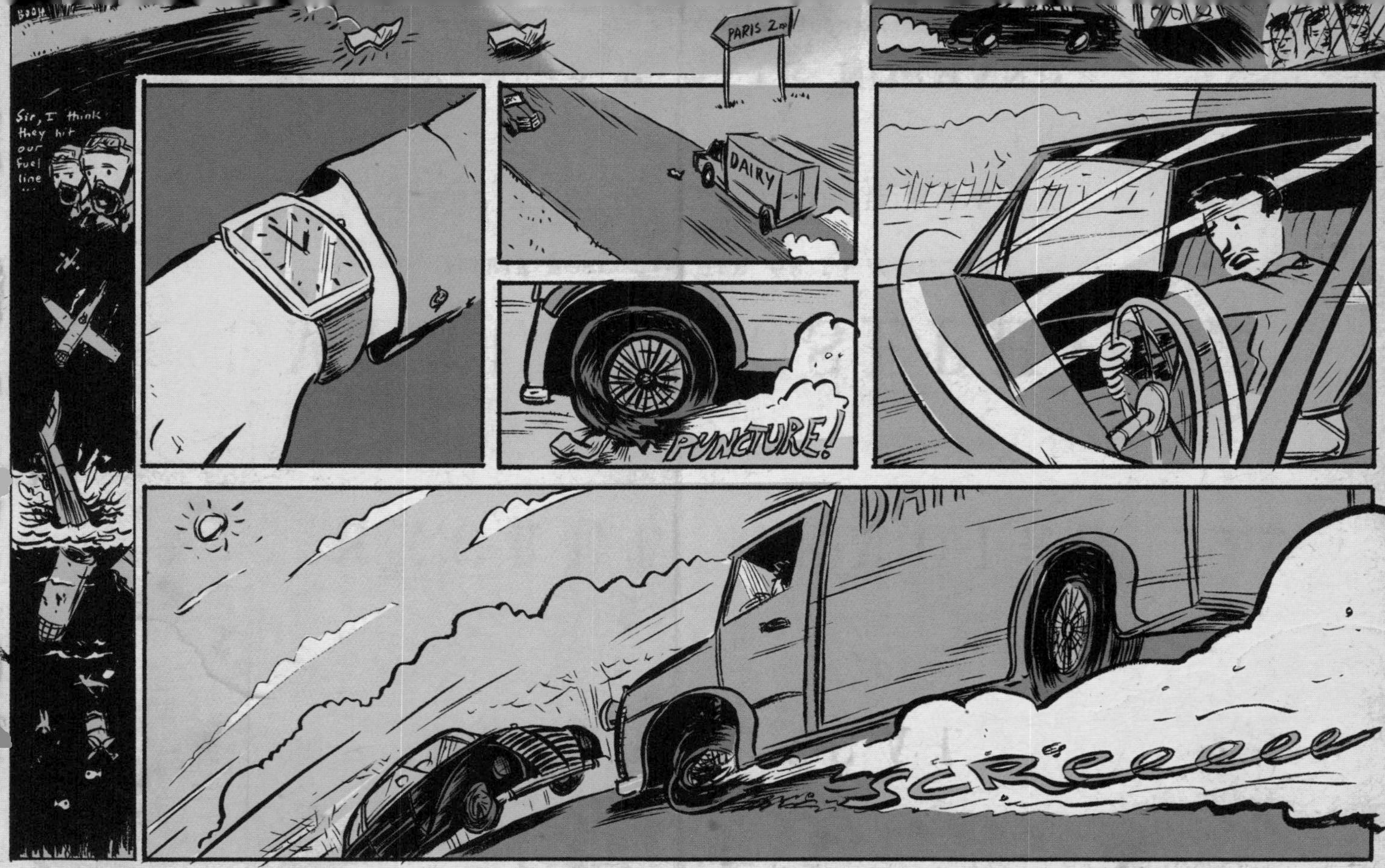
Sir, I think they hit our fuel line ...
PARIS 2
DAIRY
PUNCTURE!
SCReeeeeee

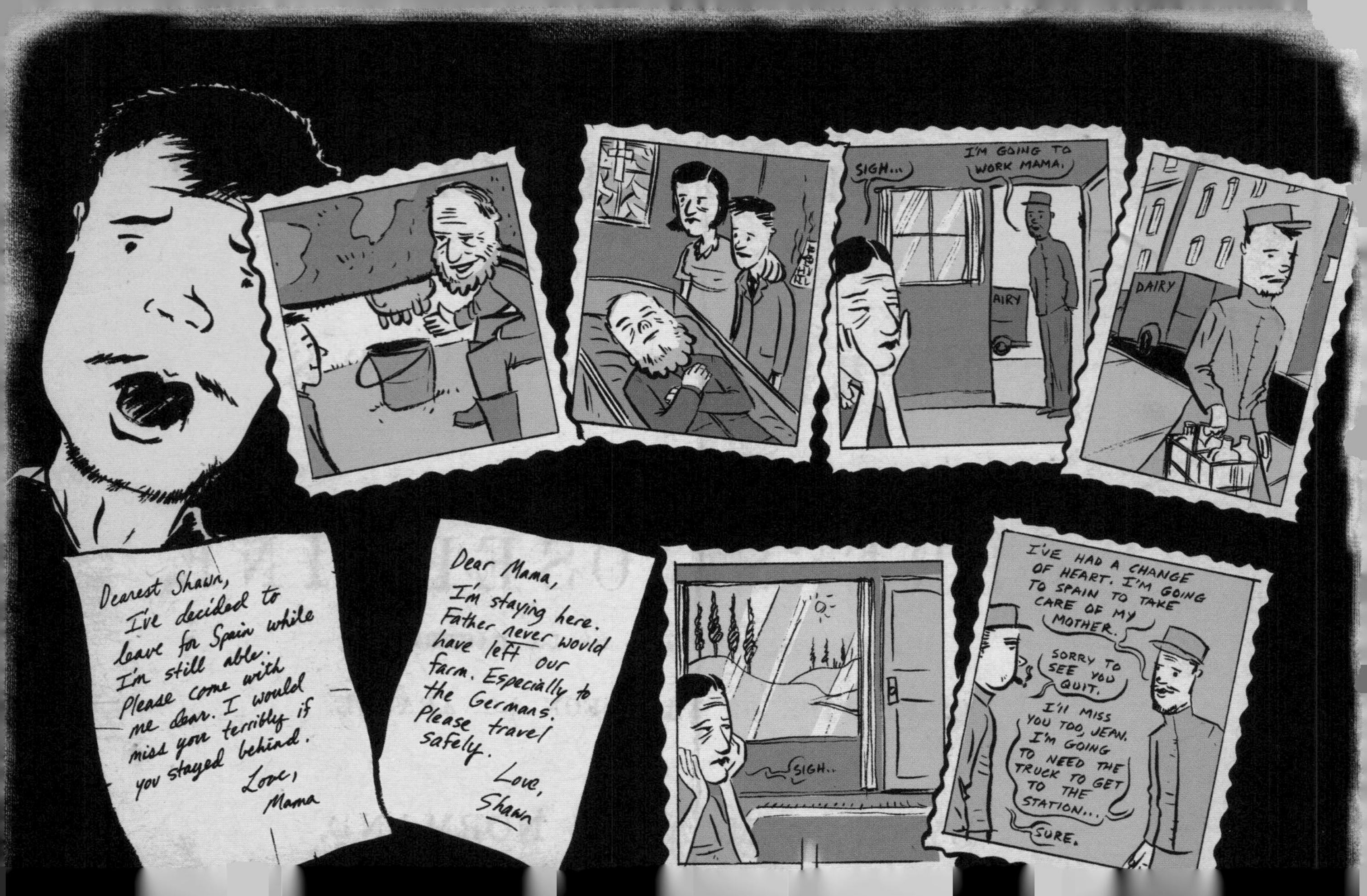
SIGH...
I'M GOING TO WORK MAMA.
DAIRY
Dearest Shawn,
I've decided to leave for Spain while I'm still able. Please come with me dear. I would miss you terribly if you stayed behind.
Love,
Mama
Dear Mama,
I'm staying here. Father never would have left our farm. Especially to the Germans. Please travel safely.
Love,
Shawn
SIGH..
I'VE HAD A CHANGE OF HEART. I'M GOING TO SPAIN TO TAKE CARE OF MY MOTHER.
SORRY TO SEE YOU QUIT.
I'LL MISS YOU TOO, JEAN. I'M GOING TO NEED THE TRUCK TO GET TO THE STATION...
SURE.

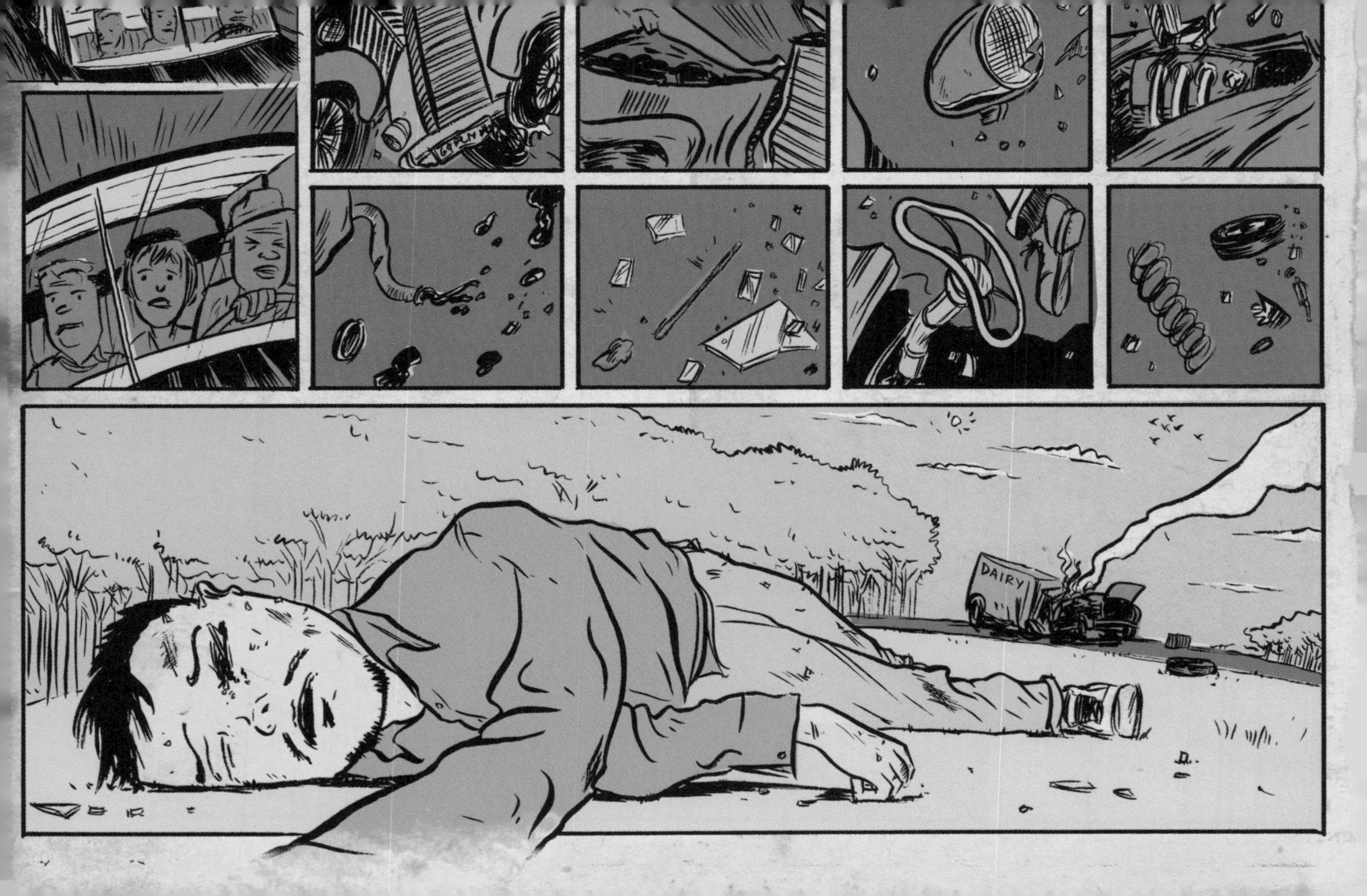
DAIRY

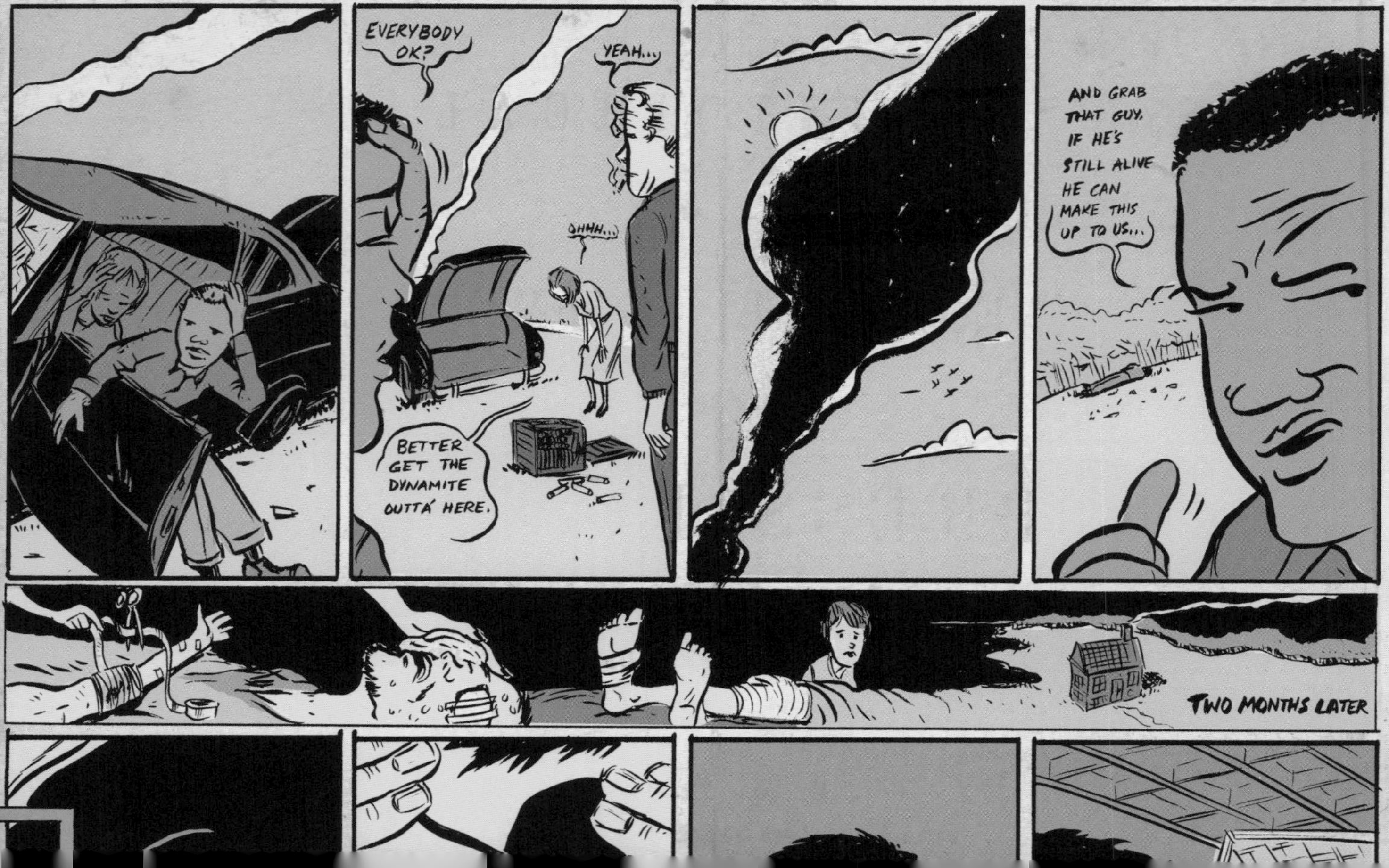
EVERYBODY OK?
YEAH...
OHHH...
BETTER GET THE DYNAMITE OUTTA' HERE.
AND GRAB THAT GUY. IF HE'S STILL ALIVE HE CAN MAKE THIS UP TO US...
TWO MONTHS LATER

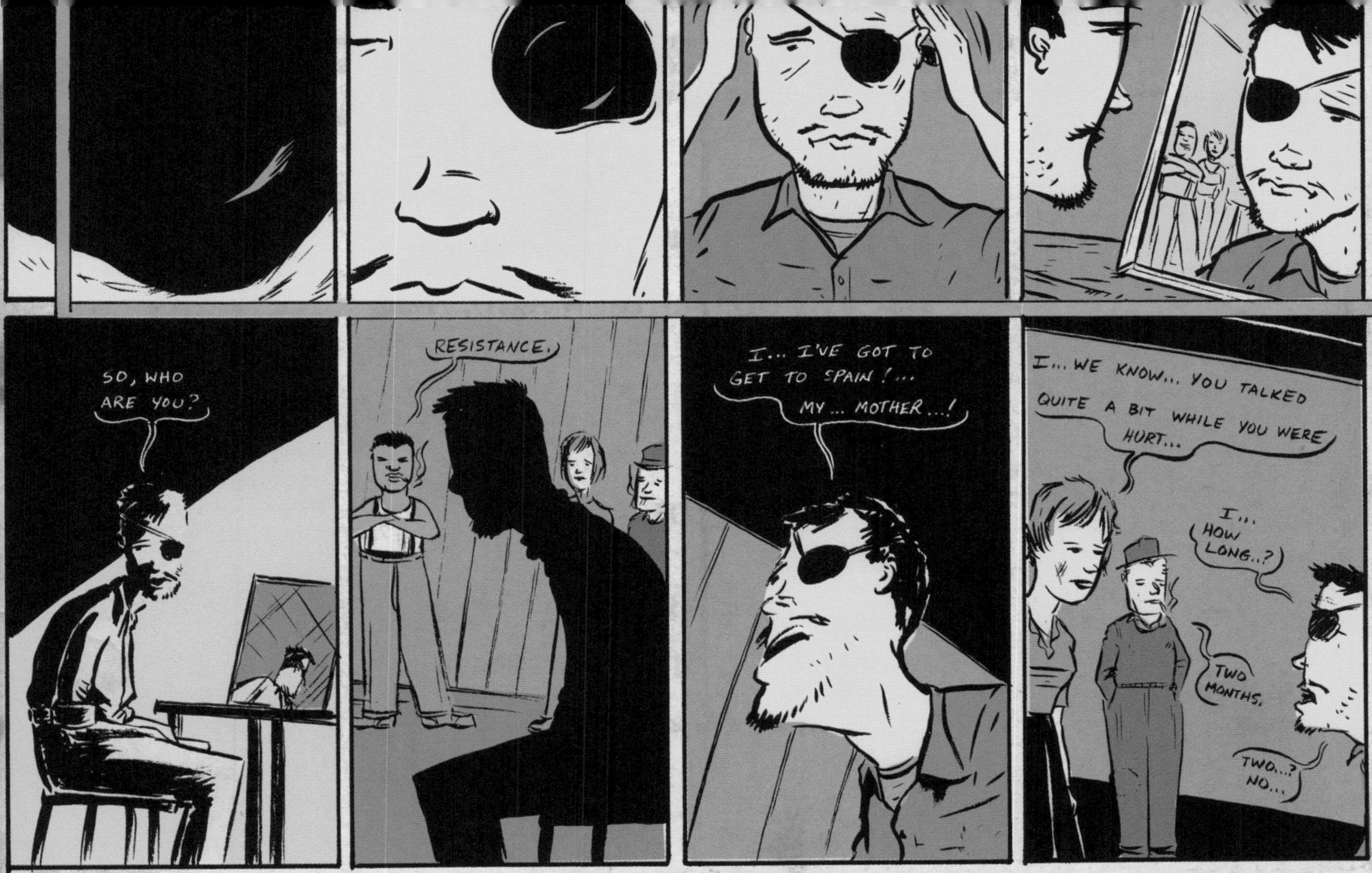
SO, WHO ARE YOU?
RESISTANCE.
I... I'VE GOT TO GET TO SPAIN!... MY... MOTHER...!
I... WE KNOW... YOU TALKED QUITE A BIT WHILE YOU WERE HURT...
I... HOW LONG..?
TWO MONTHS.
TWO...? NO...

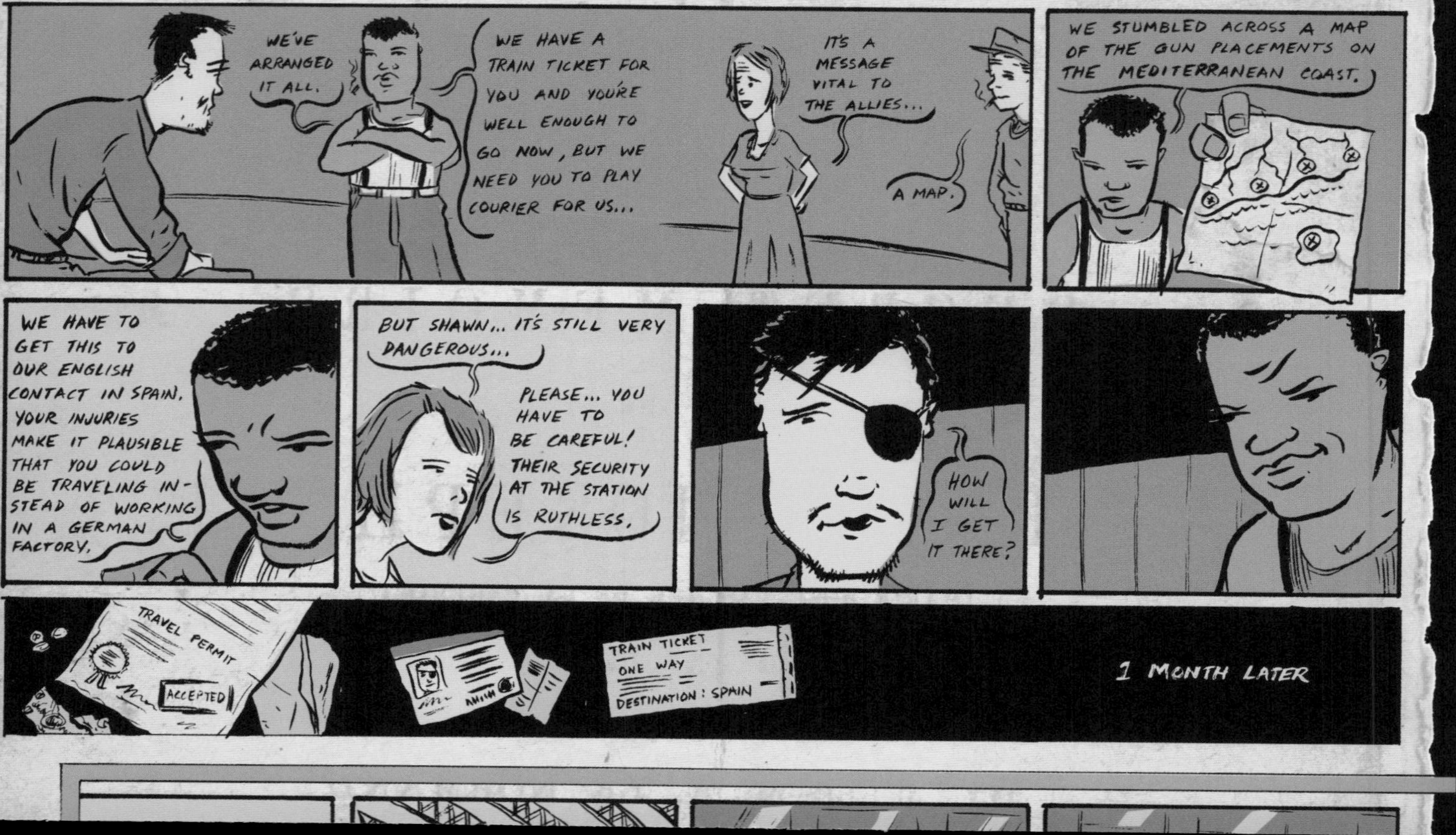
WE'VE ARRANGED IT ALL.
WE HAVE A TRAIN TICKET FOR YOU AND YOU'RE WELL ENOUGH TO GO NOW, BUT WE NEED YOU TO PLAY COURIER FOR US...
IT'S A MESSAGE VITAL TO THE ALLIES...
A MAP.
WE STUMBLED ACROSS A MAP OF THE GUN PLACEMENTS ON THE MEDITERRANEAN COAST.
WE HAVE TO GET THIS TO OUR ENGLISH CONTACT IN SPAIN. YOUR INJURIES MAKE IT PLAUSIBLE THAT YOU COULD BE TRAVELING IN-STEAD OF WORKING IN A GERMAN FACTORY.
BUT SHAWN... IT'S STILL VERY DANGEROUS...
PLEASE... YOU HAVE TO BE CAREFUL! THEIR SECURITY AT THE STATION IS RUTHLESS.
HOW WILL I GET IT THERE?
TRAVEL PERMIT
ACCEPTED
TRAIN TICKET
ONE WAY
DESTINATION : SPAIN
1 MONTH LATER

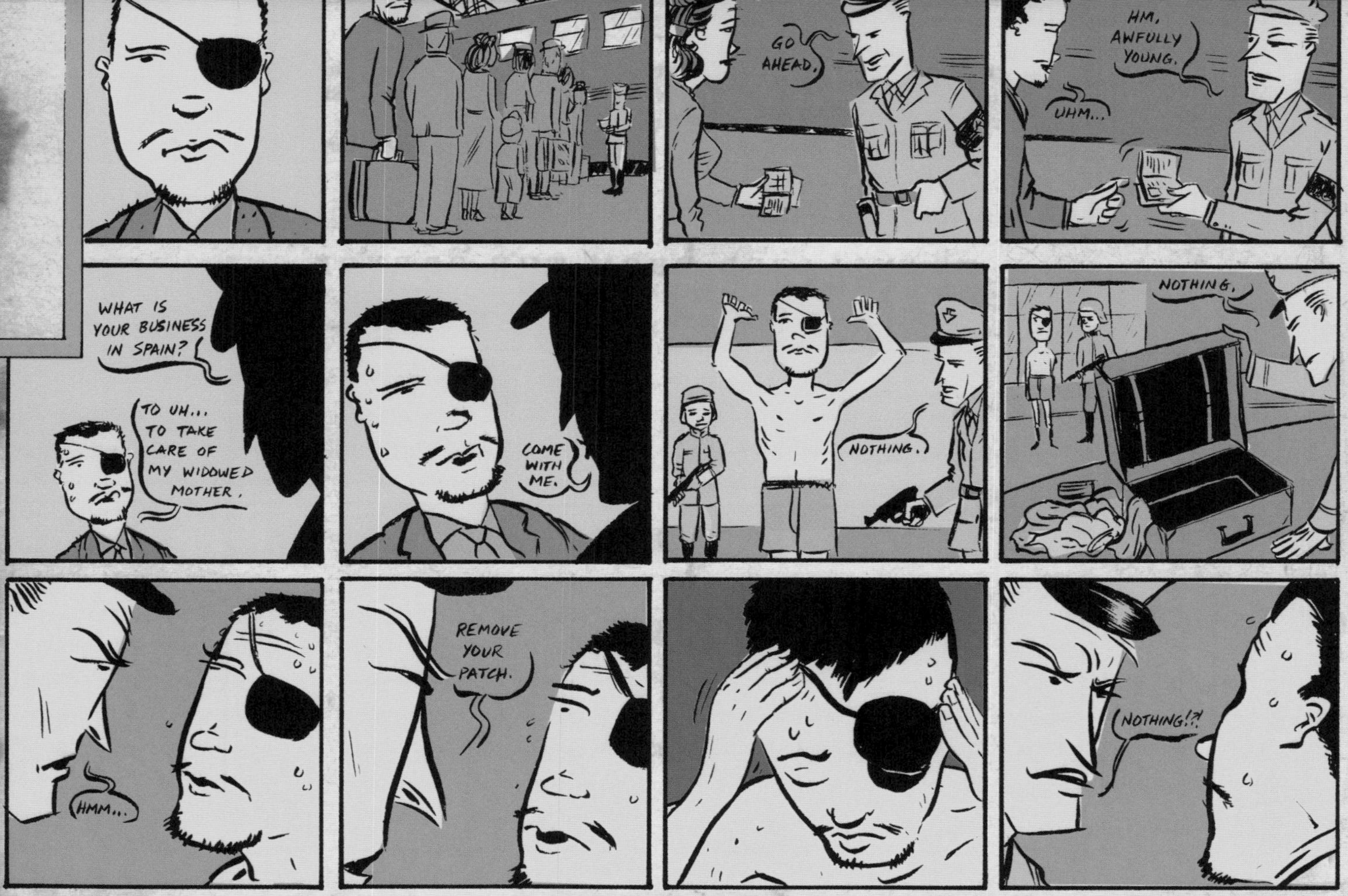
GO AHEAD.
UHM...
HM, AWFULLY YOUNG.
WHAT IS YOUR BUSINESS IN SPAIN?
TO UH... TO TAKE CARE OF MY WIDOWED MOTHER.
COME WITH ME.
NOTHING.
NOTHING.
HMM...
REMOVE YOUR PATCH.
NOTHING!?!

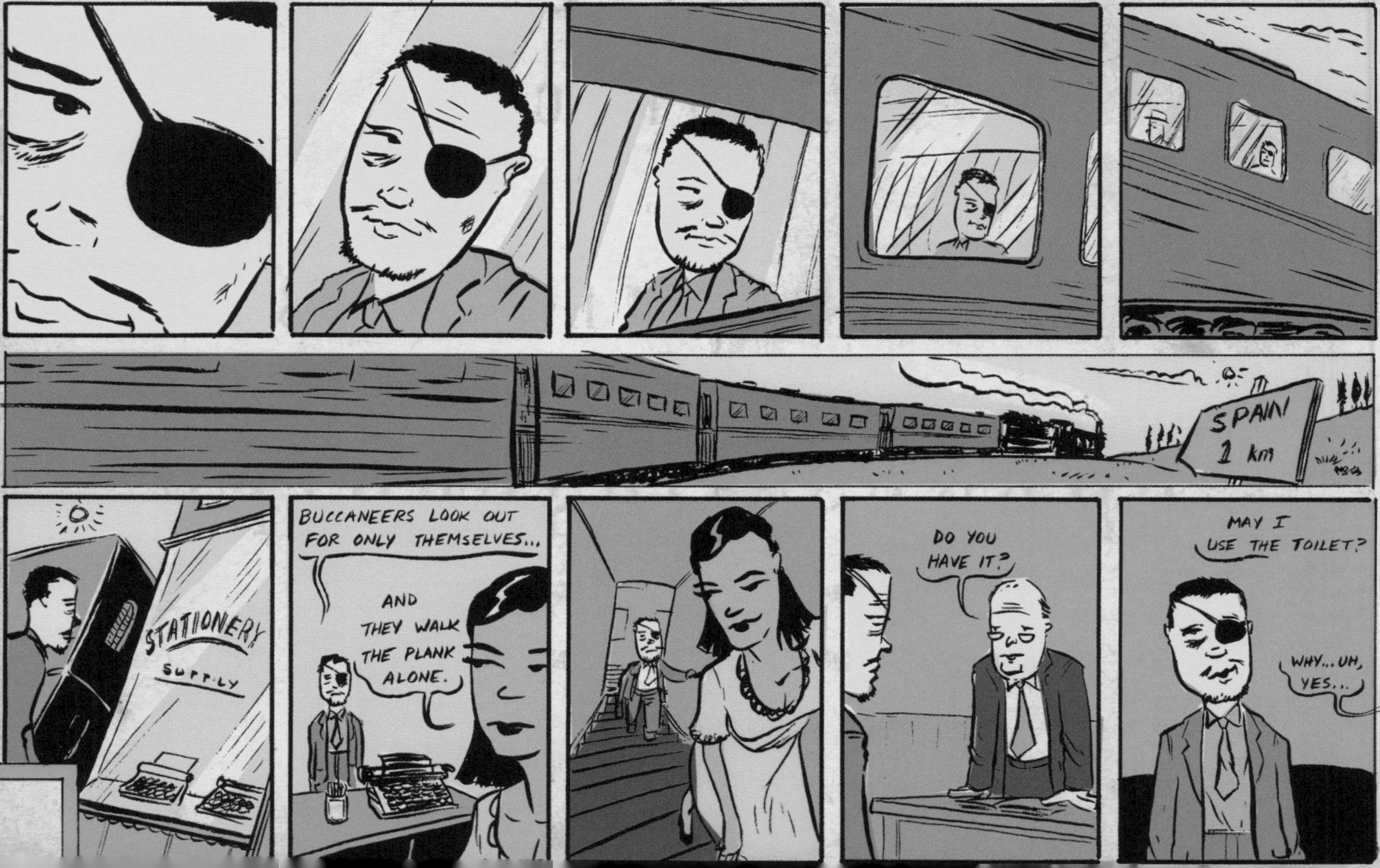
SPAIN
1 km
STATIONERY
SUPPLY
BUCCANEERS LOOK OUT FOR ONLY THEMSELVES...
AND THEY WALK THE PLANK ALONE.
DO YOU HAVE IT?
MAY I USE THE TOILET?
WHY... UH, YES...

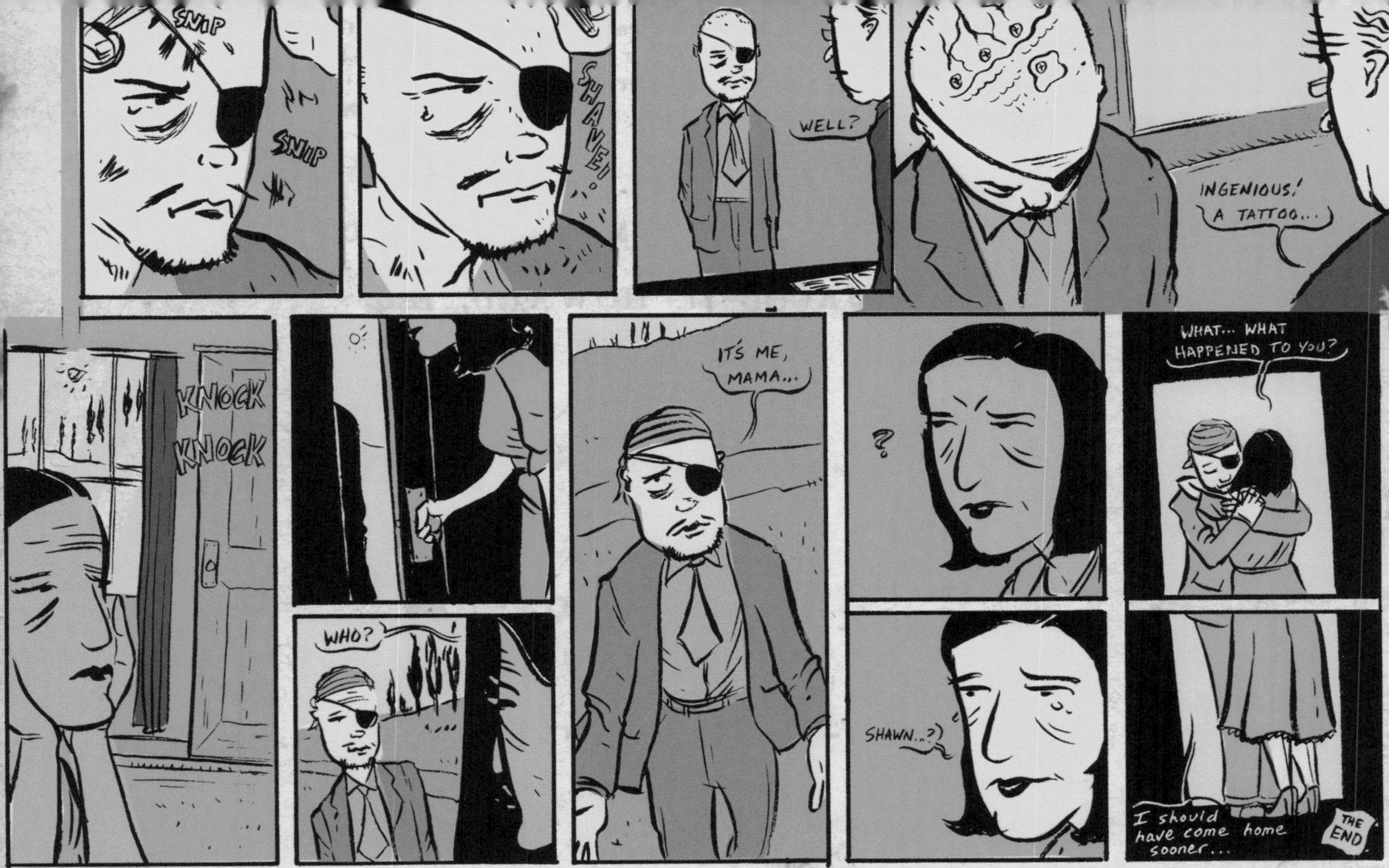
SNIP
SNIP
SHAVE!
WELL?
INGENIOUS! A TATTOO...
KNOCK
KNOCK
WHO?
IT'S ME, MAMA...
?
SHAWN..?
WHAT... WHAT HAPPENED TO YOU?
I should have come home sooner...
THE END

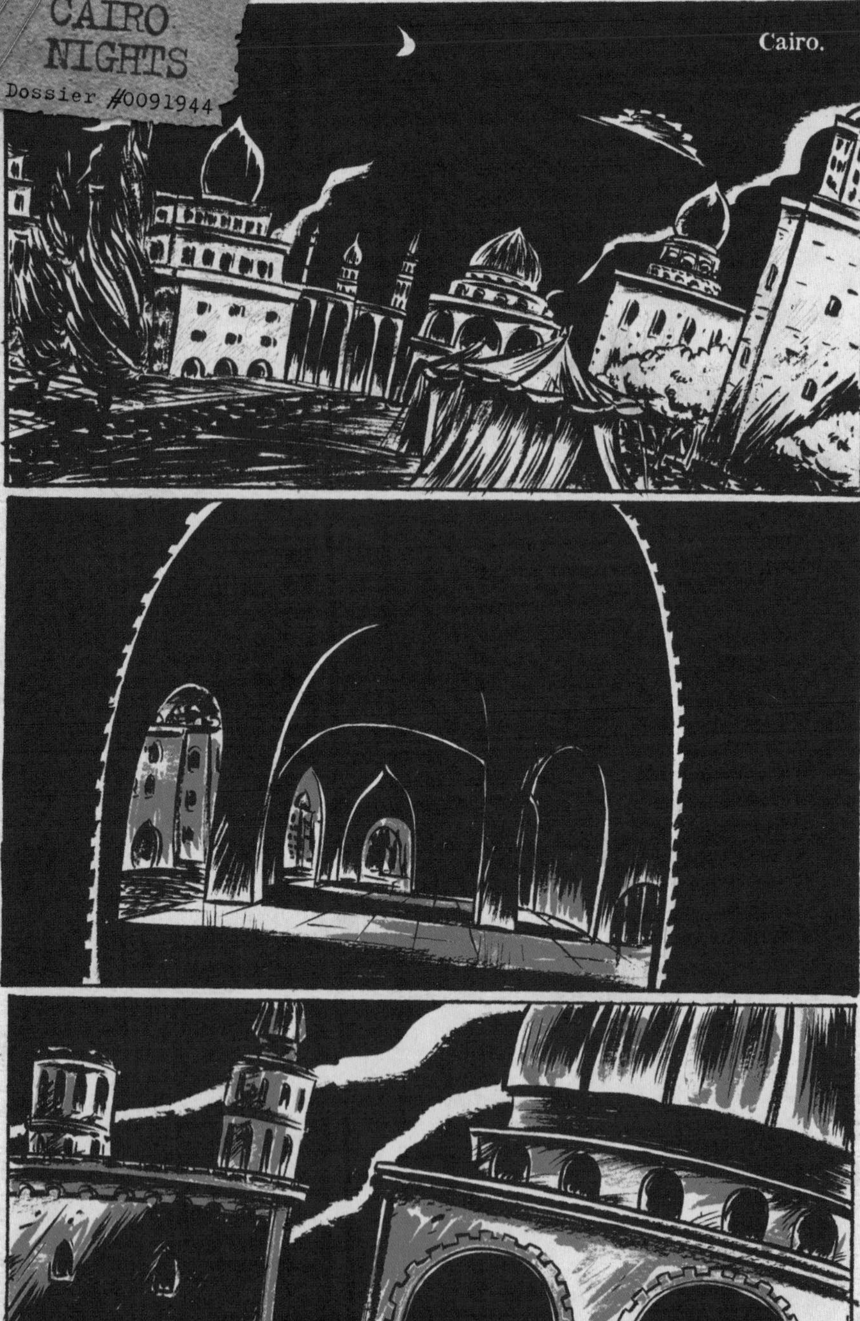
Cairo.

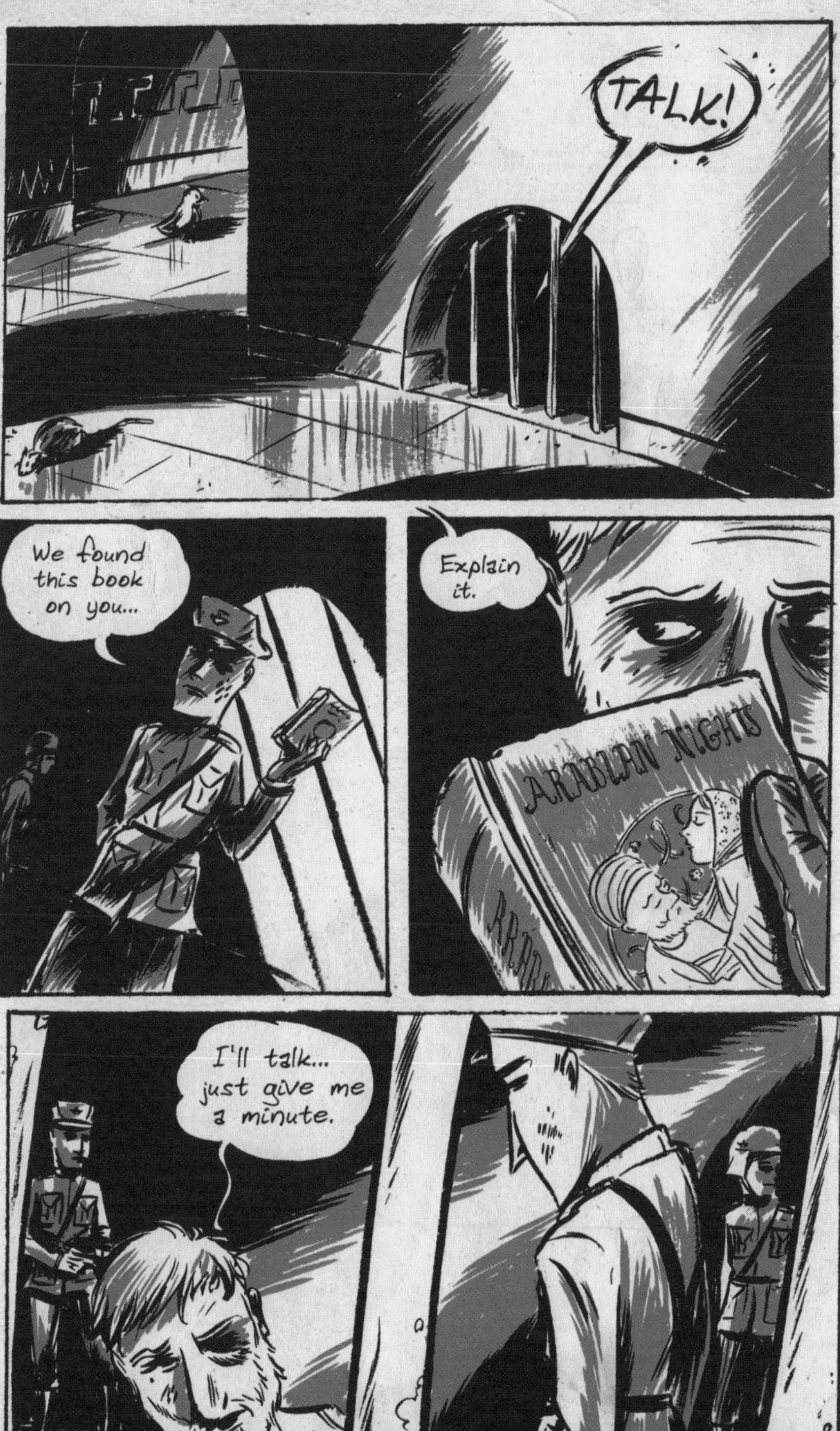
TALK!
We found this book on you...
Explain it.
ARABIAN NIGHTS
I'll talk... just give me a minute.

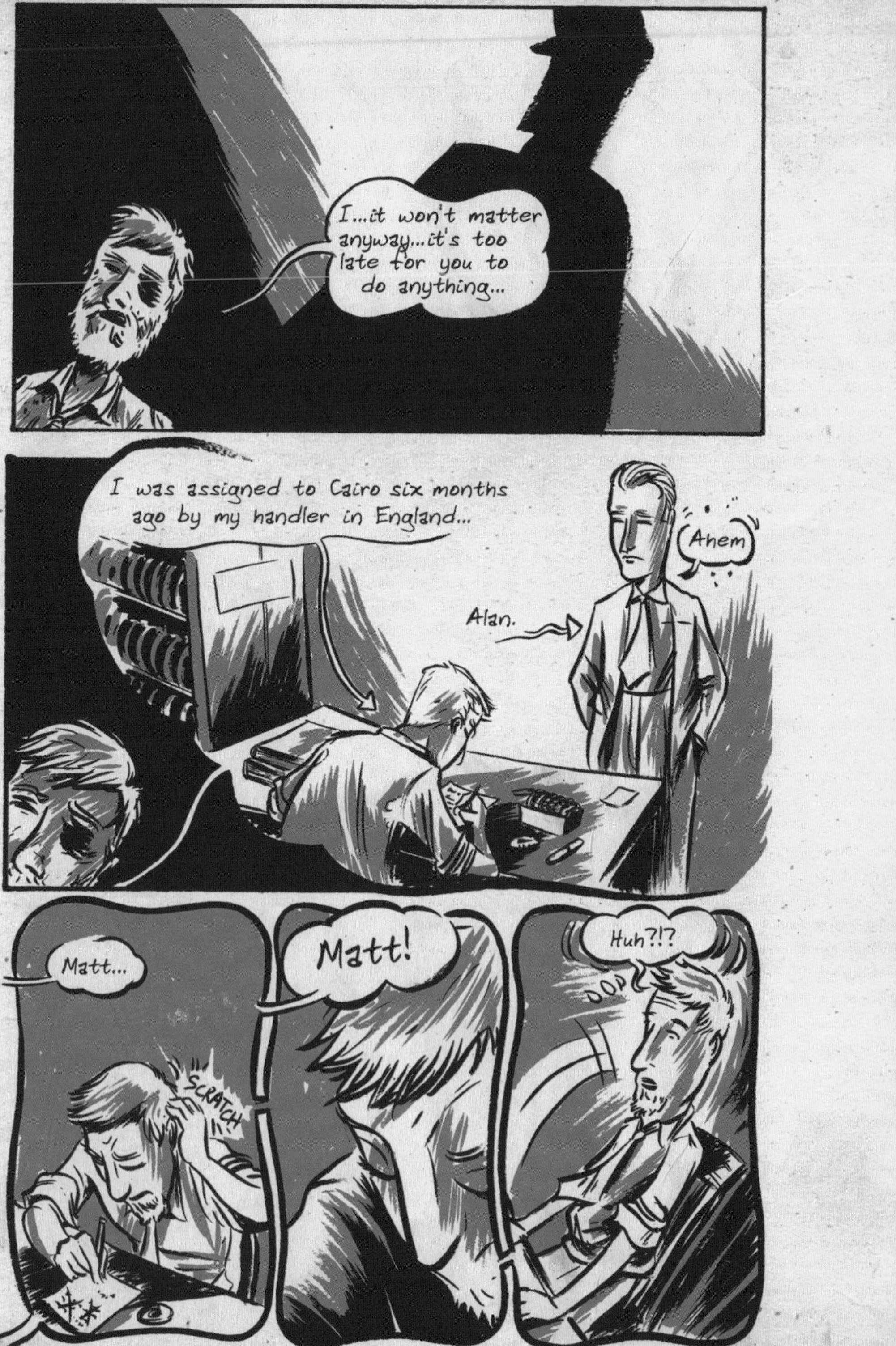
I...it won't matter anyway...it's too late for you to do anything...
I was assigned to Cairo six months ago by my handler in England...
Ahem
Alan.
Matt...
SCRATCH
Matt!
Huh?!?
OOP

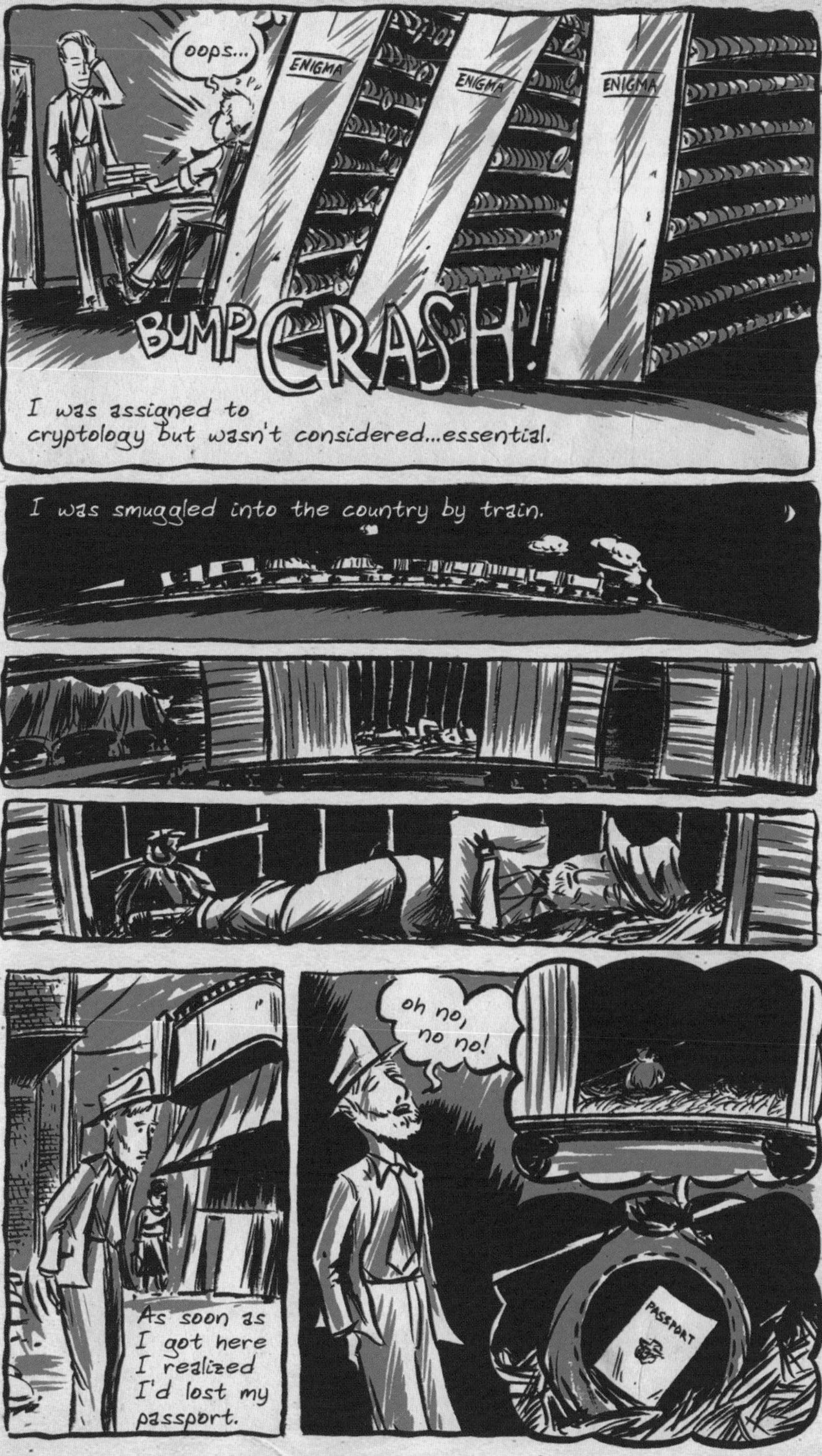
oops...
ENIGMA
ENIGMA
ENIGMA
BUMP
CRASH!
I was assigned to cryptology but wasn't considered...essential.
I was smuggled into the country by train.
As soon as I got here I realized I'd lost my passport.
oh no, no no!
PASSPORT

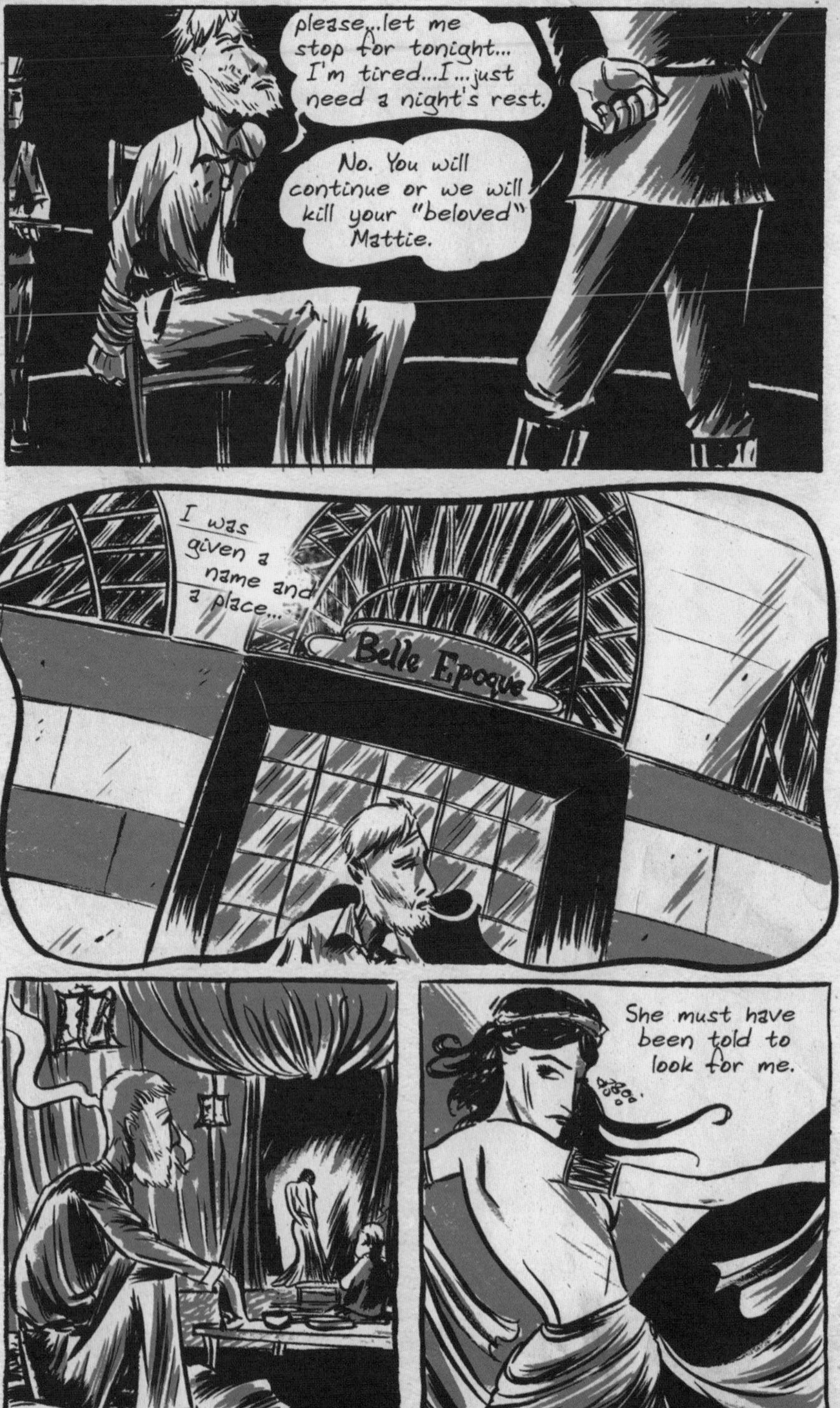
please...let me stop for tonight... I'm tired...I...just need a night's rest.
No. You will continue or we will kill your "beloved" Mattie.
I was given a name and a place...
Belle Epoque
She must have been told to look for me.

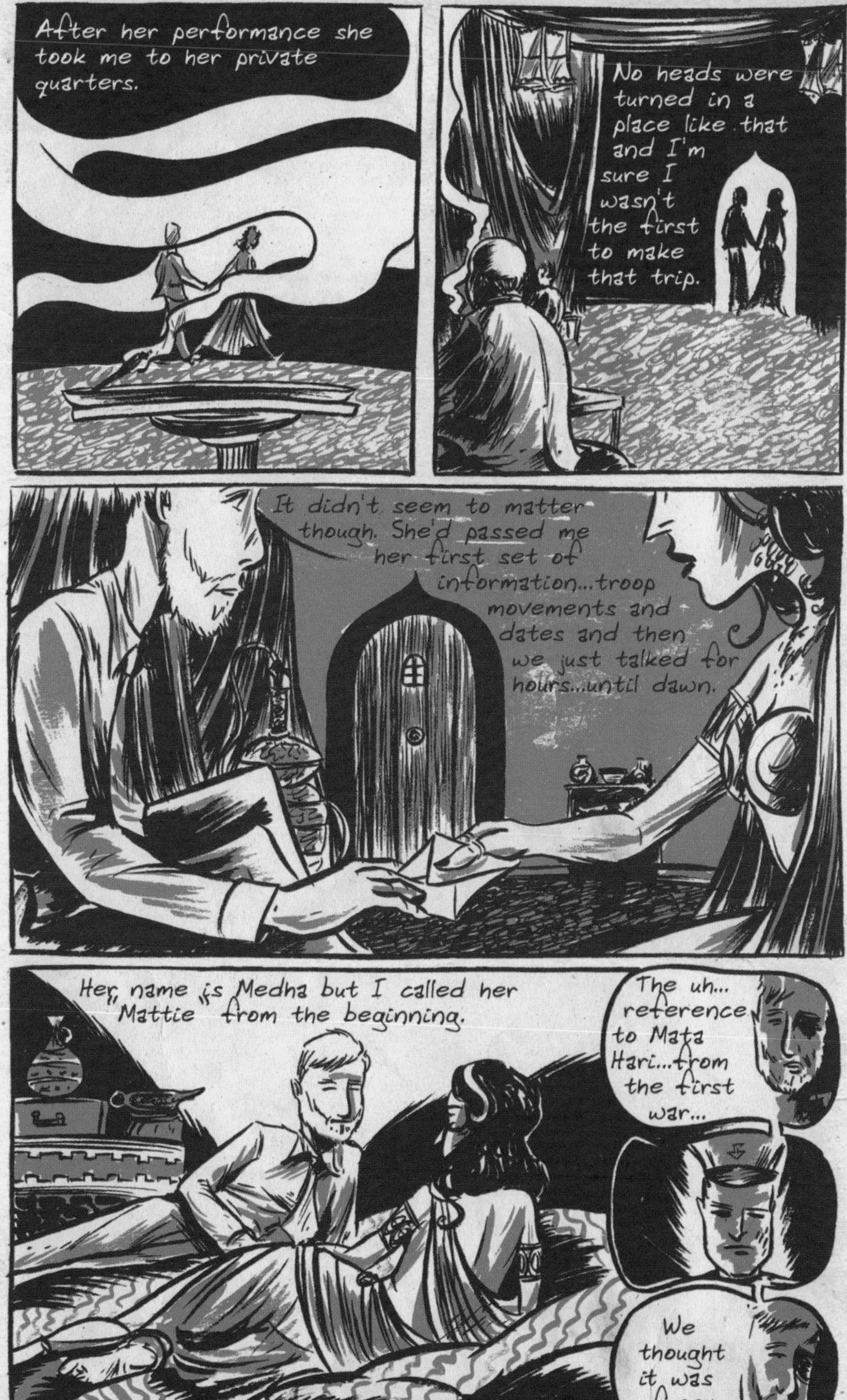
After her performance she took me to her private quarters.
No heads were turned in a place like that and I'm sure I wasn't the first to make that trip.
It didn't seem to matter though. She'd passed me her first set of information...troop movements and dates and then we just talked for hours...until dawn.
Her name is Medha but I called her "Mattie" from the beginning.
The uh... reference to Mata Hari...from the first war...
We thought it was funny.

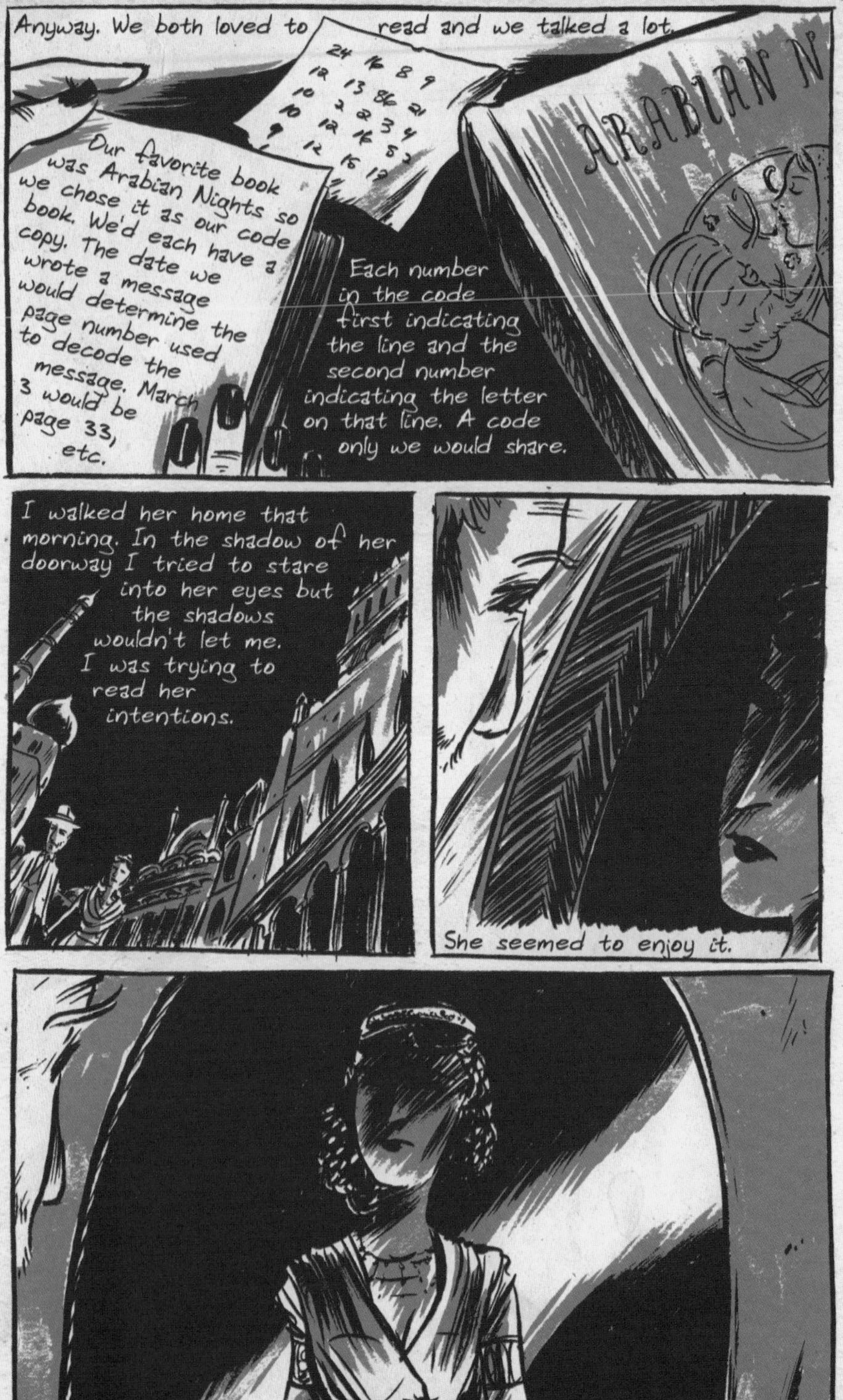
Anyway. We both loved to read and we talked a lot.
ARABIAN N
Our favorite book was Arabian Nights so we chose it as our code book. We'd each have a copy. The date we wrote a message would determine the page number used to decode the message. March 3 would be page 33, etc.
Each number in the code first indicating the line and the second number indicating the letter on that line. A code only we would share.
I walked her home that morning. In the shadow of her doorway I tried to stare into her eyes but the shadows wouldn't let me. I was trying to read her intentions.
She seemed to enjoy it.

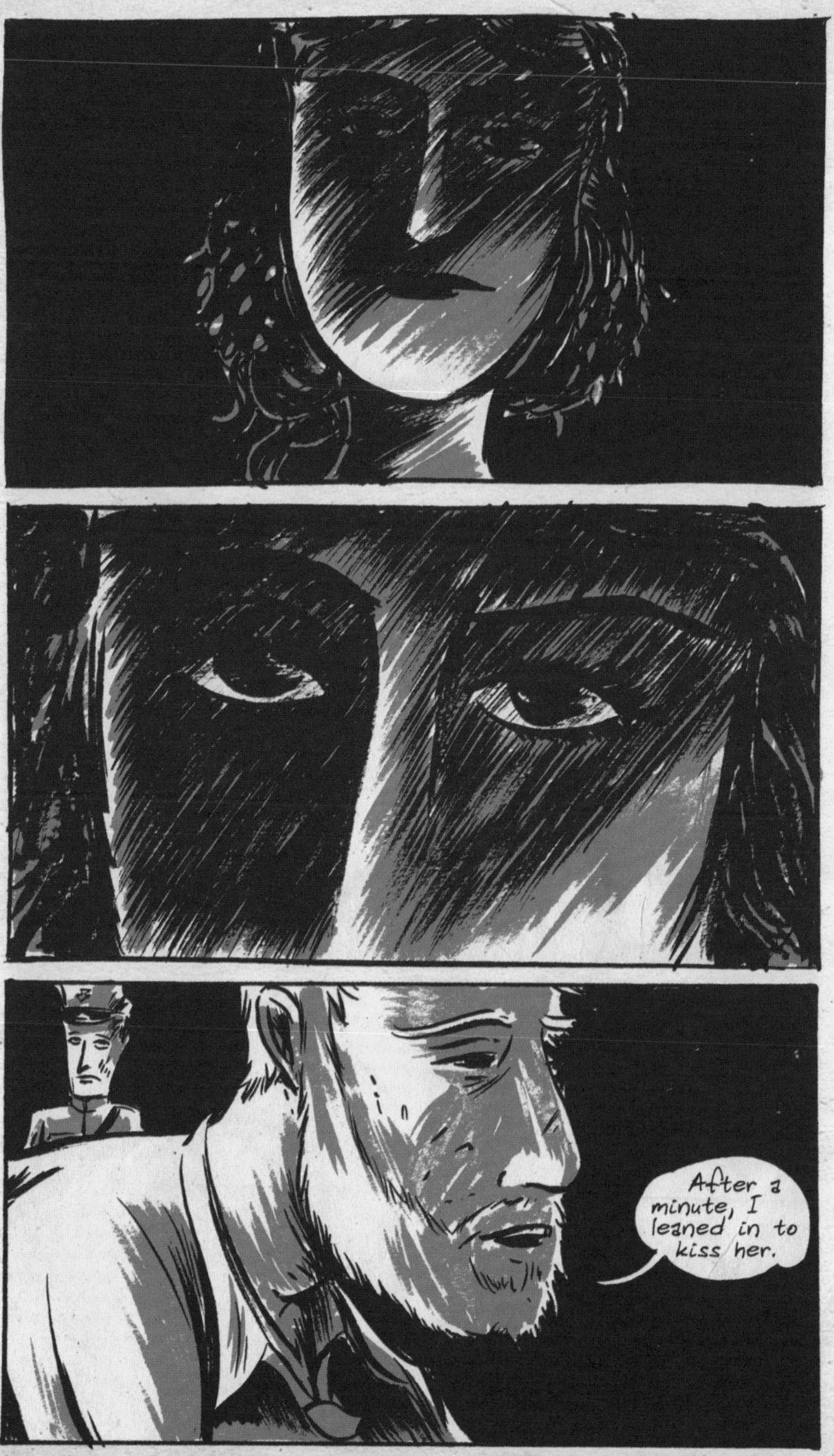
After a minute, I leaned in to kiss her.

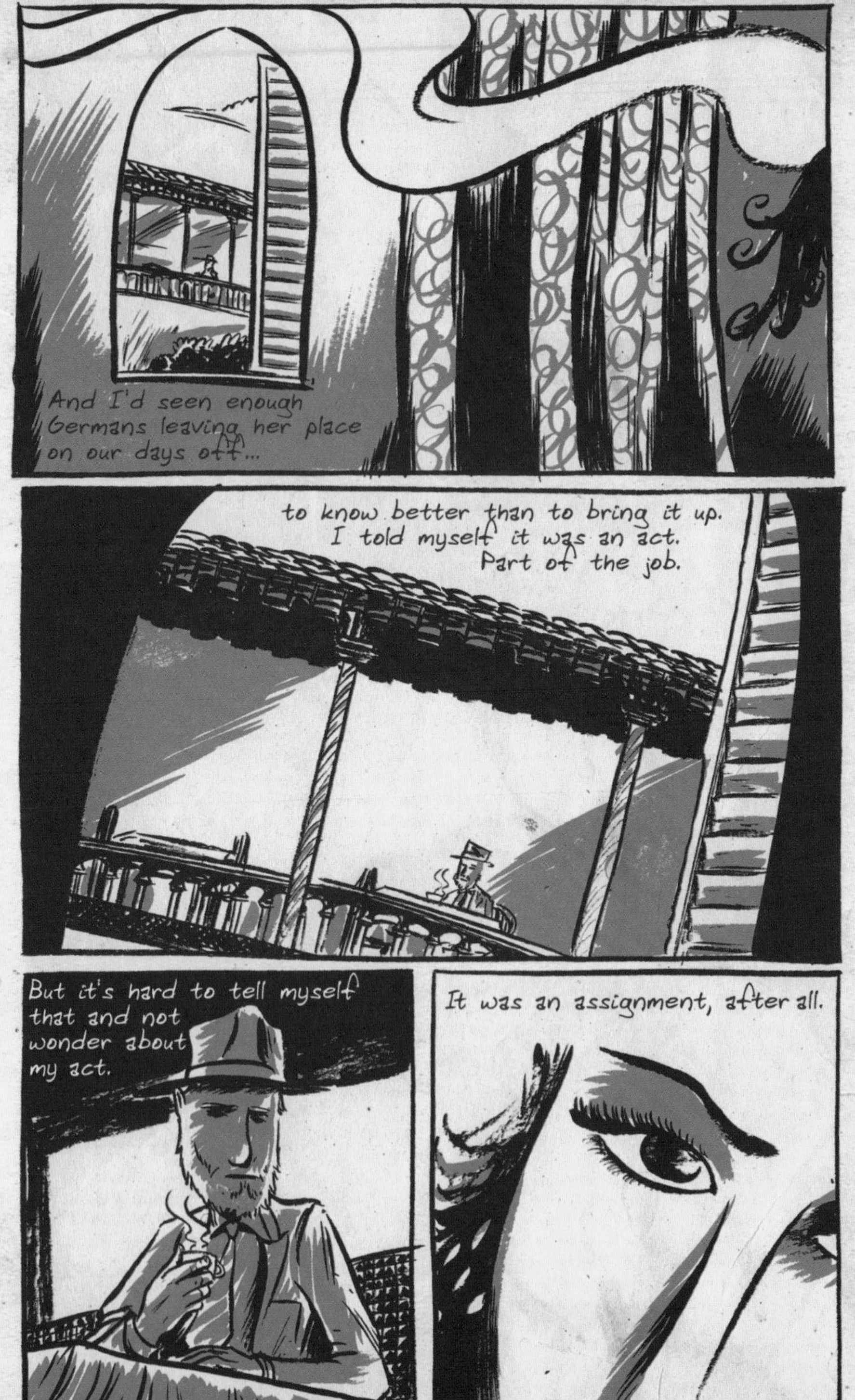
And I'd seen enough Germans leaving her place on our days off...
to know better than to bring it up. I told myself it was an act. Part of the job.
But it's hard to tell myself that and not wonder about my act.
It was an assignment, after all.

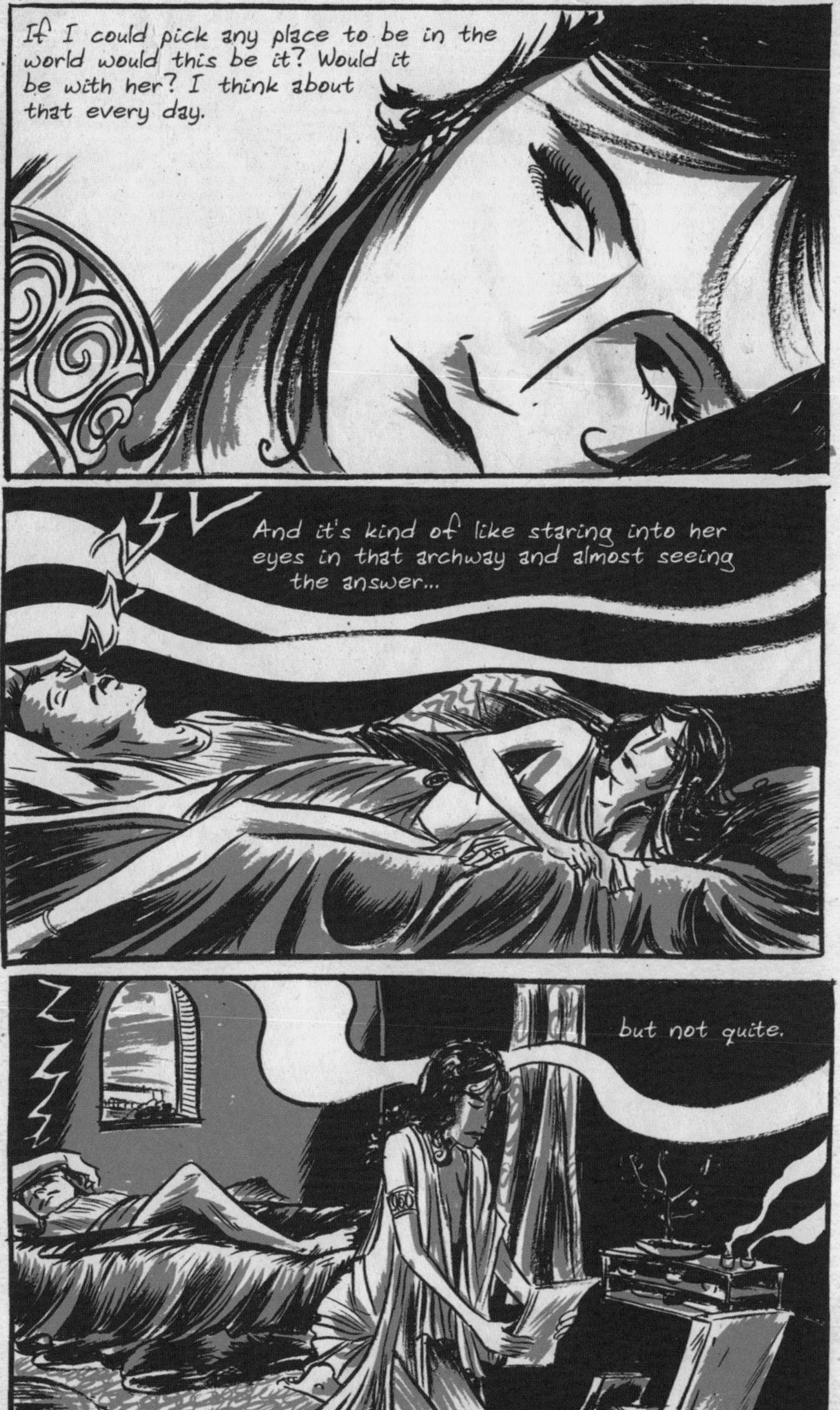
If I could pick any place to be in the world would this be it? Would it be with her? I think about that every day.
And it's kind of like staring into her eyes in that archway and almost seeing the answer...
but not quite.

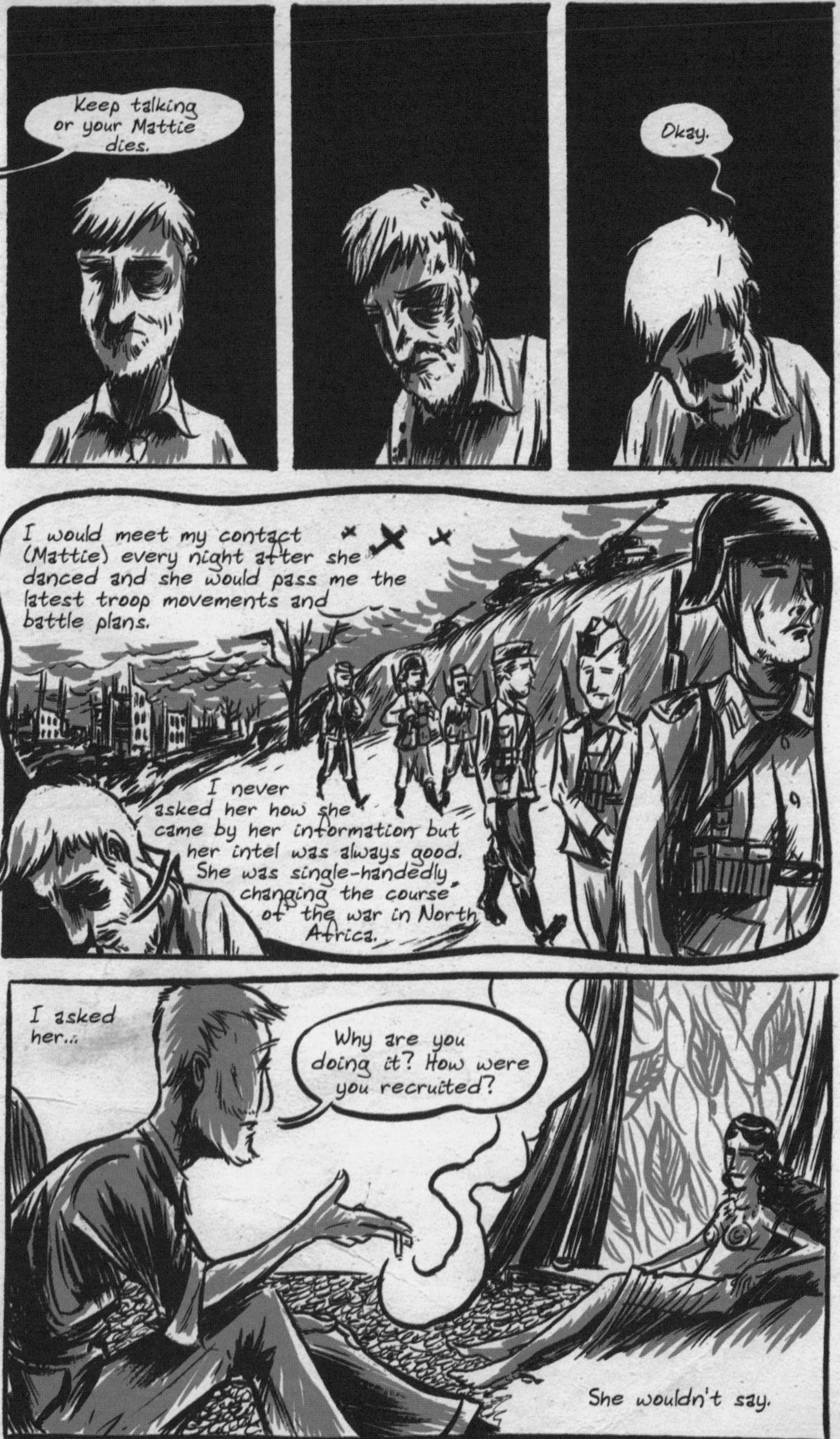
Keep talking or your Mattie dies.
Okay.
I would meet my contact (Mattie) every night after she danced and she would pass me the latest troop movements and battle plans.
I never asked her how she came by her information but her intel was always good. She was single-handedly changing the course of the war in North Africa.
I asked her...
Why are you doing it? How were you recruited?
She wouldn't say.

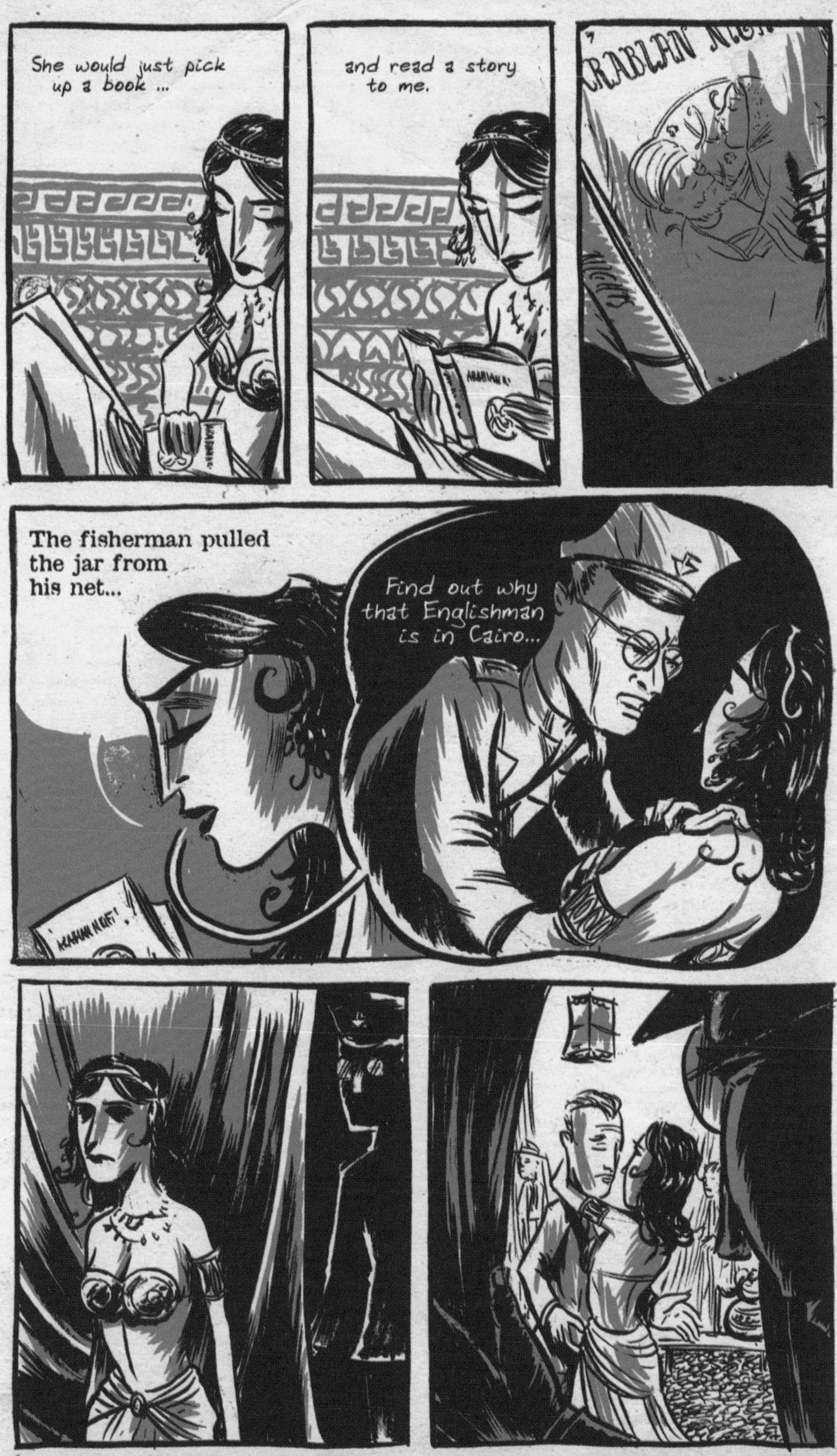
She would just pick up a book ...
and read a story to me.
The fisherman pulled the jar from his net...
Find out why that Englishman is in Cairo...

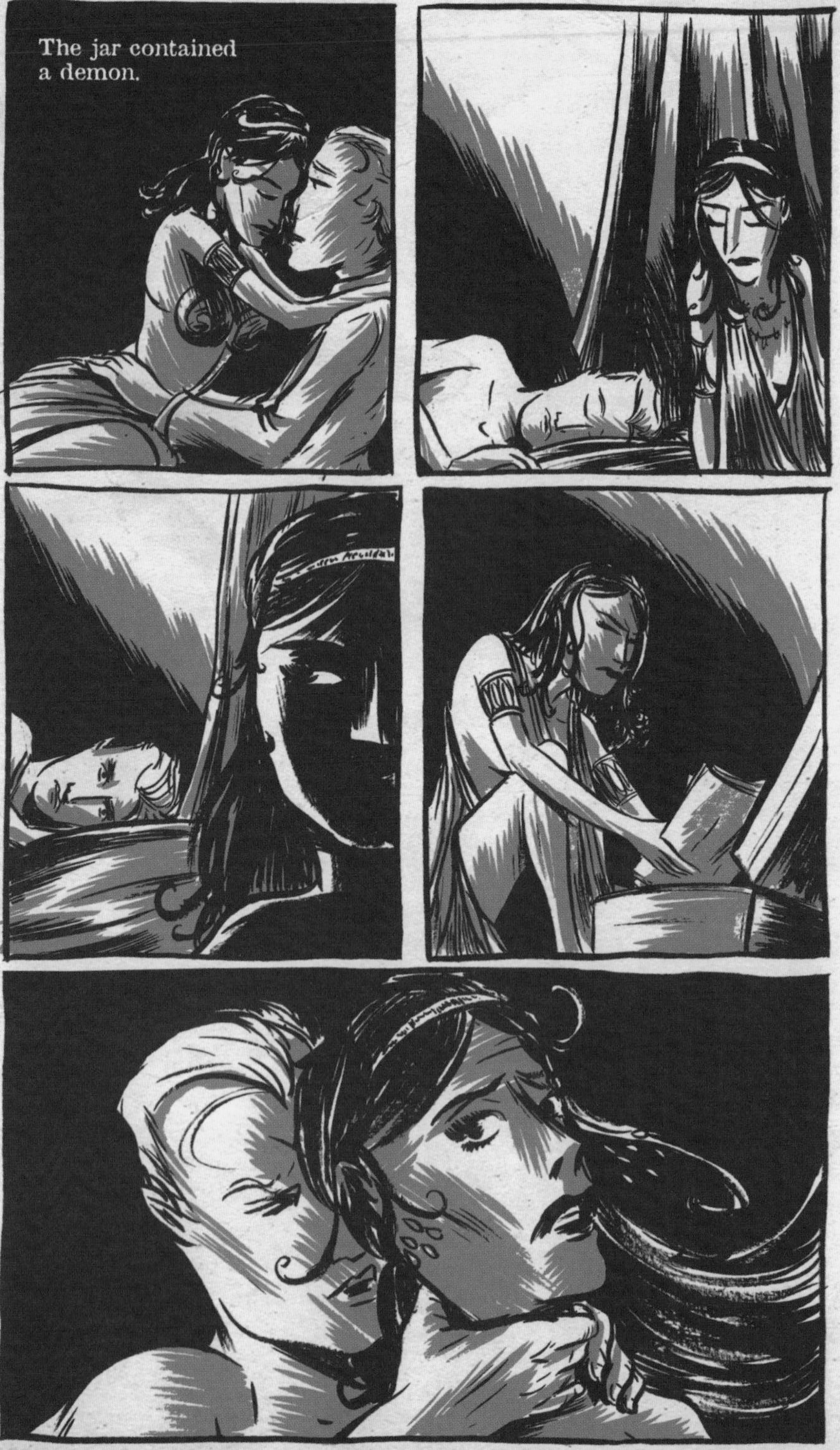
The jar contained
a demon.

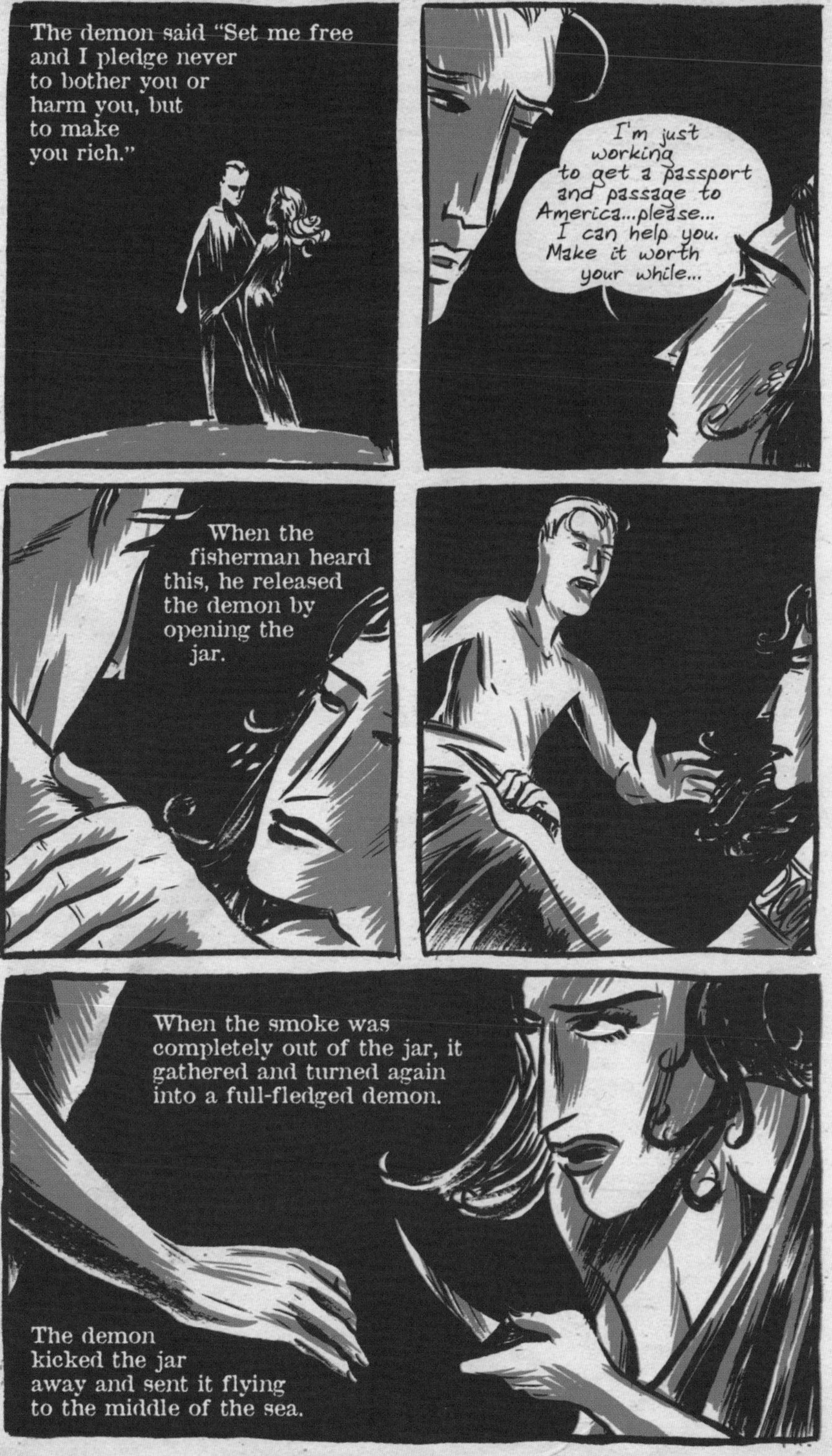
The demon said "Set me free and I pledge never to bother you or harm you, but to make you rich."
I'm just working to get a passport and passage to America...please... I can help you. Make it worth your while...
When the fisherman heard this, he released the demon by opening the jar.
When the smoke was completely out of the jar, it gathered and turned again into a full-fledged demon.
The demon kicked the jar away and sent it flying to the middle of the sea.

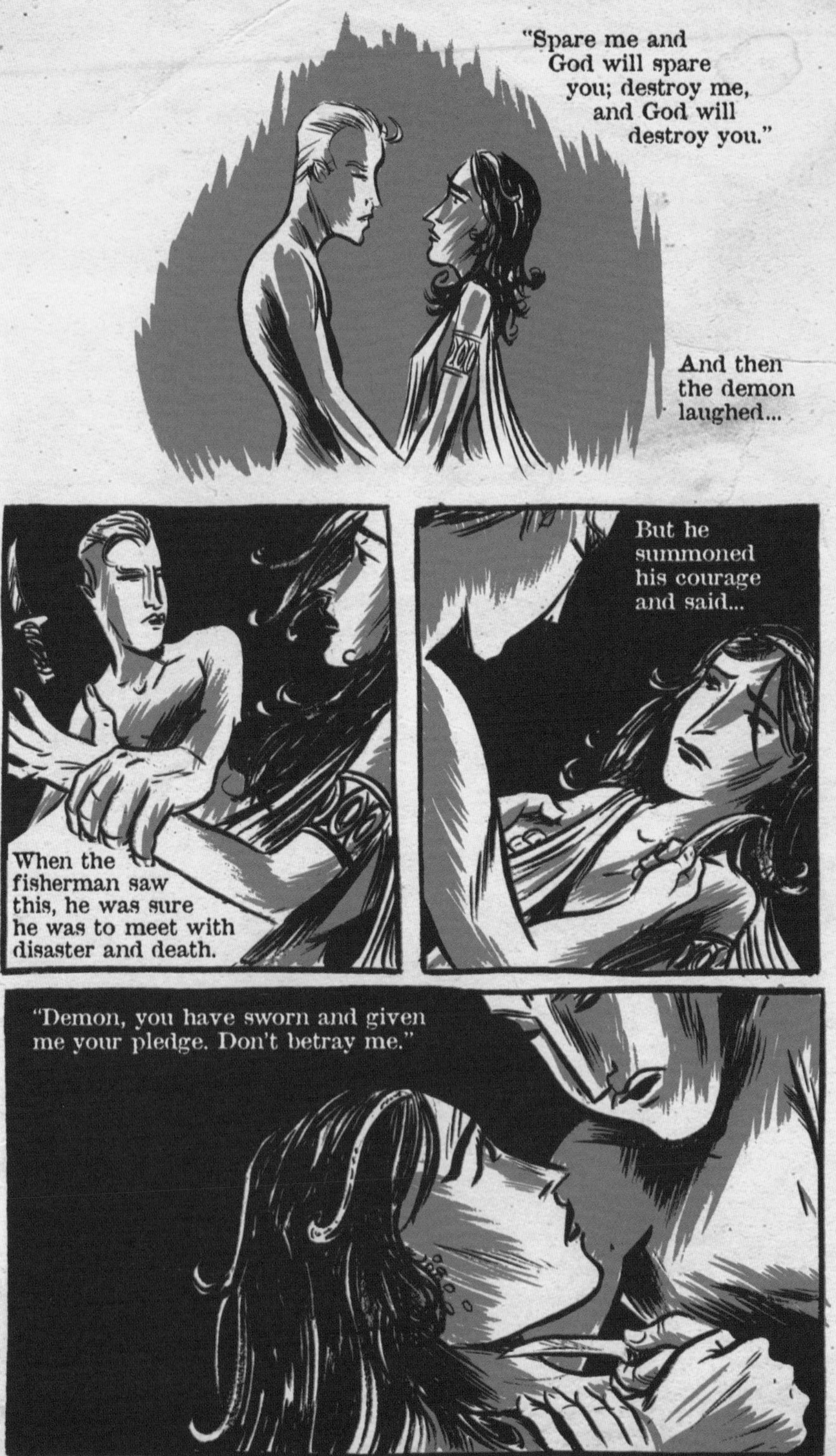
"Spare me and God will spare you; destroy me, and God will destroy you."
And then the demon laughed...
When the fisherman saw this, he was sure he was to meet with disaster and death.
But he summoned his courage and said...
"Demon, you have sworn and given me your pledge. Don't betray me."

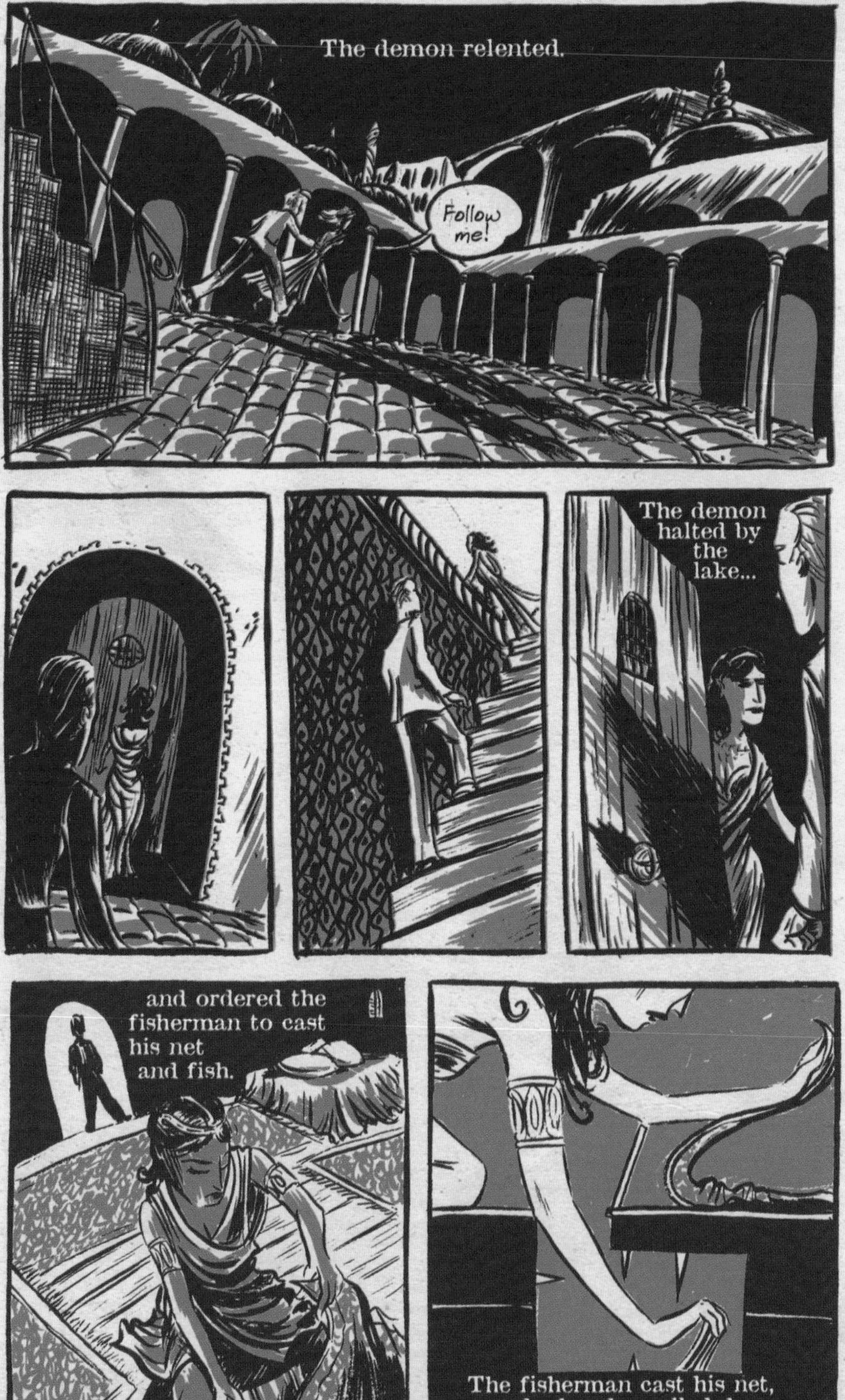
The demon relented.
Follow me!
The demon halted by the lake...
and ordered the fisherman to cast his net and fish.
The fisherman cast his net, and when he pulled, he found four fish inside...

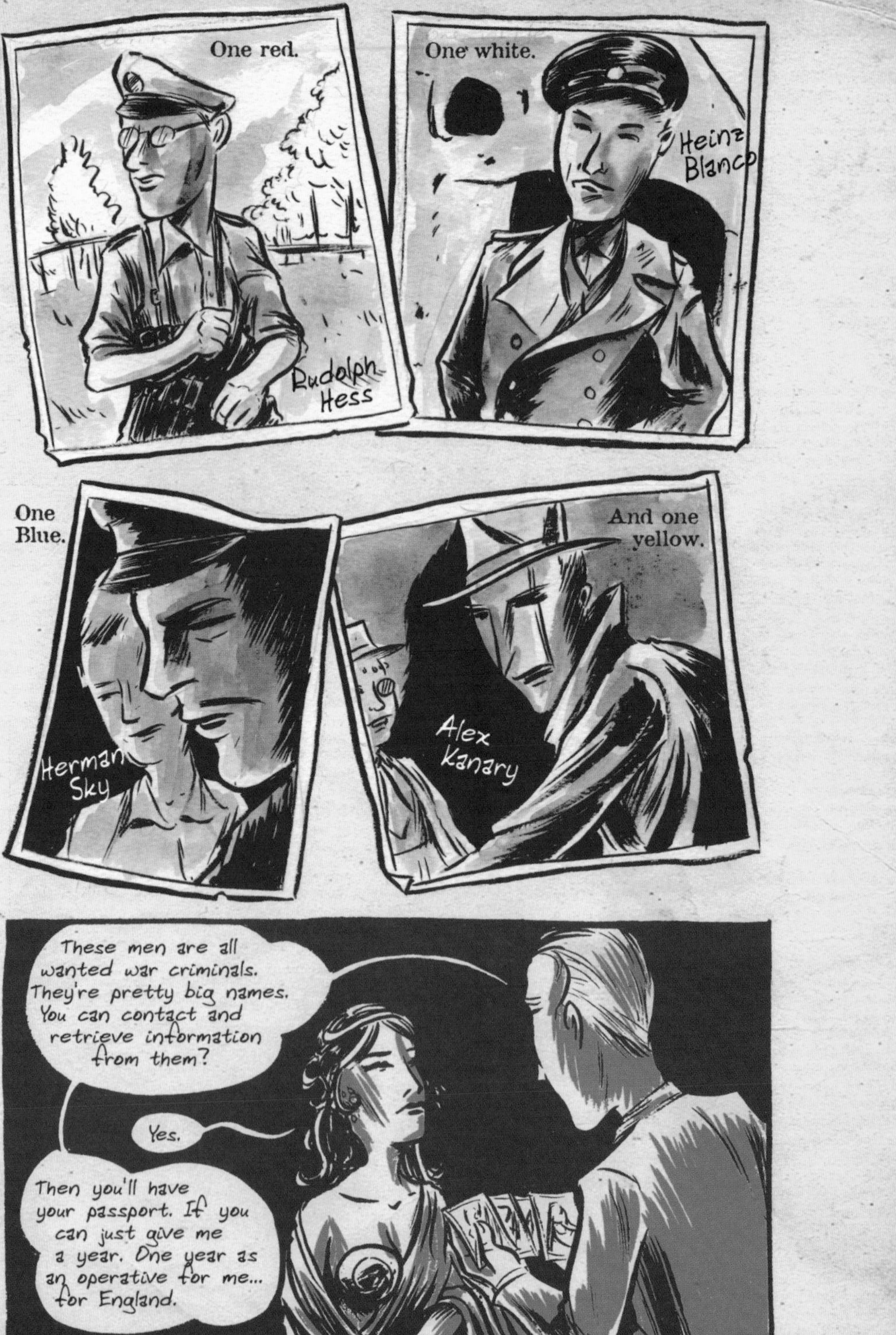
One red.
Rudolph Hess
One white.
Heinz Blanco
One Blue.
Herman Sky
And one yellow.
Alex Kanary
These men are all wanted war criminals. They're pretty big names. You can contact and retrieve information from them?
Yes.
Then you'll have your passport. If you can just give me a year. One year as an operative for me... for England.

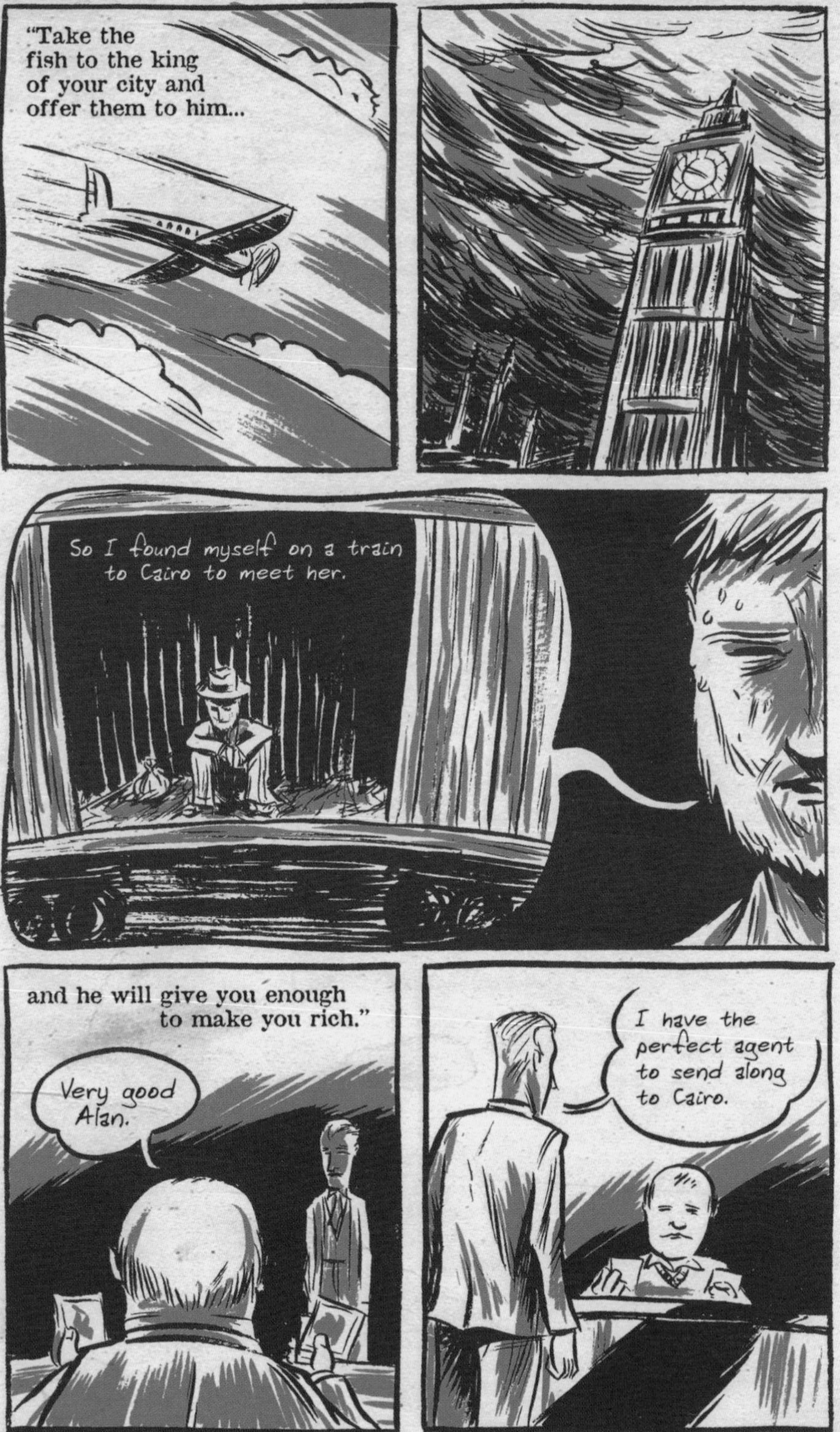
"Take the fish to the king of your city and offer them to him...
So I found myself on a train to Cairo to meet her.
and he will give you enough to make you rich."
Very good Alan.
I have the perfect agent to send along to Cairo.

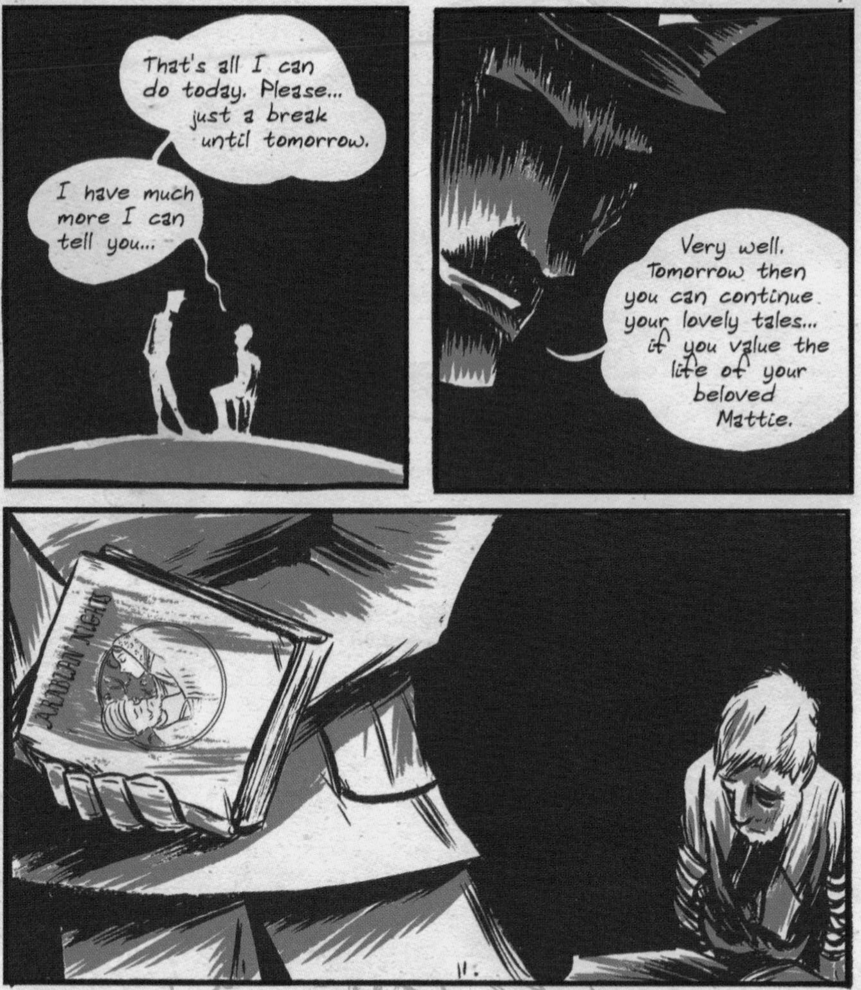
That's all I can do today. Please... just a break until tomorrow.
I have much more I can tell you...
Very well. Tomorrow then you can continue your lovely tales... if you value the life of your beloved Mattie.
ARABIAN NIGHTS

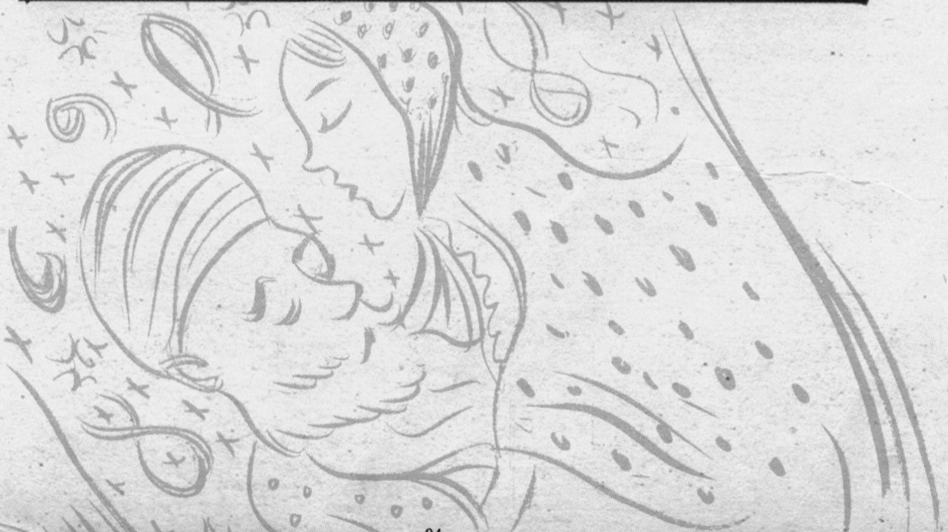

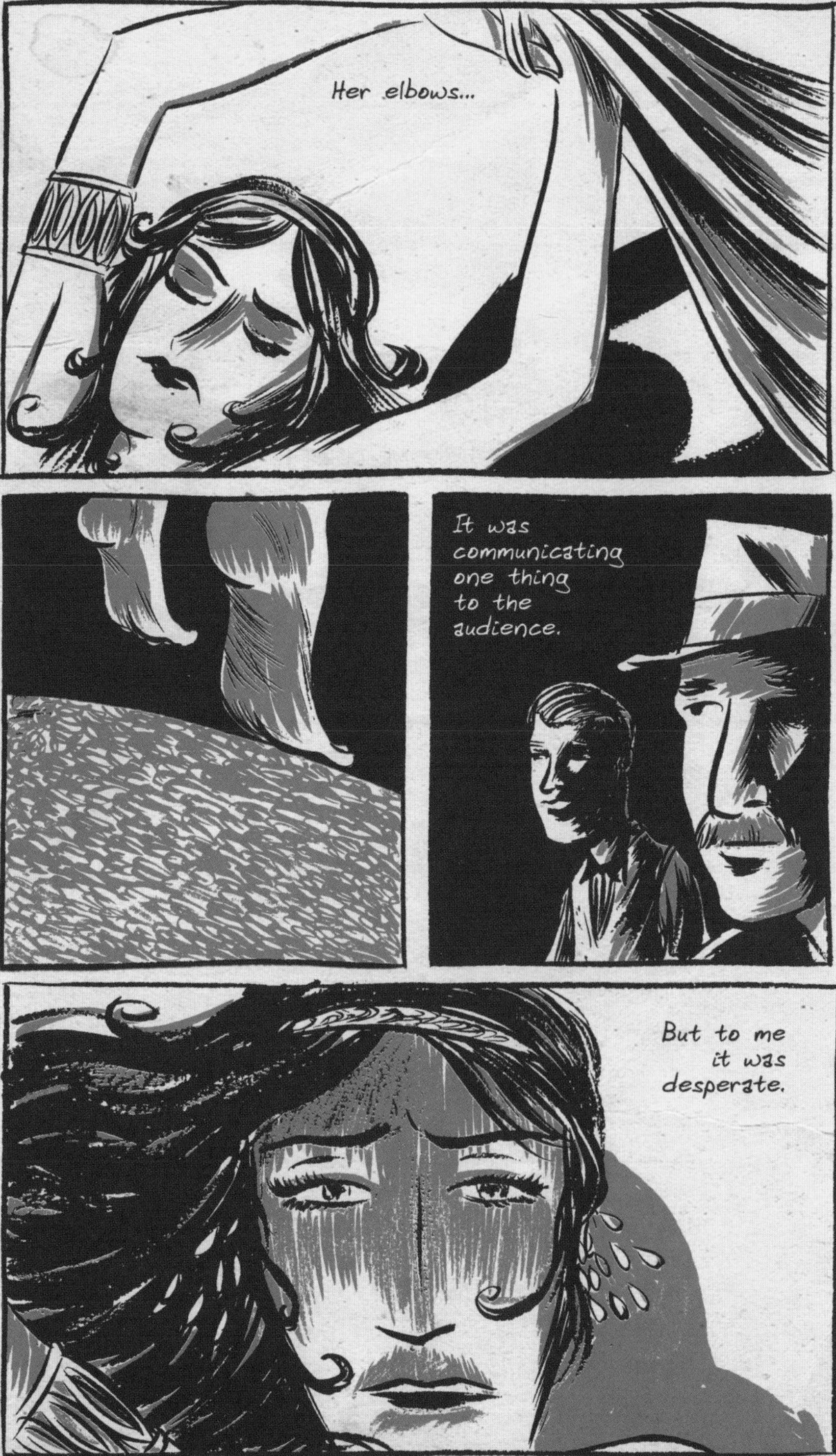
Her elbows...
It was communicating one thing to the audience.
But to me it was desperate.

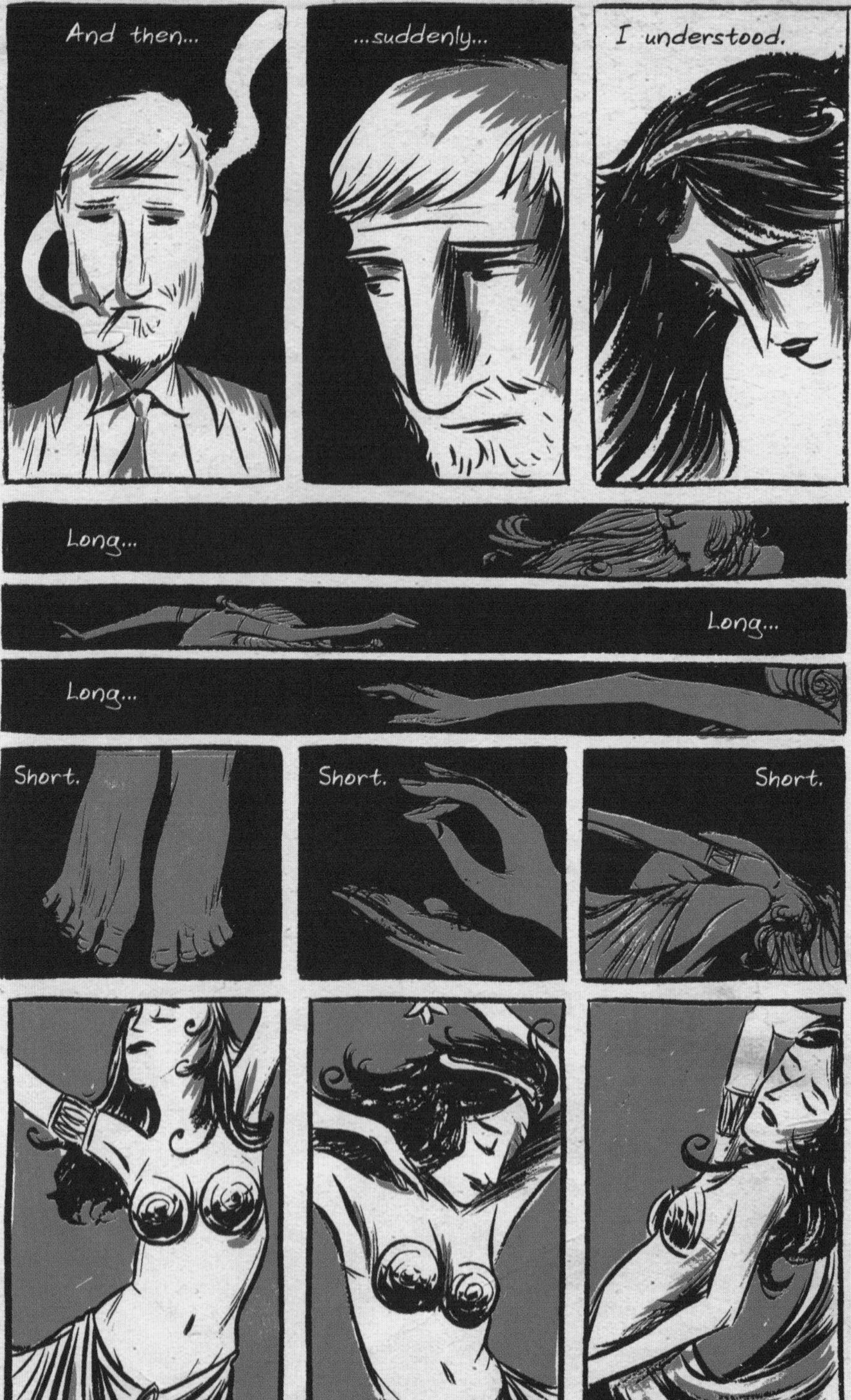
And then...
...suddenly...
I understood.
Long...
Long...
Long...
Short.
Short.
Short.

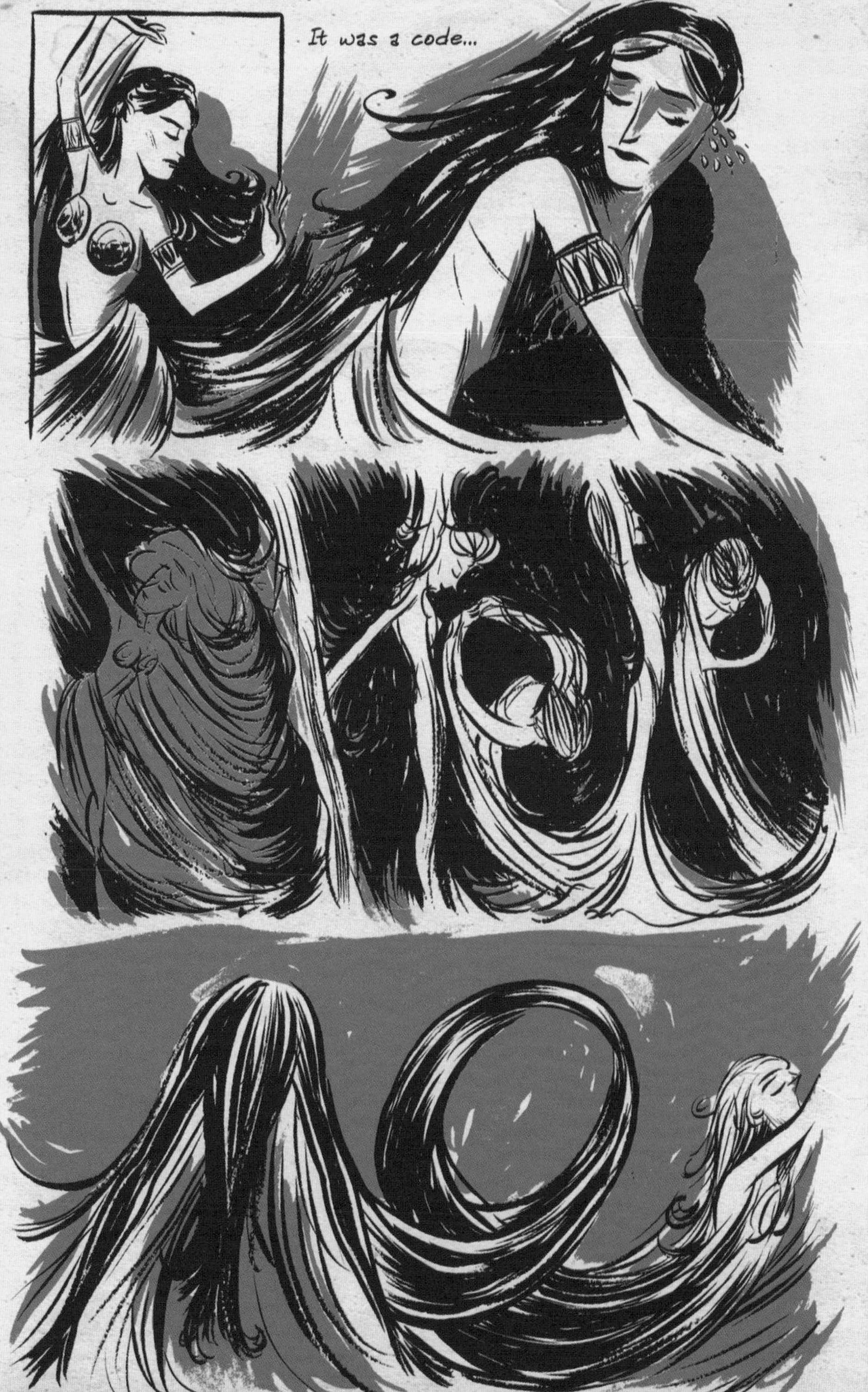
It was a code...

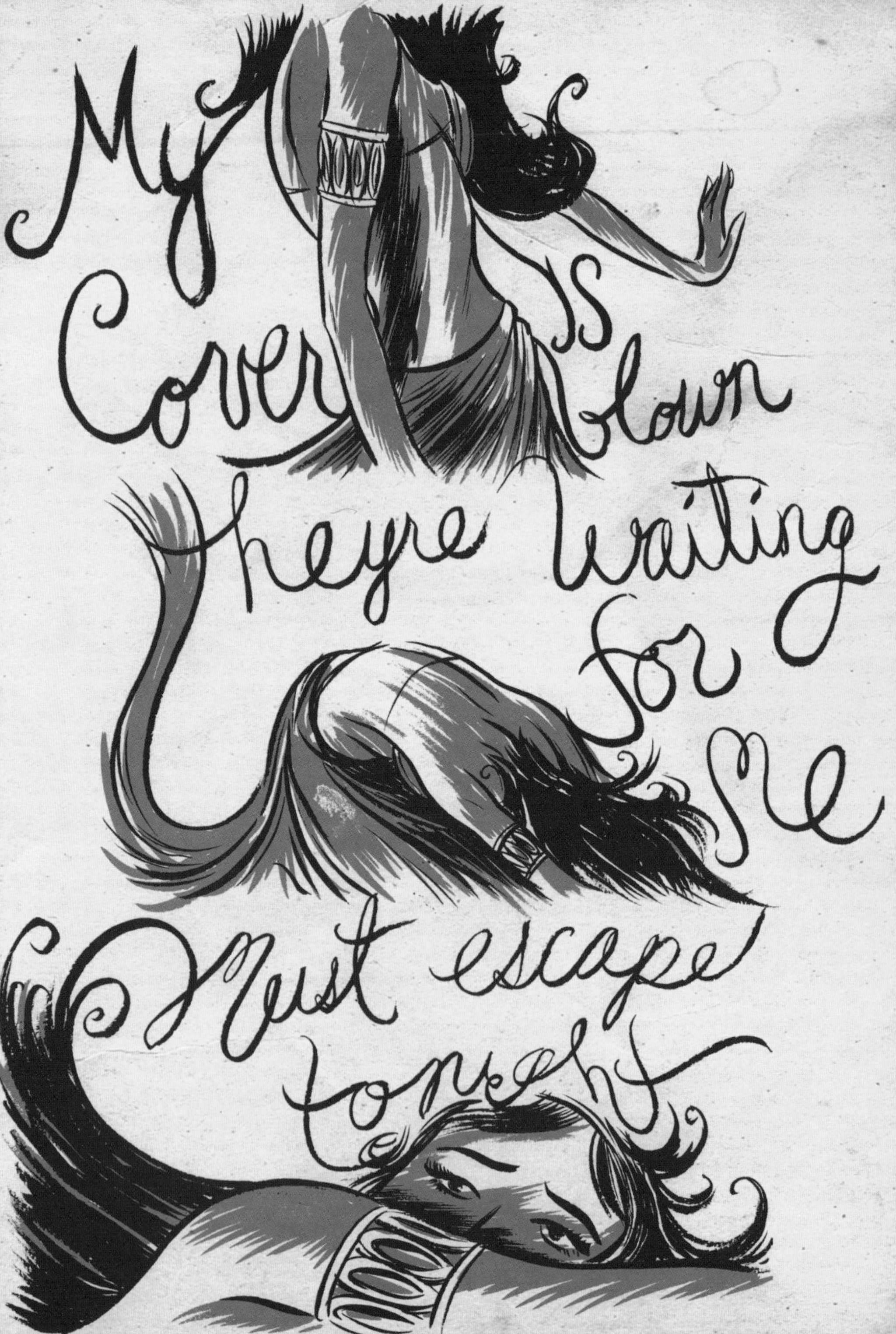
My Cover is blown
Theyre waiting for me
Must escape tonight

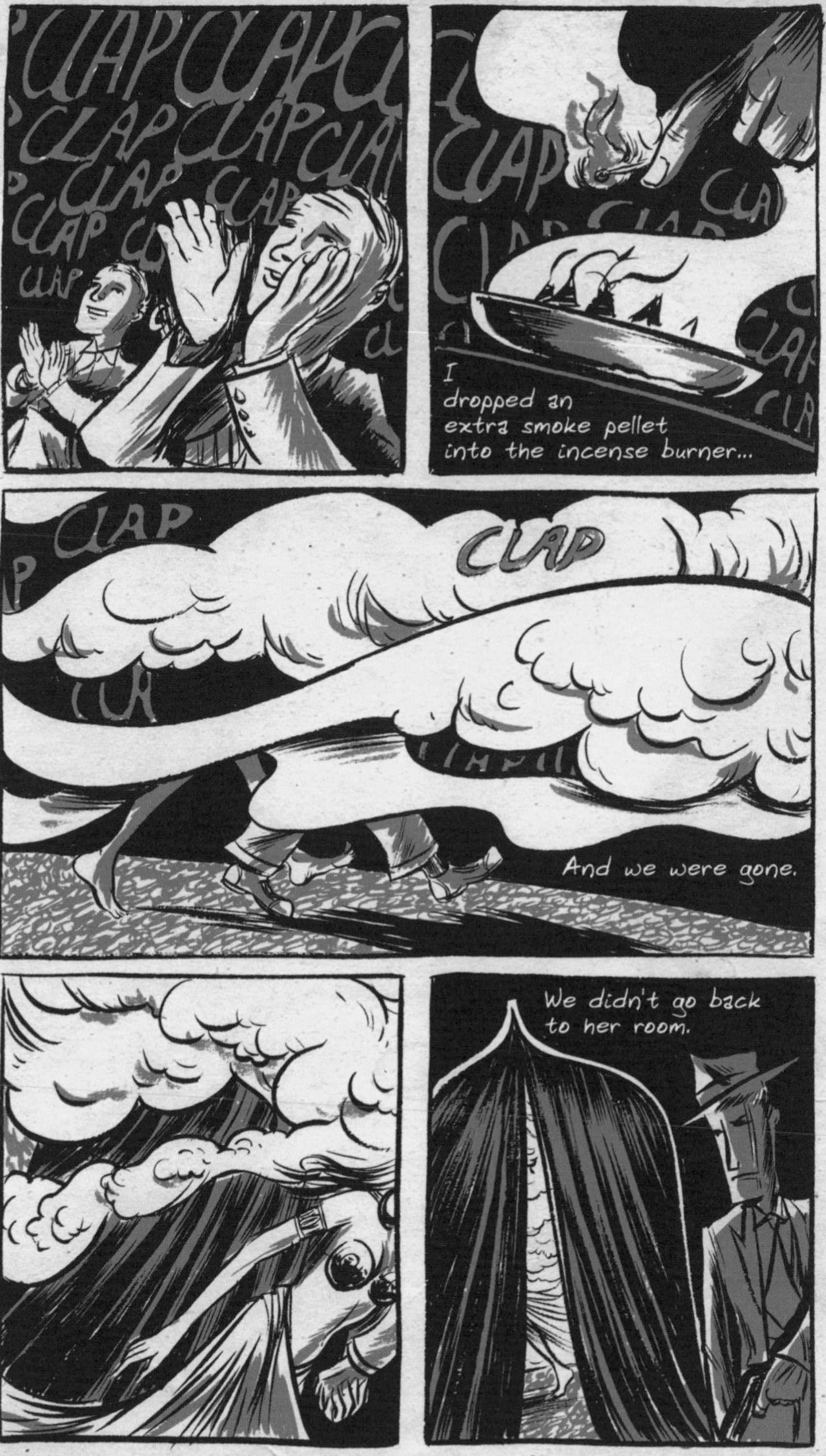
CLAP CLAP CLAP
CLAP CLAP CLAP
CLAP CLAP
CLAP CLAP
CLAP
CLAP
CLAP
I dropped an extra smoke pellet into the incense burner...
CLAP
CLAP
And we were gone.
We didn't go back to her room.

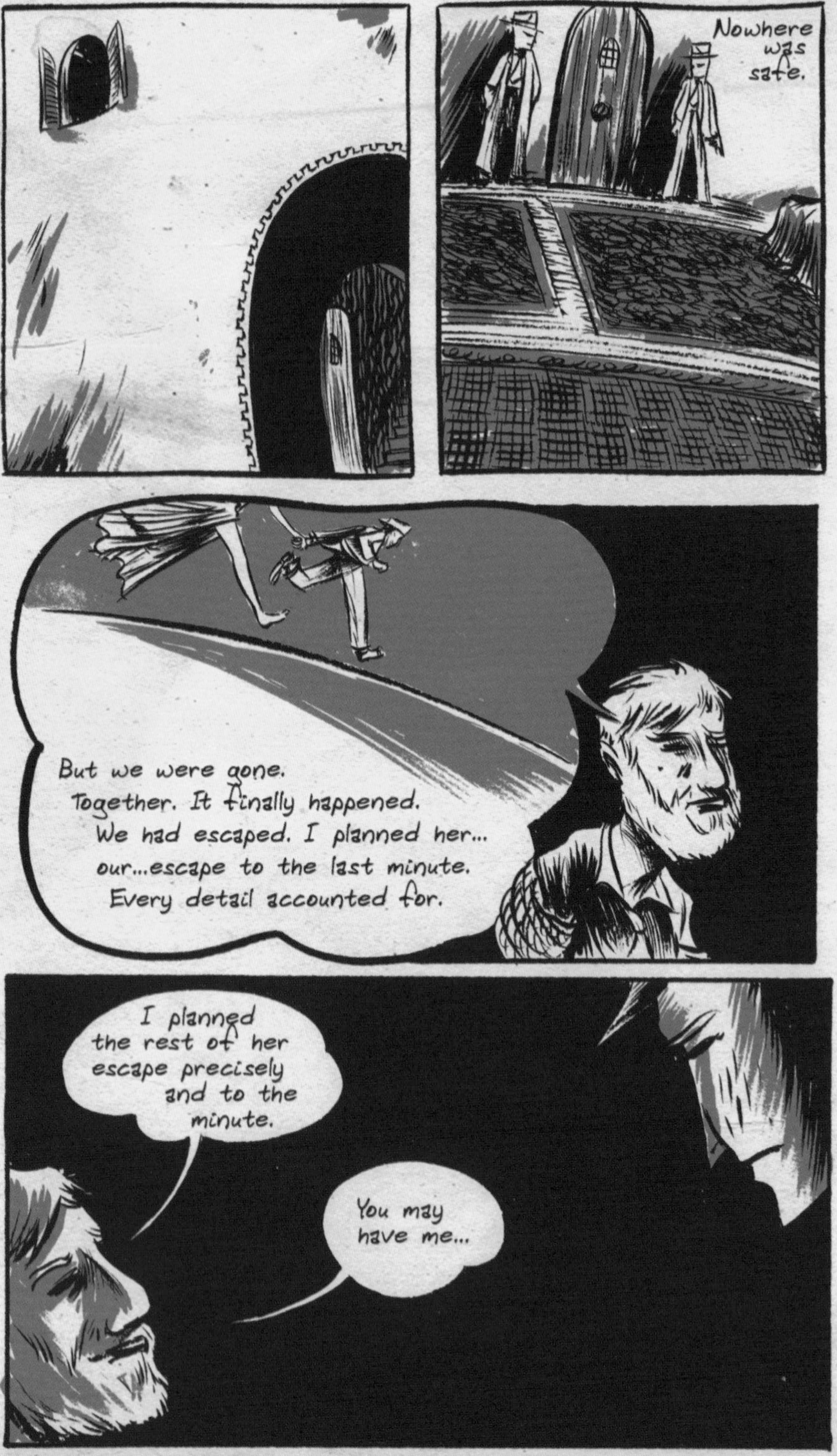
Nowhere was safe.
But we were gone. Together. It finally happened. We had escaped. I planned her... our...escape to the last minute. Every detail accounted for.
I planned the rest of her escape precisely and to the minute.
You may have me...

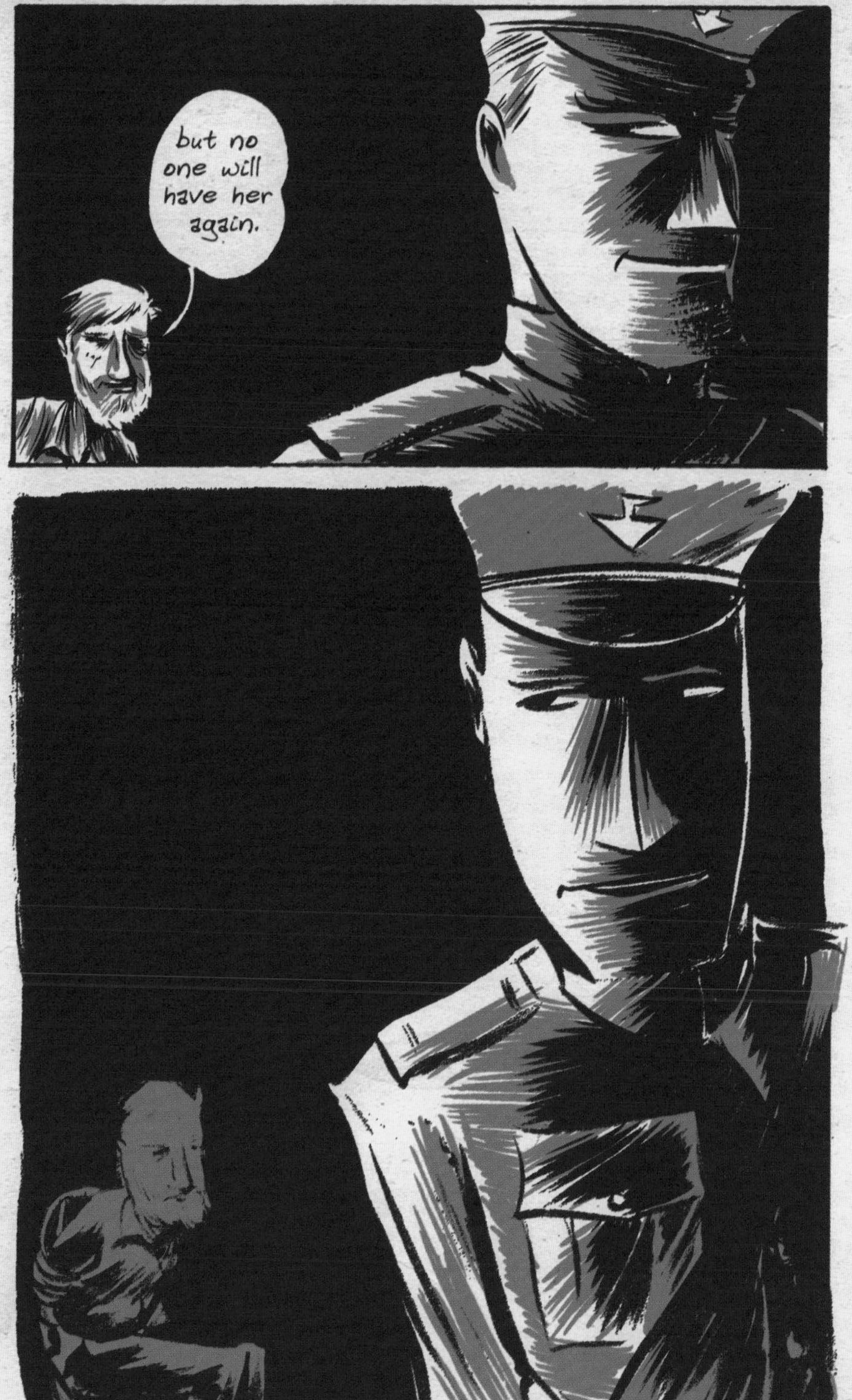
but no one will have her again.

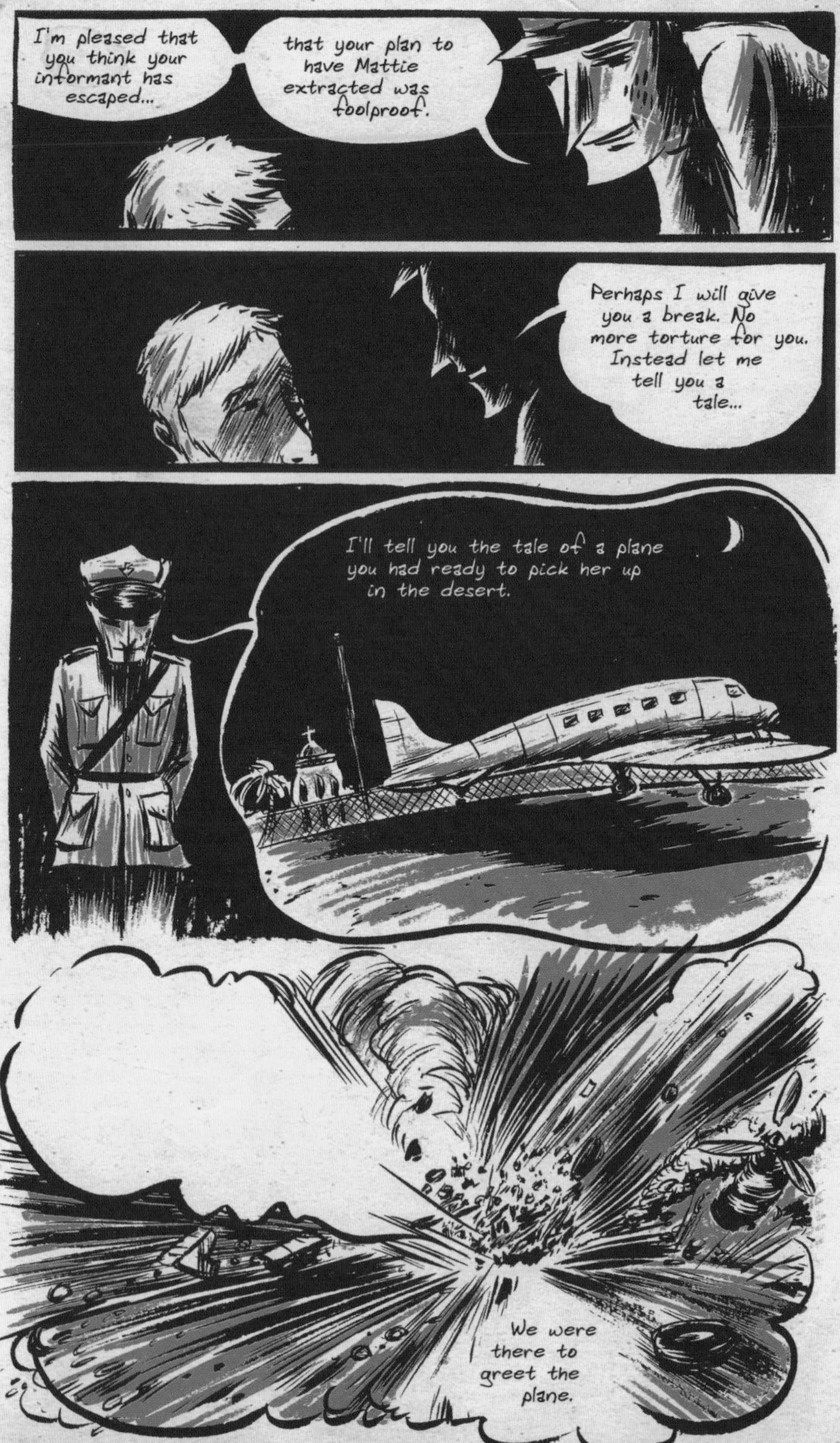
I'm pleased that you think your informant has escaped...
that your plan to have Mattie extracted was foolproof.
Perhaps I will give you a break. No more torture for you. Instead let me tell you a tale...
I'll tell you the tale of a plane you had ready to pick her up in the desert.
We were there to greet the plane.

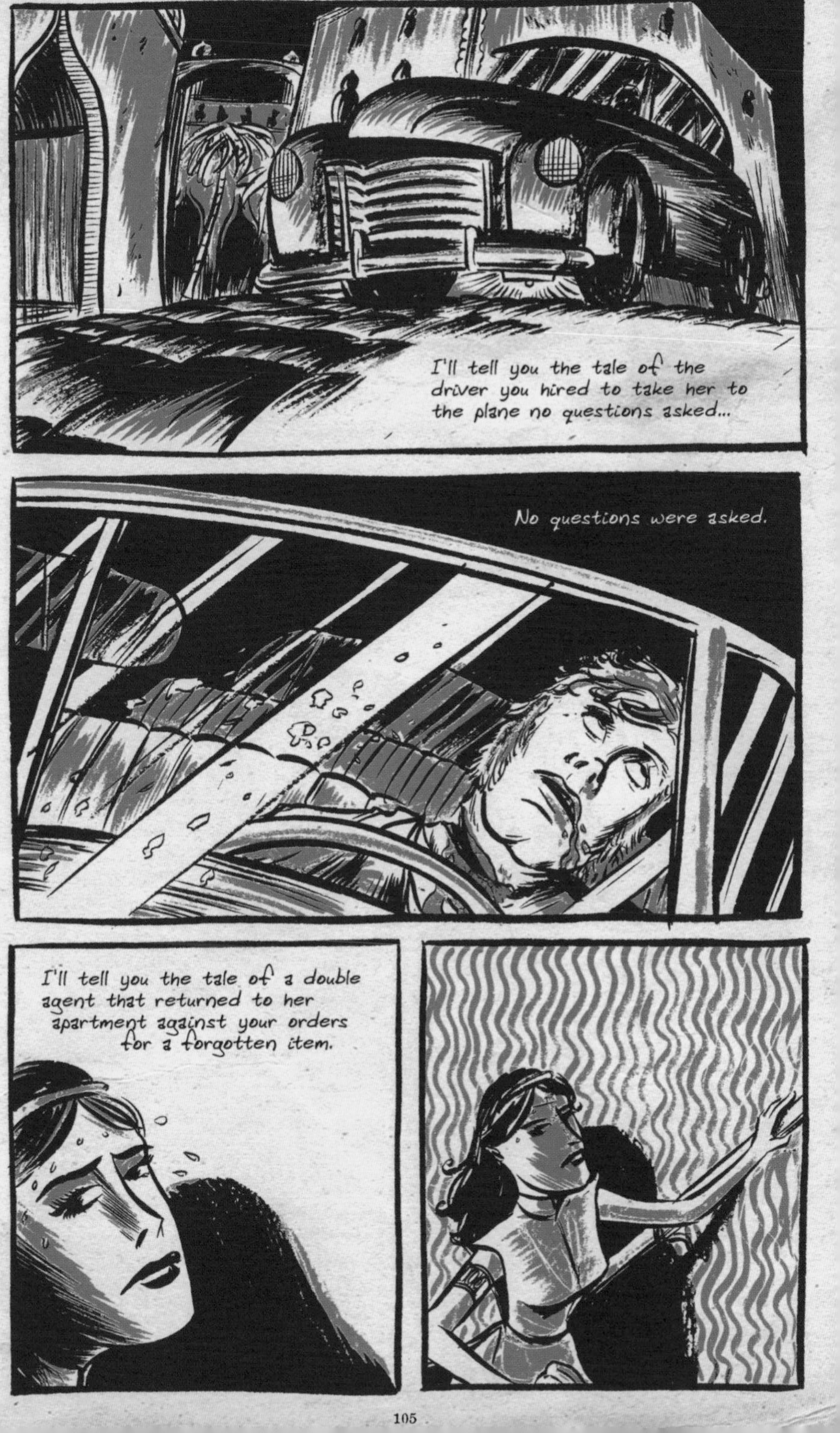
I'll tell you the tale of the driver you hired to take her to the plane no questions asked...
No questions were asked.
I'll tell you the tale of a double agent that returned to her apartment against your orders for a forgotten item.

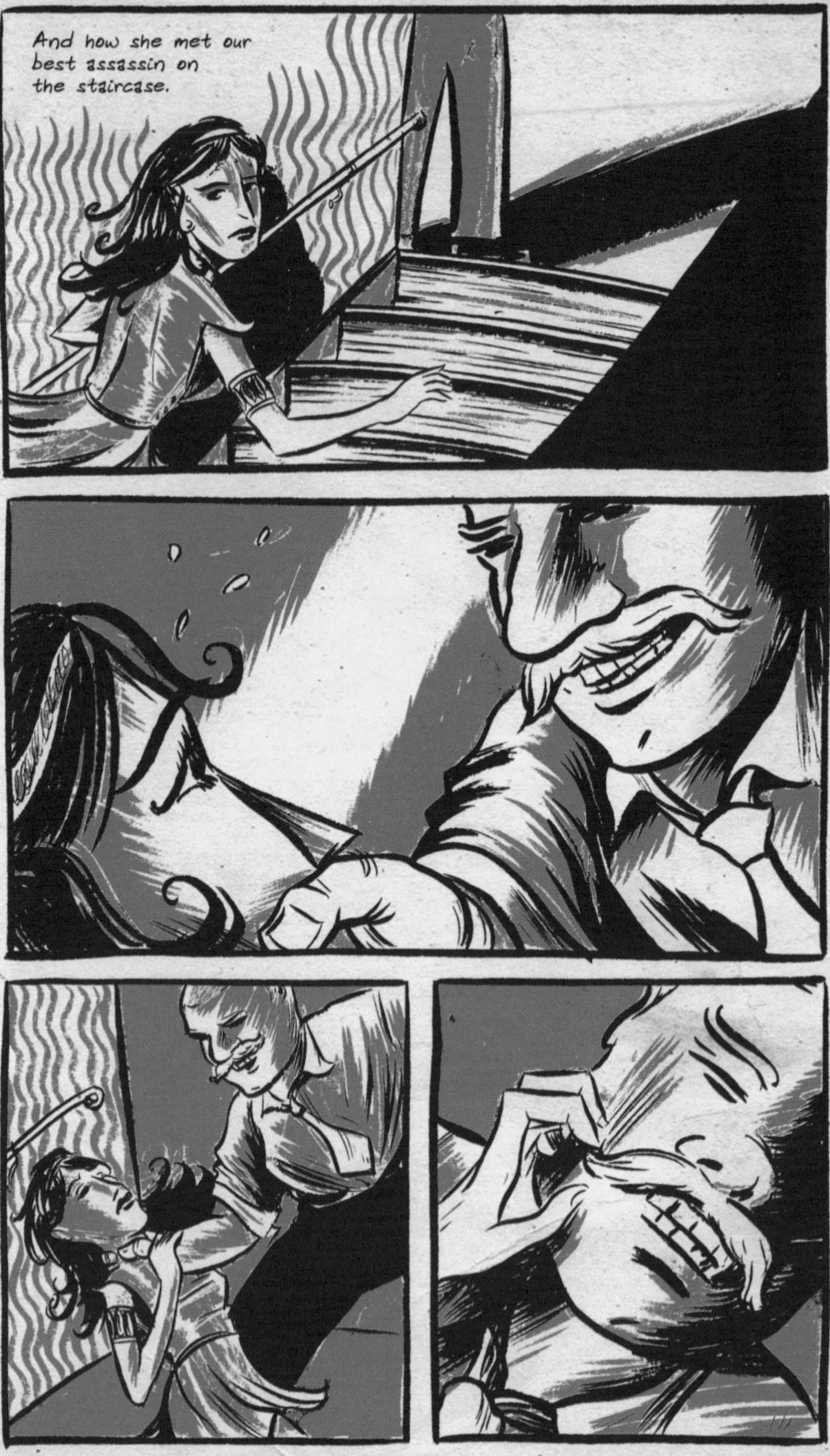
And how she met our best assassin on the staircase.

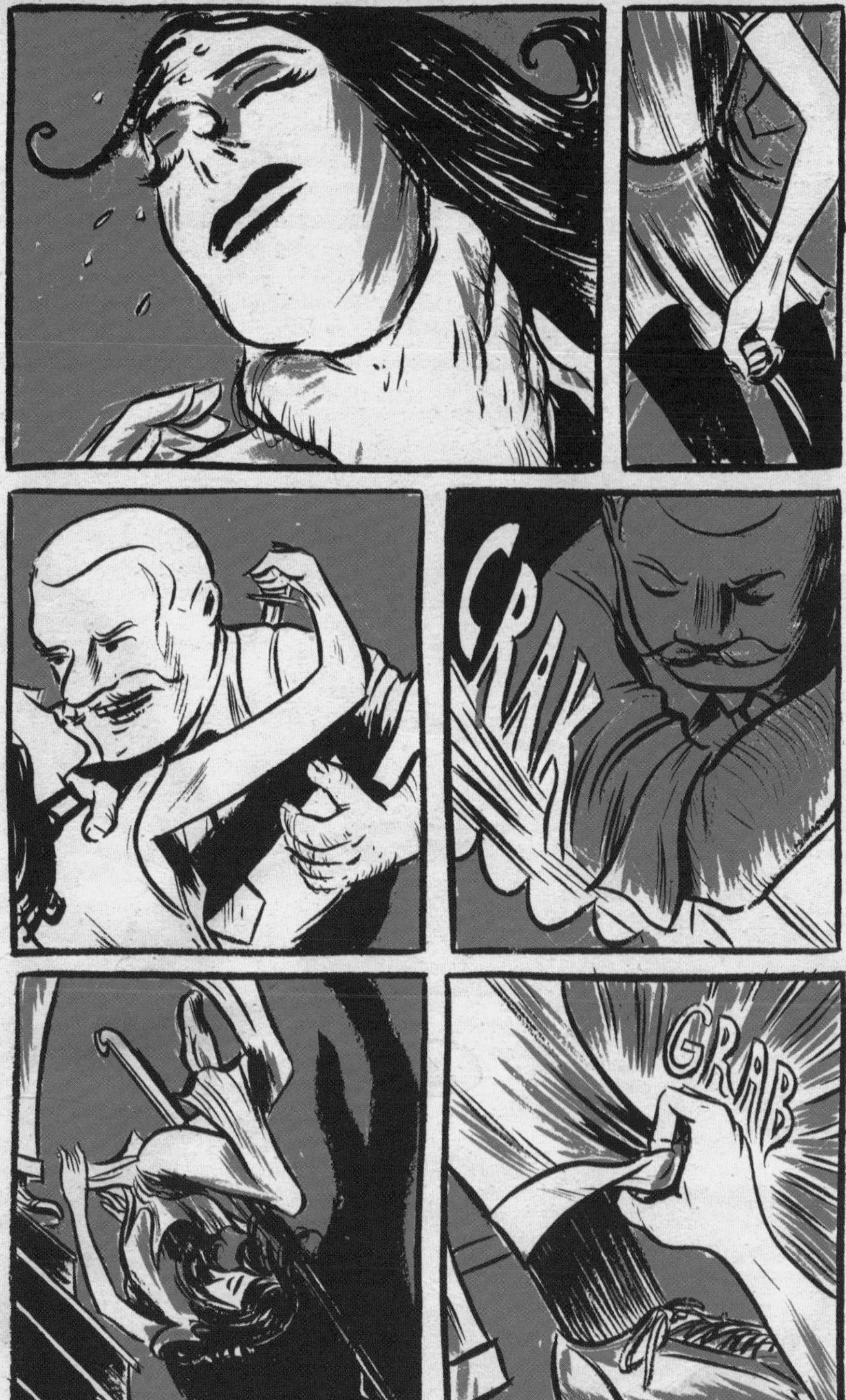
CRAK
GRAB

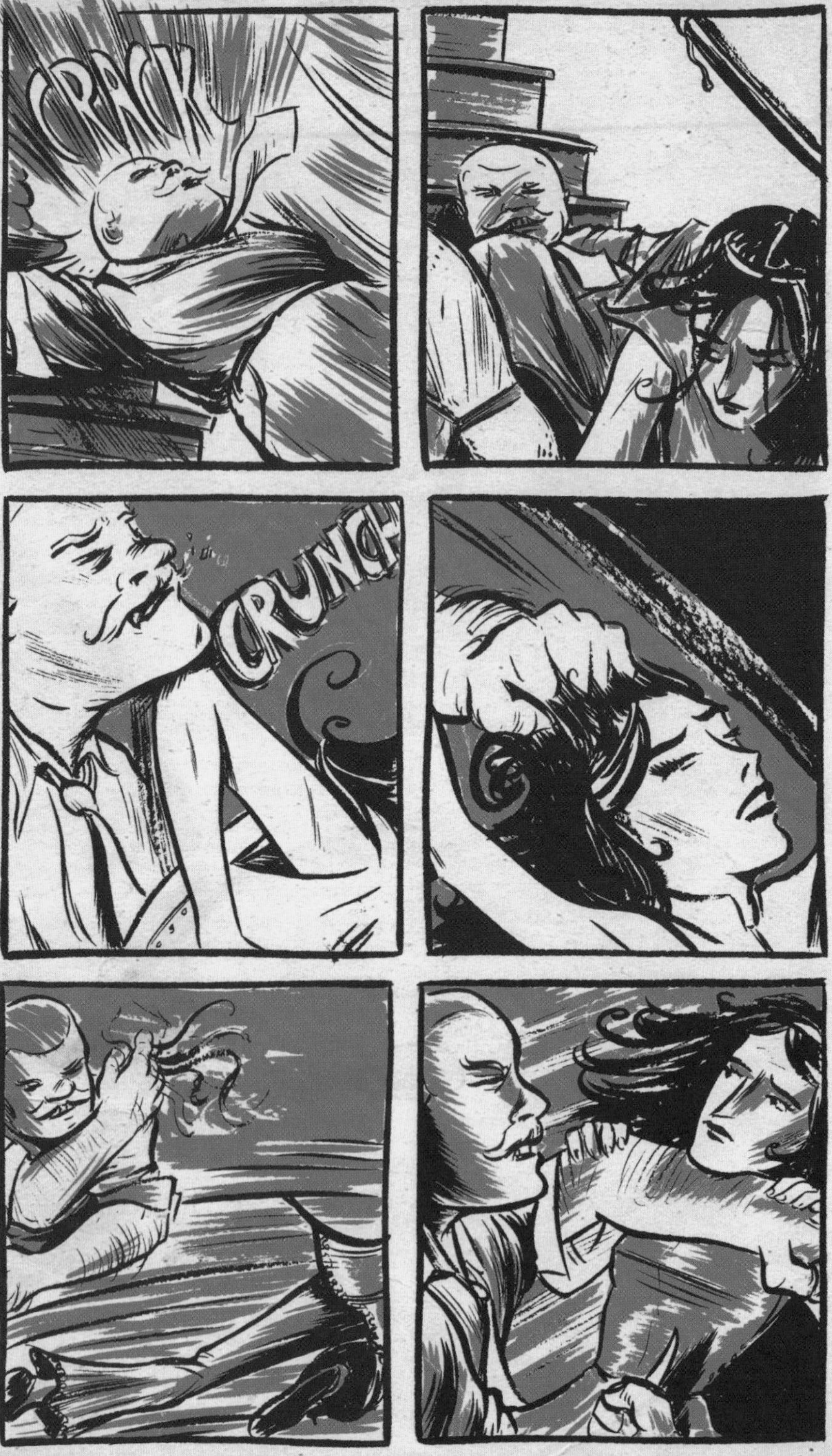
CRACK
CRUNCH

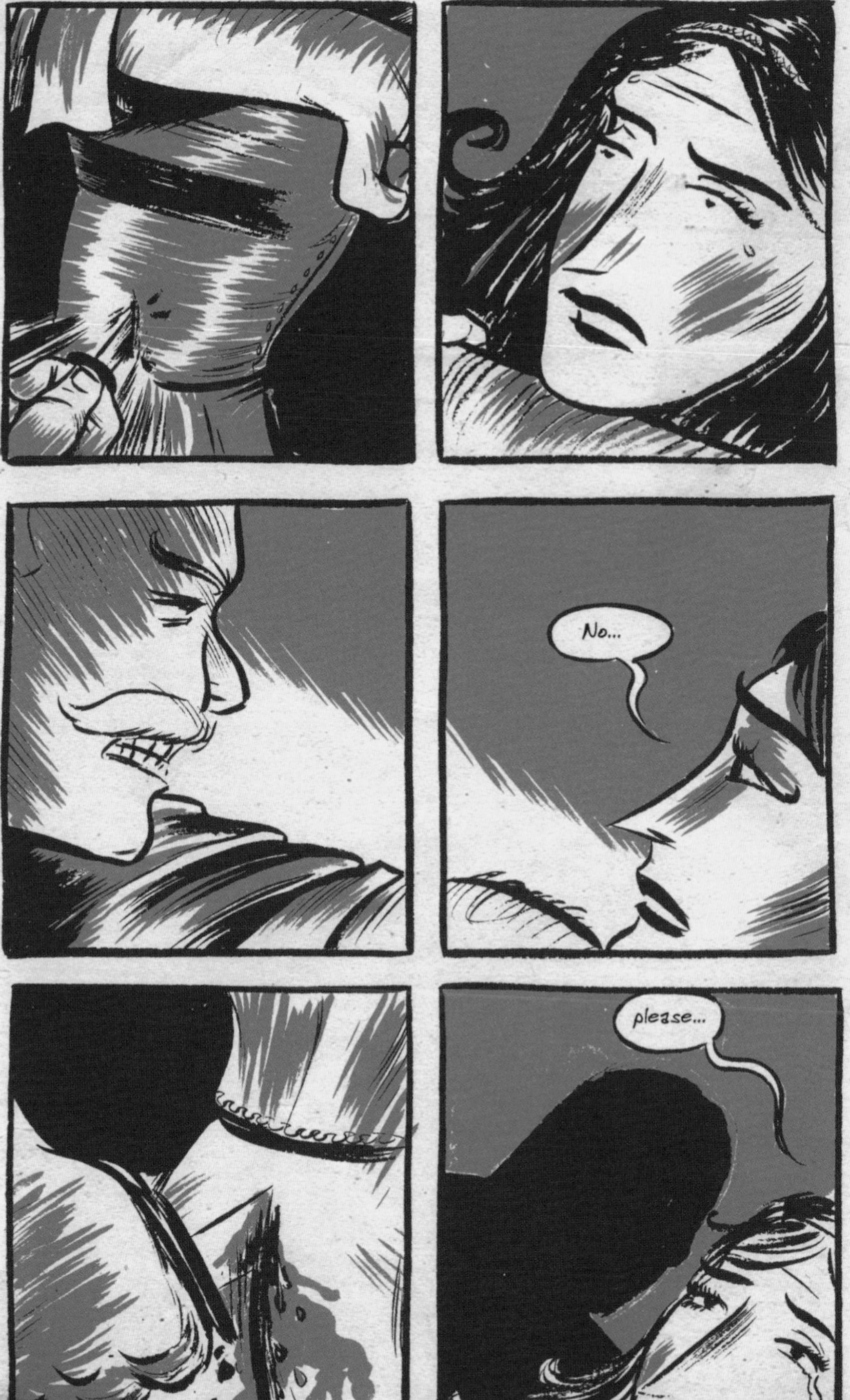
No...
please...

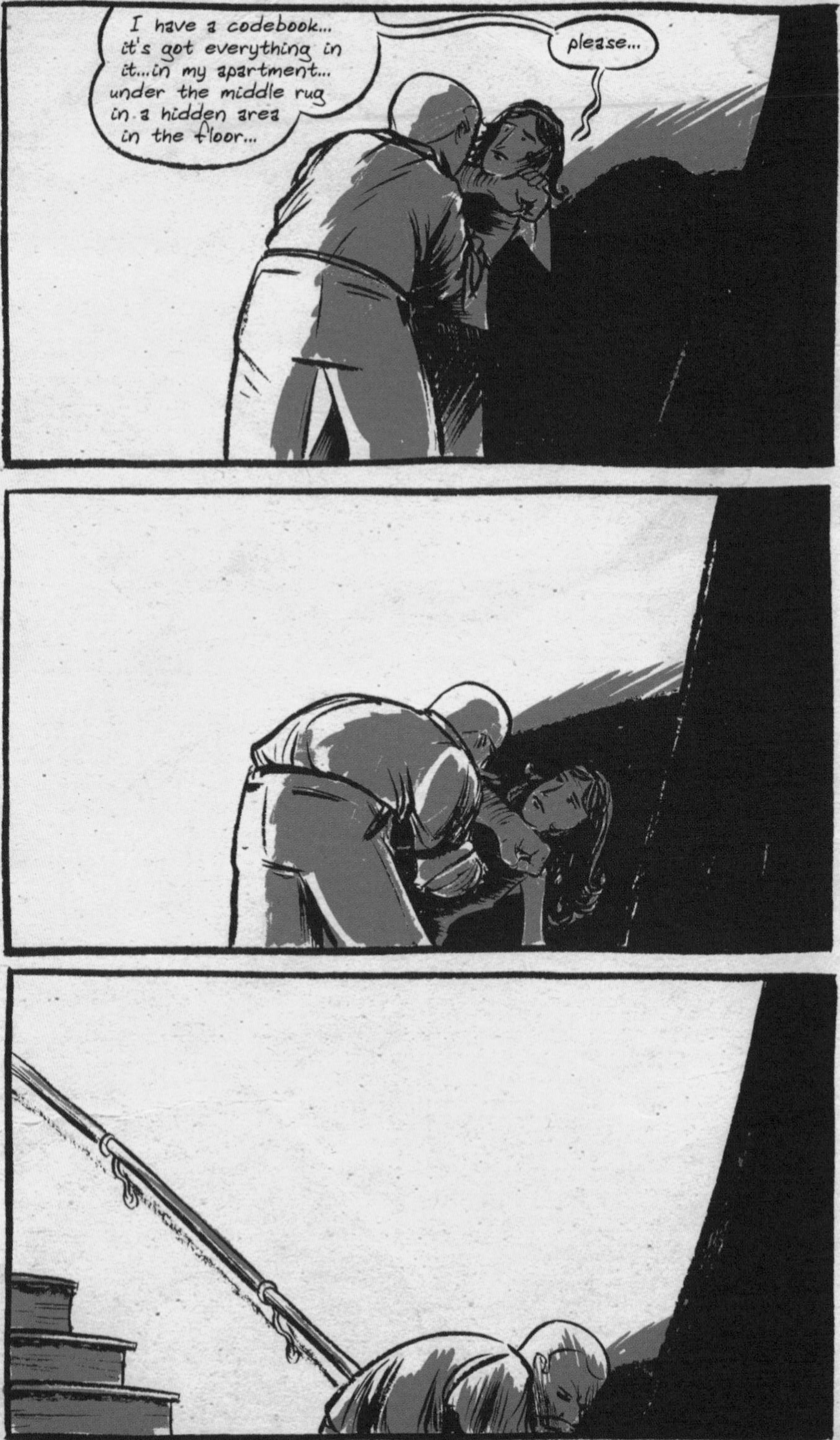
I have a codebook... it's got everything in it...in my apartment... under the middle rug in a hidden area in the floor...
please...

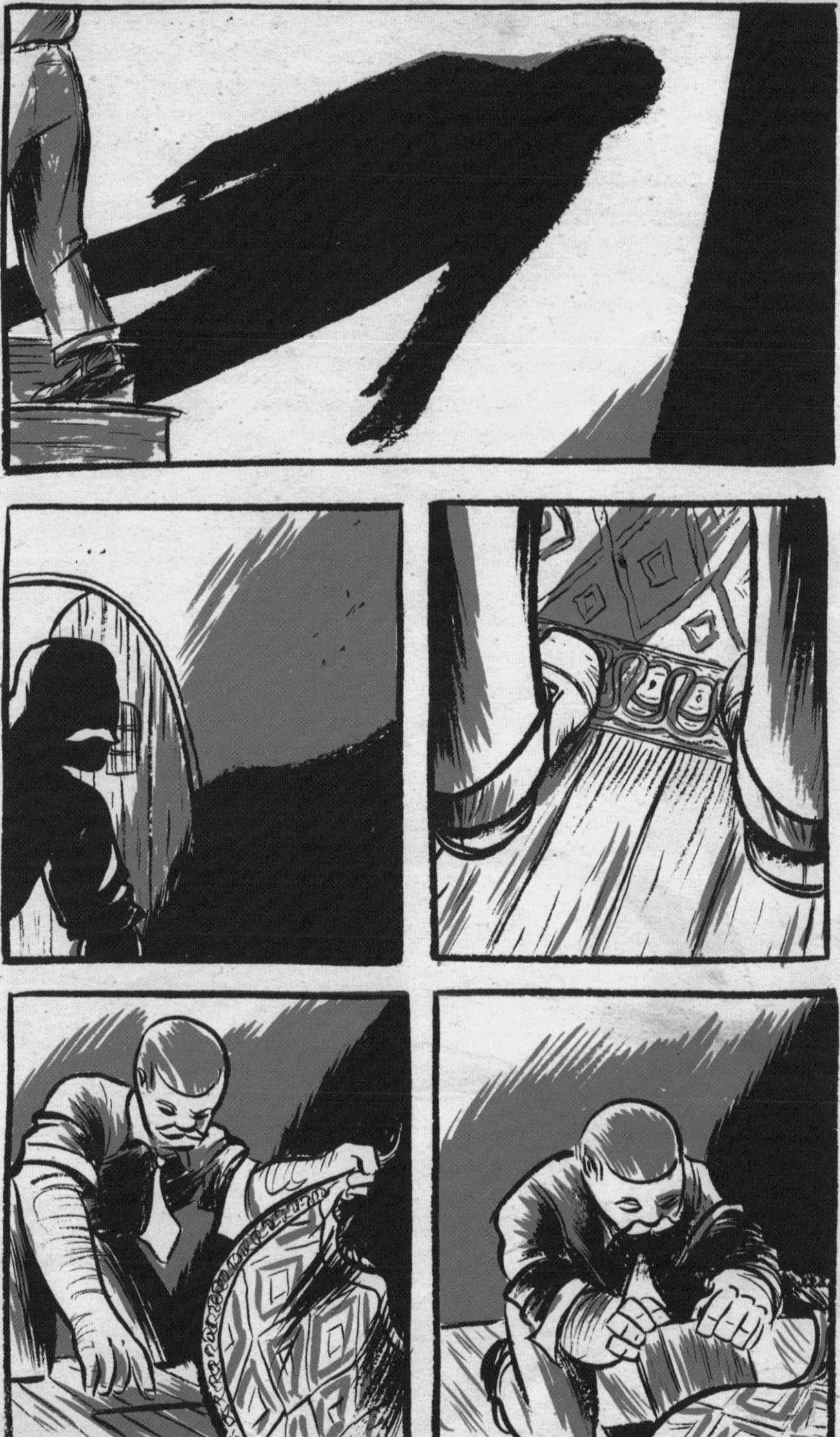

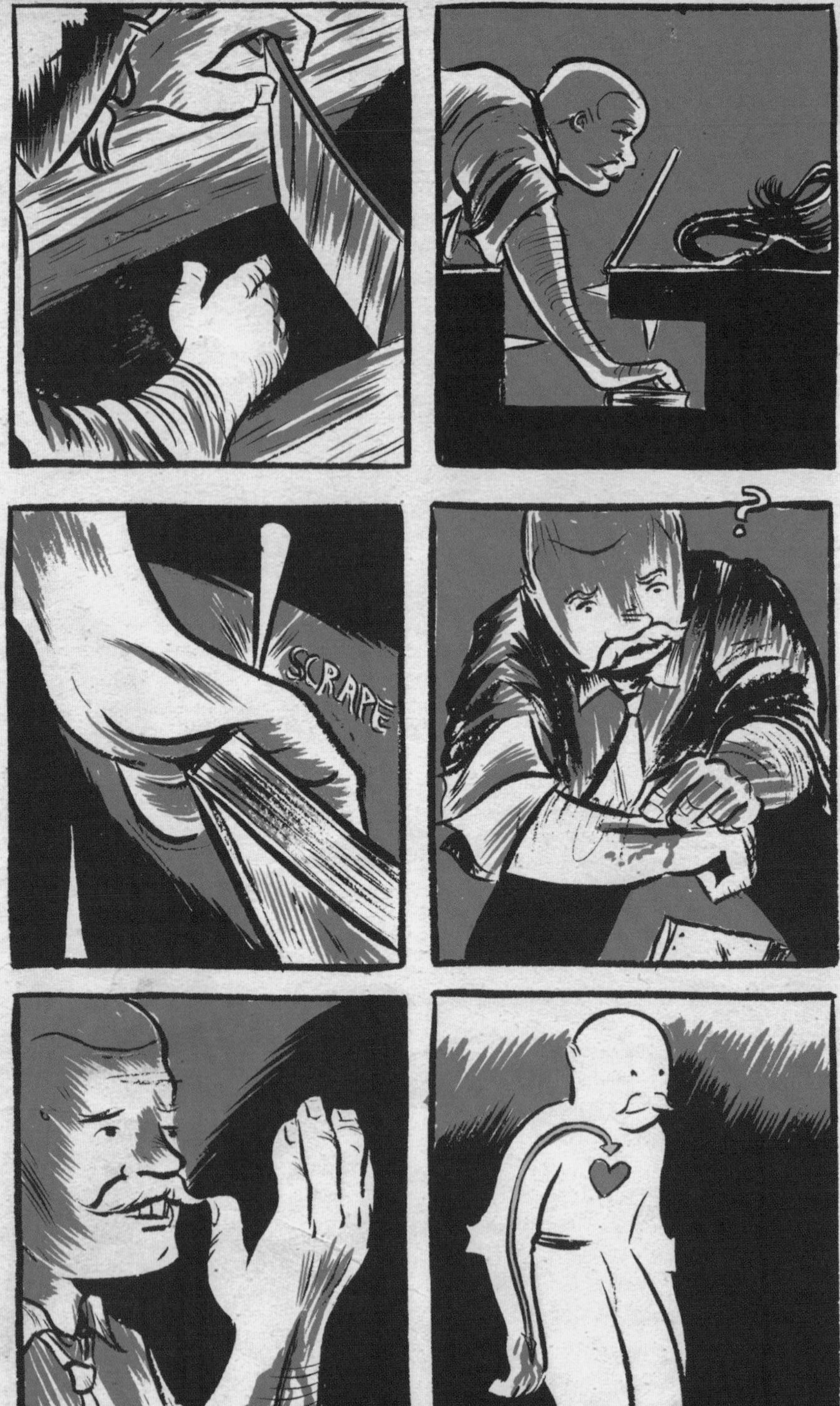
SCRAPE
?

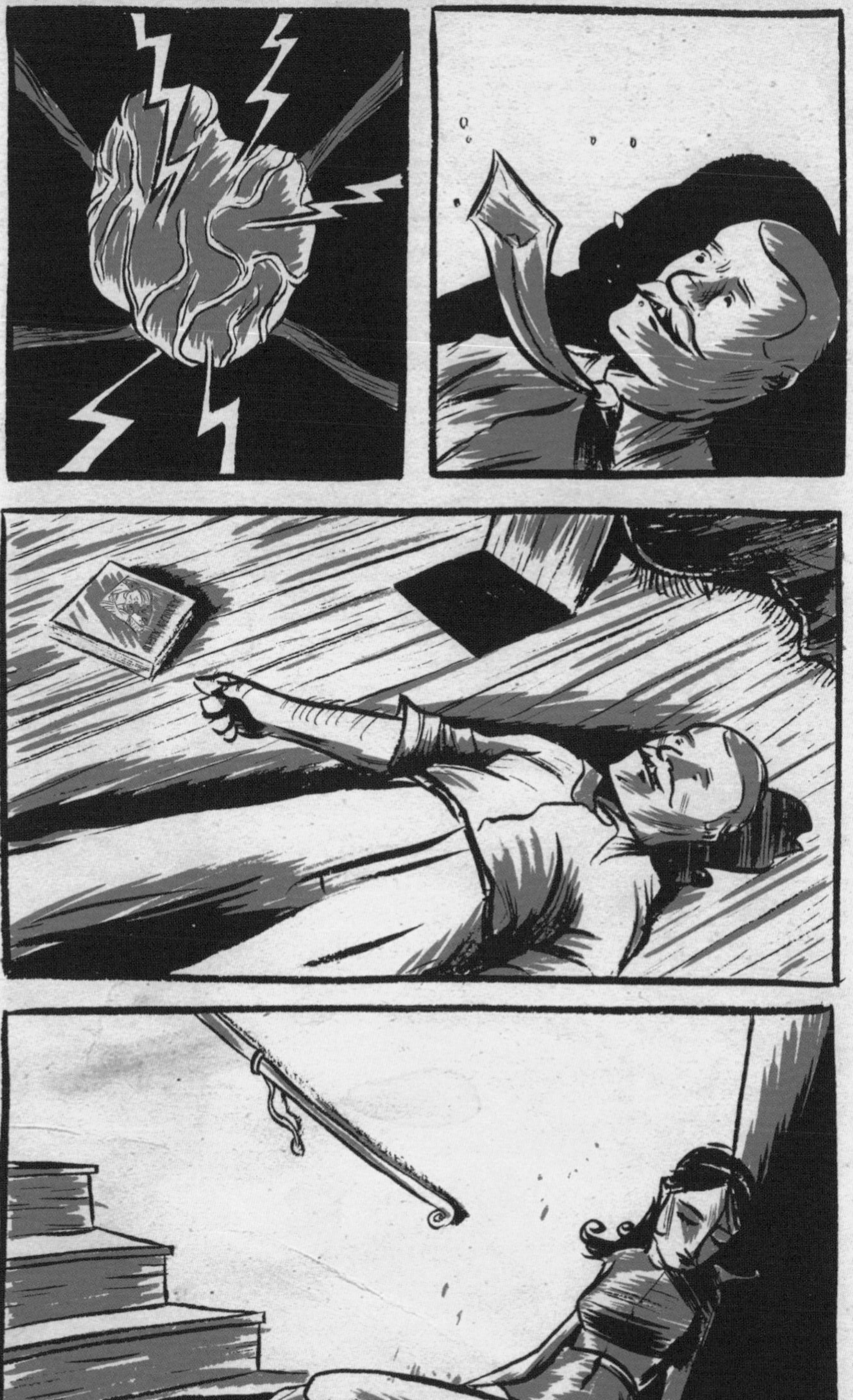

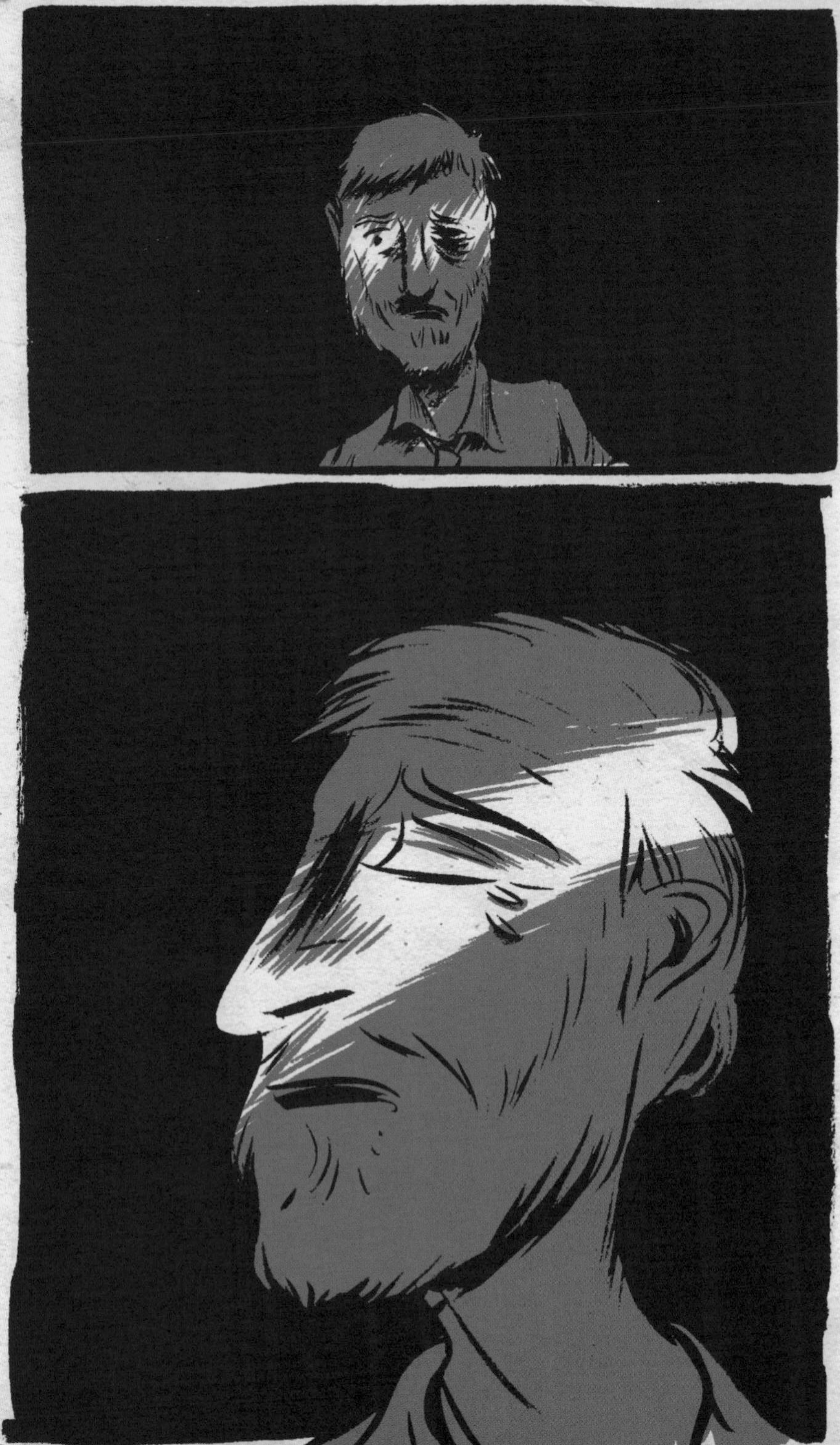

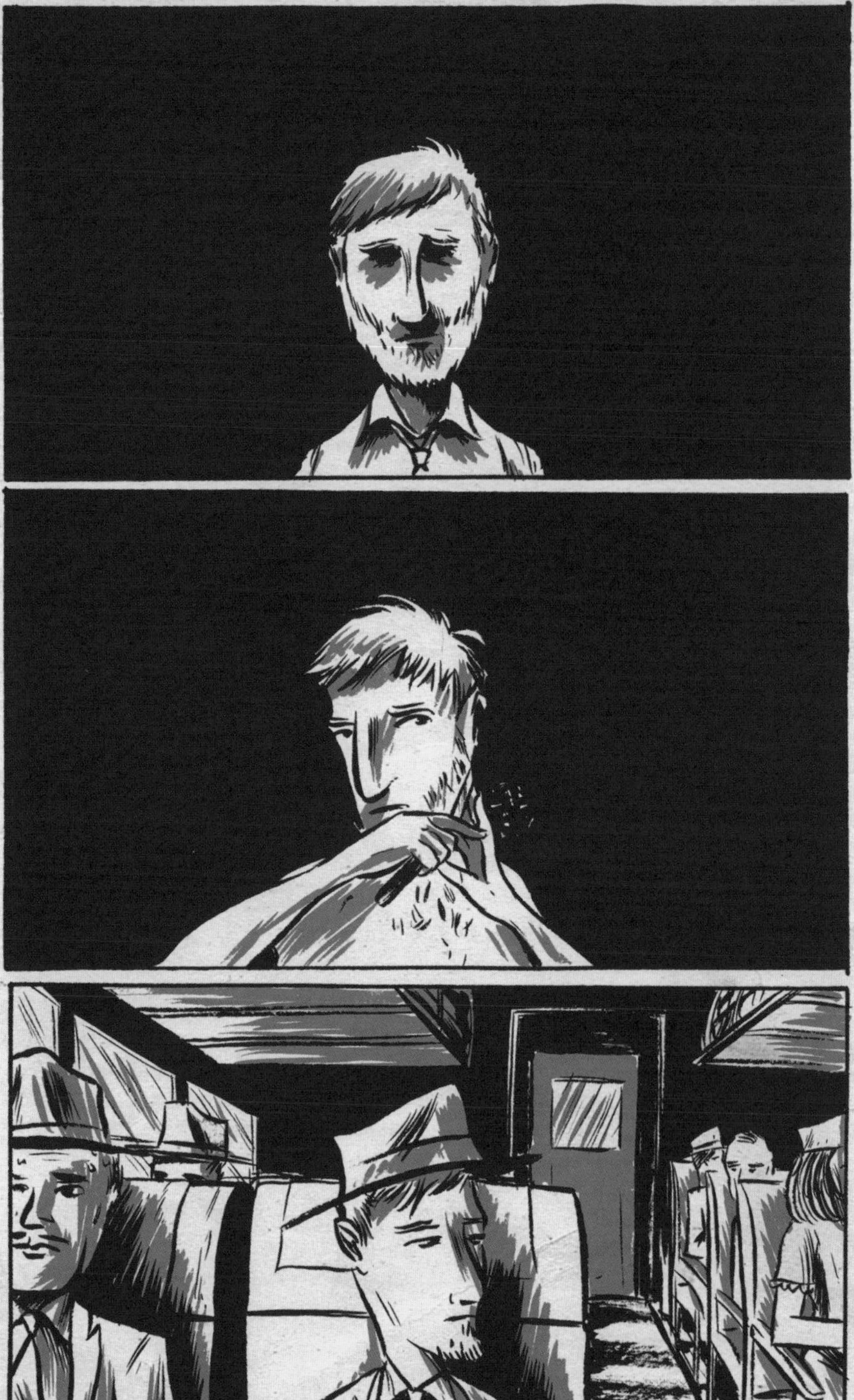

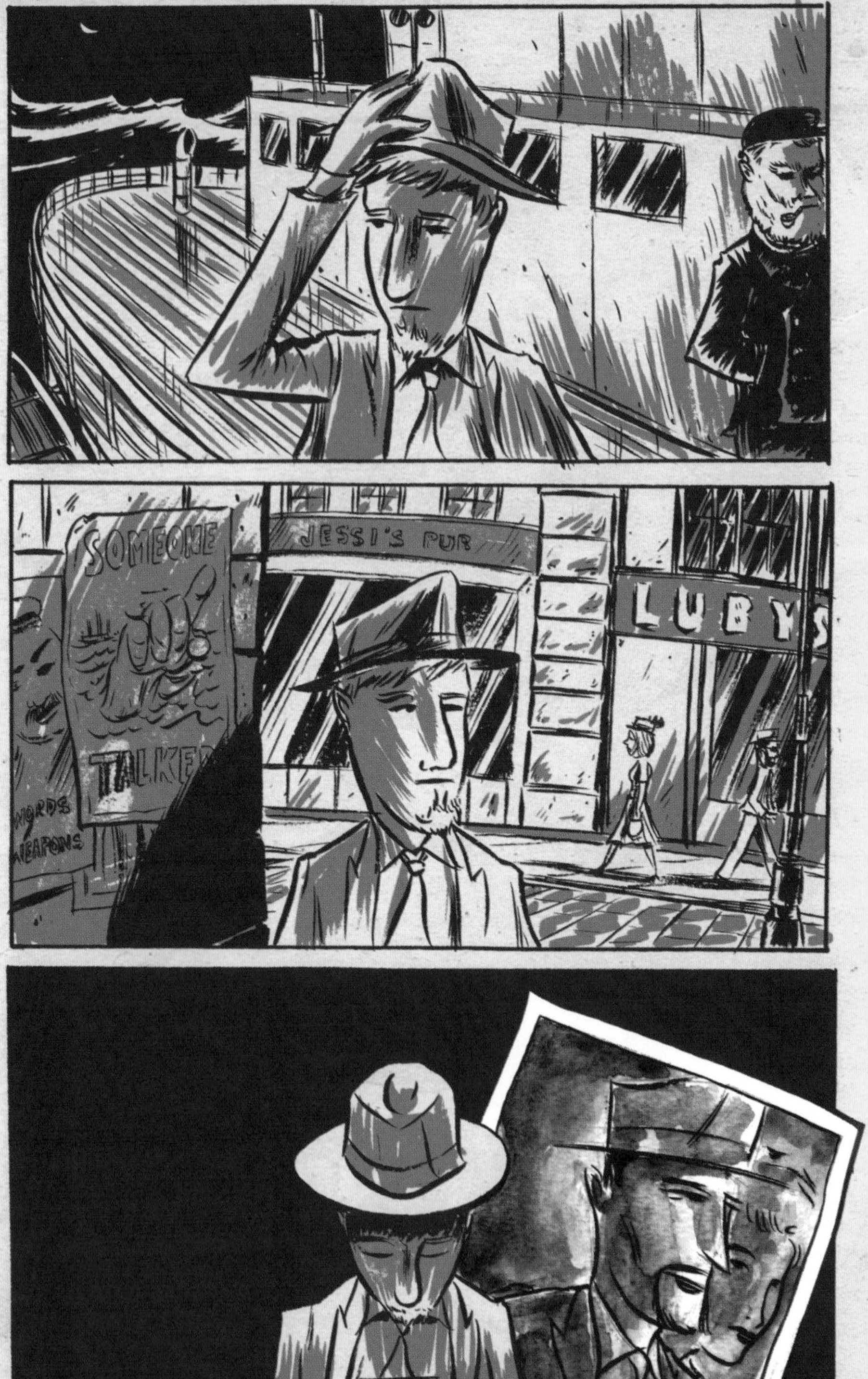

SOMEONE
JESSI'S PUB

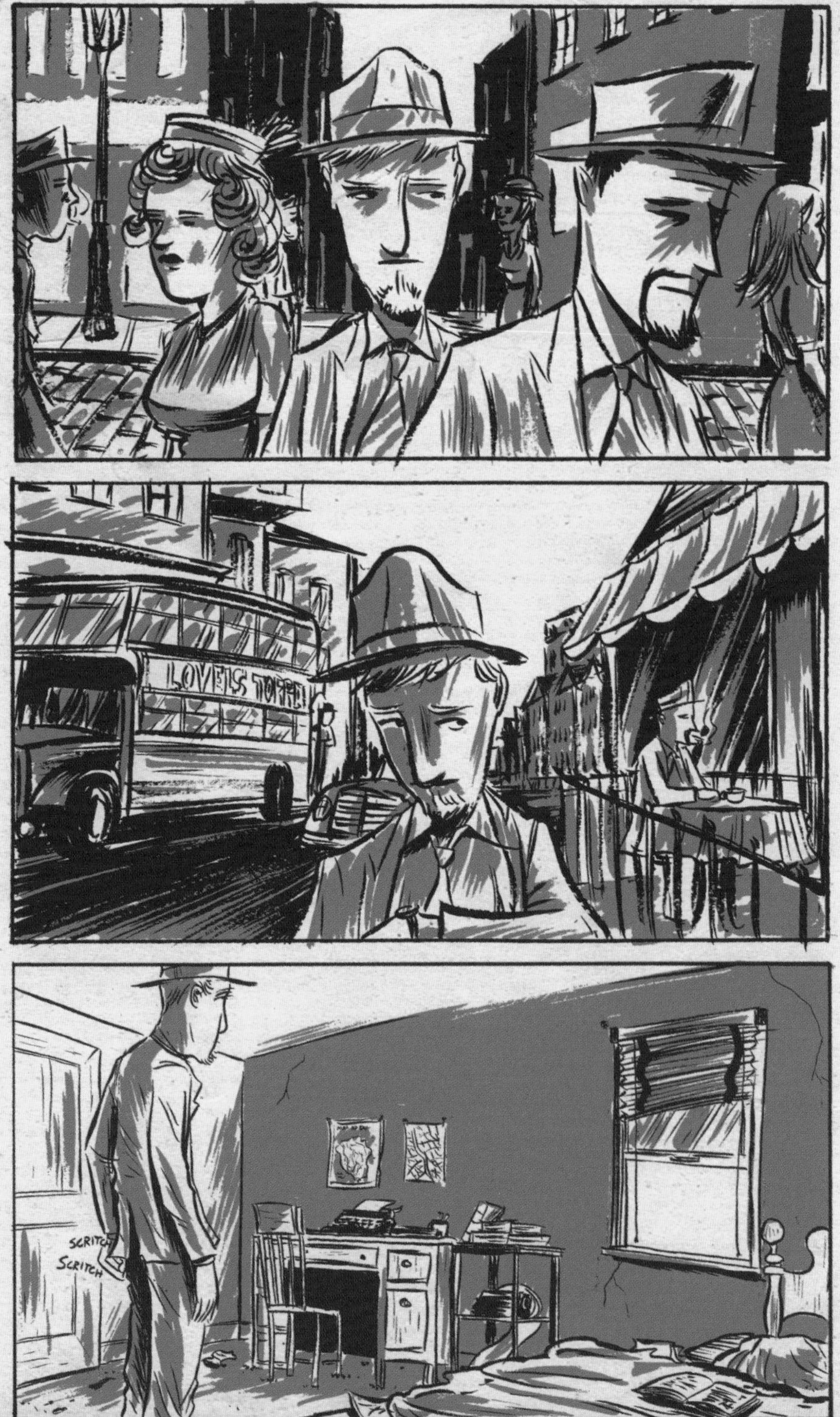

LOVEL'S
SCRITCH
SCRITCH

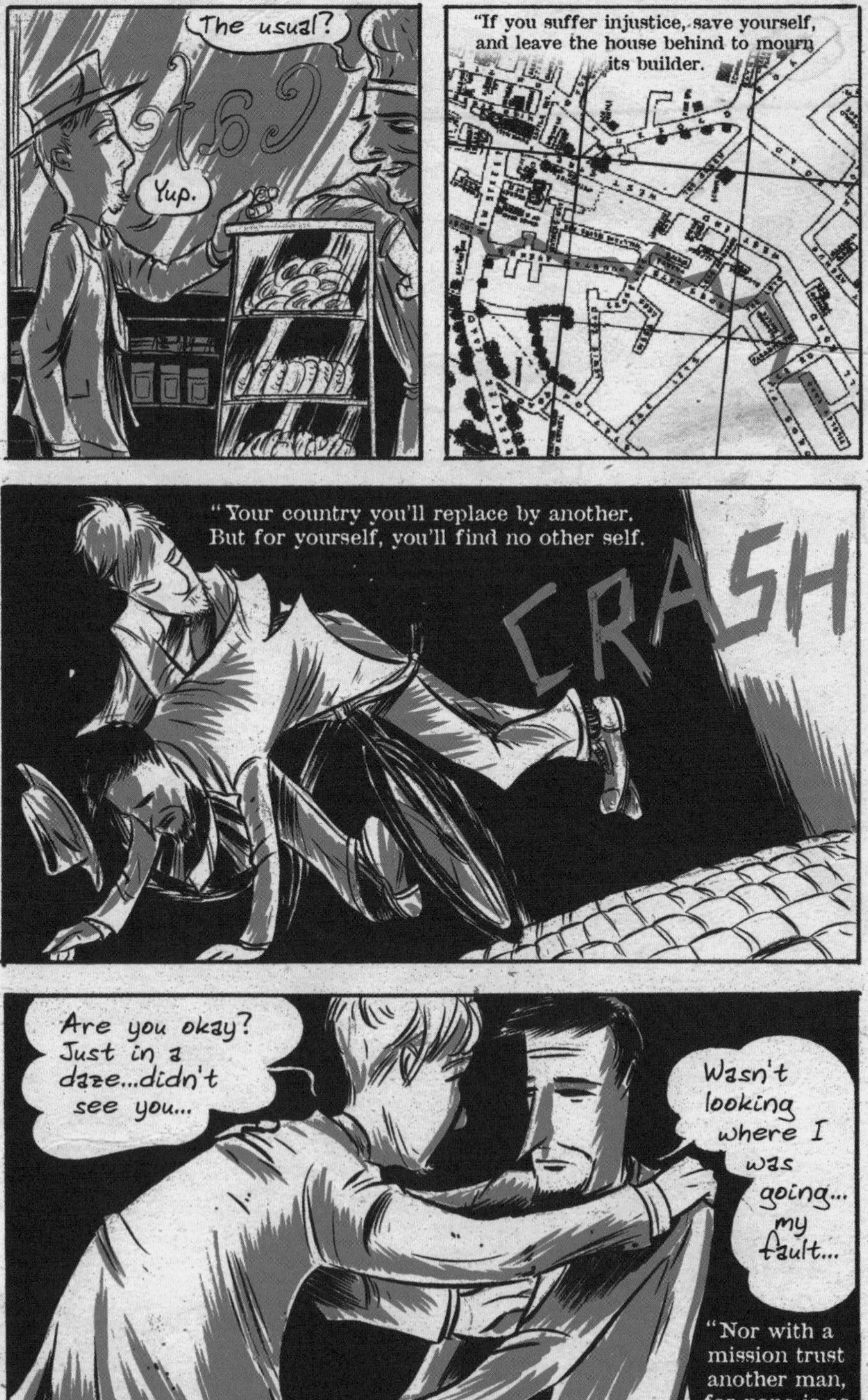
The usual?
Yup.
"If you suffer injustice, save yourself, and leave the house behind to mourn its builder.
"Your country you'll replace by another. But for yourself, you'll find no other self.
CRASH
Are you okay? Just in a daze...didn't see you...
Wasn't looking where I was going... my fault...
"Nor with a mission trust another man, for none is as loyal as you yourself.

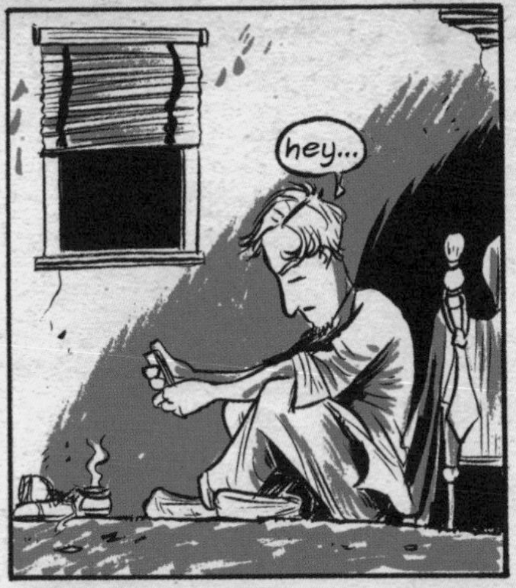
hey...

“And did the lion
not struggle by himself,
He would not prowl
with such a mighty mane.”

—The Arabian Nights

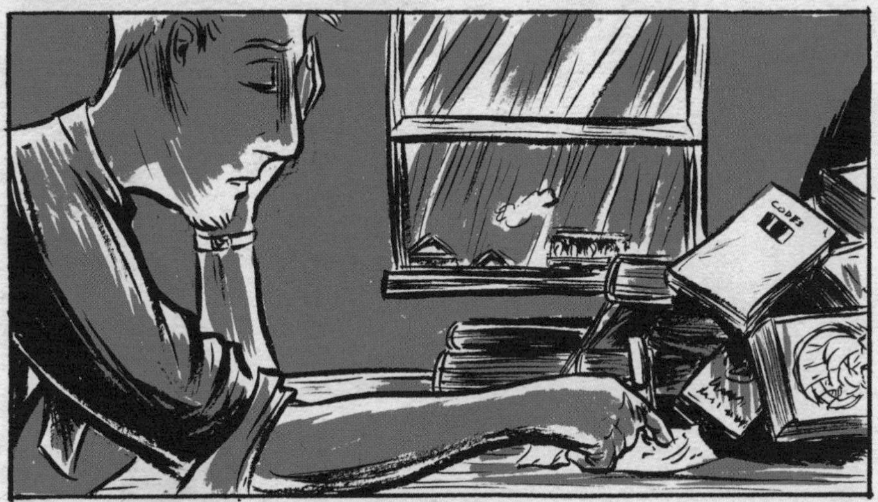
CODES

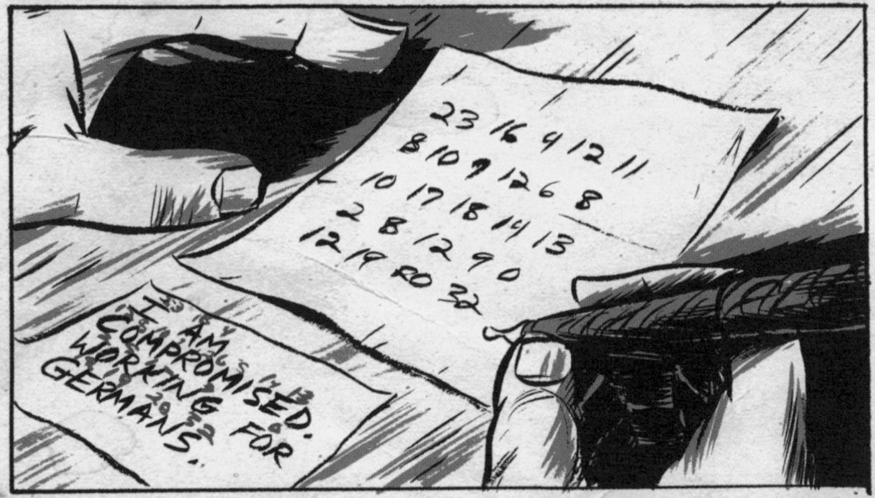
23 16 4 12 11
8 10 9 12 6 8
10 17 18 14 13
2 8 12 9 0
12 19 20 32
I AM COMPROMISED. WORKING FOR GERMANS.

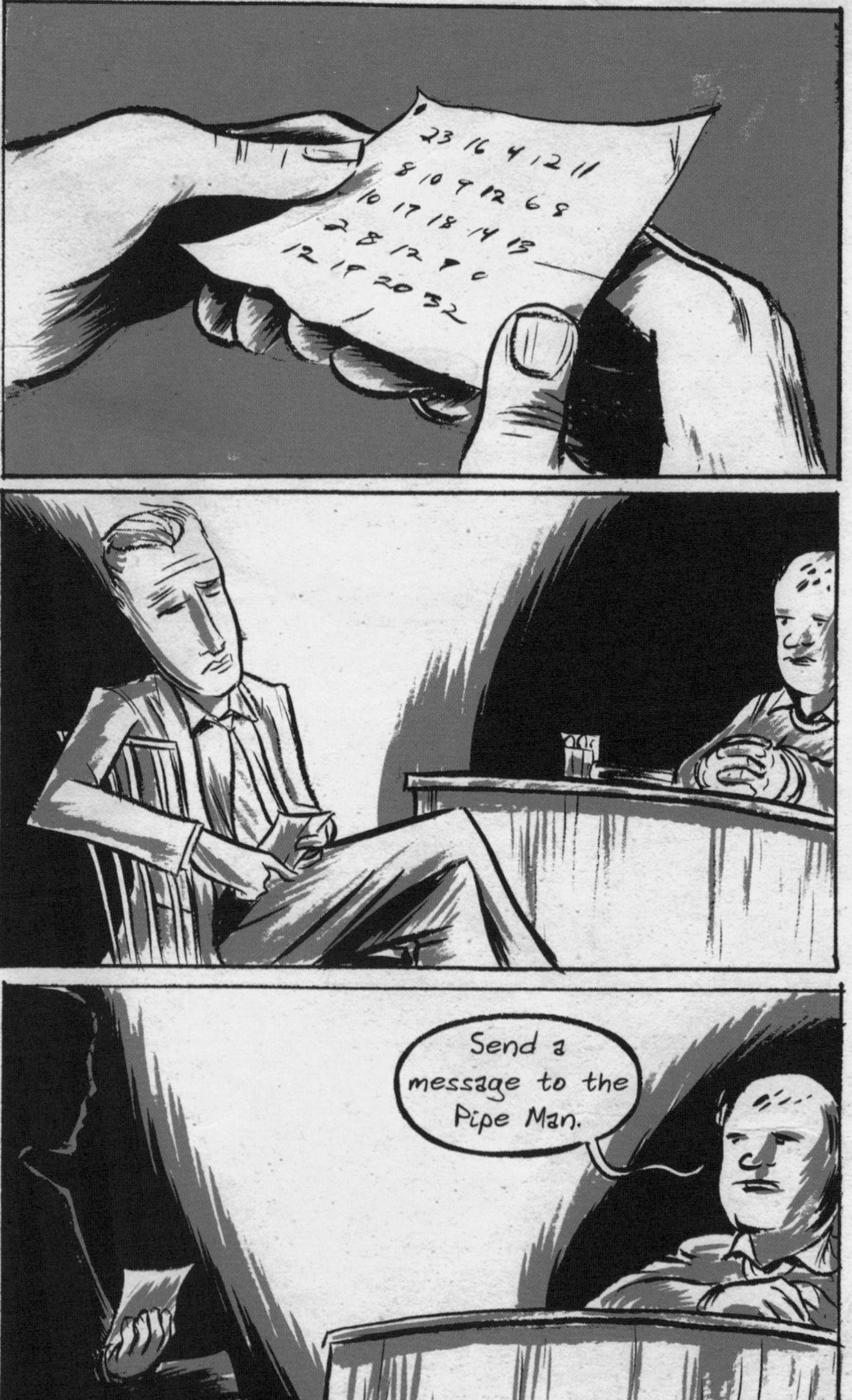
Send a message to the Pipe Man.

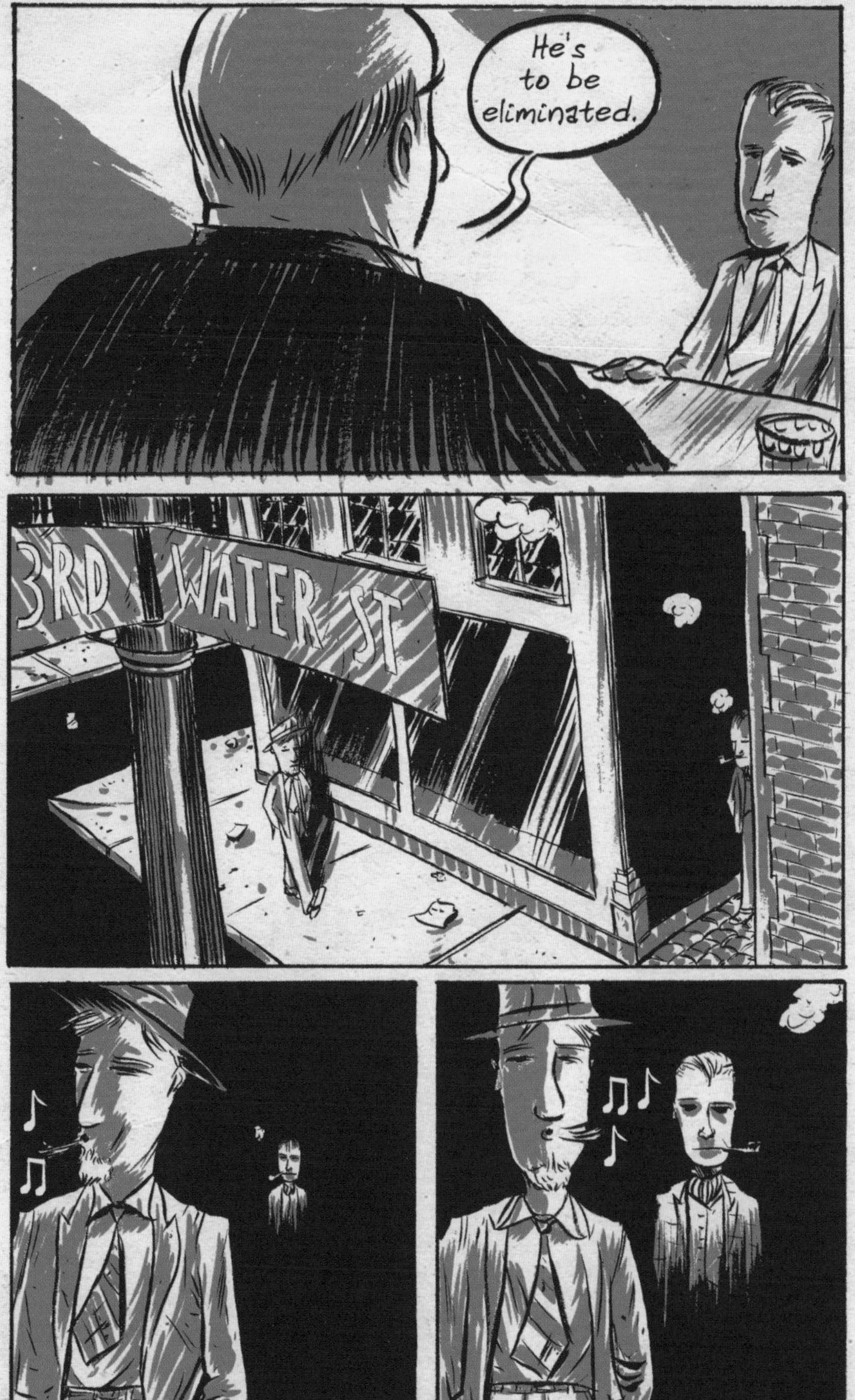
He's to be eliminated.
3RD
WATER ST

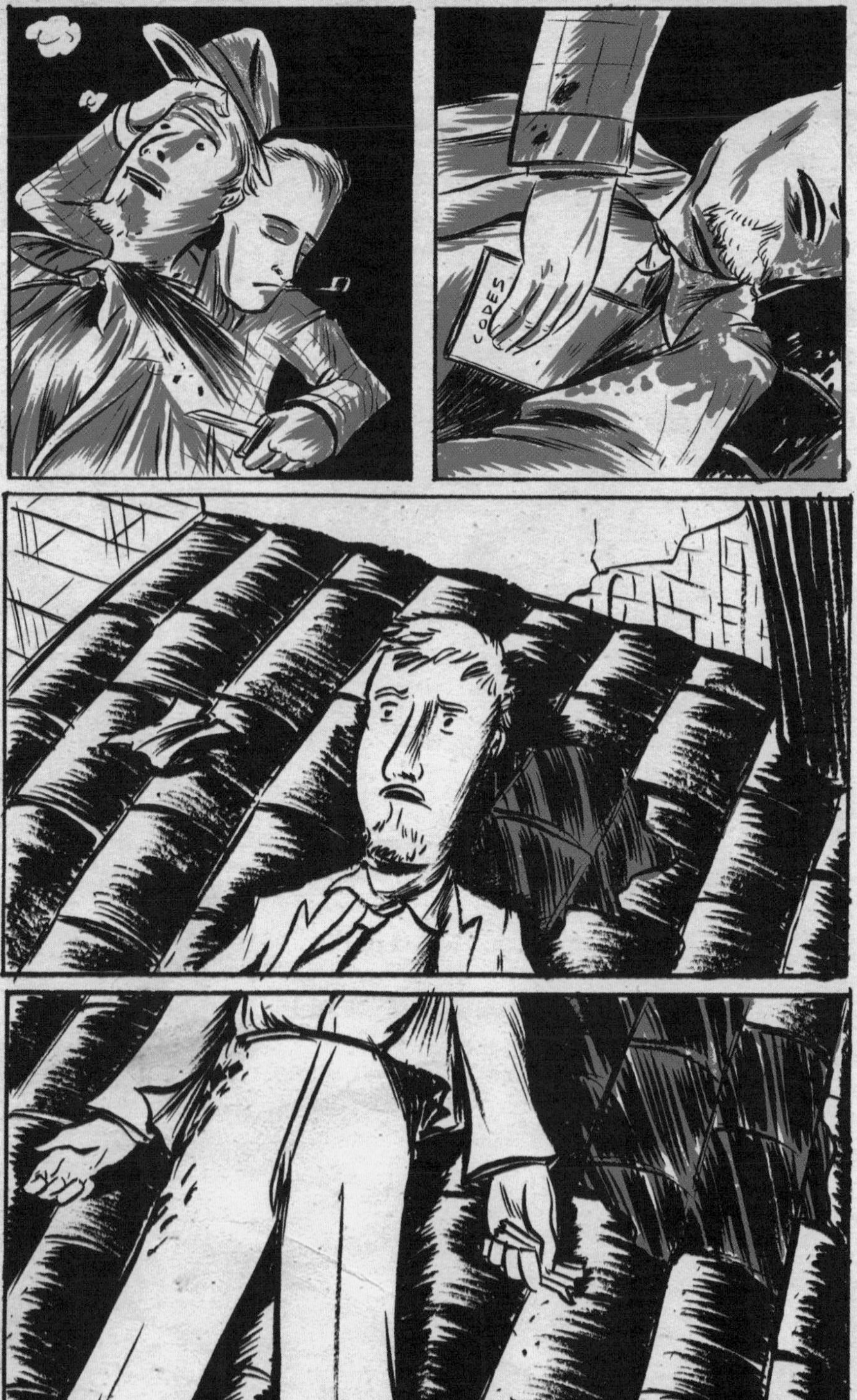
CODES

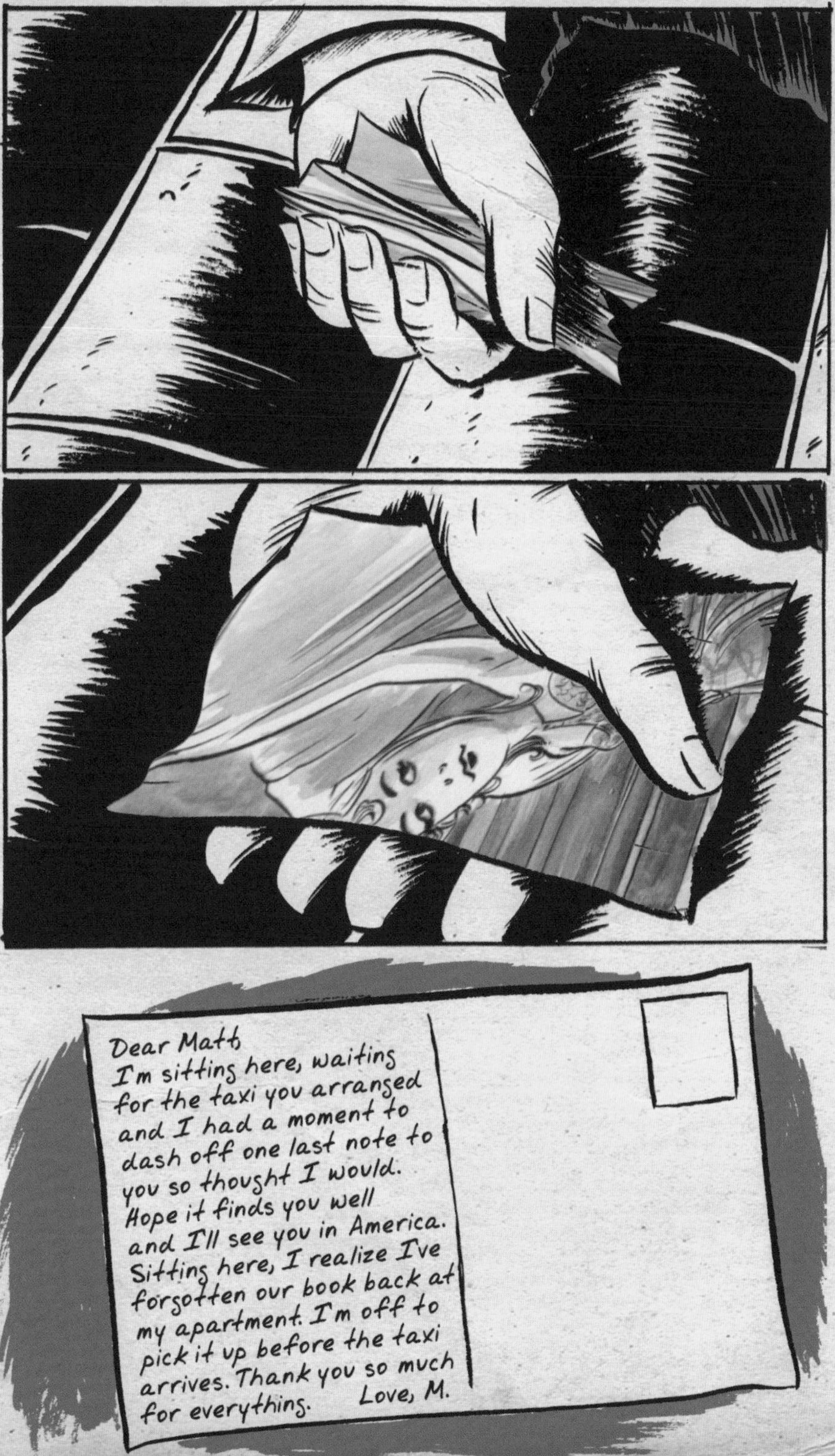
Dear Matt,
I'm sitting here, waiting for the taxi you arranged and I had a moment to dash off one last note to you so thought I would. Hope it finds you well and I'll see you in America. Sitting here, I realize I've forgotten our book back at my apartment. I'm off to pick it up before the taxi arrives. Thank you so much for everything.
Love, M.

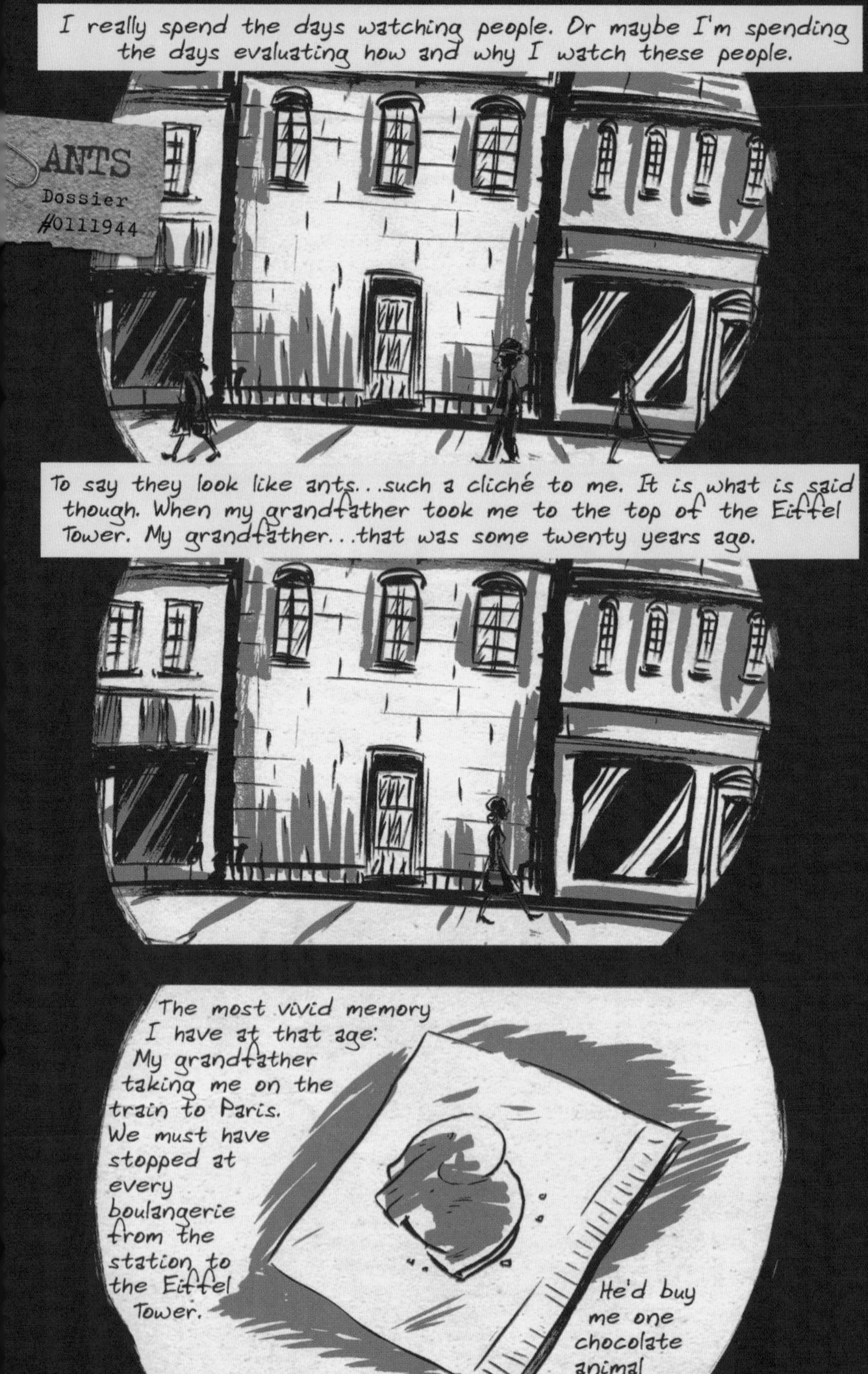
ANTS
Dossier
#0111944
I really spend the days watching people. Or maybe I'm spending the days evaluating how and why I watch these people.
To say they look like ants...such a cliché to me. It is what is said though. When my grandfather took me to the top of the Eiffel Tower. My grandfather...that was some twenty years ago.
The most vivid memory I have at that age: My grandfather taking me on the train to Paris. We must have stopped at every boulangerie from the station to the Eiffel Tower.
He'd buy me one chocolate animal cookie.

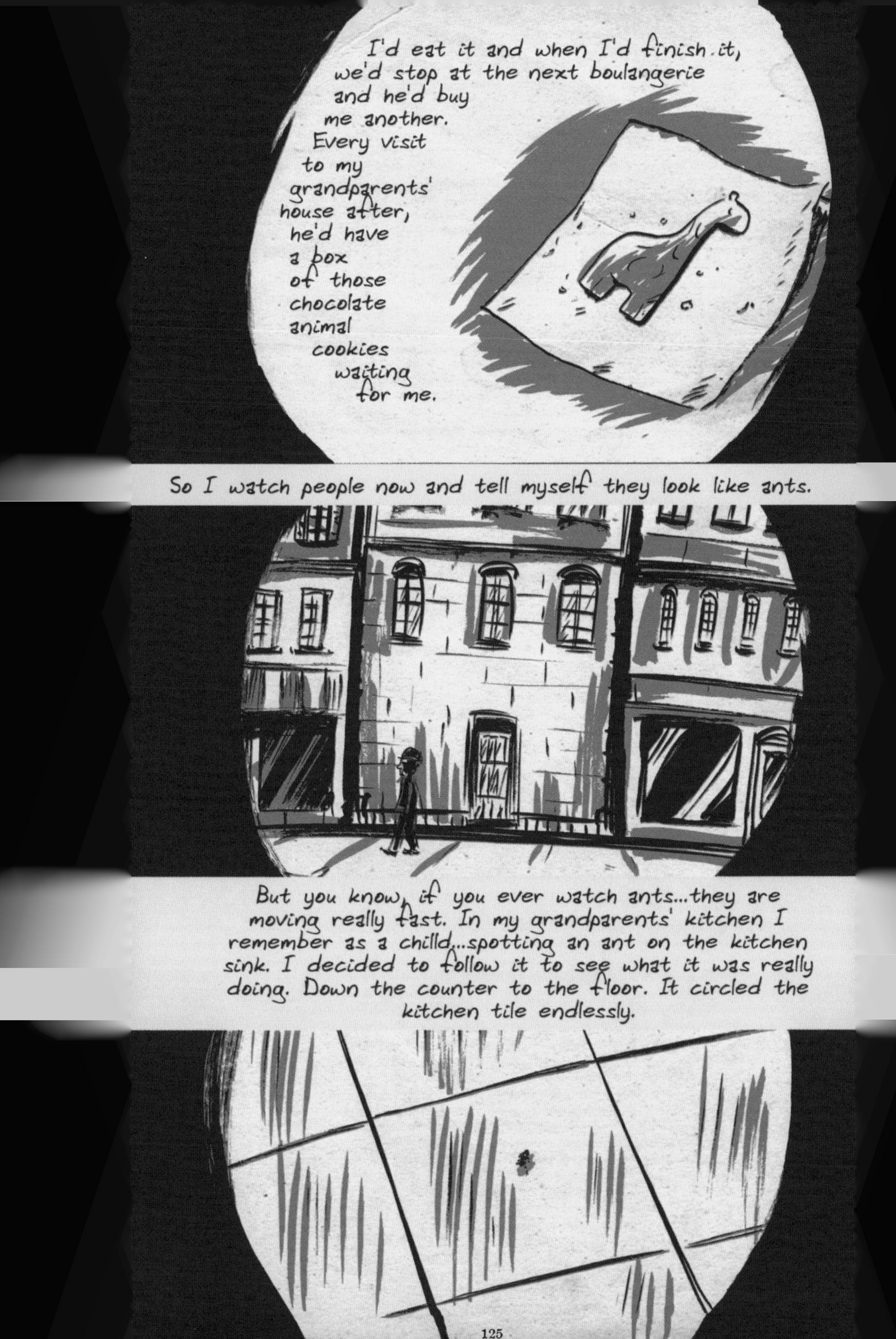
I'd eat it and when I'd finish it, we'd stop at the next boulangerie and he'd buy me another. Every visit to my grandparents' house after, he'd have a box of those chocolate animal cookies waiting for me.
So I watch people now and tell myself they look like ants.
But you know, if you ever watch ants...they are moving really fast. In my grandparents' kitchen I remember as a chilld...spotting an ant on the kitchen sink. I decided to follow it to see what it was really doing. Down the counter to the floor. It circled the kitchen tile endlessly.

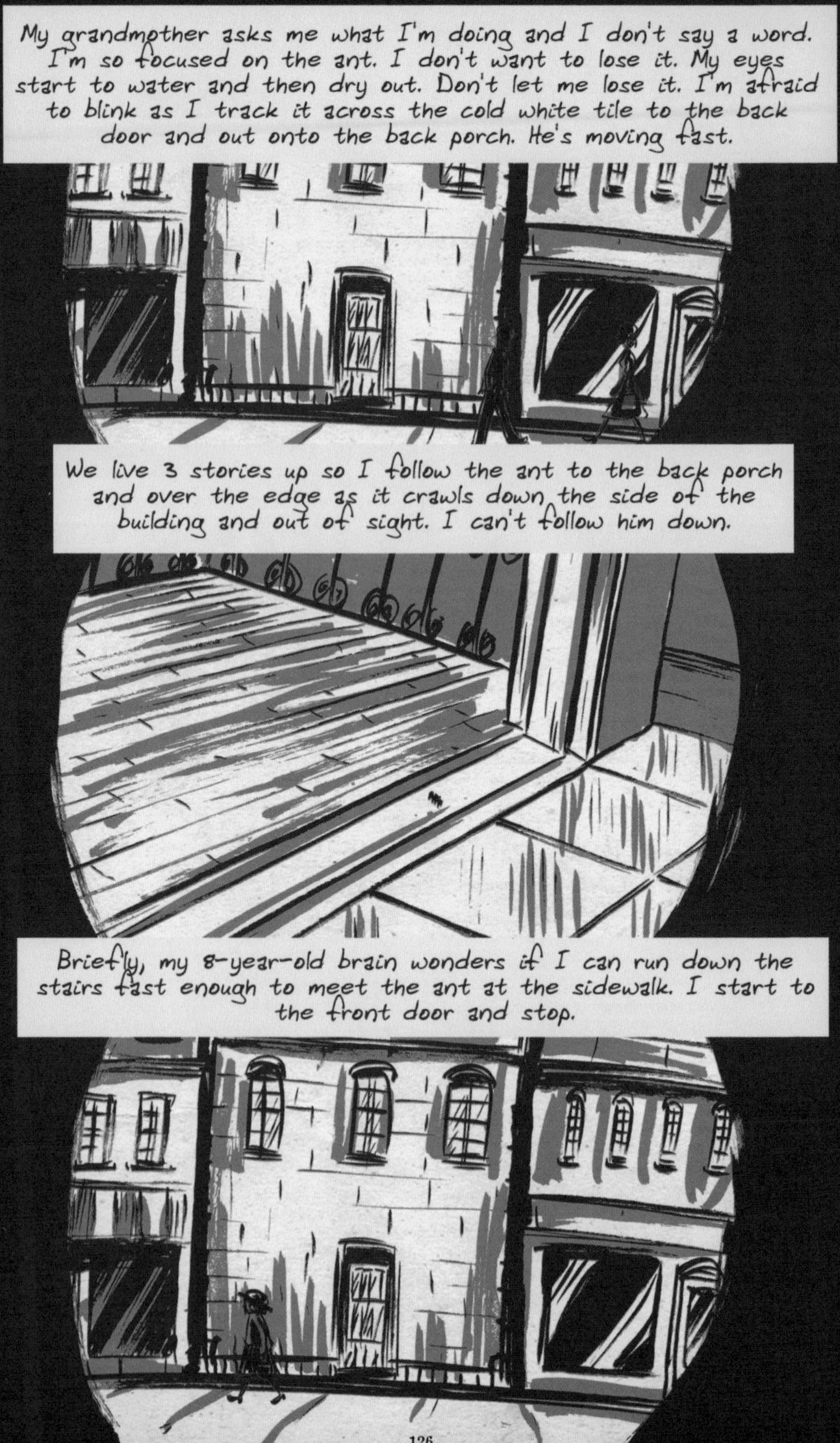
My grandmother asks me what I'm doing and I don't say a word. I'm so focused on the ant. I don't want to lose it. My eyes start to water and then dry out. Don't let me lose it. I'm afraid to blink as I track it across the cold white tile to the back door and out onto the back porch. He's moving fast.
We live 3 stories up so I follow the ant to the back porch and over the edge as it crawls down the side of the building and out of sight. I can't follow him down.
Briefly, my 8-year-old brain wonders if I can run down the stairs fast enough to meet the ant at the sidewalk. I start to the front door and stop.

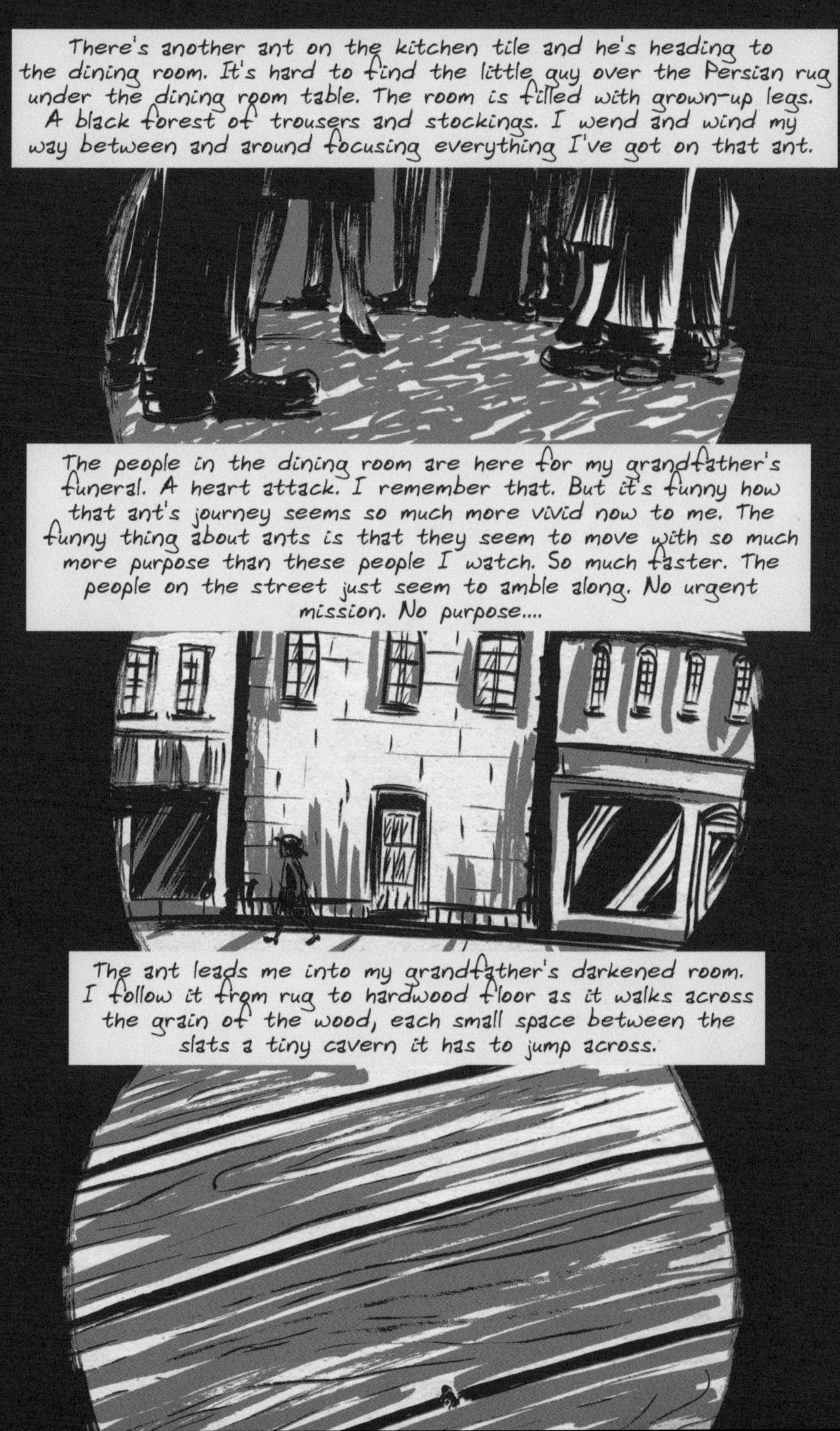
There's another ant on the kitchen tile and he's heading to the dining room. It's hard to find the little guy over the Persian rug under the dining room table. The room is filled with grown-up legs. A black forest of trousers and stockings. I wend and wind my way between and around focusing everything I've got on that ant.
The people in the dining room are here for my grandfather's funeral. A heart attack. I remember that. But it's funny how that ant's journey seems so much more vivid now to me. The funny thing about ants is that they seem to move with so much more purpose than these people I watch. So much faster. The people on the street just seem to amble along. No urgent mission. No purpose....
The ant leads me into my grandfather's darkened room. I follow it from rug to hardwood floor as it walks across the grain of the wood, each small space between the slats a tiny cavern it has to jump across.

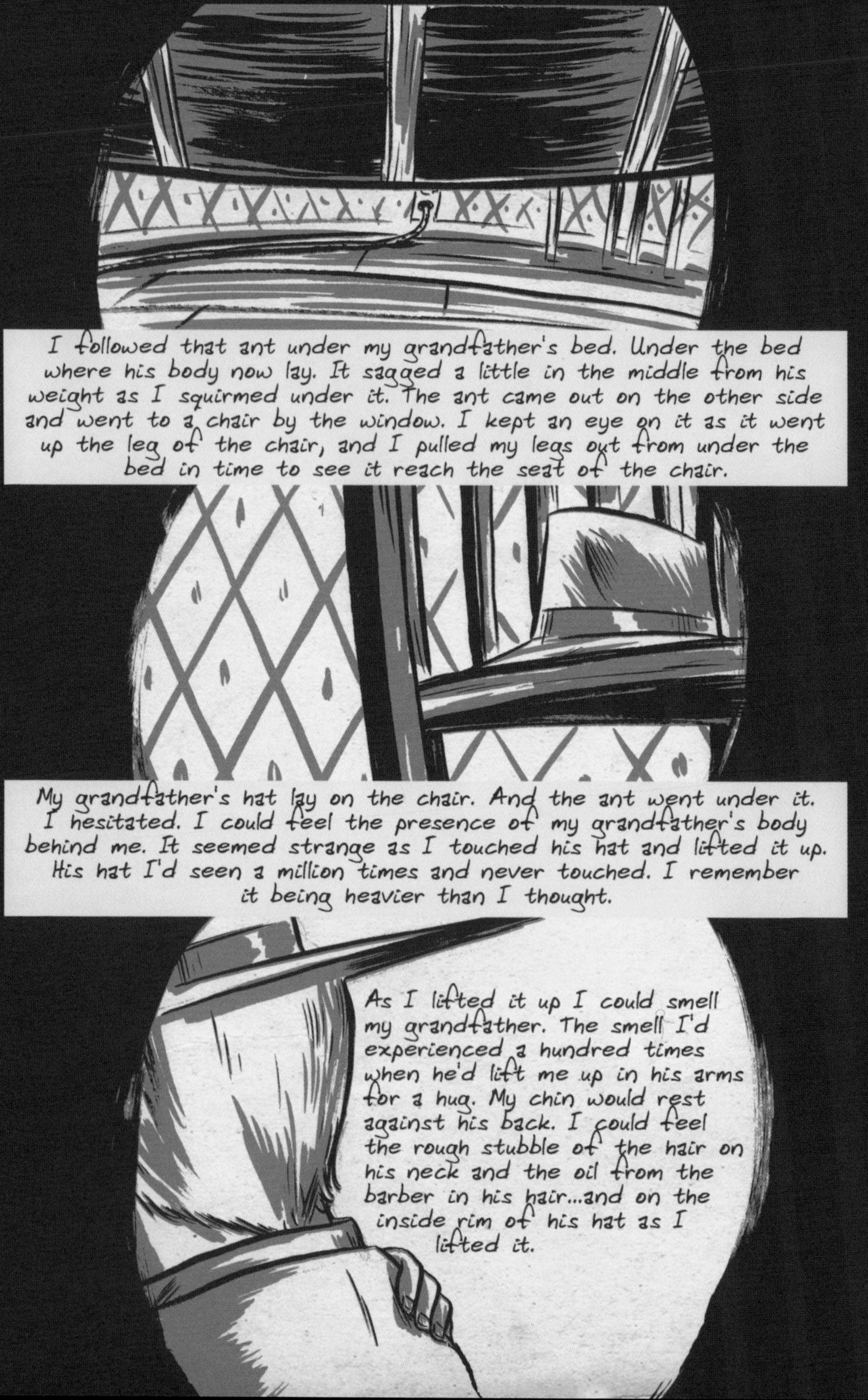
I followed that ant under my grandfather's bed. Under the bed where his body now lay. It sagged a little in the middle from his weight as I squirmed under it. The ant came out on the other side and went to a chair by the window. I kept an eye on it as it went up the leg of the chair, and I pulled my legs out from under the bed in time to see it reach the seat of the chair.
My grandfather's hat lay on the chair. And the ant went under it. I hesitated. I could feel the presence of my grandfather's body behind me. It seemed strange as I touched his hat and lifted it up. His hat I'd seen a million times and never touched. I remember it being heavier than I thought.
As I lifted it up I could smell my grandfather. The smell I'd experienced a hundred times when he'd lift me up in his arms for a hug. My chin would rest against his back. I could feel the rough stubble of the hair on his neck and the oil from the barber in his hair...and on the inside rim of his hat as I lifted it.

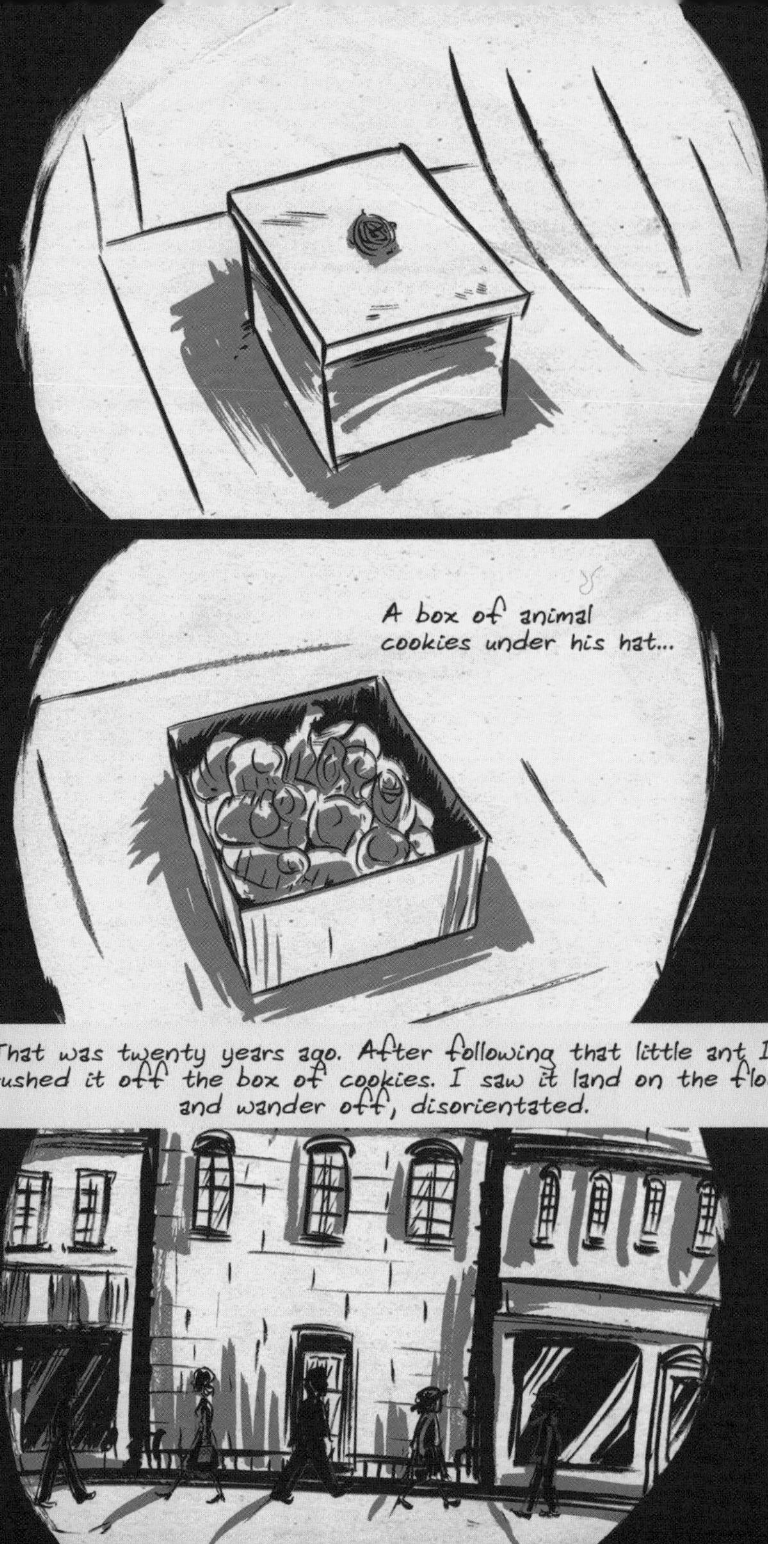
A box of animal cookies under his hat...
That was twenty years ago. After following that little ant I brushed it off the box of cookies. I saw it land on the floor and wander off, disorientated.

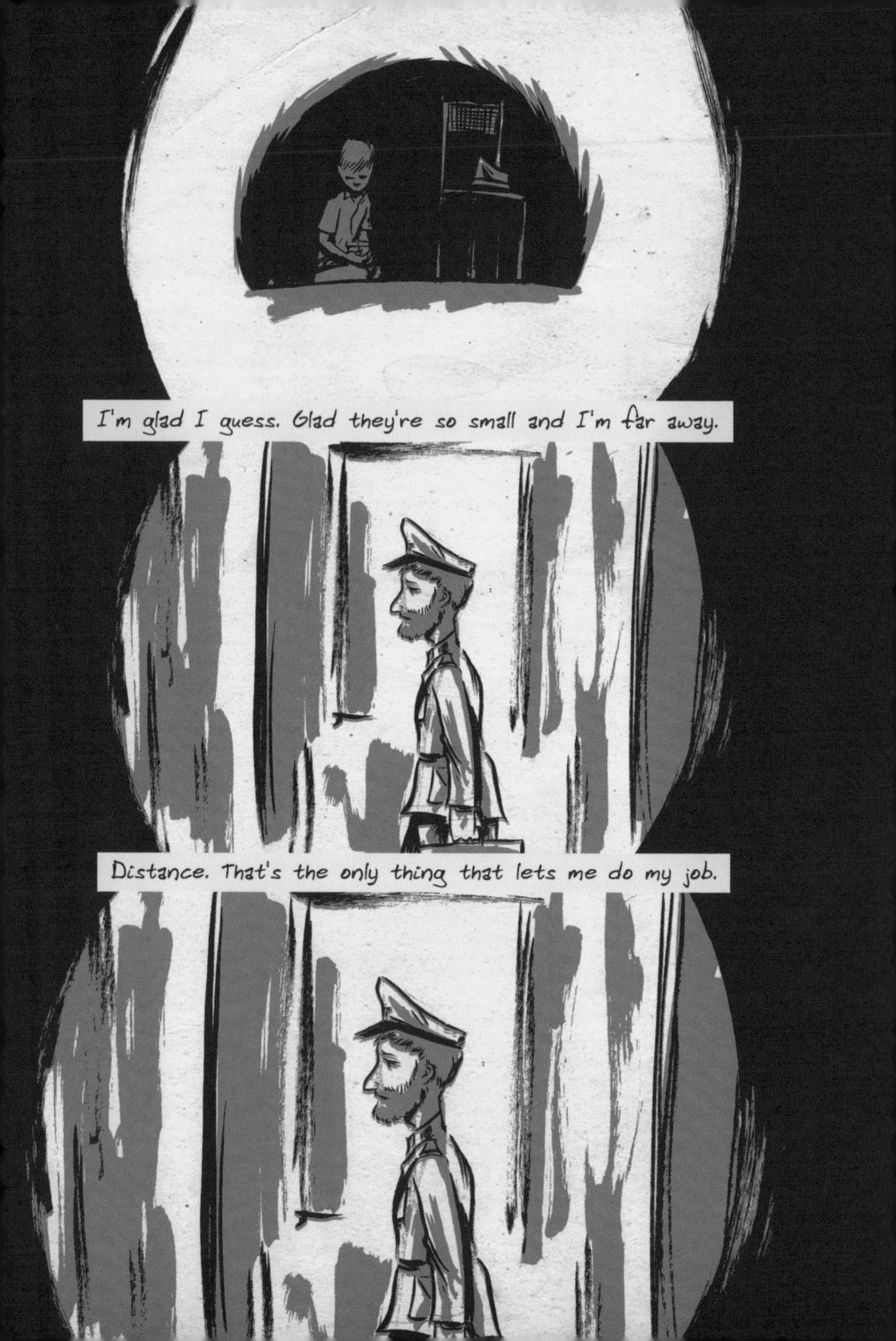
I'm glad I guess. Glad they're so small and I'm far away.
Distance. That's the only thing that lets me do my job.

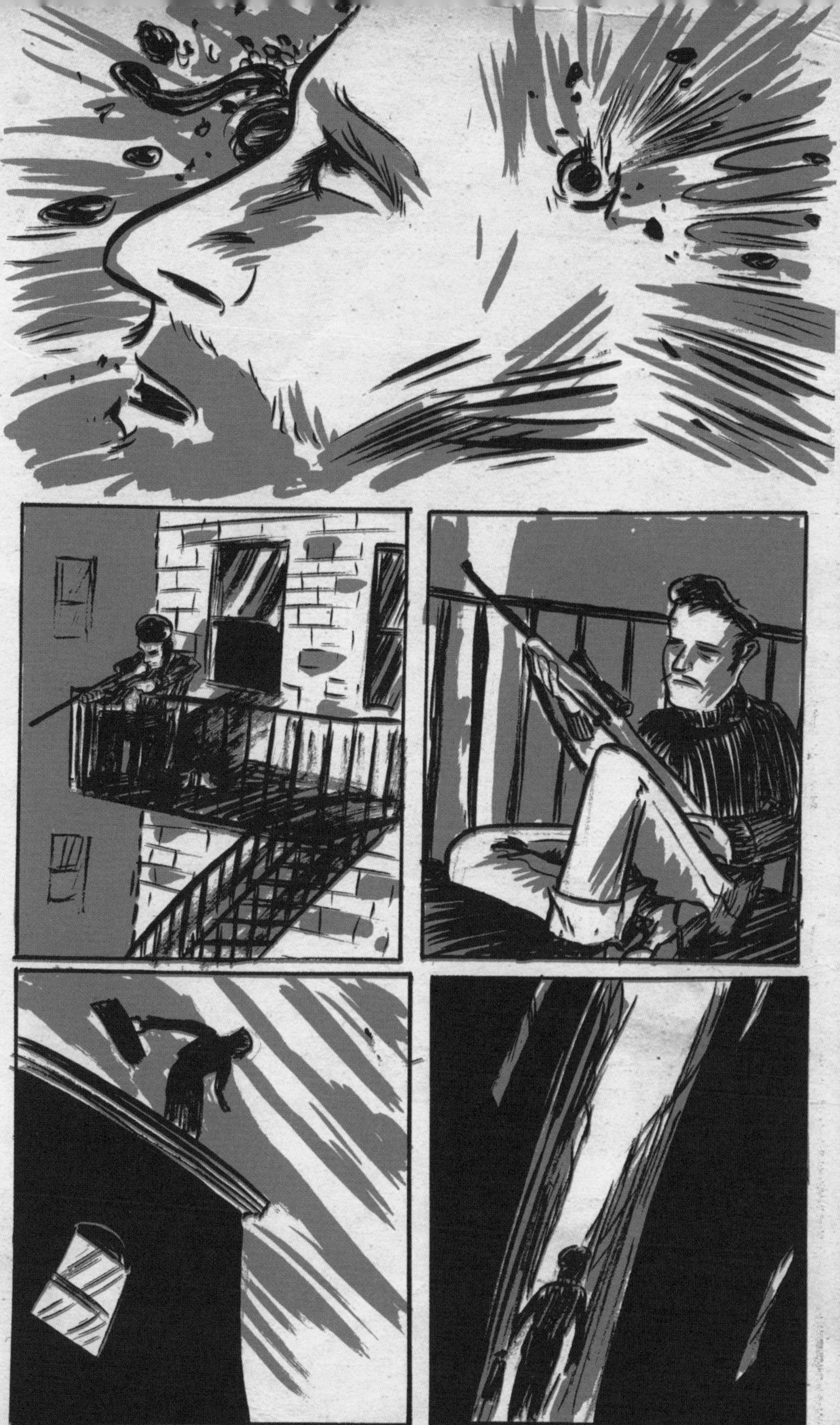

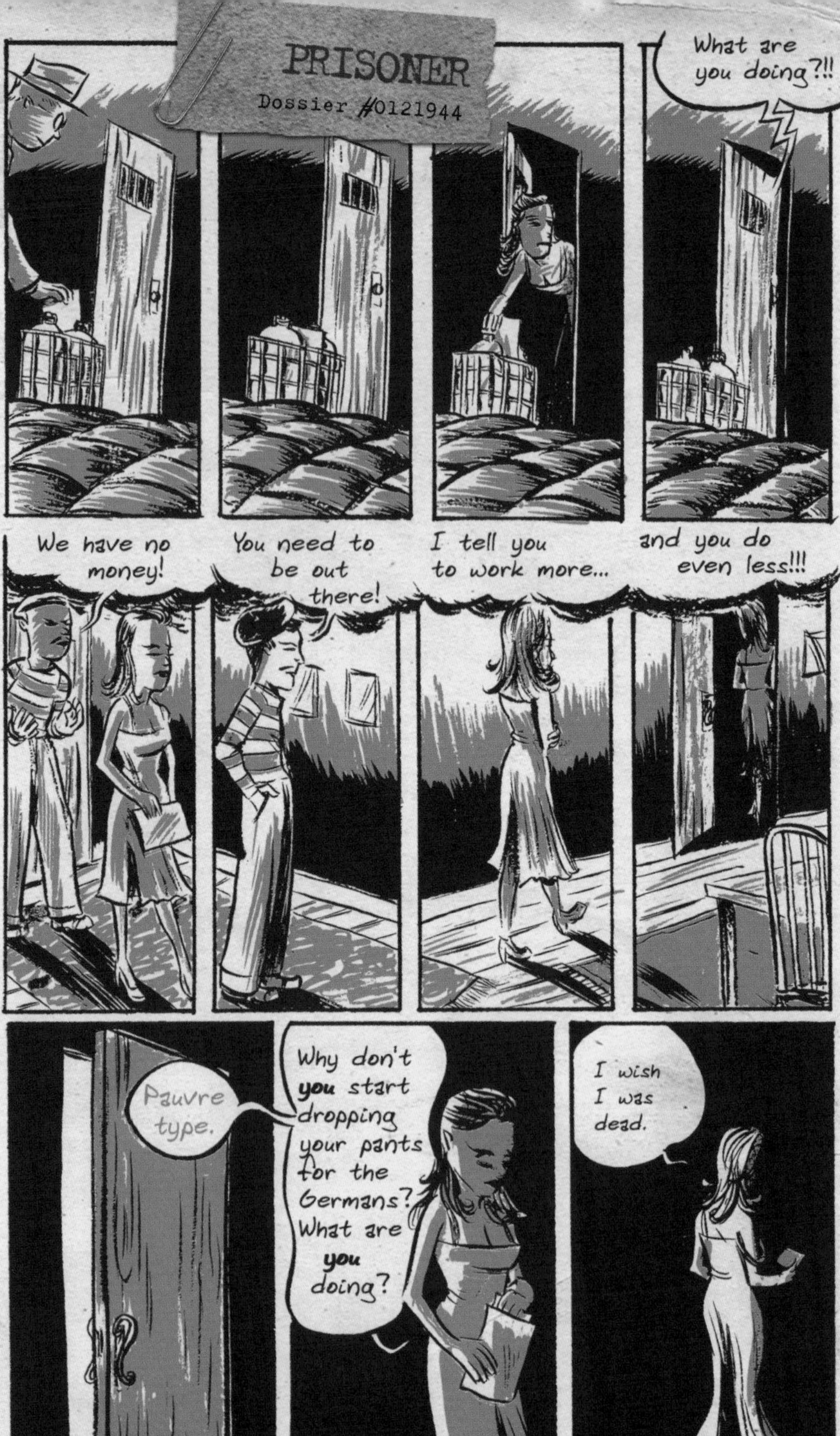
PRISONER
Dossier #0121944
What are you doing?!!
We have no money!
You need to be out there!
I tell you to work more...
and you do even less!!!
Pauvre type.
Why don't **you** start dropping your pants for the Germans? What are **you** doing?
I wish I was dead.

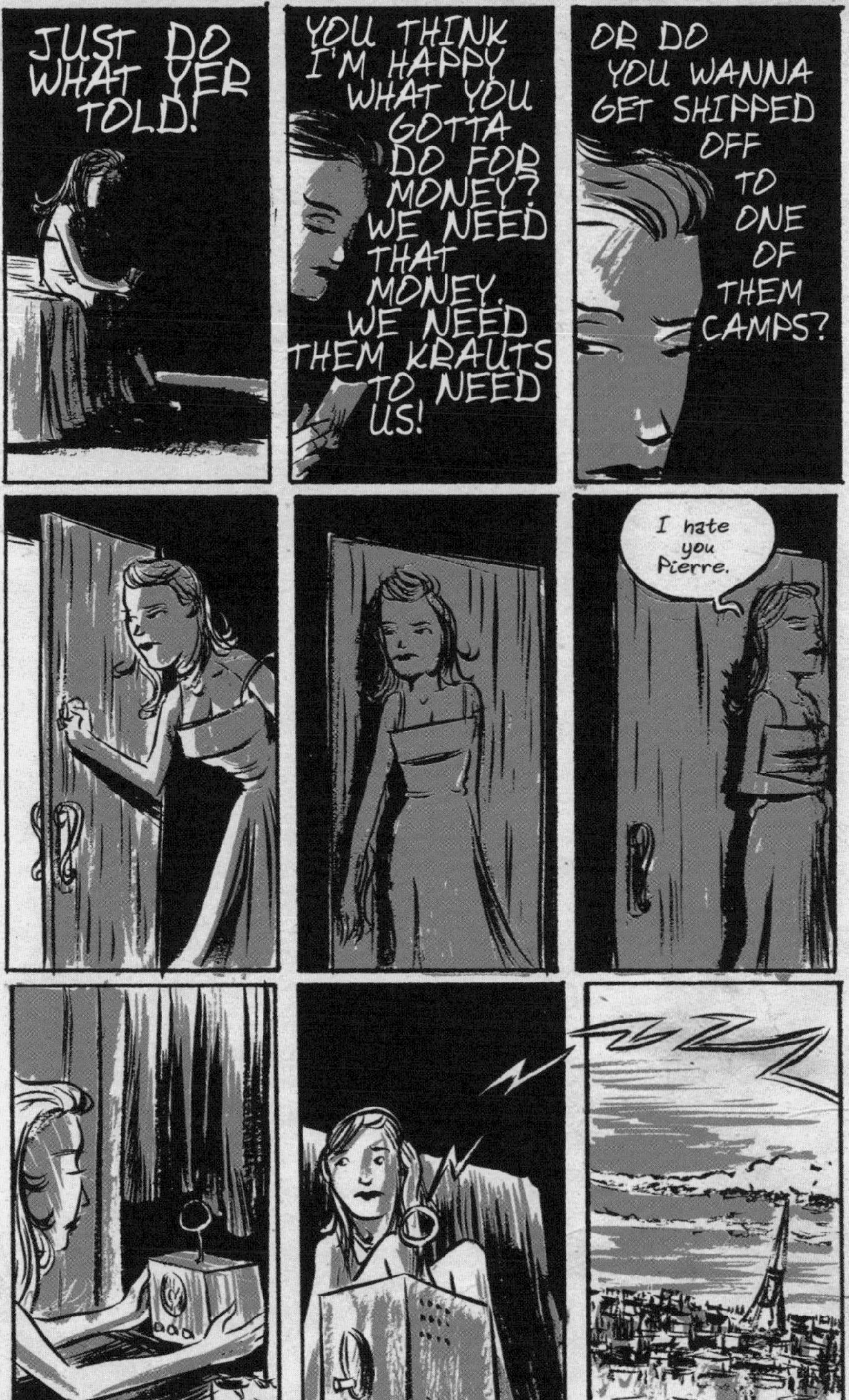
JUST DO WHAT YER TOLD!
YOU THINK I'M HAPPY WHAT YOU GOTTA DO FOR MONEY? WE NEED THAT MONEY. WE NEED THEM KRAUTS TO NEED US!
OR DO YOU WANNA GET SHIPPED OFF TO ONE OF THEM CAMPS?
I hate you Pierre.

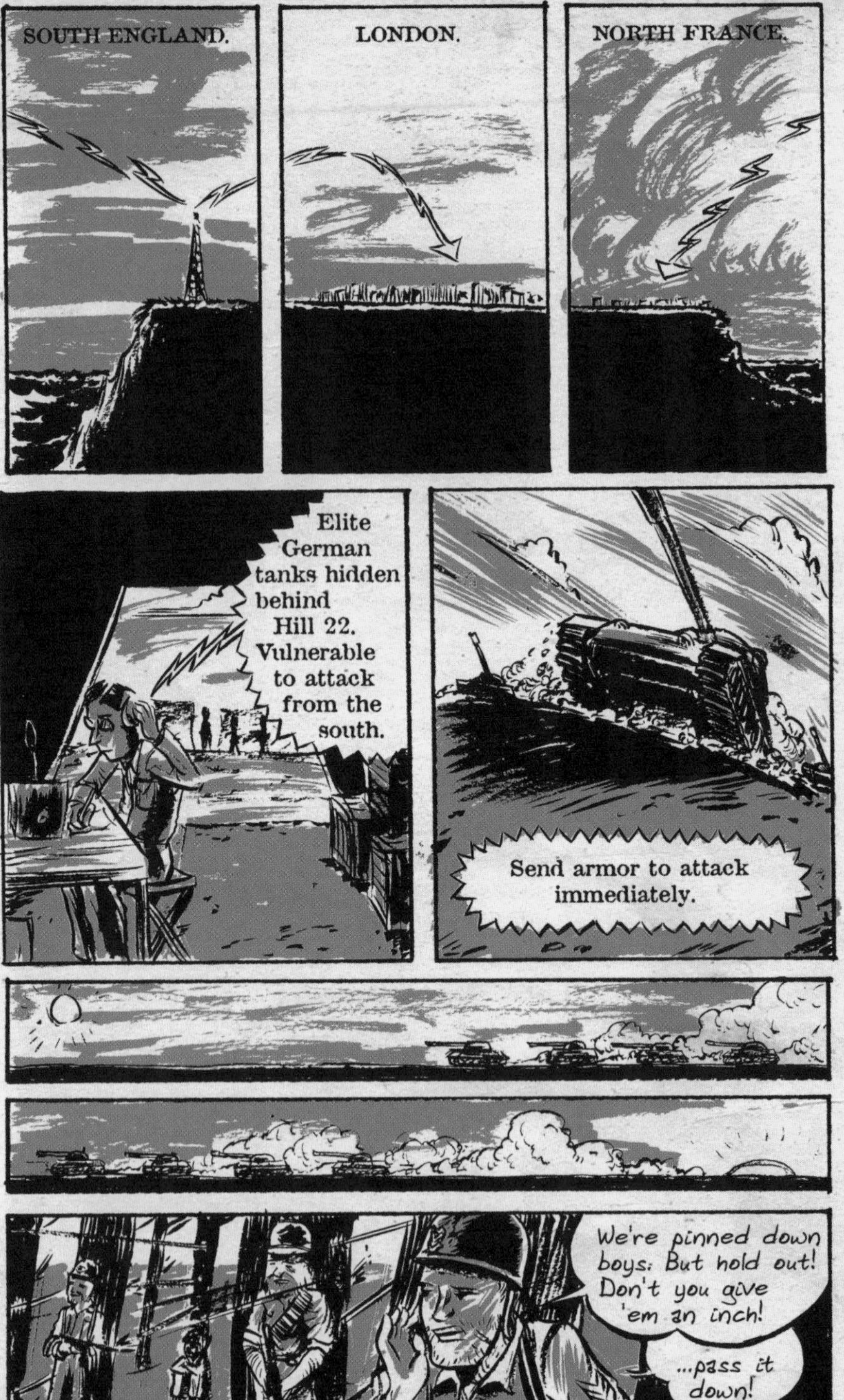
SOUTH ENGLAND.
LONDON.
NORTH FRANCE.
Elite German tanks hidden behind Hill 22. Vulnerable to attack from the south.
Send armor to attack immediately.
We're pinned down boys. But hold out! Don't you give 'em an inch!
...pass it down!

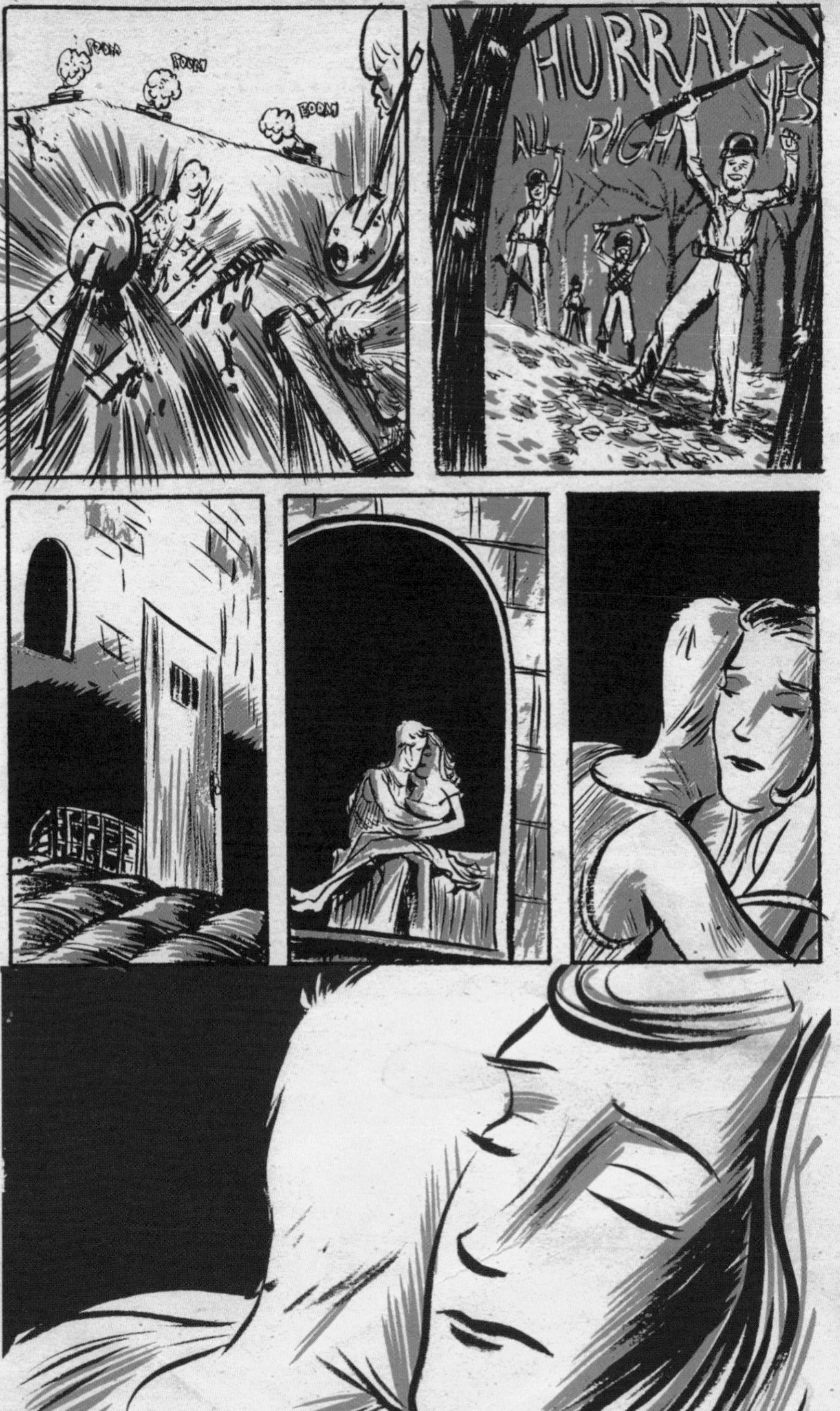
BOOM
BOOM
HURRAY
YES
ALL RIGH

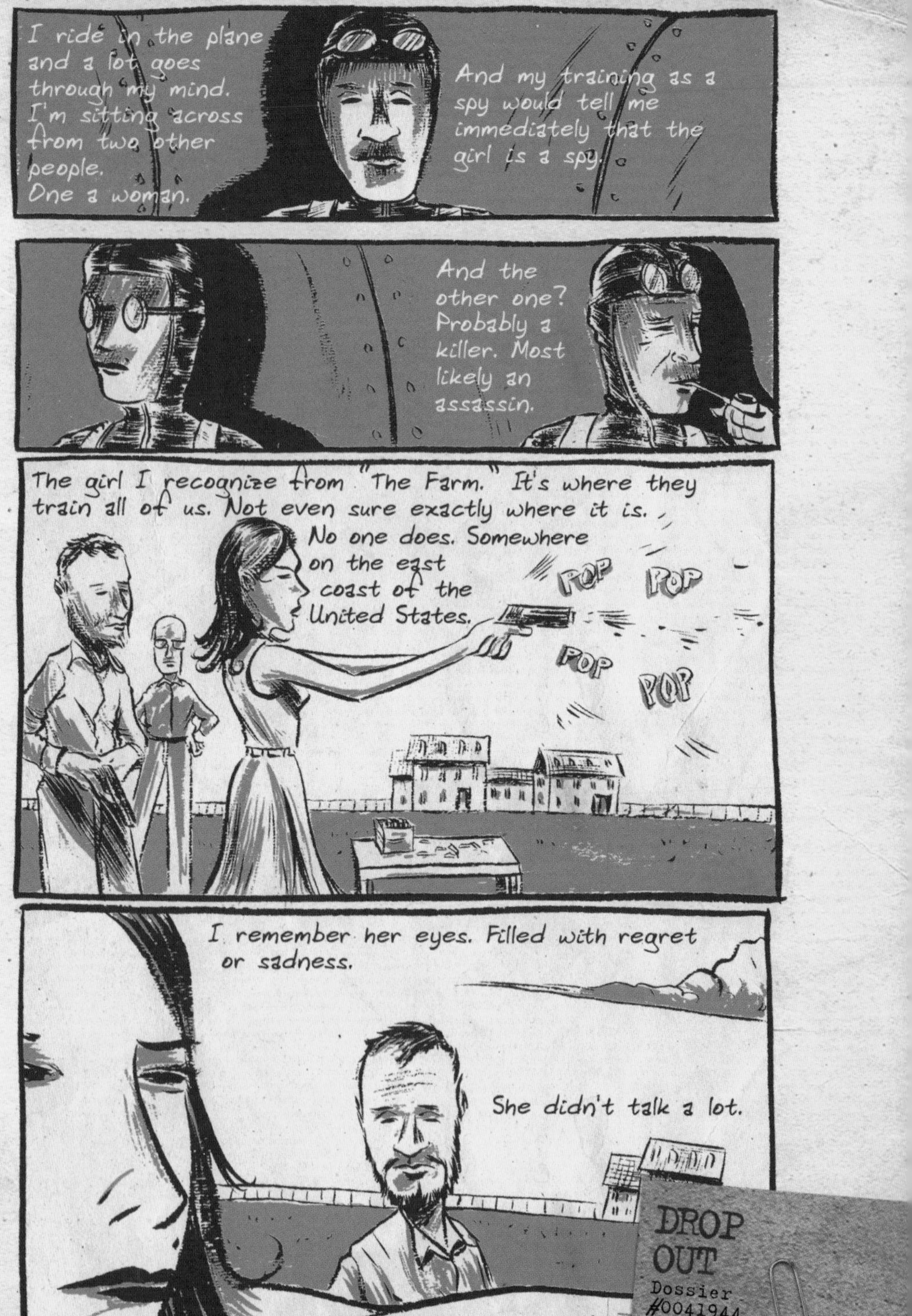
I ride in the plane and a lot goes through my mind. I'm sitting across from two other people. One a woman.
And my training as a spy would tell me immediately that the girl is a spy.
And the other one? Probably a killer. Most likely an assassin.
The girl I recognize from "The Farm." It's where they train all of us. Not even sure exactly where it is. No one does. Somewhere on the east coast of the United States.
POP
POP
POP
POP
I remember her eyes. Filled with regret or sadness.
She didn't talk a lot.
DROP OUT
Dossier #0041944

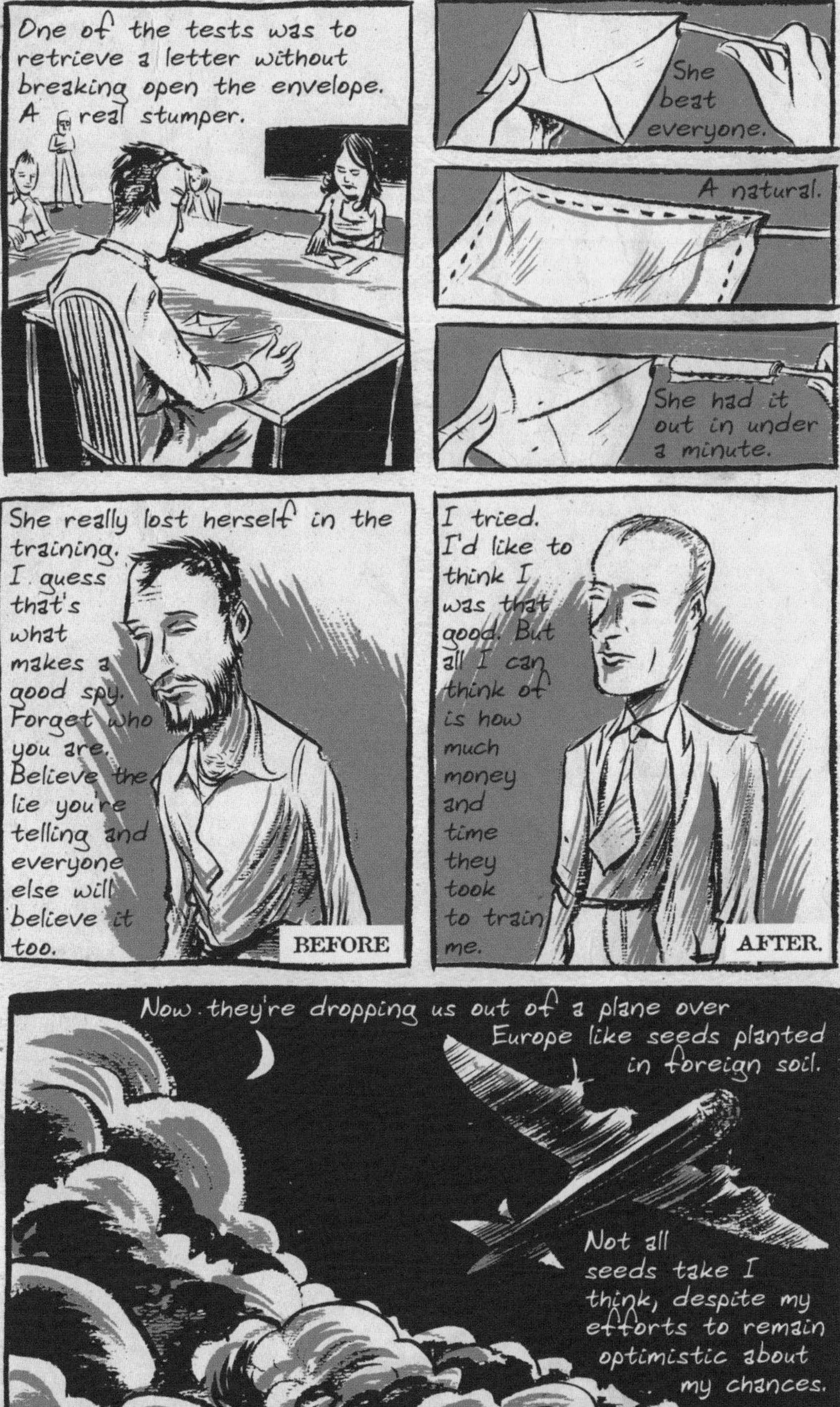
One of the tests was to retrieve a letter without breaking open the envelope. A real stumper.
She beat everyone.
A natural.
She had it out in under a minute.
She really lost herself in the training. I guess that's what makes a good spy. Forget who you are. Believe the lie you're telling and everyone else will believe it too.
BEFORE
I tried. I'd like to think I was that good. But all I can think of is how much money and time they took to train me.
AFTER.
Now they're dropping us out of a plane over Europe like seeds planted in foreign soil.
Not all seeds take I think, despite my efforts to remain optimistic about my chances.

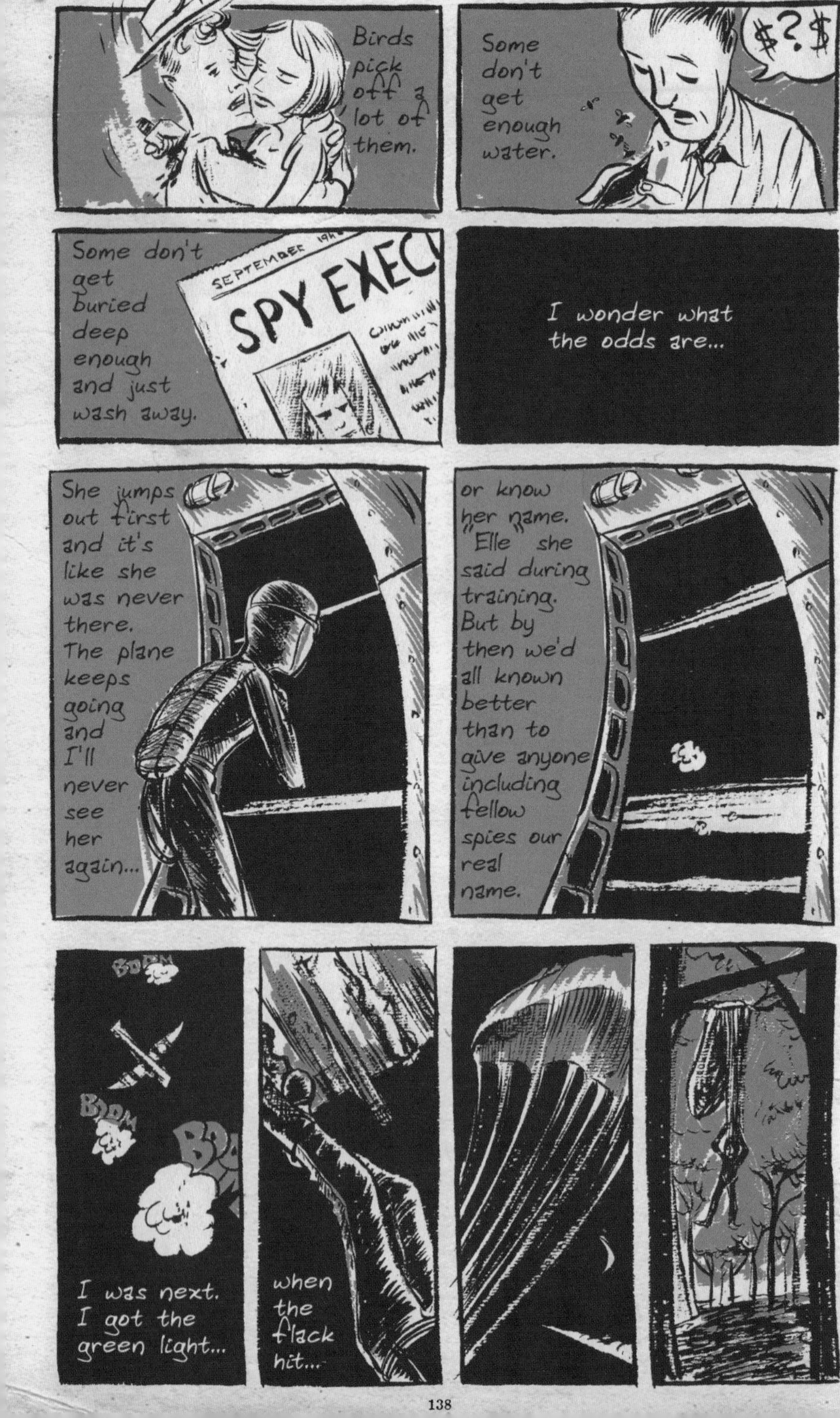
Birds pick off a lot of them.
Some don't get enough water.
$?$
Some don't get buried deep enough and just wash away.
SPY EXEC
I wonder what the odds are...
She jumps out first and it's like she was never there. The plane keeps going and I'll never see her again...
or know her name. "Elle" she said during training. But by then we'd all known better than to give anyone including fellow spies our real name.
I was next. I got the green light...
when the flack hit...

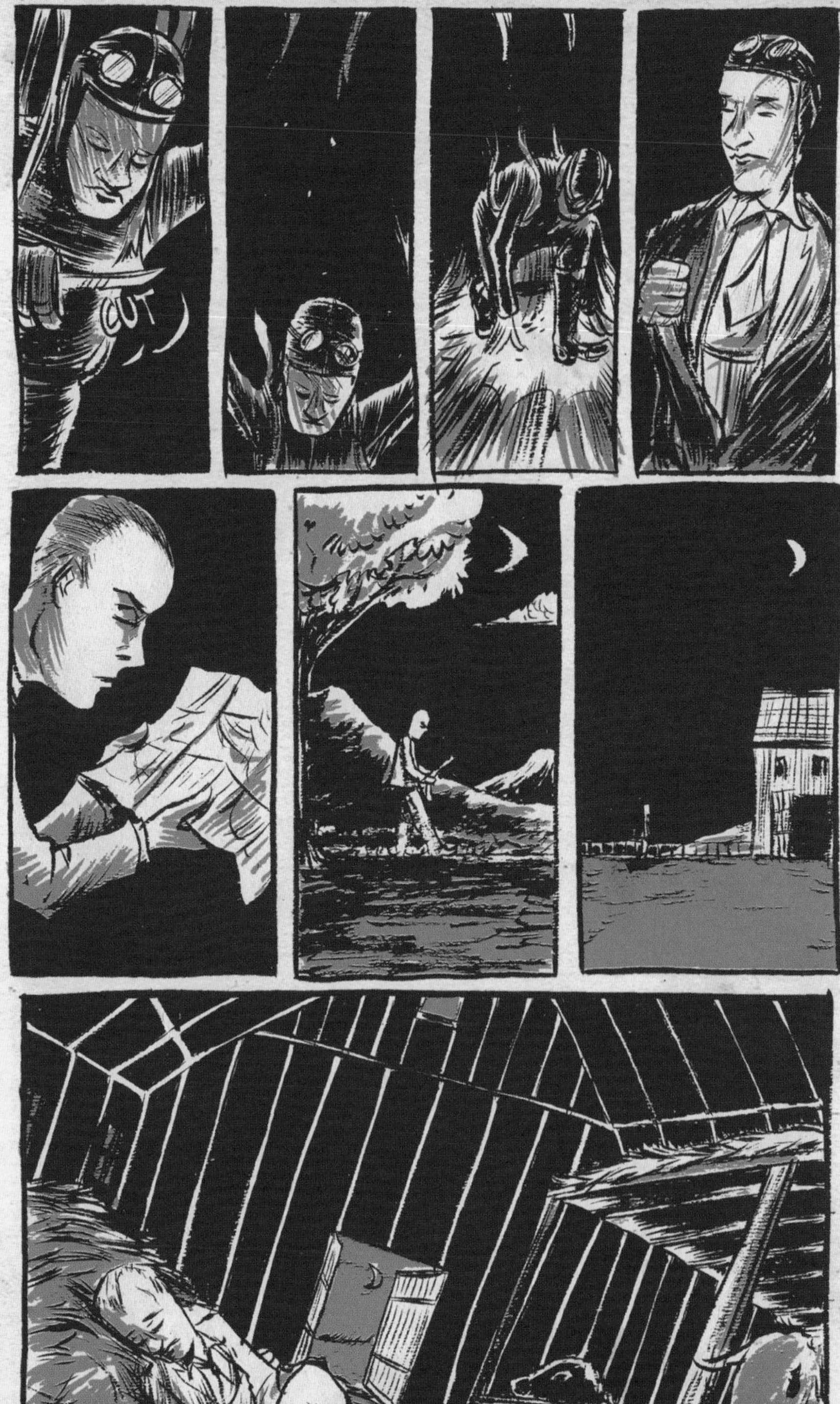
CUT

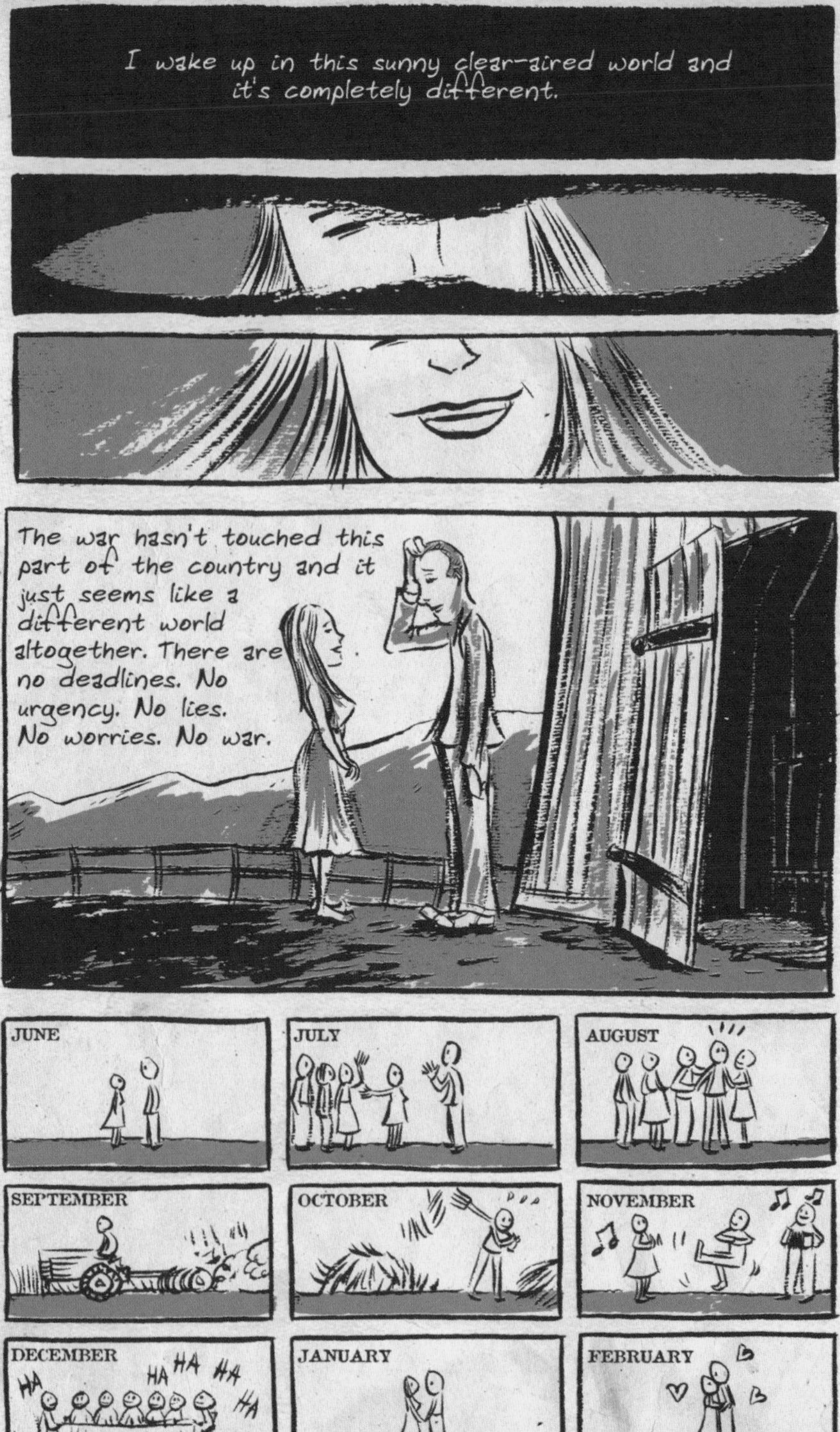
I wake up in this sunny clear-aired world and it's completely different.
The war hasn't touched this part of the country and it just seems like a different world altogether. There are no deadlines. No urgency. No lies. No worries. No war.
JUNE
JULY
AUGUST
SEPTEMBER
OCTOBER
NOVEMBER
DECEMBER
HA HA HA HA HA HA
JANUARY
FEBRUARY

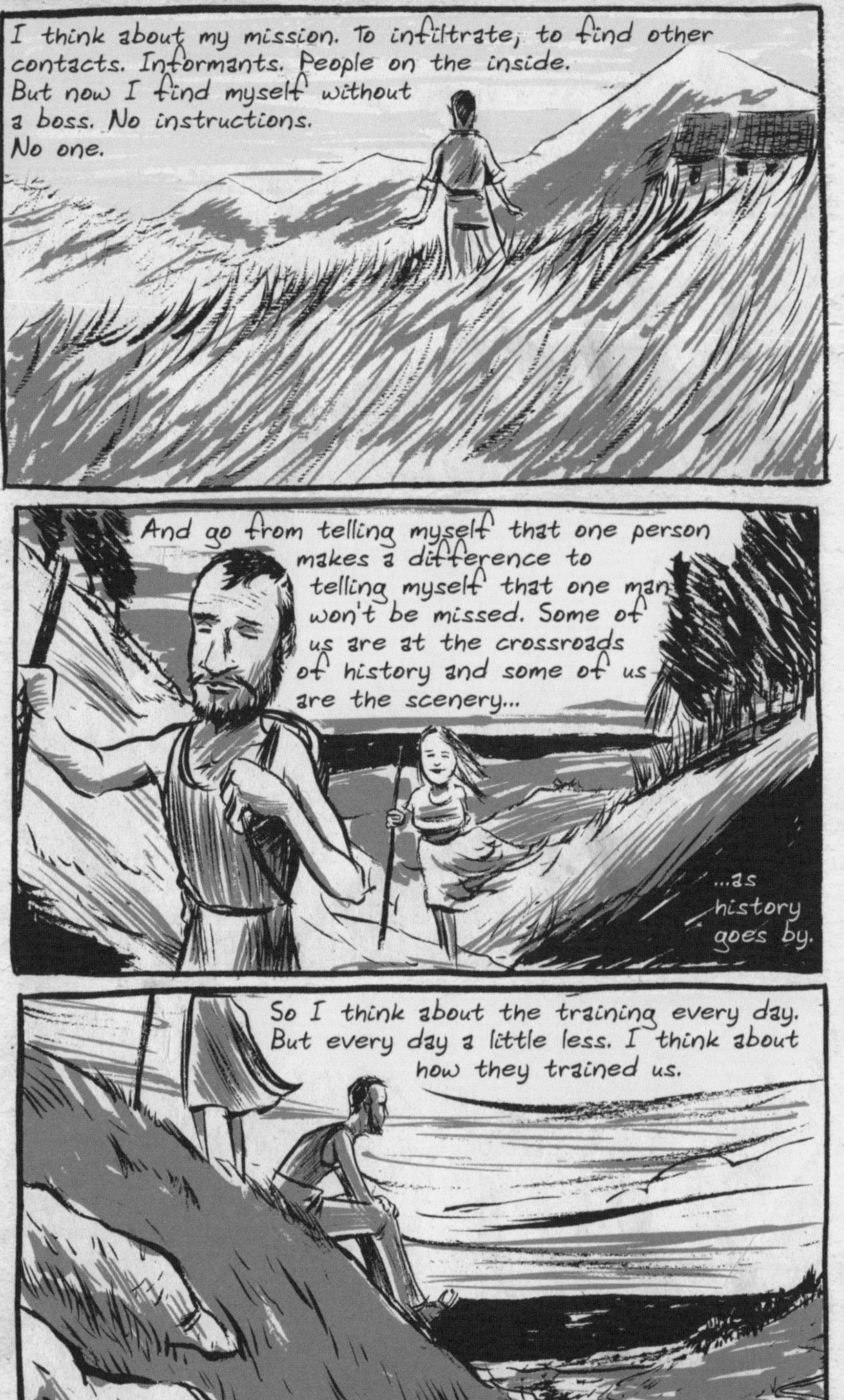
I think about my mission. To infiltrate, to find other contacts. Informants. People on the inside. But now I find myself without a boss. No instructions. No one.
And go from telling myself that one person makes a difference to telling myself that one man won't be missed. Some of us are at the crossroads of history and some of us are the scenery...
...as history goes by.
So I think about the training every day. But every day a little less. I think about how they trained us.

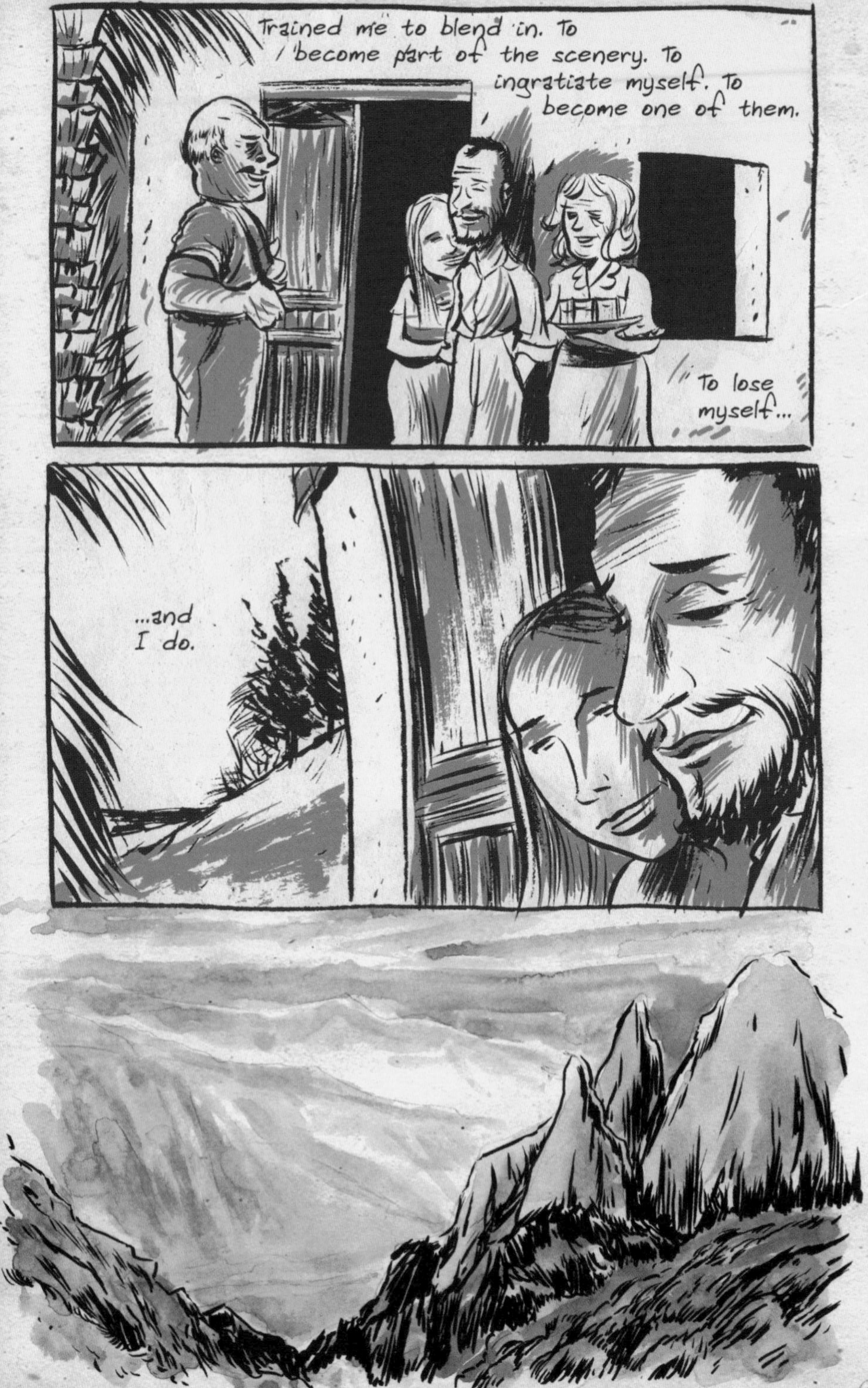
Trained me to blend in. To become part of the scenery. To ingratiate myself. To become one of them.
To lose myself...
...and I do.

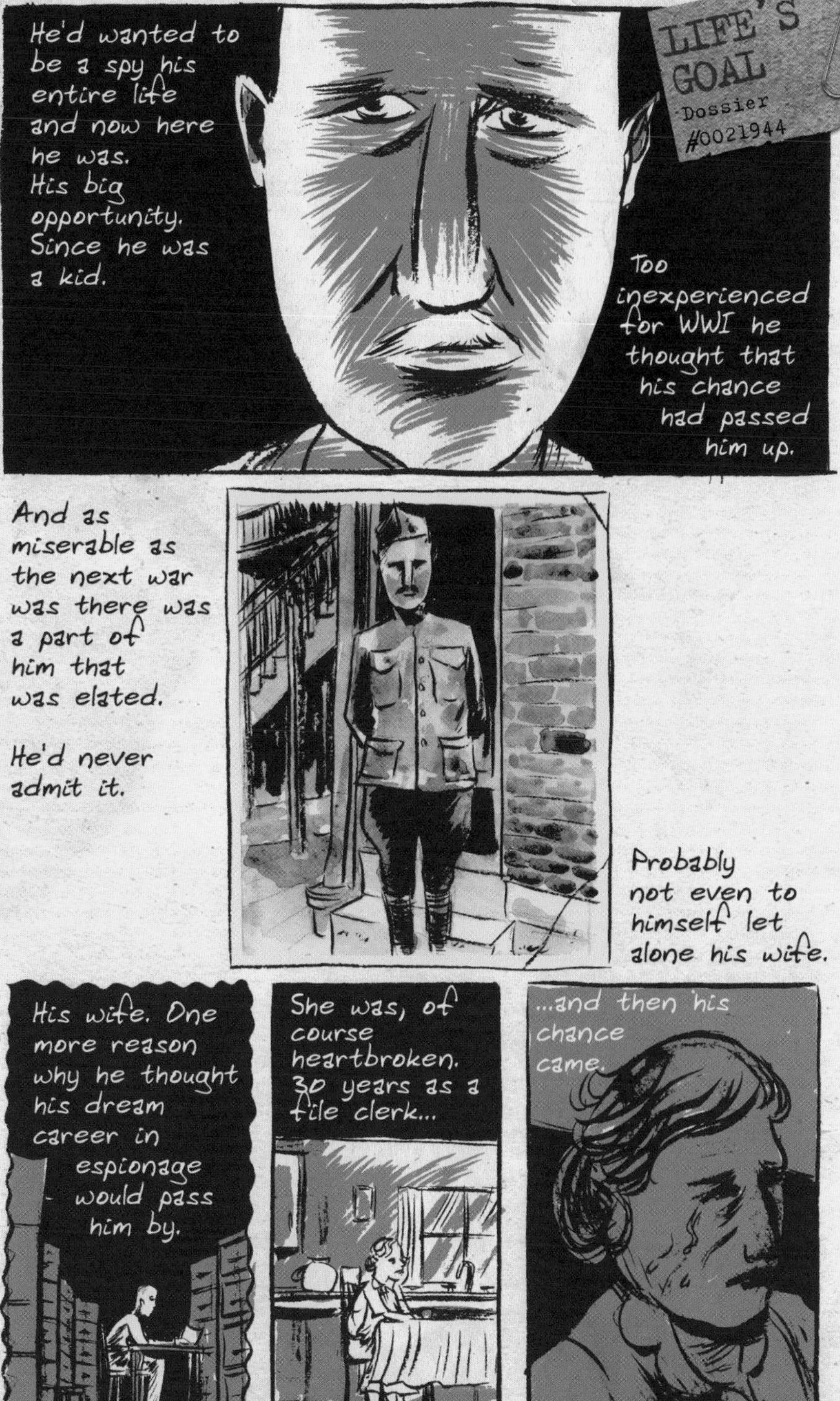
LIFE'S GOAL
Dossier #0021944
He'd wanted to be a spy his entire life and now here he was. His big opportunity. Since he was a kid.
Too inexperienced for WWI he thought that his chance had passed him up.
And as miserable as the next war was there was a part of him that was elated.
He'd never admit it.
Probably not even to himself let alone his wife.
His wife. One more reason why he thought his dream career in espionage would pass him by.
She was, of course heartbroken. 30 years as a file clerk...
...and then his chance came.

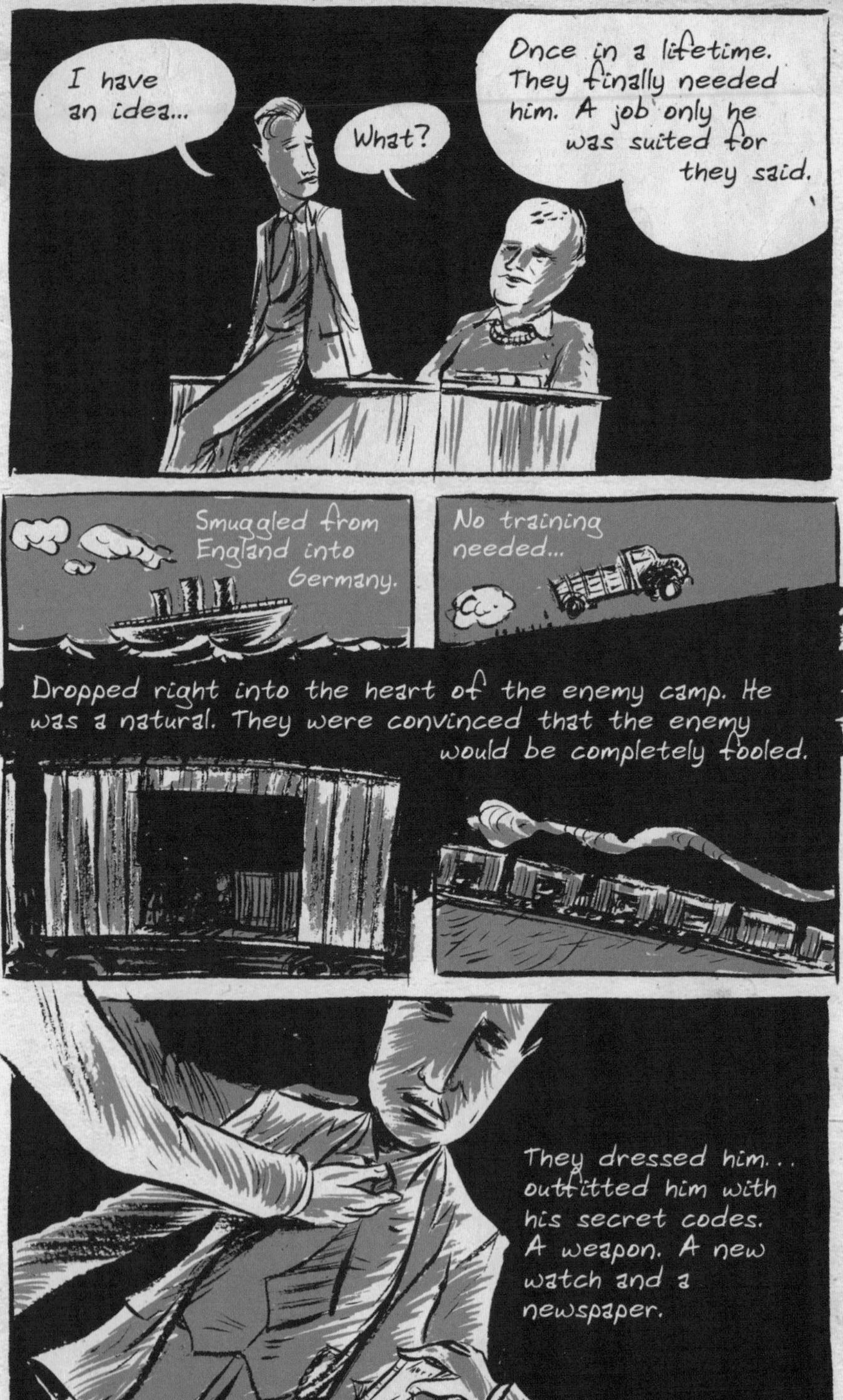

I have an idea...
What?
Once in a lifetime. They finally needed him. A job only he was suited for they said.
Smuggled from England into Germany.
No training needed...
Dropped right into the heart of the enemy camp. He was a natural. They were convinced that the enemy would be completely fooled.
They dressed him... outfitted him with his secret codes. A weapon. A new watch and a newspaper.

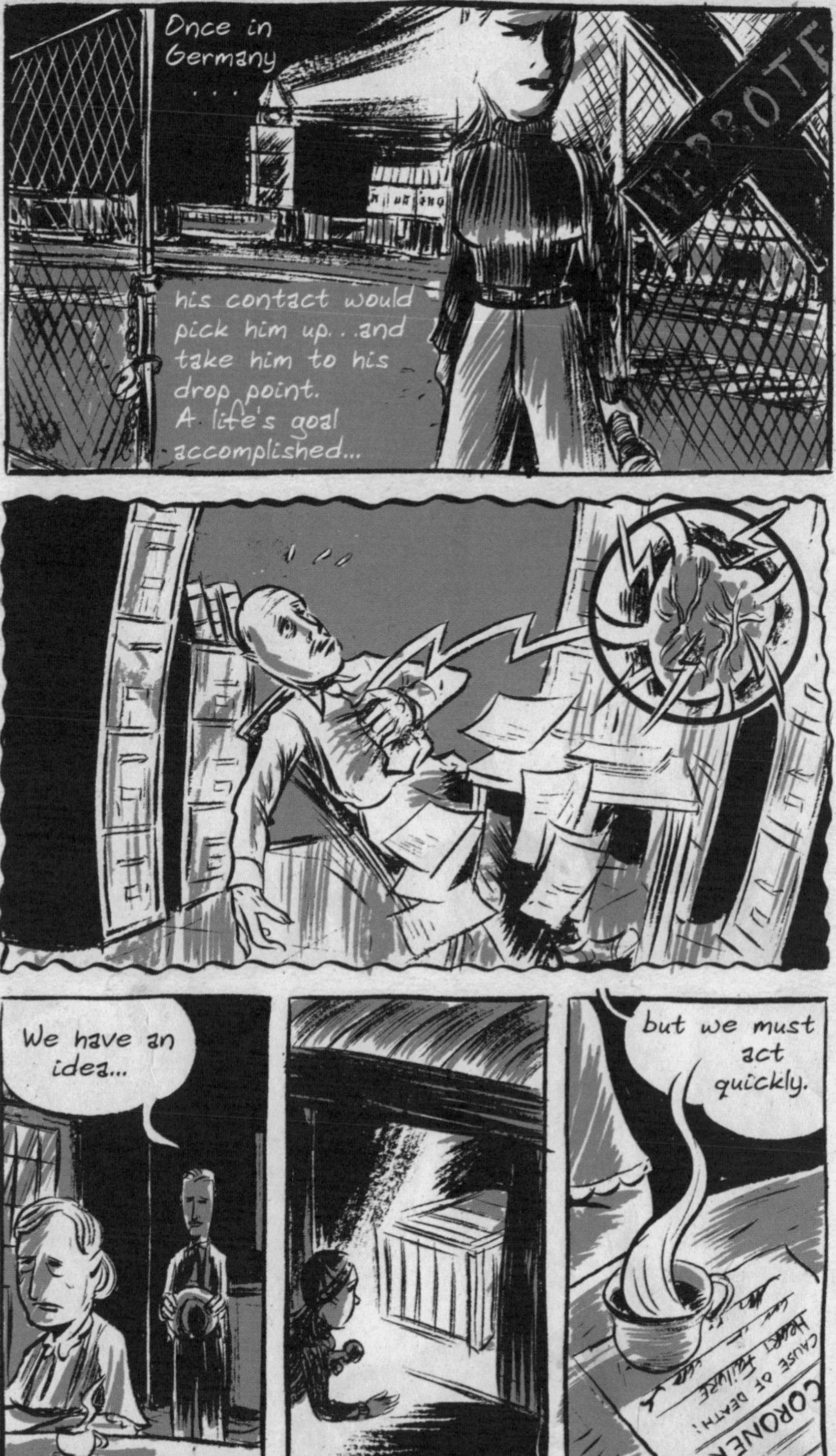
Once in Germany . . .
his contact would pick him up...and take him to his drop point. A life's goal accomplished...
We have an idea...
but we must act quickly.
CAUSE OF DEATH: HEART FAILURE

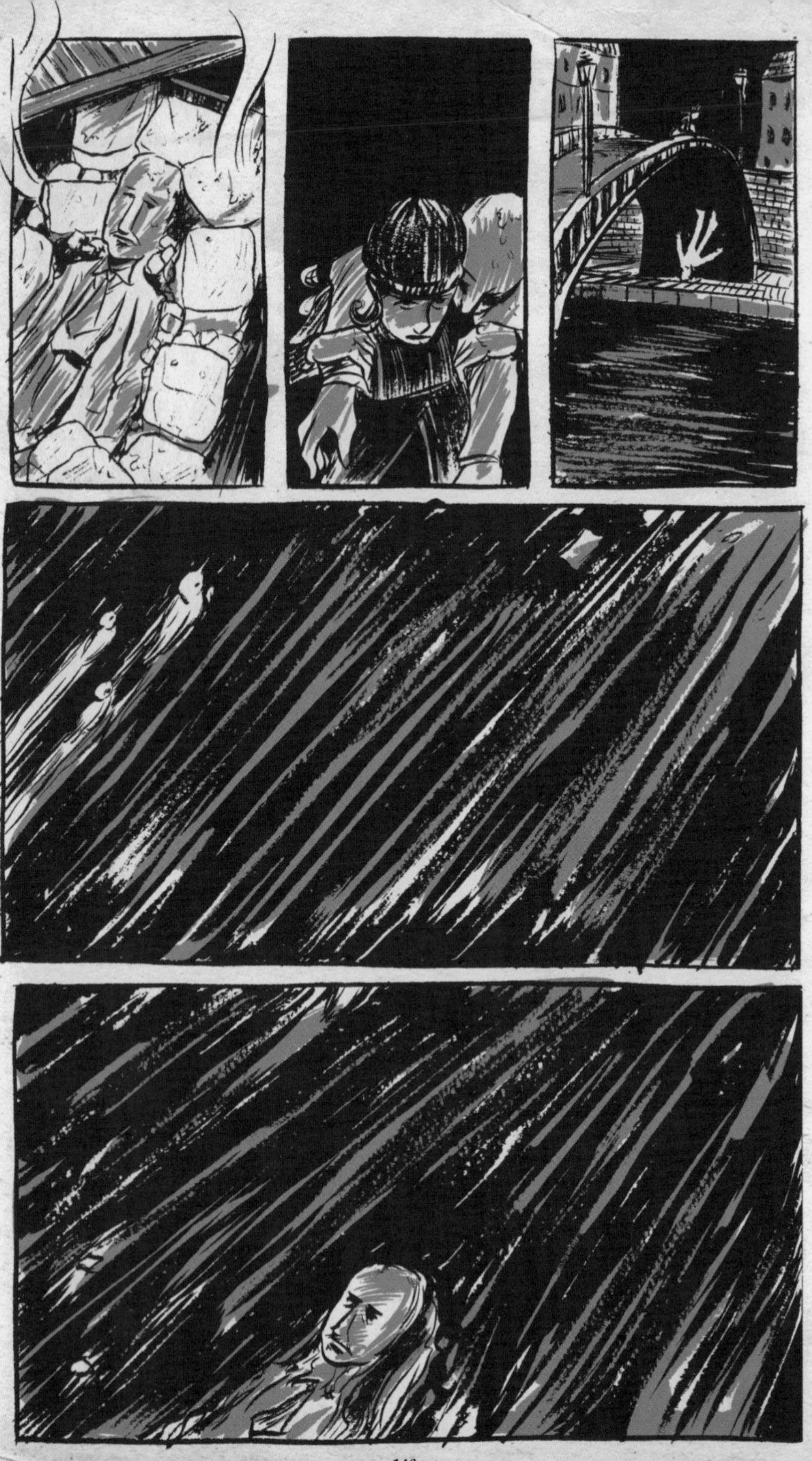

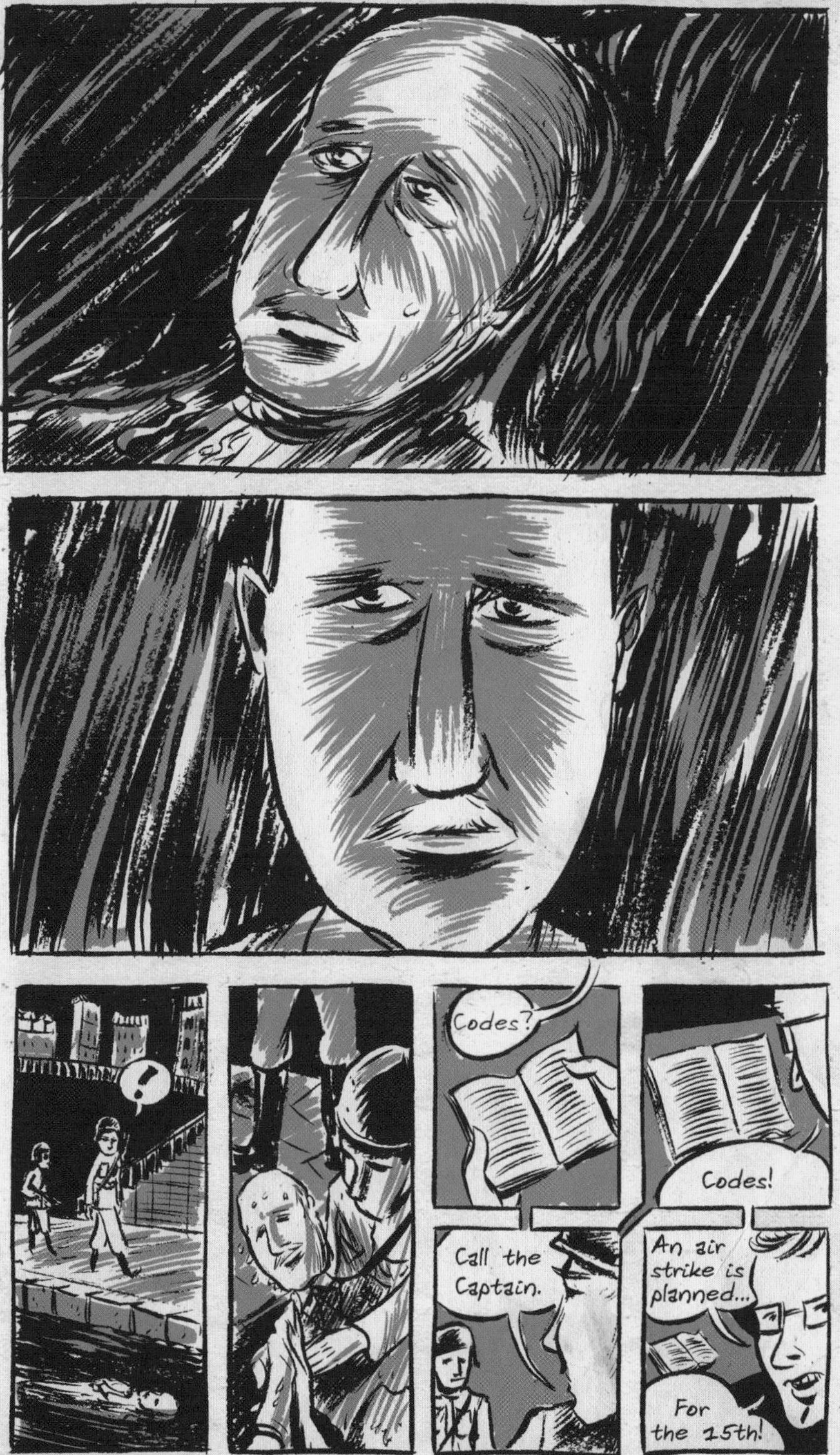

!
Codes?
Codes!
Call the Captain.
An air strike is planned...
For the 15th!

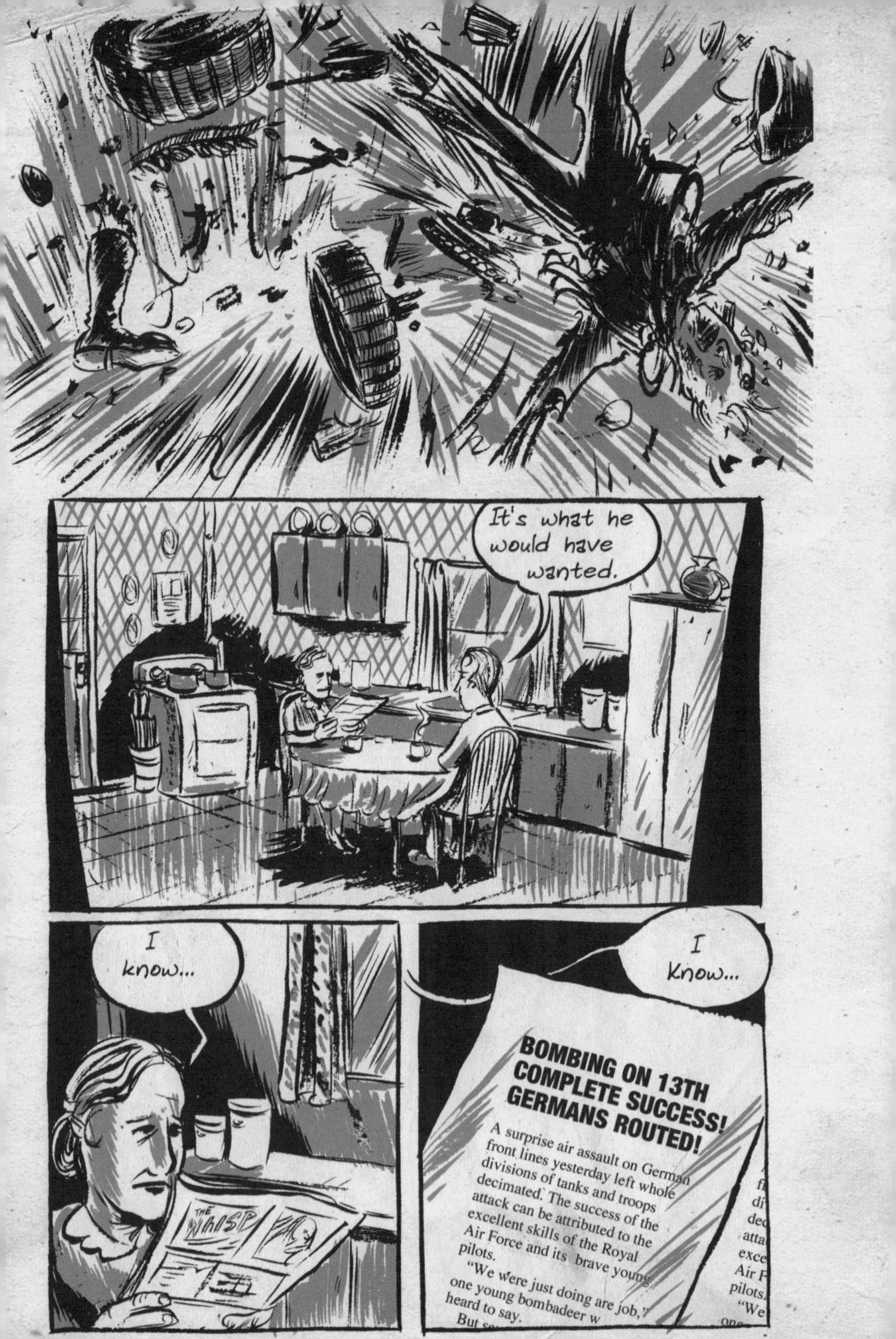
It's what he would have wanted.
I know...
I know...
BOMBING ON 13TH COMPLETE SUCCESS! GERMANS ROUTED!
A surprise air assault on German front lines yesterday left whole divisions of tanks and troops decimated. The success of the attack can be attributed to the excellent skills of the Royal Air Force and its brave young pilots.
"We were just doing are job," one young bombadeer w heard to say.

EAVESDROP
Dossier
#0151944
Rent room above suspected enemy agent codenamed "Satin". Put under surveillance and report suspicious activities.
YOU THINK I'M HAPPY WHAT YOU GOTTA DO FOR MONEY? WE NEED THAT MONEY. WE NEED THEM KRAUTS TO NEED US!
OR DO YOU WANNA GET SHIPPED OFF TO ONE OF THEM CAMPS?
I hate you Pierre.

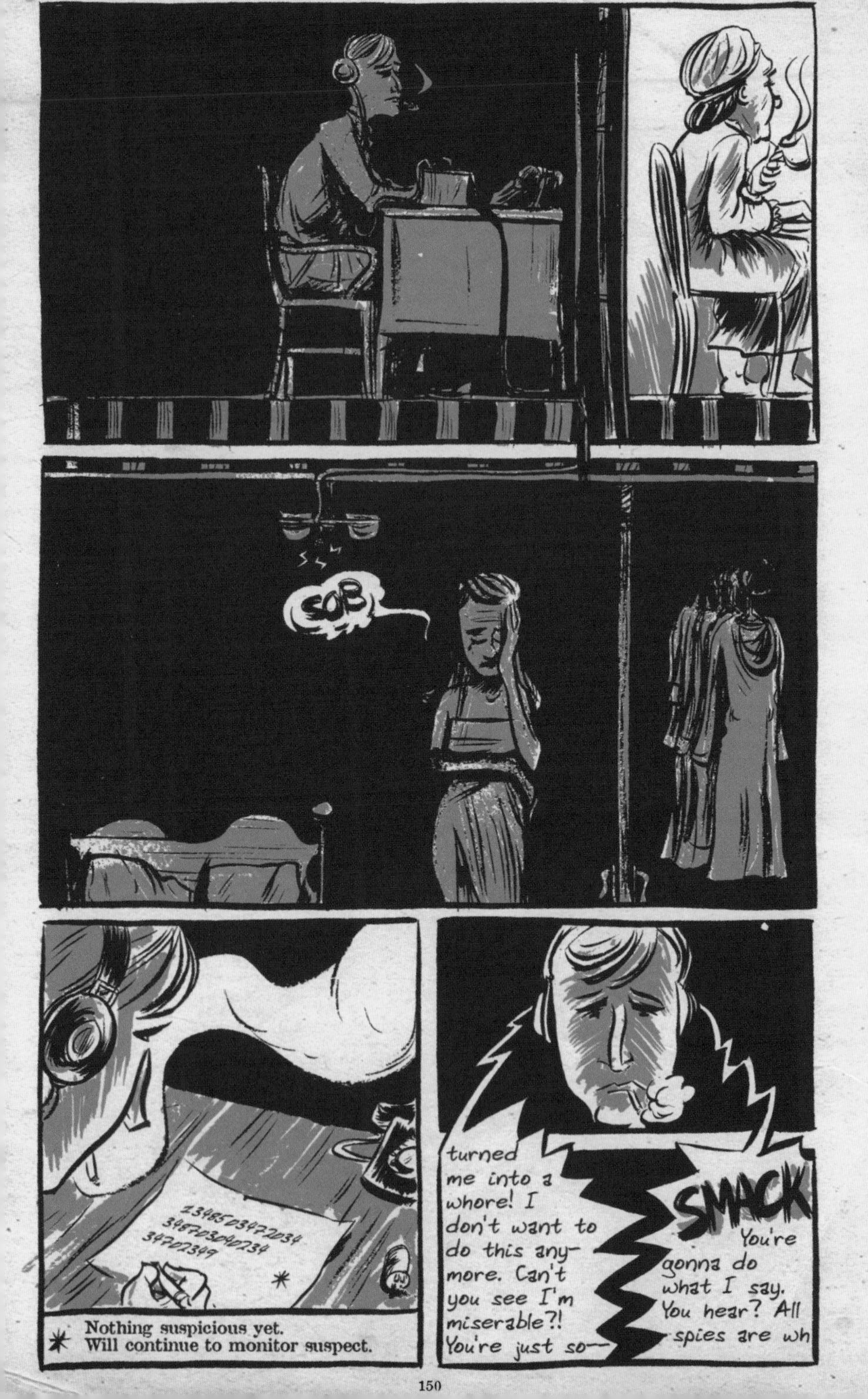
SOB
* Nothing suspicious yet.
Will continue to monitor suspect.
turned me into a whore! I don't want to do this any-more. Can't you see I'm miserable?! You're just so—
SMACK
You're gonna do what I say. You hear? All spies are wh

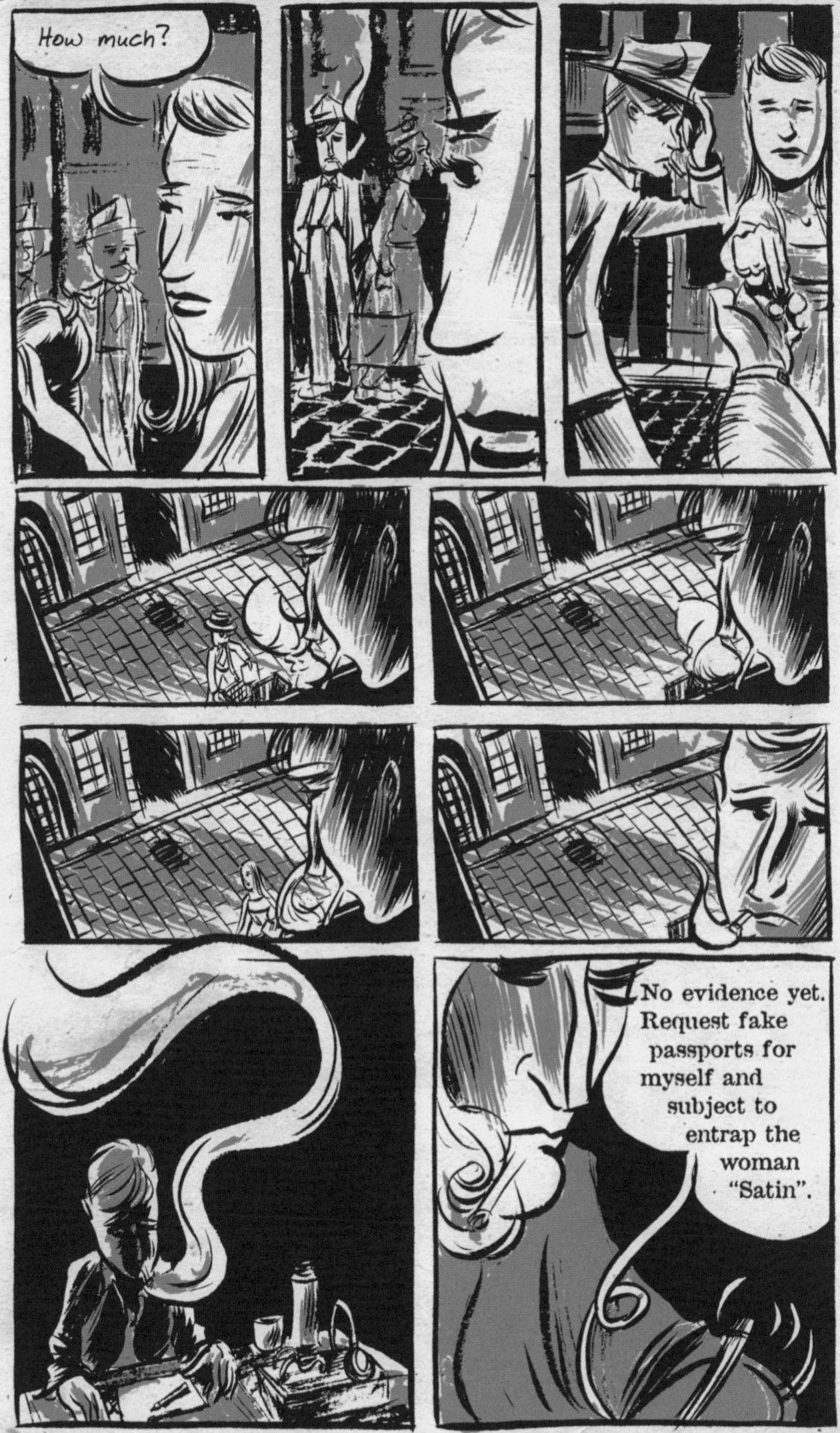
How much?
No evidence yet. Request fake passports for myself and subject to entrap the woman "Satin".

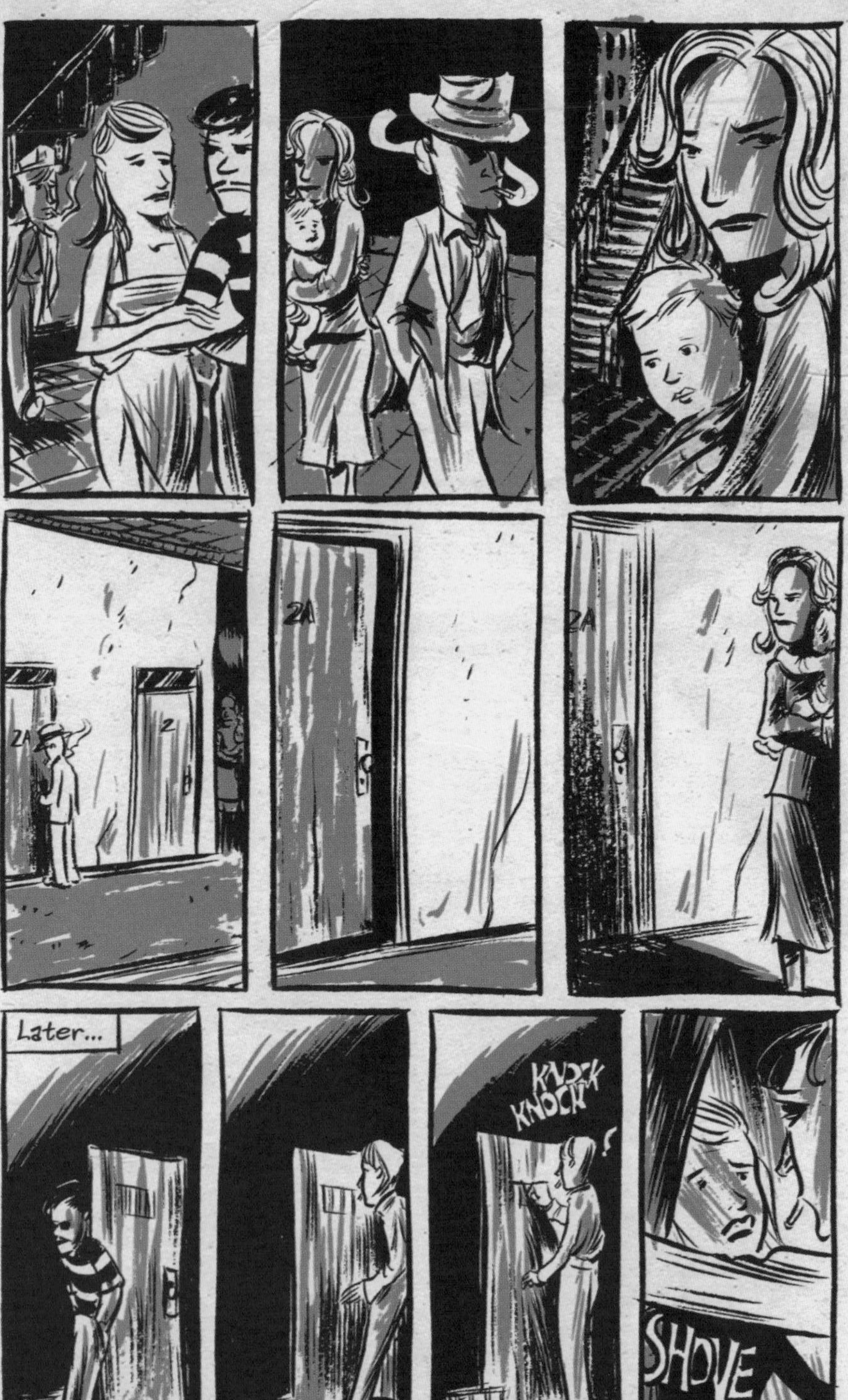
2A
2
2A
2A
Later...
KNOCK KNOCK
SHOVE

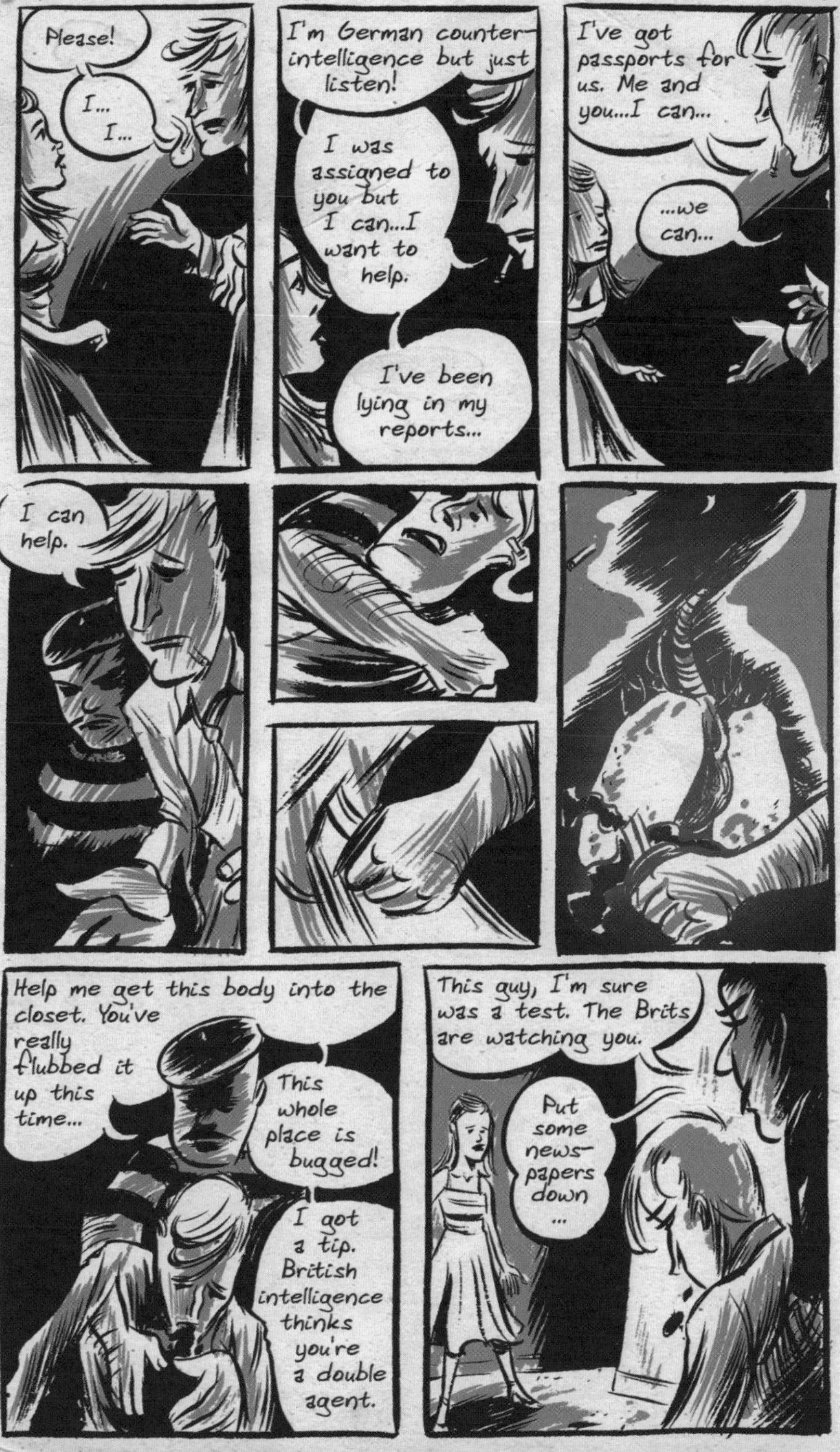
Please!
I... I...
I'm German counter-intelligence but just listen!
I was assigned to you but I can...I want to help.
I've been lying in my reports...
I've got passports for us. Me and you...I can...
...we can...
I can help.
Help me get this body into the closet. You've really flubbed it up this time...
This whole place is bugged!
I got a tip. British intelligence thinks you're a double agent.
This guy, I'm sure was a test. The Brits are watching you.
Put some news-papers down ...

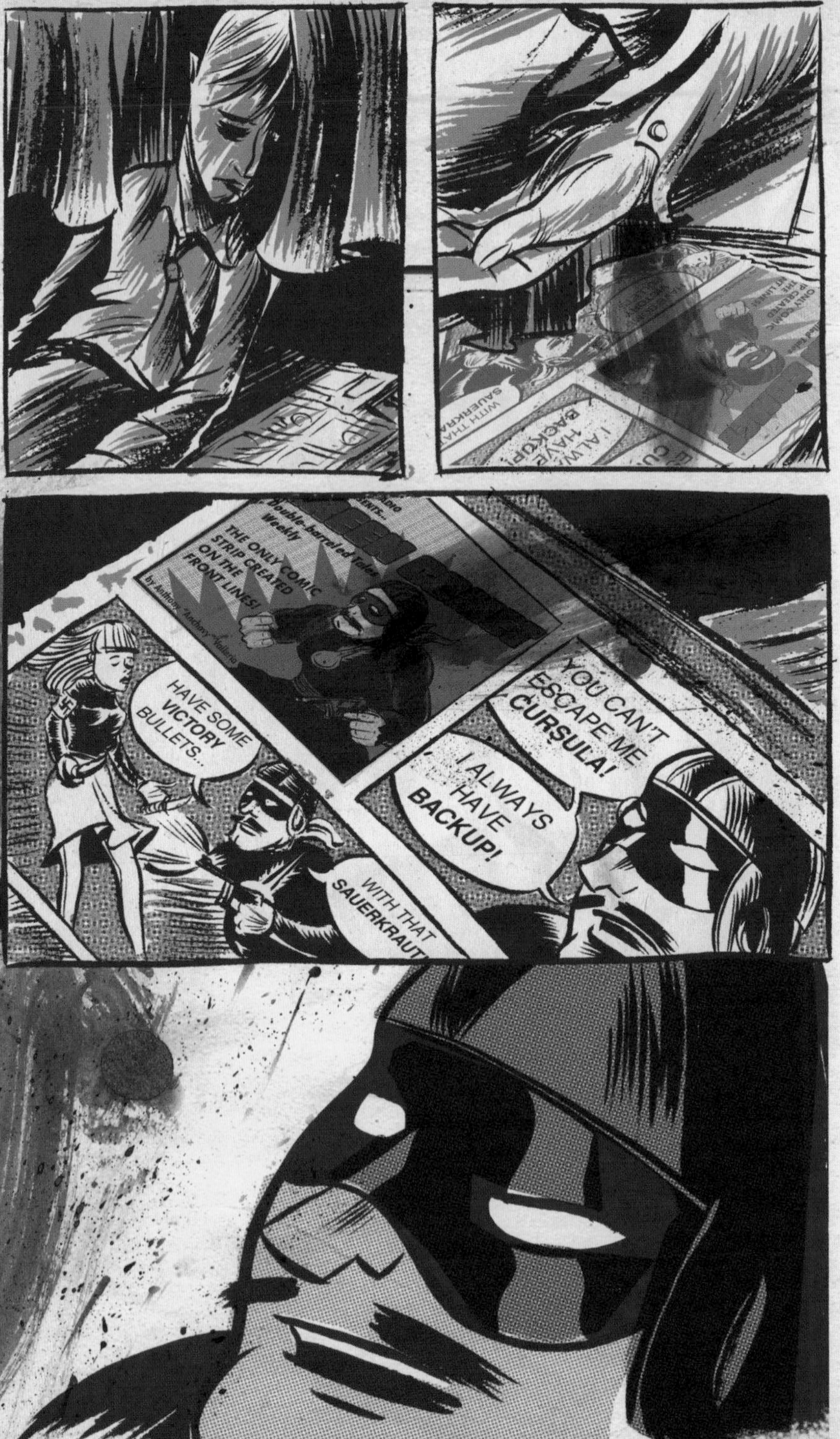
Double-barreled Tales Weekly
THE ONLY COMIC STRIP CREATED ON THE FRONT LINES!
HAVE SOME VICTORY BULLETS...
WITH THAT SAUERKRAUT
YOU CAN'T ESCAPE ME ÇURŞULA!
I ALWAYS HAVE BACKUP!

DISTRACTION
Dossier #0131944

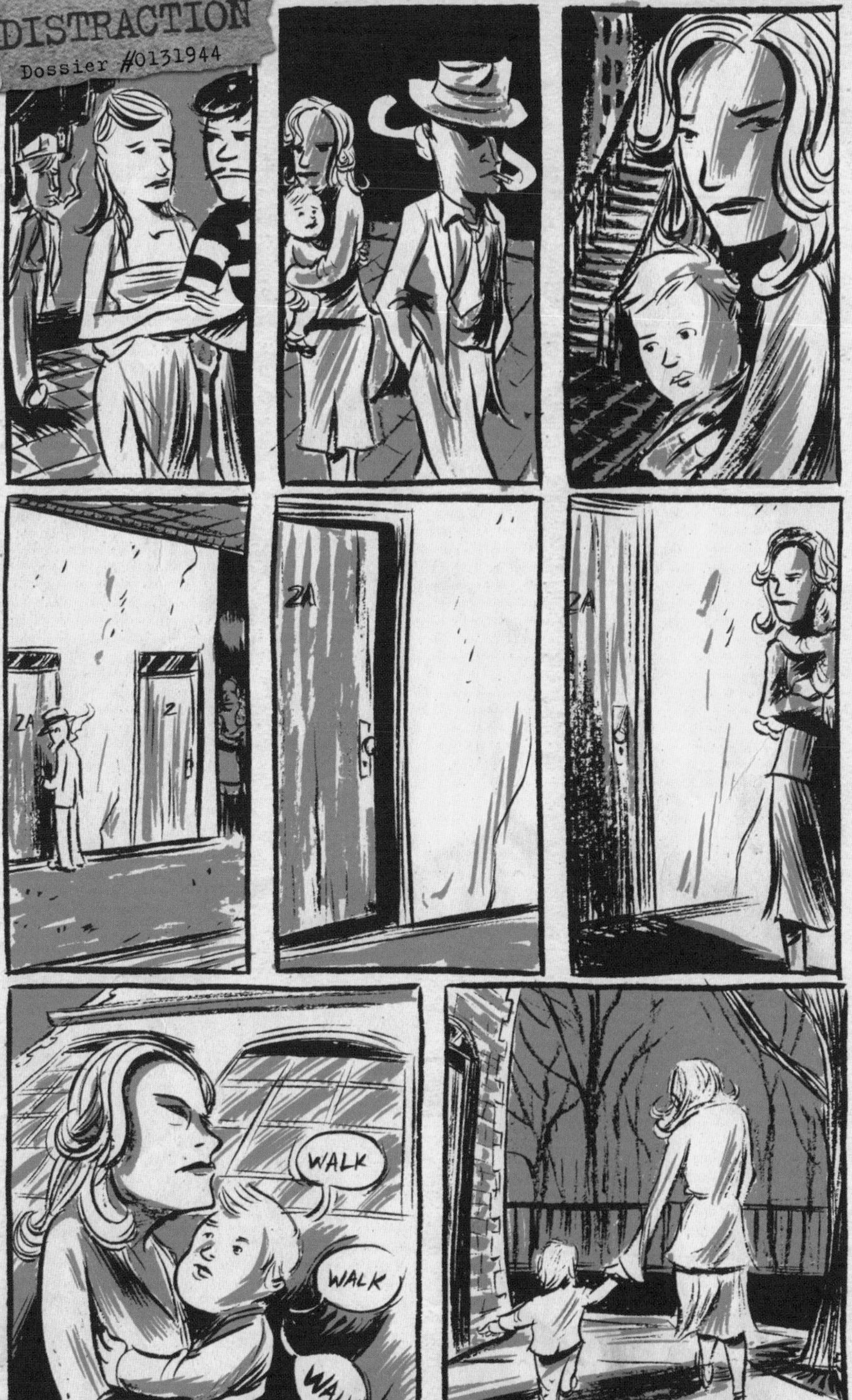
2A
2
2A
2A
WALK
WALK
WALK

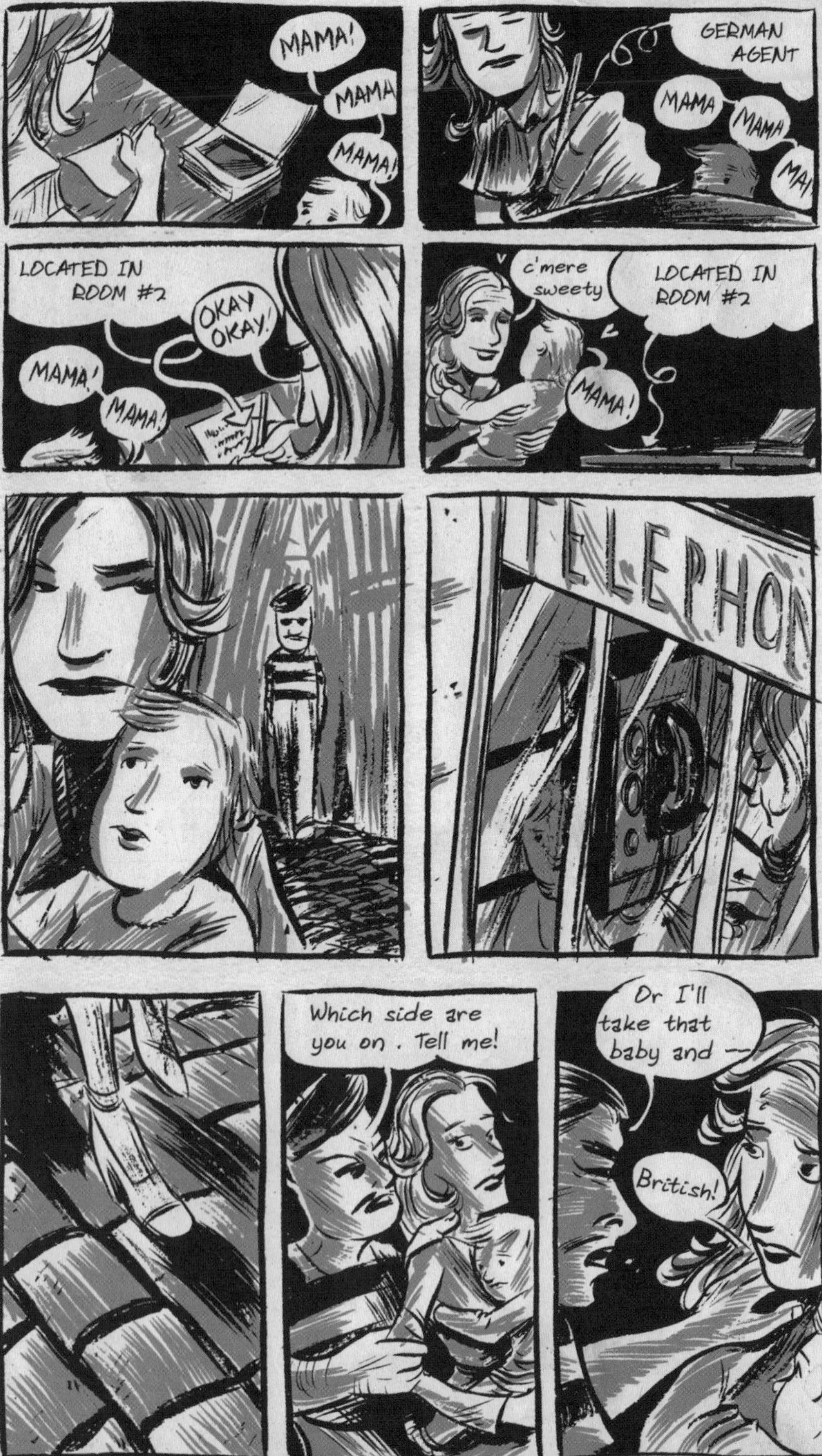
MAMA!
MAMA
MAMA!
GERMAN AGENT
MAMA
MAMA
LOCATED IN ROOM #2
OKAY OKAY!
MAMA!
MAMA!
c'mere sweety
LOCATED IN ROOM #2
MAMA!
TELEPHON
Which side are you on. Tell me!
Or I'll take that baby and —
British!

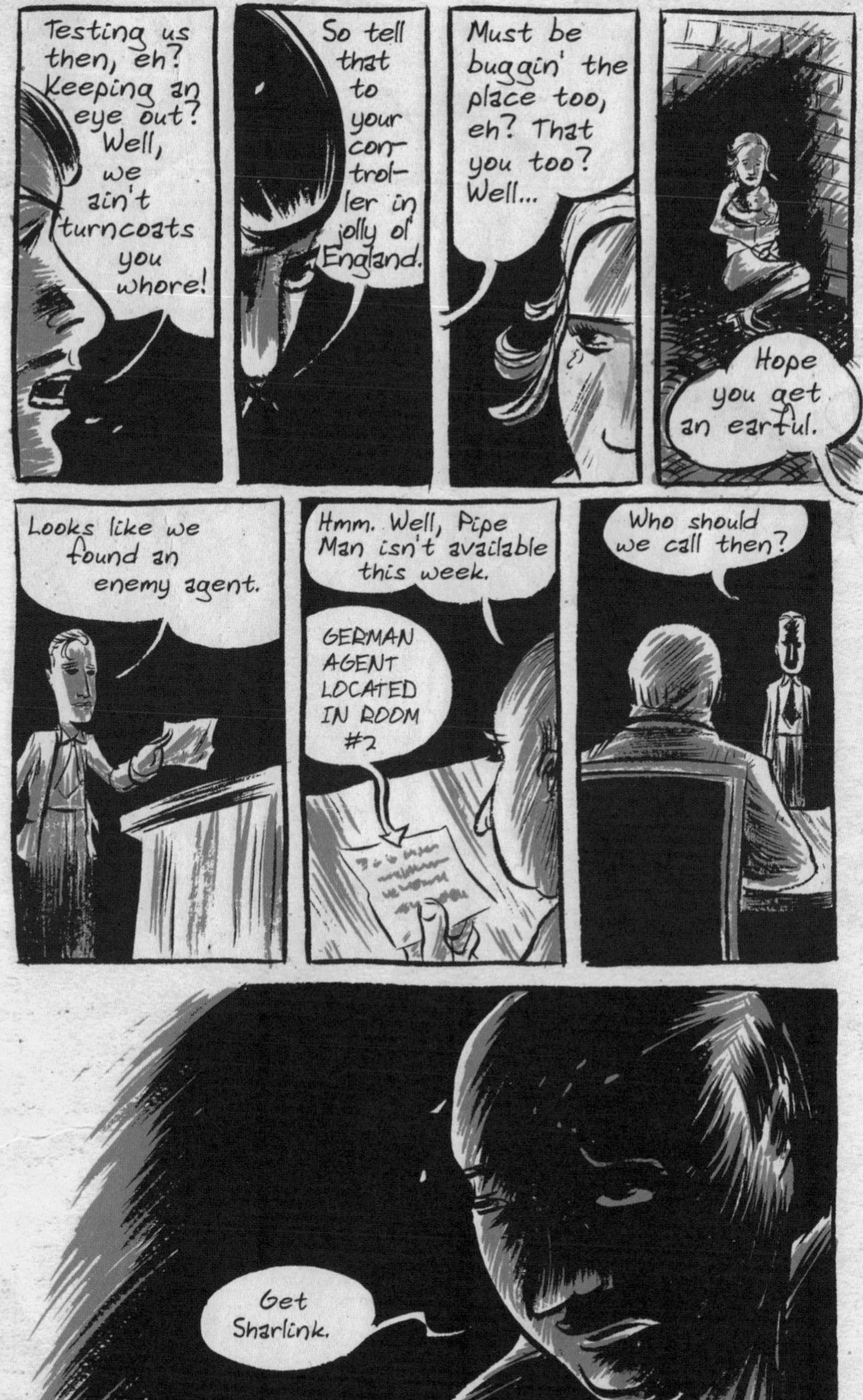
Testing us then, eh? Keeping an eye out? Well, we ain't turncoats you whore!
So tell that to your con-trol-ler in jolly ol' England.
Must be buggin' the place too, eh? That you too? Well...
Hope you get an earful.
Looks like we found an enemy agent.
Hmm. Well, Pipe Man isn't available this week.
GERMAN AGENT LOCATED IN ROOM #2
Who should we call then?
Get Sharlink.

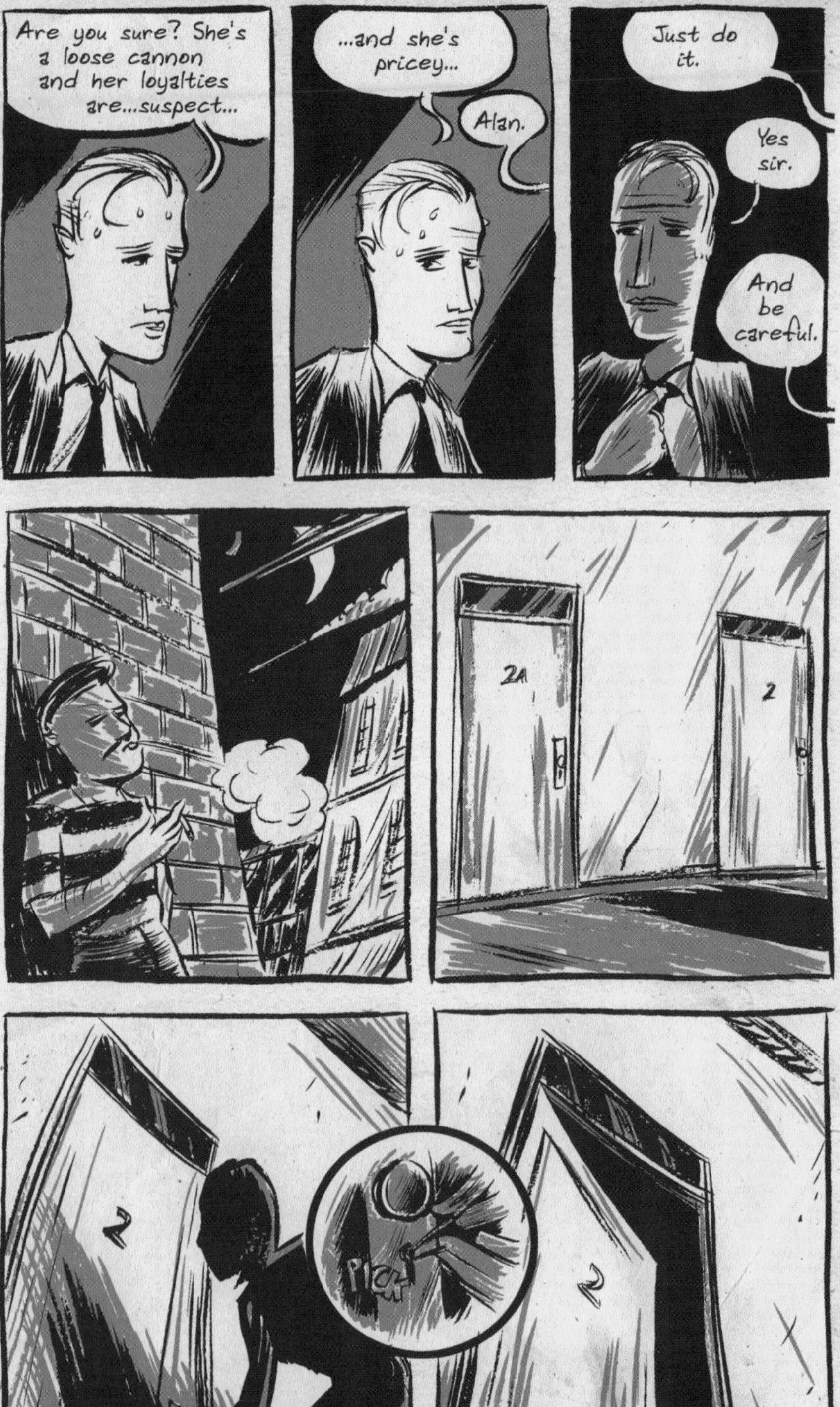
Are you sure? She's a loose cannon and her loyalties are...suspect...
...and she's pricey...
Alan.
Just do it.
Yes sir.
And be careful.
2A
2
2
2

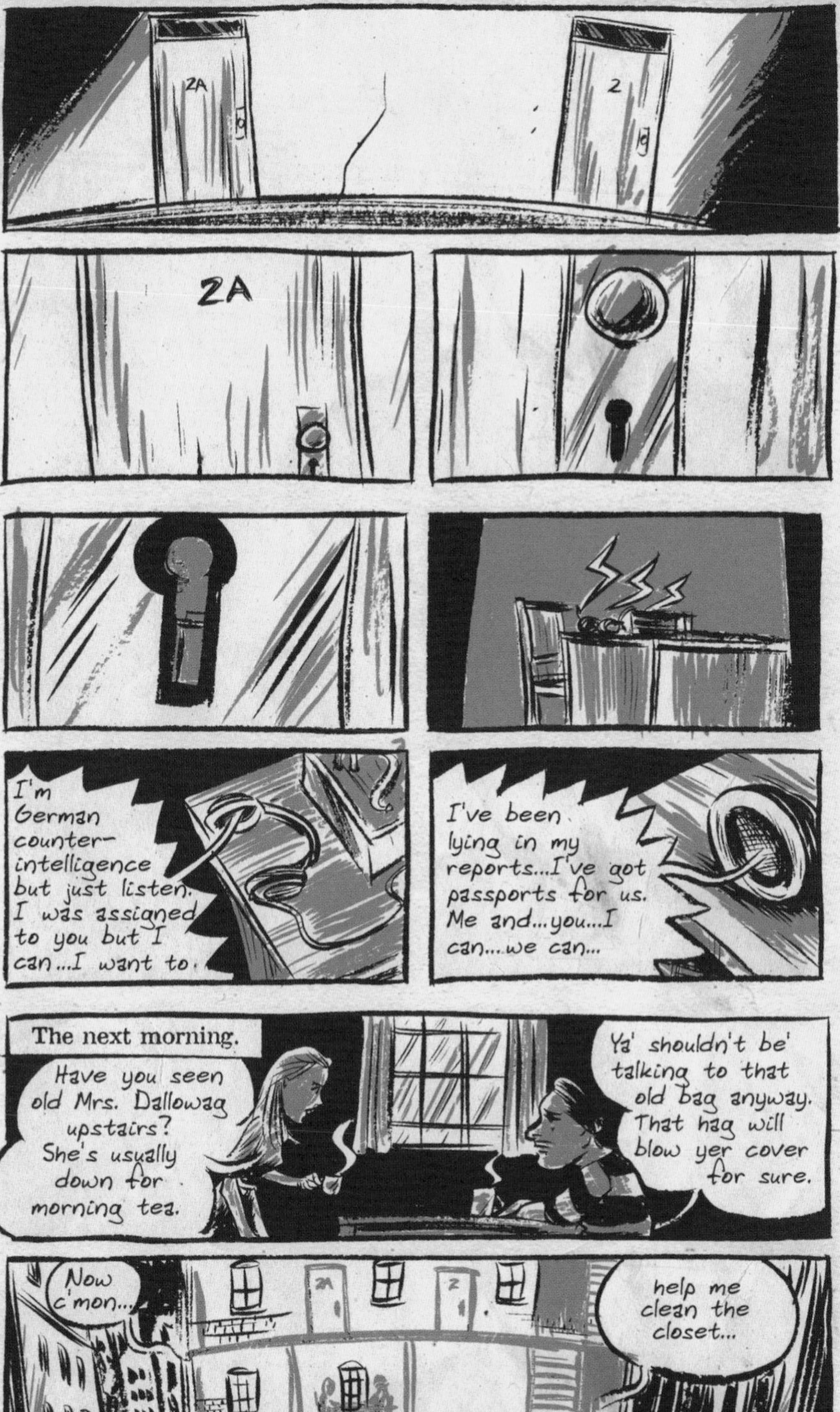
2A
2
2A
I'm German counter-intelligence but just listen. I was assigned to you but I can...I want to.
I've been lying in my reports...I've got passports for us. Me and...you...I can....we can...
The next morning.
Have you seen old Mrs. Dallowag upstairs? She's usually down for morning tea.
Ya' shouldn't be' talking to that old bag anyway. That hag will blow yer cover for sure.
Now c'mon...
2A
2
help me clean the closet...

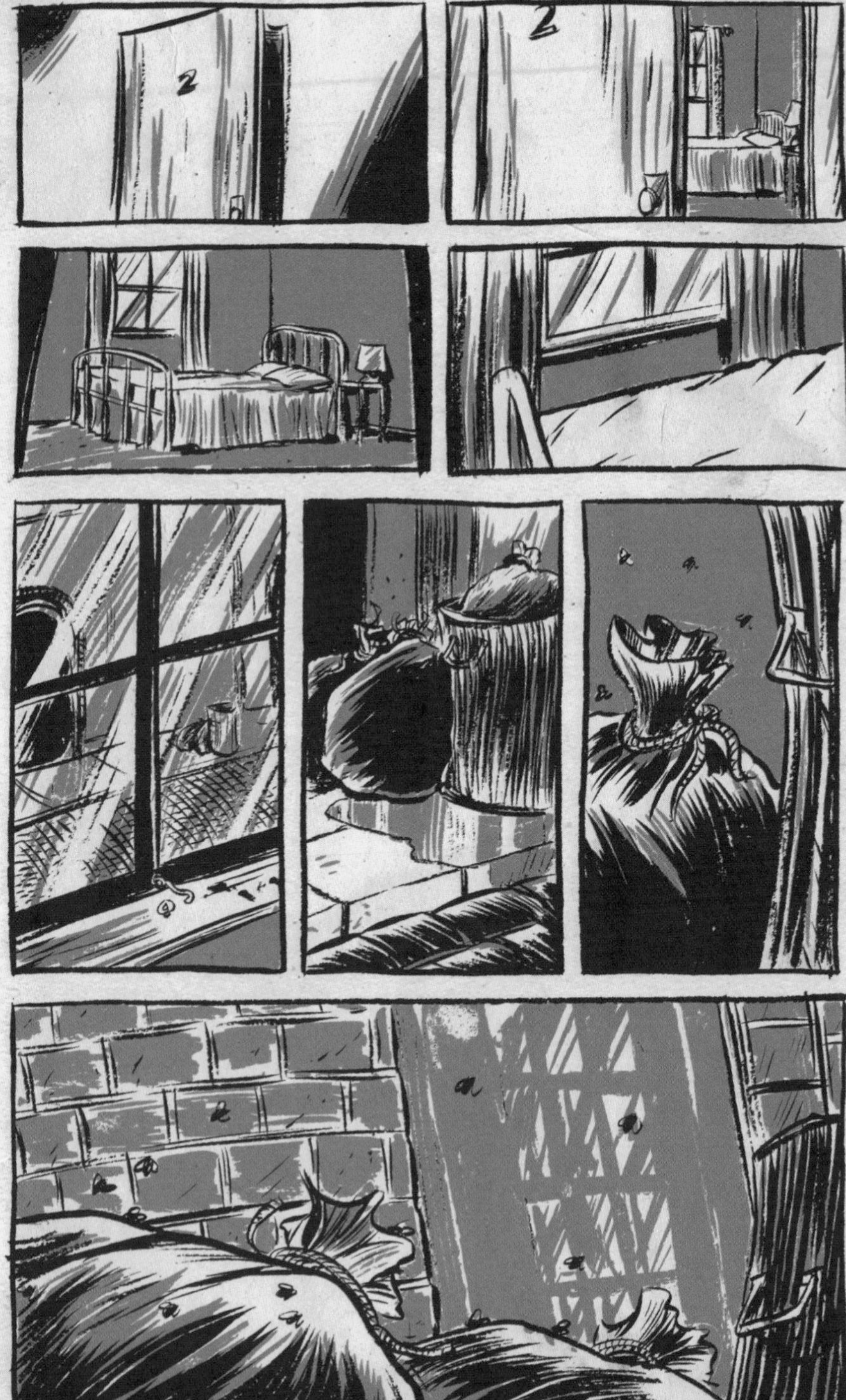
2
2

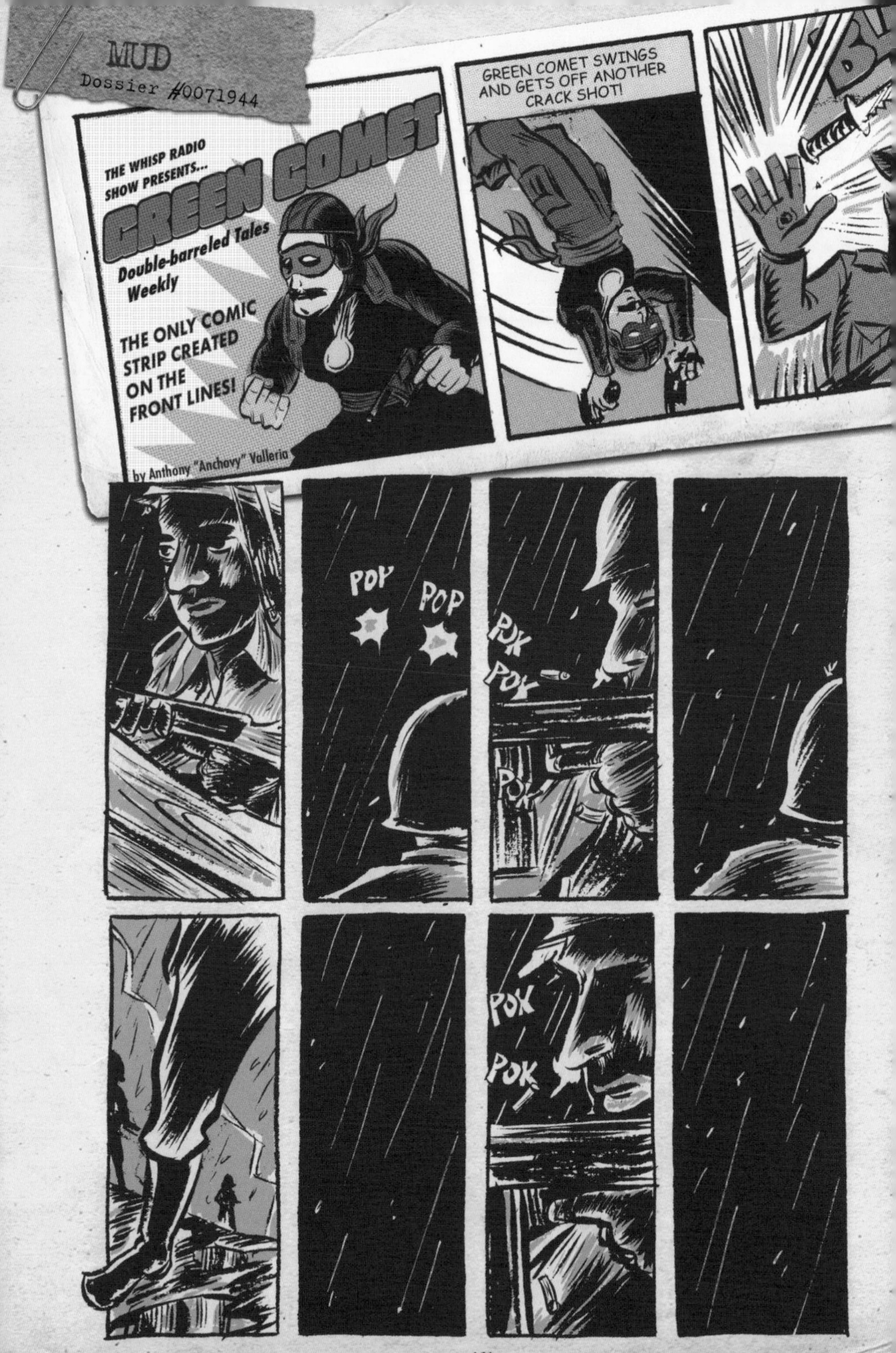
MUD
Dossier #0071944
THE WHISP RADIO SHOW PRESENTS...
GREEN COMET
Double-barreled Tales Weekly
THE ONLY COMIC STRIP CREATED ON THE FRONT LINES!
by Anthony "Anchovy" Valleria
GREEN COMET SWINGS AND GETS OFF ANOTHER CRACK SHOT!
POP
POP
POK
POK
POK
POK
POK

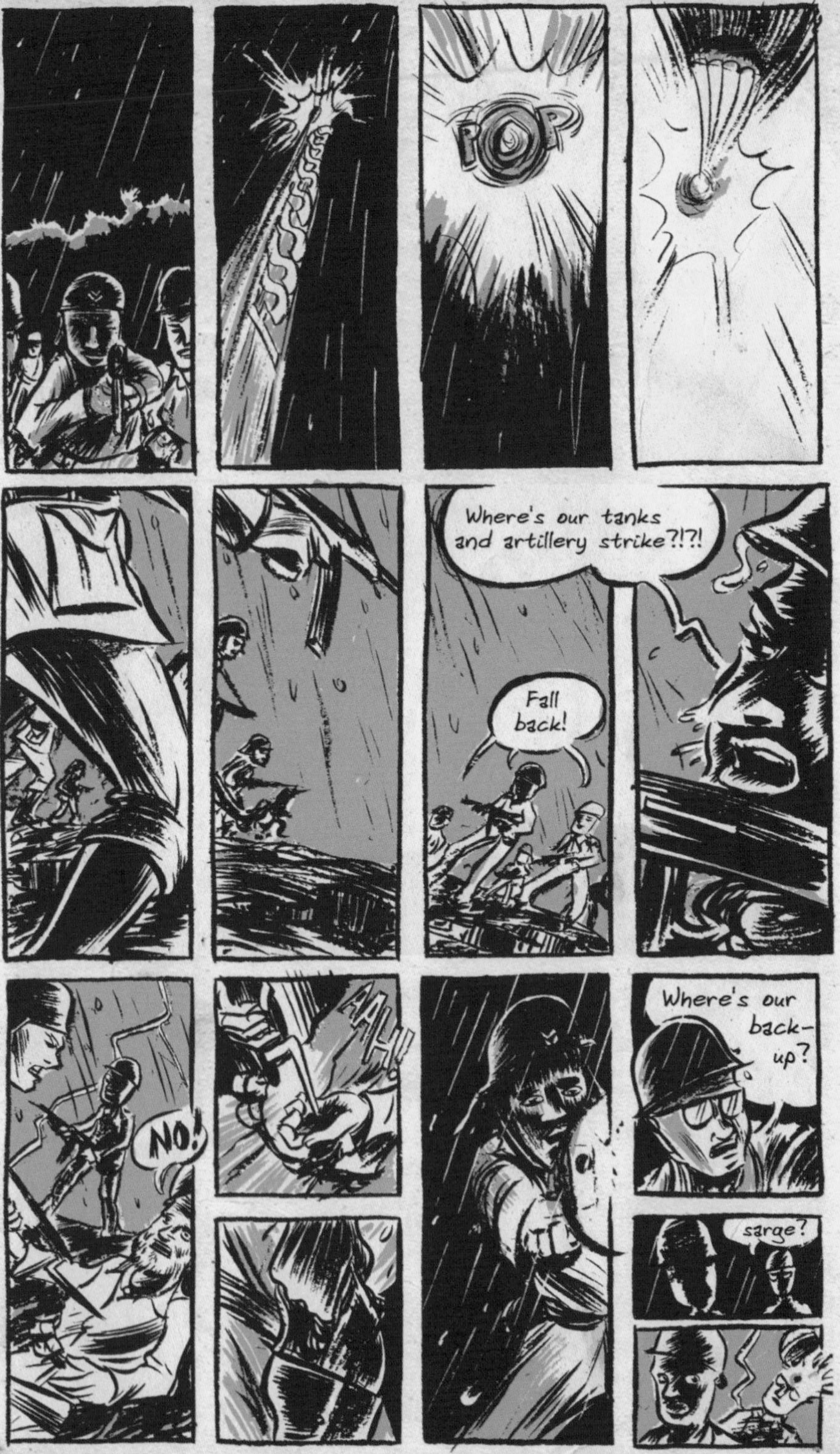
SSSSSS
POP
Where's our tanks and artillery strike?!?!
Fall back!
NO!
AAH!
Where's our back-up?
sarge?

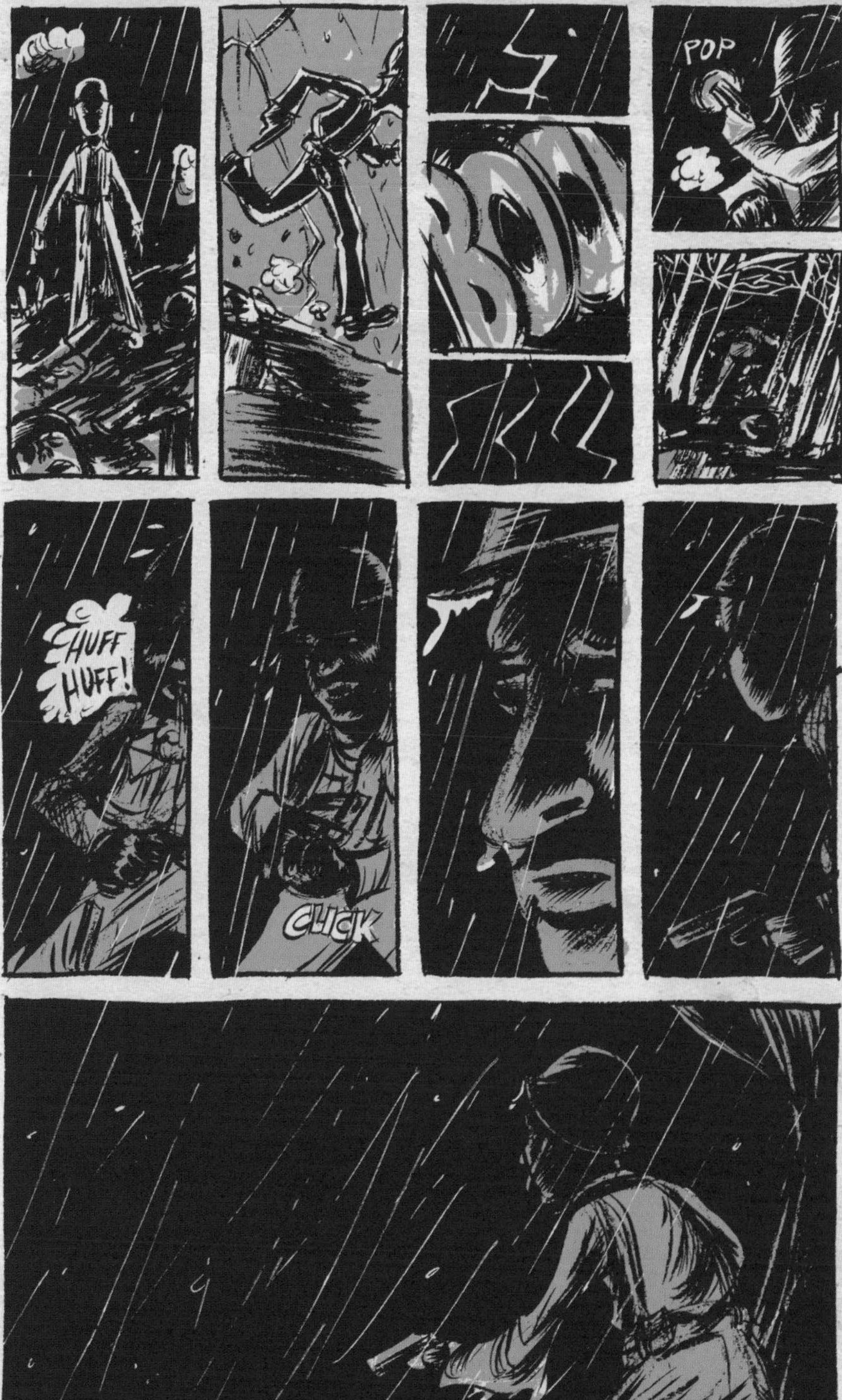
POP
BOOM
HUFF HUFF!
CLICK

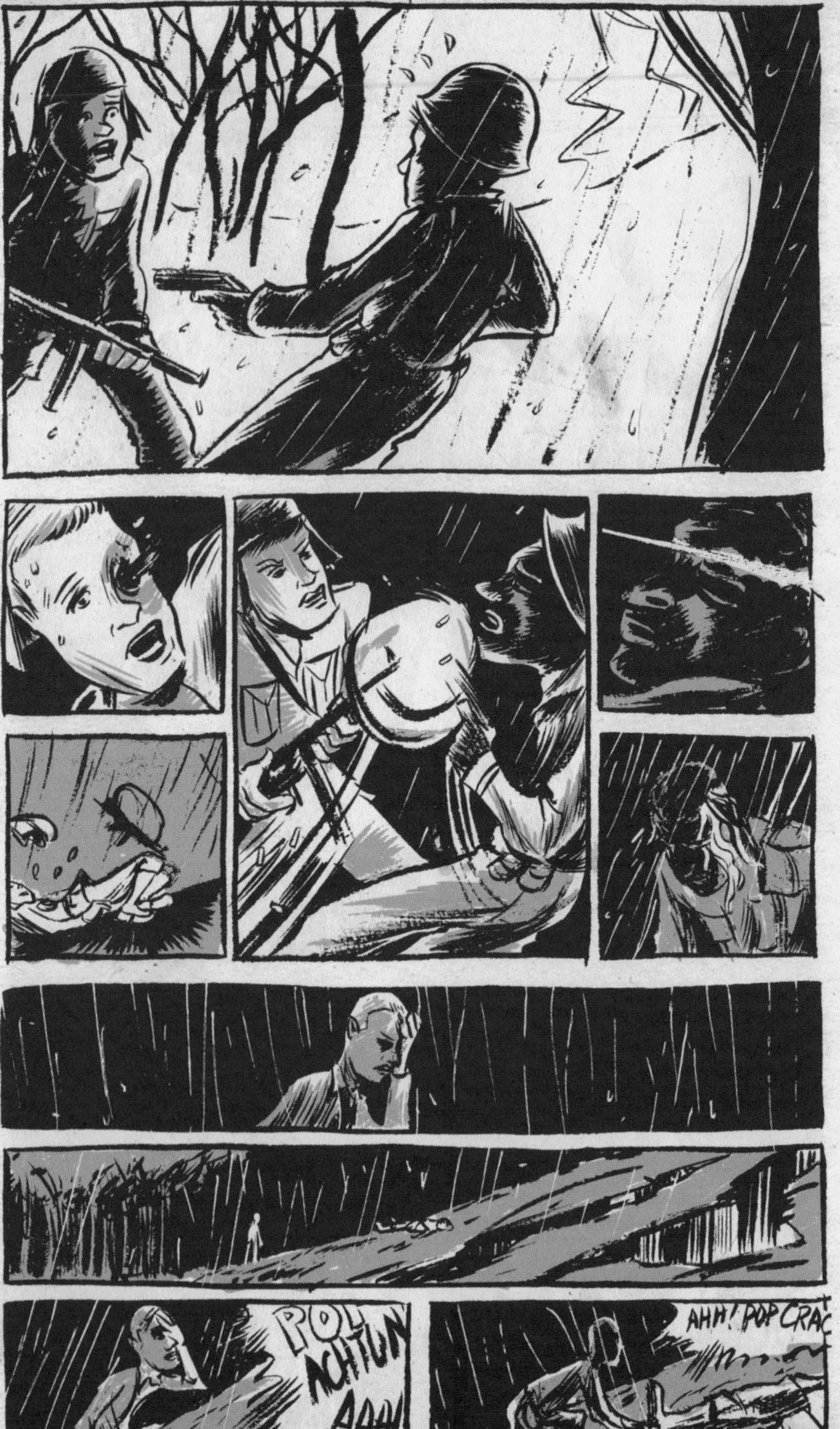
POL
ACHTUN
AAH
AHH! POP CRAC

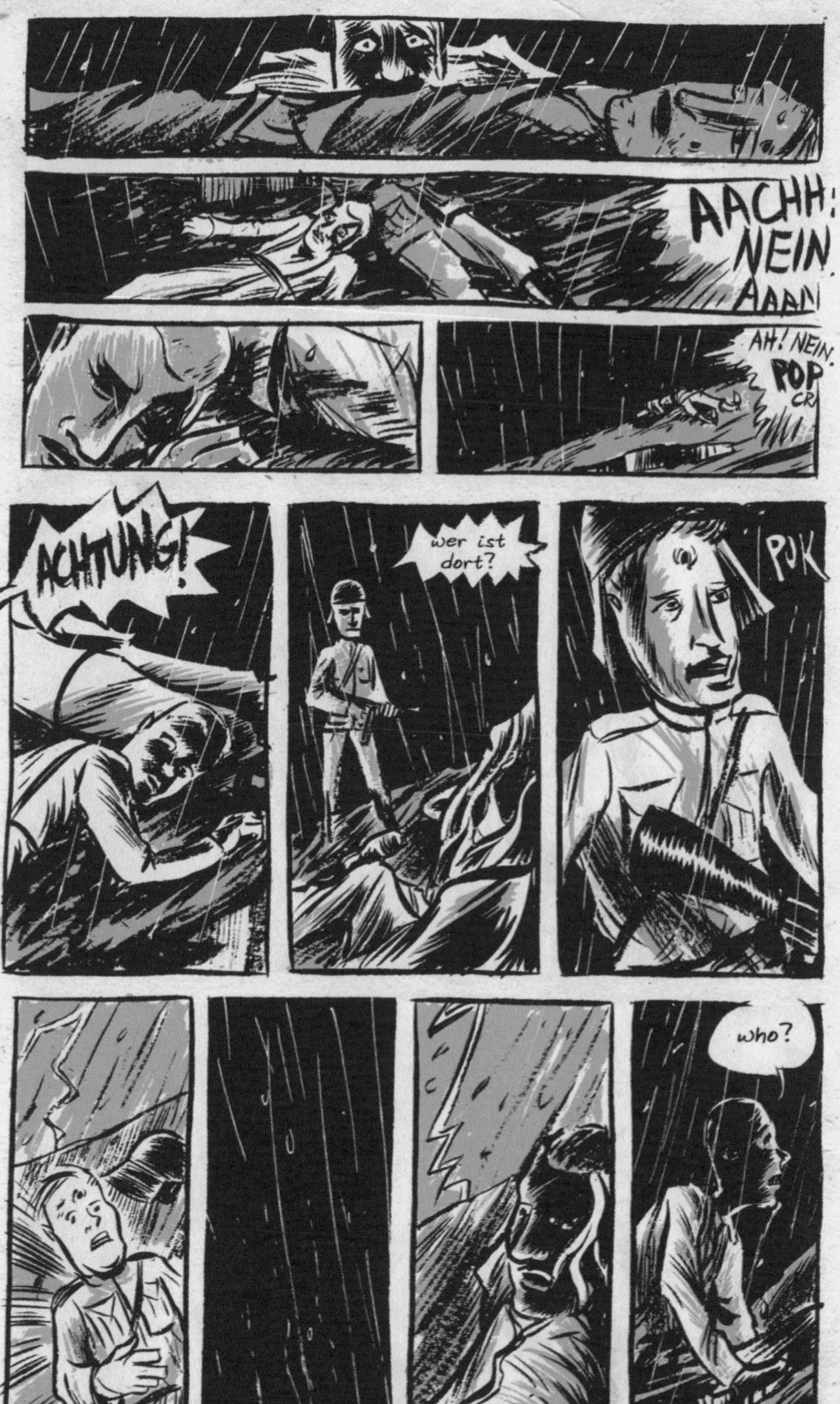
AACHH
NEIN
AH! NEIN.
POP
ACHTUNG!
wer ist dort?
POK
who?

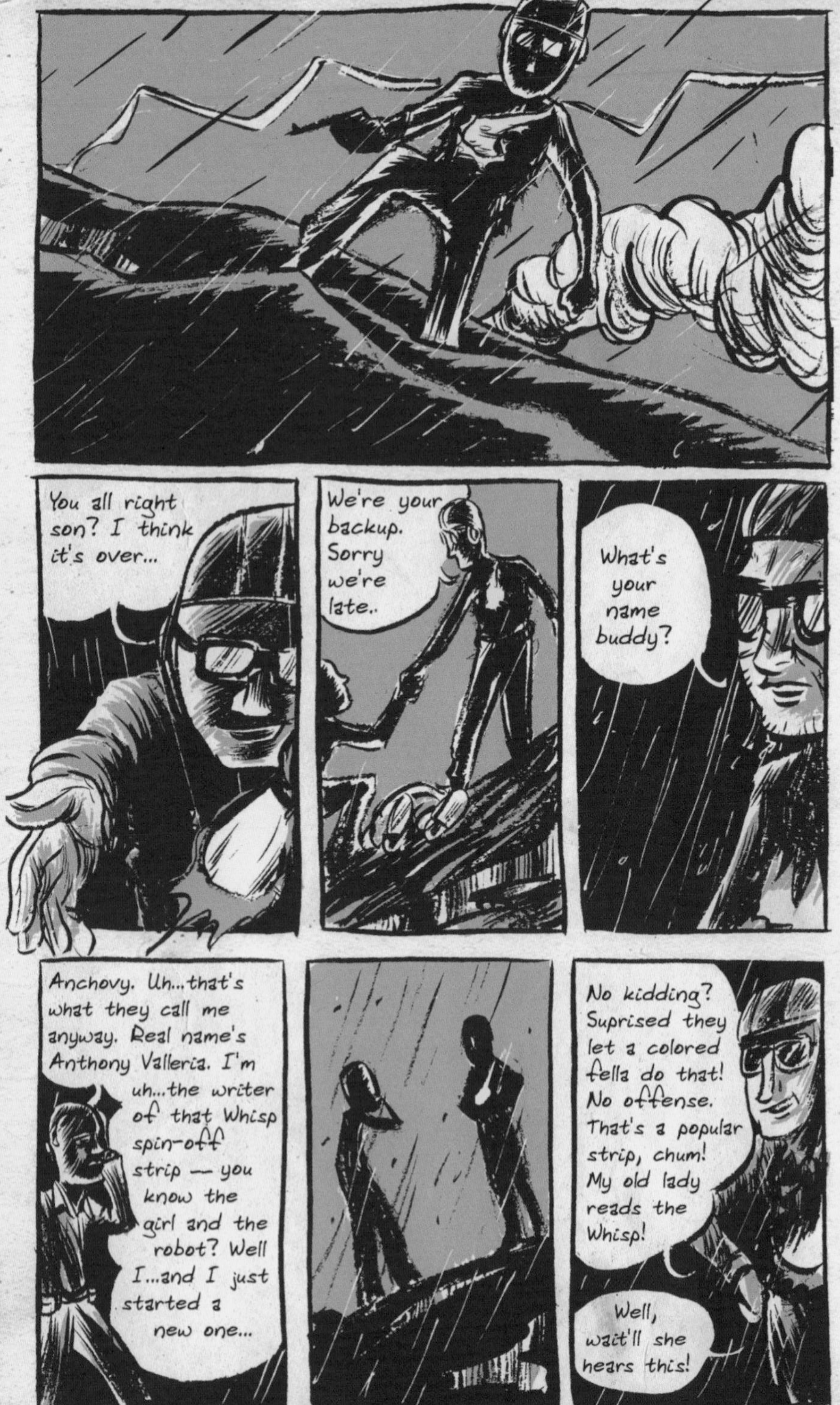
You all right son? I think it's over...
We're your backup. Sorry we're late..
What's your name buddy?
Anchovy. Uh...that's what they call me anyway. Real name's Anthony Valleria. I'm uh...the writer of that Whisp spin-off strip — you know the girl and the robot? Well I...and I just started a new one...
No kidding? Suprised they let a colored fella do that! No offense. That's a popular strip, chum! My old lady reads the Whisp!
Well, wait'll she hears this!

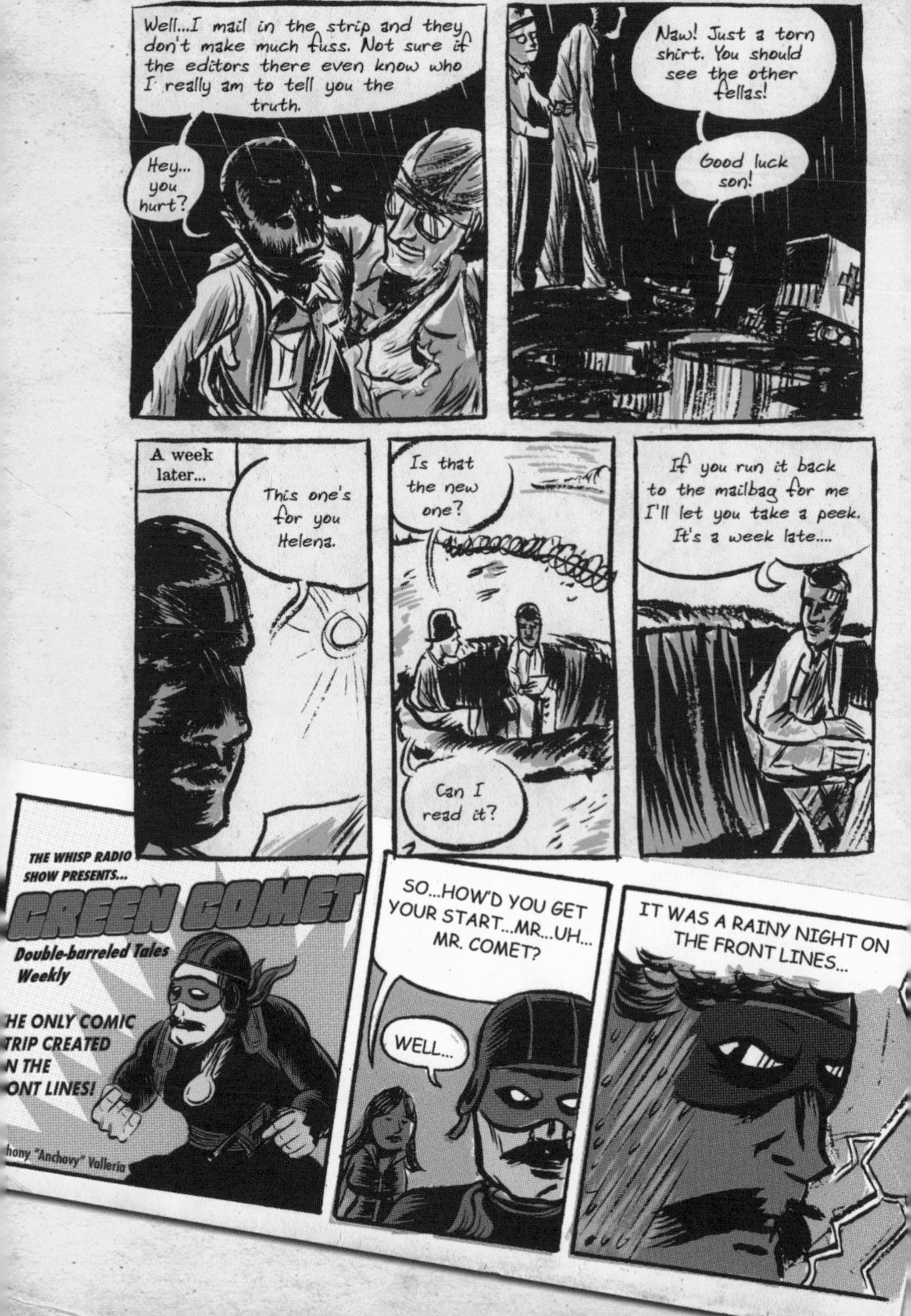
Well...I mail in the strip and they don't make much fuss. Not sure if the editors there even know who I really am to tell you the truth.
Hey... you hurt?
Naw! Just a torn shirt. You should see the other fellas!
Good luck son!
A week later...
This one's for you Helena.
Is that the new one?
Can I read it?
If you run it back to the mailbag for me I'll let you take a peek. It's a week late....
THE WHISP RADIO SHOW PRESENTS...
GREEN COMET
Double-barreled Tales Weekly
HE ONLY COMIC
TRIP CREATED
N THE
ONT LINES!
hony "Anchovy" Valleria
SO...HOW'D YOU GET YOUR START...MR...UH... MR. COMET?
WELL...
IT WAS A RAINY NIGHT ON THE FRONT LINES...

I ask the German interrogator to reach one of my cigarettes for me. The least he can do really. He's had me in his torture cell for a week now and still hasn't gotten it out of me.
I'm surprised really. I haven't had any training in espionage but I can keep my mouth shut that's for sure. He slips the cigarette between my lips and even lights it for me. What a courtesy. I'd spit in his eye if my mouth wasn't so dry.

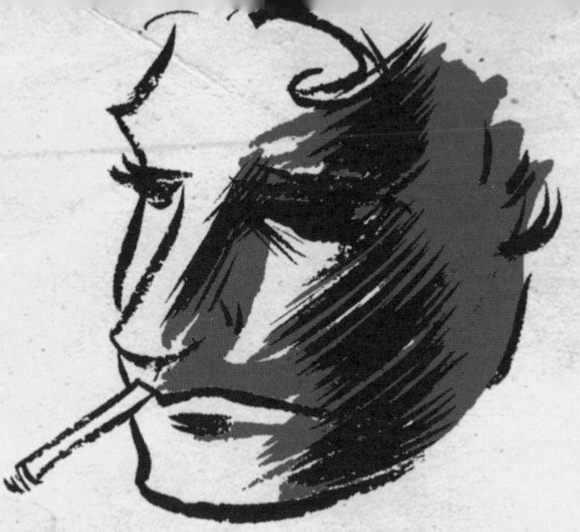

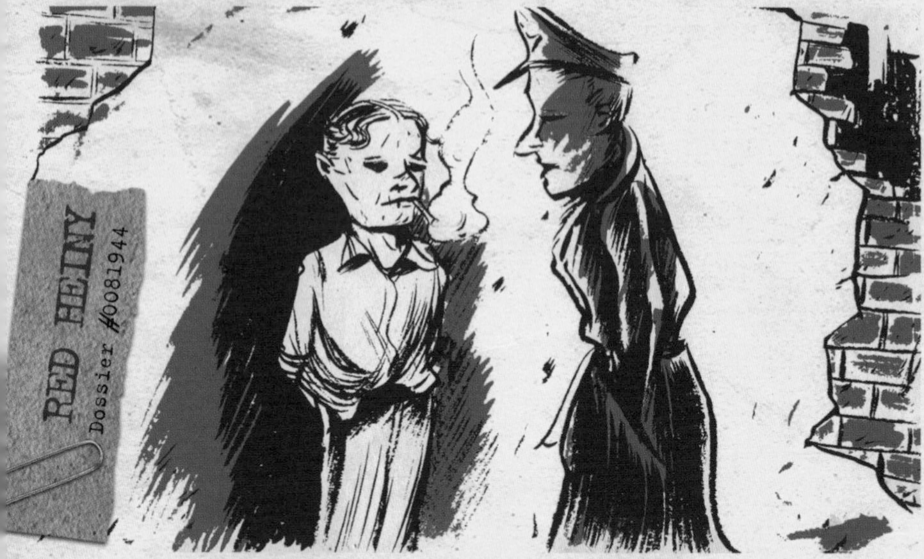
RED HEINY
Dossier #0081944

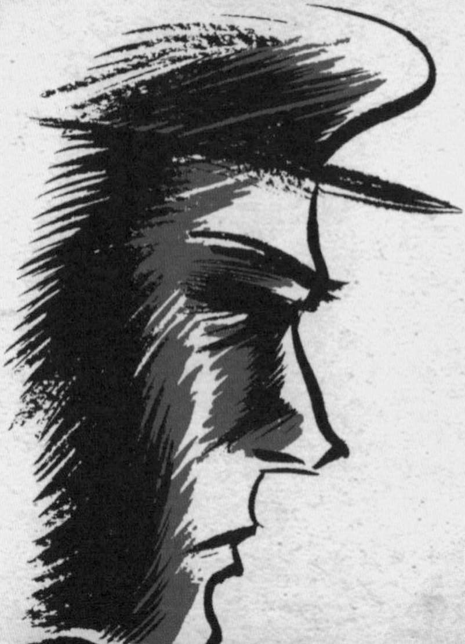

He yells at me one last time to talk. I know enough now not to smile or make a joke. It took me a few fingernails to figure out that he doesn't like that.

I don't react so he keeps yelling and I let him. Drawing in a deep breath of the terrible German brand cigarette. He shouts again and I flinch. He wants the secret messages I was supposed to be taking back to England. Well, he probably could have had them but he took Muriel away. What worse could he do to me?

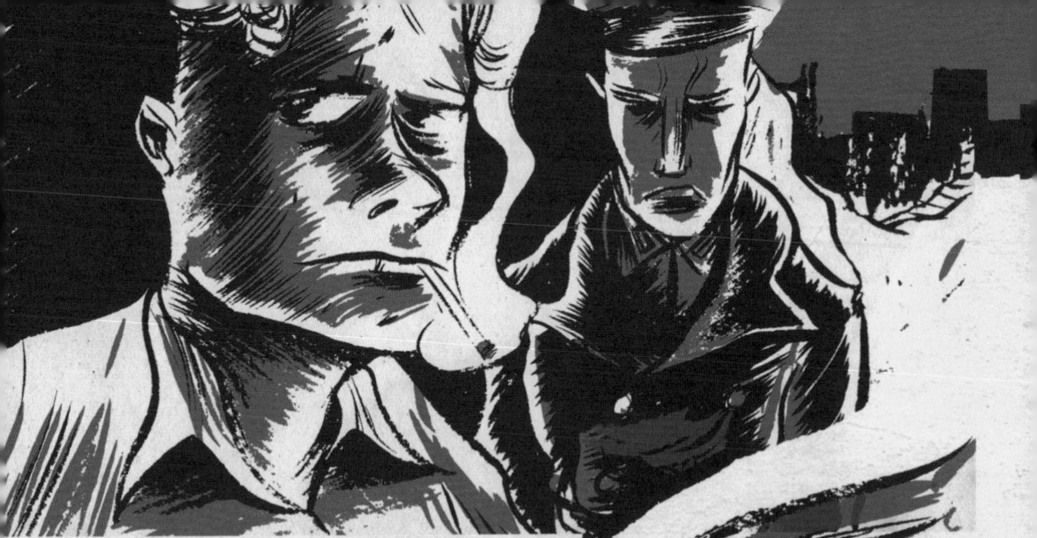

He had the only card he needed to make me hand over the secret documents and he didn't even use it. Just killed her. So I'll be damned if he'll get anything out of me. And then it occurs to me. I'll have a little fun with him.

"Sure," I say. "I'll tell you where the stuff is," as I kill time. Suddenly his eyes light up and I almost laugh.

Almost.

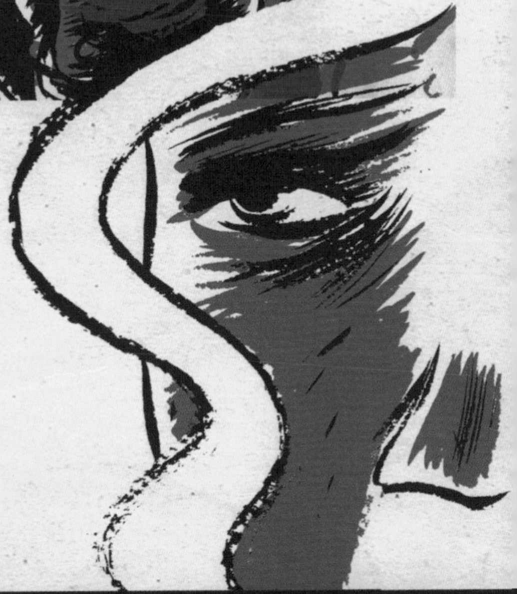

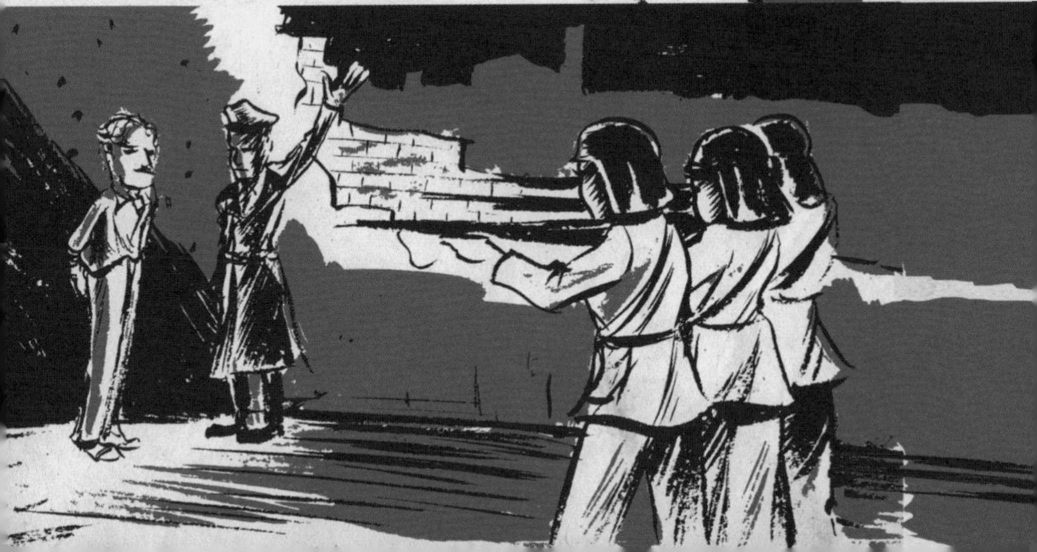

So then I start to talk. I tell him everything. And as I tell him I watch his eyes. I see them turn from bright to dark and angry and then I do laugh. I let the cigarette butt drop from my mouth and close my eyes and wait for the last word I'll ever hear.

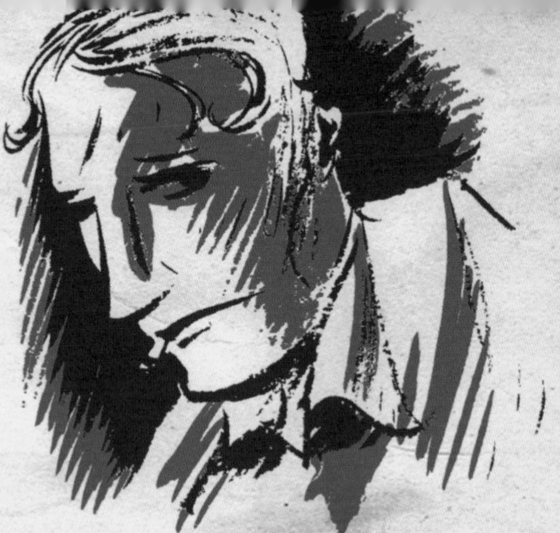

Fire.

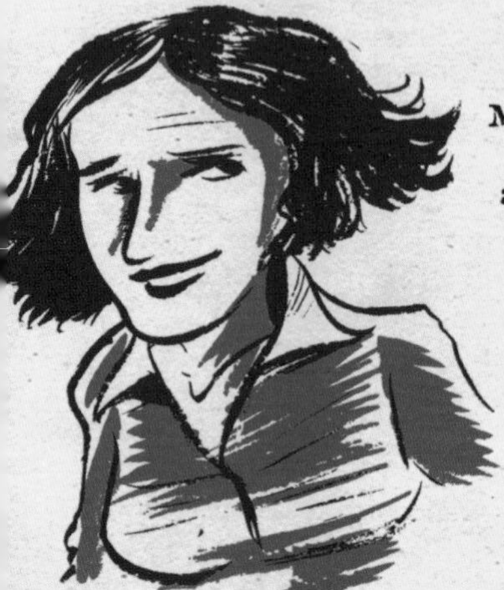

My last words describe Muriel. Muriel and I in occupied France and it was perfect. I met her at a café and we both knew it was right.

In one night we found out everything about each other and I found out she was part of the French Resistance. I didn't care either way but I was sick of smoking the terrible German cigarettes so I was on her side.

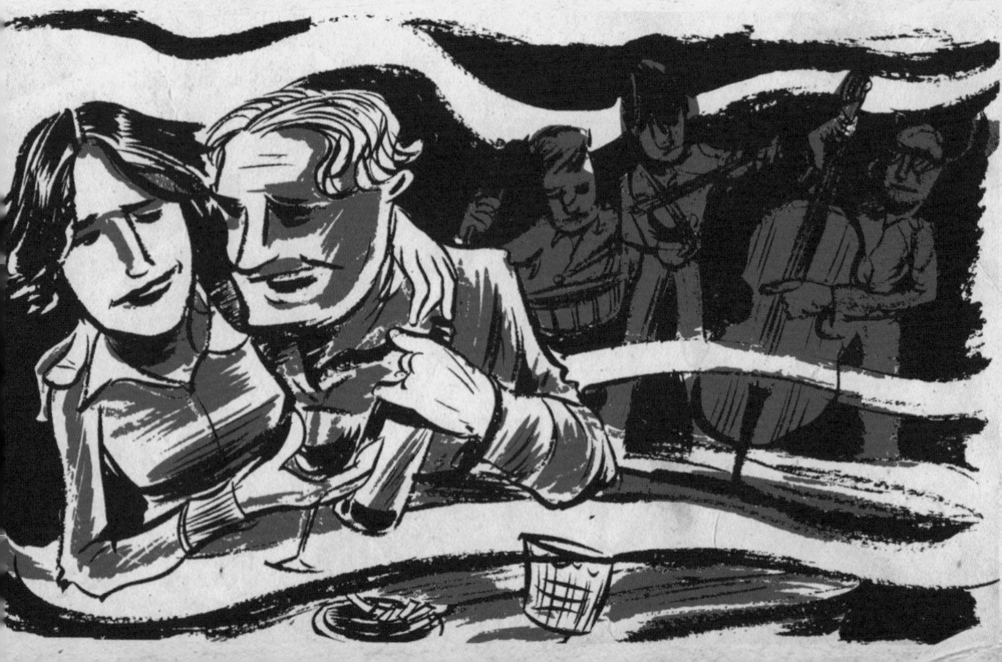

I wasn't complicated and neither were we. Most of the time we spent was trying to drown out the sounds of the war by watching jazz bands at The Hole and listening to records. She didn't talk much about her work and I didn't ask. She didn't involve me except the one time. She wanted me to carry some secret papers to England with a fake passport. Sure. I'd be back in a couple weeks and we'd continue. Until the Nazi's men broke our door in.

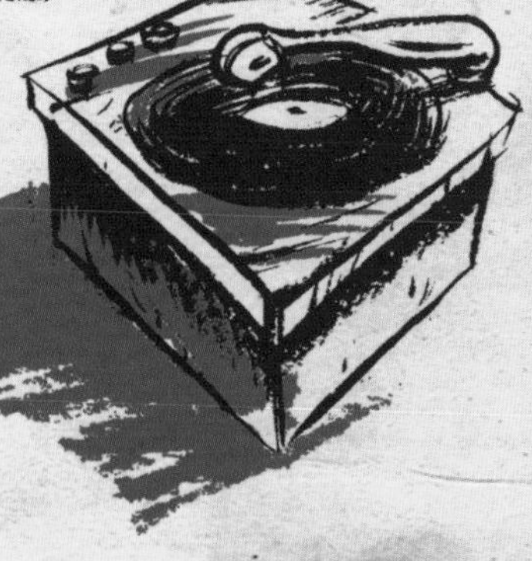

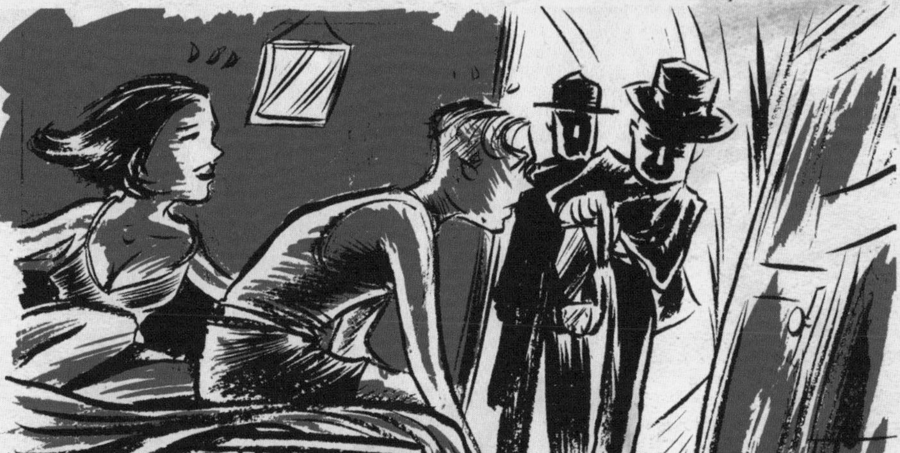

Yes. She asked me to take the coded messages and I did. But where to hide them? Wouldn't I be searched if I was caught and executed as a spy? And the messages discovered? She already had it planned out.

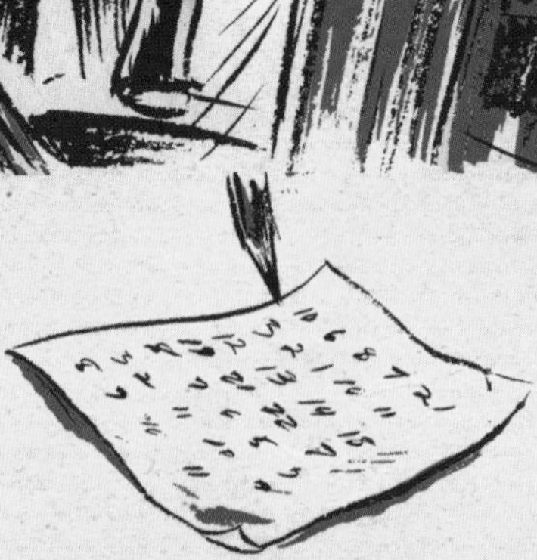

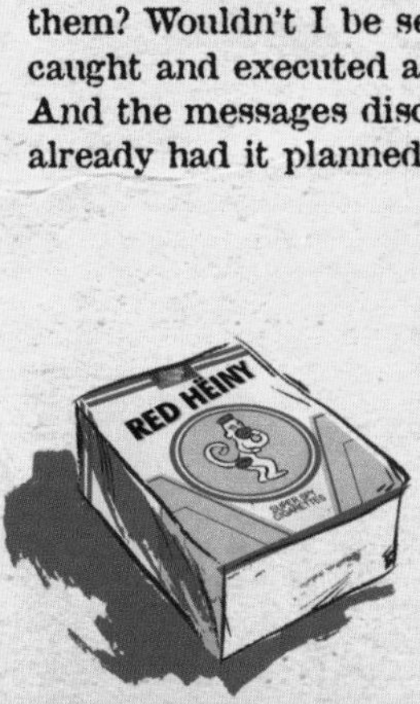
RED HEINY

The secret messages rolled around an awful German cigarette. Who really smoked those anyway? And who would ask to bum one from me if they saw me carrying the pack? It was foolproof.

The cigarette butt falls from my mouth as the firing squad opens fire.

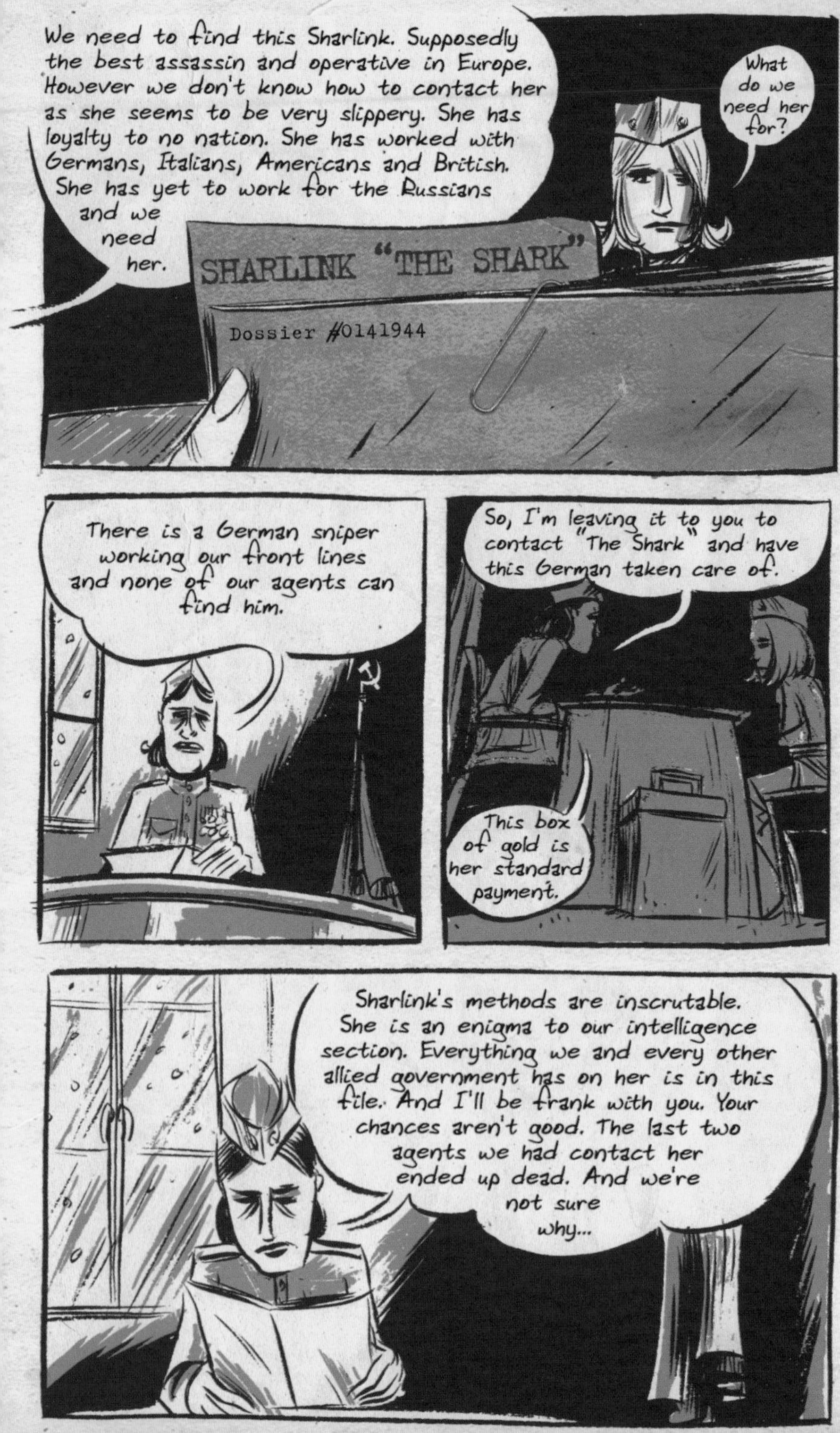

We need to find this Sharlink. Supposedly the best assassin and operative in Europe. However we don't know how to contact her as she seems to be very slippery. She has loyalty to no nation. She has worked with Germans, Italians, Americans and British. She has yet to work for the Russians and we need her.
What do we need her for?
SHARLINK "THE SHARK"
Dossier #0141944
There is a German sniper working our front lines and none of our agents can find him.
So, I'm leaving it to you to contact "The Shark" and have this German taken care of.
This box of gold is her standard payment.
Sharlink's methods are inscrutable. She is an enigma to our intelligence section. Everything we and every other allied government has on her is in this file. And I'll be frank with you. Your chances aren't good. The last two agents we had contact her ended up dead. And we're not sure why...

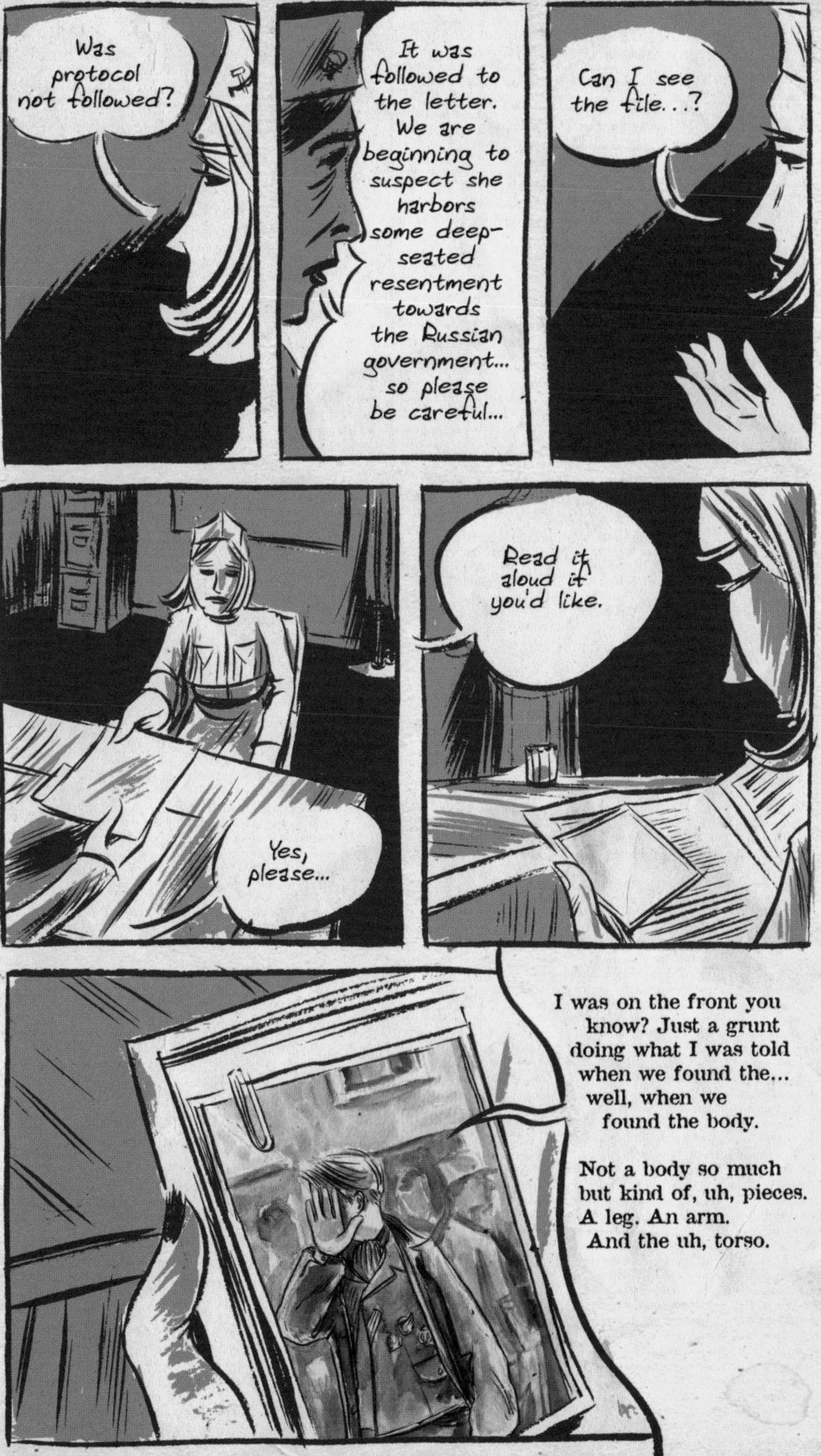

Was protocol not followed?
It was followed to the letter. We are beginning to suspect she harbors some deep-seated resentment towards the Russian government... so please be careful...
Can I see the file...?
Read it aloud if you'd like.
Yes, please...
I was on the front you know? Just a grunt doing what I was told when we found the... well, when we found the body.
Not a body so much but kind of, uh, pieces. A leg. An arm. And the uh, torso.

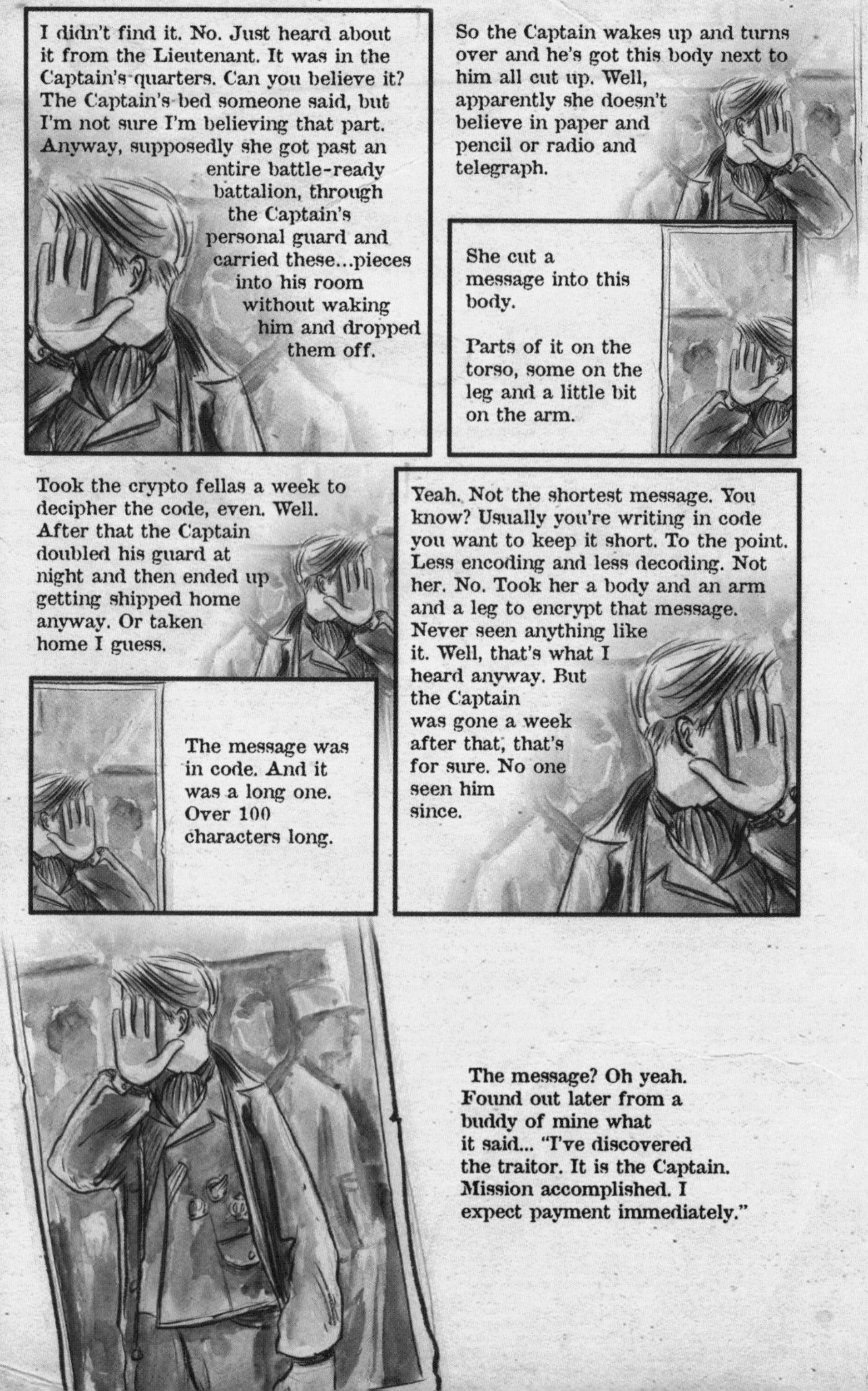
I didn't find it. No. Just heard about it from the Lieutenant. It was in the Captain's quarters. Can you believe it? The Captain's bed someone said, but I'm not sure I'm believing that part. Anyway, supposedly she got past an entire battle-ready battalion, through the Captain's personal guard and carried these...pieces into his room without waking him and dropped them off.
So the Captain wakes up and turns over and he's got this body next to him all cut up. Well, apparently she doesn't believe in paper and pencil or radio and telegraph.
She cut a message into this body.
Parts of it on the torso, some on the leg and a little bit on the arm.
Took the crypto fellas a week to decipher the code, even. Well. After that the Captain doubled his guard at night and then ended up getting shipped home anyway. Or taken home I guess.
The message was in code. And it was a long one. Over 100 characters long.
Yeah. Not the shortest message. You know? Usually you're writing in code you want to keep it short. To the point. Less encoding and less decoding. Not her. No. Took her a body and an arm and a leg to encrypt that message. Never seen anything like it. Well, that's what I heard anyway. But the Captain was gone a week after that, that's for sure. No one seen him since.
The message? Oh yeah. Found out later from a buddy of mine what it said... "I've discovered the traitor. It is the Captain. Mission accomplished. I expect payment immediately."

So I walk into the Café. It's our rendezvous point. Every last Wednesday of the month at noon. So Francois walks in – what? Yeah. Francois, I know. Anyway, he walks in like normal but something's wrong, I can see it in his eyes. He doesn't say anything and I know something is terribly wrong. But he sits down and I think, well, it's not urgent.

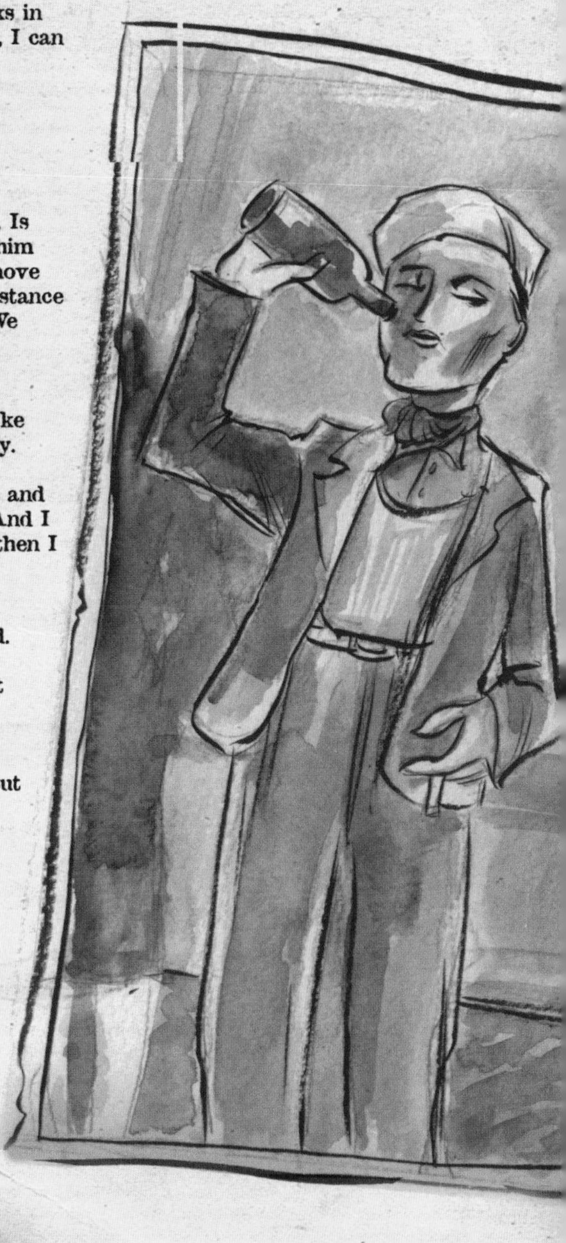

Whatever it is we can figure it out. Is his cover blown? Well, we can get him out. There's always time. We can move on it. We'd been setting up the resistance in Paris since Poland, you know? We saw it coming and we were ready. Ready for anything.

Well, he looks at me and it looks like he's about to cry. "What is it?" I say. But I can tell he is having trouble talking. I ask him if he was caught and he says "not really, I don't know". And I know he's been compromised and then I just want to get out of there.

But I wait a minute. He's my friend. We were in it from the beginning. Then he tells me he's not sure what happened. He went to sleep at the safe house and then woke up in a basement room tied up. He was expecting to be tortured or killed but he wasn't. He saw nothing – just shadows on the wall. A woman he thought because of the hair. Long dark hair. Unusually long hair. Anyway, he blacked out or maybe chloroform. He couldn't tell. But he woke up in an alleyway in pain.

He pulled up his shirt and saw about 50 or 60 stitches in his belly. He wasn't sure what day it was but went back to the safe house and realized it was Wednesday. Our meeting day. He had just enough time to get there and so there we were. "What happened? Whattaya make of that?" he asked me with tears in his eyes. He was desperate.

At this point I'm looking around and realizing that I'm sure he's compromised and now I probably am too. That's when I notice it. On his neck nearly hidden by his collar. "What is that?" I ask. "What?" he says. On his neck. He pulls his collar back and I see a tiny red scar on his neck. Just about the size of a franc. A fresh scar, like somebody just took a pin and scraped into his skin. It was an "S". It took a second for it to register. Just a second.

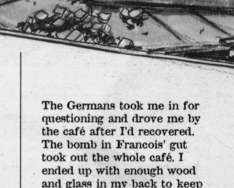

An S carved onto his neck? He looked at me and felt his neck and I knew it was over. I got up and started to walk away. Trying not to panic. I got to the door when he doubled over in pain clutching his stomach. And he screamed.

That's all I remember.

The Germans took me in for questioning and drove me by the café after I'd recovered. The bomb in Francois' gut took out the whole café. I ended up with enough wood and glass in my back to keep me out of the German interrogation room for a few weeks. By the time I recovered the Germans had figure out that me and Francois weren't even the real targets.

Apparently some British spook hit the same café as us. We had no idea. Well, they found nothing but pieces of that British agent and I ended up flipping sides. The Germans had me. What could I do? That's all I have.

Never saw her.

Just the letter "S".

Had no idea it was her. Just another in a line of women that the higher-ups would send me. I guess she got what she wanted. Should have been more cautious I guess.

I remember the scar though. A thick ugly scar from the corner of her mouth up to her temple. She hid it well, the hair cut in just a way where you couldn't see it unless you really looked. I asked her where she got it. "Shark bite," she said. That was it. I think I laughed. Don't think she liked that but the way she said it, it just seemed ridiculous.

But when a woman comes in that's supposedly recommended by the Führer...I don't know. You just don't ask that many questions. Anyway, it was one night. She came in and that was it. Gone in the morning.

Guess she didn't think it was funny. Woke up the next morning with her on top of me. Took my eyes out. I still wonder if maybe it was ordered from higher up. But who knows?
The war's over for me. That's it.

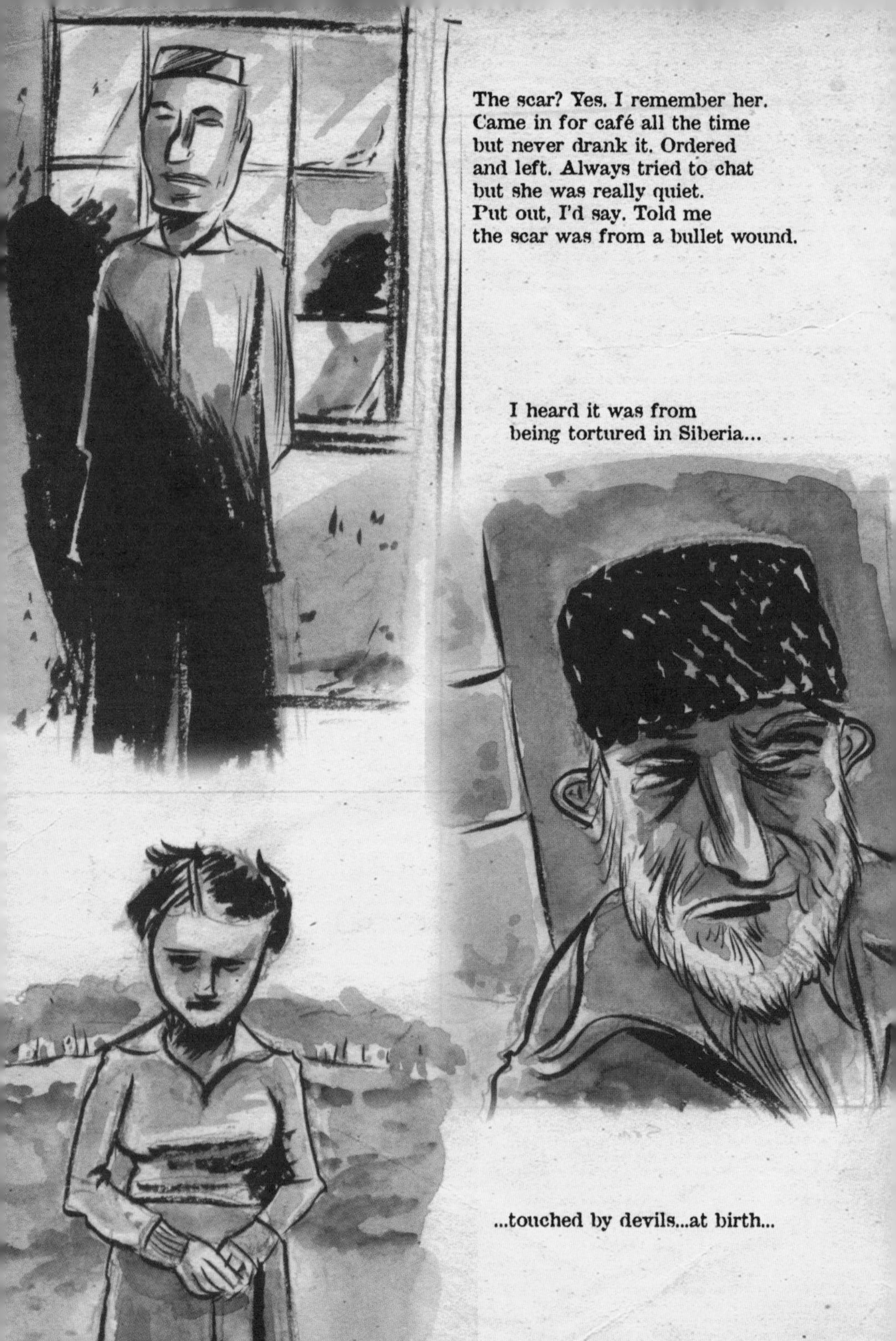
The scar? Yes. I remember her. Came in for café all the time but never drank it. Ordered and left. Always tried to chat but she was really quiet. Put out, I'd say. Told me the scar was from a bullet wound.
I heard it was from being tortured in Siberia...
...touched by devils...at birth...

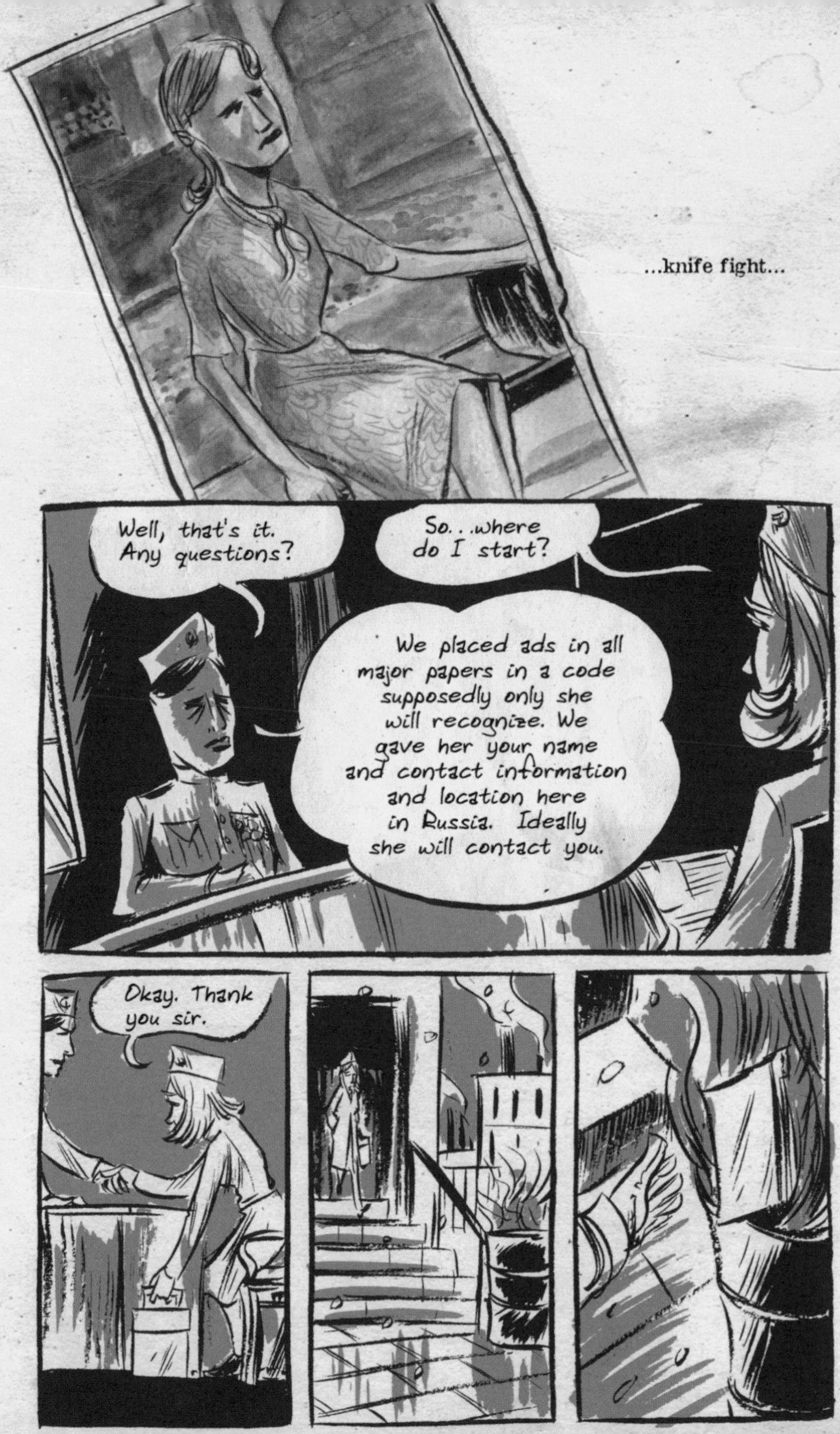
...knife fight...
Well, that's it. Any questions?
So...where do I start?
We placed ads in all major papers in a code supposedly only she will recognize. We gave her your name and contact information and location here in Russia. Ideally she will contact you.
Okay. Thank you sir.

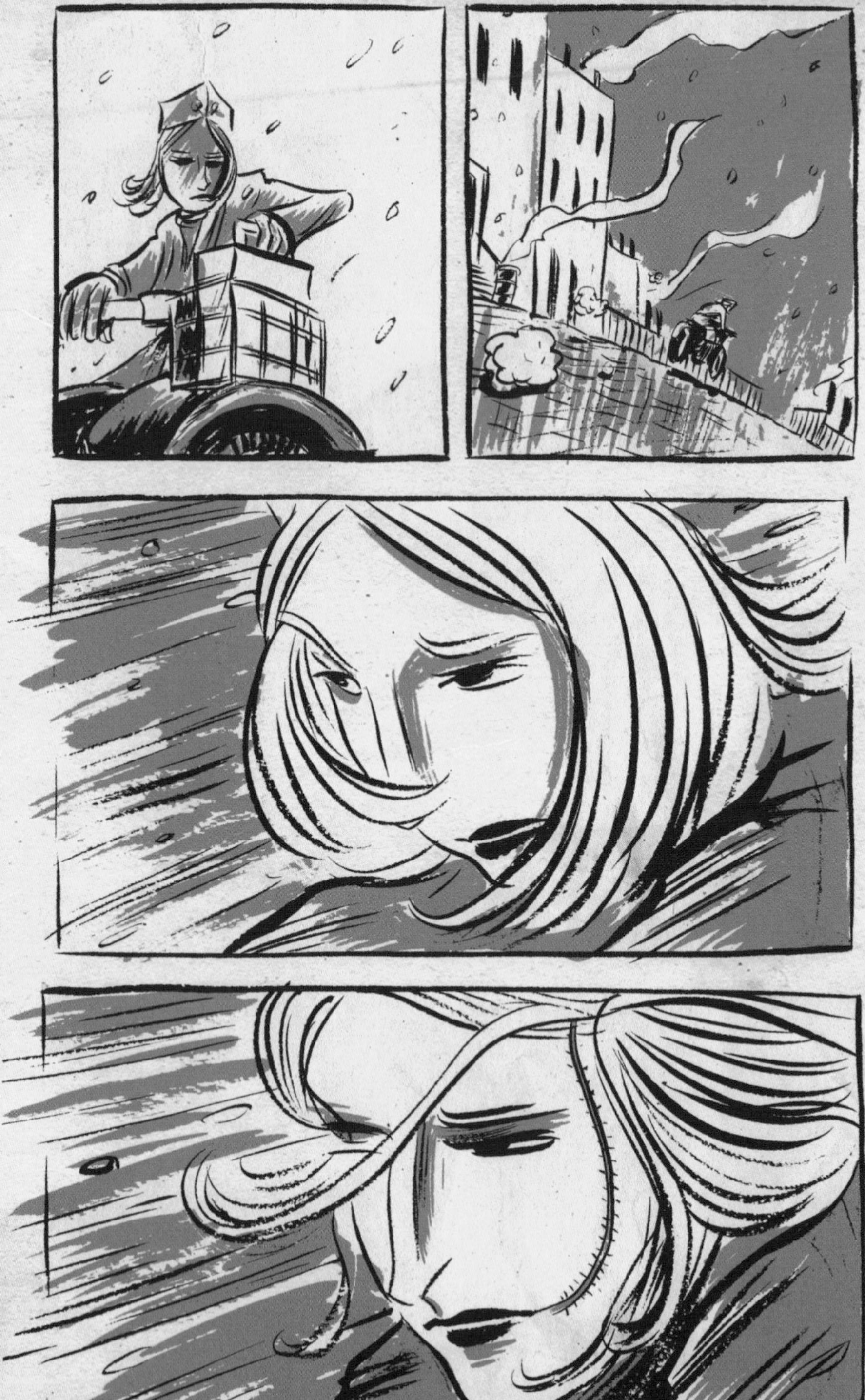

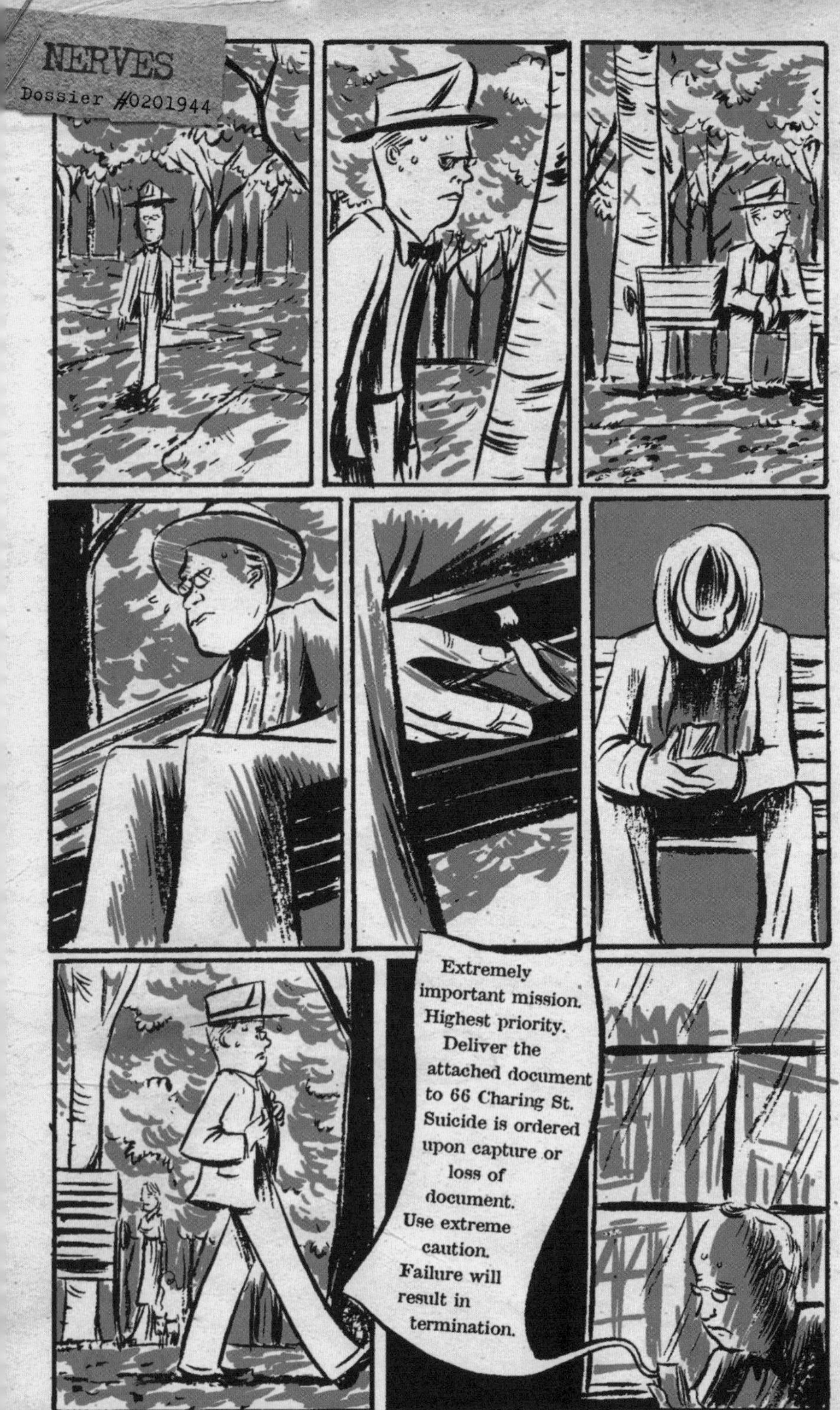
NERVES
Dossier #0201944
Extremely important mission. Highest priority. Deliver the attached document to 66 Charing St. Suicide is ordered upon capture or loss of document. Use extreme caution. Failure will result in termination.

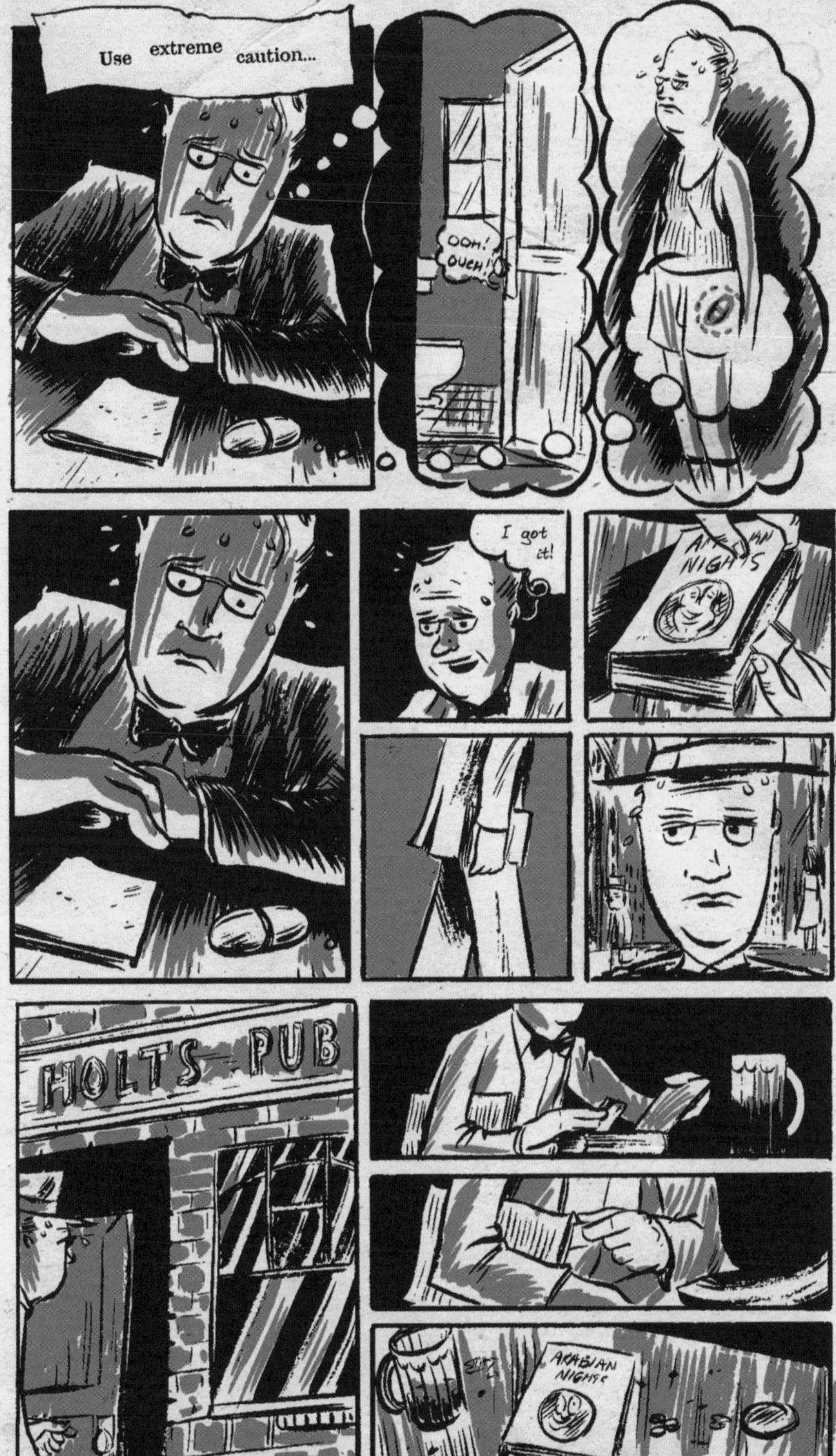
Use extreme caution...
OOH! OUCH!
I got it!
ARABIAN NIGHTS
HOLTS PUB
ARABIAN NIGHTS

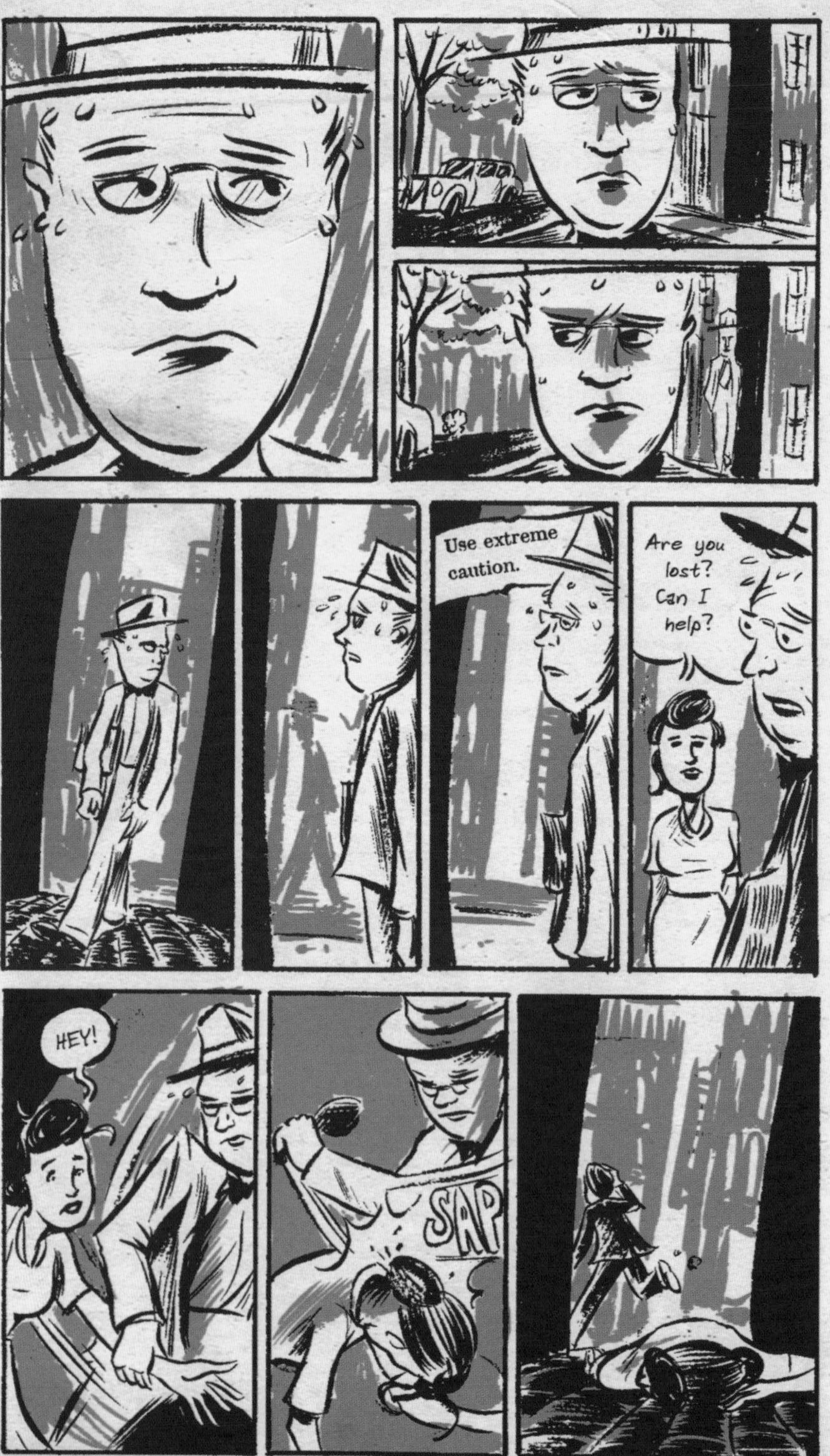
Use extreme caution.
Are you lost? Can I help?
HEY!
SAP

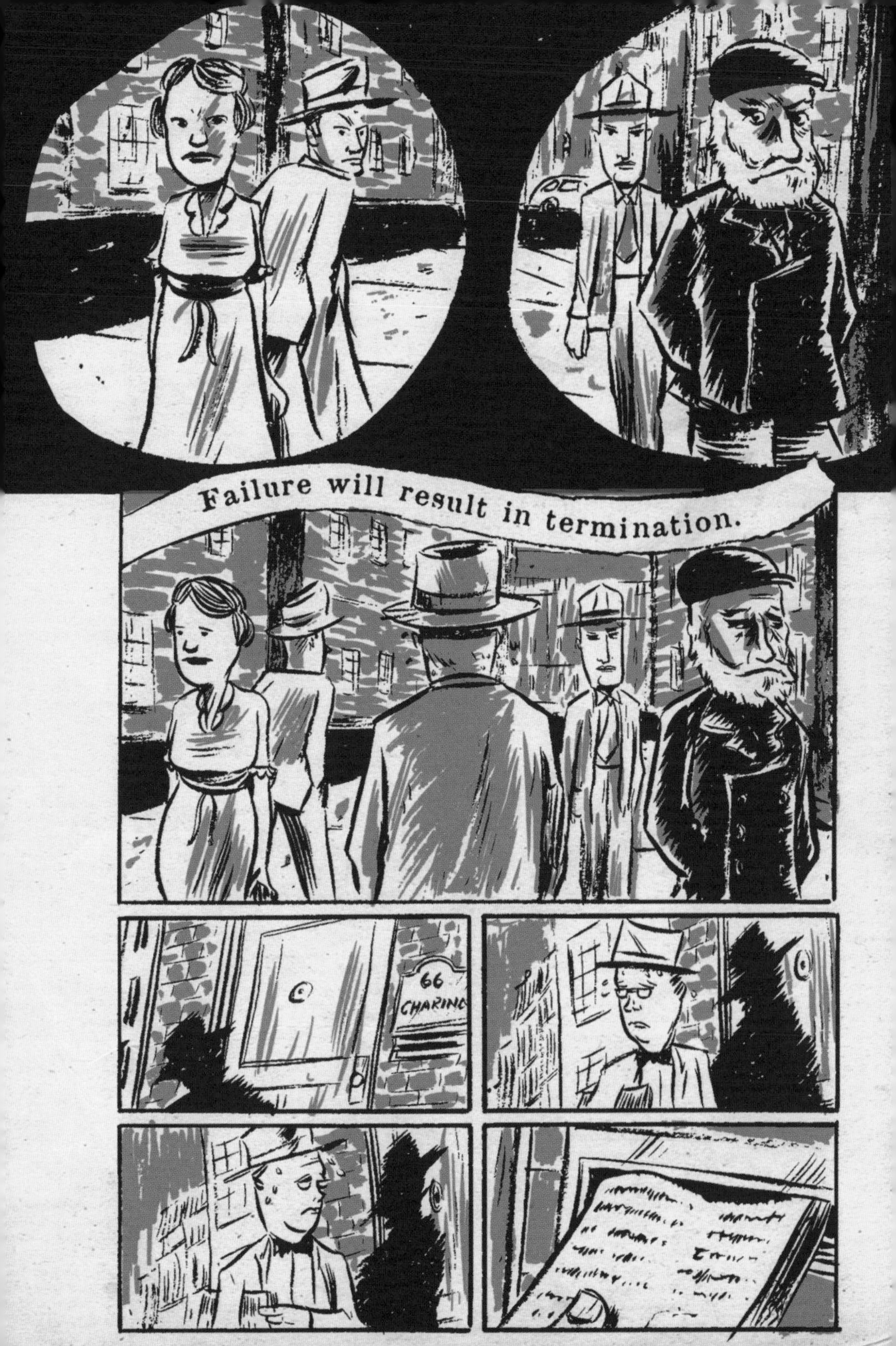
Failure will result in termination.
66
CHARING

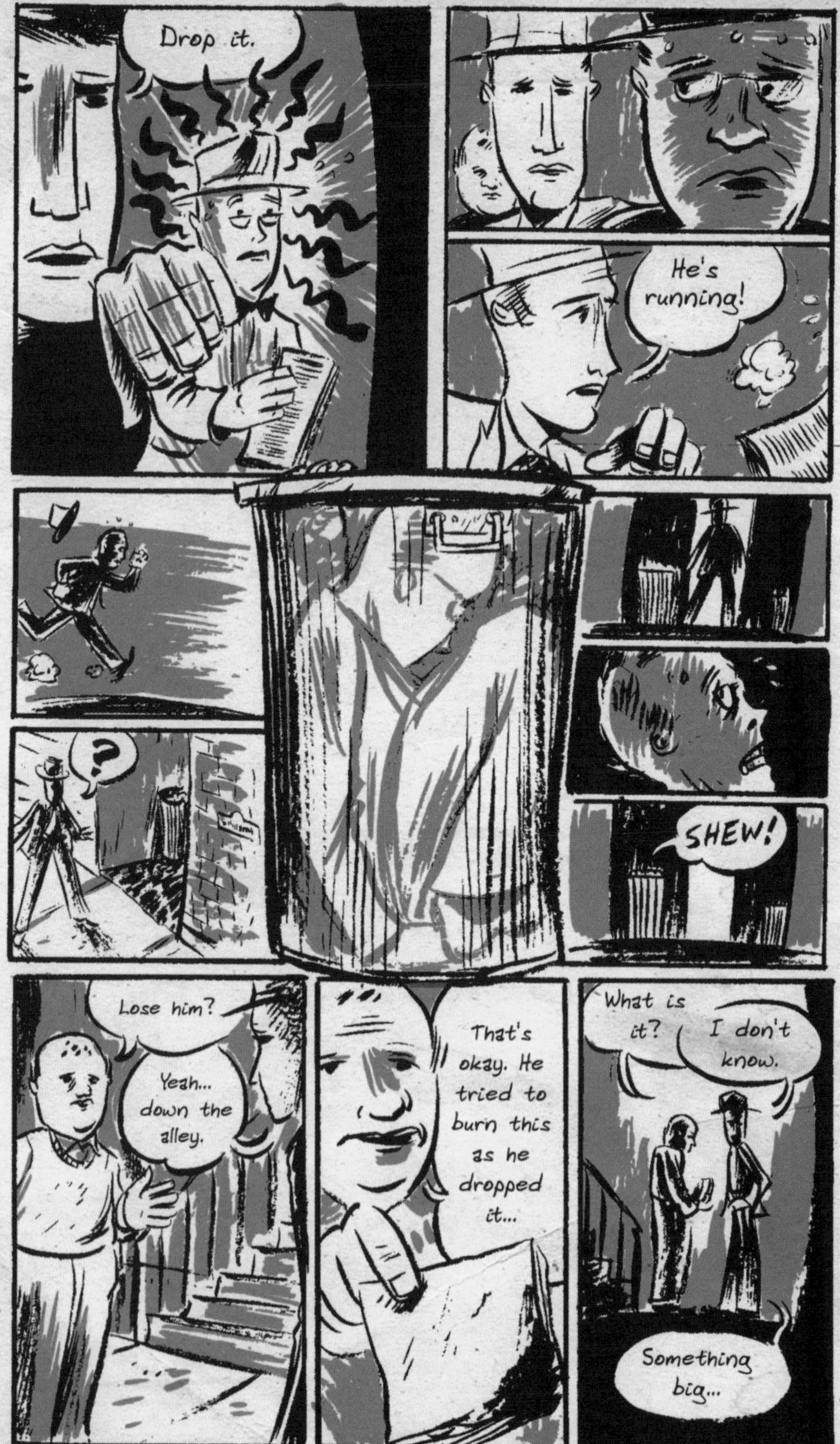
Drop it.
He's running!
?
SHEW!
Lose him?
Yeah... down the alley.
That's okay. He tried to burn this as he dropped it...
What is it?
I don't know.
Something big...

Something big.

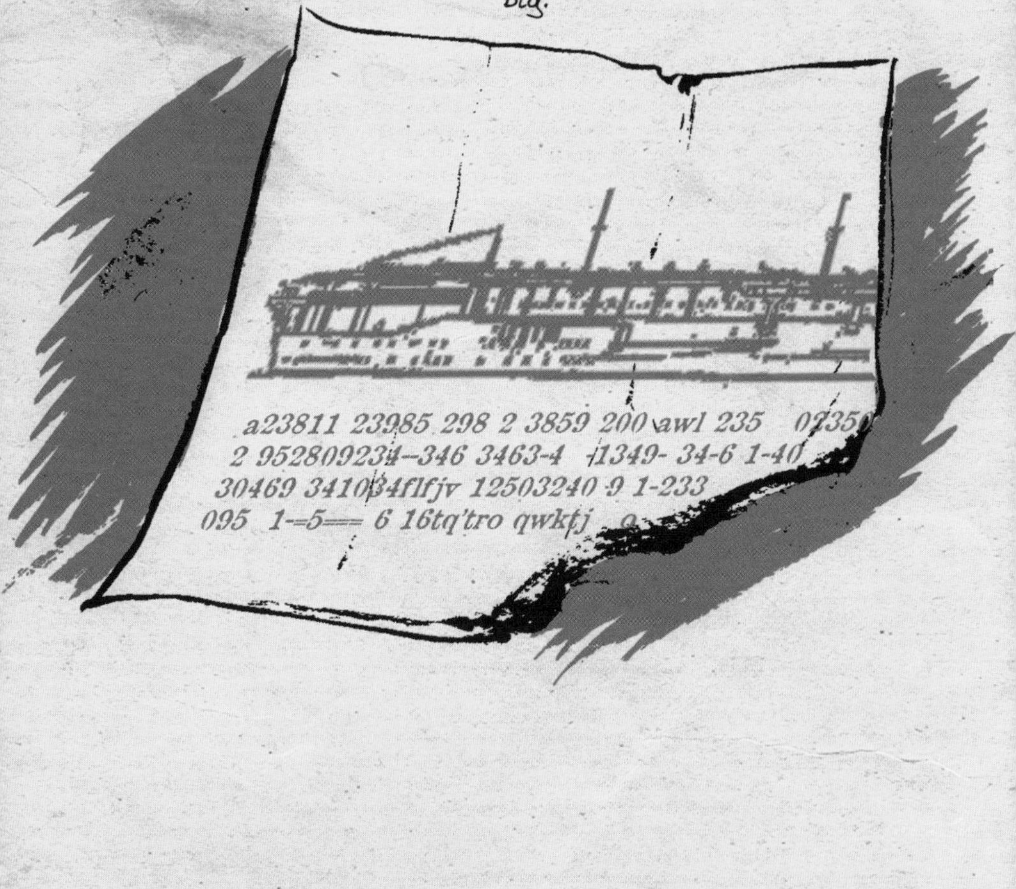
a23811 23985 298 2 3859 200 awl 235
2 952809234-346 3463-4 1349- 34-6 1-40
30469 341034flfjv 12503240 9 1-233
095 1-=5== 6 16tq'tro qwktj

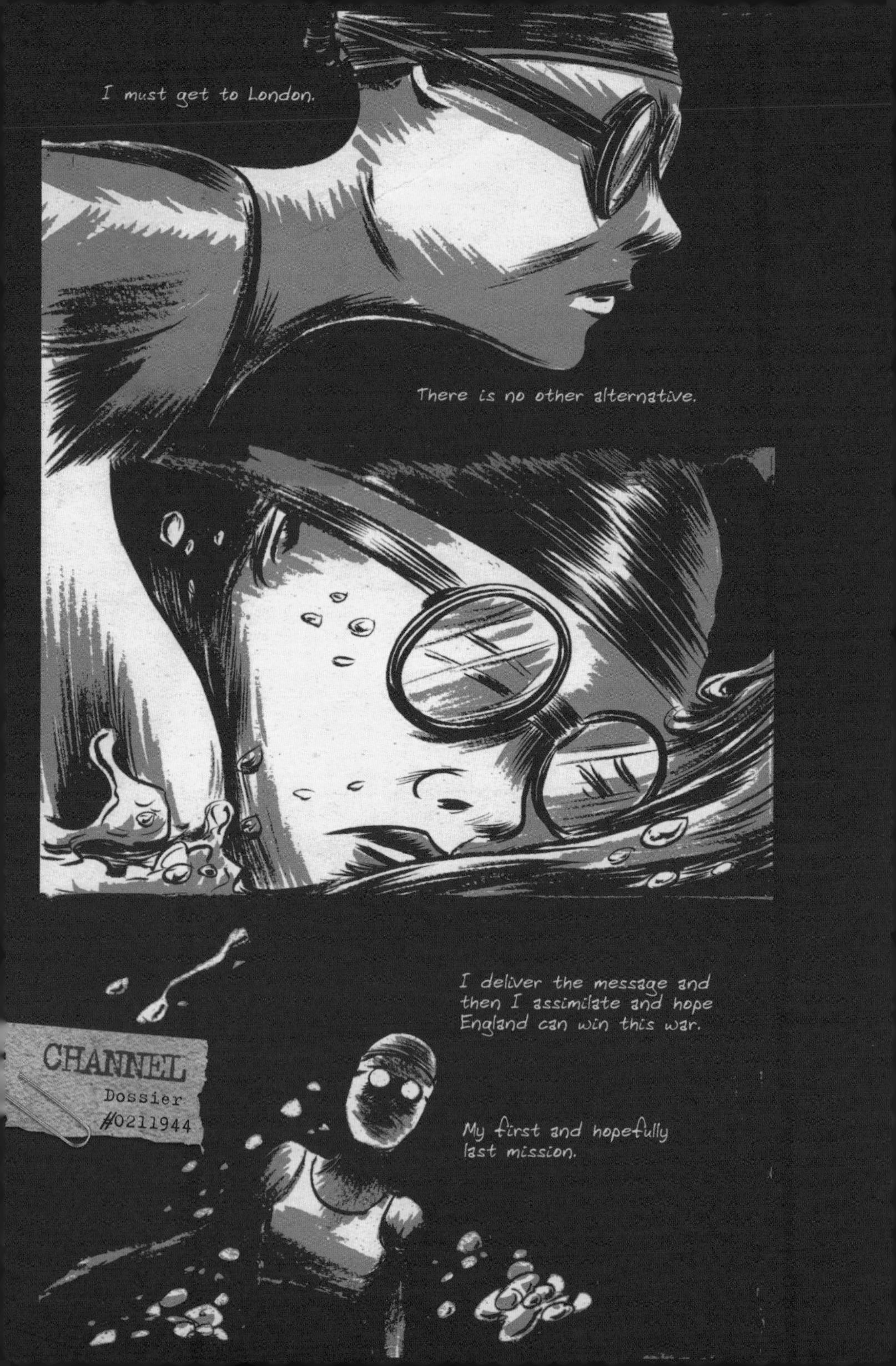
I must get to London.
There is no other alternative.
I deliver the message and then I assimilate and hope England can win this war.
CHANNEL
Dossier
#0211944
My first and hopefully last mission.

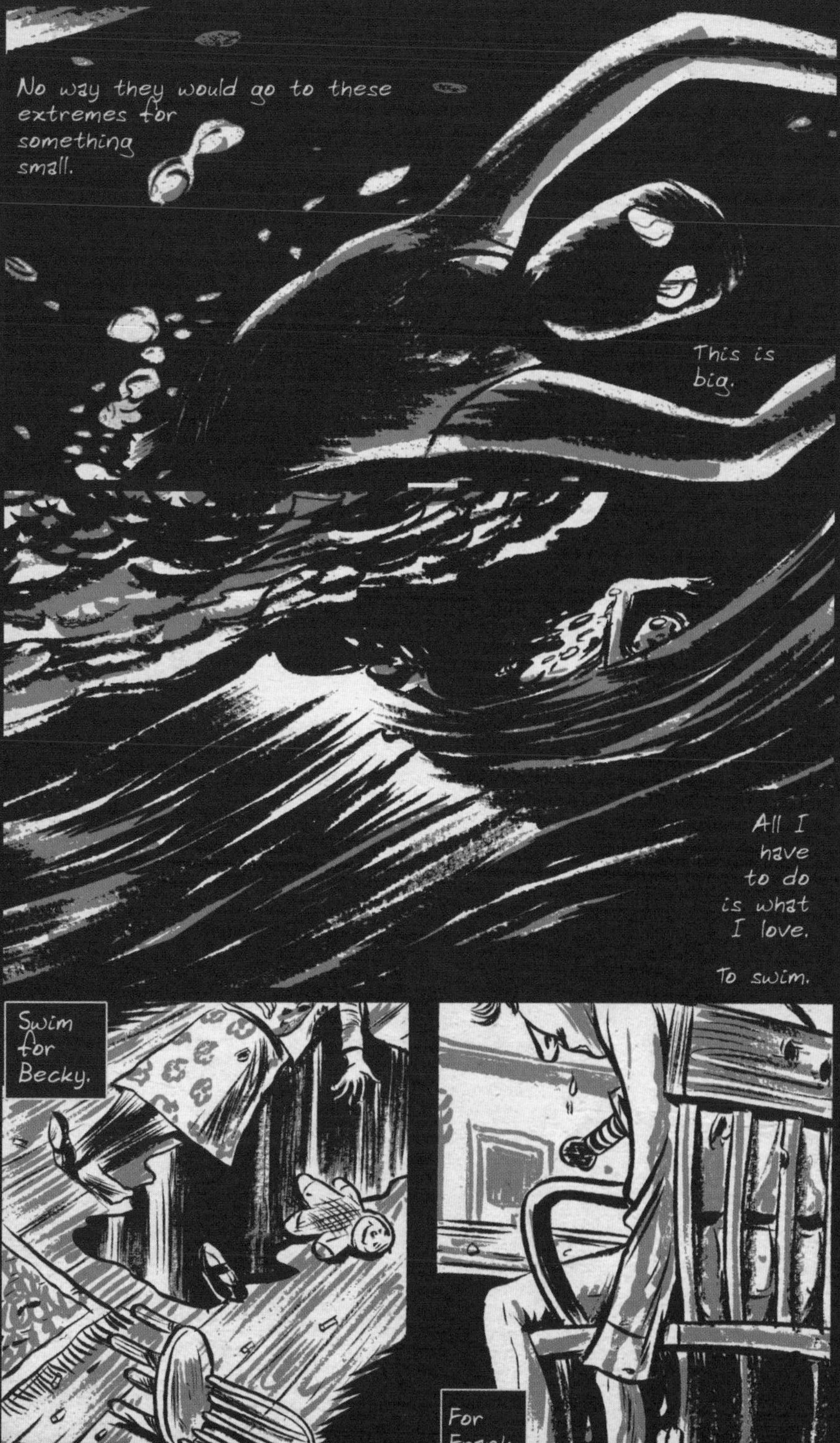
No way they would go to these extremes for something small.
This is big.
All I have to do is what I love.
To swim.
Swim for Becky.
For Frank.

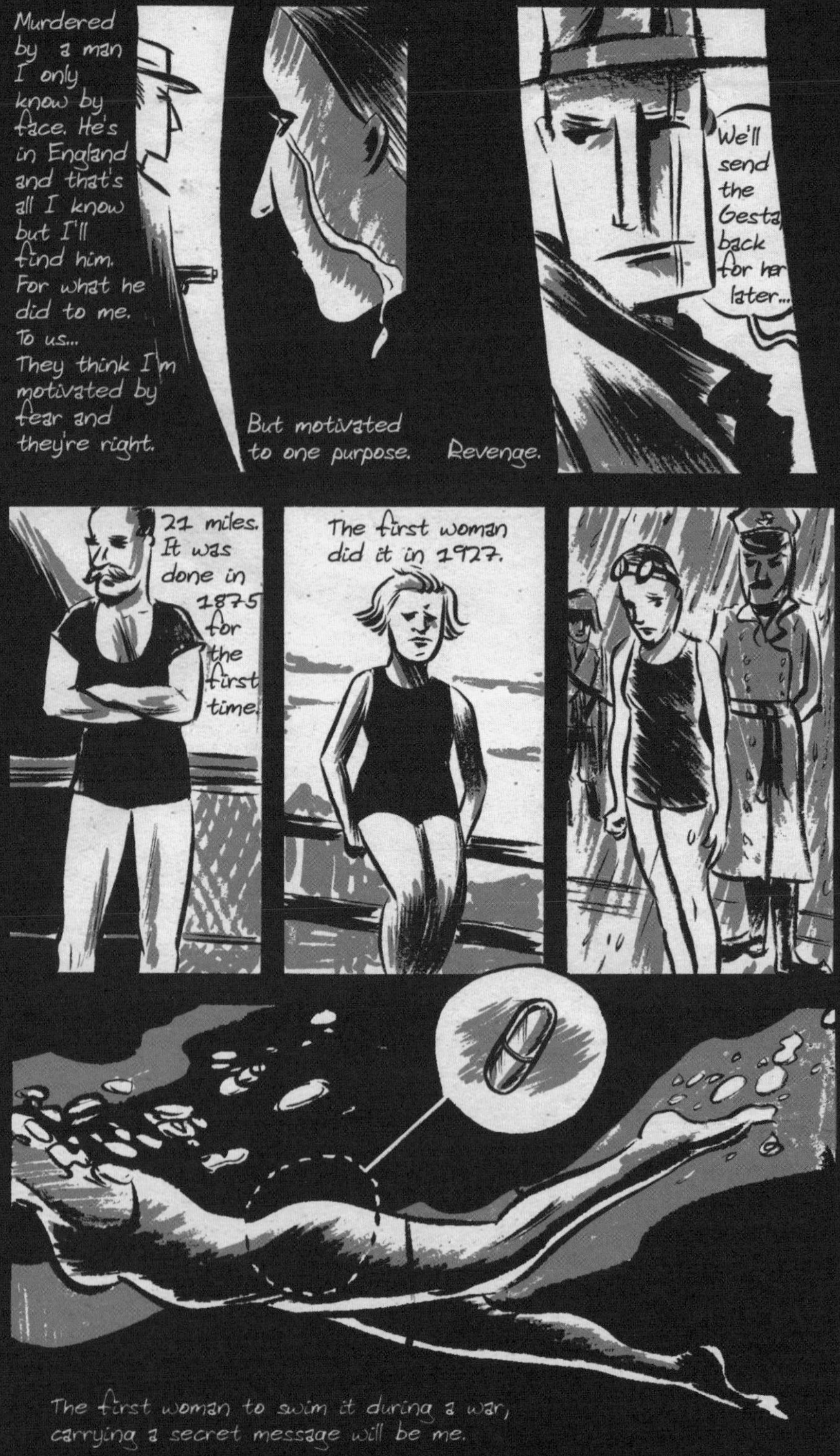
Murdered by a man I only know by face. He's in England and that's all I know but I'll find him. For what he did to me. To us... They think I'm motivated by fear and they're right.
But motivated to one purpose.
Revenge.
We'll send the Gesta back for her later...
21 miles. It was done in 1875 for the first time.
The first woman did it in 1927.
The first woman to swim it during a war, carrying a secret message will be me.

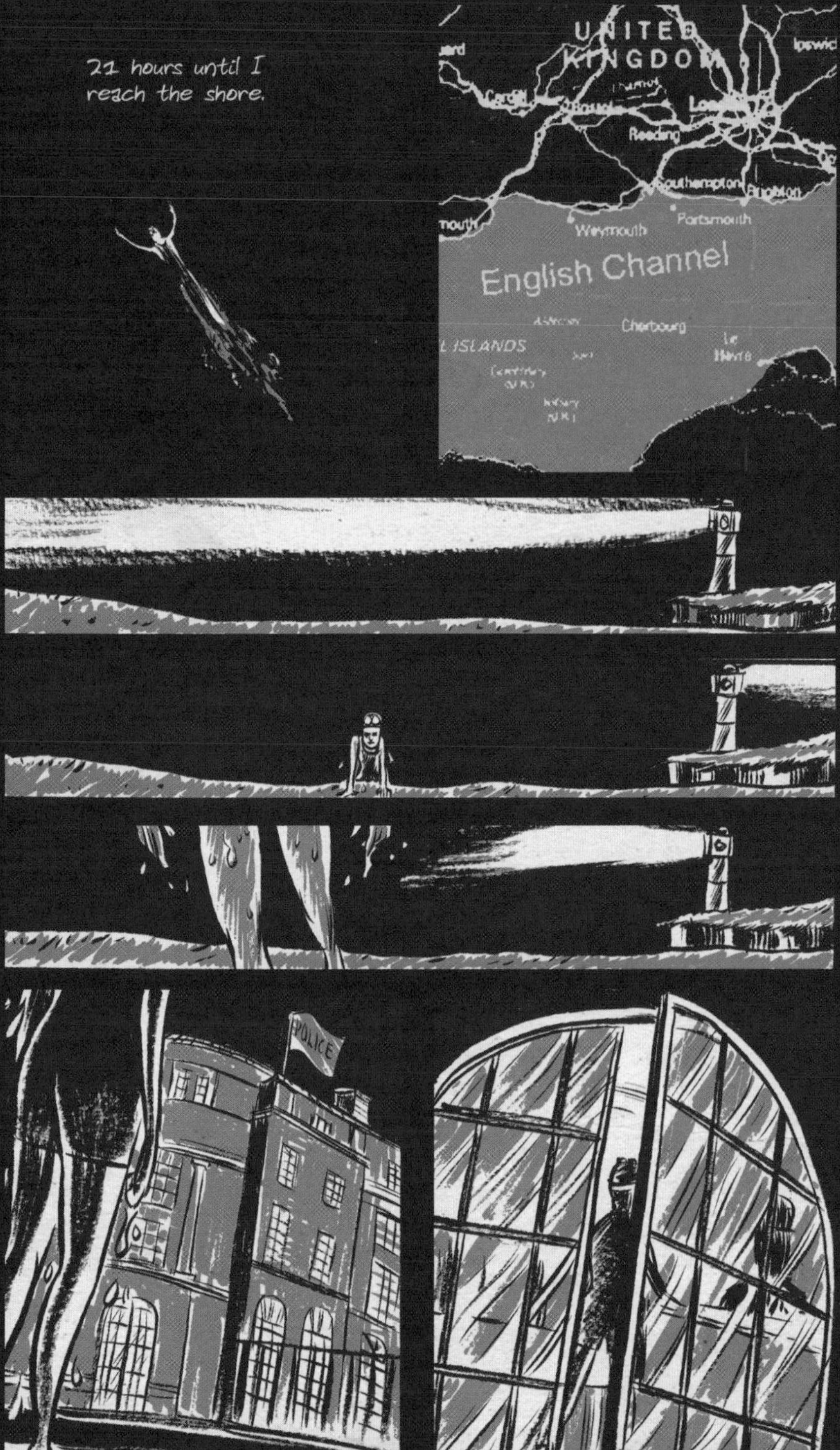
21 hours until I reach the shore.
UNITED KINGDOM
Reading
Southampton
Weymouth
Portsmouth
English Channel
Cherbourg
Le Havre
POLICE

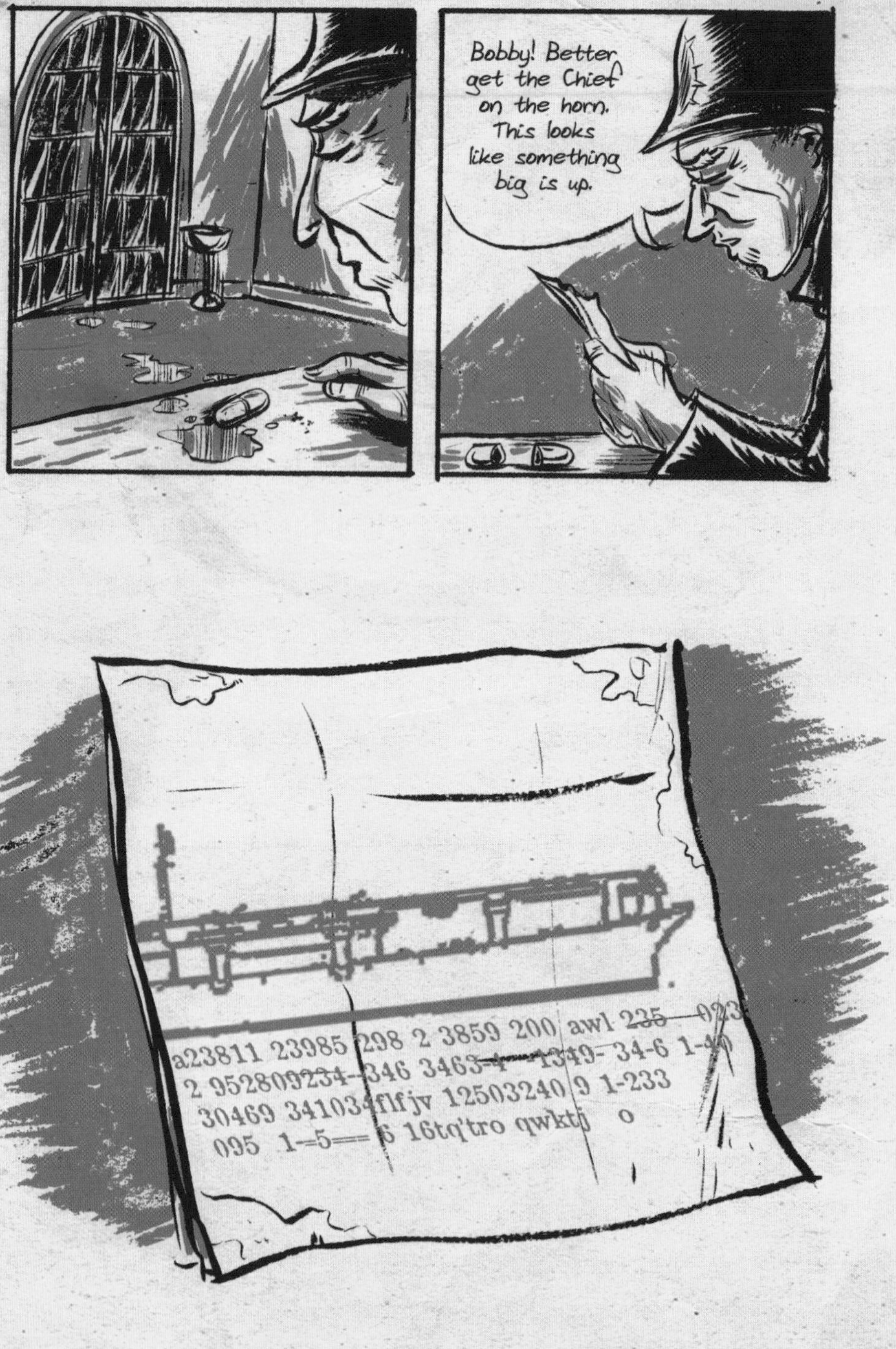
Bobby! Better get the Chief on the horn. This looks like something big is up.
awl 235
a23811 23985 298 2 3859 200
2 952809234--346 3463-4 1349- 34-6 1-40
30469 341034flfjv 12503240 9 1-233
095 1-=5=== 6 16tq'tro qwktj o

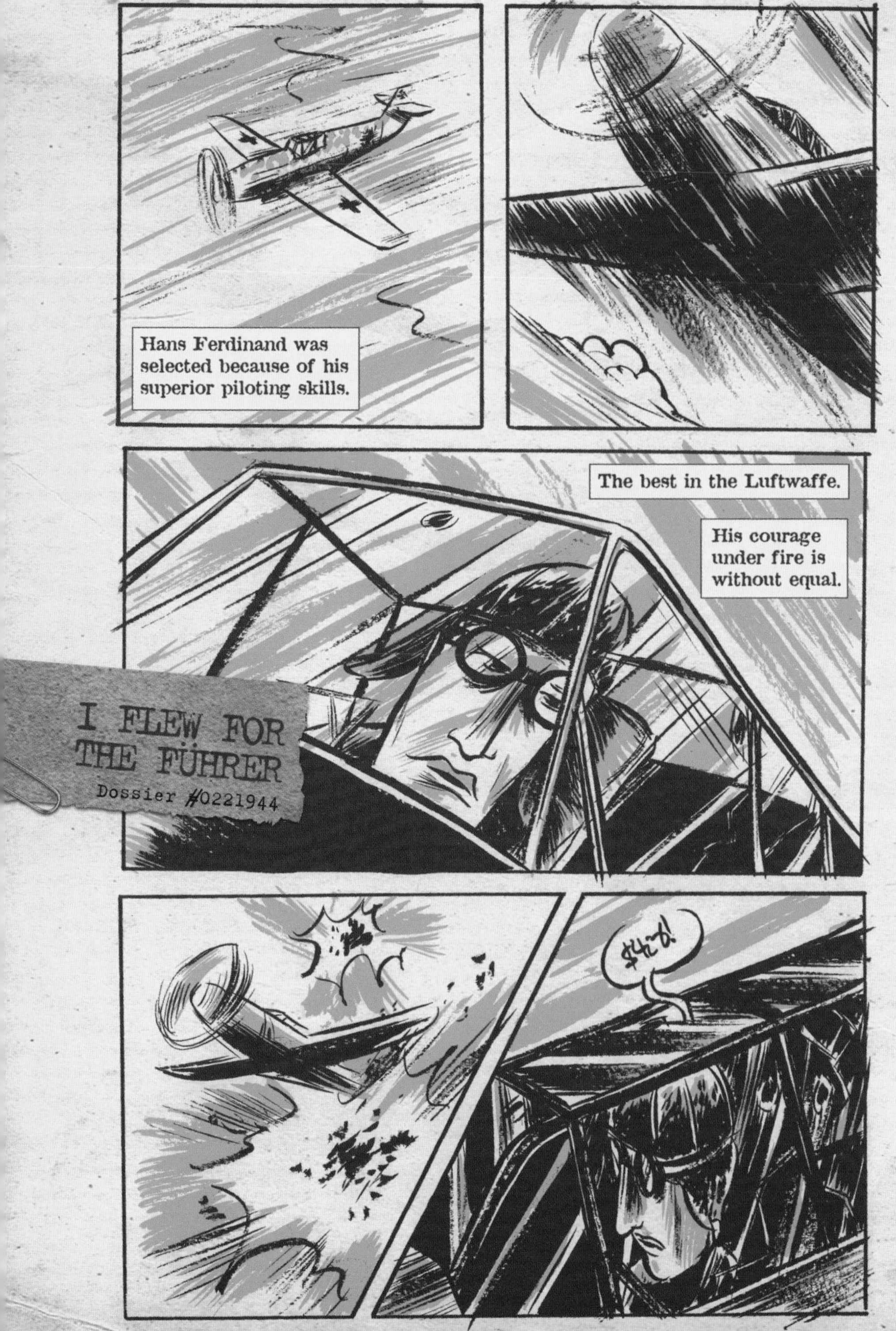

Hans Ferdinand was selected because of his superior piloting skills.
The best in the Luftwaffe.
His courage under fire is without equal.
I FLEW FOR THE FÜHRER
Dossier #0221944

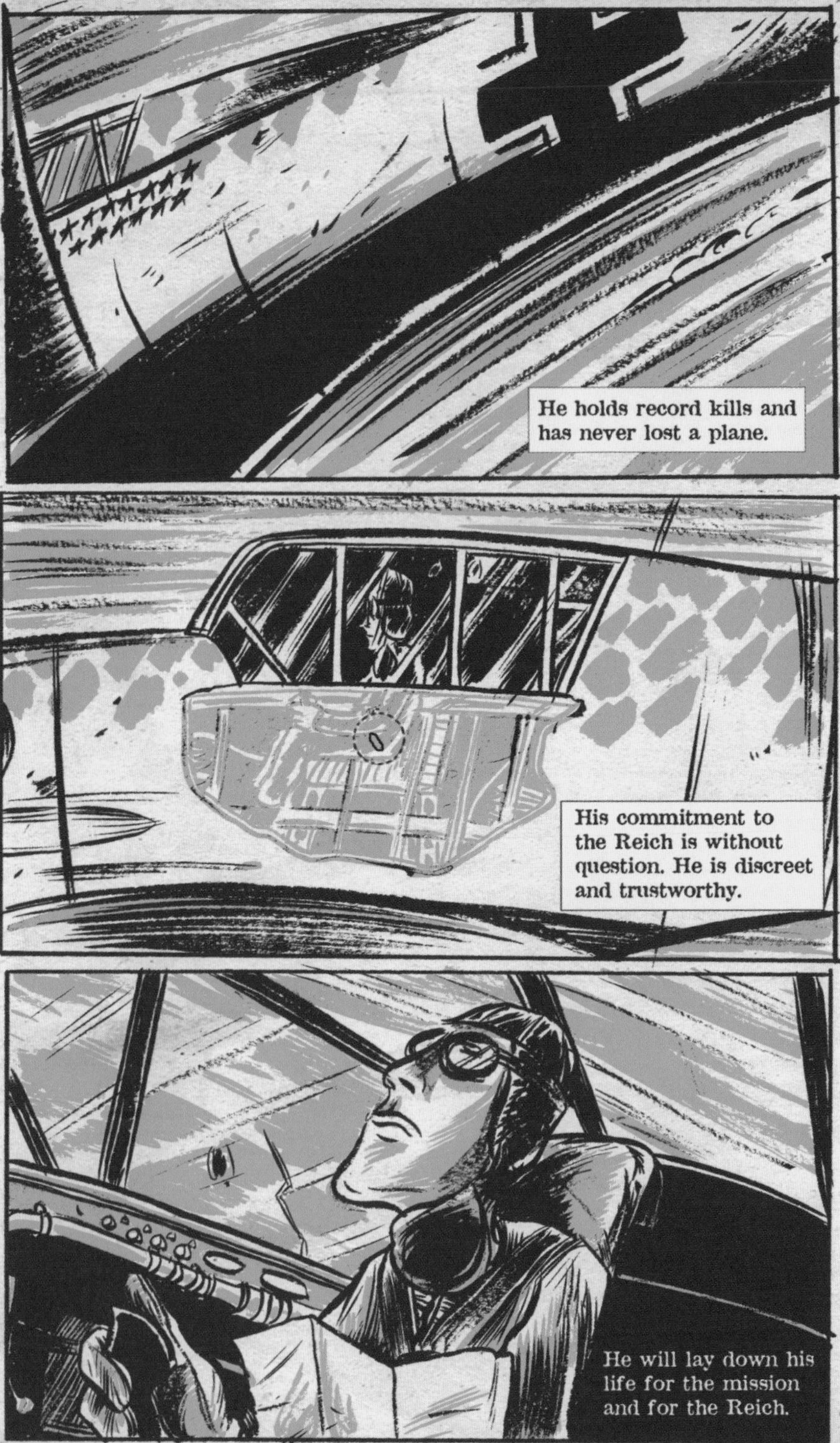
He holds record kills and has never lost a plane.
His commitment to the Reich is without question. He is discreet and trustworthy.
He will lay down his life for the mission and for the Reich.

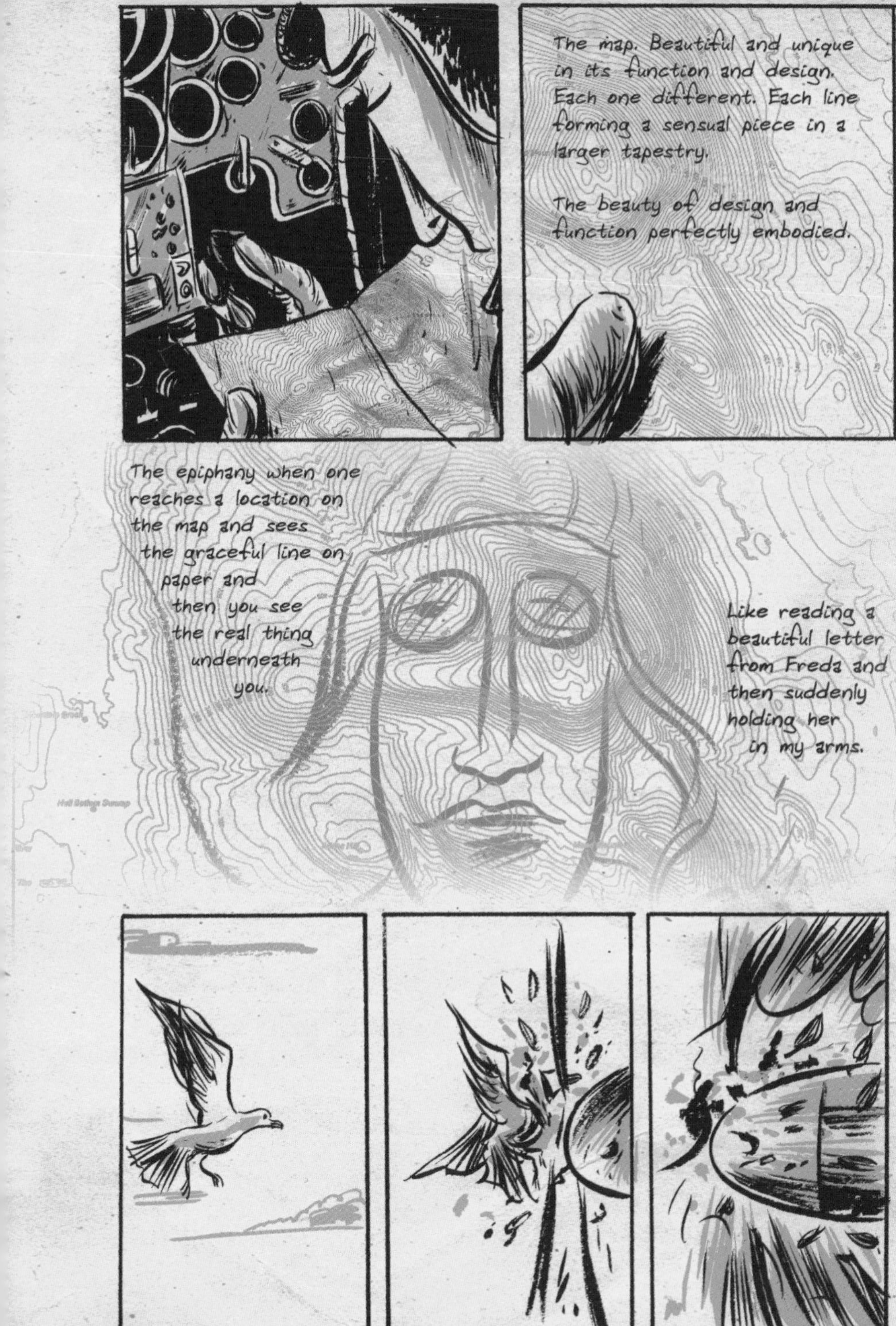
The map. Beautiful and unique in its function and design. Each one different. Each line forming a sensual piece in a larger tapestry.
The beauty of design and function perfectly embodied.
The epiphany when one reaches a location on the map and sees the graceful line on paper and then you see the real thing underneath you.
Like reading a beautiful letter from Freda and then suddenly holding her in my arms.

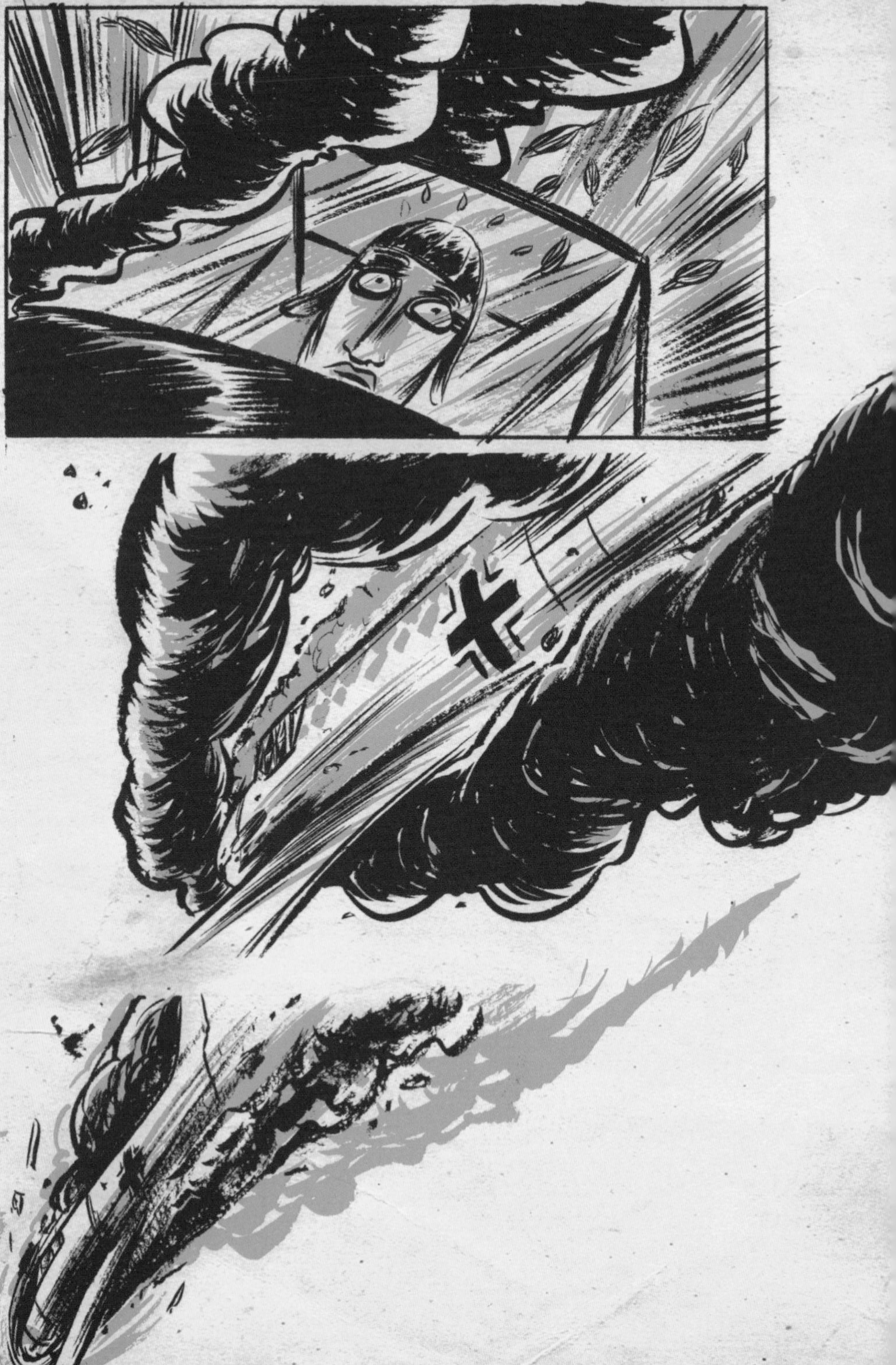

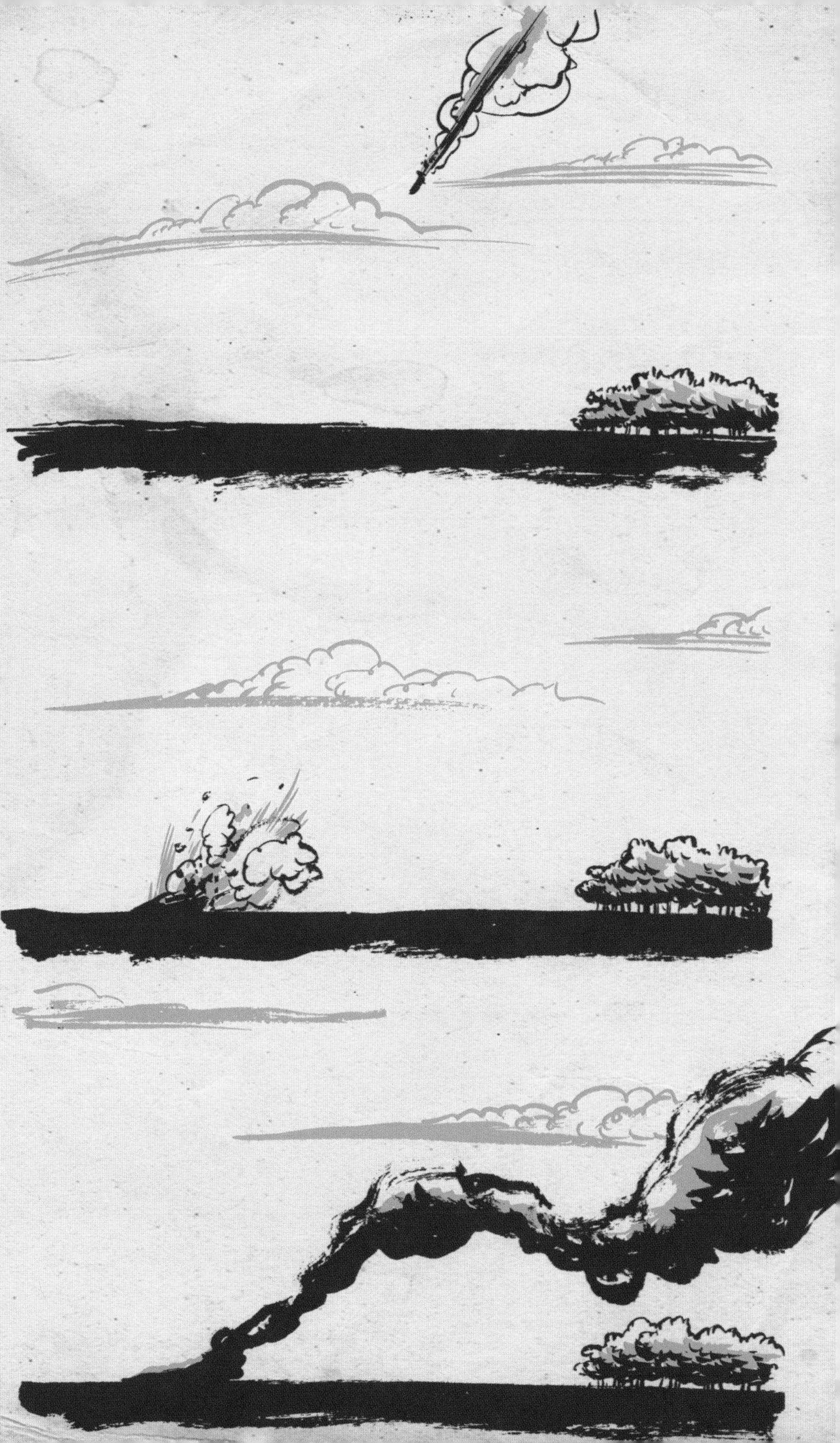

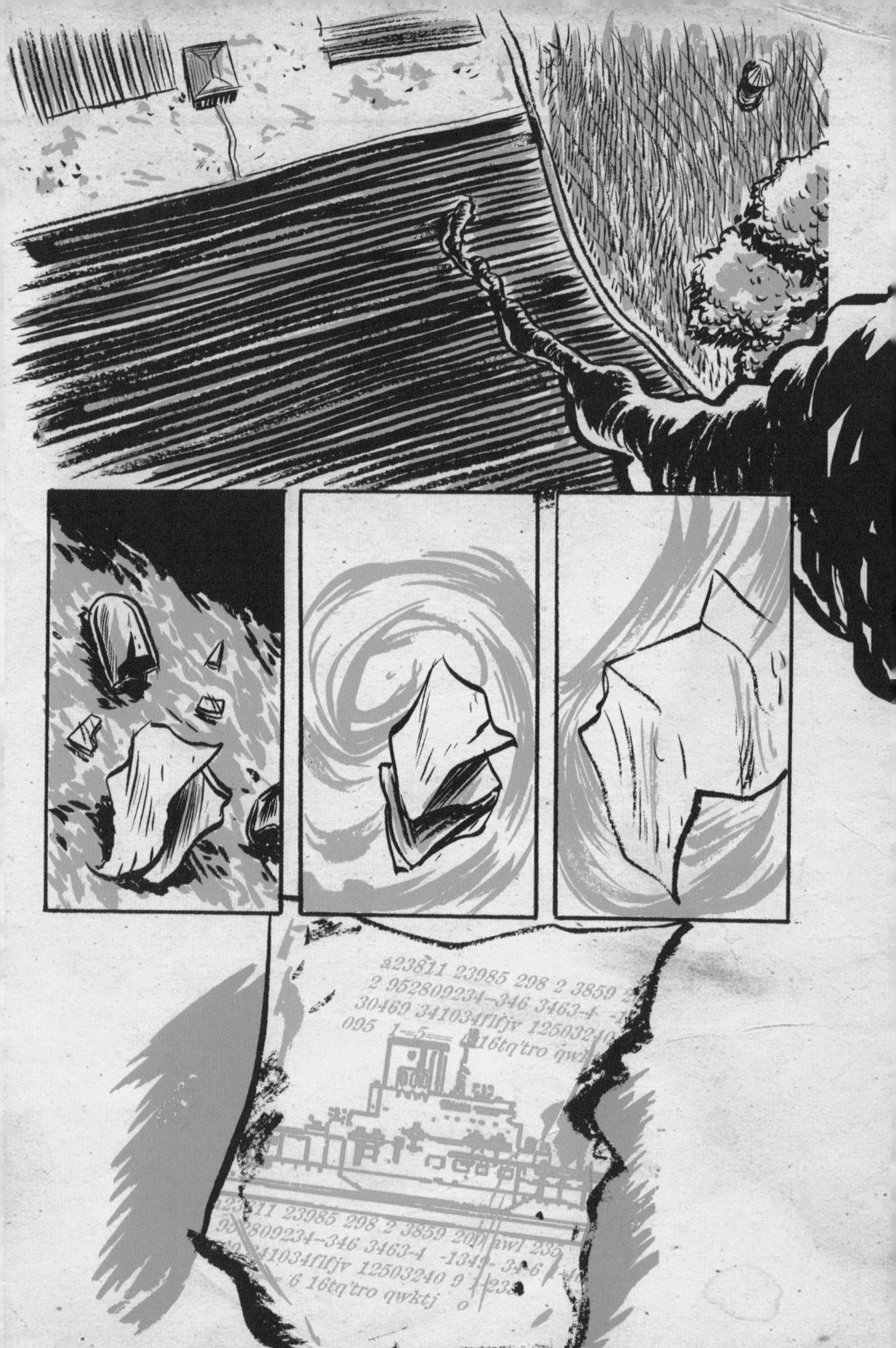
a23811 23985 298 2 3859
2 952809234–346 3463-4
30469 341034flfjv 12503240
095 1–5 16tq'tro qwk
23985 298 2 3859 200 awl 235
09234–346 3463-4 -134
341034flfjv 12503240 9
16tq'tro qwktj o

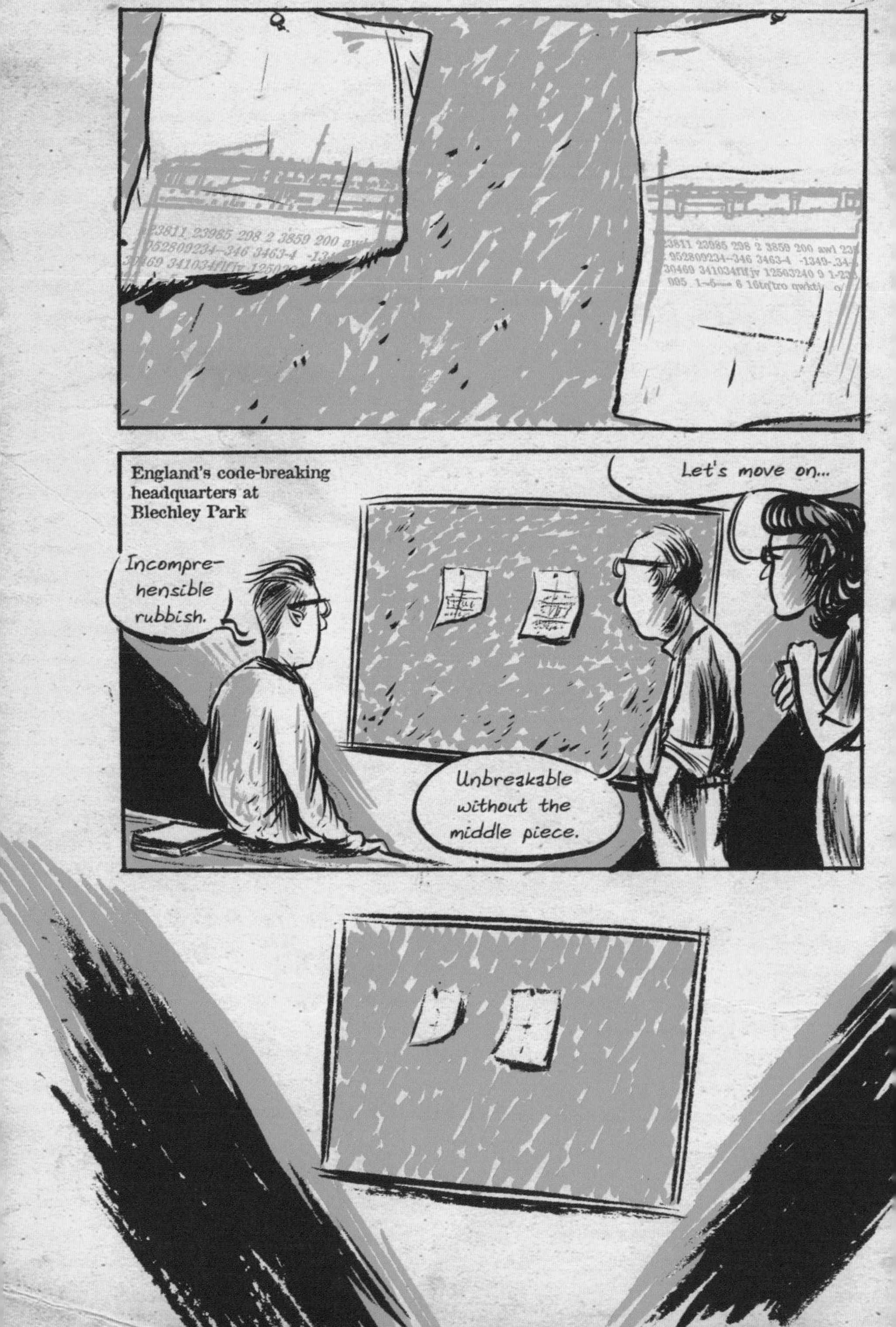
England's code-breaking headquarters at Blechley Park
Incomprehensible rubbish.
Let's move on...
Unbreakable without the middle piece.

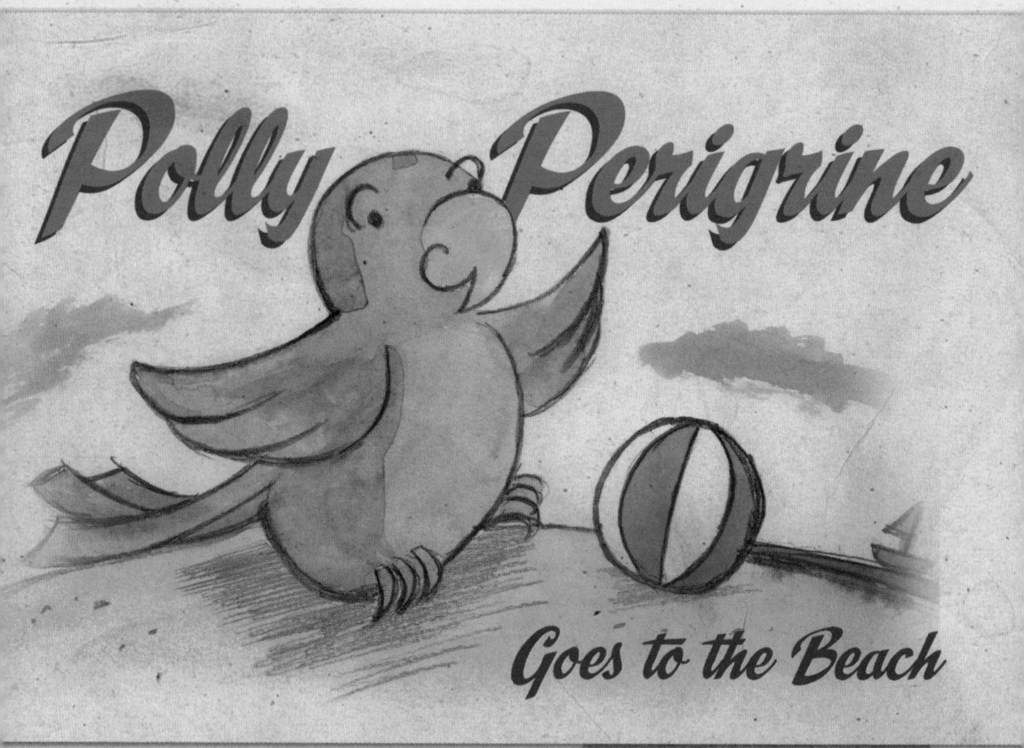
Polly Perigrine
Goes to the Beach

Dossier #0161944

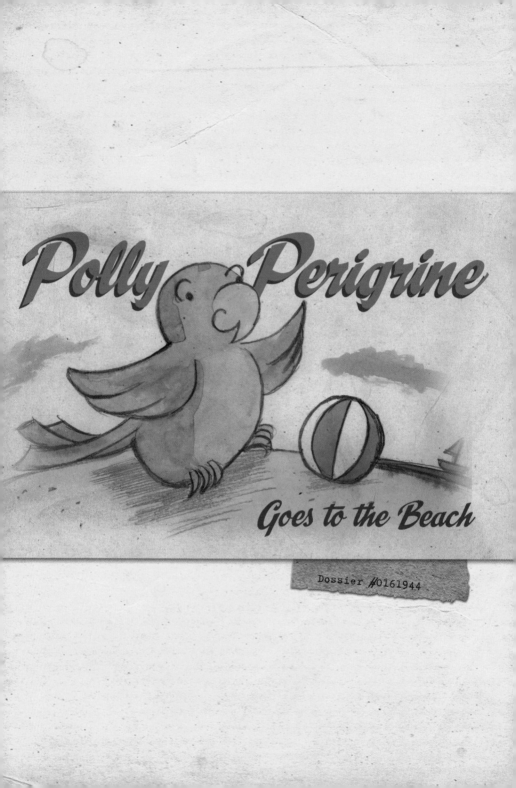

The old man in the straw hat decided to take his beloved pet Polly to the beach one day.

Polly was so excited she couldn't help but flap her wings all the way there.

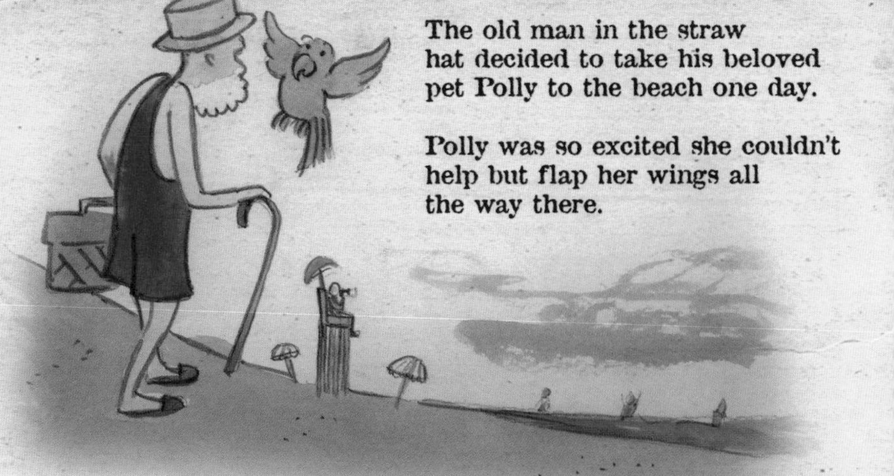

Polly and the old man had a wonderful time. Polly learned how to play catch!

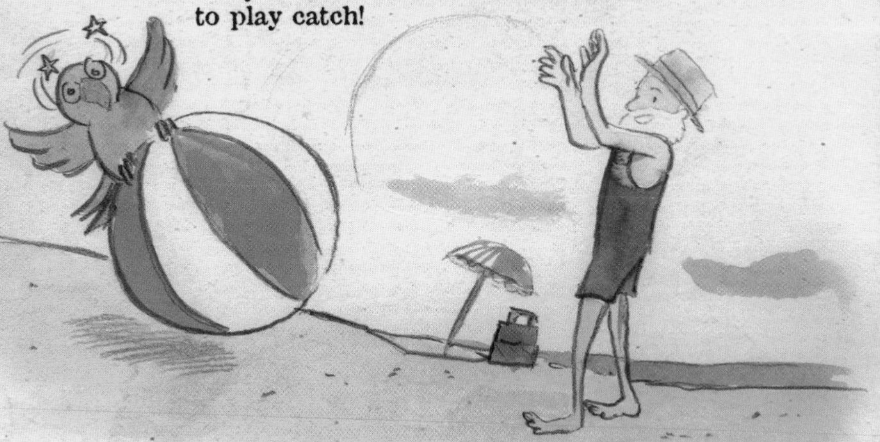

The old man played a trick on Polly and buried her in the sand all the way up to her beak!

Then he ran off to play with his girlfriend, Betsy.

Poor Polly was all alone.

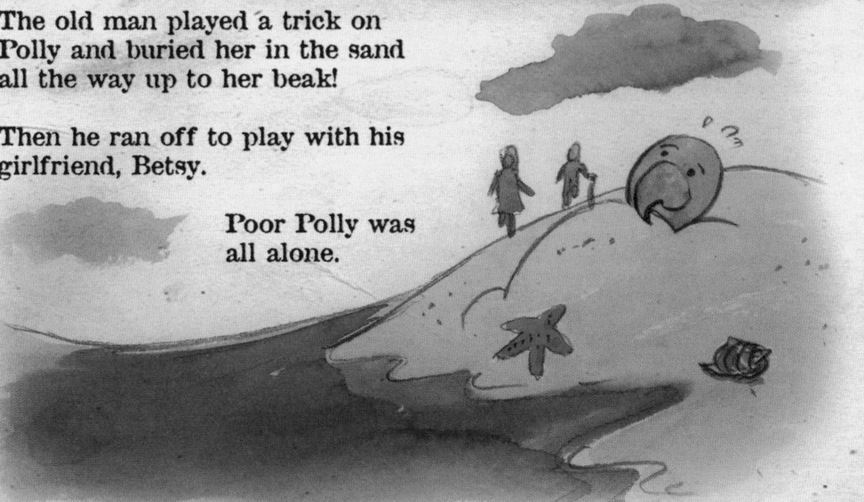

All alone, Polly decided to make some friends. She took all of the sandwiches out of the old man's picnic basket and shared them with the sandpipers.

Sandpipers love peanut butter and jelly!

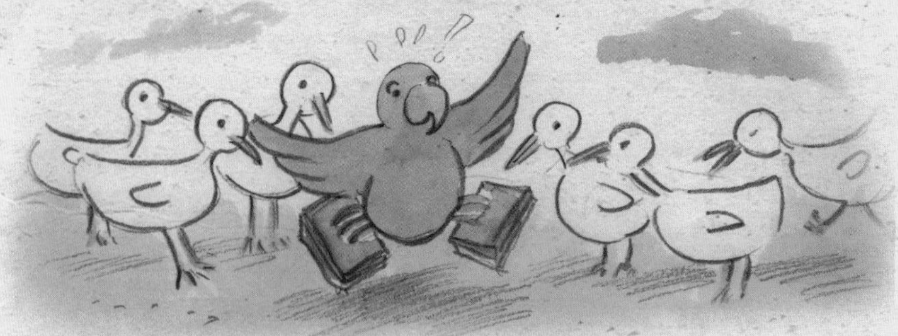

When the old man got back he was shocked! All of the food was gone and the picnic was ruined!

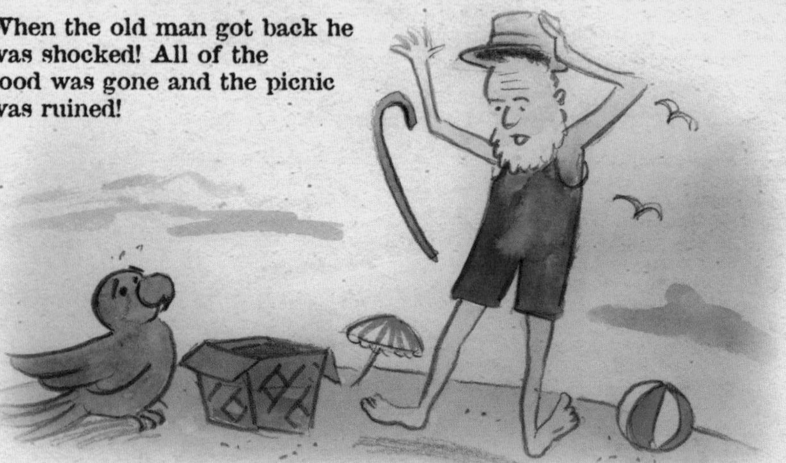

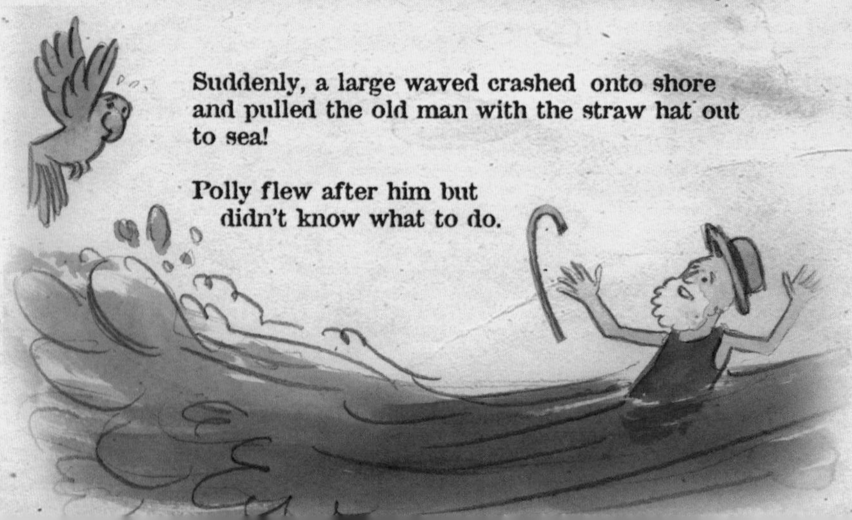

Suddenly, a large waved crashed onto shore and pulled the old man with the straw hat out to sea!

Polly flew after him but didn't know what to do.

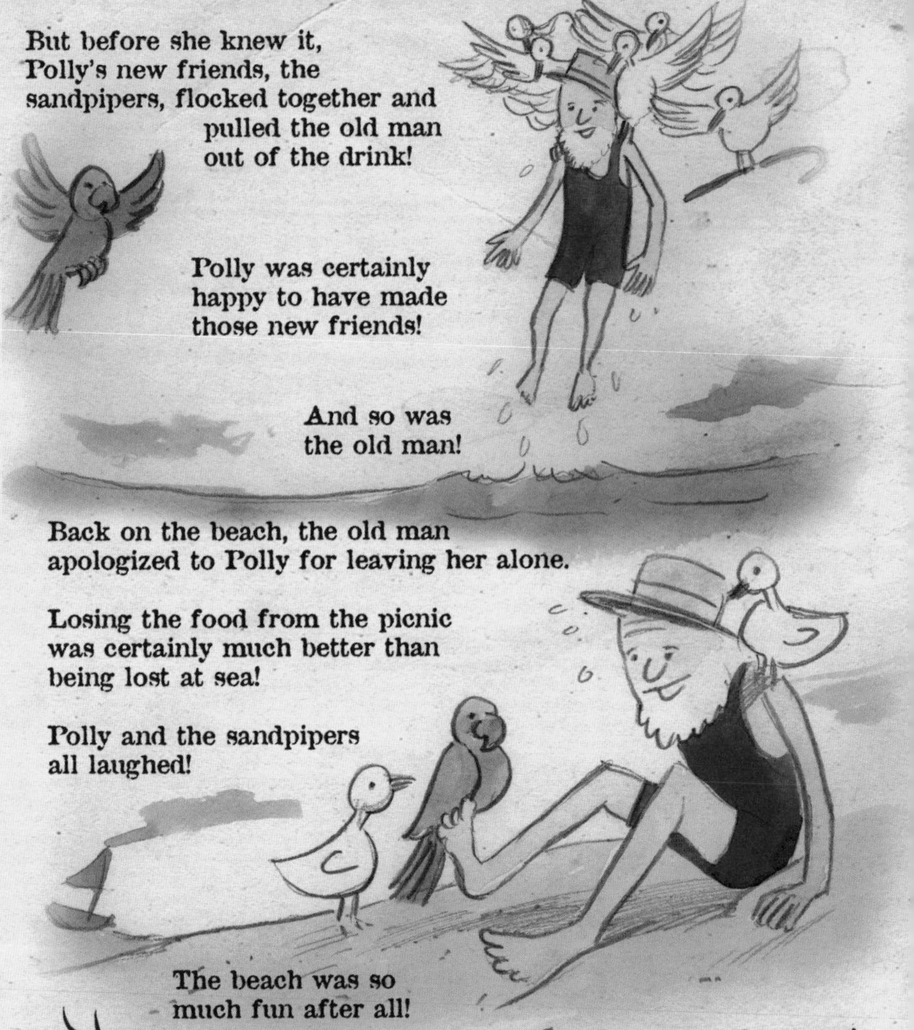
But before she knew it,
Polly's new friends, the
sandpipers, flocked together and
pulled the old man
out of the drink!
Polly was certainly
happy to have made
those new friends!
And so was
the old man!
Back on the beach, the old man
apologized to Polly for leaving her alone.
Losing the food from the picnic
was certainly much better than
being lost at sea!
Polly and the sandpipers
all laughed!
The beach was so
much fun after all!

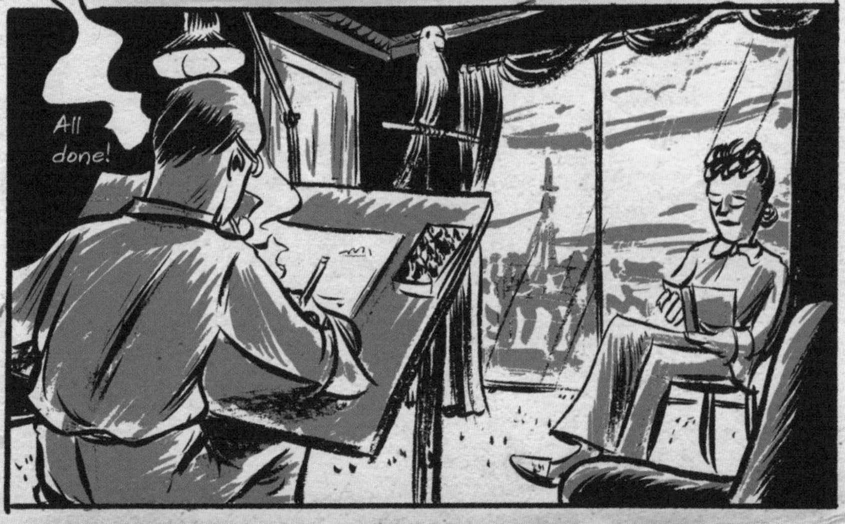
All
done!

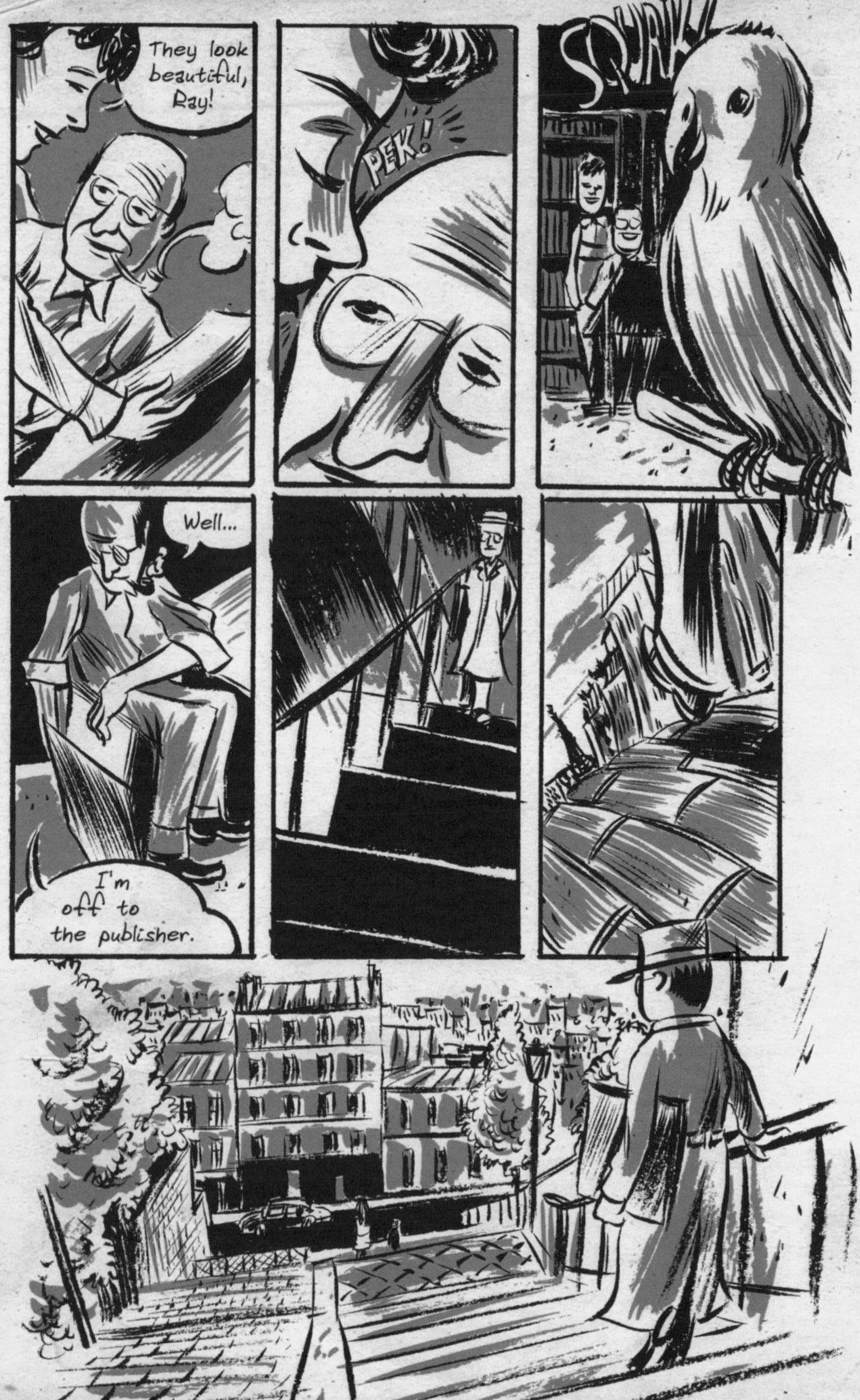
They look beautiful, Ray!
PEK!
SQUAWK!
Well...
I'm off to the publisher.

LAPIN PUBLISH
Ça va?
Ça va.
They are magnifique!
Polly Peregrine
Spain...

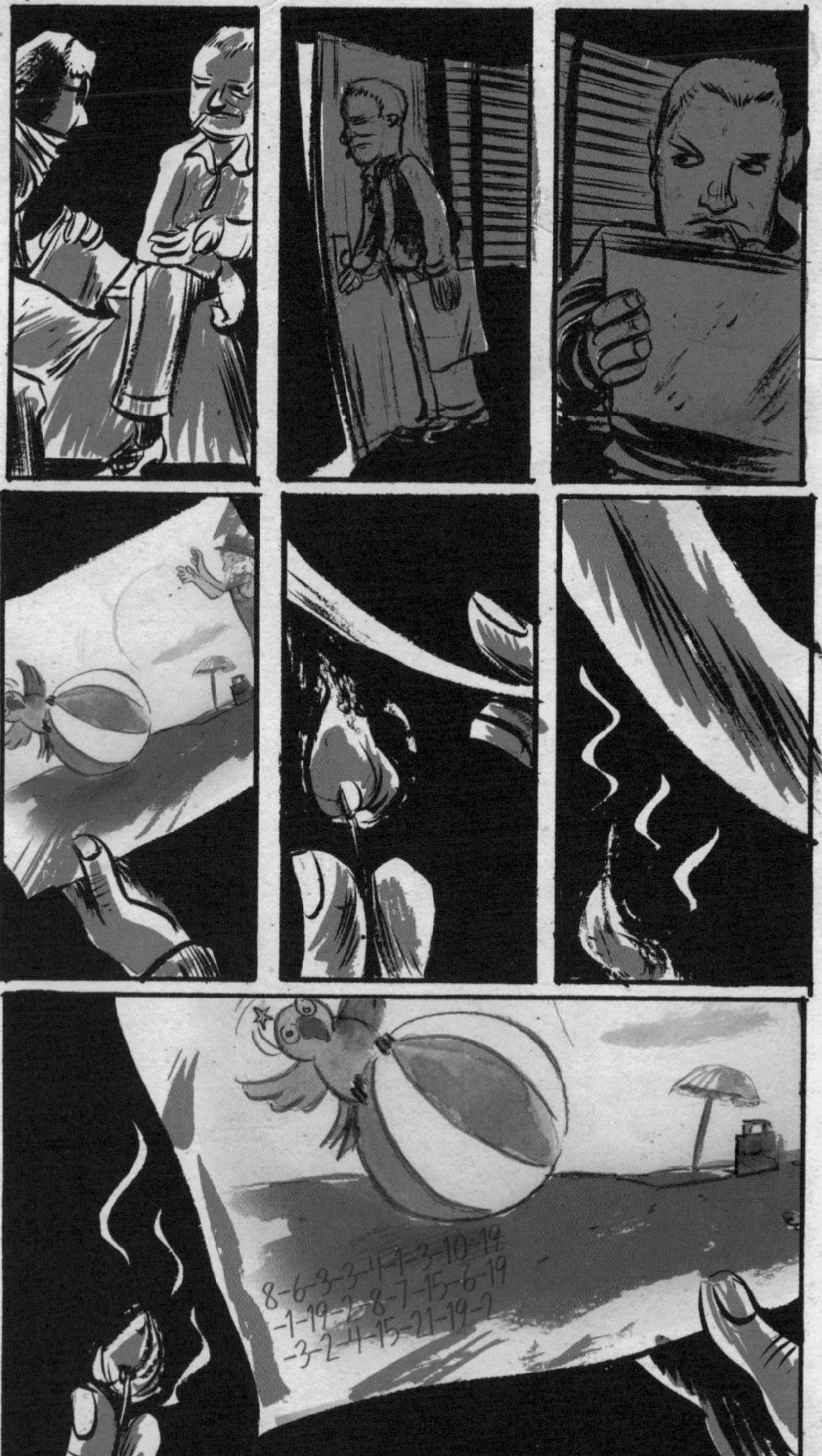
8-6-3-3-4-1-3-10-19
-1-19-2-8-7-15-6-19
-3-2-4-15-21-19-2

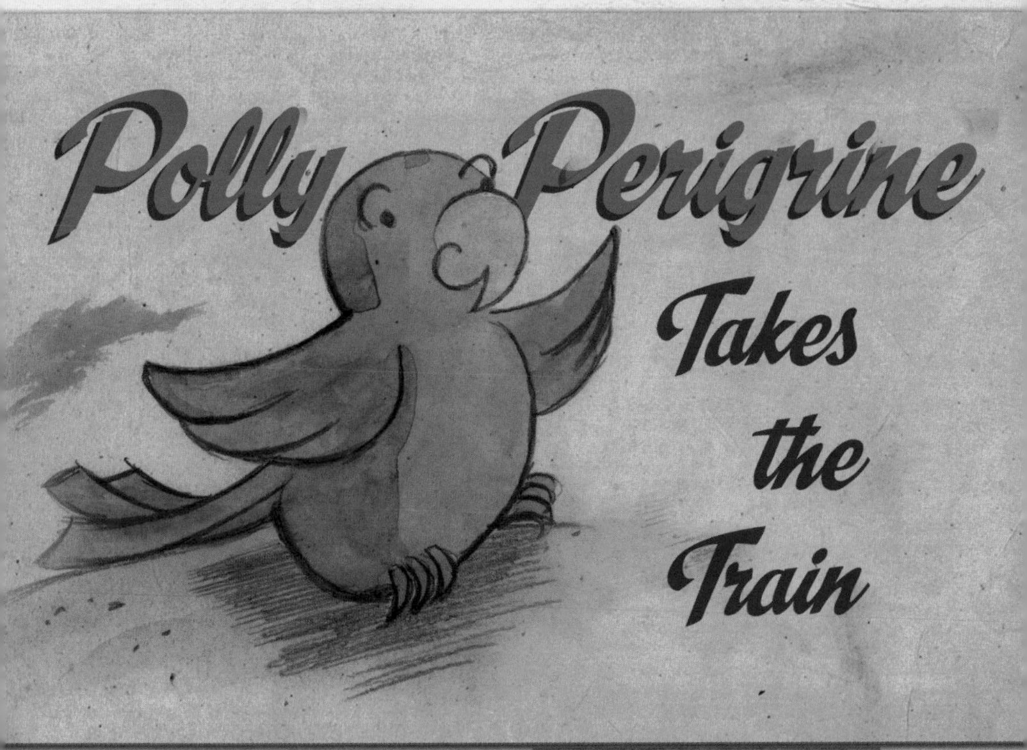
Polly Perigrine
Takes the Train

Dossier #0171944

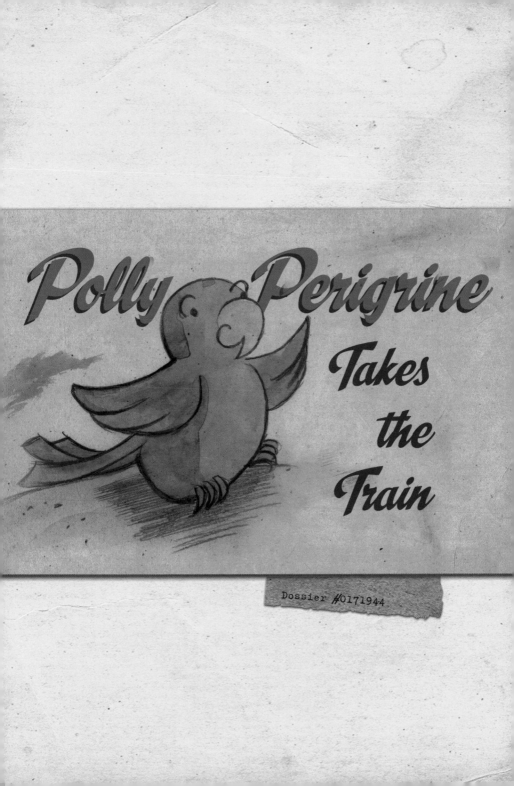

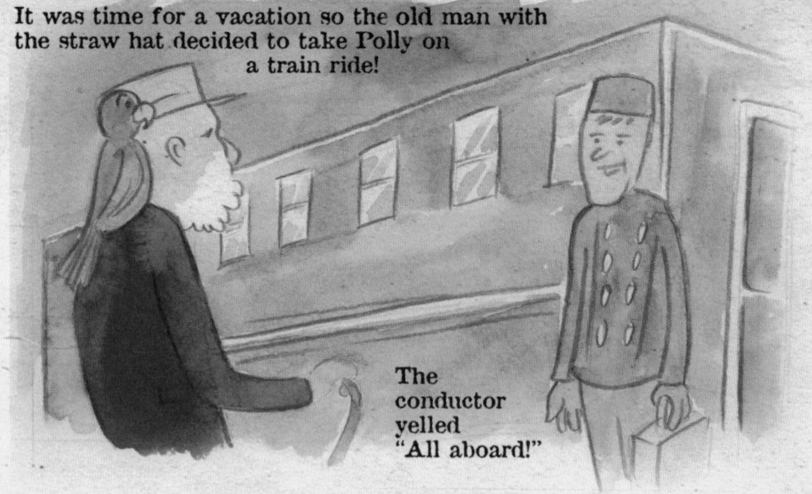
It was time for a vacation so the old man with the straw hat decided to take Polly on a train ride!
The conductor yelled "All aboard!"

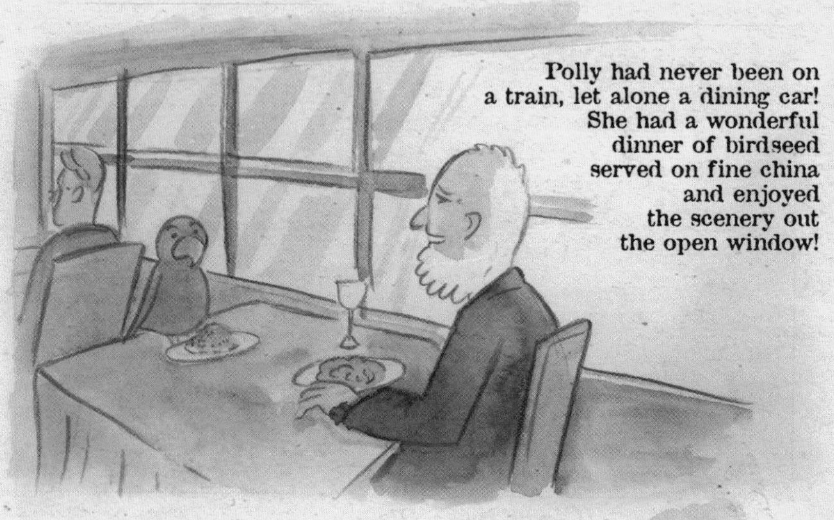
Polly had never been on a train, let alone a dining car! She had a wonderful dinner of birdseed served on fine china and enjoyed the scenery out the open window!

Suddenly Polly got swept out of the open window of the train!

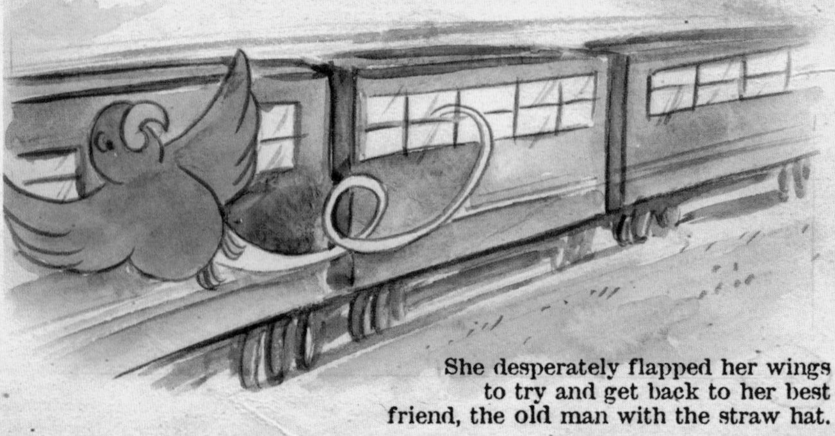
She desperately flapped her wings to try and get back to her best friend, the old man with the straw hat.

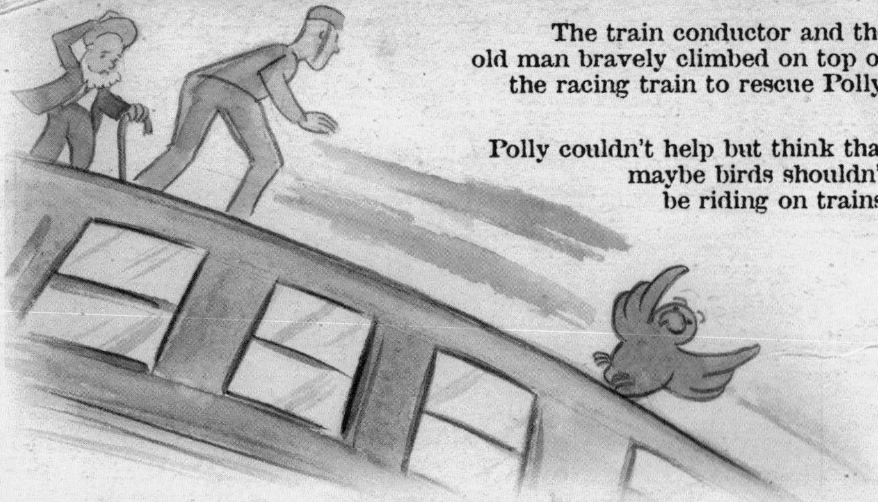

The train conductor and the old man bravely climbed on top of the racing train to rescue Polly!

Polly couldn't help but think that maybe birds shouldn't be riding on trains.

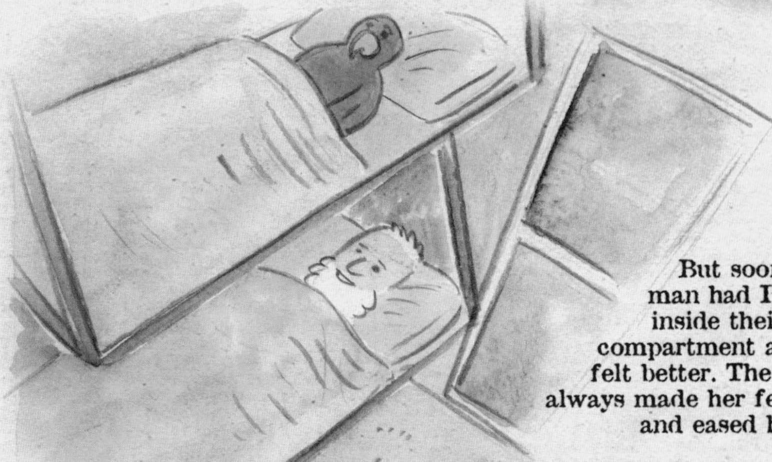

But soon the old man had Polly safe inside their sleeper compartment and Polly felt better. The old man always made her feel better and eased her fears.

Sleeping on the train was the most fun Polly had ever had!

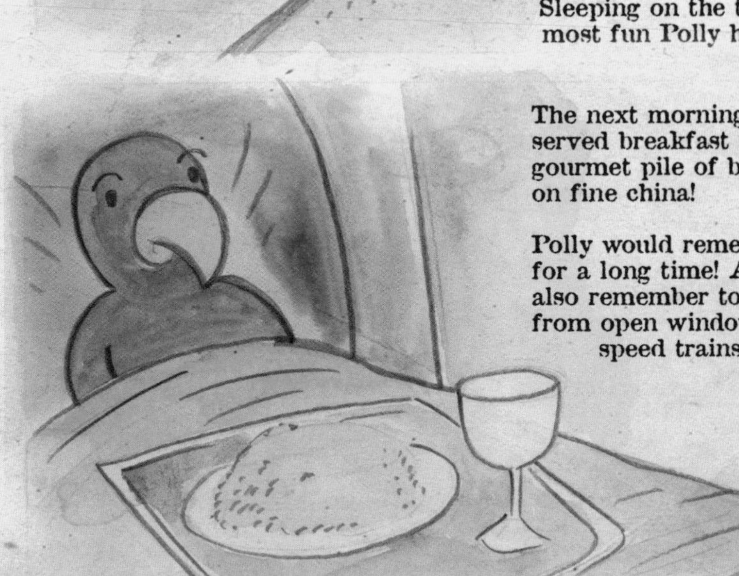

The next morning Polly was served breakfast in bed! A gourmet pile of birdseed served on fine china!

Polly would remember this trip for a long time! And she would also remember to stay away from open windows on high-speed trains!

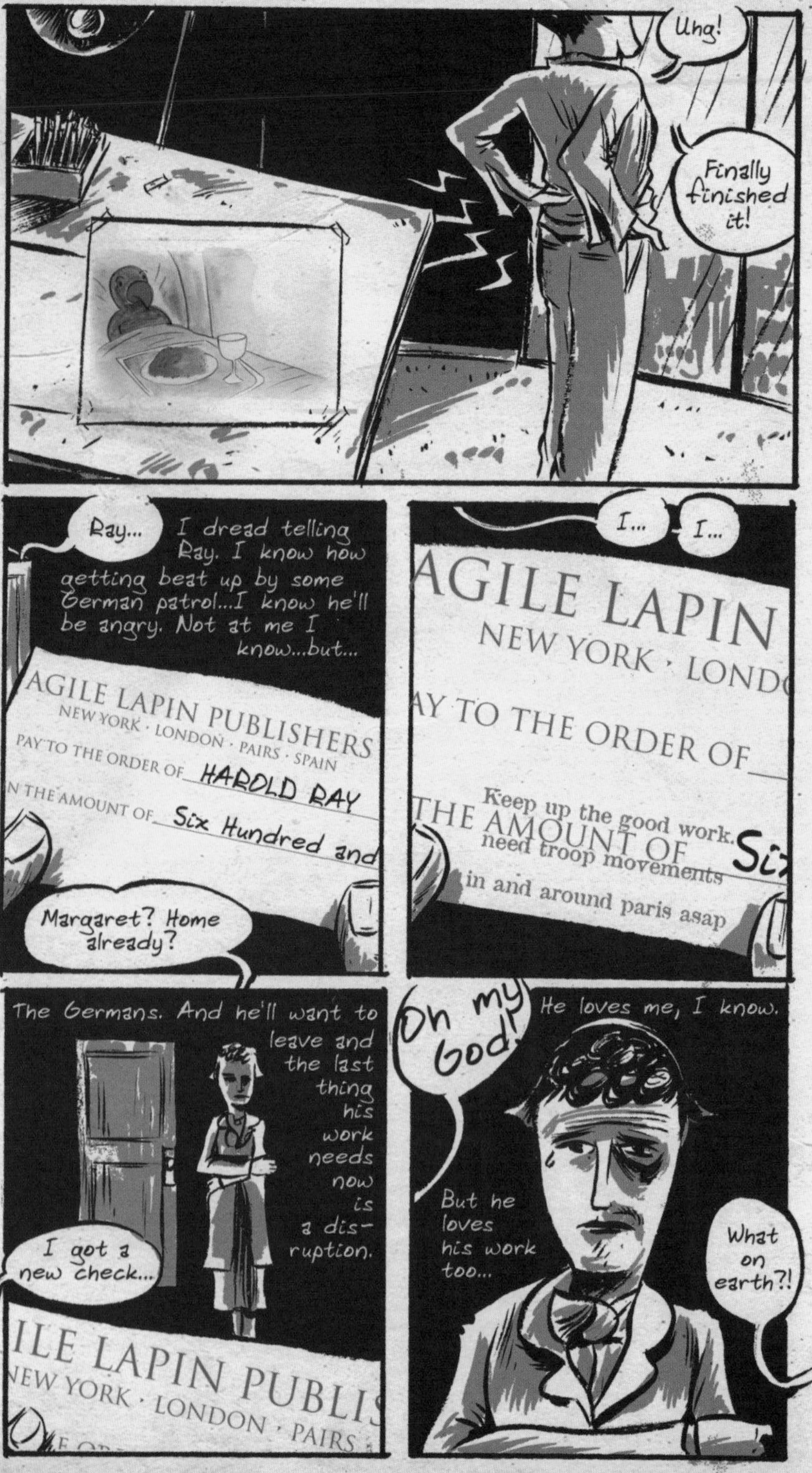

Ung!
Finally finished it!
Ray...
I dread telling Ray. I know how getting beat up by some German patrol...I know he'll be angry. Not at me I know...but...
AGILE LAPIN PUBLISHERS
NEW YORK · LONDON · PAIRS · SPAIN
PAY TO THE ORDER OF HAROLD RAY
IN THE AMOUNT OF Six Hundred and
Margaret? Home already?
I...
I...
AGILE LAPIN
NEW YORK · LONDO
AY TO THE ORDER OF
THE AMOUNT OF Six
Keep up the good work.
need troop movements
in and around paris asap
The Germans. And he'll want to leave and the last thing his work needs now is a dis-ruption.
I got a new check...
ILE LAPIN PUBLIS
NEW YORK · LONDON · PAIRS
Oh my God!
He loves me, I know.
But he loves his work too...
What on earth?!

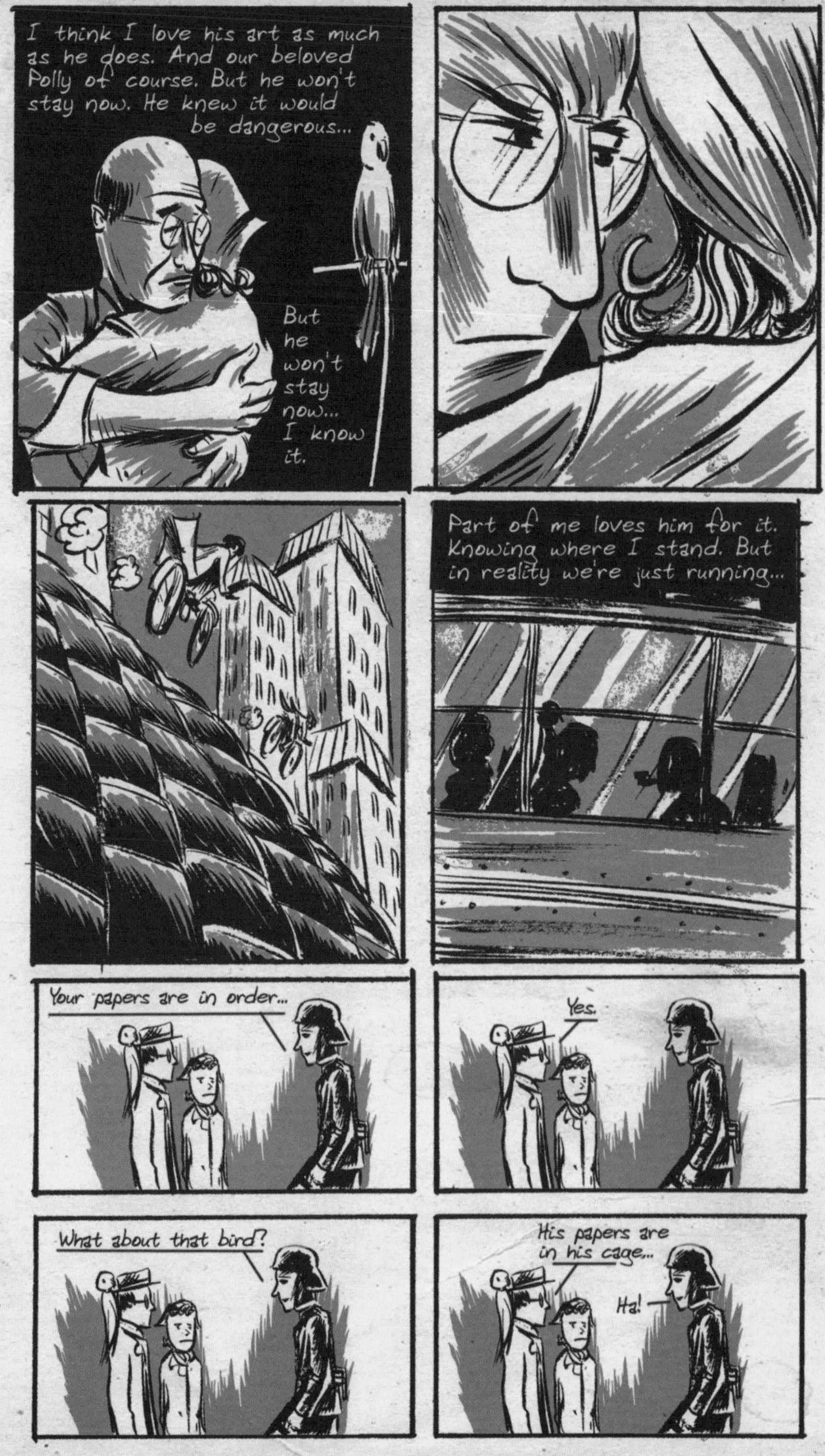
I think I love his art as much as he does. And our beloved Polly of course. But he won't stay now. He knew it would be dangerous...
But he won't stay now... I know it.
Part of me loves him for it. Knowing where I stand. But in reality we're just running...
Your papers are in order...
Yes.
What about that bird?
His papers are in his cage...
Ha!

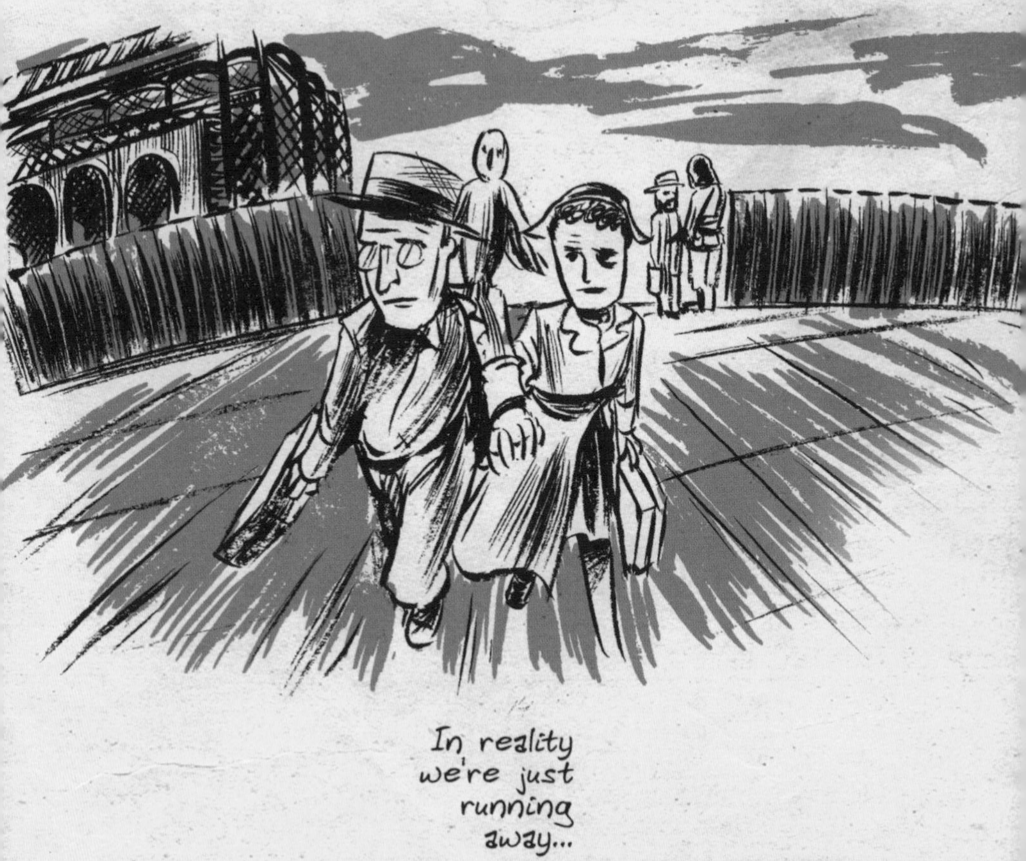
In reality we're just running away...

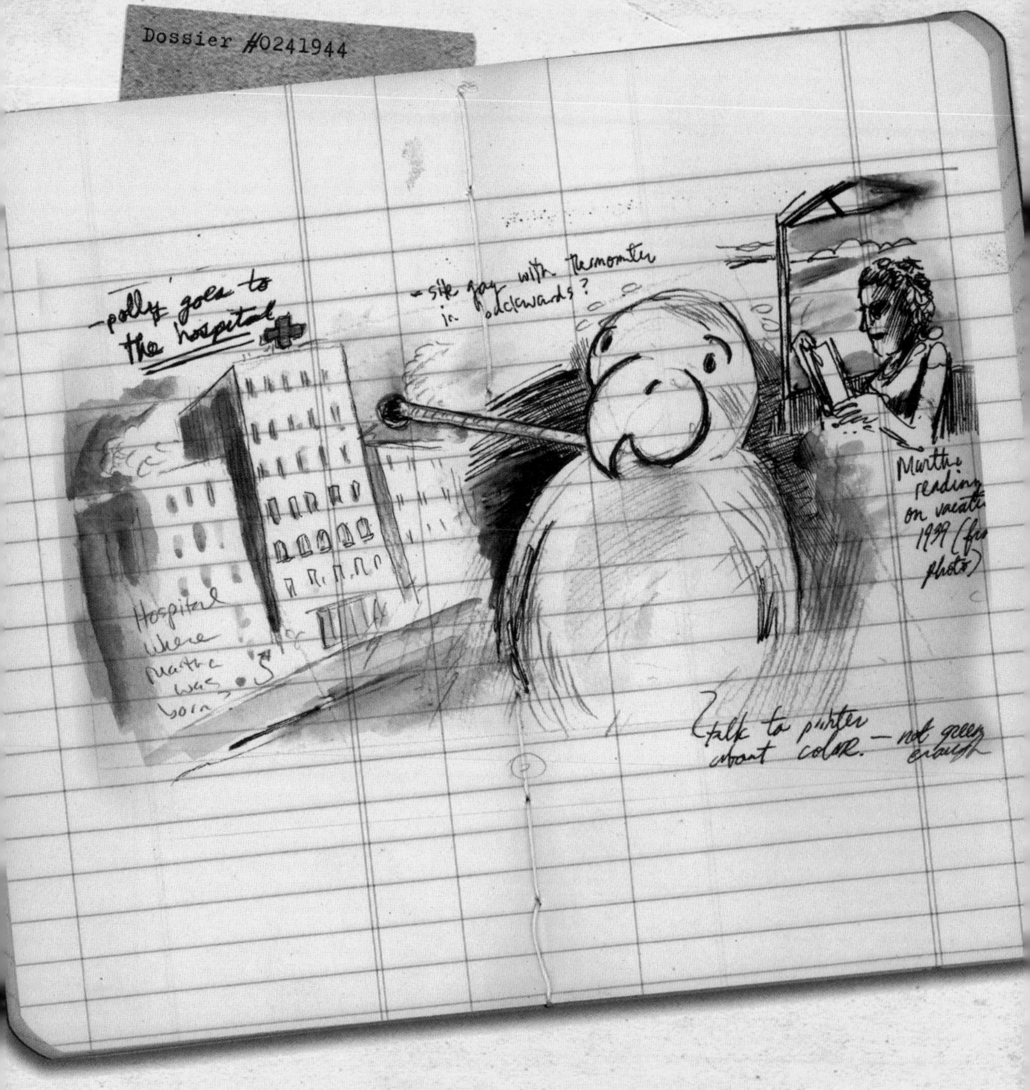
Dossier #0241944
-polly goes to the hospital
-sick guy with thermometer in backwards?
Hospital where martha was born
Martha reading on vacati 1939 (fr photo)
talk to printer about color. — not green enough

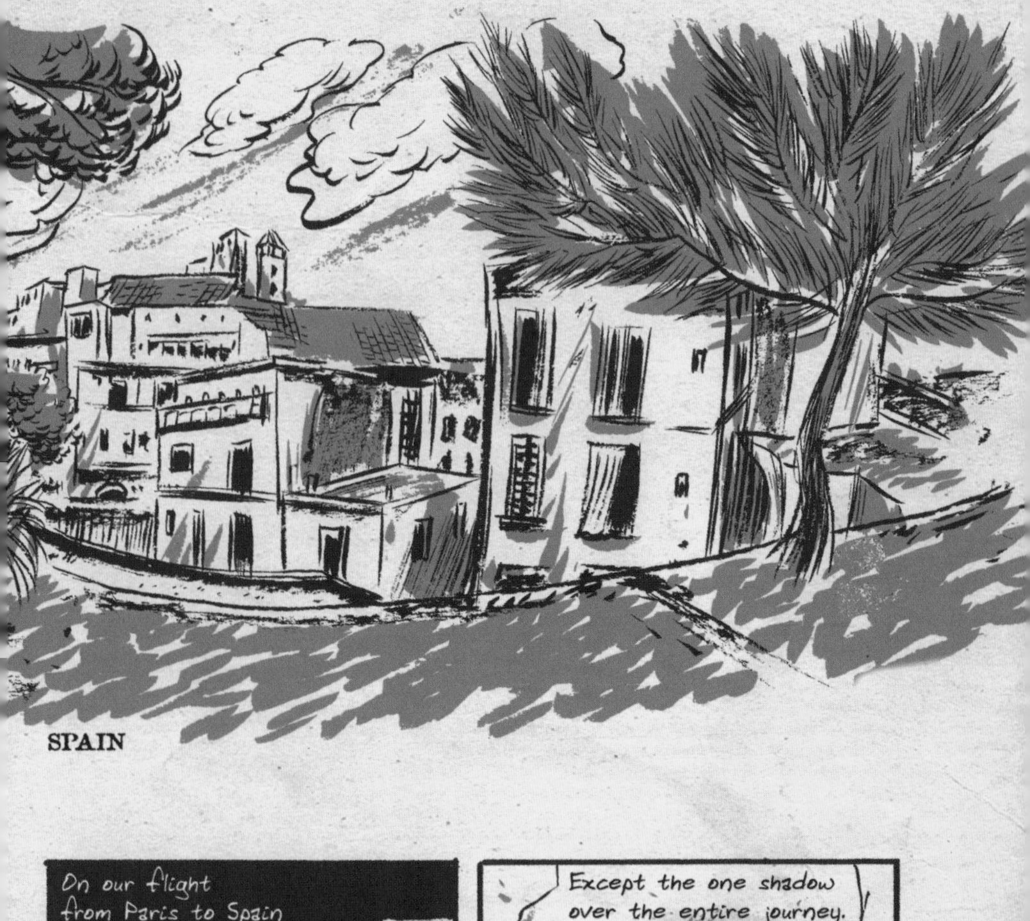

SPAIN

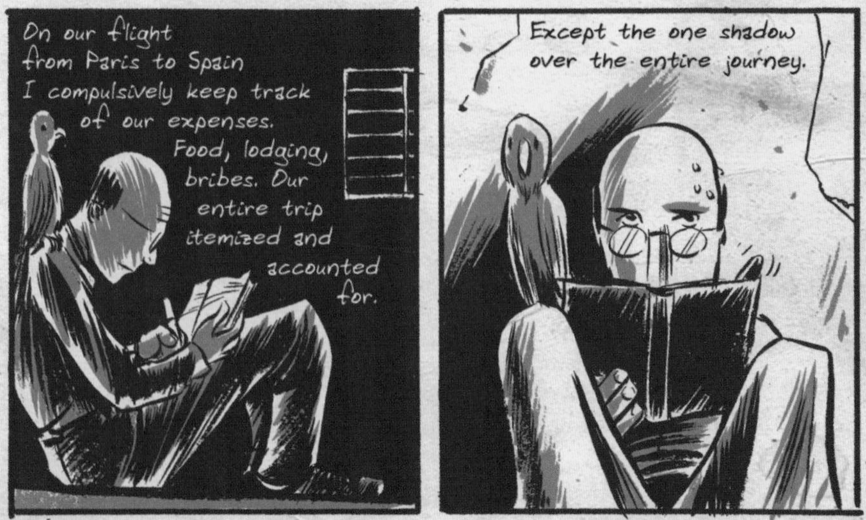
On our flight from Paris to Spain I compulsively keep track of our expenses.
Food, lodging, bribes. Our entire trip itemized and accounted for.
Except the one shadow over the entire journey.

France

9/10	bananas		1 f
9/10	grapefruit		2 f
9/10	cigarettes		3 f
9/11	bird food		2 f 9
9/13	train tickets		600 f
9/13	flowers		.50
9/13	ink		7 f
9/13	paper		2 f

Spain

Walker lunch | 3 f

Squeak! *

* meal ticket

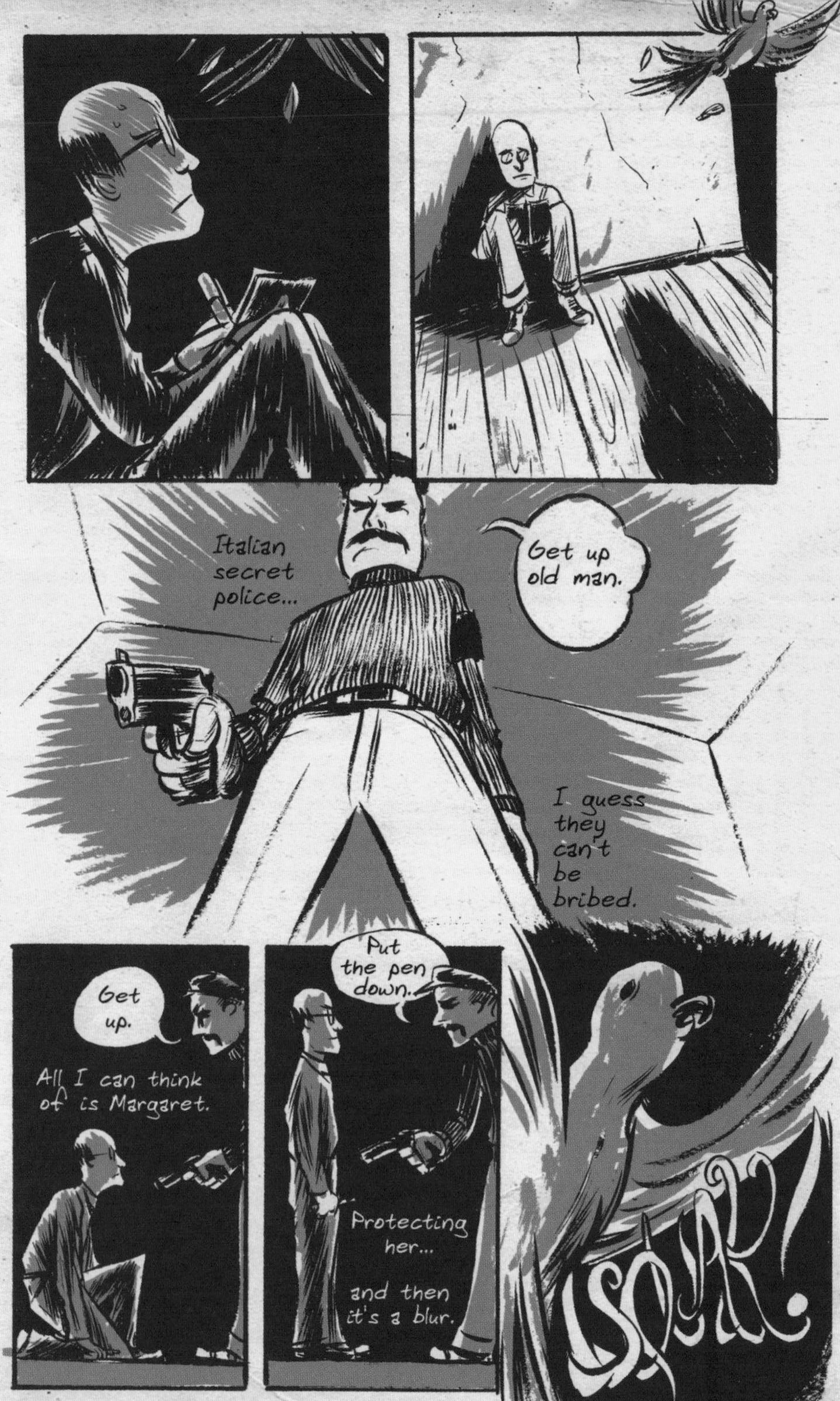
Italian secret police...
Get up old man.
I guess they can't be bribed.
Get up.
All I can think of is Margaret.
Put the pen down.
Protecting her...
and then it's a blur.

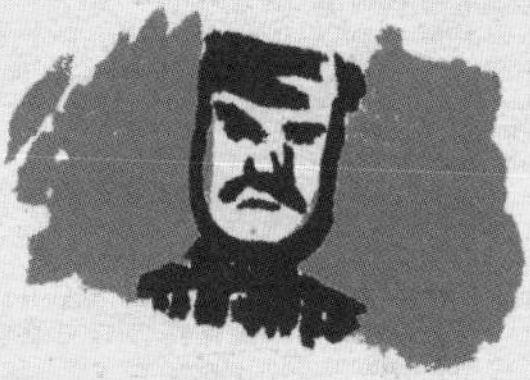
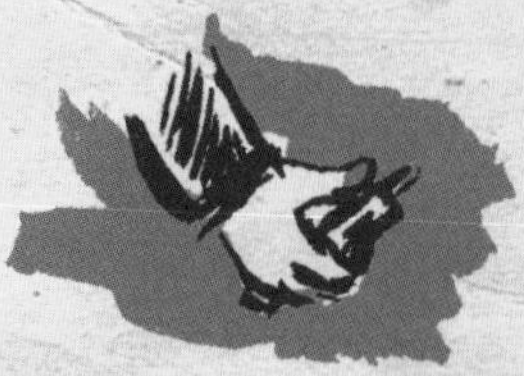
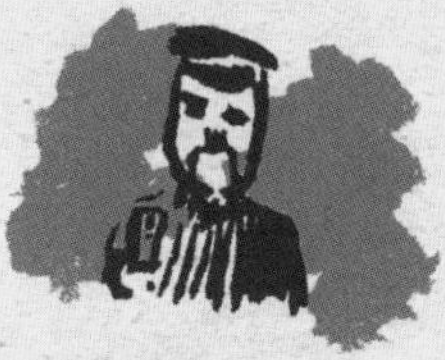
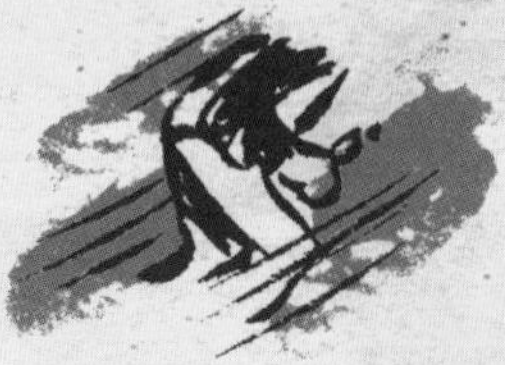
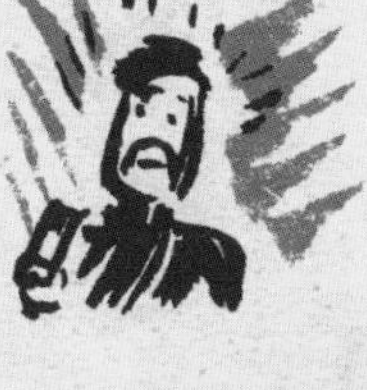
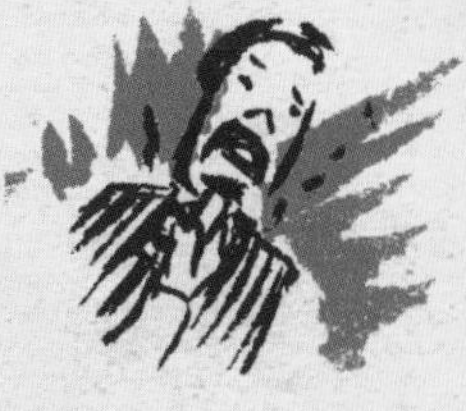
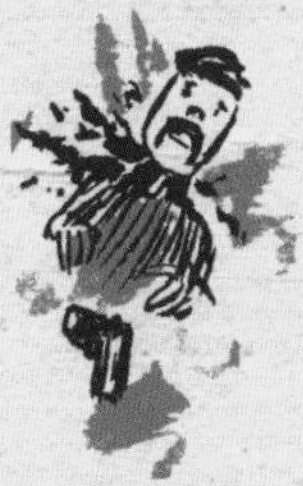
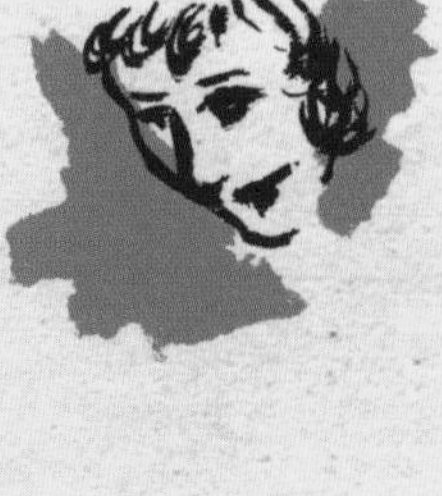

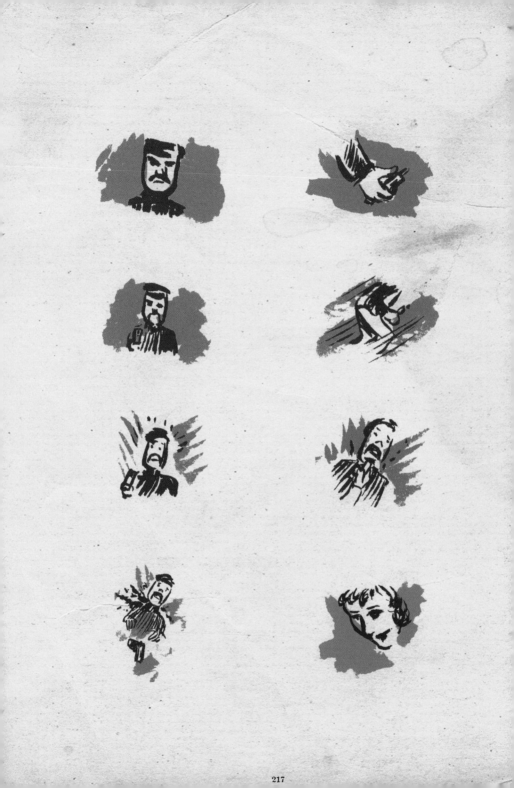

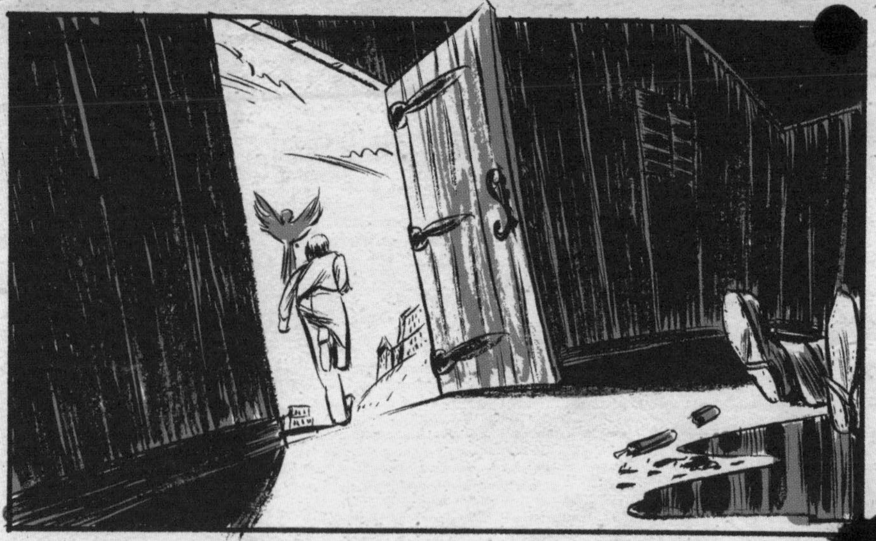

I find her in the market and she's okay. The world falls away and I know I'll never tell her.

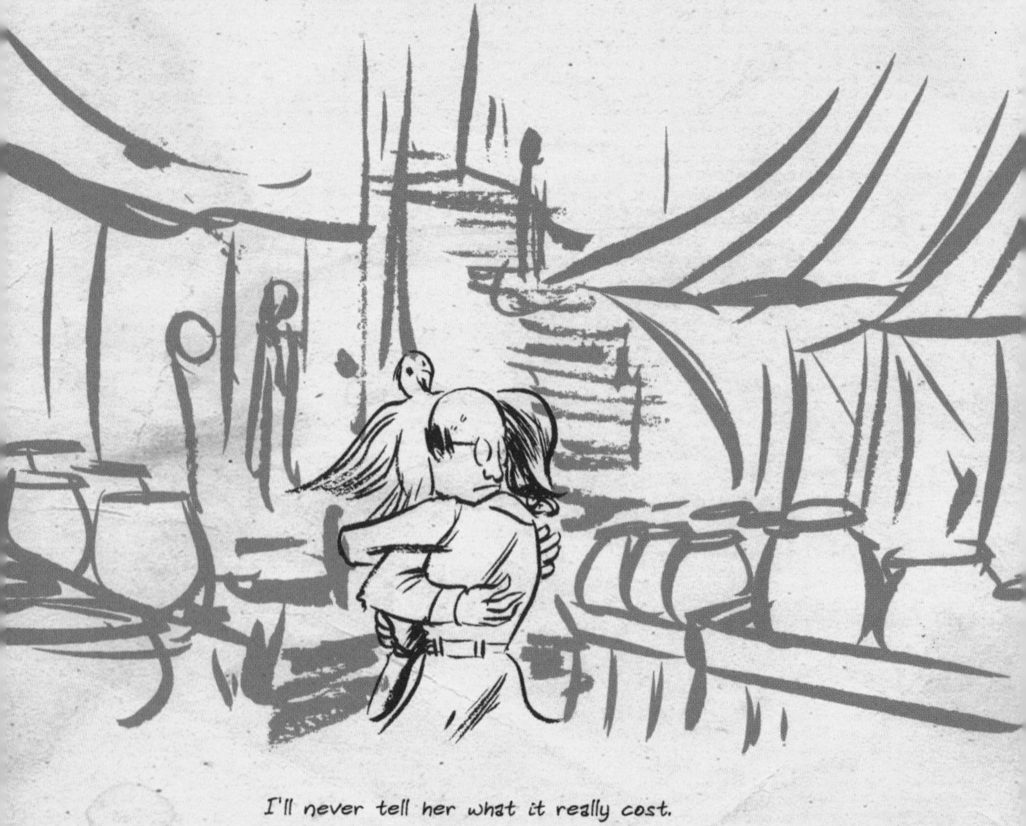

I'll never tell her what it really cost.

Something's come
between us.

whatever do
your mean?

10/11	new pen	75 f.
10/11	paper	2 f.
10/12	lemon juice	.50 f
10/12	bleach	7 f.
10/13	candles	.50
10/14	firewood	2 f
10/15	flowers	.50

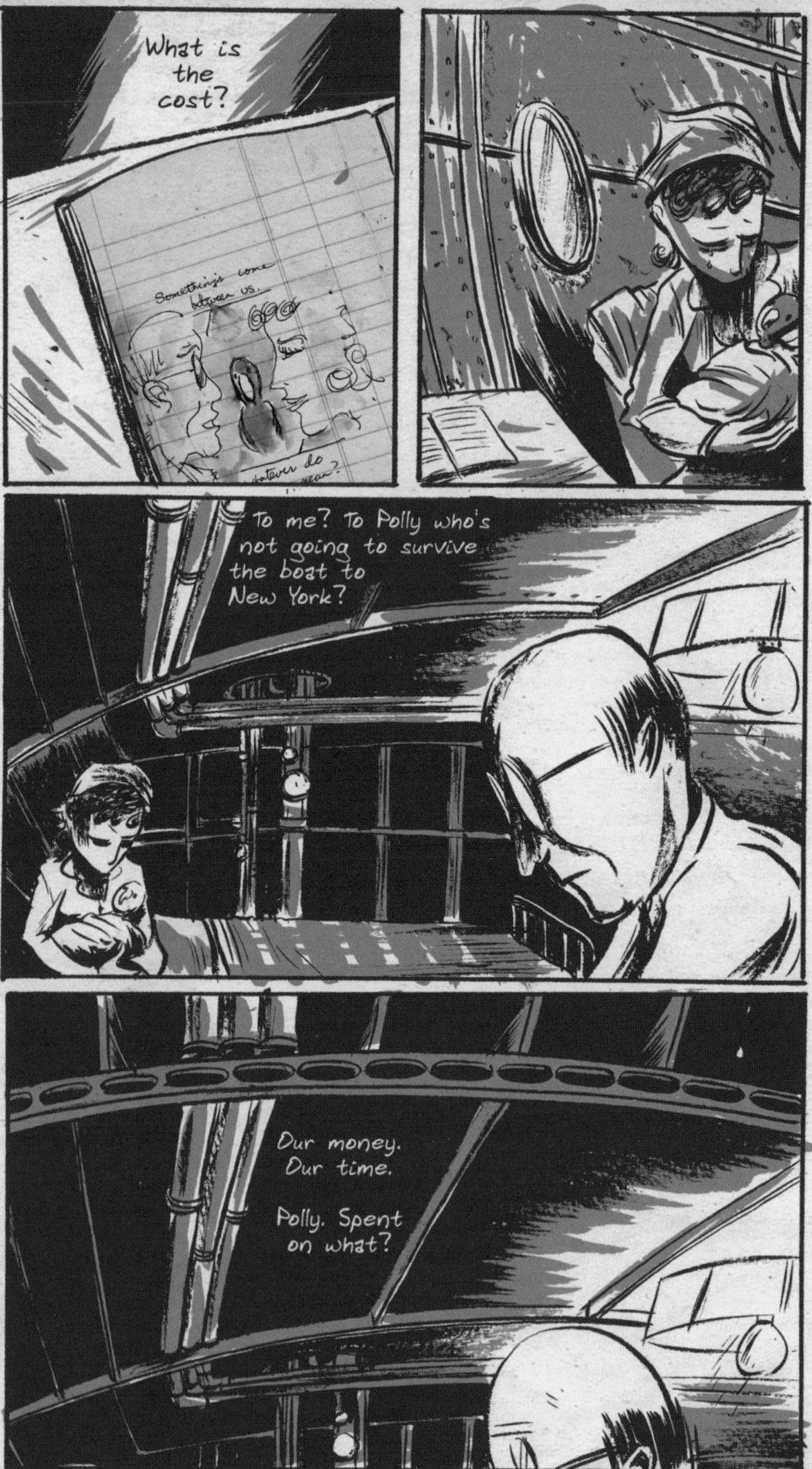
What is the cost?
Something's come between us.
To me? To Polly who's not going to survive the boat to New York?
Our money. Our time.
Polly. Spent on what?

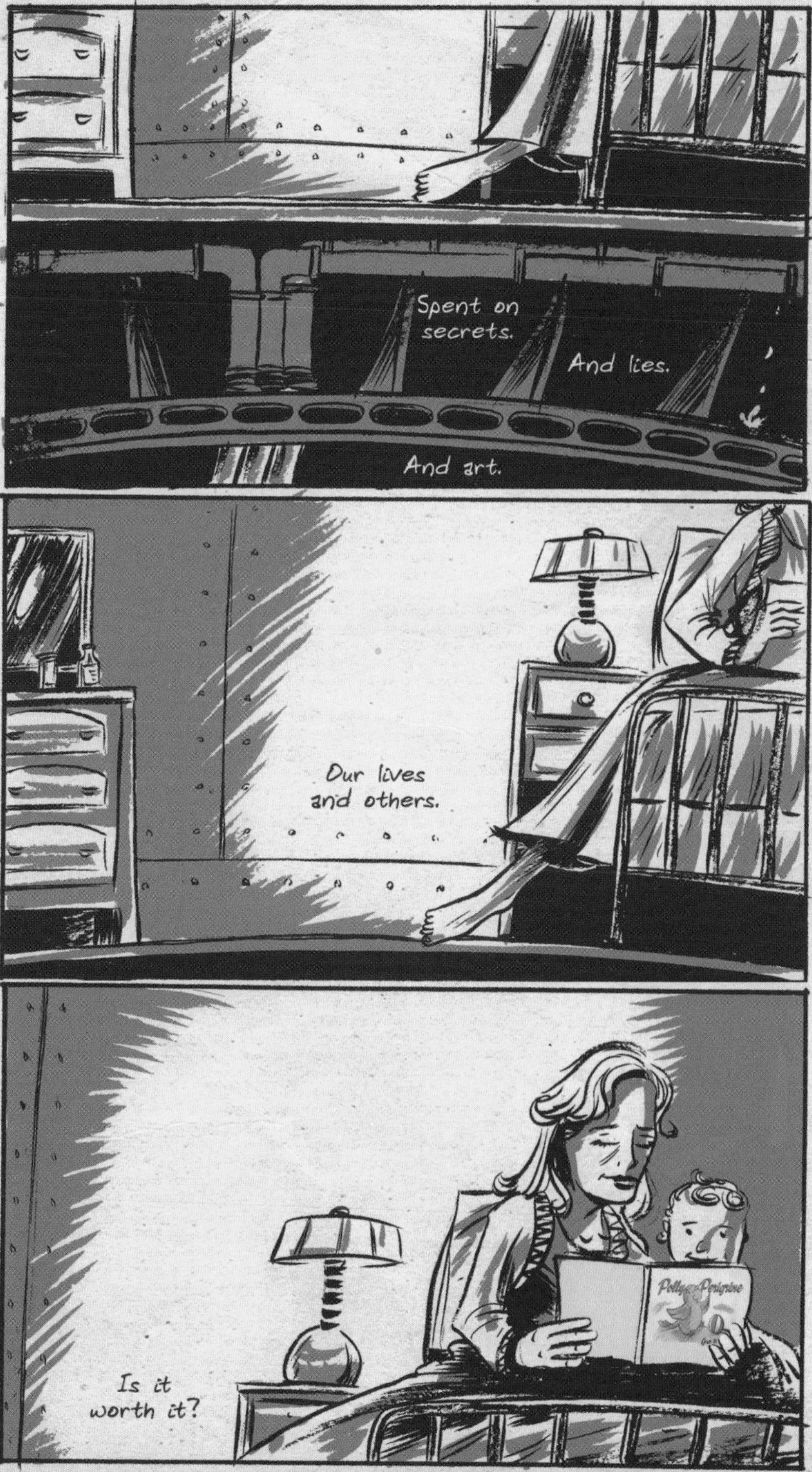
Spent on secrets.
And lies.
And art.
Our lives and others.
Is it worth it?

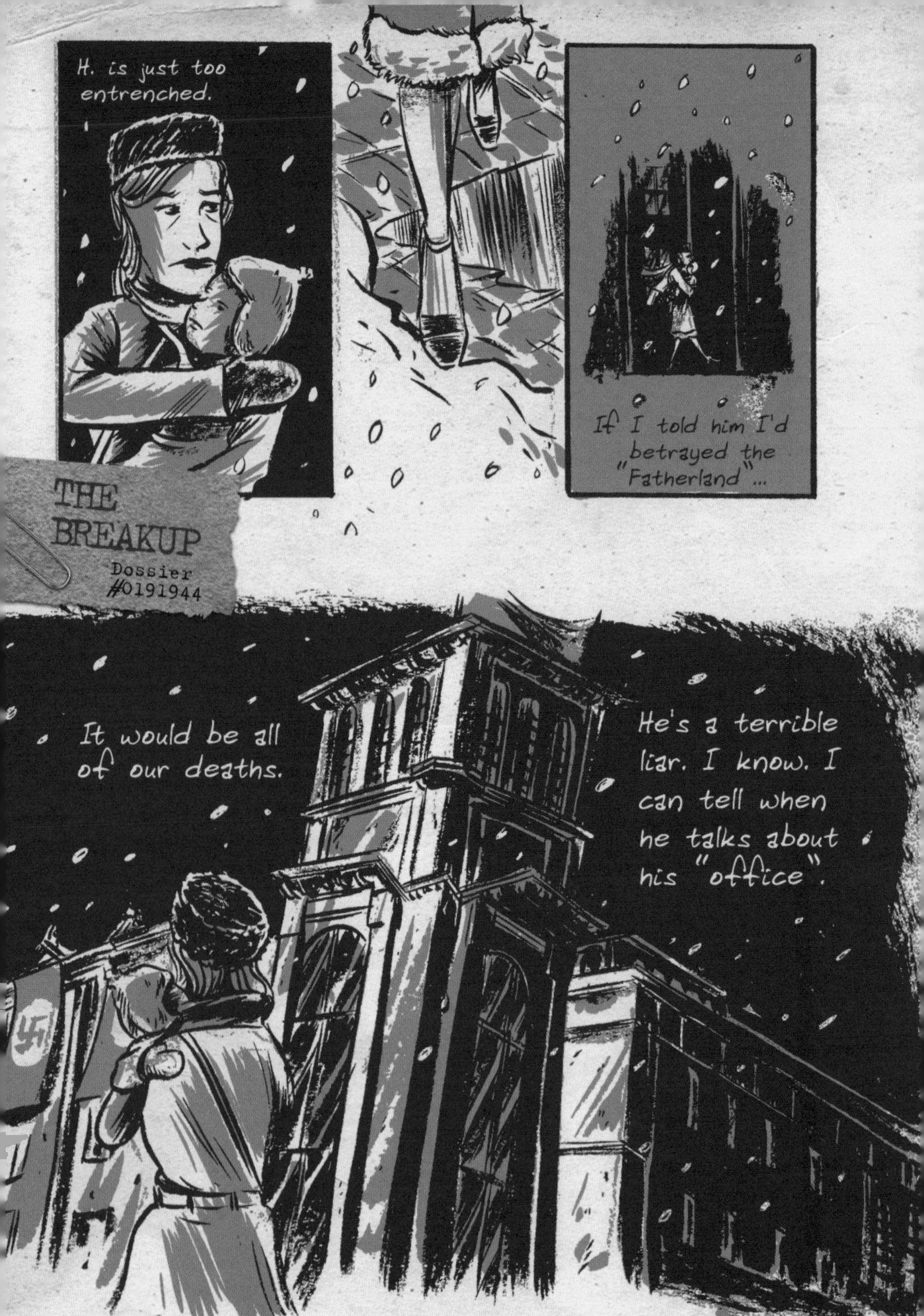
H. is just too entrenched.
If I told him I'd betrayed the "Fatherland"...
THE BREAKUP
Dossier #0191944
It would be all of our deaths.
He's a terrible liar. I know. I can tell when he talks about his "office".

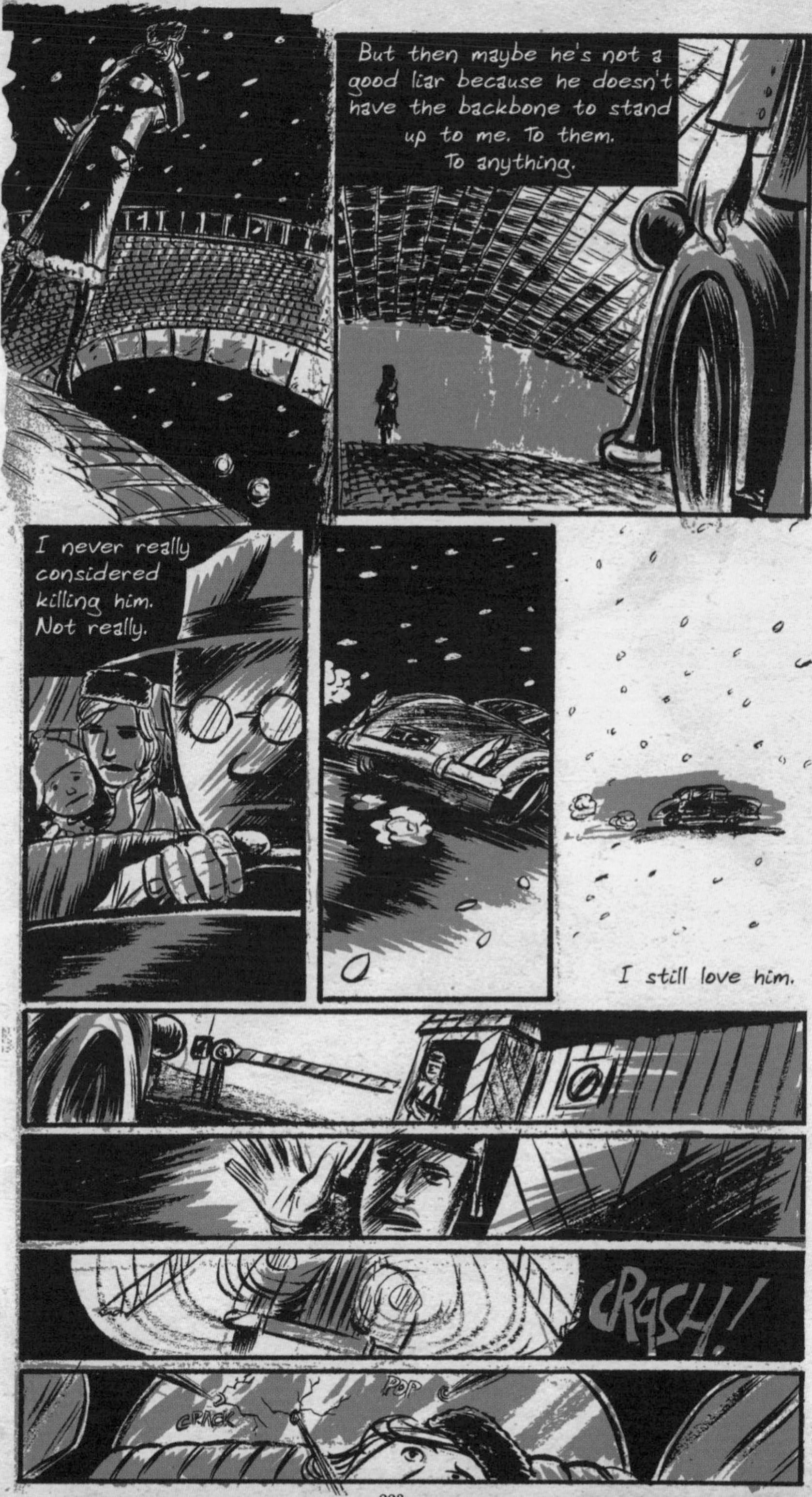
But then maybe he's not a good liar because he doesn't have the backbone to stand up to me. To them. To anything.
I never really considered killing him. Not really.
I still love him.
CRASH!
POP
CRACK

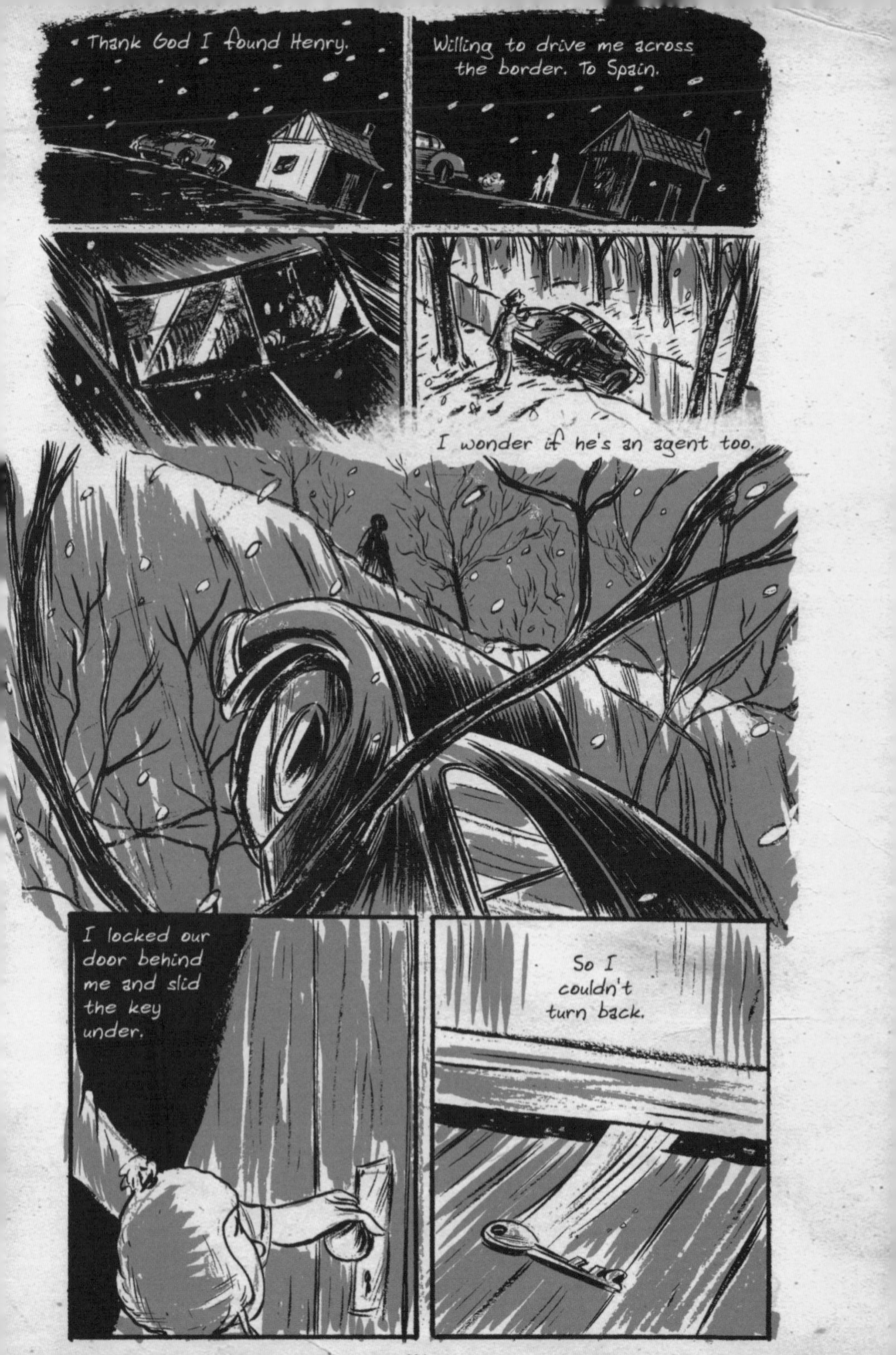
Thank God I found Henry.
Willing to drive me across the border. To Spain.
I wonder if he's an agent too.
I locked our door behind me and slid the key under.
So I couldn't turn back.

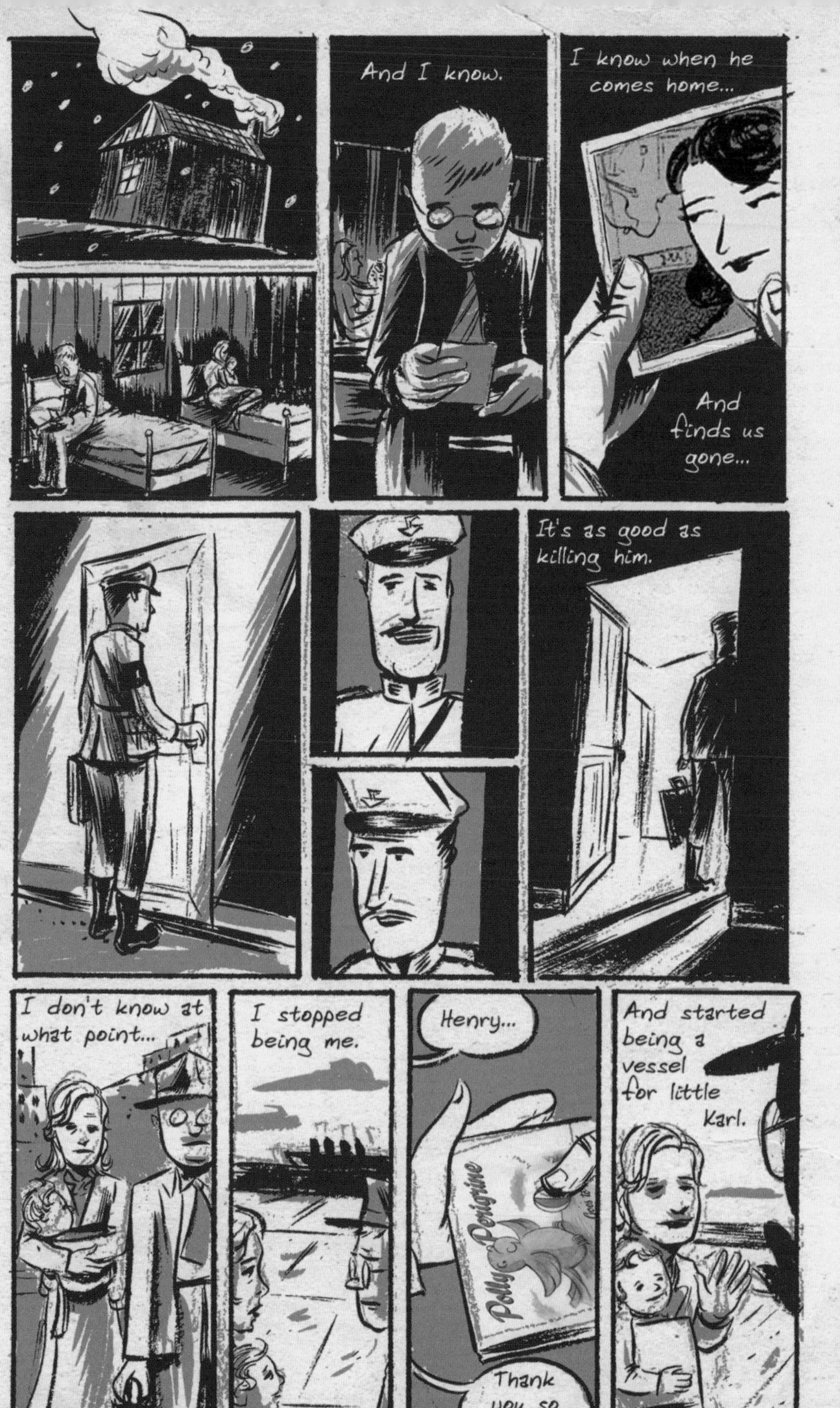
And I know.
I know when he comes home...
And finds us gone...
It's as good as killing him.
I don't know at what point...
I stopped being me.
Henry...
Thank you so much.
And started being a vessel for little Karl.

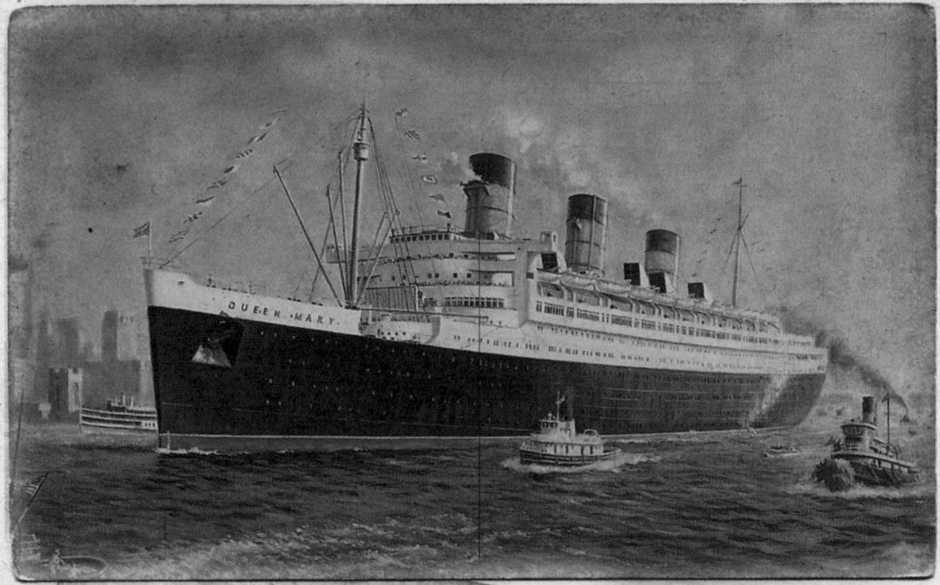
QUEEN MARY

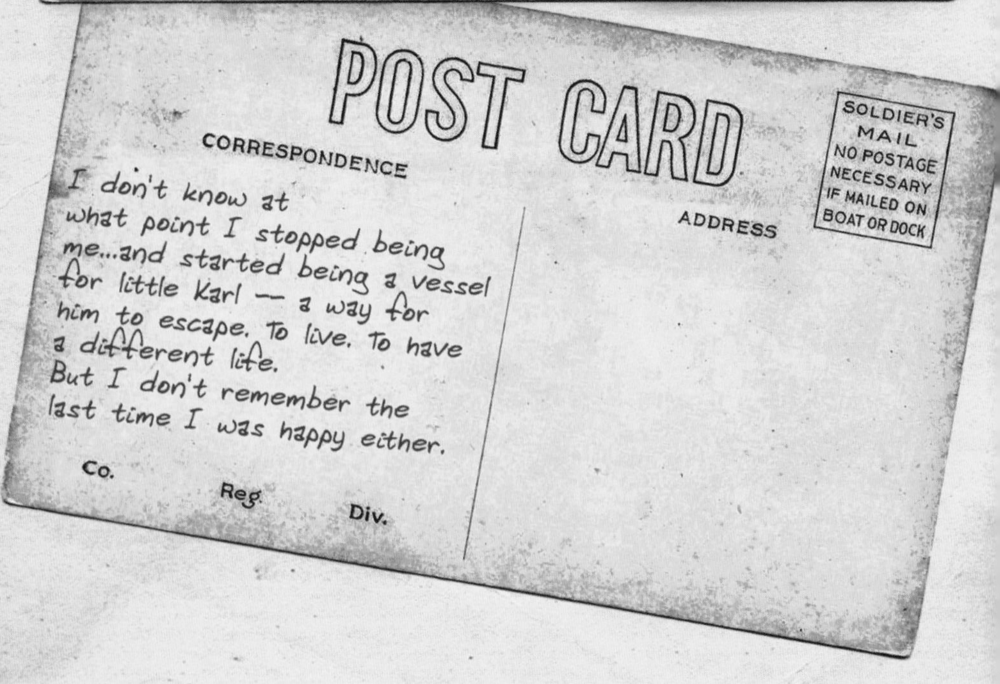
POST CARD

CORRESPONDENCE

I don't know at
what point I stopped being
me...and started being a vessel
for little Karl — a way for
him to escape. To live. To have
a different life.
But I don't remember the
last time I was happy either.

Co.

Reg.

Div.

ADDRESS

SOLDIER'S
MAIL
NO POSTAGE
NECESSARY
IF MAILED ON
BOAT OR DOCK

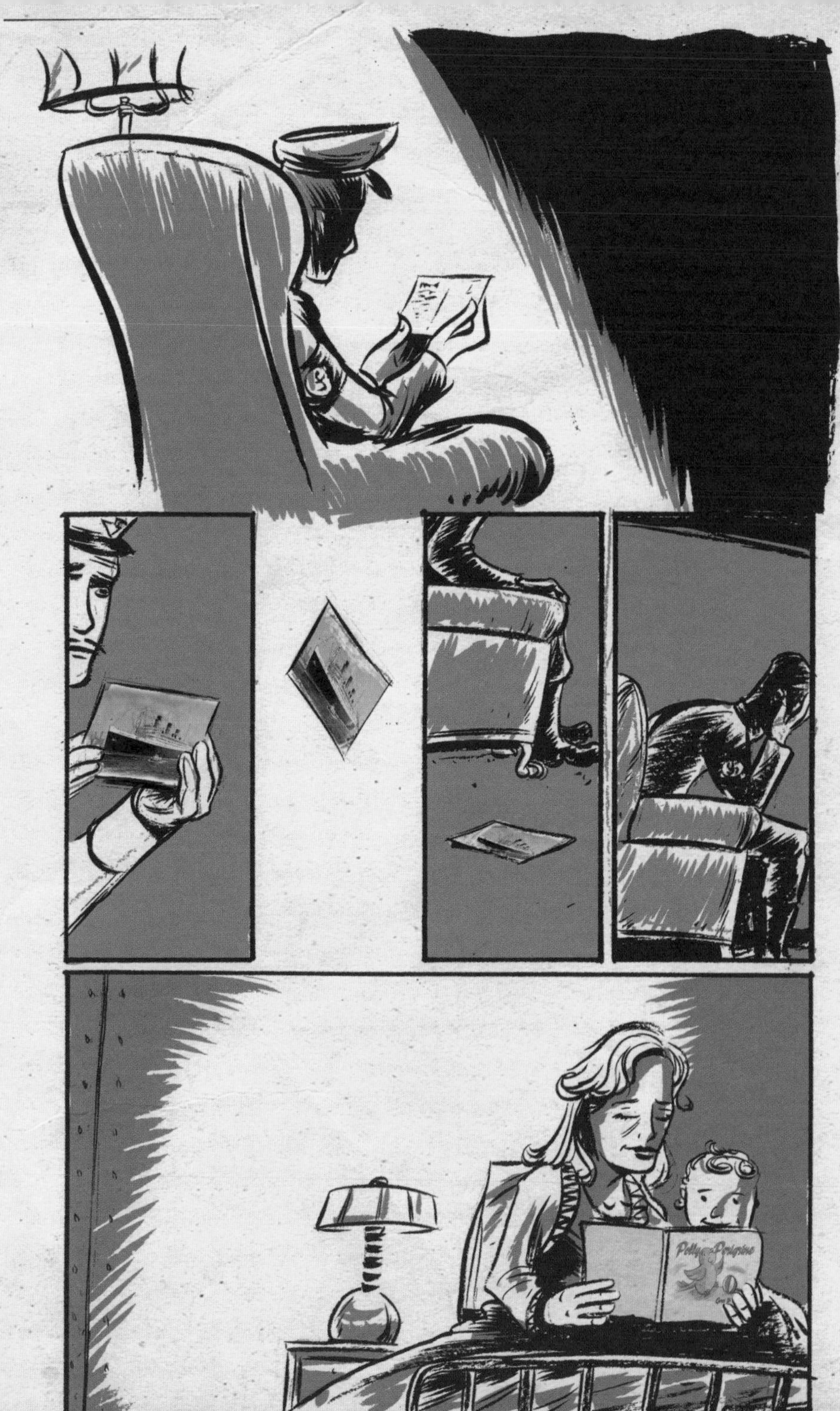

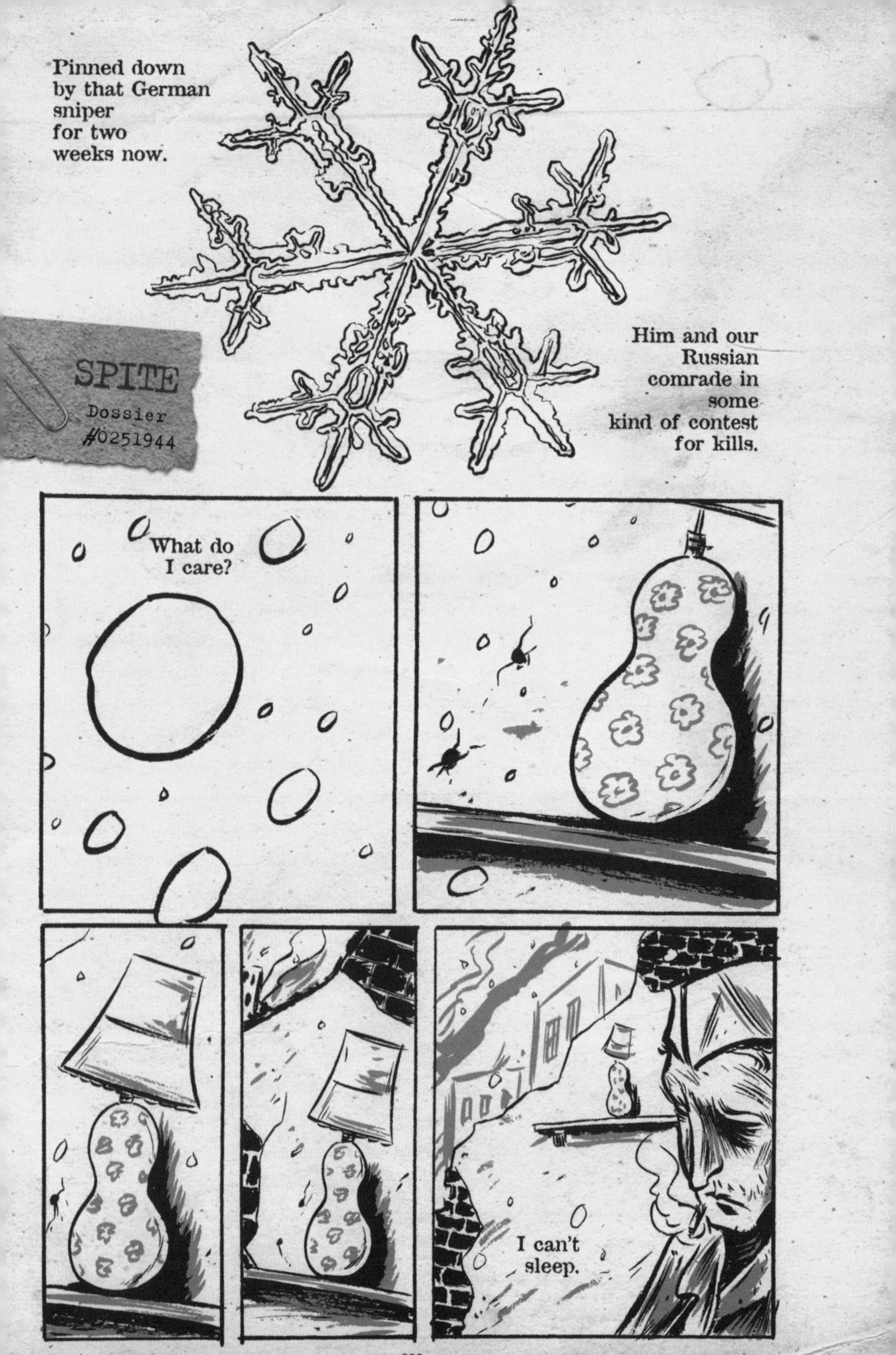
Pinned down by that German sniper for two weeks now.
SPITE
Dossier #0251944
Him and our Russian comrade in some kind of contest for kills.
What do I care?
I can't sleep.

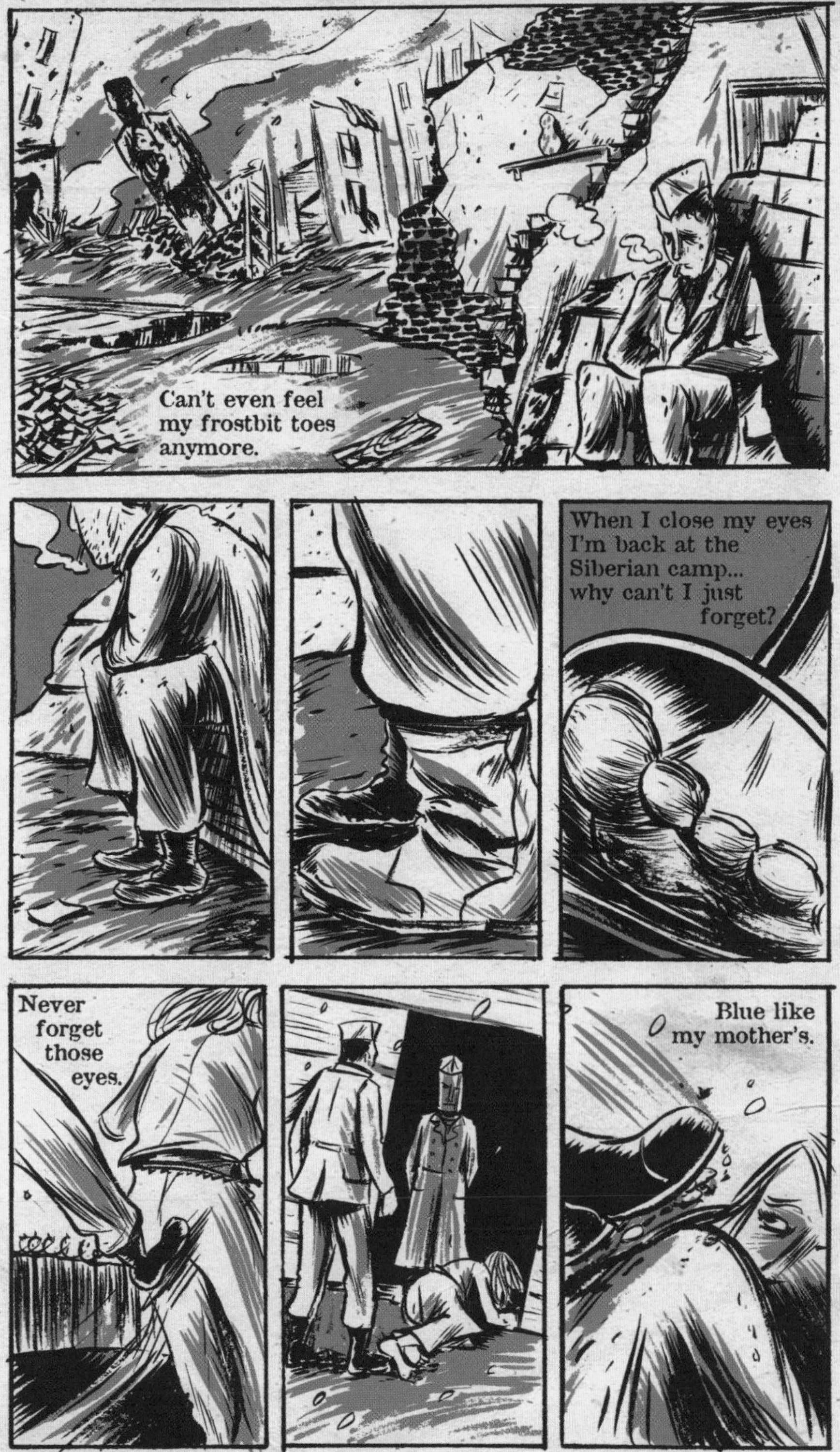
Can't even feel
my frostbit toes
anymore.
When I close my eyes
I'm back at the
Siberian camp...
why can't I just
forget?
Never
forget
those
eyes.
Blue like
my mother's.

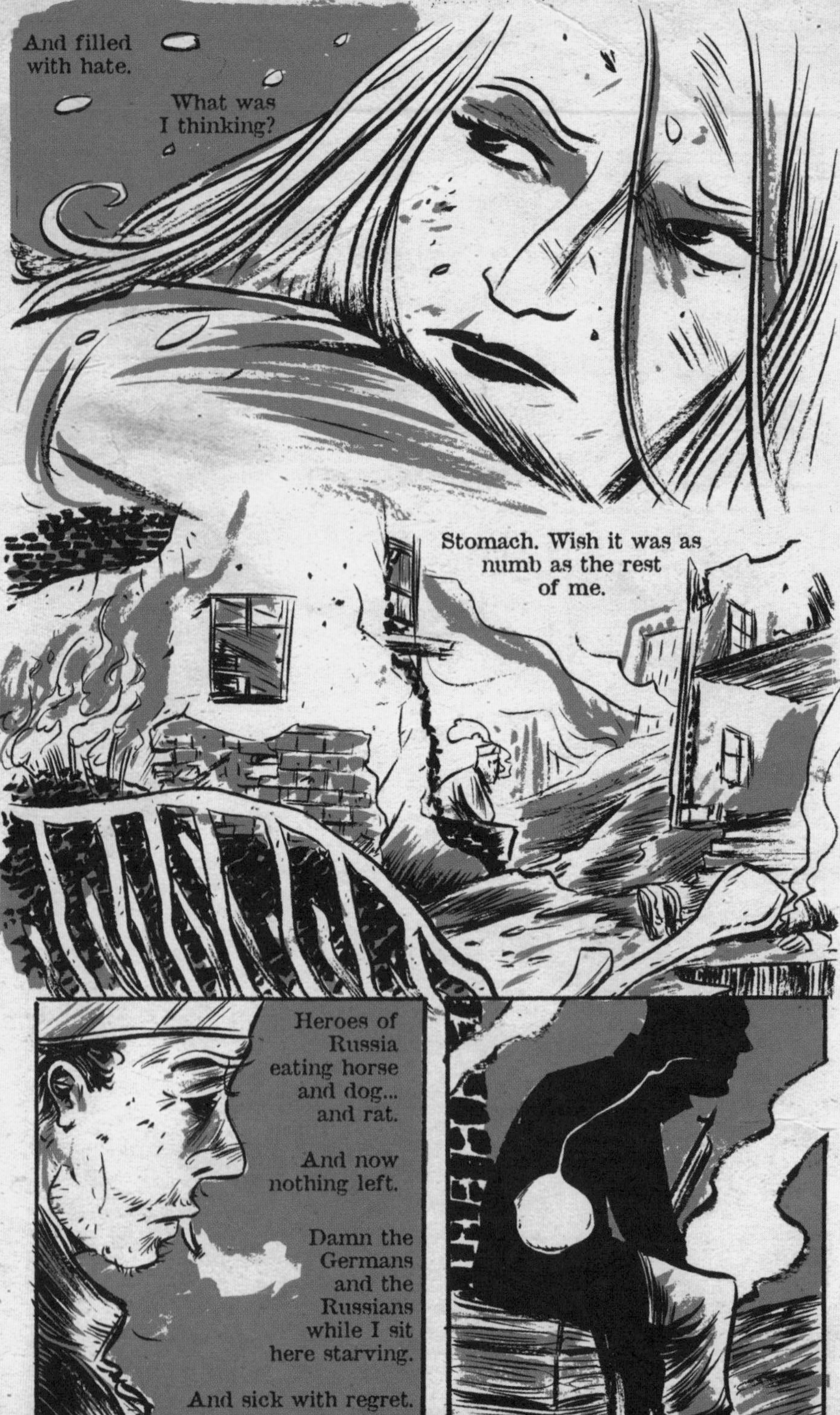
And filled with hate.
What was I thinking?
Stomach. Wish it was as numb as the rest of me.
Heroes of Russia eating horse and dog... and rat.
And now nothing left.
Damn the Germans and the Russians while I sit here starving.
And sick with regret.

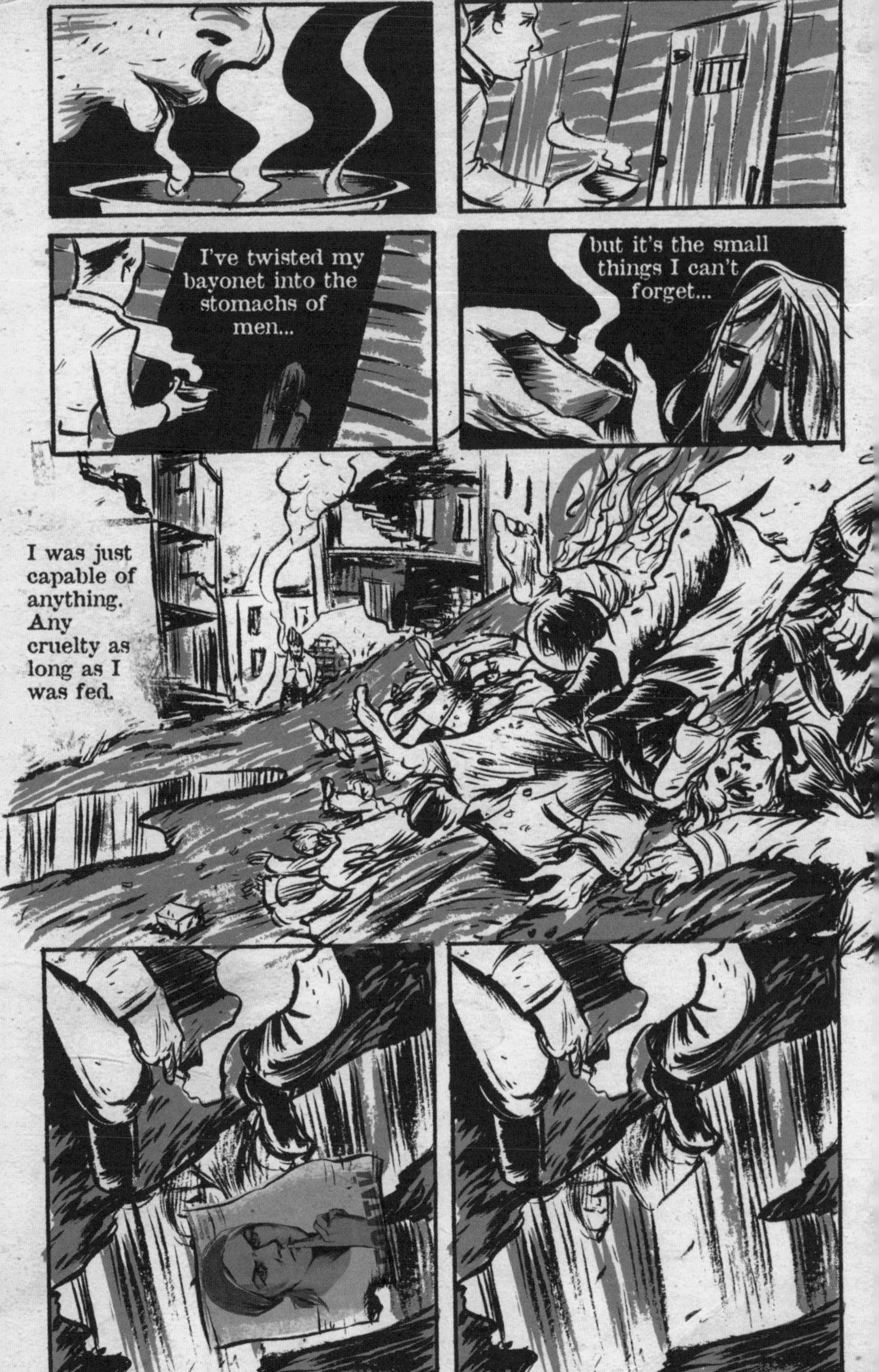
I've twisted my bayonet into the stomachs of men...
but it's the small things I can't forget...
I was just capable of anything. Any cruelty as long as I was fed.

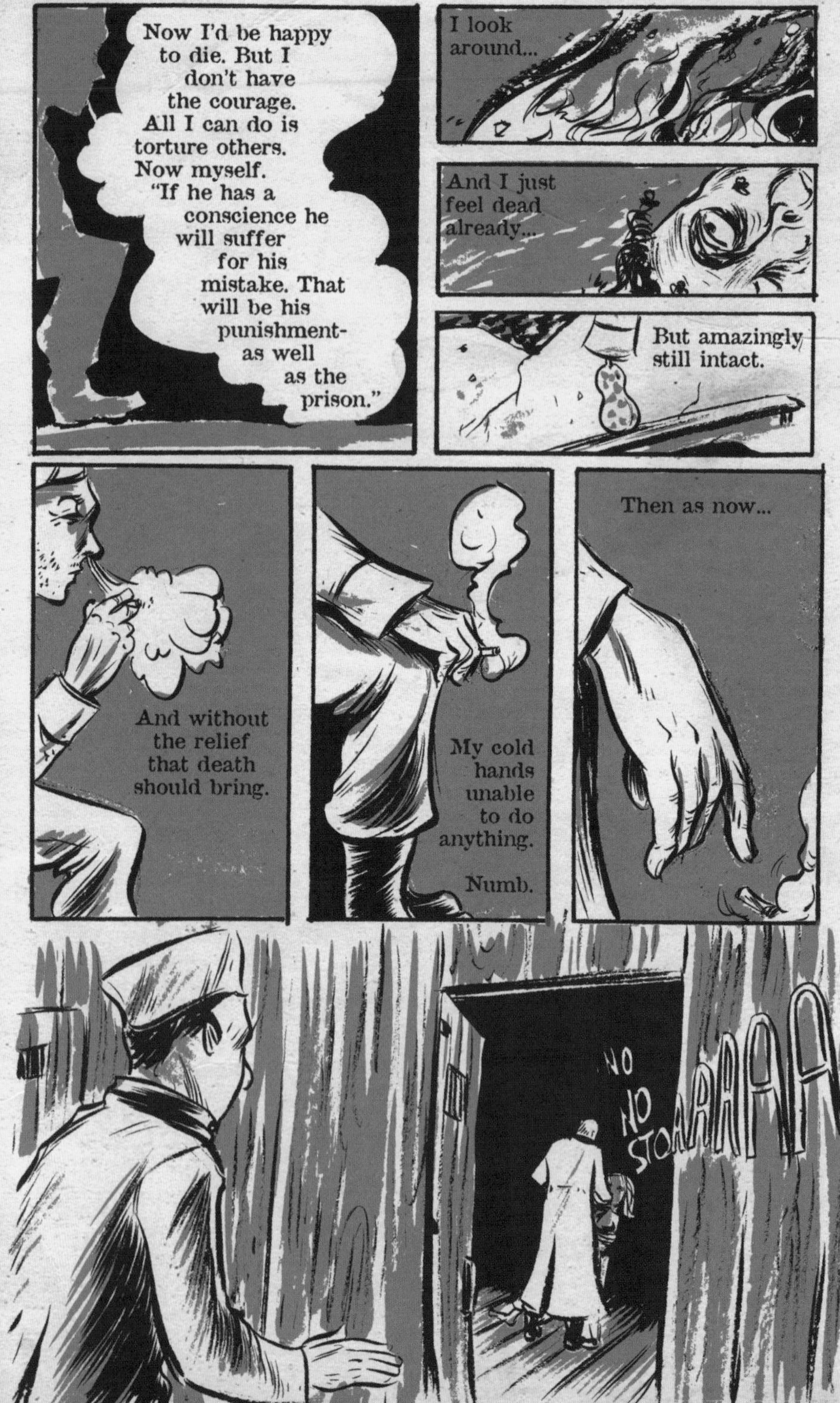

Now I'd be happy to die. But I don't have the courage. All I can do is torture others. Now myself. "If he has a conscience he will suffer for his mistake. That will be his punishment- as well as the prison."
I look around...
And I just feel dead already...
But amazingly still intact.
And without the relief that death should bring.
My cold hands unable to do anything.
Numb.
Then as now...
NO
NO
STOAAAAAA

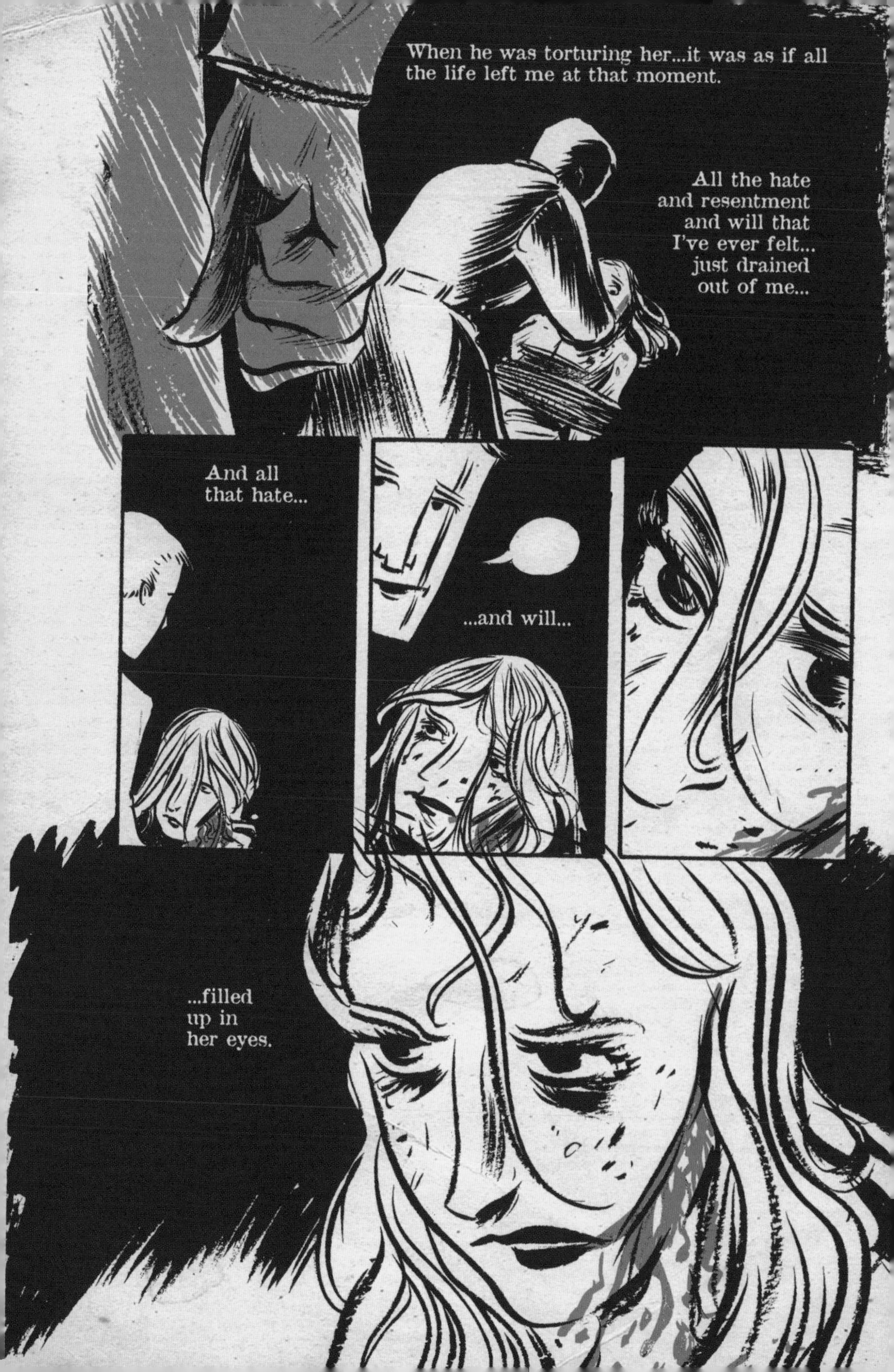

When he was torturing her...it was as if all the life left me at that moment.
All the hate and resentment and will that I've ever felt... just drained out of me...
And all that hate...
...and will...
...filled up in her eyes.

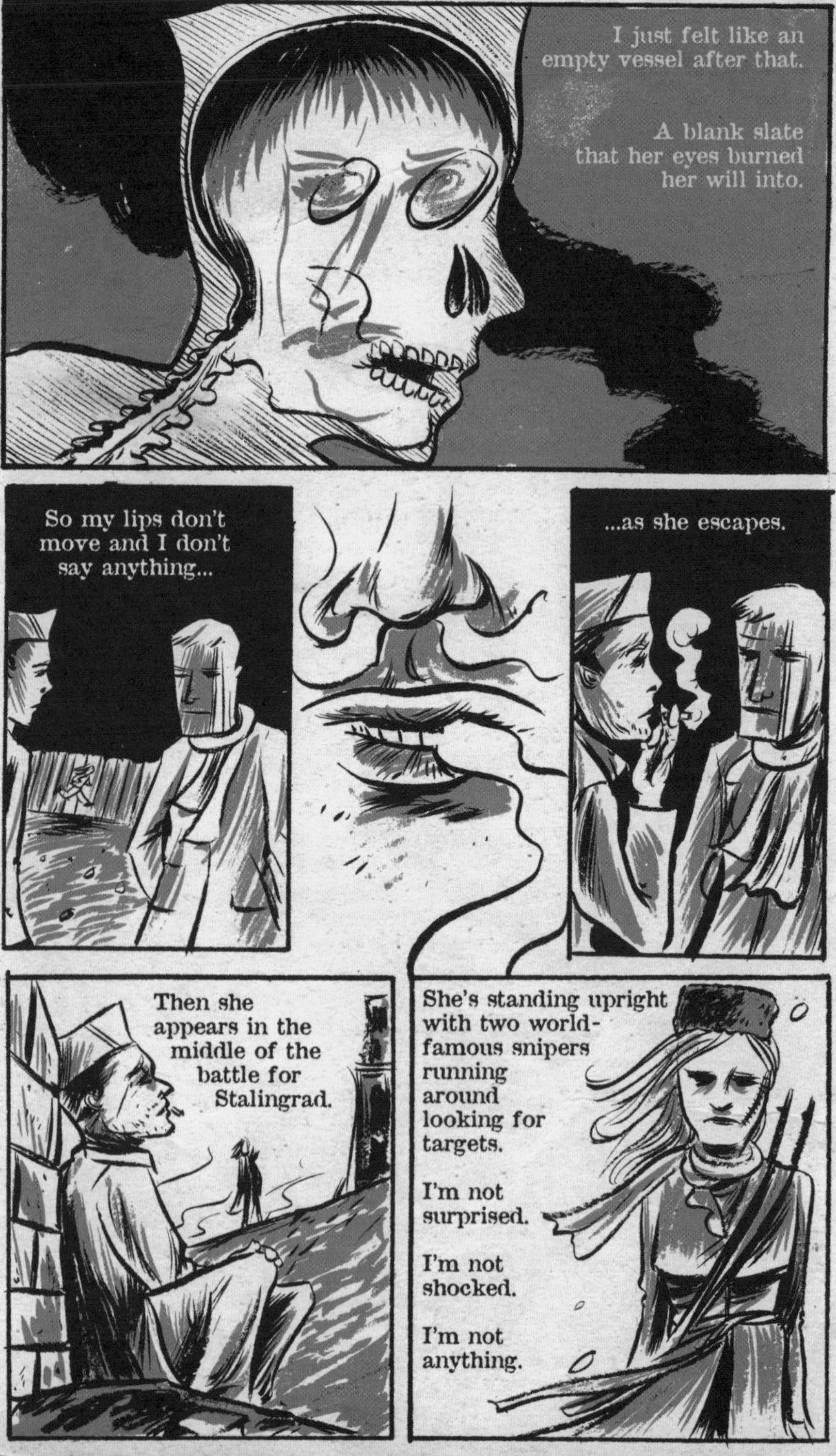
I just felt like an empty vessel after that.
A blank slate that her eyes burned her will into.
So my lips don't move and I don't say anything...
...as she escapes.
Then she appears in the middle of the battle for Stalingrad.
She's standing upright with two world-famous snipers running around looking for targets.
I'm not surprised.
I'm not shocked.
I'm not anything.

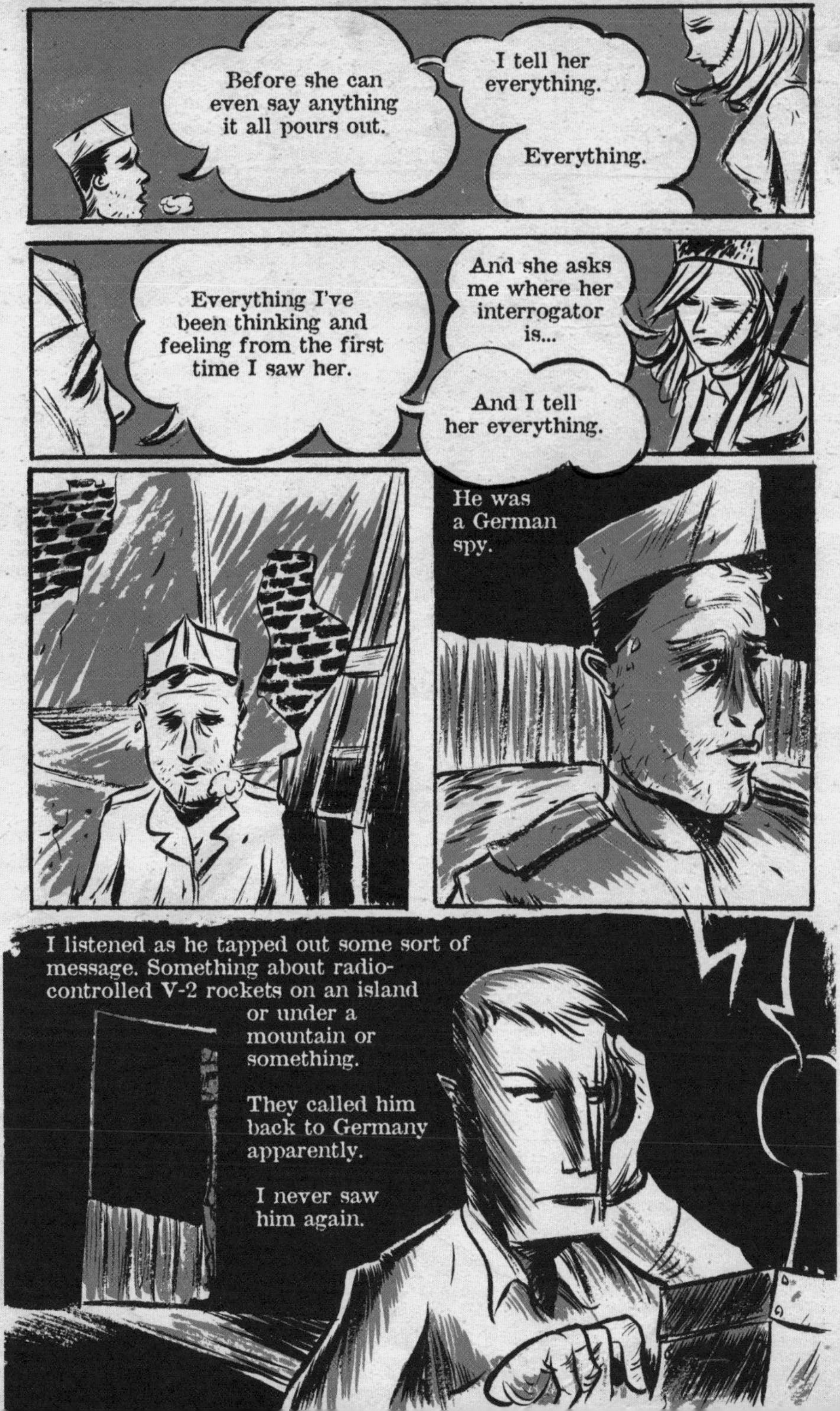
Before she can even say anything it all pours out.
I tell her everything.
Everything.
Everything I've been thinking and feeling from the first time I saw her.
And she asks me where her interrogator is...
And I tell her everything.
He was a German spy.
I listened as he tapped out some sort of message. Something about radio-controlled V-2 rockets on an island or under a mountain or something.
They called him back to Germany apparently.
I never saw him again.

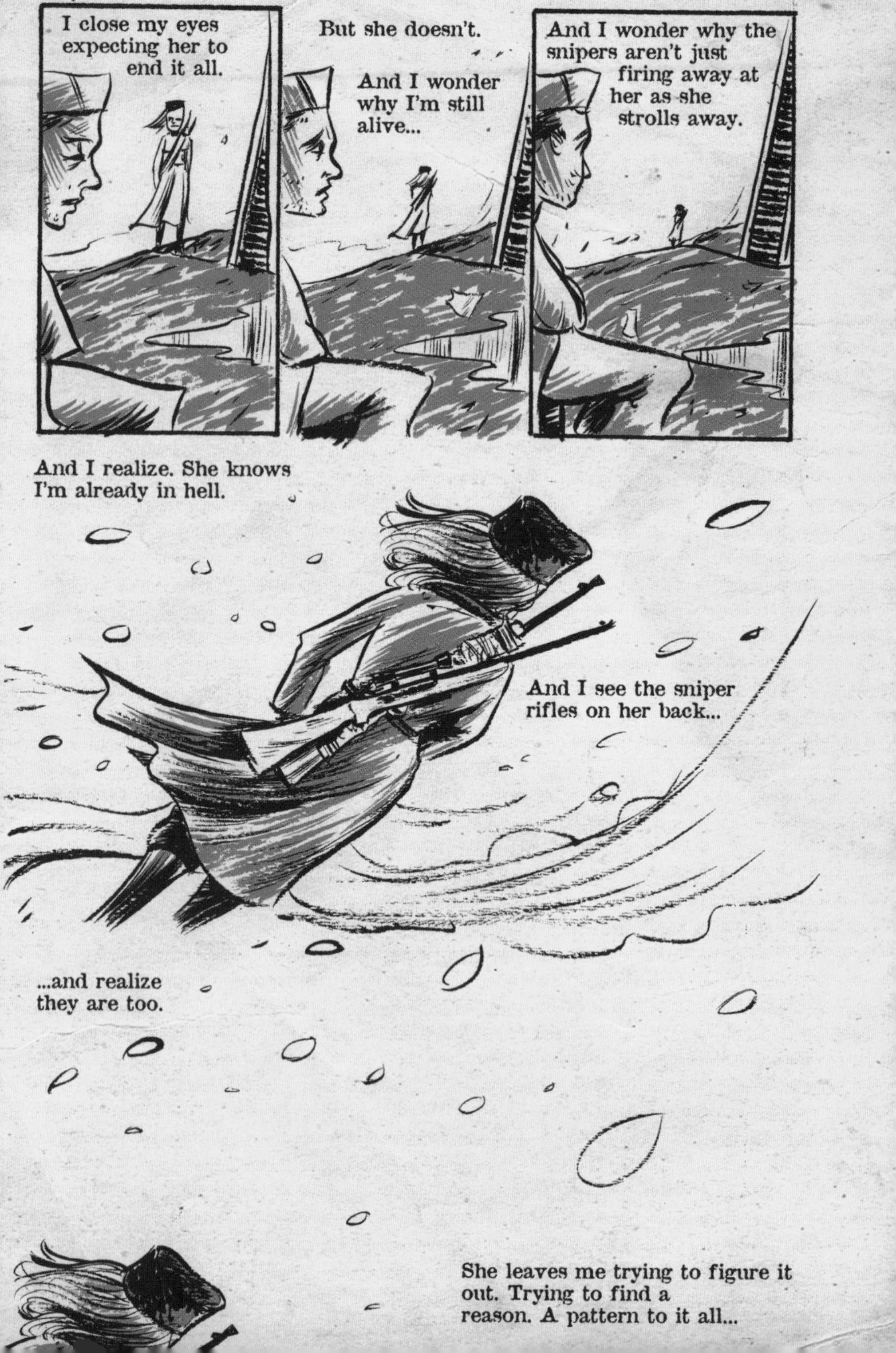
I close my eyes expecting her to end it all.
But she doesn't.
And I wonder why I'm still alive...
And I wonder why the snipers aren't just firing away at her as she strolls away.
And I realize. She knows I'm already in hell.
And I see the sniper rifles on her back...
...and realize they are too.
She leaves me trying to figure it out. Trying to find a reason. A pattern to it all...

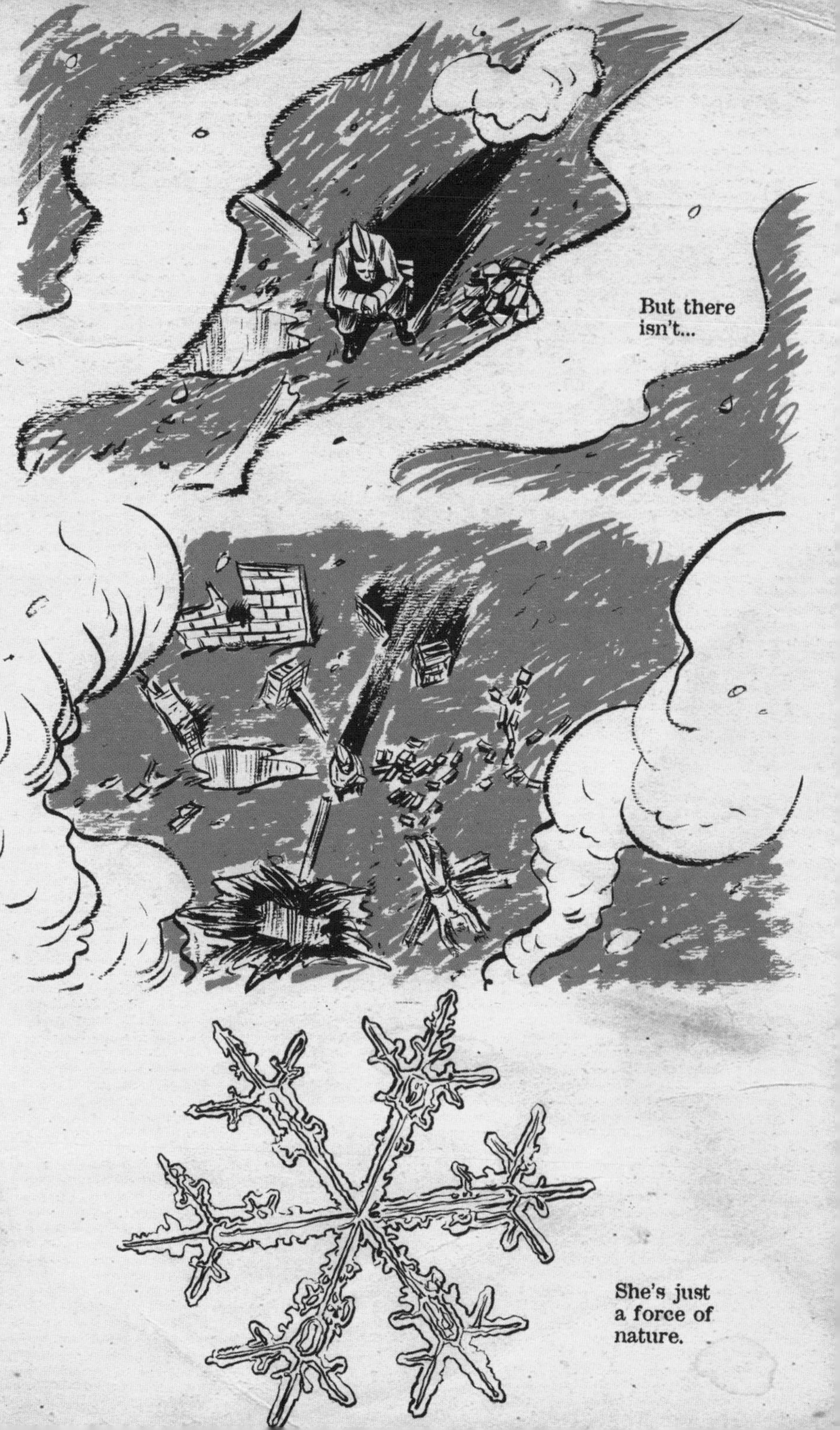
But there isn't...
She's just a force of nature.

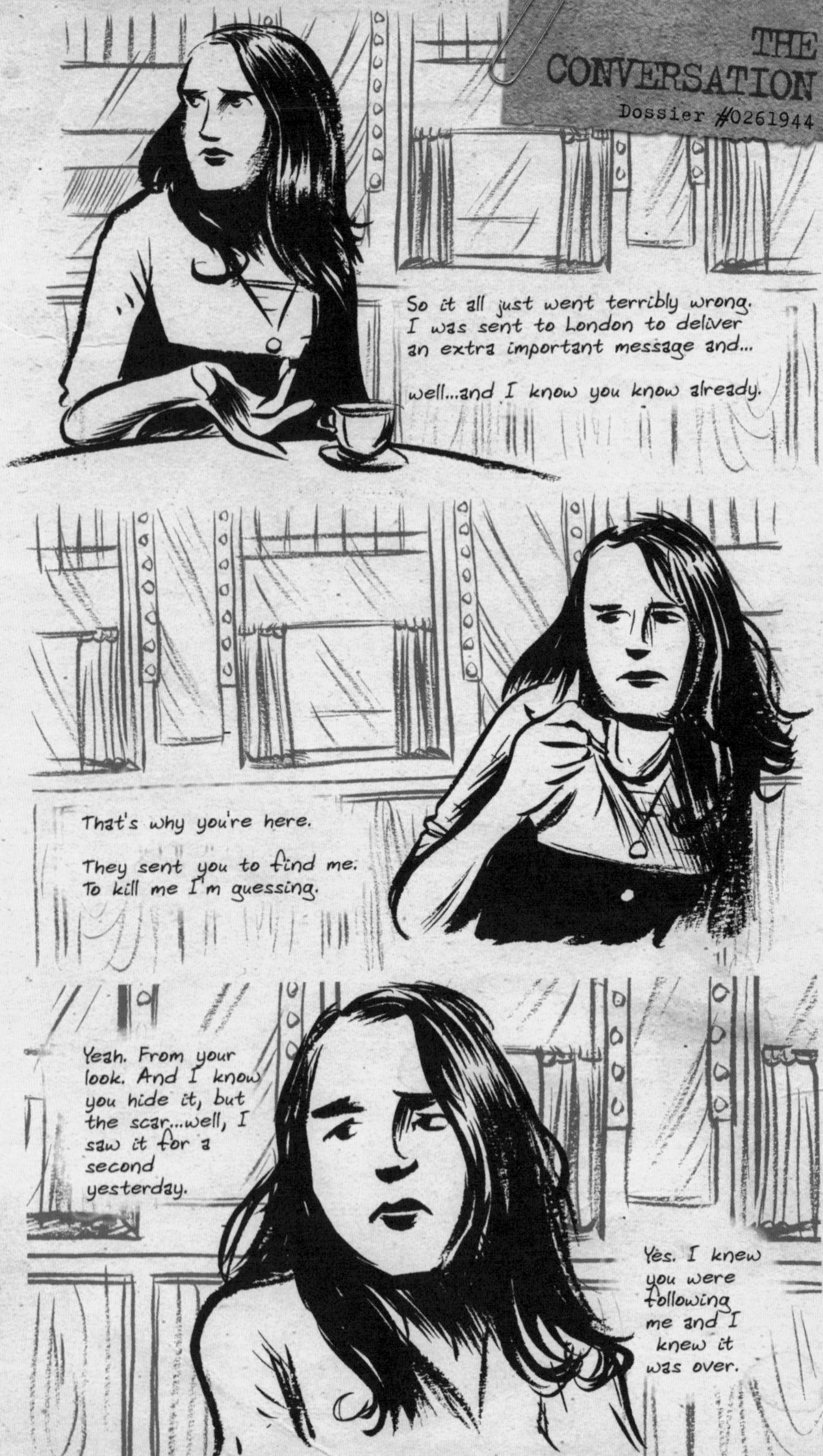
THE CONVERSATION
Dossier #0261944
So it all just went terribly wrong. I was sent to London to deliver an extra important message and...
well...and I know you know already.
That's why you're here.
They sent you to find me. To kill me I'm guessing.
Yeah. From your look. And I know you hide it, but the scar...well, I saw it for a second yesterday.
Yes. I knew you were following me and I knew it was over.

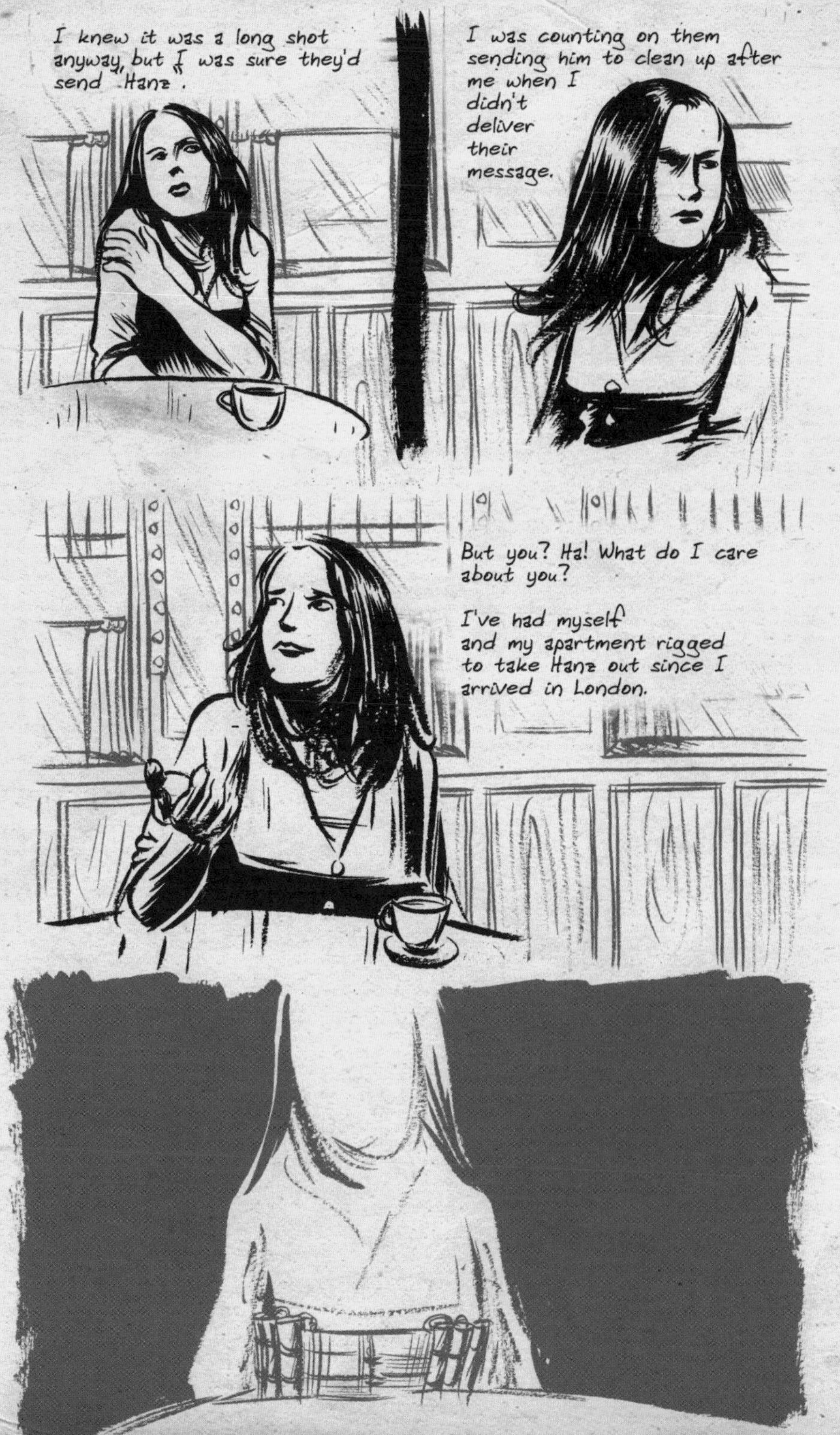
I knew it was a long shot anyway, but I was sure they'd send "Hanz".
I was counting on them sending him to clean up after me when I didn't deliver their message.
But you? Ha! What do I care about you?
I've had myself and my apartment rigged to take Hanz out since I arrived in London.

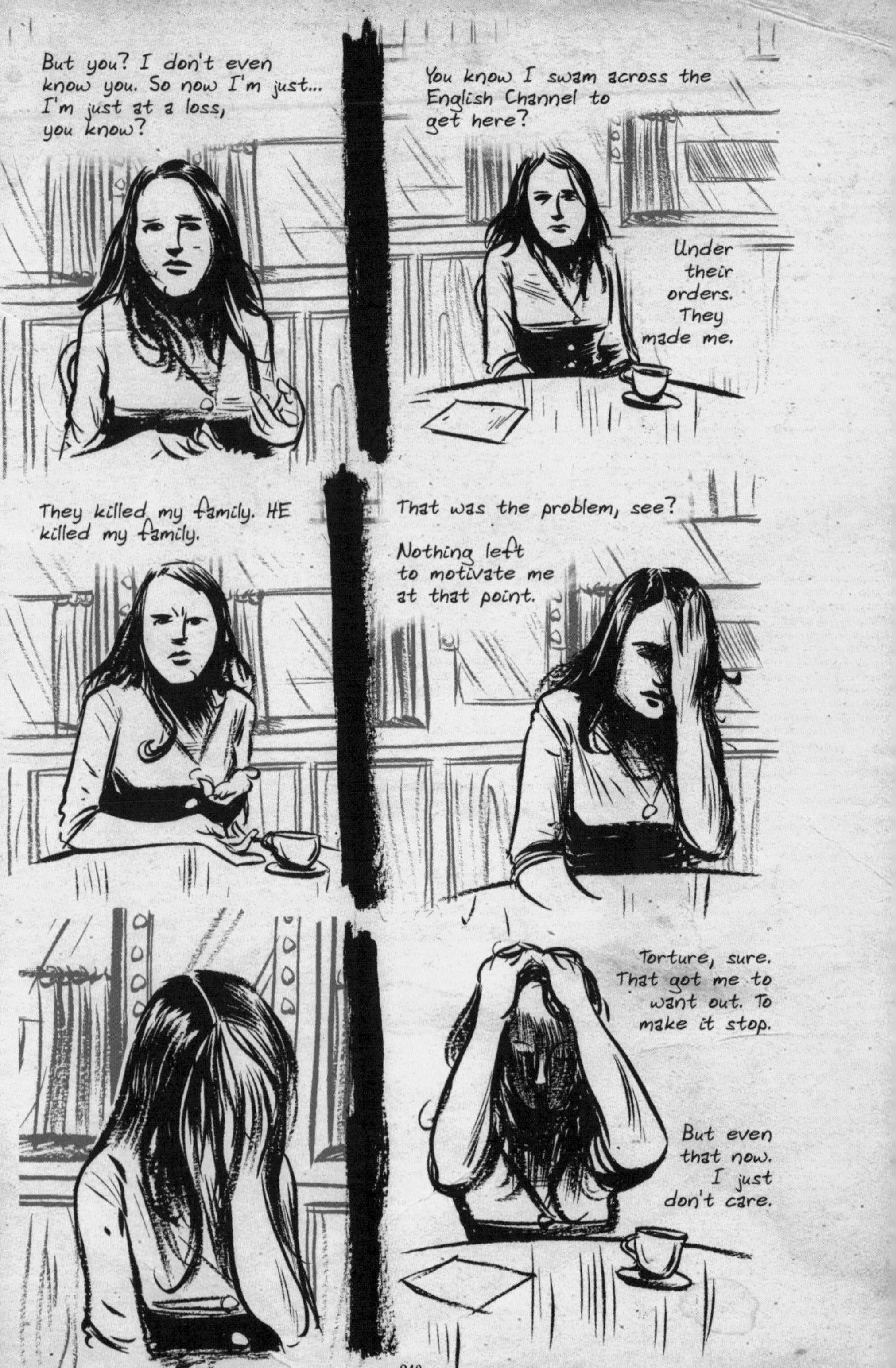
But you? I don't even know you. So now I'm just... I'm just at a loss, you know?
You know I swam across the English Channel to get here?
Under their orders. They made me.
They killed my family. HE killed my family.
That was the problem, see?
Nothing left to motivate me at that point.
Torture, sure. That got me to want out. To make it stop.
But even that now. I just don't care.

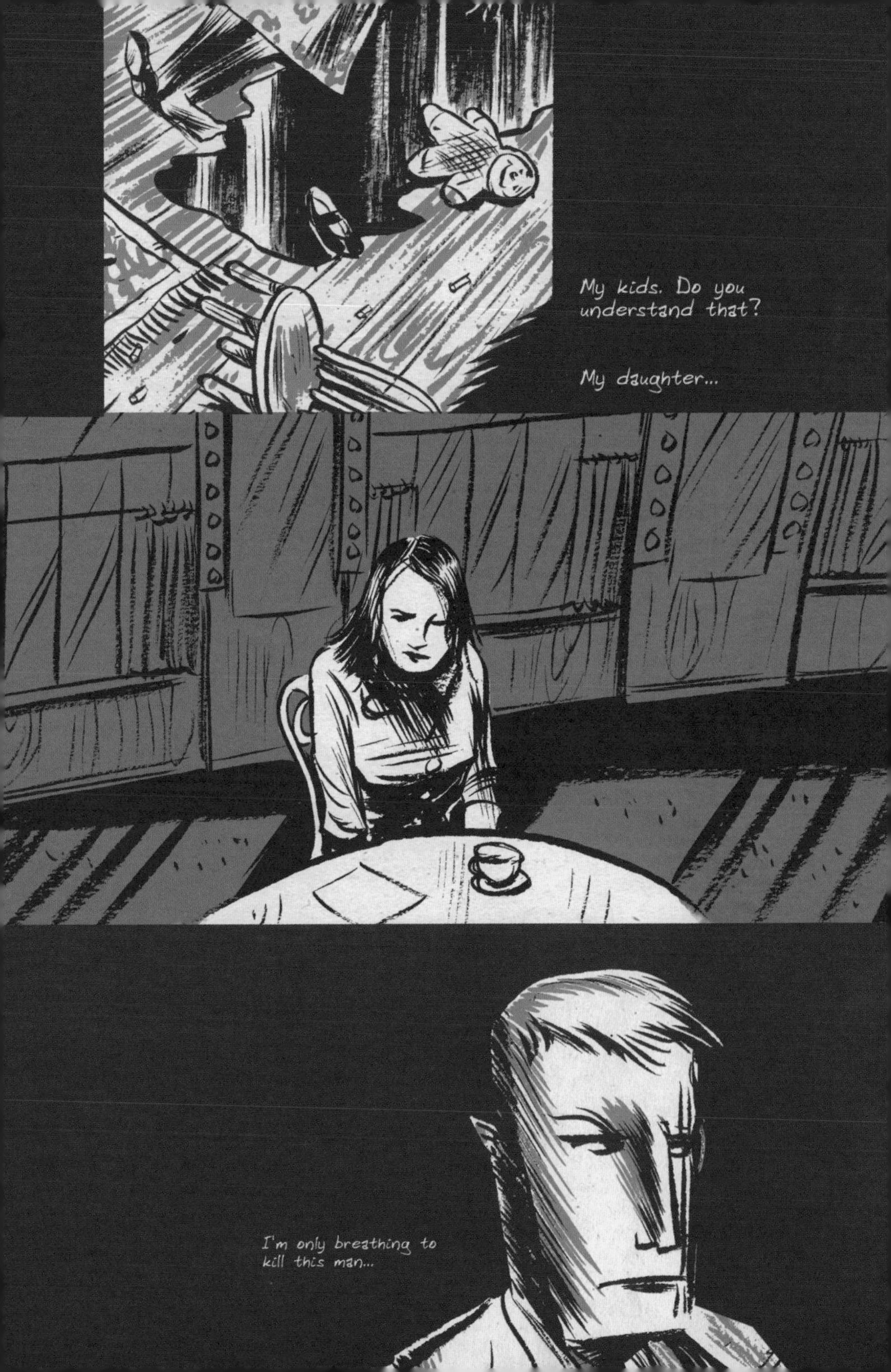
My kids. Do you understand that?
My daughter...
I'm only breathing to kill this man...

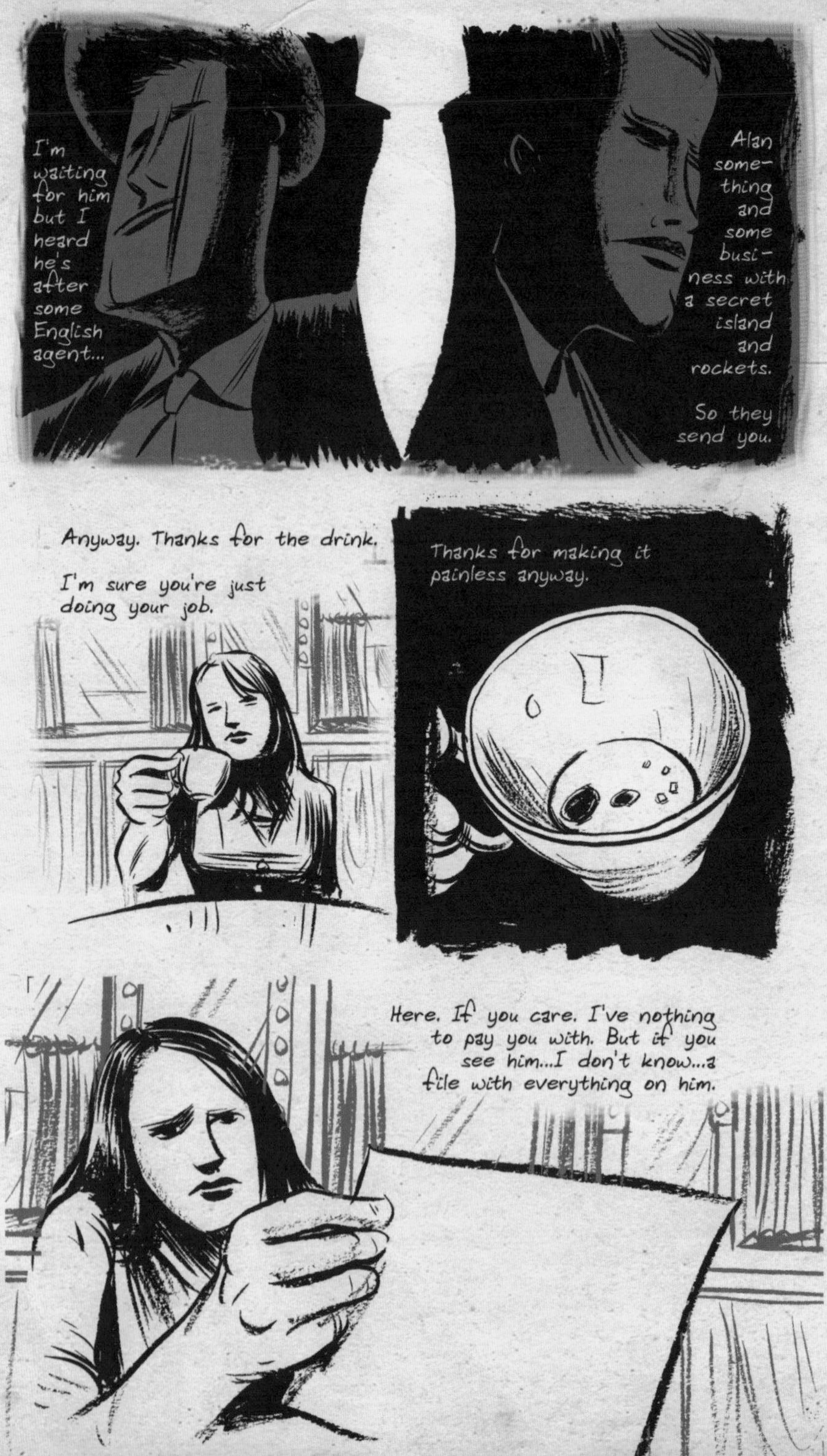

I'm waiting for him but I heard he's after some English agent...
Alan something and some business with a secret island and rockets.
So they send you.
Anyway. Thanks for the drink.
I'm sure you're just doing your job.
Thanks for making it painless anyway.
Here. If you care. I've nothing to pay you with. But if you see him...I don't know...a file with everything on him.

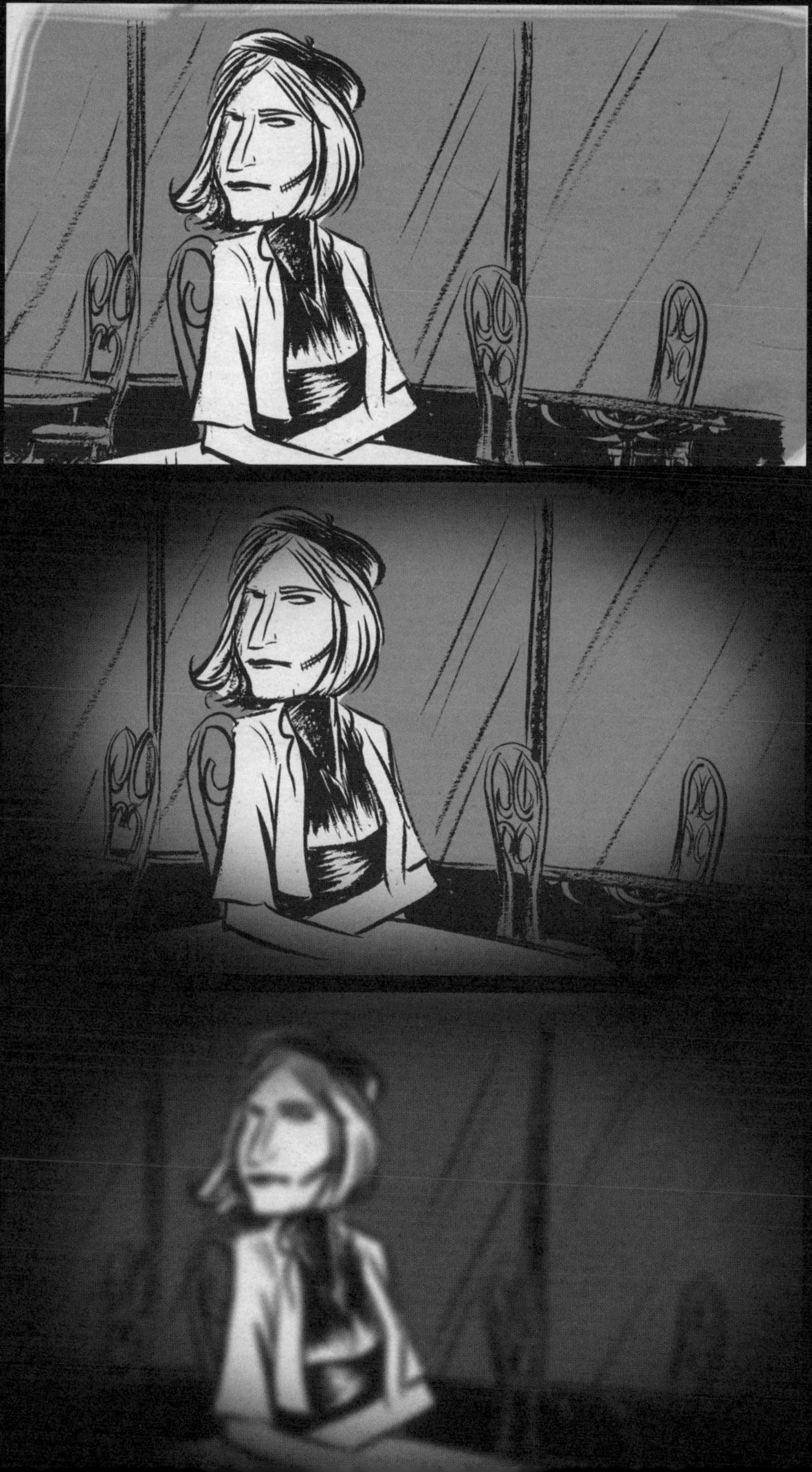

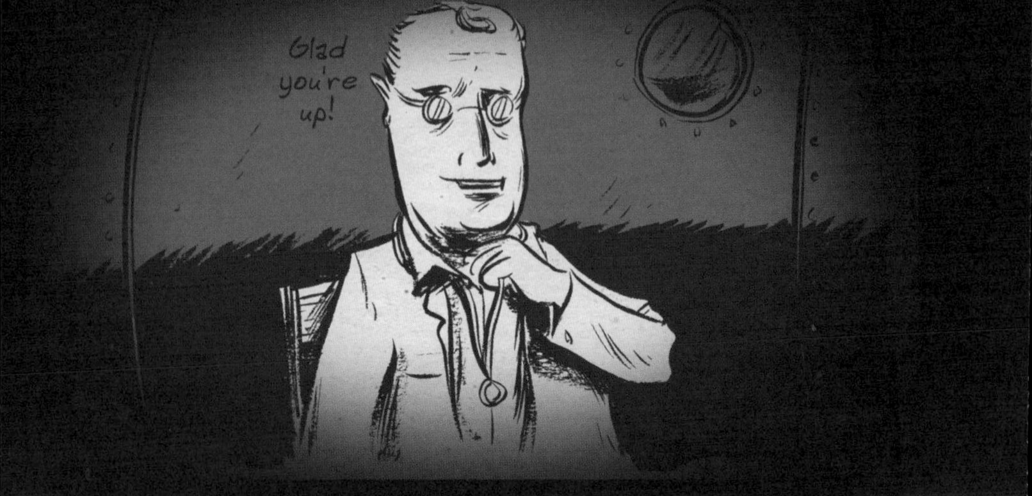
Glad you're up!

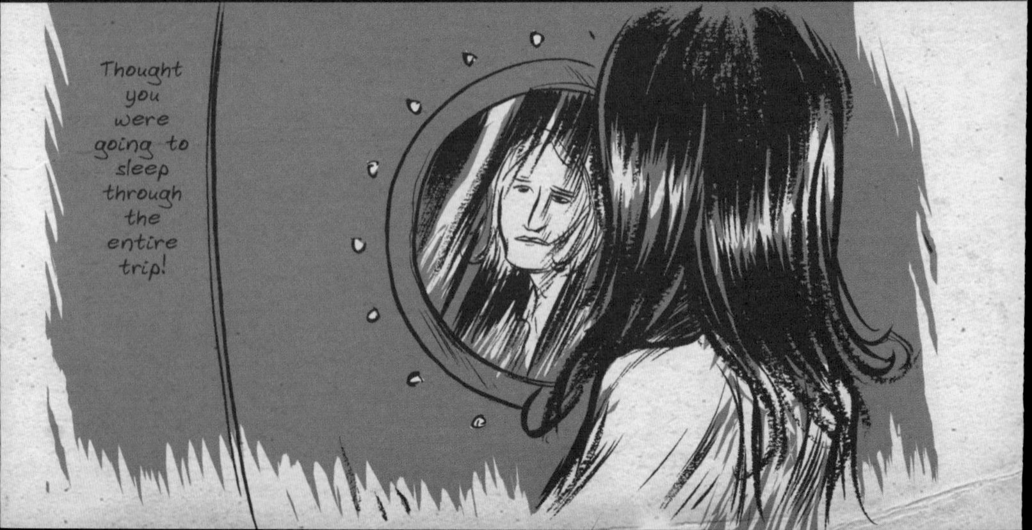
Thought you were going to sleep through the entire trip!

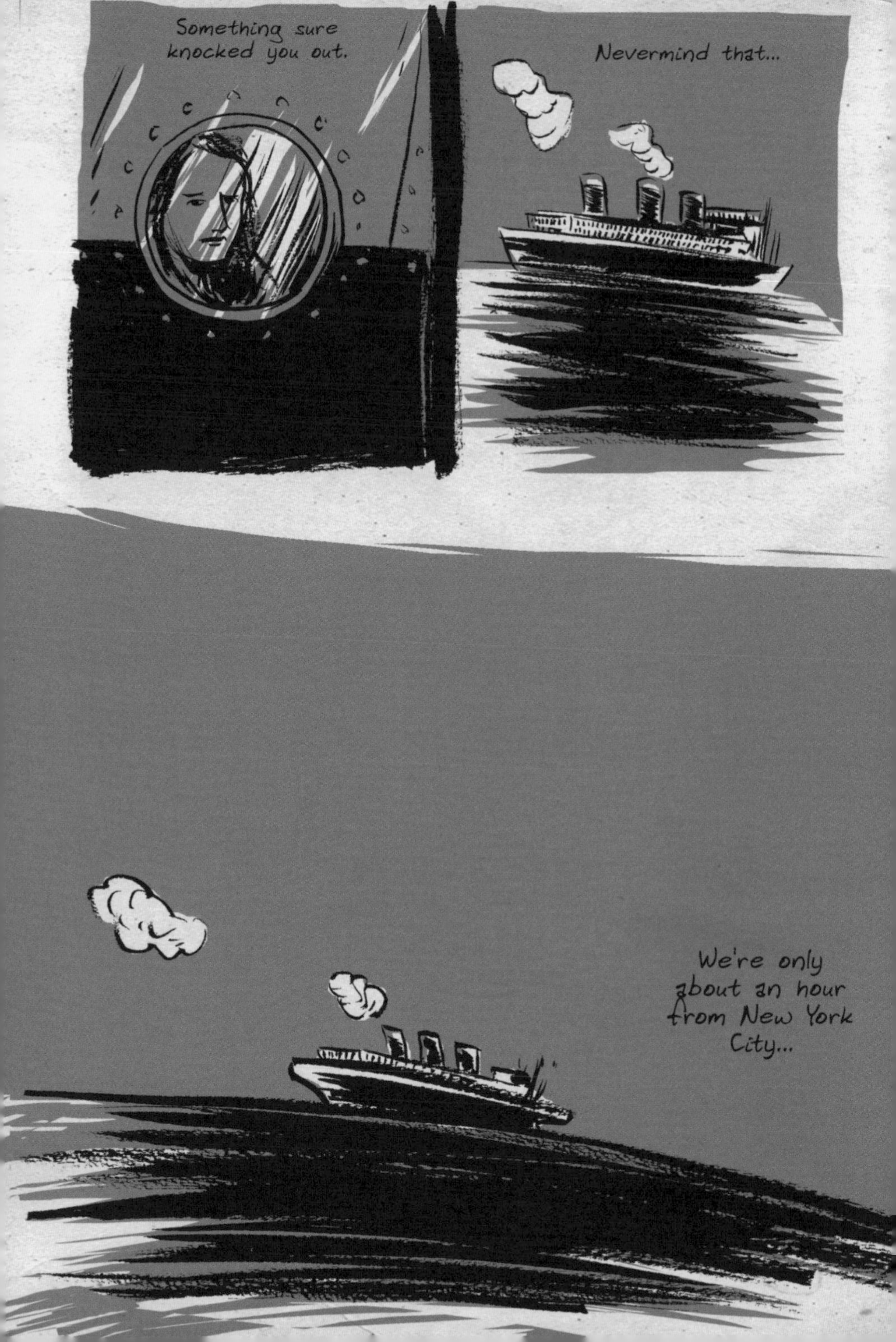
Something sure knocked you out.
Nevermind that...
We're only about an hour from New York City...

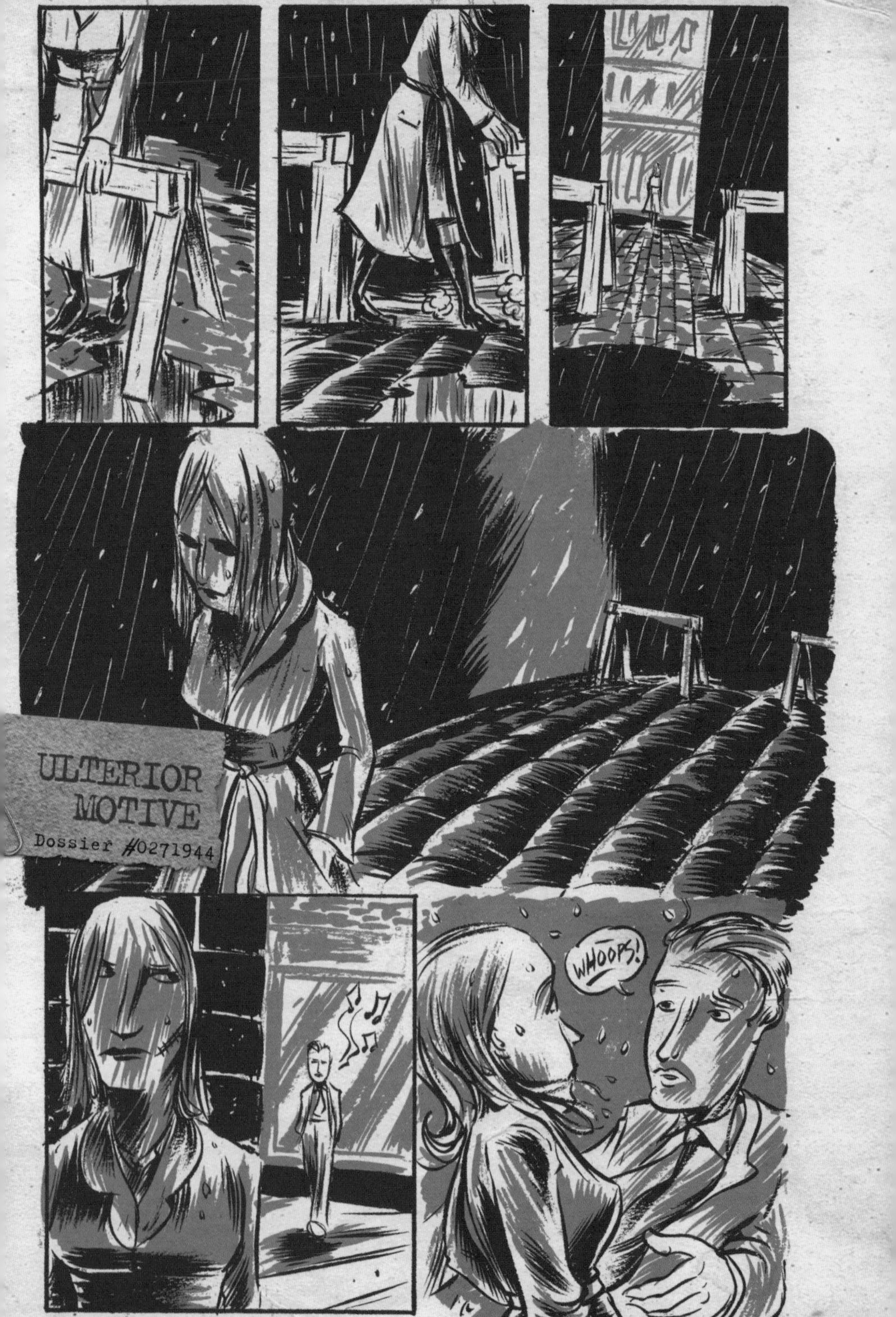
ULTERIOR MOTIVE
Dossier #0271944
WHOOPS!

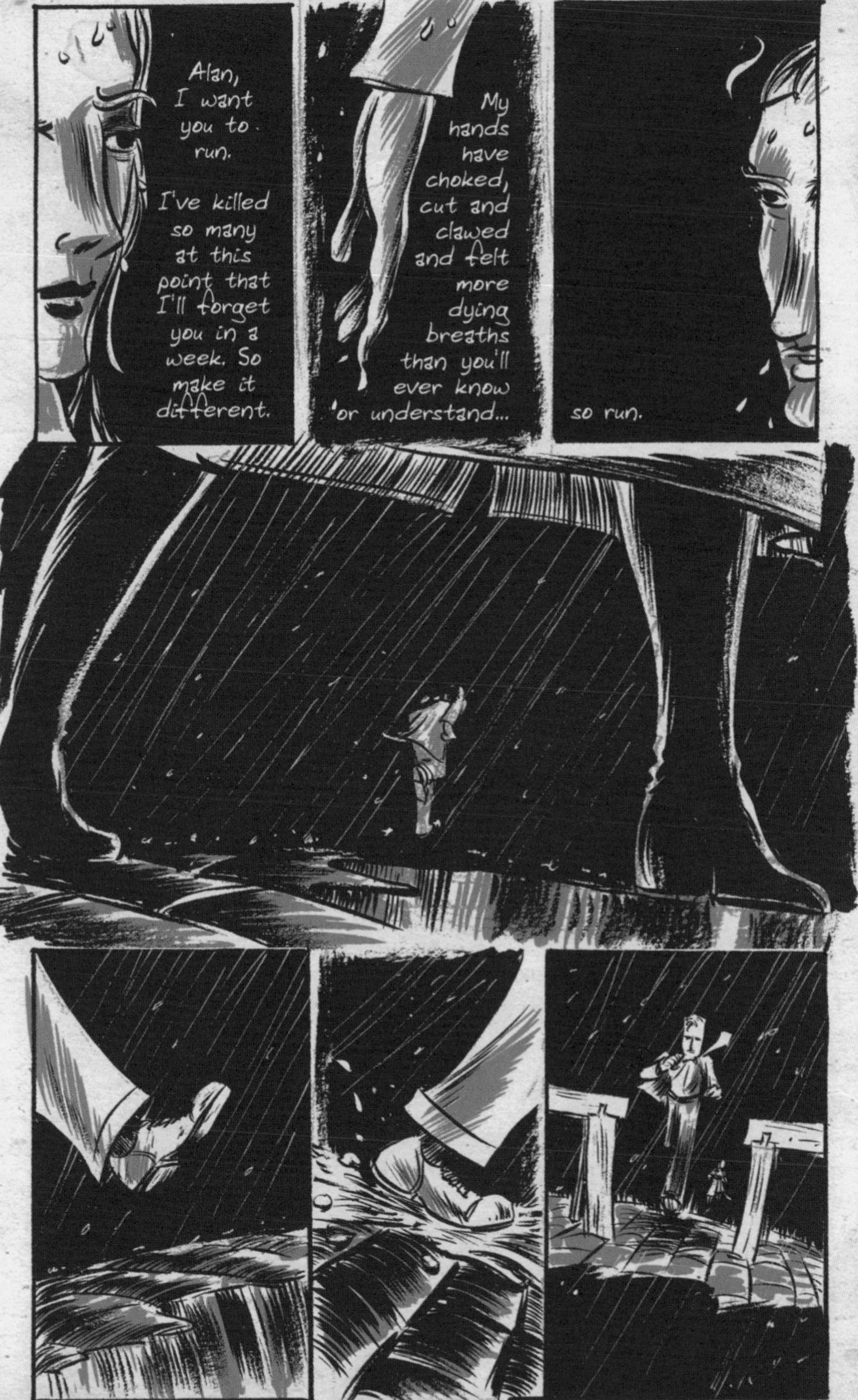
Alan, I want you to run.
I've killed so many at this point that I'll forget you in a week. So make it different.
My hands have choked, cut and clawed and felt more dying breaths than you'll ever know or understand...
so run.

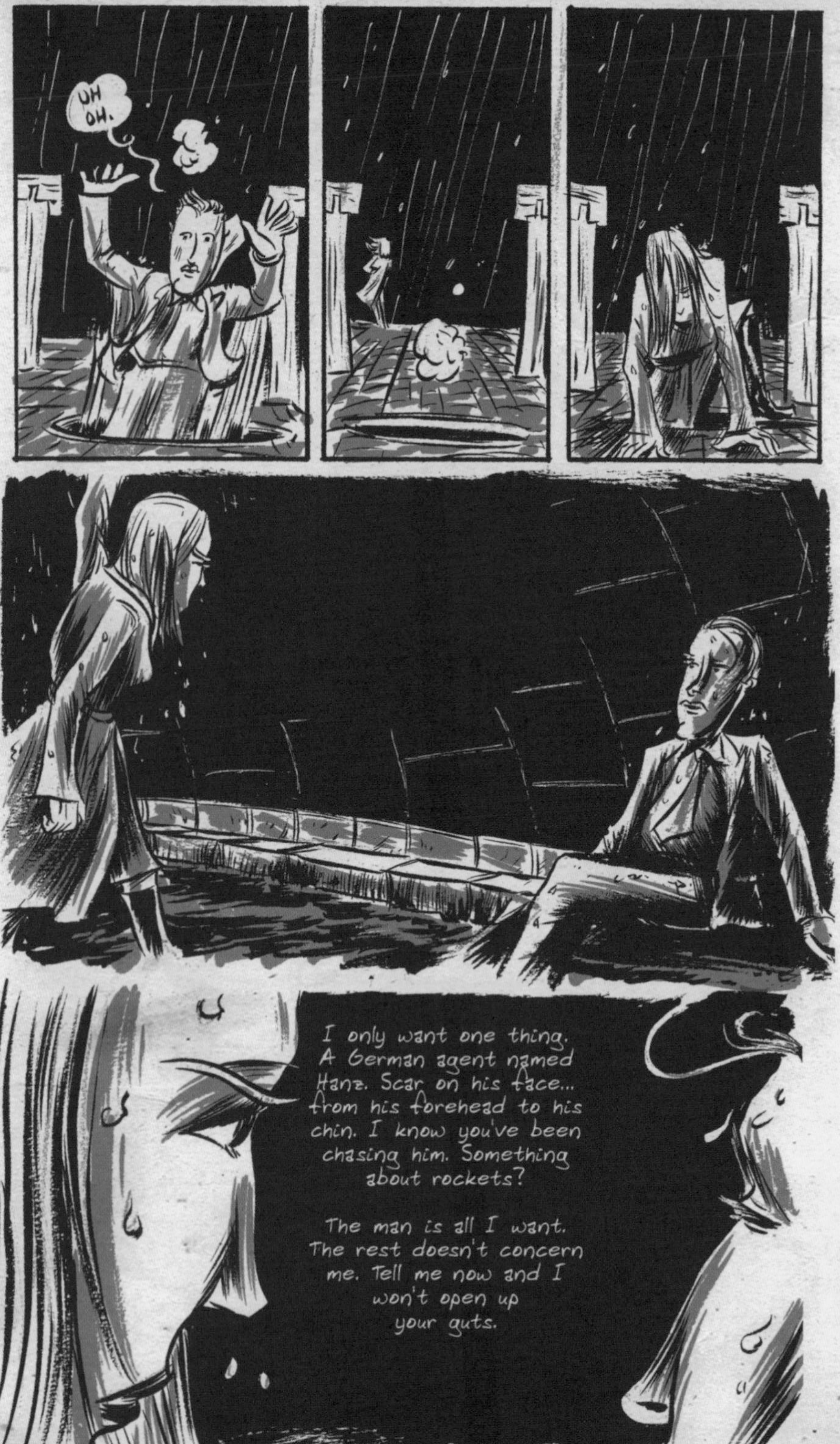
UH OH.
I only want one thing. A German agent named Hanz. Scar on his face... from his forehead to his chin. I know you've been chasing him. Something about rockets?
The man is all I want. The rest doesn't concern me. Tell me now and I won't open up your guts.

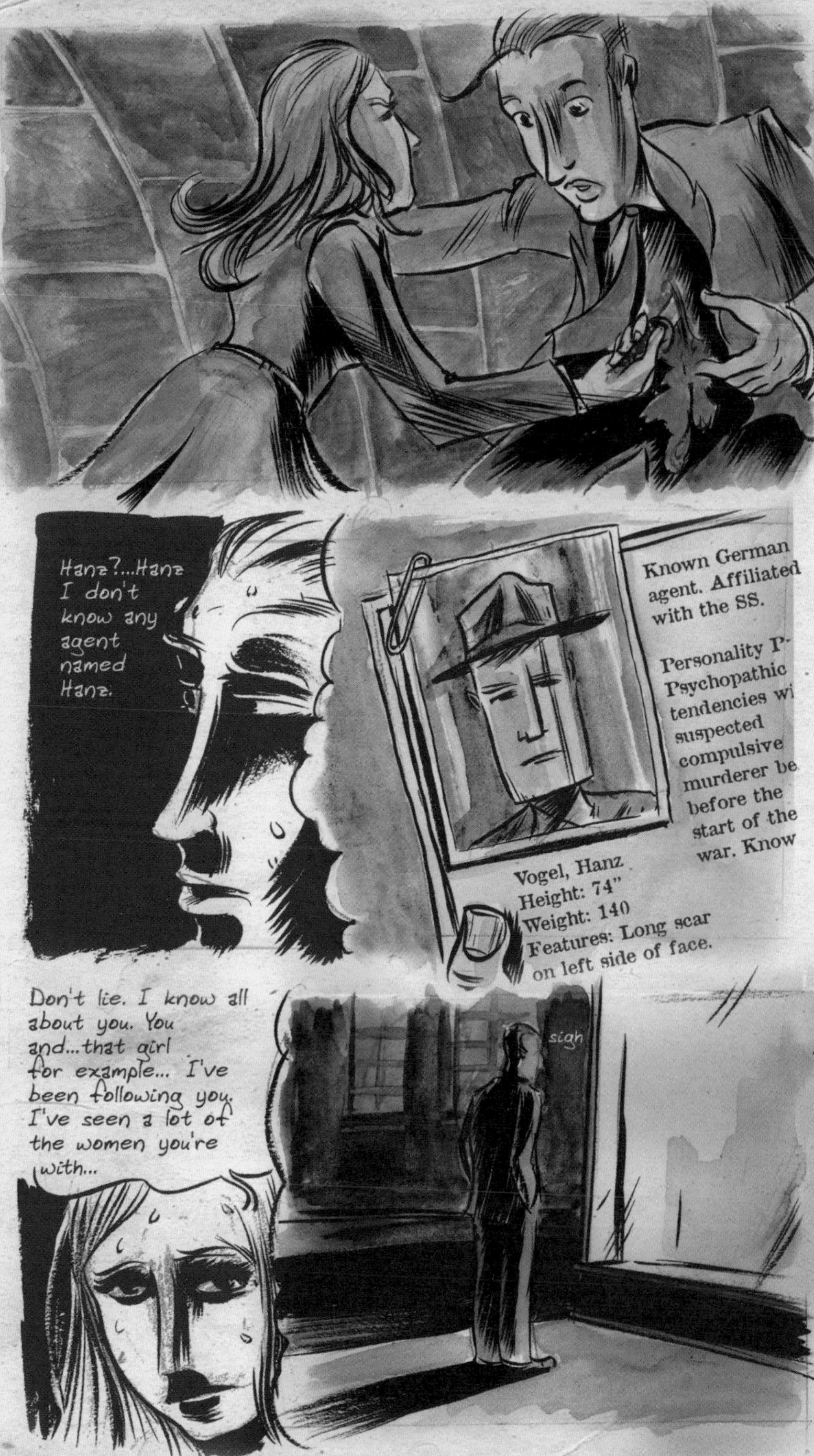

Hanz?....Hanz I don't know any agent named Hanz.
Known German agent. Affiliated with the SS.
Personality P-
Psychopathic tendencies wi
suspected compulsive murderer be
before the start of the war. Know
Vogel, Hanz
Height: 74"
Weight: 140
Features: Long scar on left side of face.
Don't lie. I know all about you. You and...that girl for example... I've been following you. I've seen a lot of the women you're with...
sigh

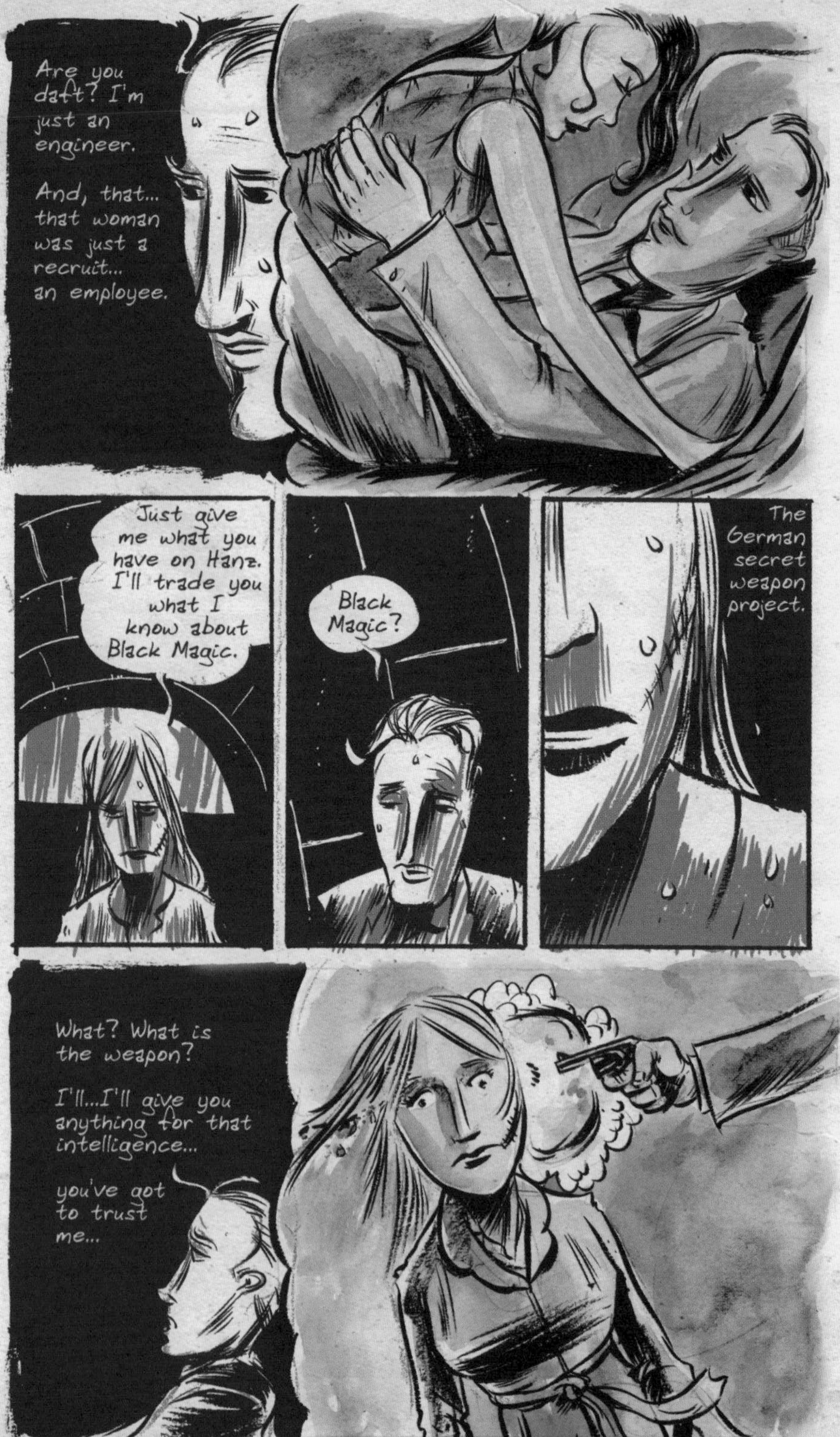
Are you daft? I'm just an engineer.
And, that... that woman was just a recruit... an employee.
Just give me what you have on Hanz. I'll trade you what I know about Black Magic.
Black Magic?
The German secret weapon project.
What? What is the weapon?
I'll...I'll give you anything for that intelligence...
you've got to trust me...

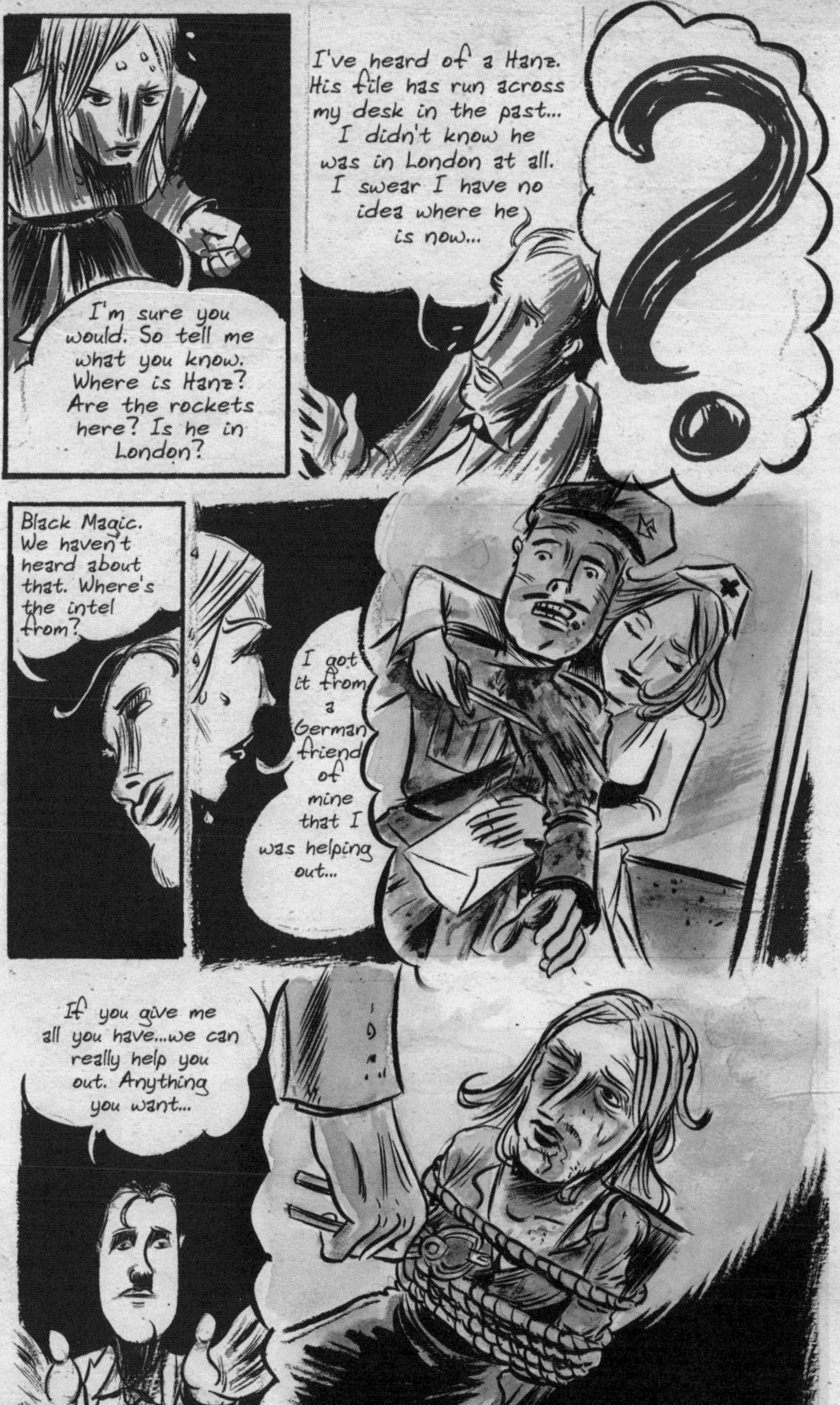
I'm sure you would. So tell me what you know. Where is Hanz? Are the rockets here? Is he in London?
I've heard of a Hanz. His file has run across my desk in the past... I didn't know he was in London at all. I swear I have no idea where he is now...
?
Black Magic. We haven't heard about that. Where's the intel from?
I got it from a German friend of mine that I was helping out...
If you give me all you have...we can really help you out. Anything you want...

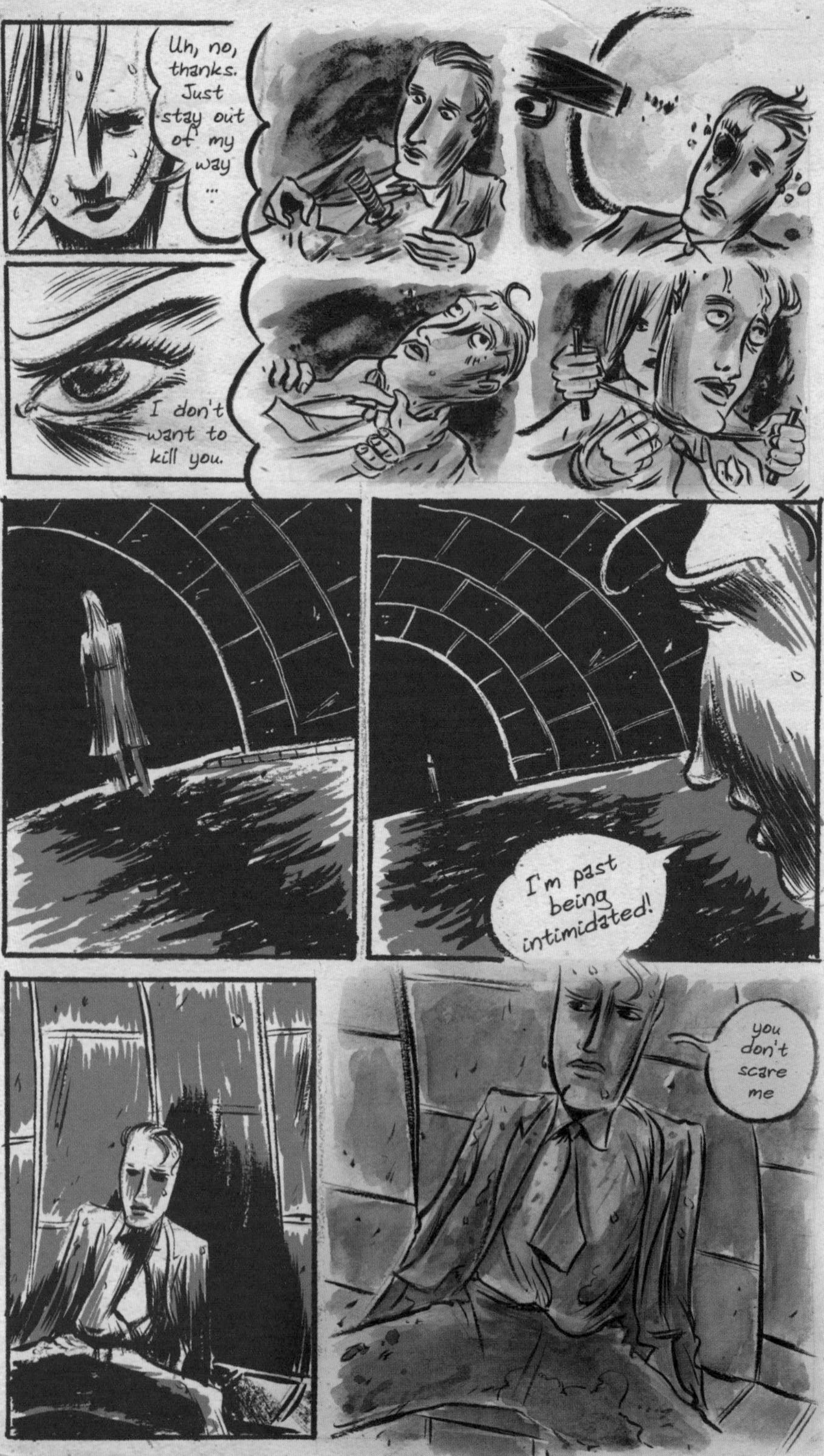
Uh, no, thanks. Just stay out of my way ...
I don't want to kill you.
I'm past being intimidated!
you don't scare me

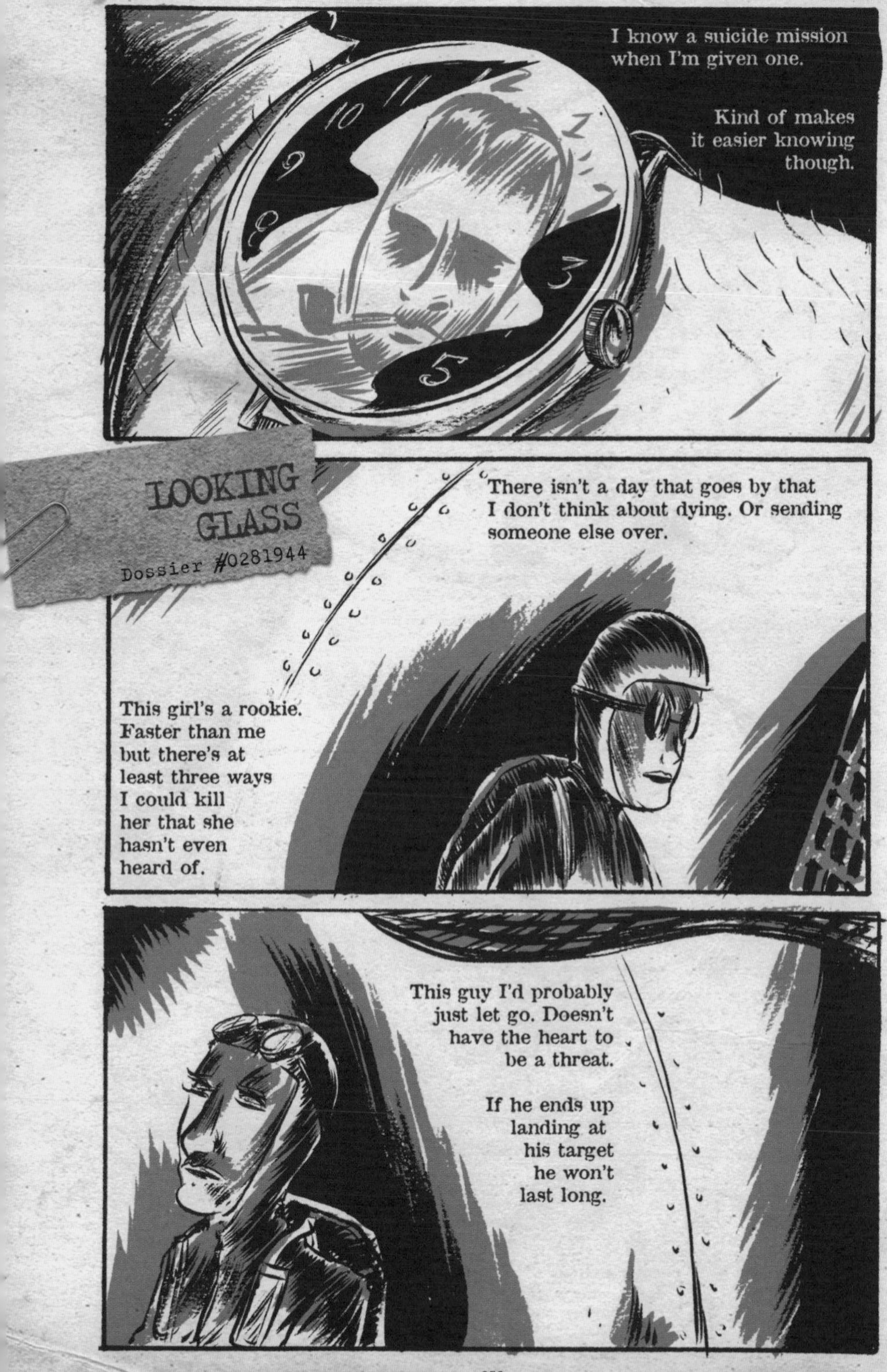
I know a suicide mission when I'm given one.
Kind of makes it easier knowing though.
LOOKING GLASS
Dossier #0281944
There isn't a day that goes by that I don't think about dying. Or sending someone else over.
This girl's a rookie. Faster than me but there's at least three ways I could kill her that she hasn't even heard of.
This guy I'd probably just let go. Doesn't have the heart to be a threat.
If he ends up landing at his target he won't last long.

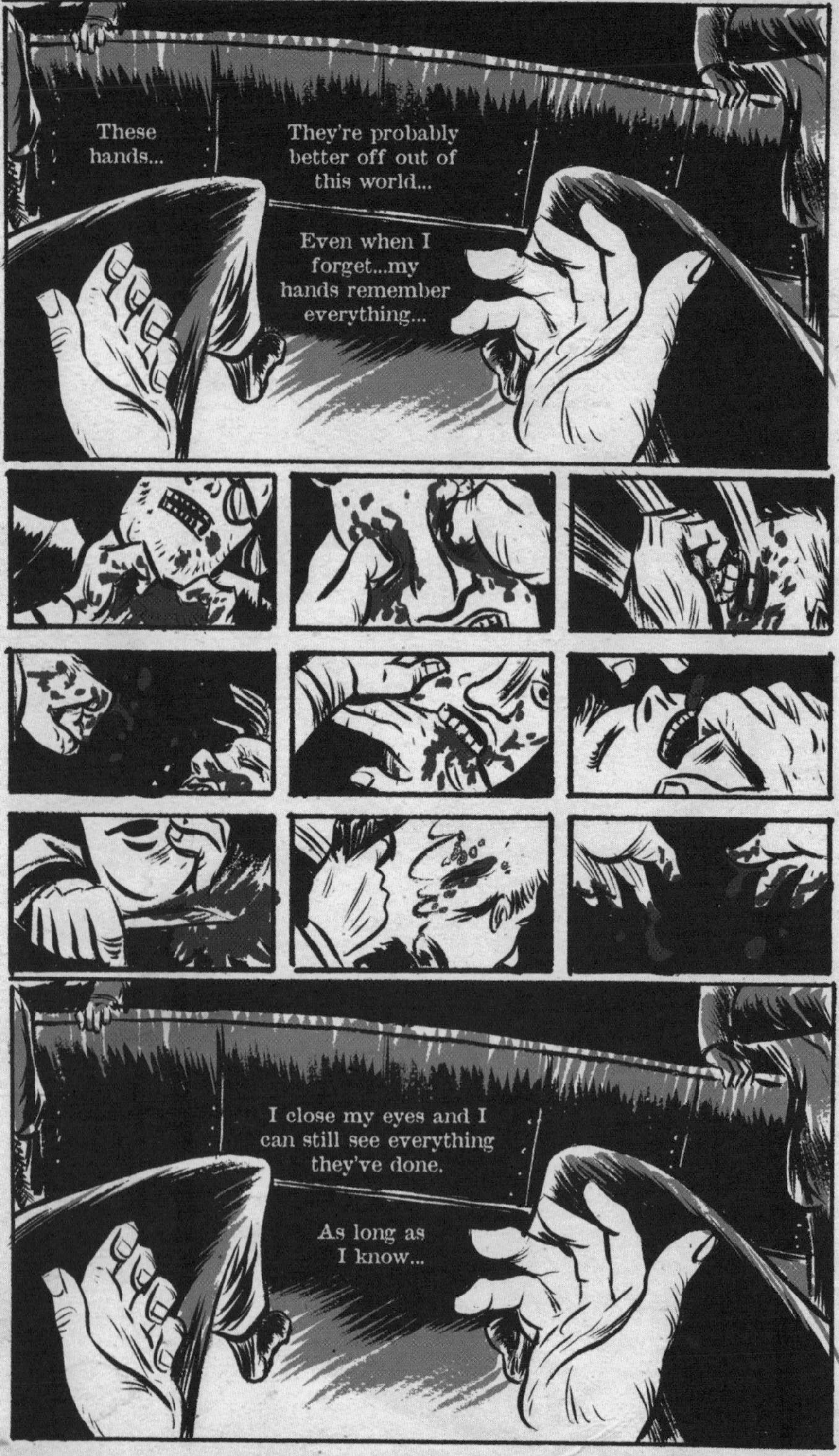
These hands...
They're probably better off out of this world...
Even when I forget...my hands remember everything...
I close my eyes and I can still see everything they've done.
As long as I know...

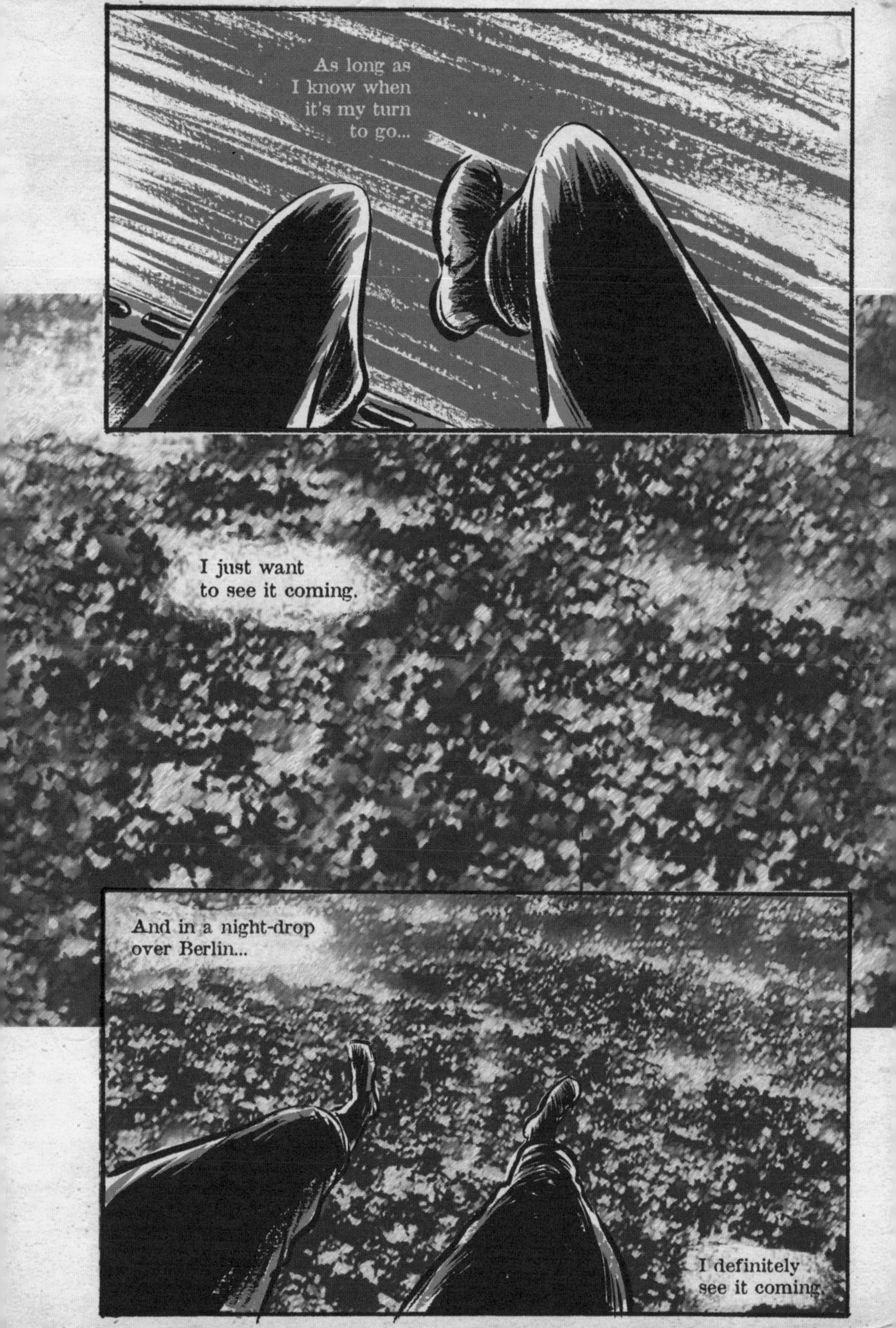
As long as I know when it's my turn to go...
I just want to see it coming.
And in a night-drop over Berlin...
I definitely see it coming.

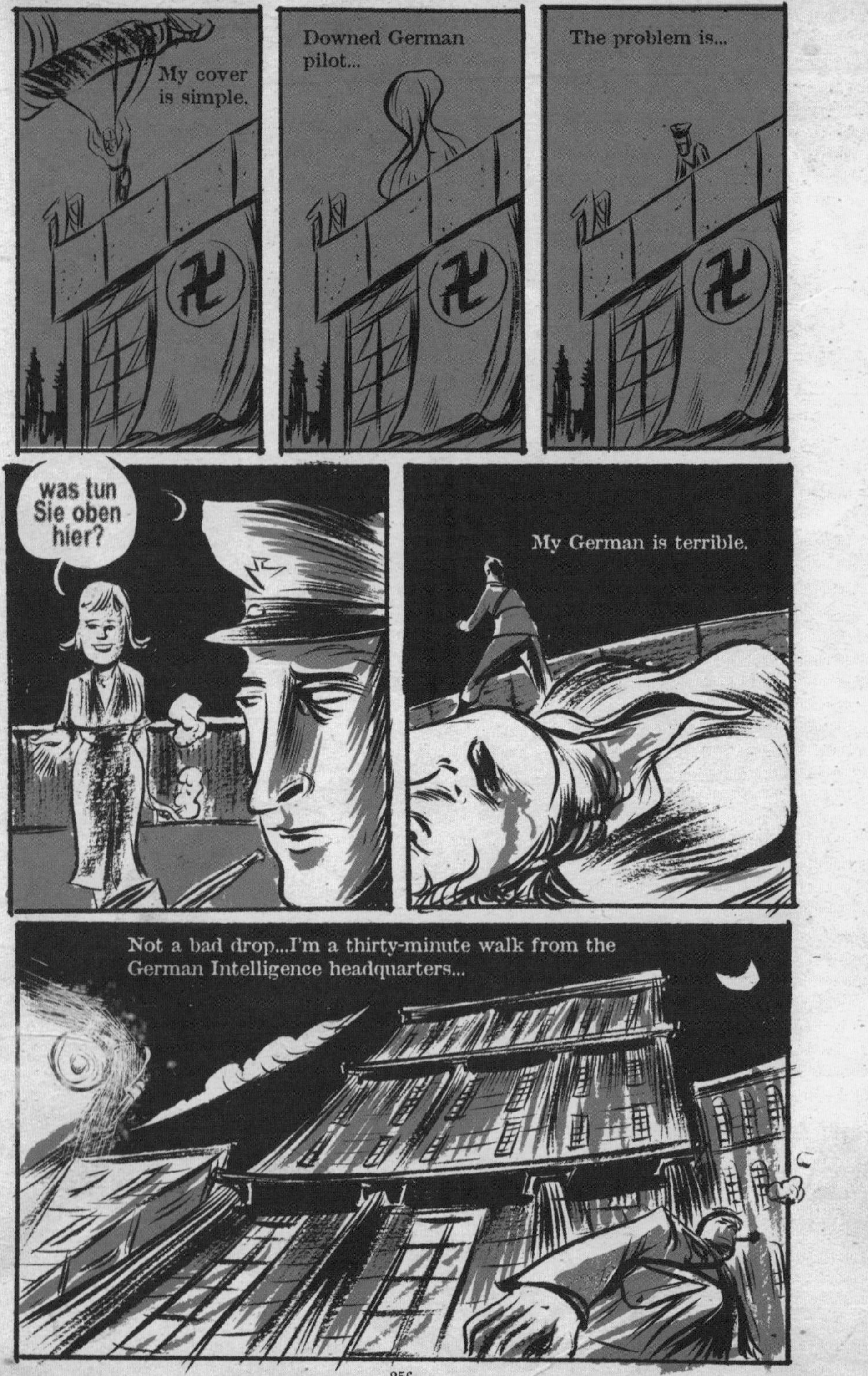
My cover is simple.
Downed German pilot...
The problem is...
was tun Sie oben hier?
My German is terrible.
Not a bad drop...I'm a thirty-minute walk from the German Intelligence headquarters...

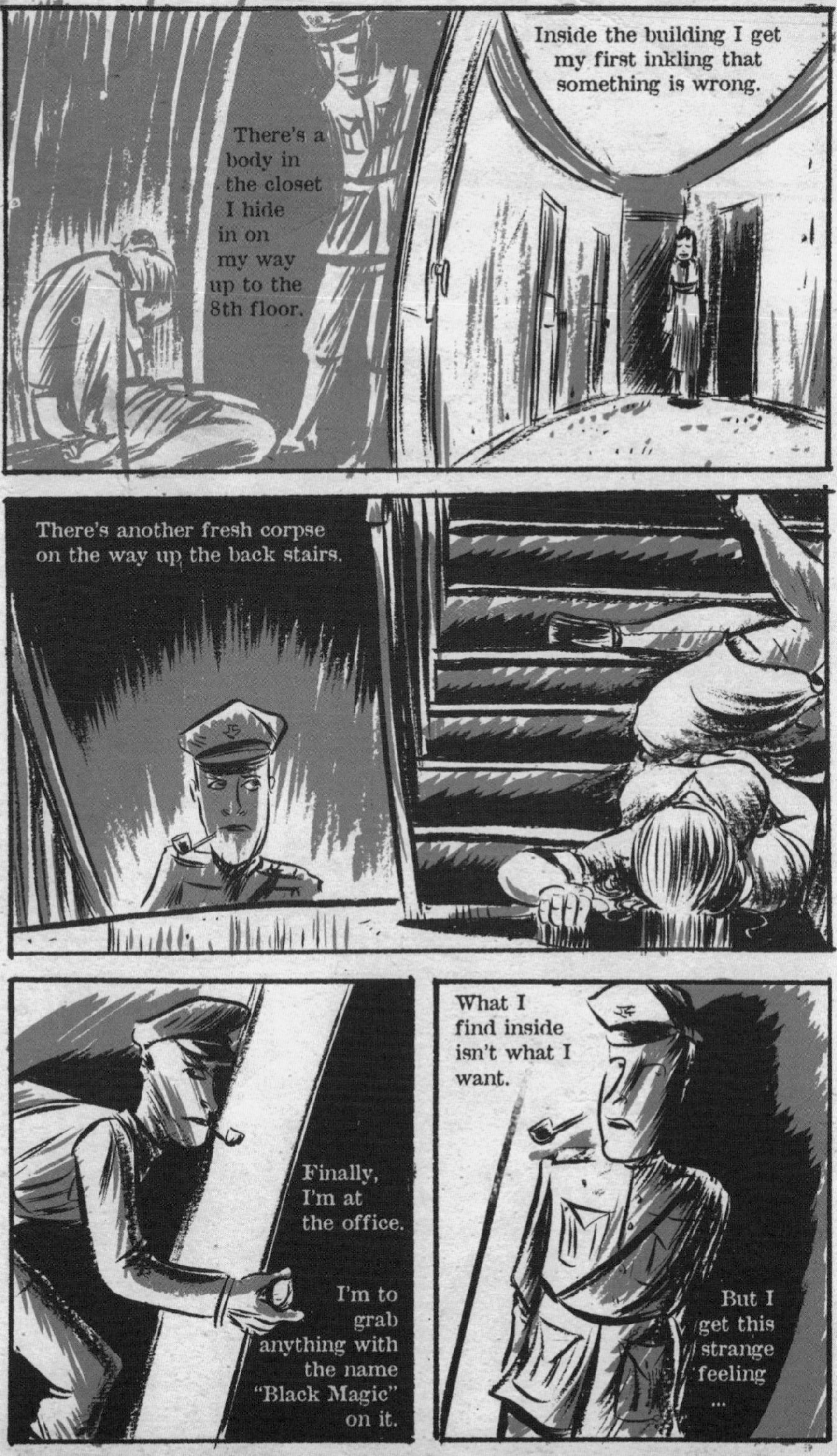
Inside the building I get my first inkling that something is wrong.
There's a body in the closet I hide in on my way up to the 8th floor.
There's another fresh corpse on the way up the back stairs.
Finally, I'm at the office.
I'm to grab anything with the name "Black Magic" on it.
What I find inside isn't what I want.
But I get this strange feeling ...

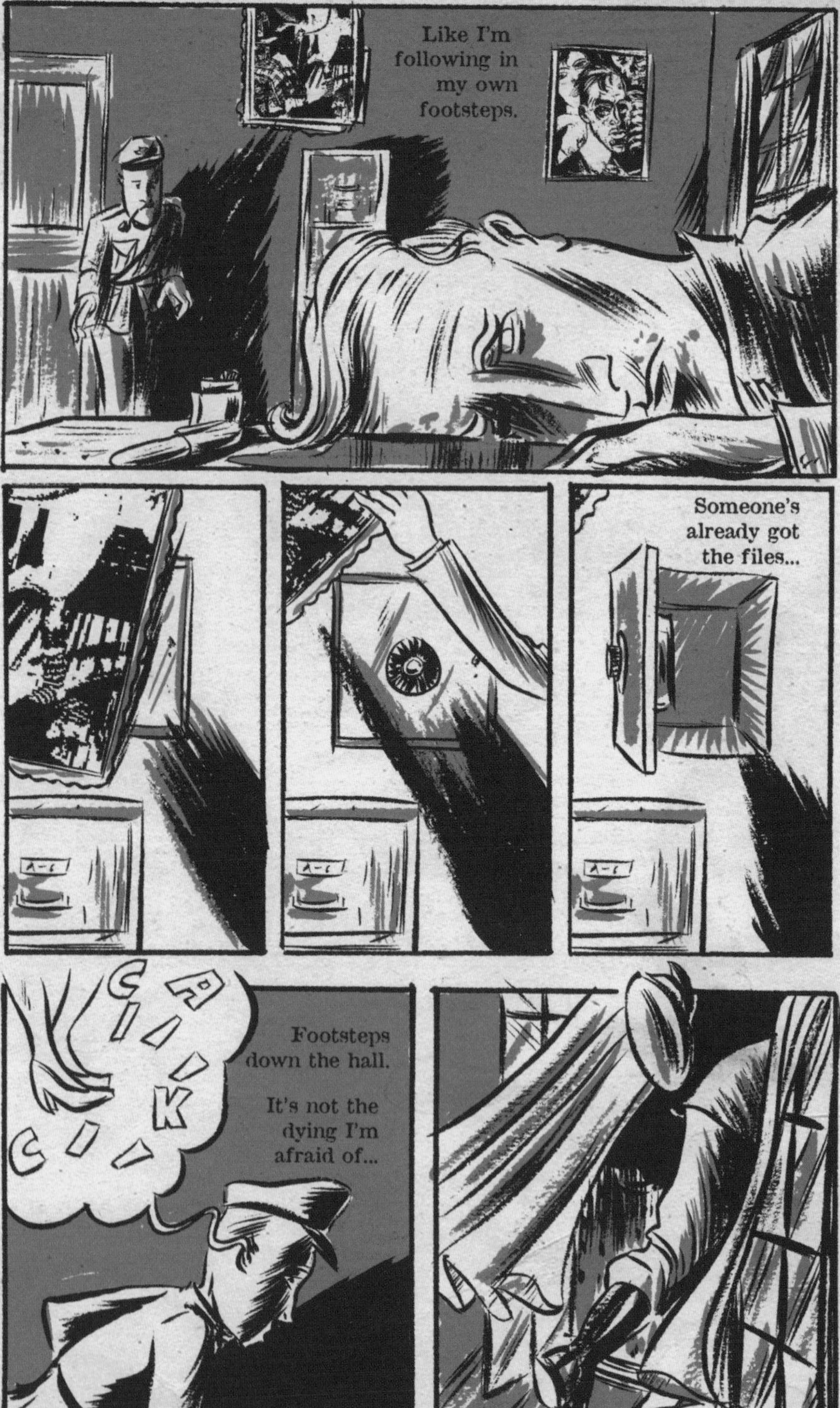
Like I'm following in my own footsteps.
Someone's already got the files...
CLICK
Footsteps down the hall.
It's not the dying I'm afraid of...

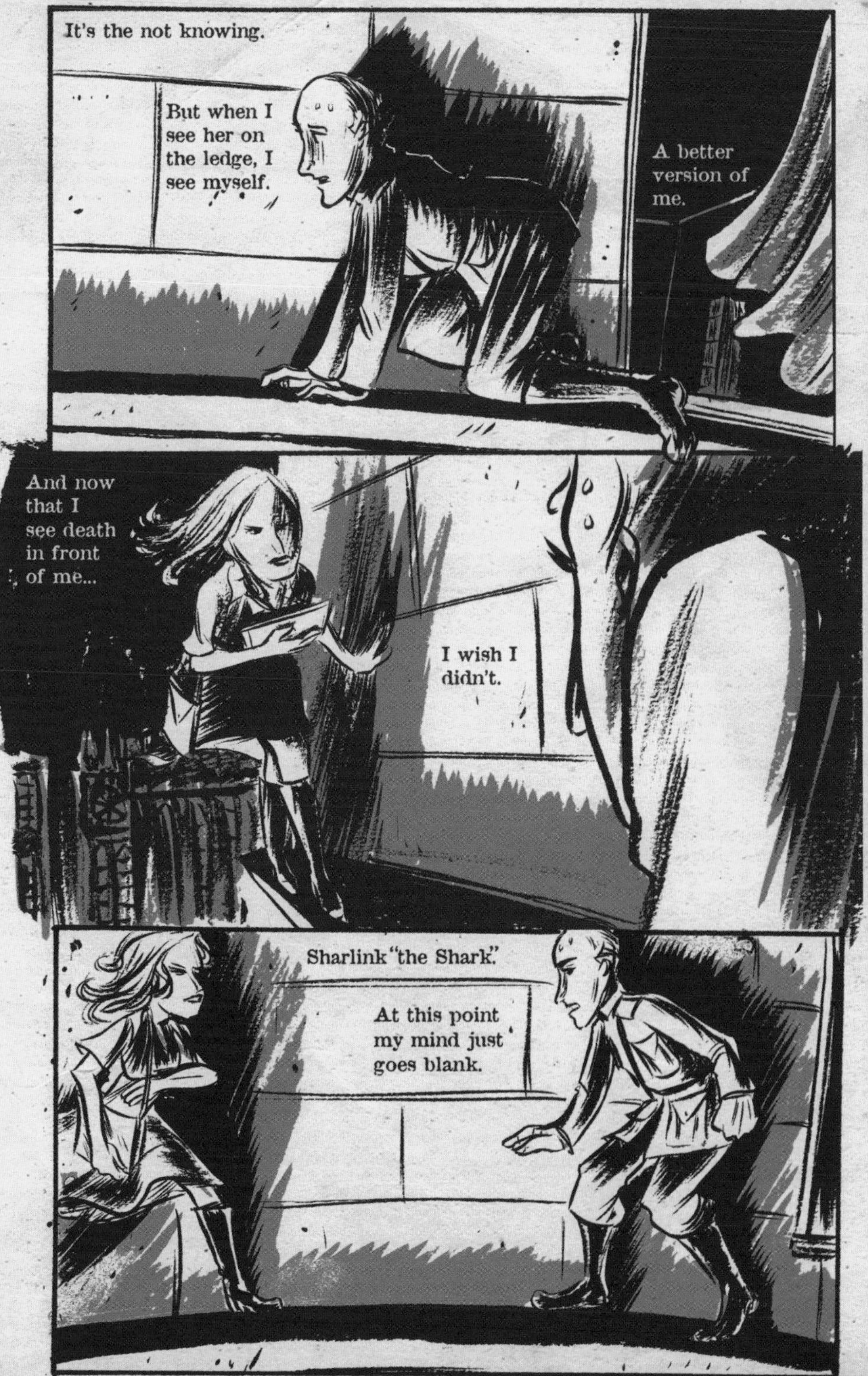
It's the not knowing.
But when I see her on the ledge, I see myself.
A better version of me.
And now that I see death in front of me...
I wish I didn't.
Sharlink "the Shark."
At this point my mind just goes blank.

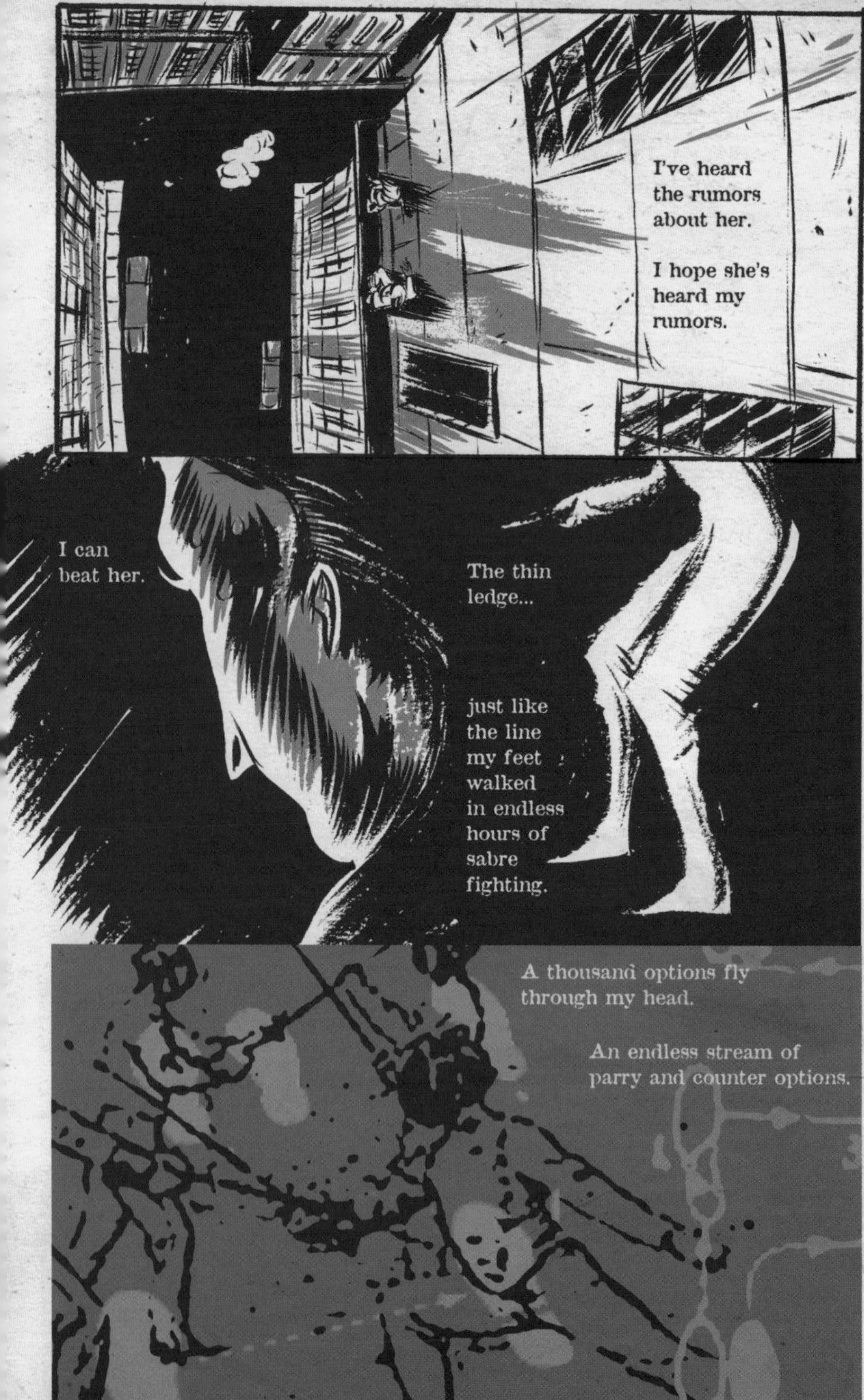
I've heard the rumors about her.
I hope she's heard my rumors.
I can beat her.
The thin ledge...
just like the line my feet walked in endless hours of sabre fighting.
A thousand options fly through my head.
An endless stream of parry and counter options.

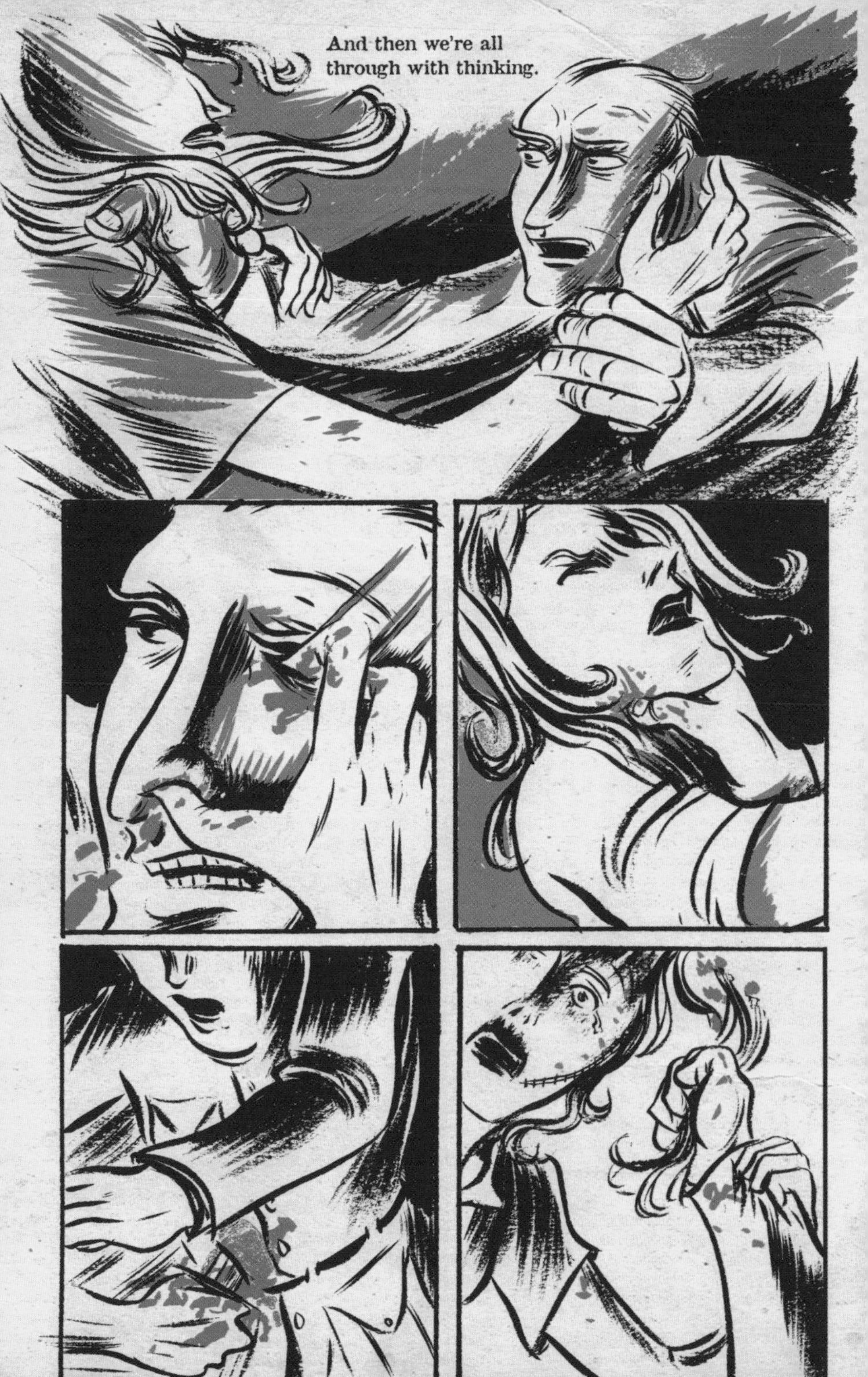
And then we're all through with thinking.

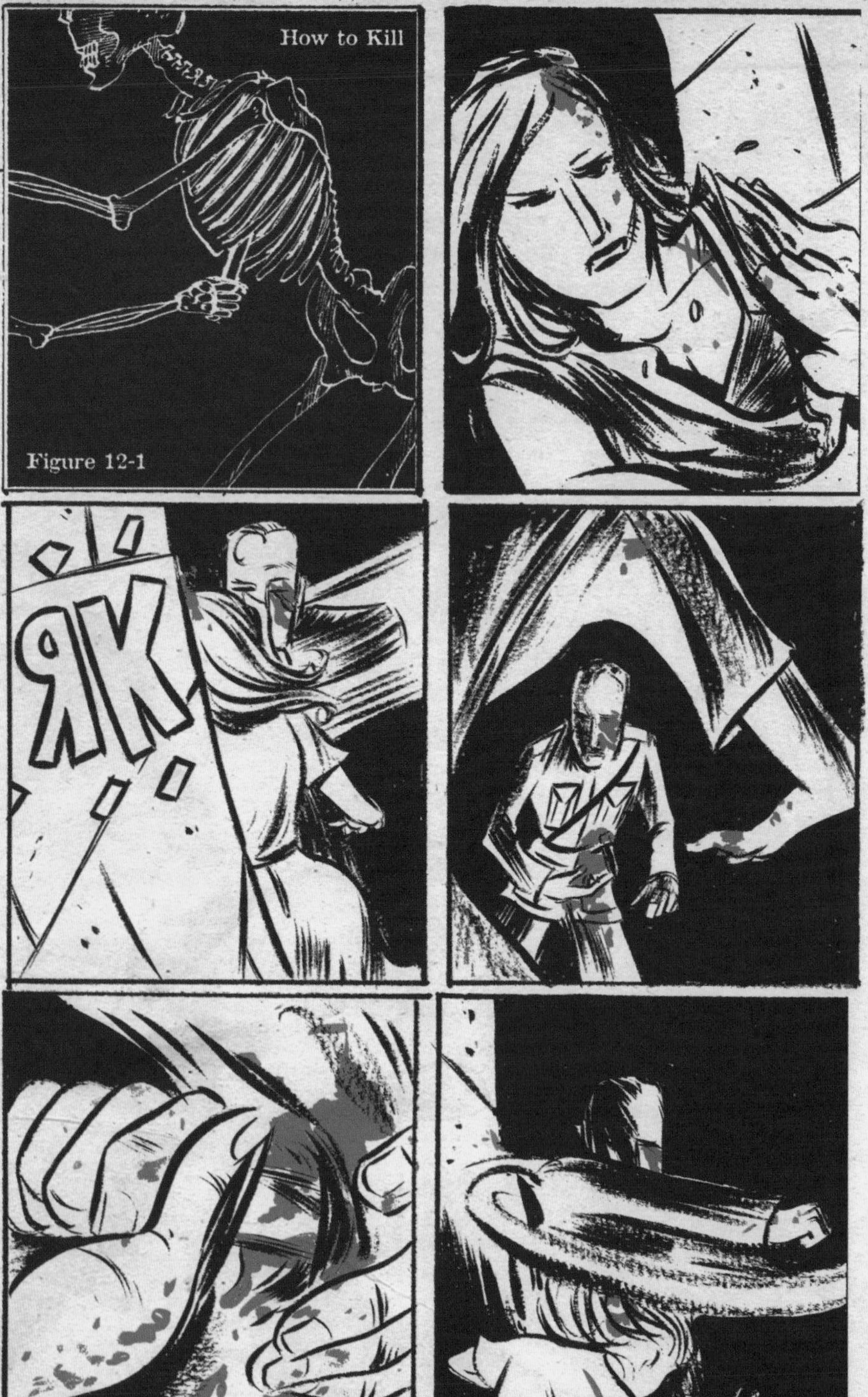
How to Kill
Figure 12-1
RK

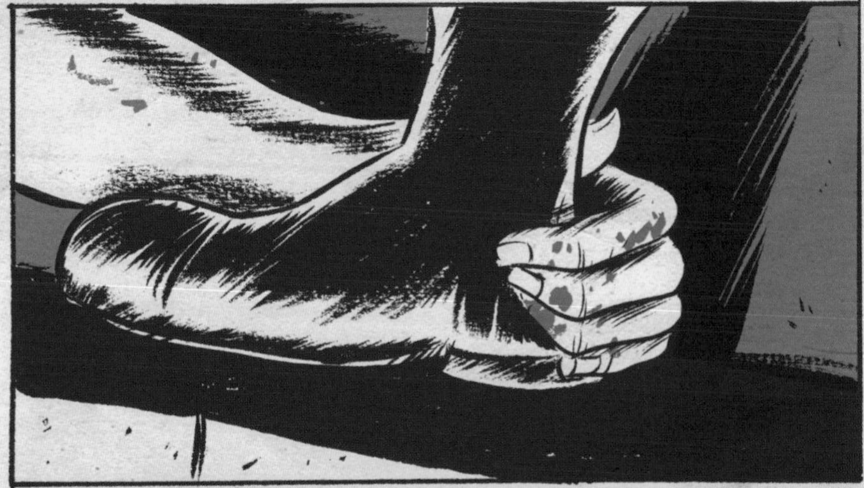

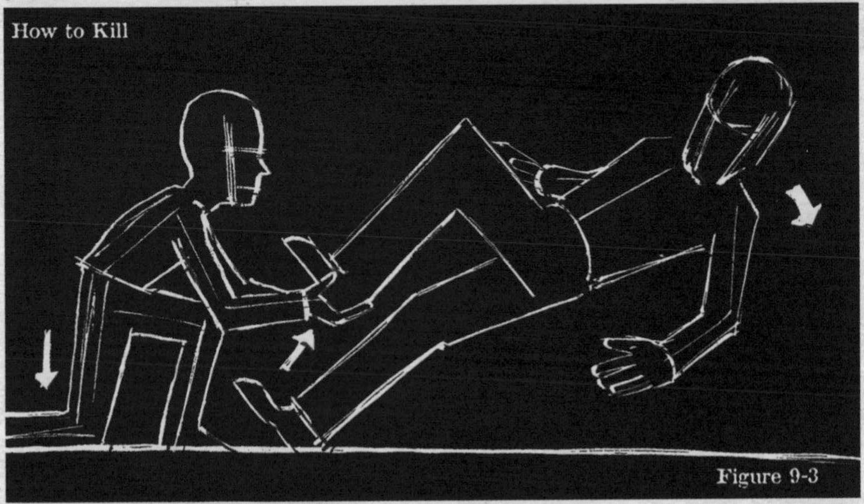
How to Kill
Figure 9-3

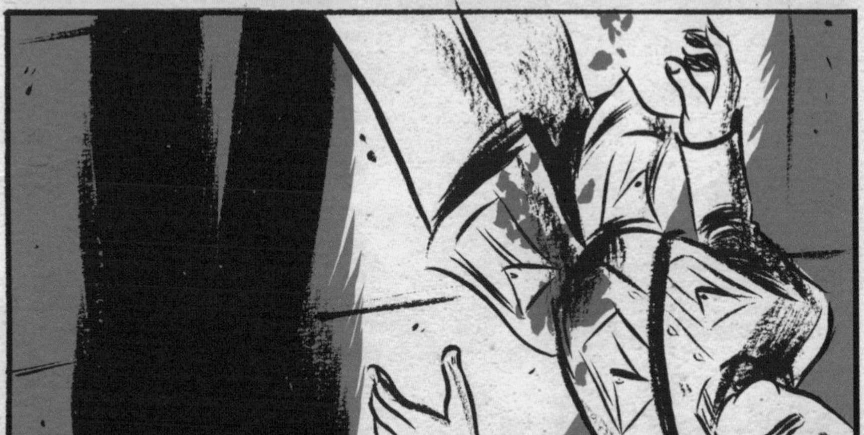

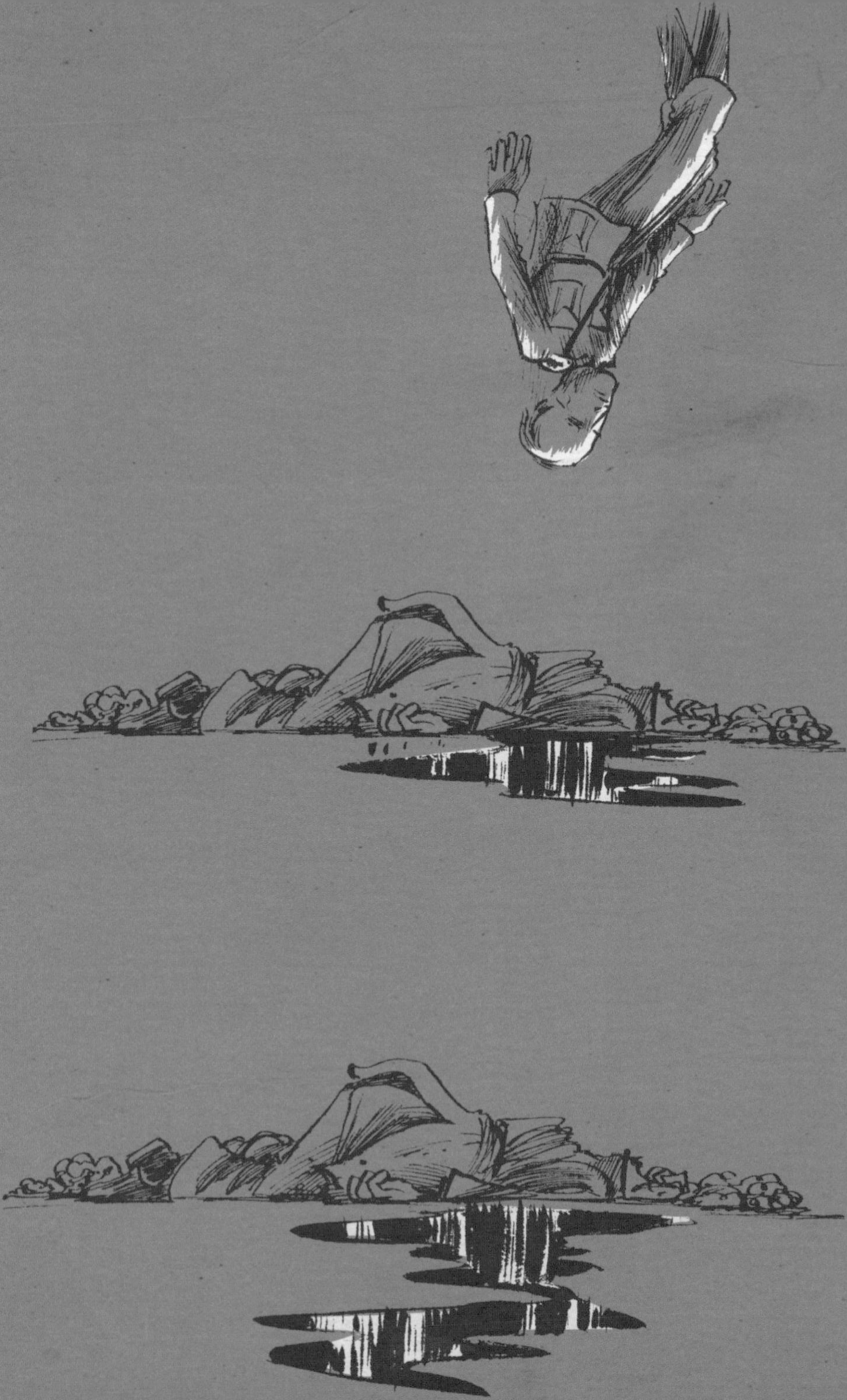

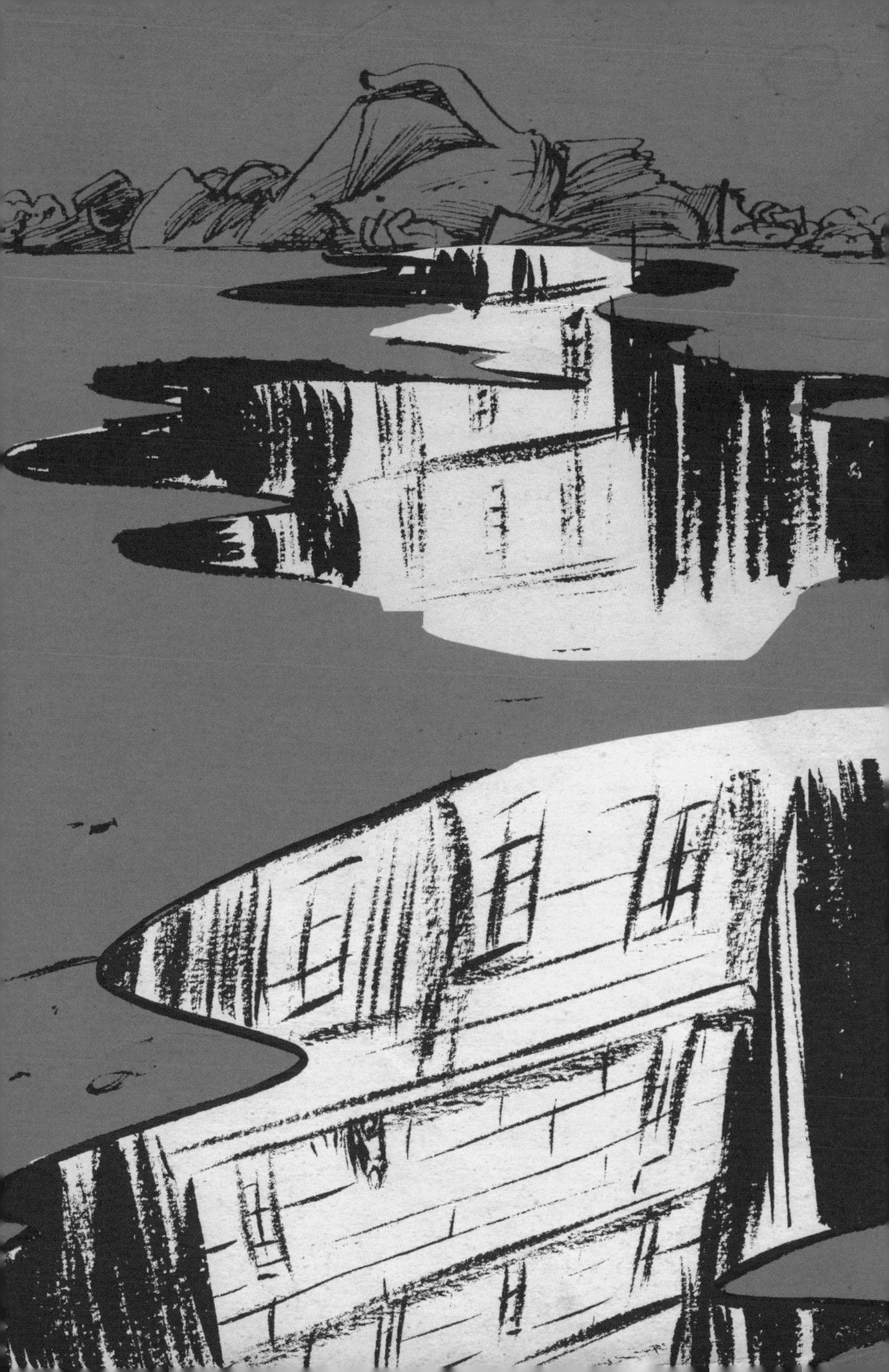

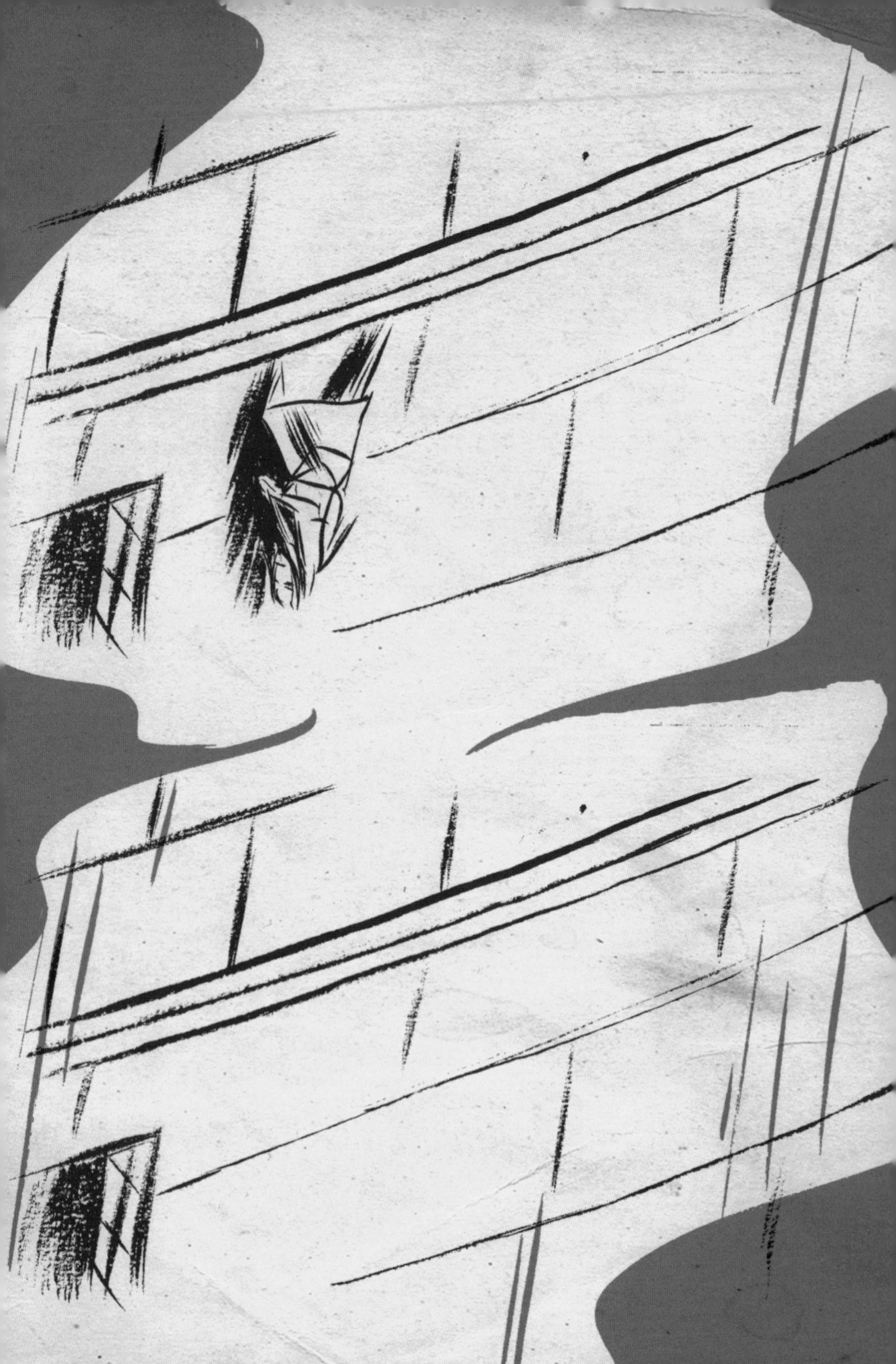

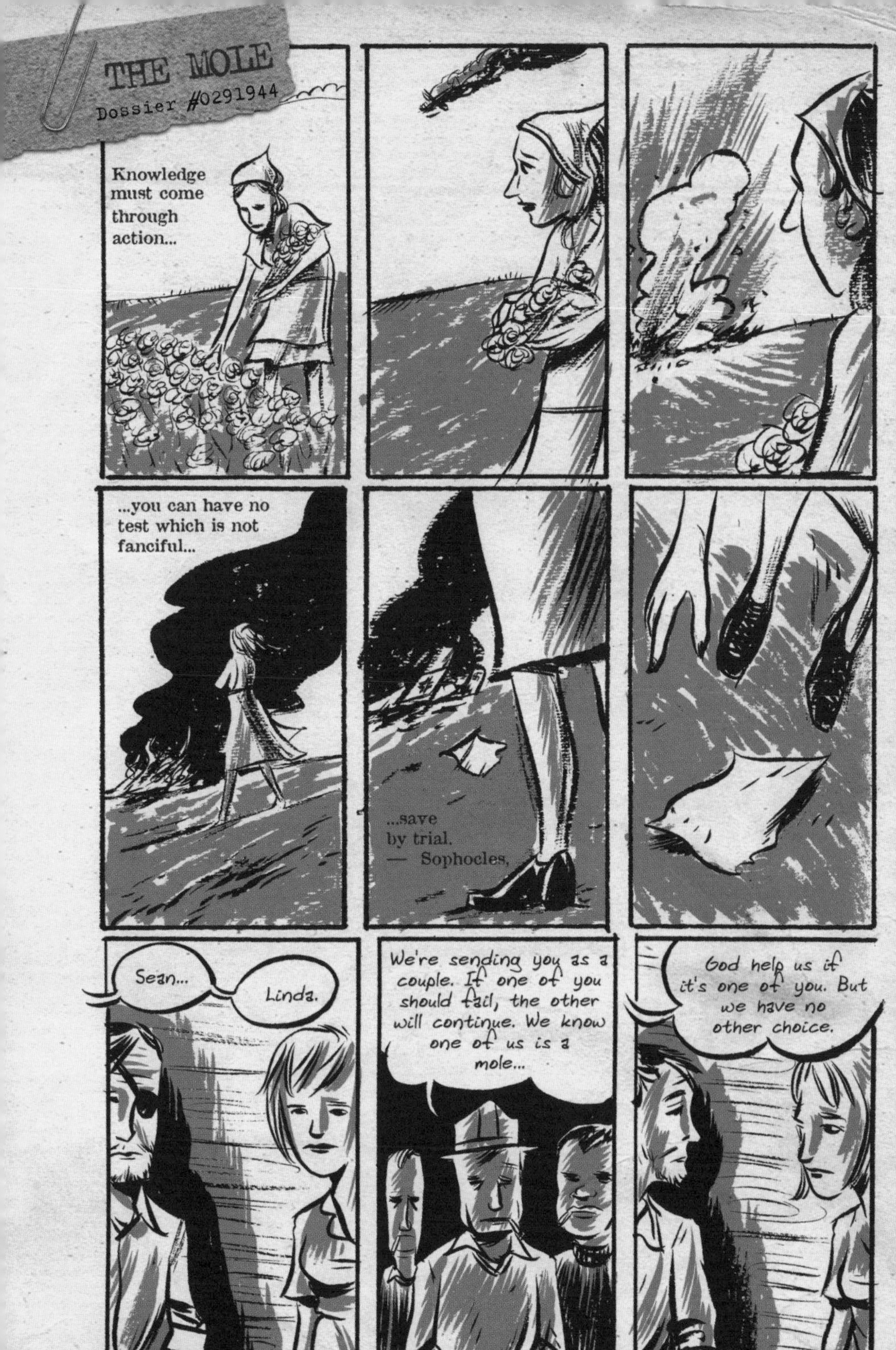
THE MOLE
Dossier #0291944
Knowledge must come through action...
...you can have no test which is not fanciful...
...save by trial.
— Sophocles.
Sean...
Linda.
We're sending you as a couple. If one of you should fail, the other will continue. We know one of us is a mole...
God help us if it's one of you. But we have no other choice.

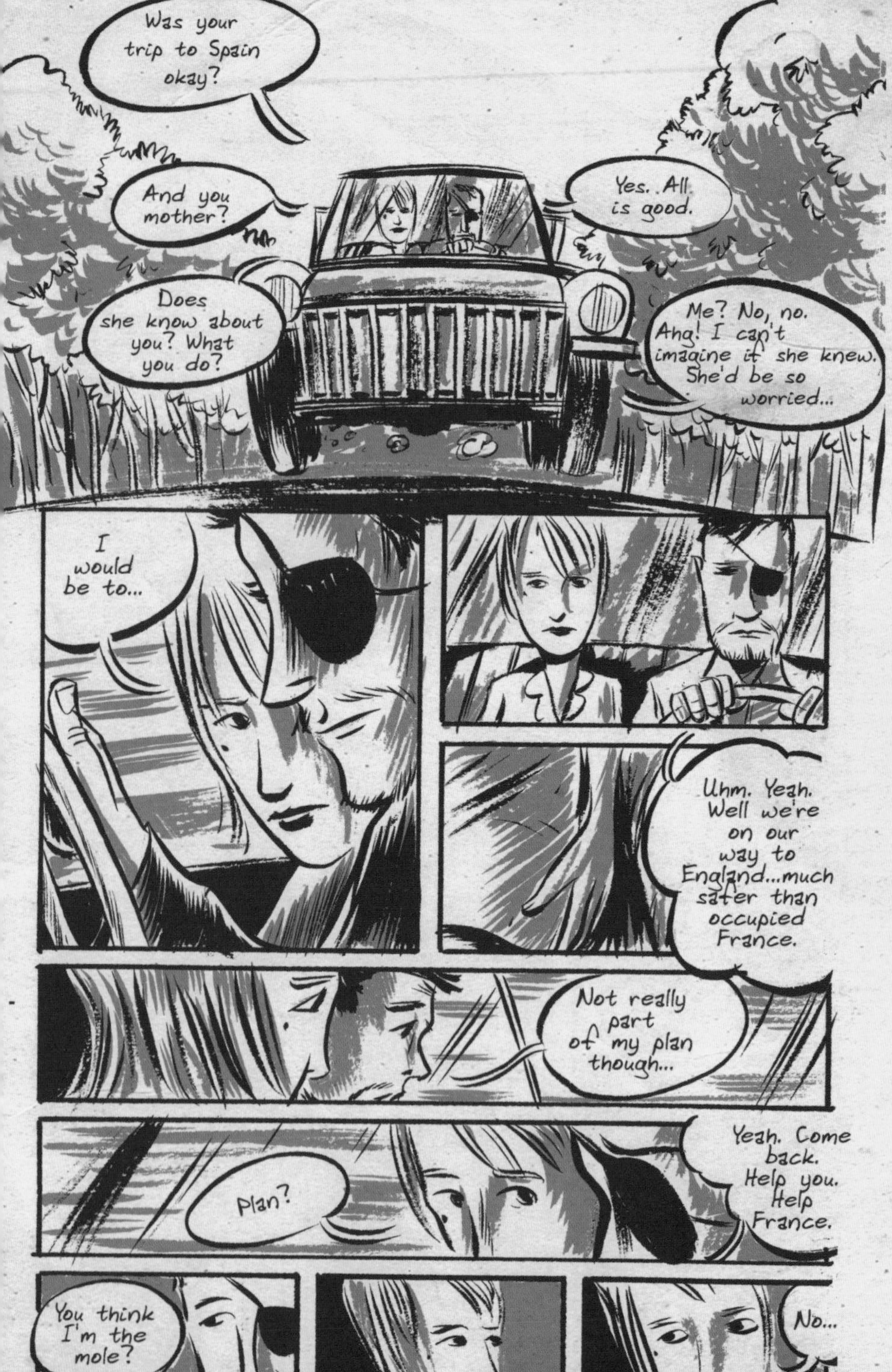
Was your trip to Spain okay?
And you mother?
Yes. All is good.
Does she know about you? What you do?
Me? No, no. Ahg! I can't imagine it she knew. She'd be so worried...
I would be to...
Uhm. Yeah. Well we're on our way to England...much safer than occupied France.
Not really part of my plan though...
Plan?
Yeah. Come back. Help you. Help France.
You think I'm the mole?
No...

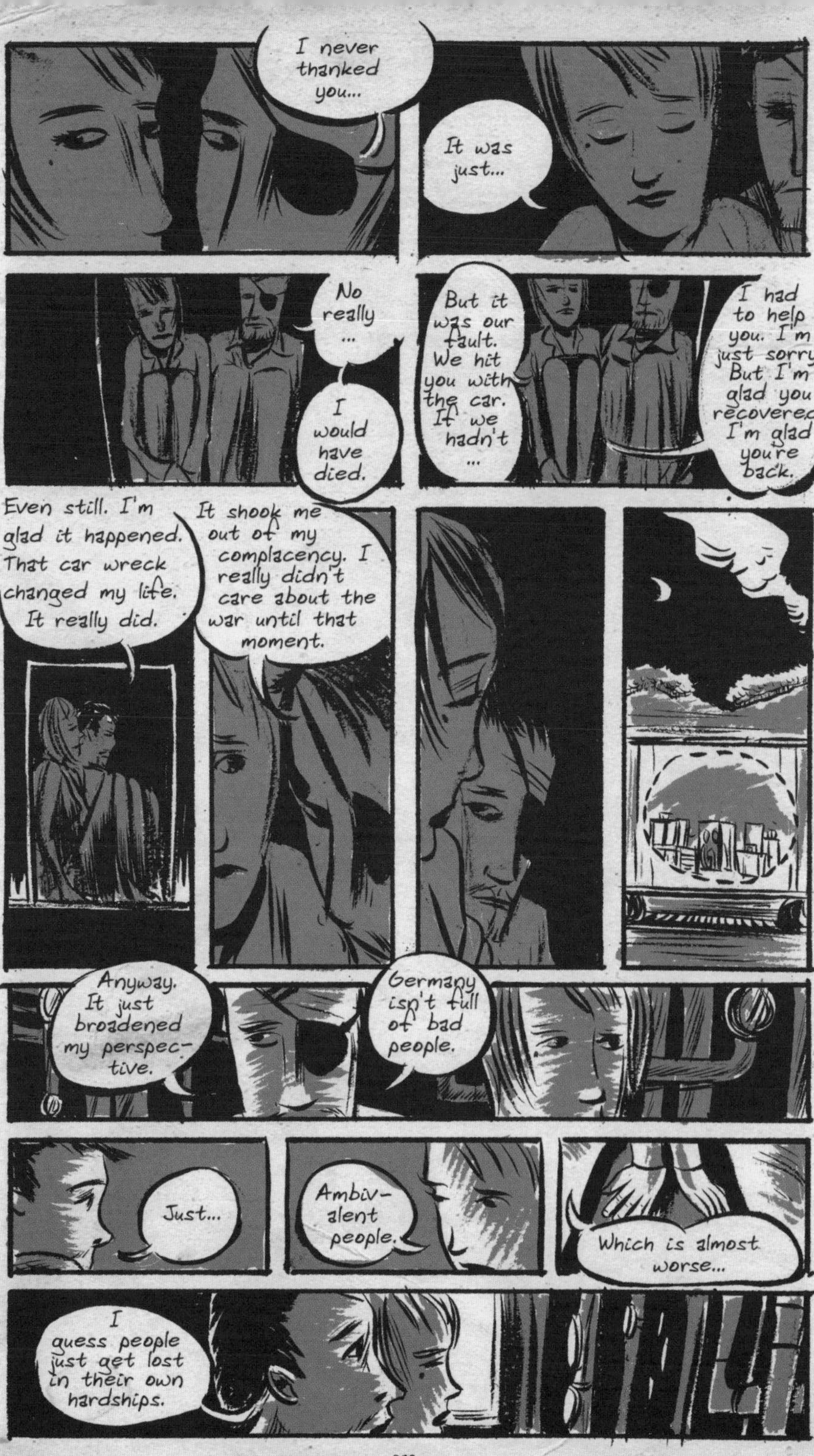
I never thanked you...
It was just...
No really ...
I would have died.
But it was our fault. We hit you with the car. If we hadn't ...
I had to help you. I'm just sorry. But I'm glad you recovered. I'm glad you're back.
Even still. I'm glad it happened. That car wreck changed my life. It really did.
It shook me out of my complacency. I really didn't care about the war until that moment.
Anyway. It just broadened my perspective.
Germany isn't full of bad people.
Just...
Ambivalent people.
Which is almost worse...
I guess people just get lost in their own hardships.

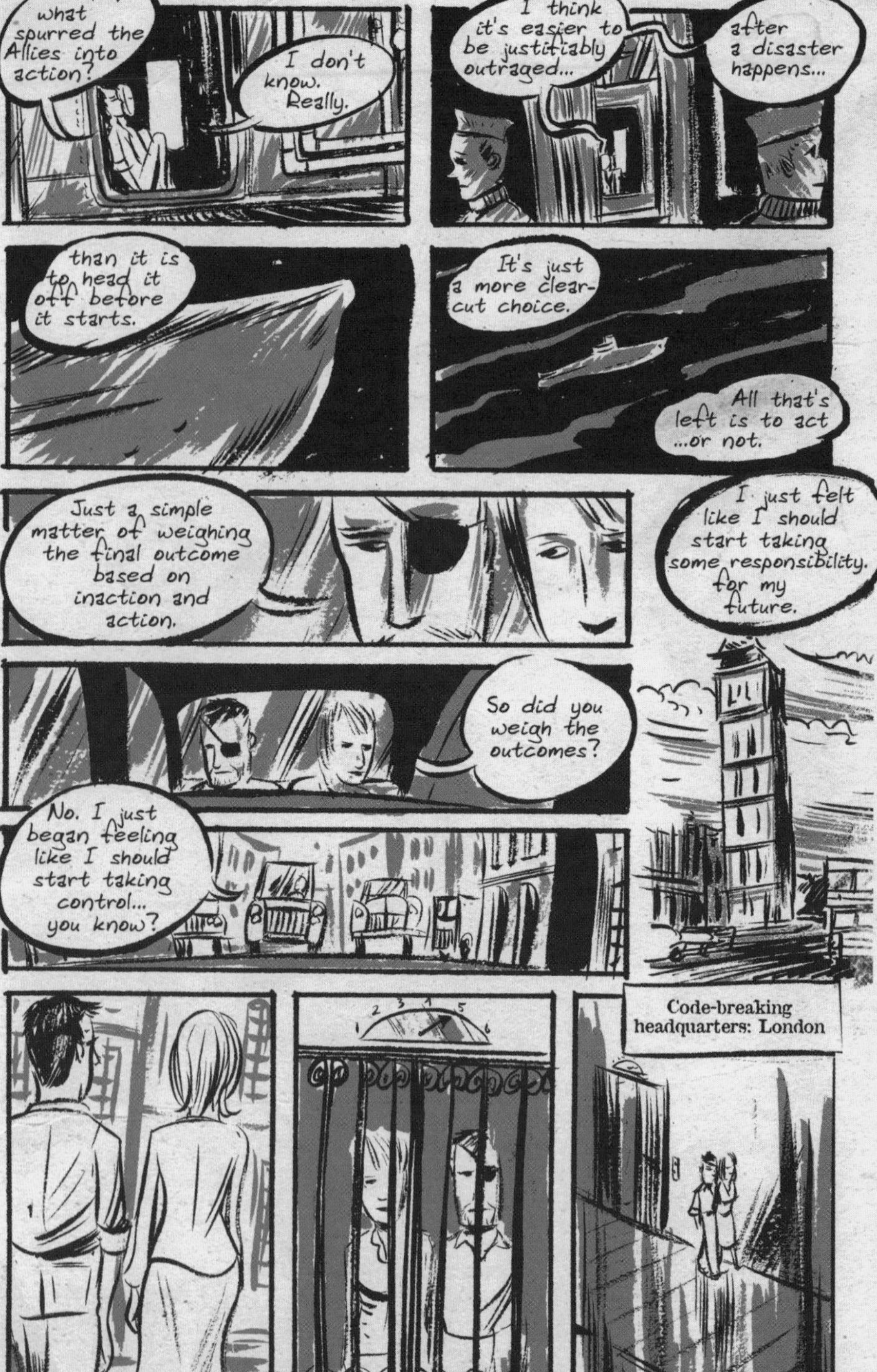
Then what spurred the Allies into action?
I don't know. Really.
I think it's easier to be justifiably outraged...
after a disaster happens...
than it is to head it off before it starts.
It's just a more clear-cut choice.
All that's left is to act ...or not.
Just a simple matter of weighing the final outcome based on inaction and action.
I just felt like I should start taking some responsibility. for my future.
So did you weigh the outcomes?
No. I just began feeling like I should start taking control... you know?
Code-breaking headquarters: London

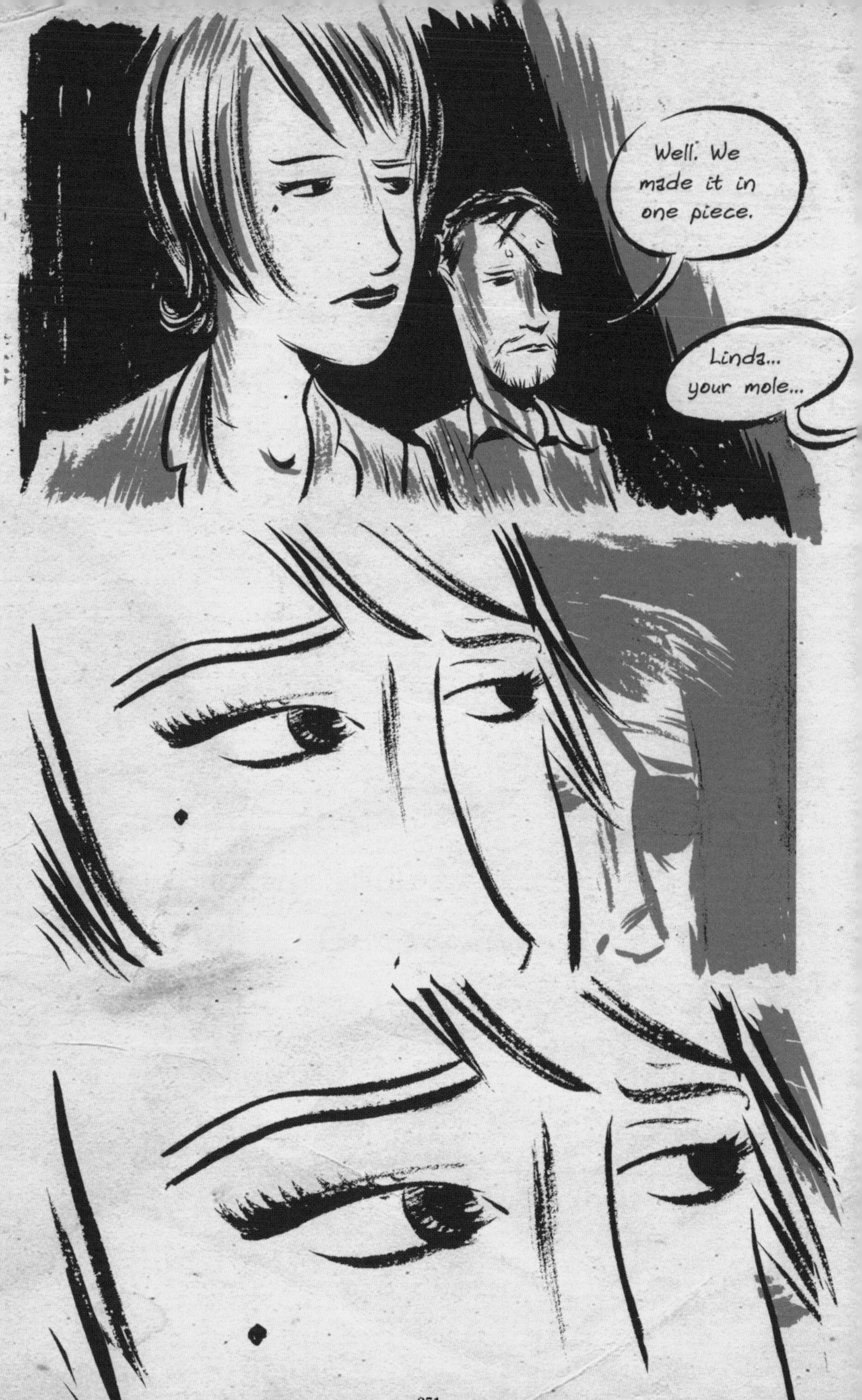
Well. We made it in one piece.
Linda... your mole...

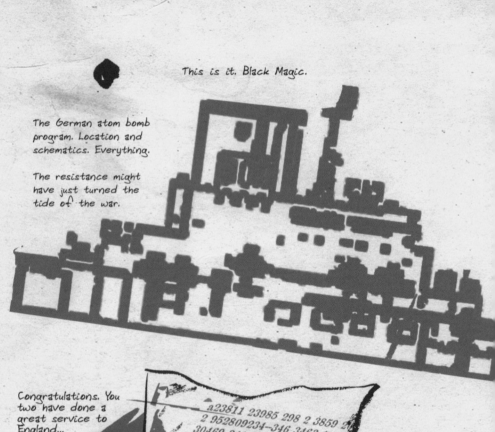

This is it. Black Magic.

The German atom bomb program. Location and schematics. Everything.

The resistance might have just turned the tide of the war.

Congratulations. You two have done a great service to England...

a23811 23985 298 2 3859 2
2 952809234-346 3463-4 -1
30469 341034flfjv 12503240
095 1—5   16tq'tro qwl

223811 23985 298 2 3859 200 awl 235
99 809234-346 3463-4 -1349 34 6 4
69 41034flfjv 12503240 9 1 233
6 16tq'tro qwktj o

to France and all of the Allies.

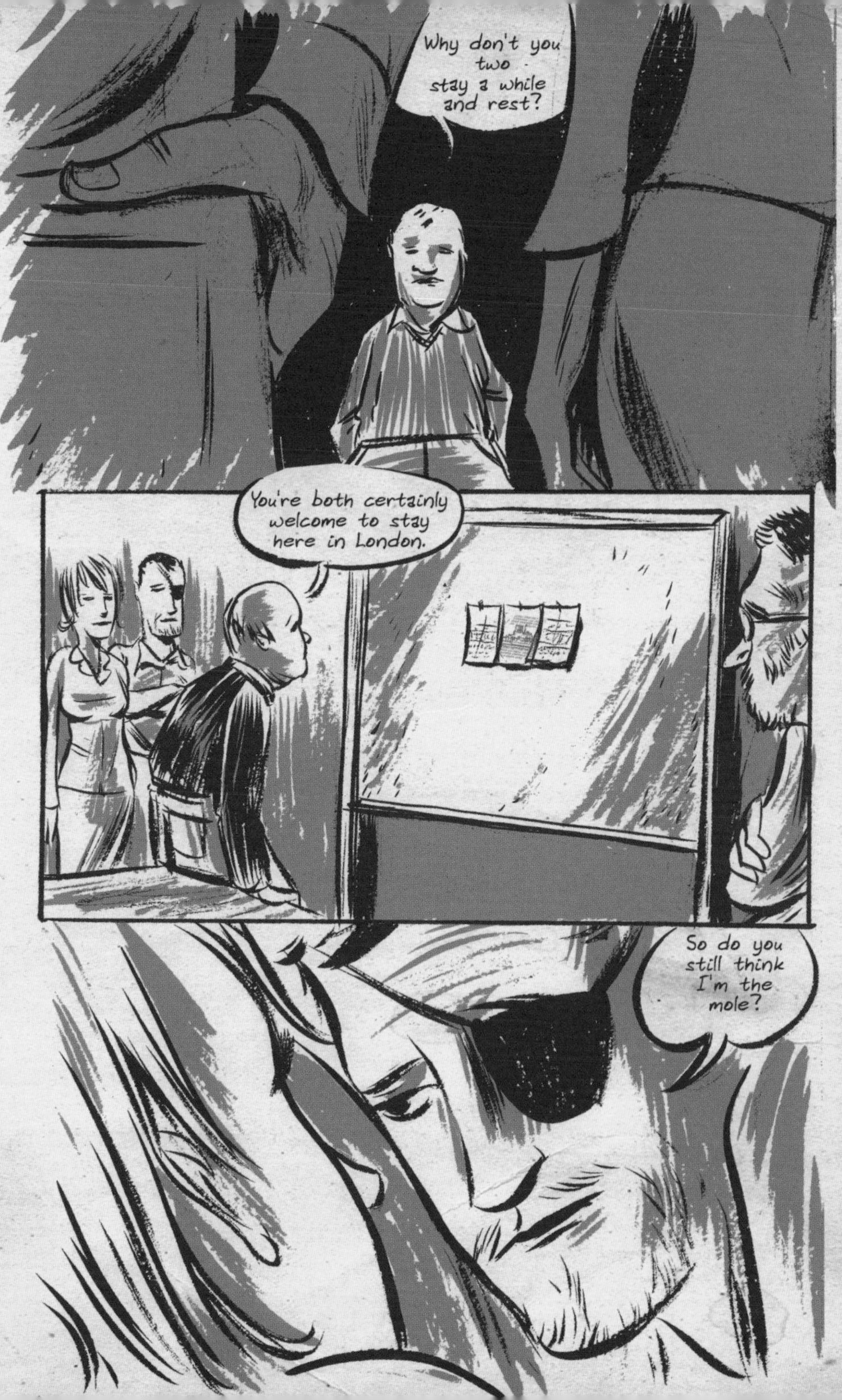
Why don't you two stay a while and rest?
You're both certainly welcome to stay here in London.
So do you still think I'm the mole?

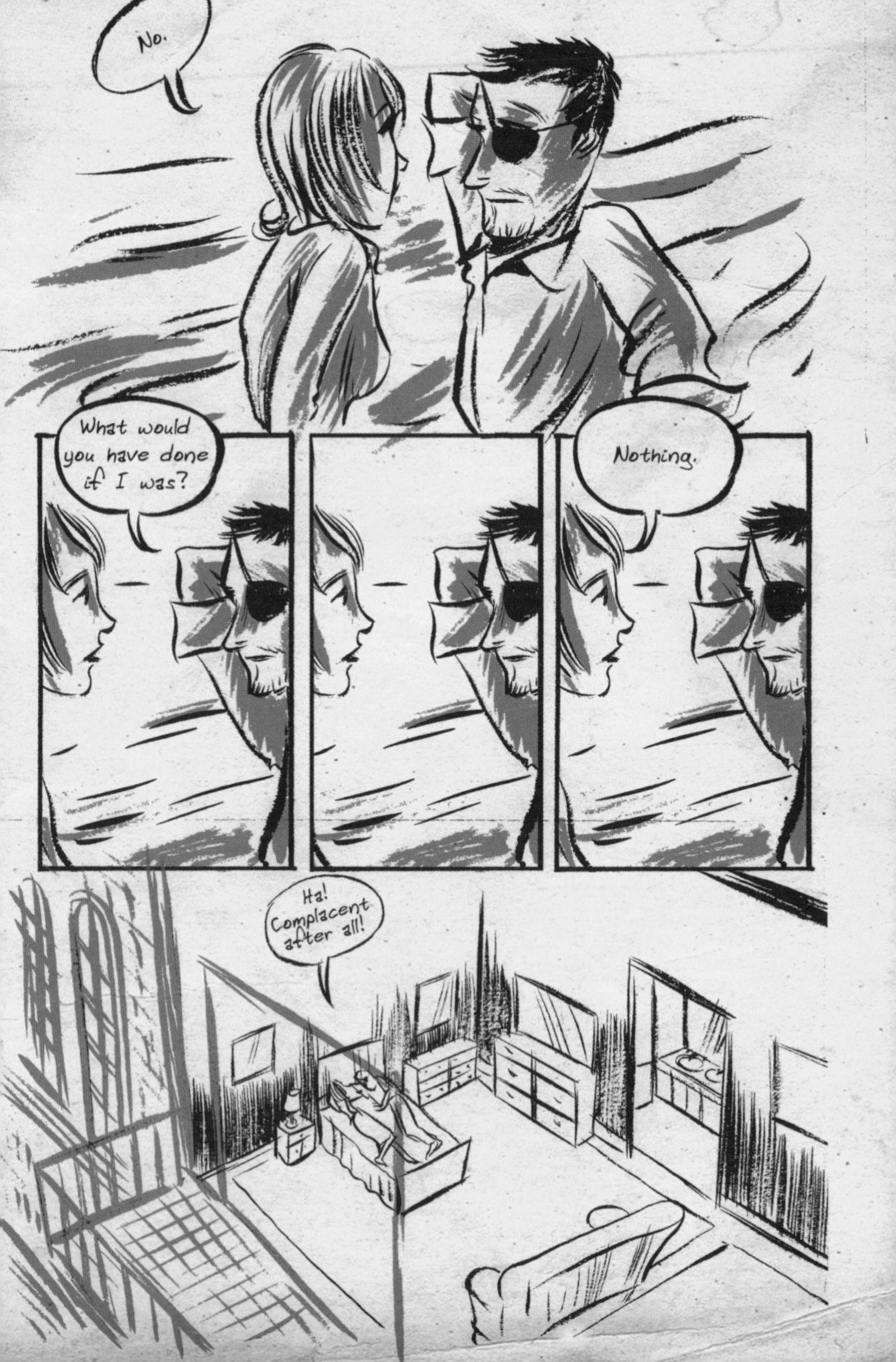
No.
What would you have done if I was?
Nothing.
Ha! Complacent after all!

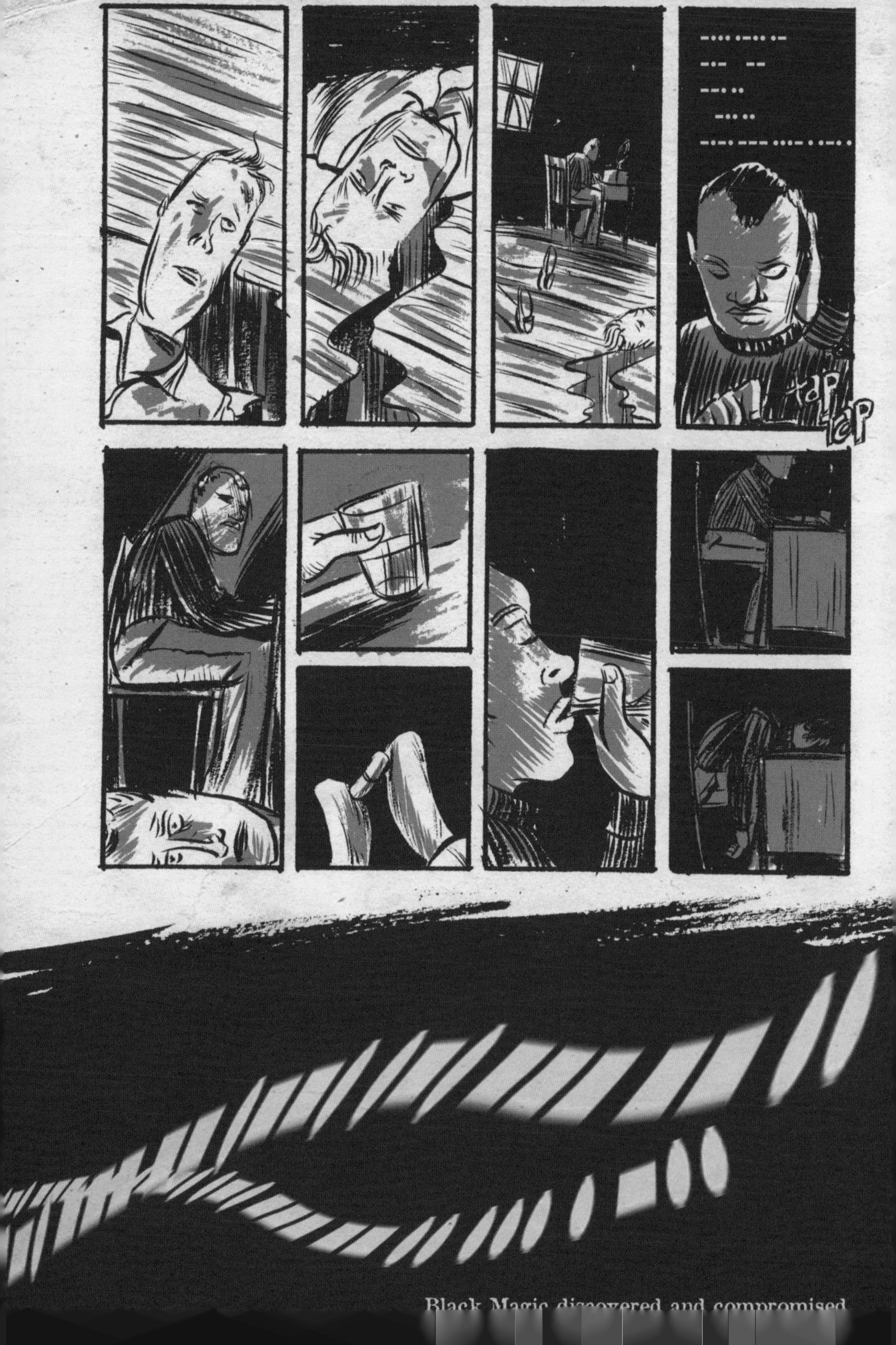
tap
tap
Black Magic discovered and compromised

Alan. My best agent. Level-headed and competent.

He had the mind of a scientist but really just wanted adventure. Travel. Love.

His death ended up being meaningless. We threw him away on nothing.

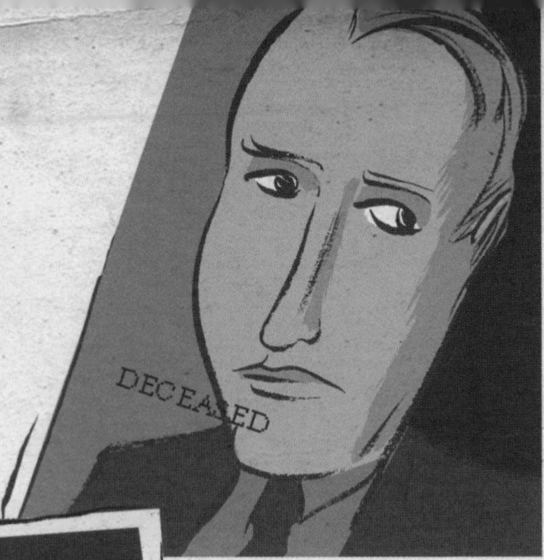
DECEASED

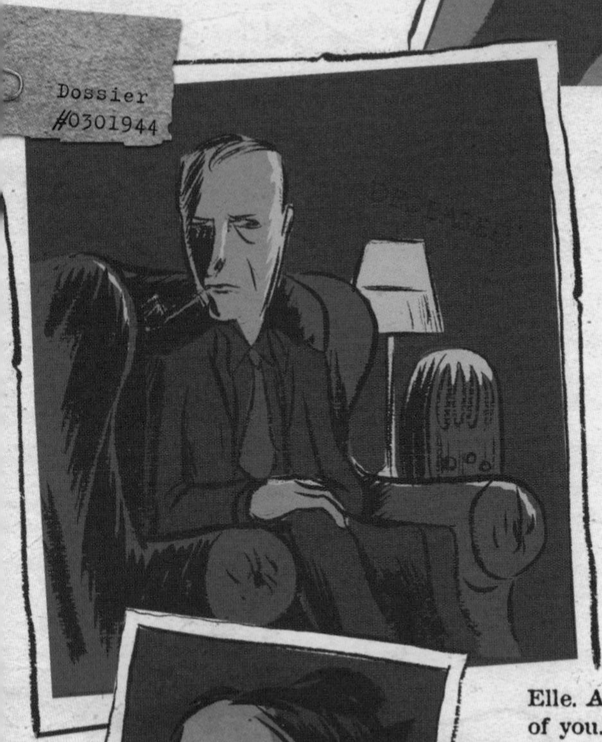
Dossier
#0301944

Richard. The "Pipe Man". Psychopathic really. Without the war I'm sure Scotland Yard would be hunting him down.

Cold-blooded. Also our best assassin. But not the best. Killed by the freelance agent, Sharlink "the Shark".

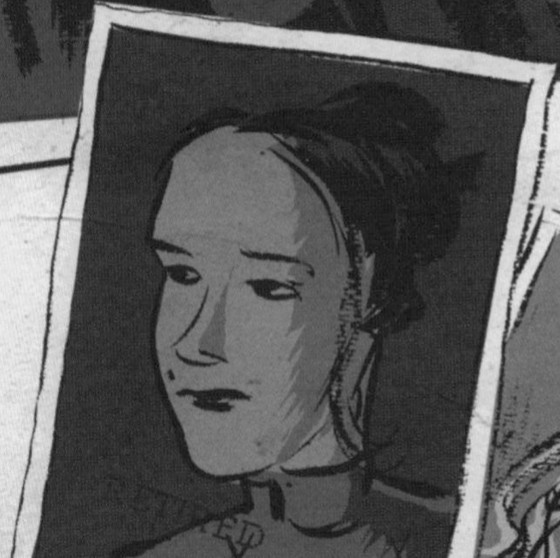

Elle. Alan thought the world of you. You might have even been a better agent than him.

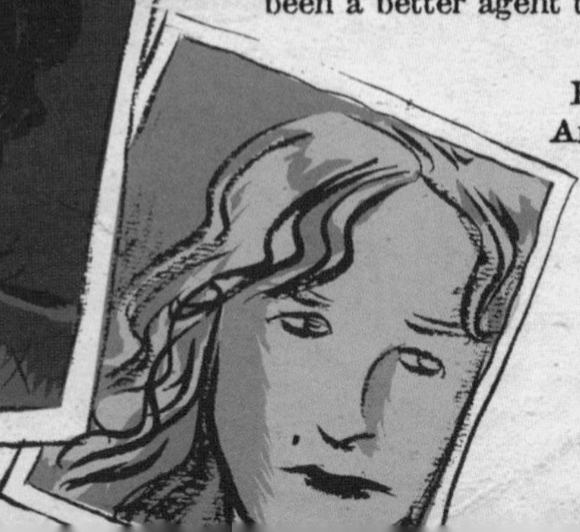

But reluctant. And ultimately too haunted to be of any use to us.

Useless after Alan's death.

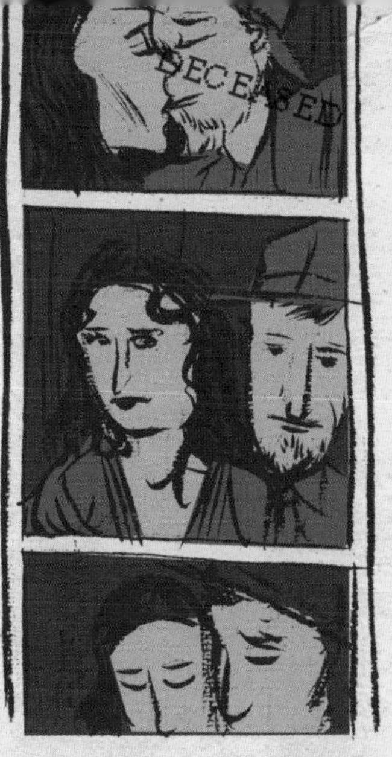
DECEASED

Matt...a mess of an agent. But ultimately ended up doing some good.

Another agent I ended up sending to his death. But if not in Cairo, somewhere else. He cared too much.

Never get involved.

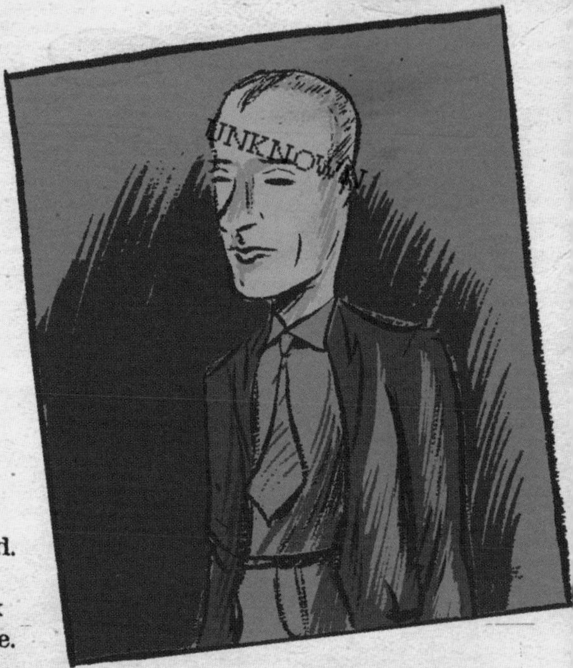
UNKNOWN

Merkel. The only enigma of all the agents I've handled.

What happened? Defected? Dead? Impeccably trained and a perfect background for espionage.

But ultimately he's too good. Too much potential to just hope he doesn't come back into play on the wrong side.

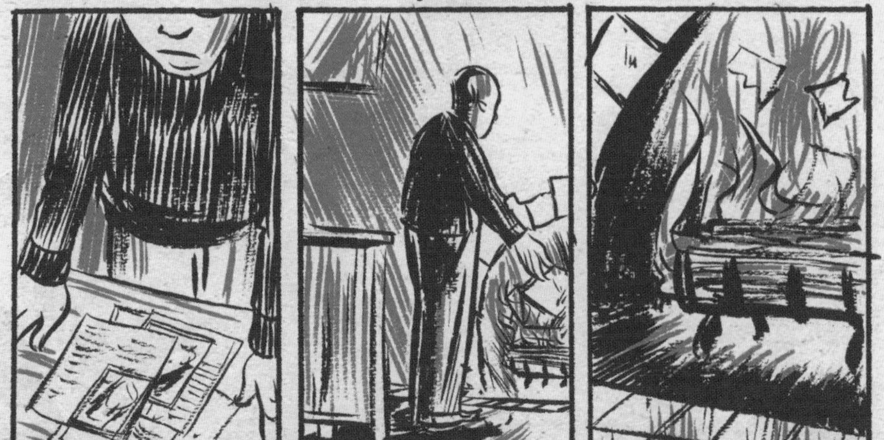

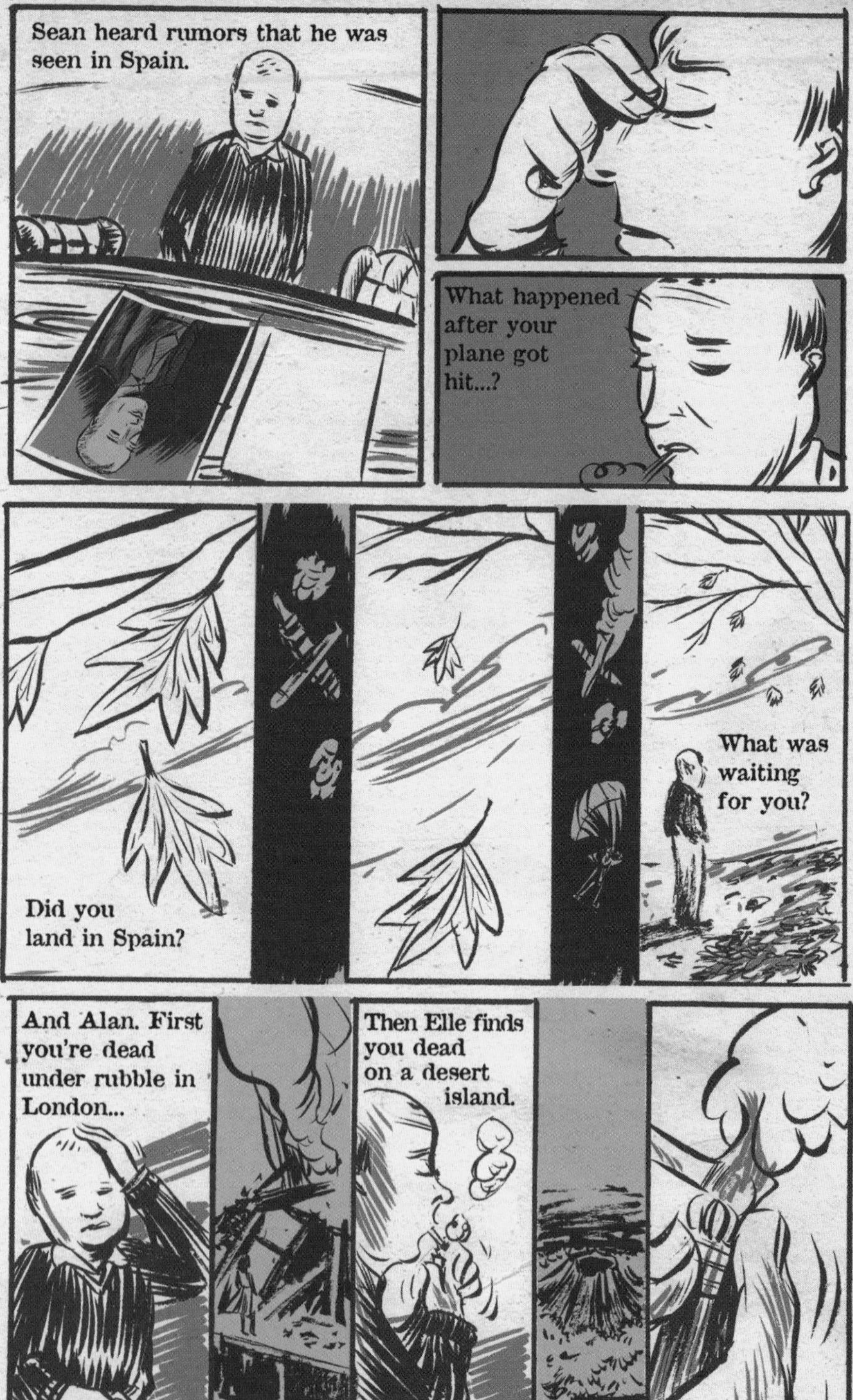
Sean heard rumors that he was seen in Spain.
What happened after your plane got hit...?
Did you land in Spain?
What was waiting for you?
And Alan. First you're dead under rubble in London...
Then Elle finds you dead on a desert island.

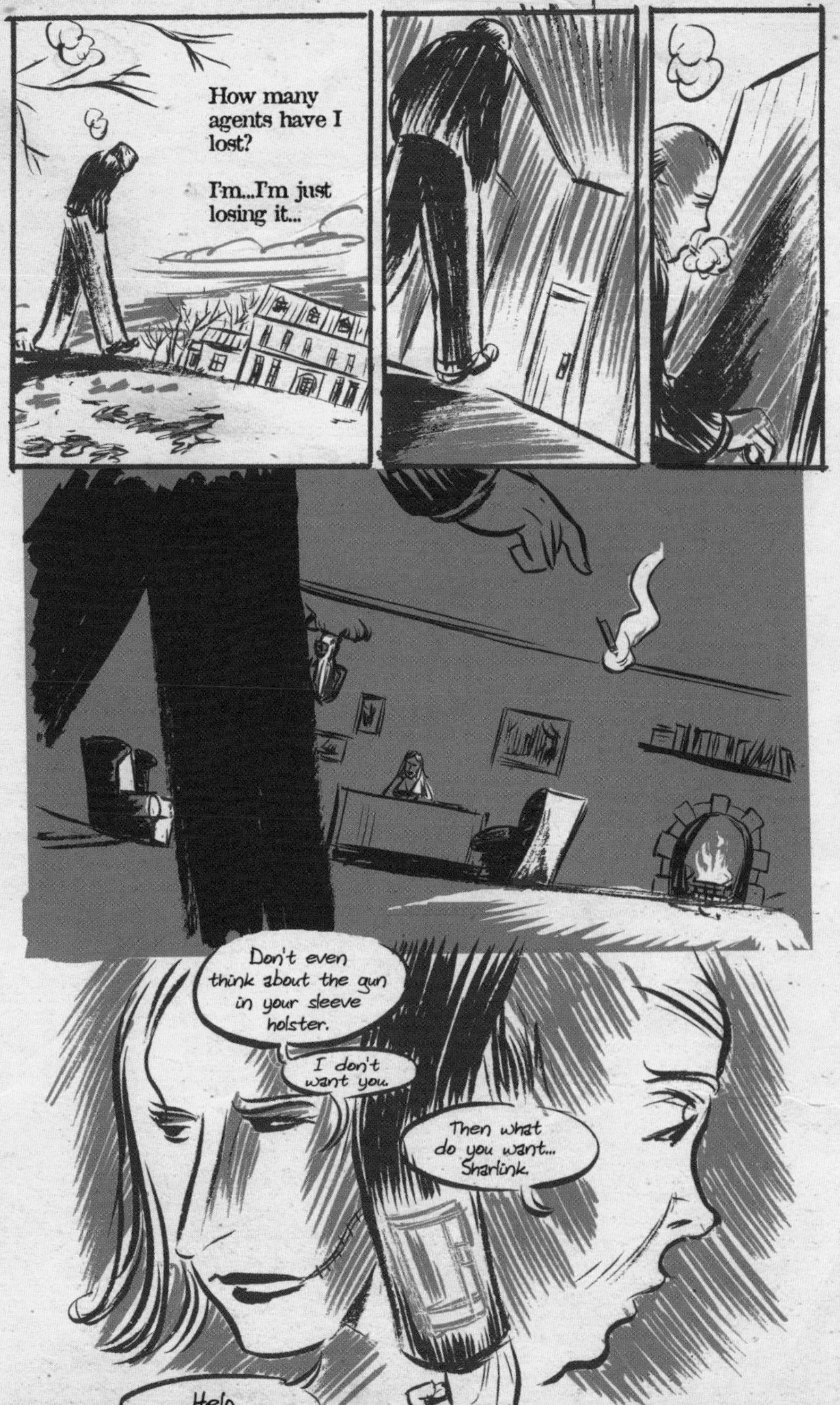
How many agents have I lost?
I'm...I'm just losing it...
Don't even think about the gun in your sleeve holster.
I don't want you.
Then what do you want... Sharlink.
Help.

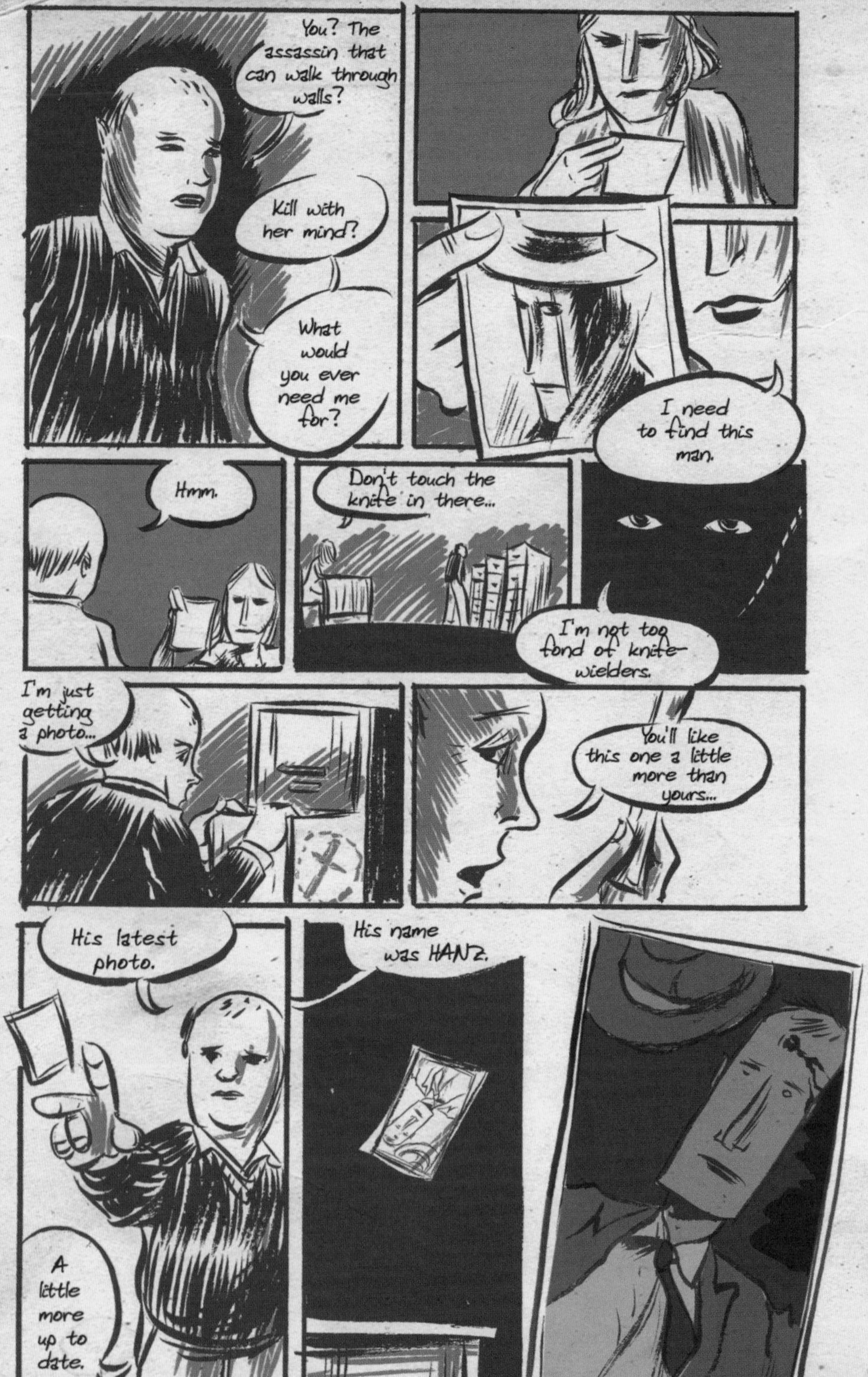
You? The assassin that can walk through walls?
Kill with her mind?
What would you ever need me for?
I need to find this man.
Hmm.
Don't touch the knife in there...
I'm not too fond of knife wielders.
I'm just getting a photo...
You'll like this one a little more than yours...
His latest photo.
A little more up to date.
His name was HANZ.

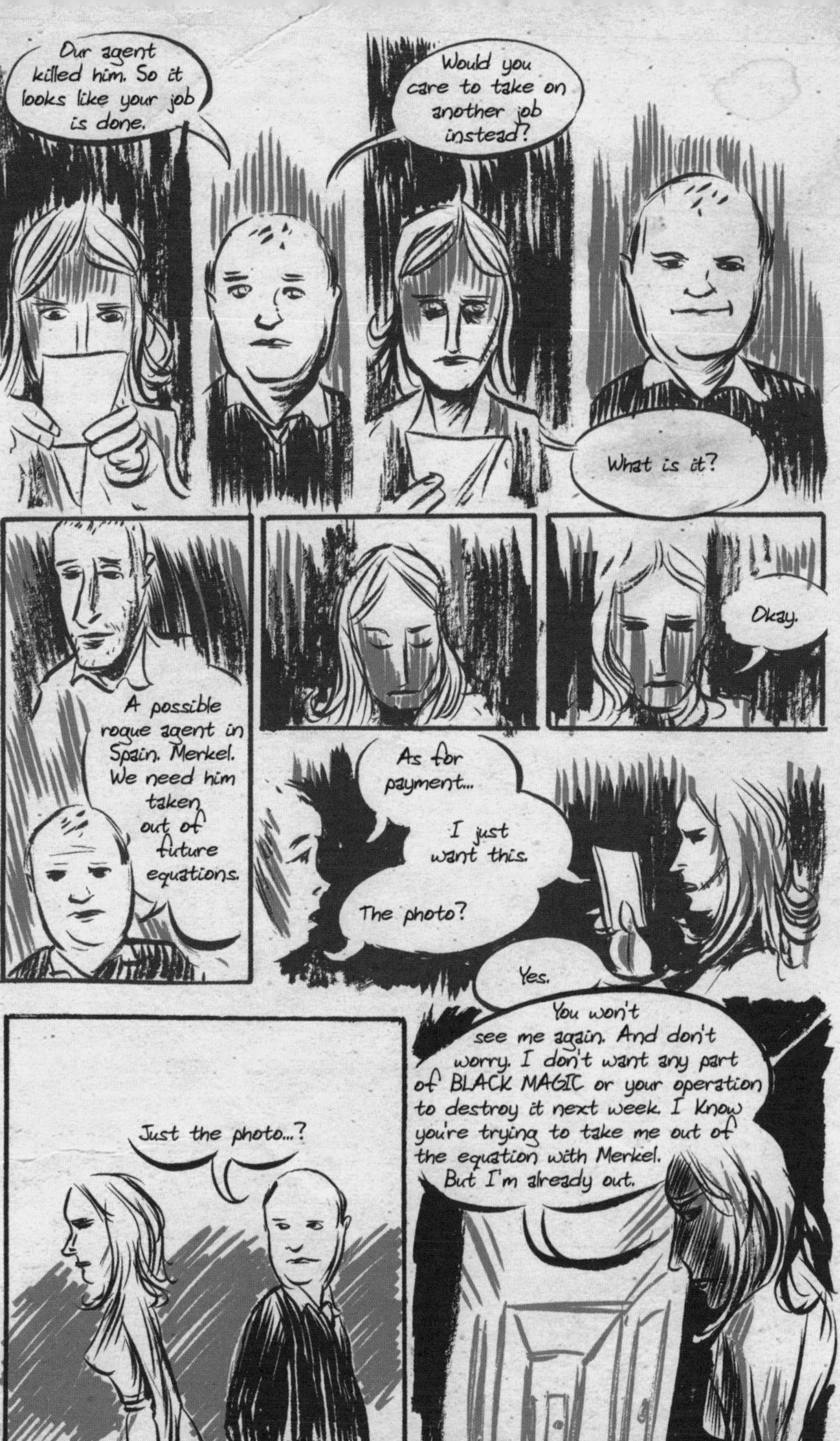

Our agent killed him. So it looks like your job is done.
Would you care to take on another job instead?
What is it?
A possible rogue agent in Spain. Merkel. We need him taken out of future equations.
Okay.
As for payment...
I just want this.
The photo?
Yes.
Just the photo...?
You won't see me again. And don't worry. I don't want any part of BLACK MAGIC or your operation to destroy it next week. I know you're trying to take me out of the equation with Merkel. But I'm already out.

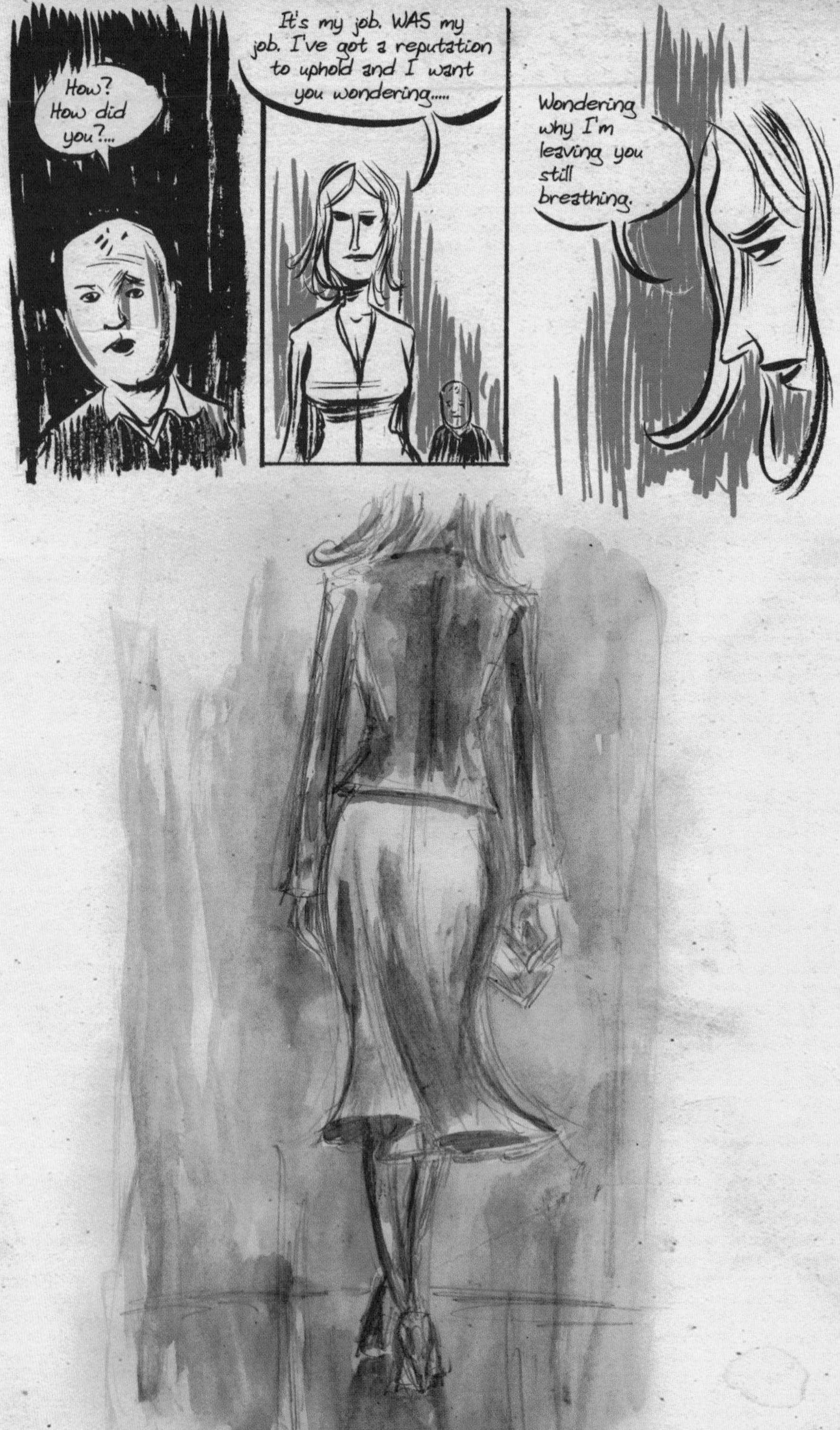
How? How did you?...
It's my job. WAS my job. I've got a reputation to uphold and I want you wondering.....
Wondering why I'm leaving you still breathing.

THE END: 1
Dossier #0361944

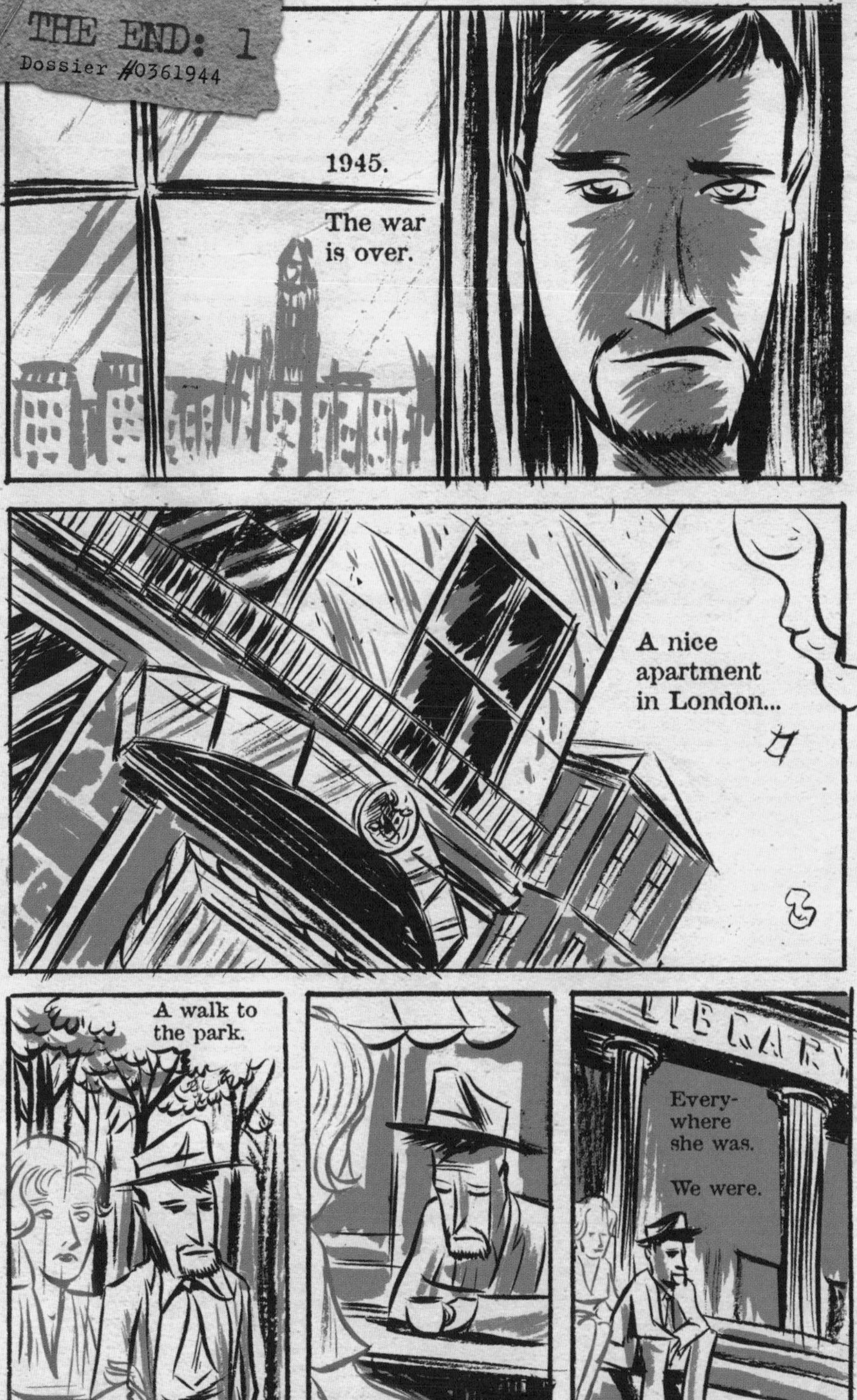
1945.
The war is over.
A nice apartment in London...
A walk to the park.
Our cafe.
Every-where she was.
We were.

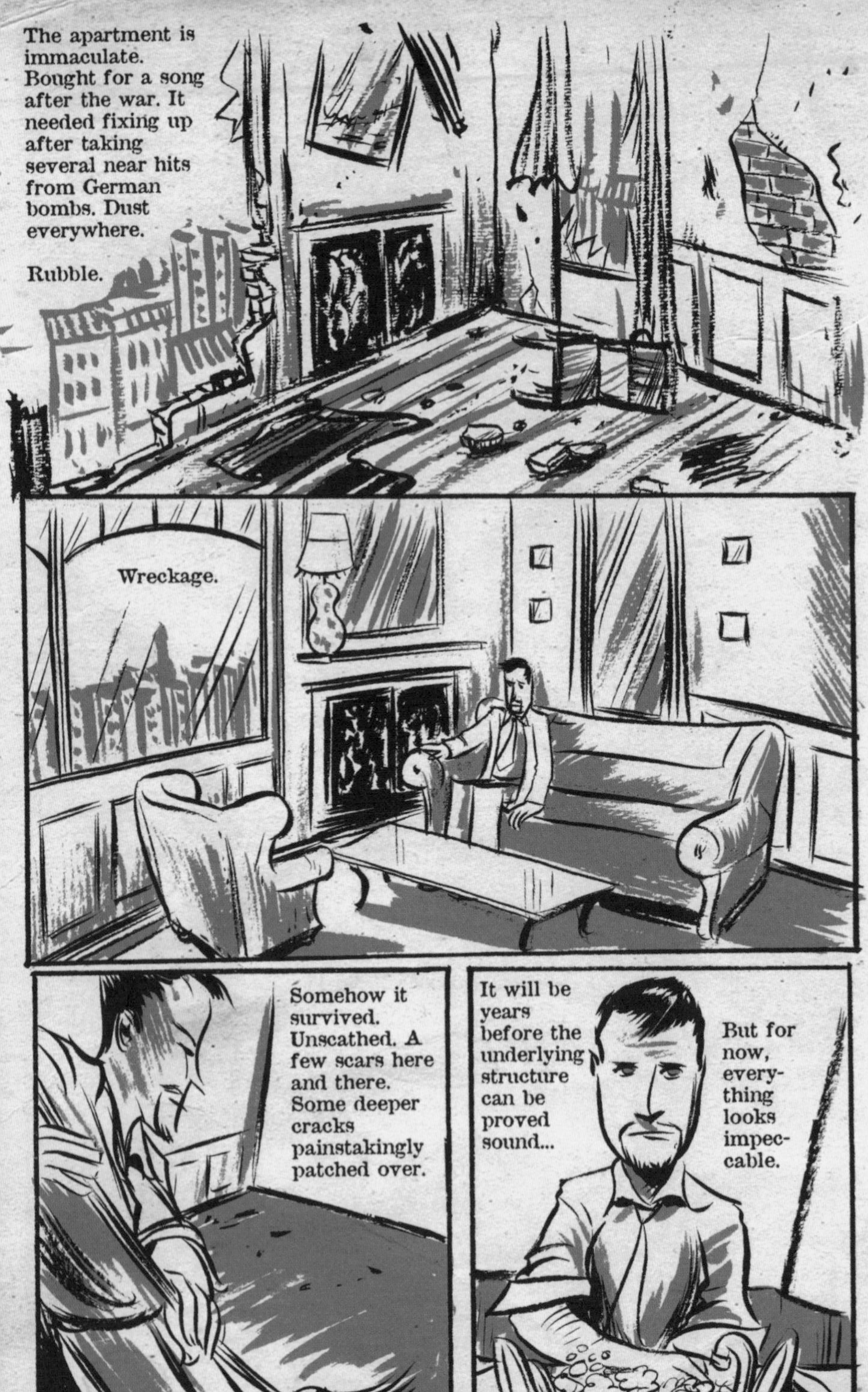
The apartment is immaculate. Bought for a song after the war. It needed fixing up after taking several near hits from German bombs. Dust everywhere.
Rubble.
Wreckage.
Somehow it survived. Unscathed. A few scars here and there. Some deeper cracks painstakingly patched over.
It will be years before the underlying structure can be proved sound...
But for now, every-thing looks impec-cable.

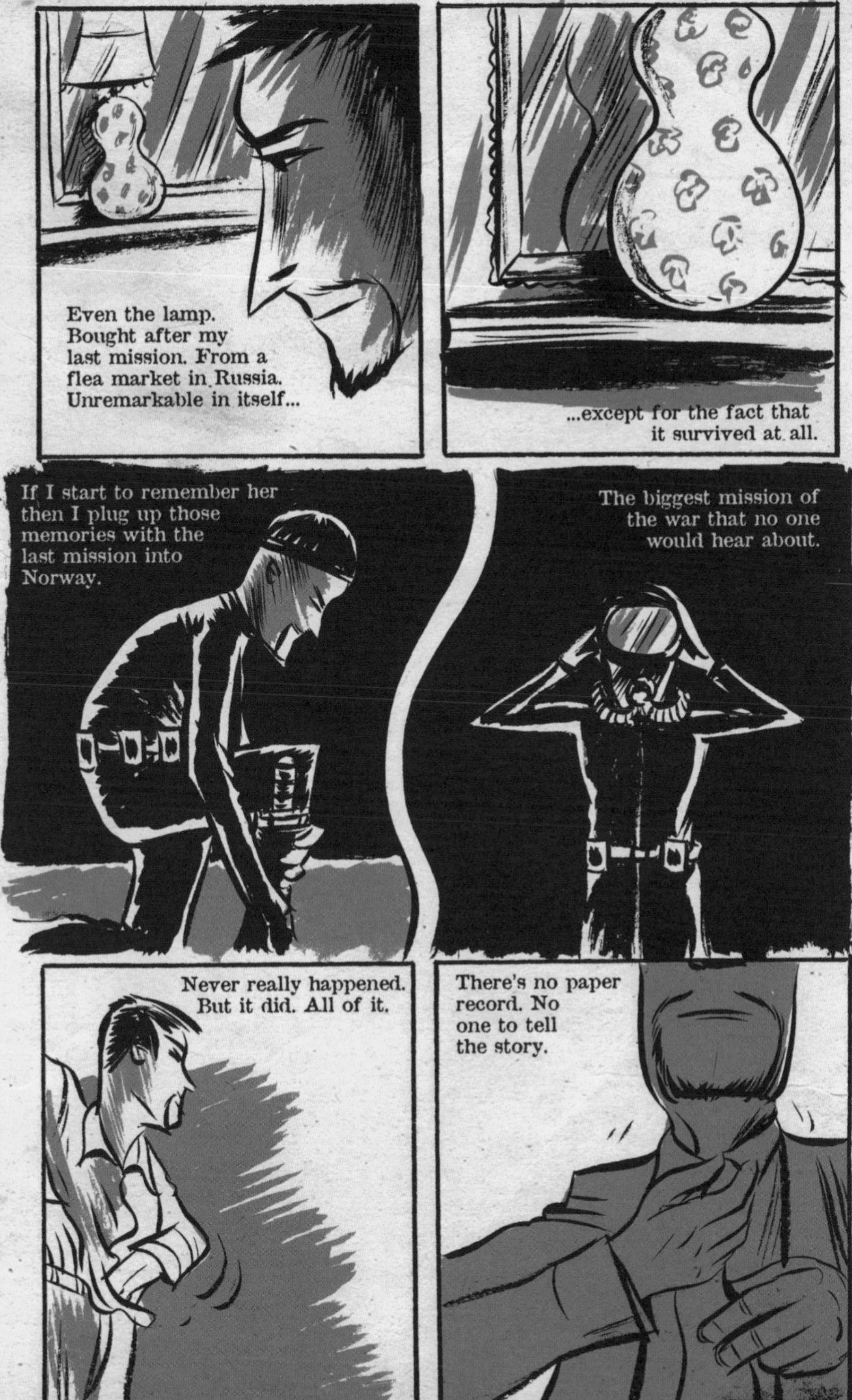
Even the lamp. Bought after my last mission. From a flea market in Russia. Unremarkable in itself...
...except for the fact that it survived at all.
If I start to remember her then I plug up those memories with the last mission into Norway.
The biggest mission of the war that no one would hear about.
Never really happened. But it did. All of it.
There's no paper record. No one to tell the story.

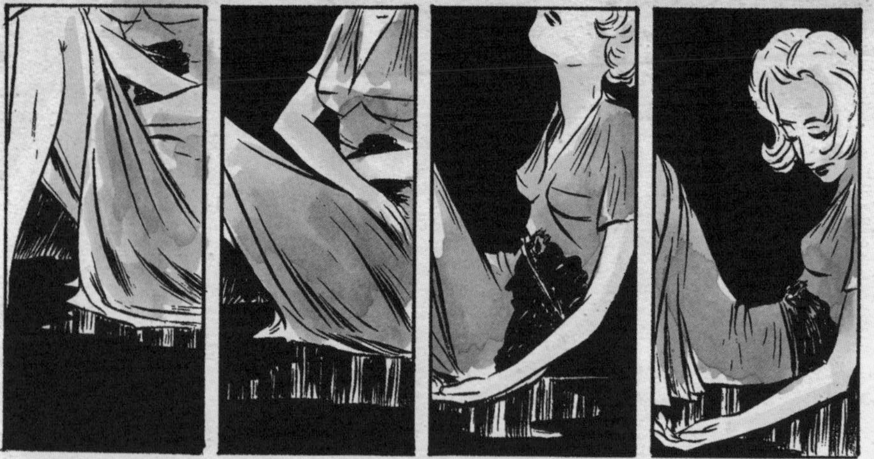

Just my memory. My memory. Of her. Dying in a closet because of me.

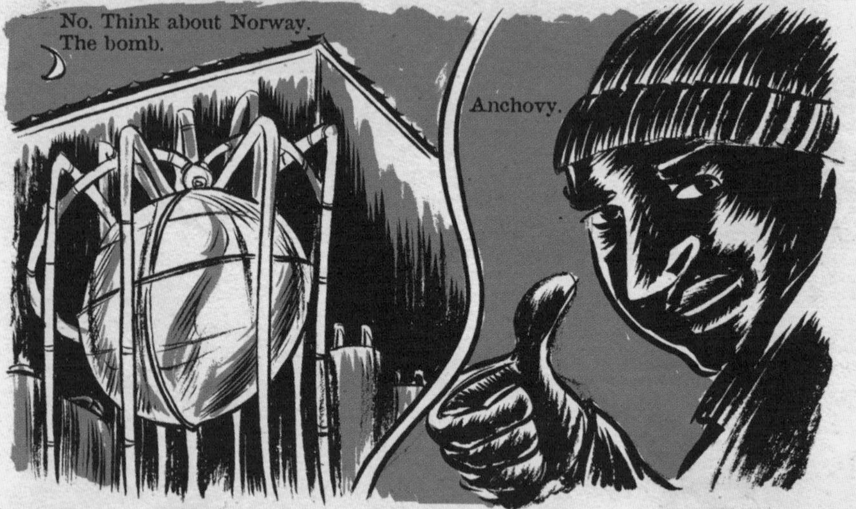
No. Think about Norway.
The bomb.
Anchovy.

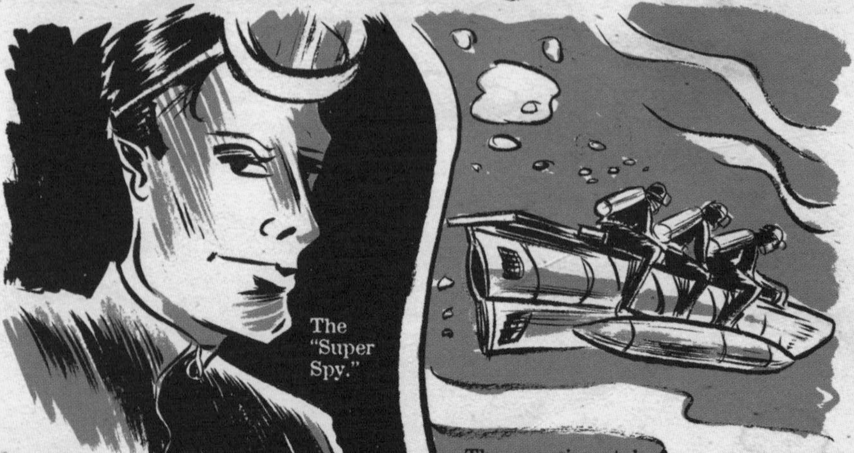
The "Super Spy."
The experimental submarine.

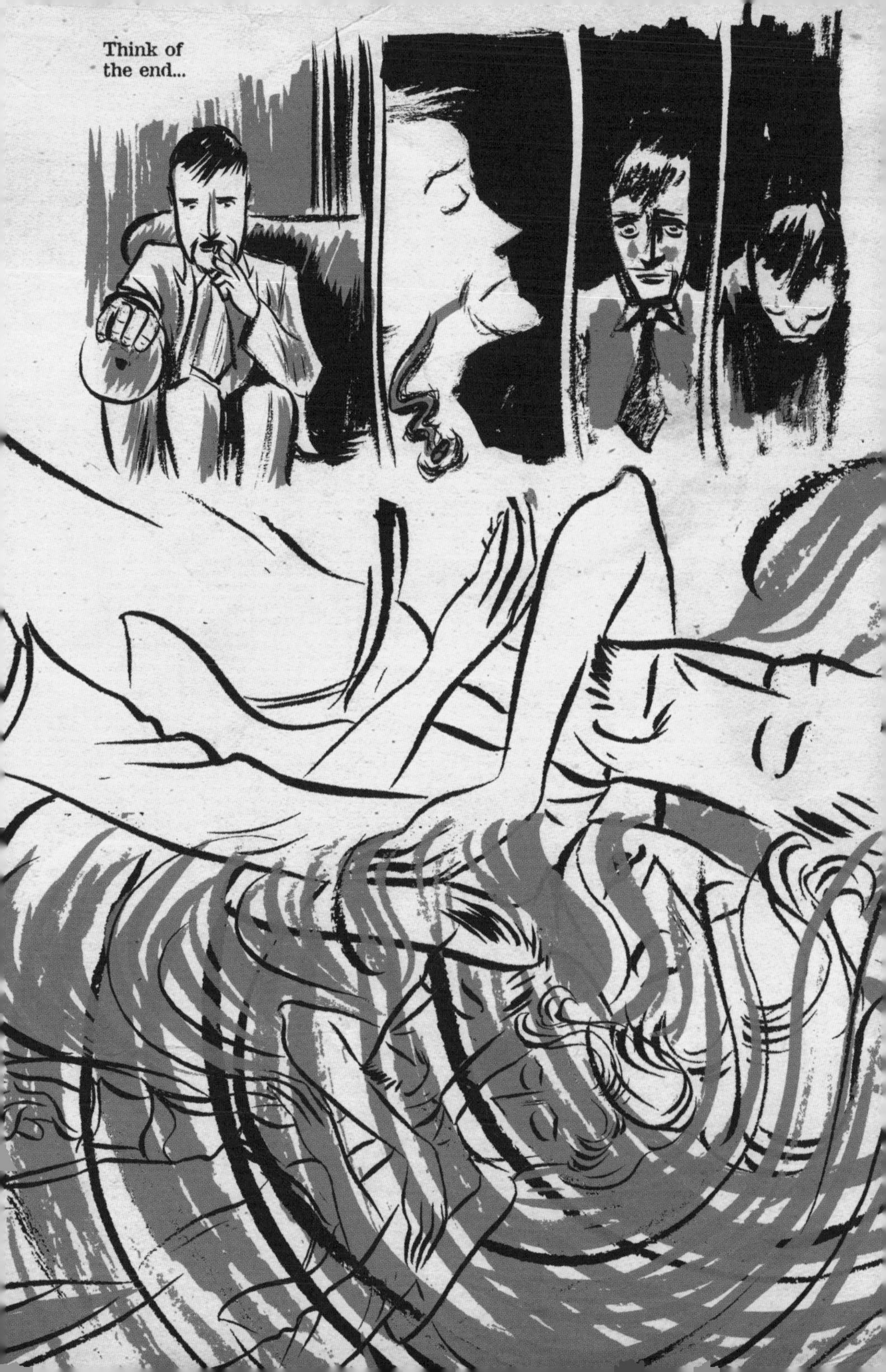
Think of
the end...

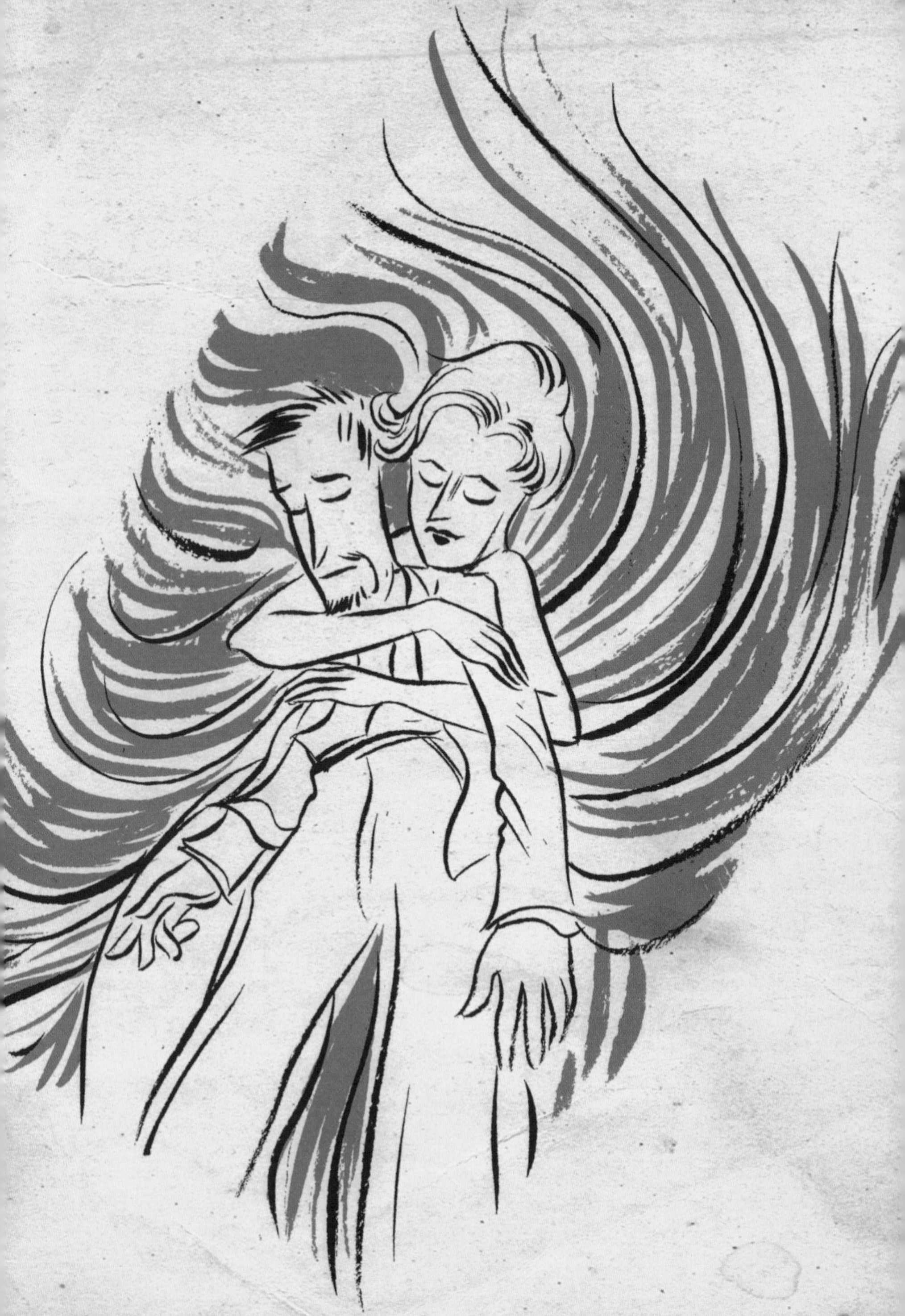

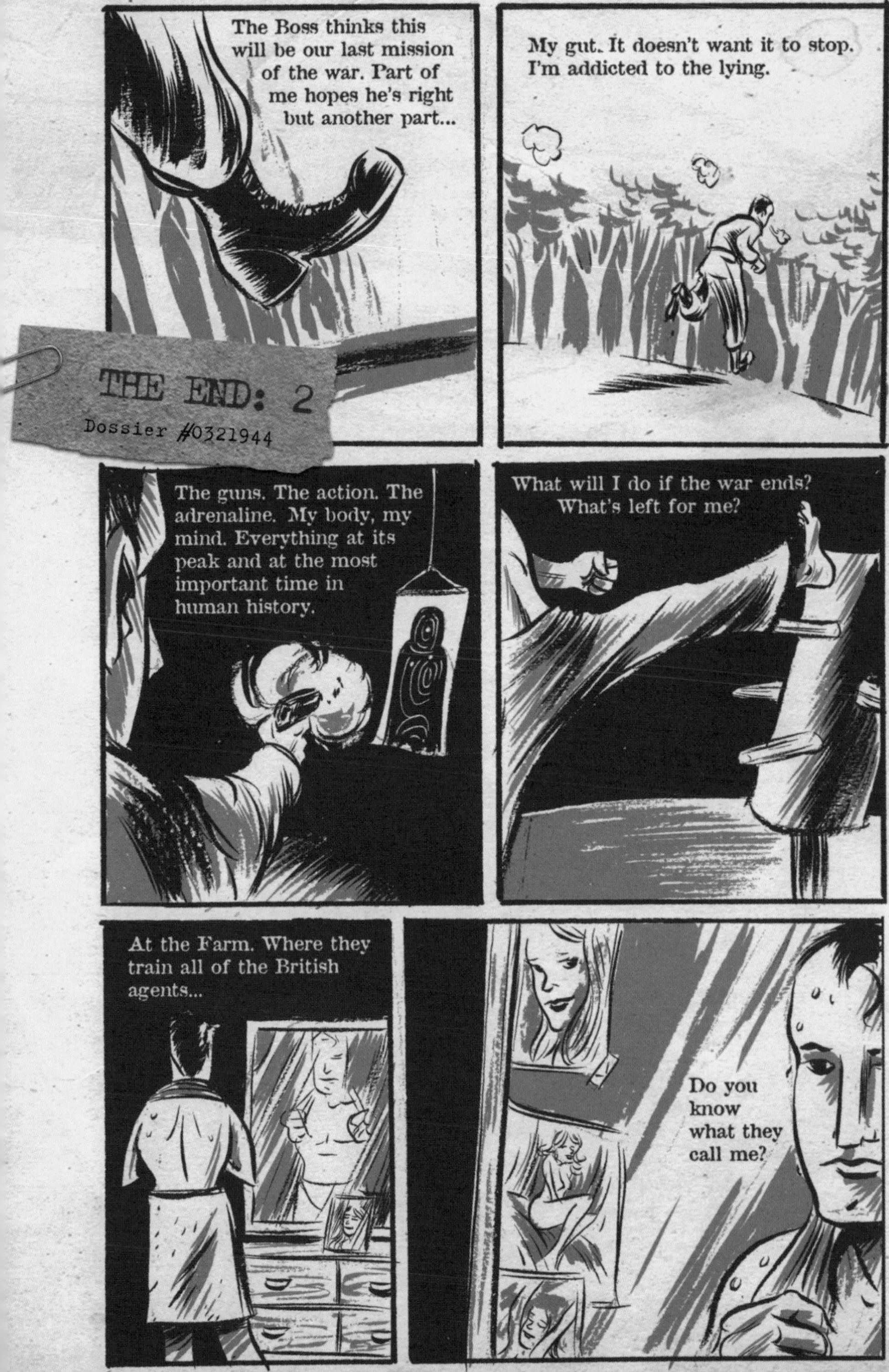

The Boss thinks this will be our last mission of the war. Part of me hopes he's right but another part...
THE END: 2
Dossier #0321944
My gut. It doesn't want it to stop. I'm addicted to the lying.
The guns. The action. The adrenaline. My body, my mind. Everything at its peak and at the most important time in human history.
What will I do if the war ends? What's left for me?
At the Farm. Where they train all of the British agents...
Do you know what they call me?

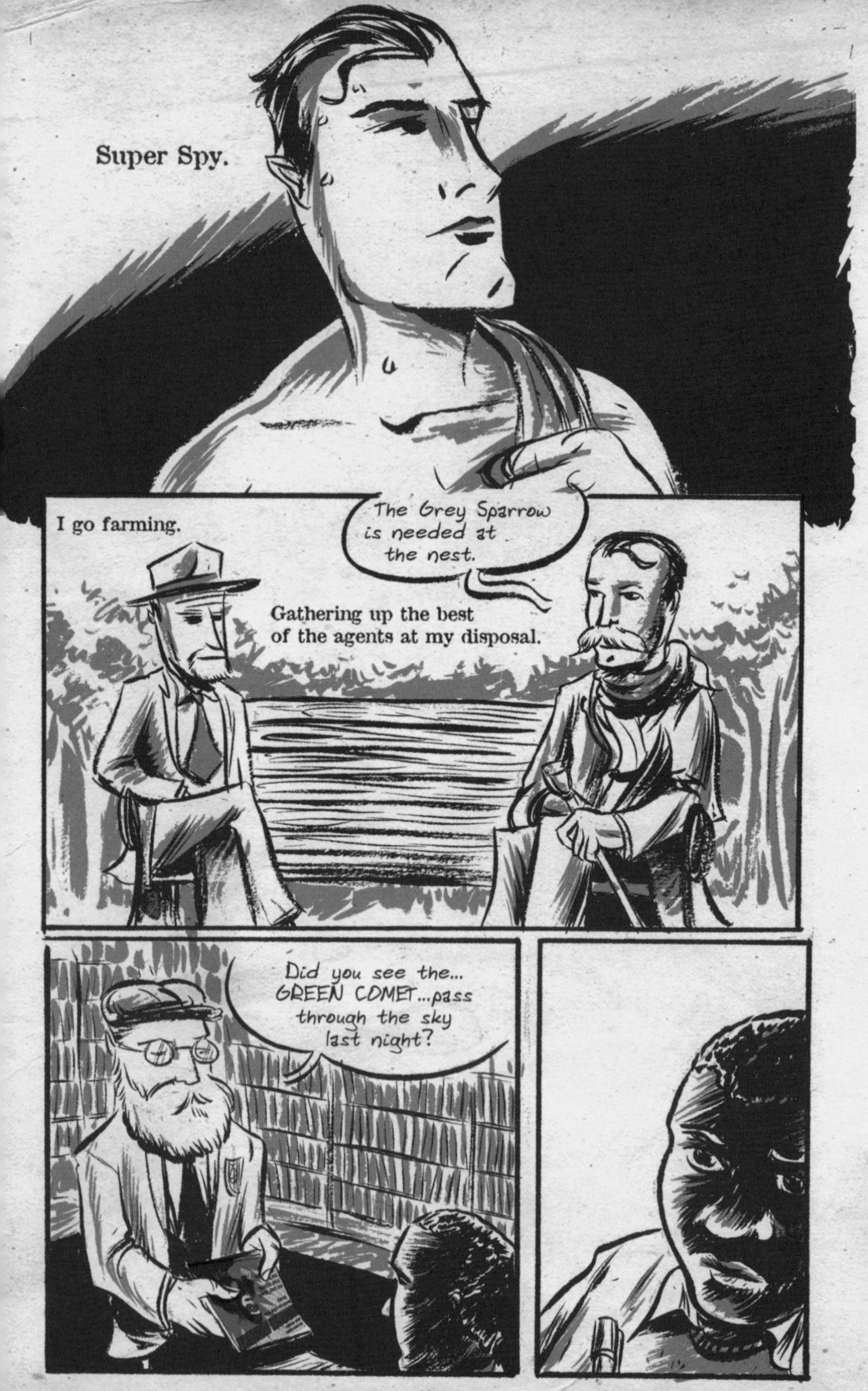
Super Spy.
I go farming.
The Grey Sparrow is needed at the nest.
Gathering up the best of the agents at my disposal.
Did you see the... GREEN COMET...pass through the sky last night?

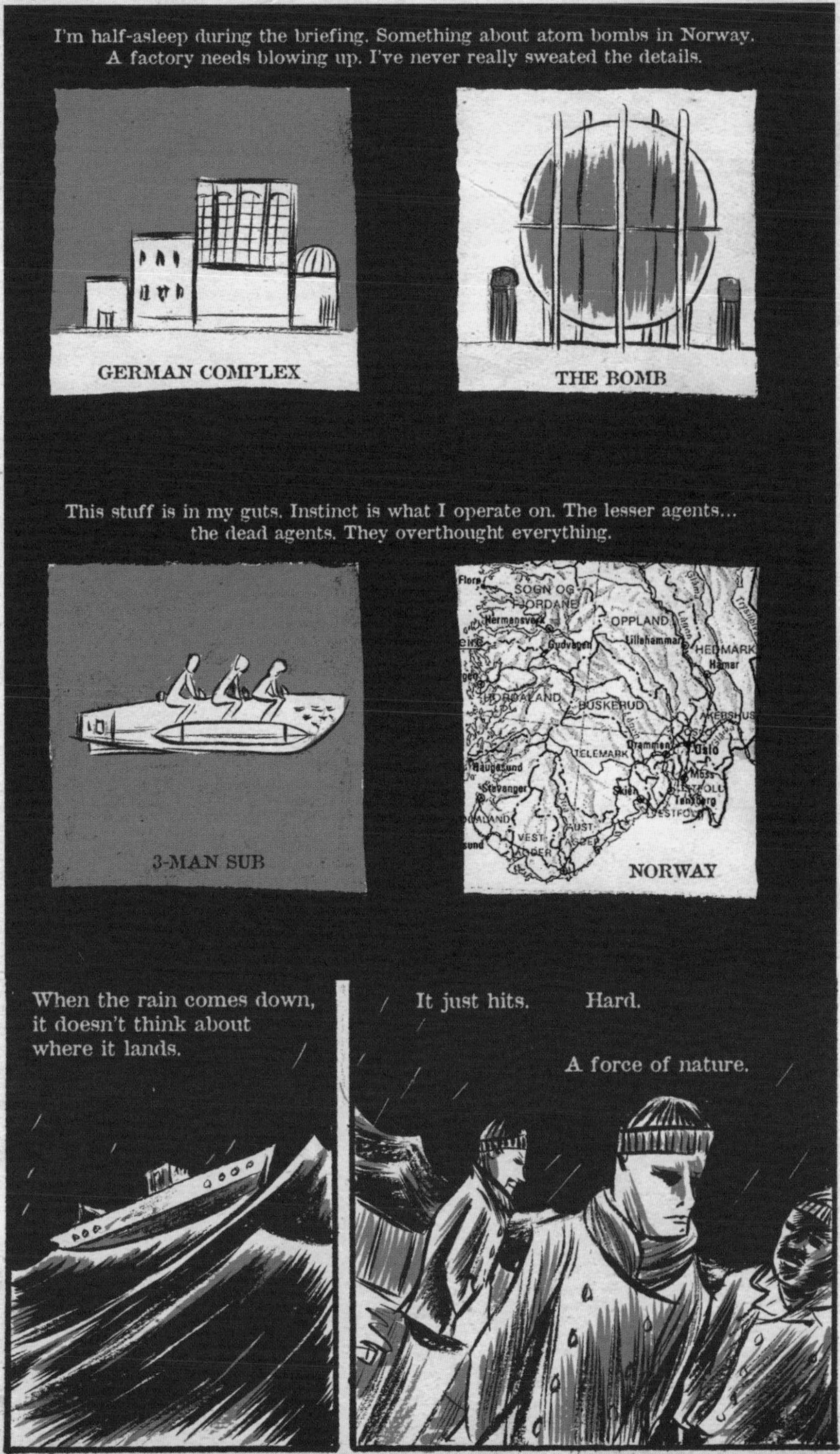

I'm half-asleep during the briefing. Something about atom bombs in Norway. A factory needs blowing up. I've never really sweated the details.
GERMAN COMPLEX
THE BOMB
This stuff is in my guts. Instinct is what I operate on. The lesser agents... the dead agents. They overthought everything.
3-MAN SUB
OPPLAND
HEDMARK
HORDALAND
BUSKERUD
TELEMARK
NORWAY
When the rain comes down, it doesn't think about where it lands.
It just hits.
Hard.
A force of nature.

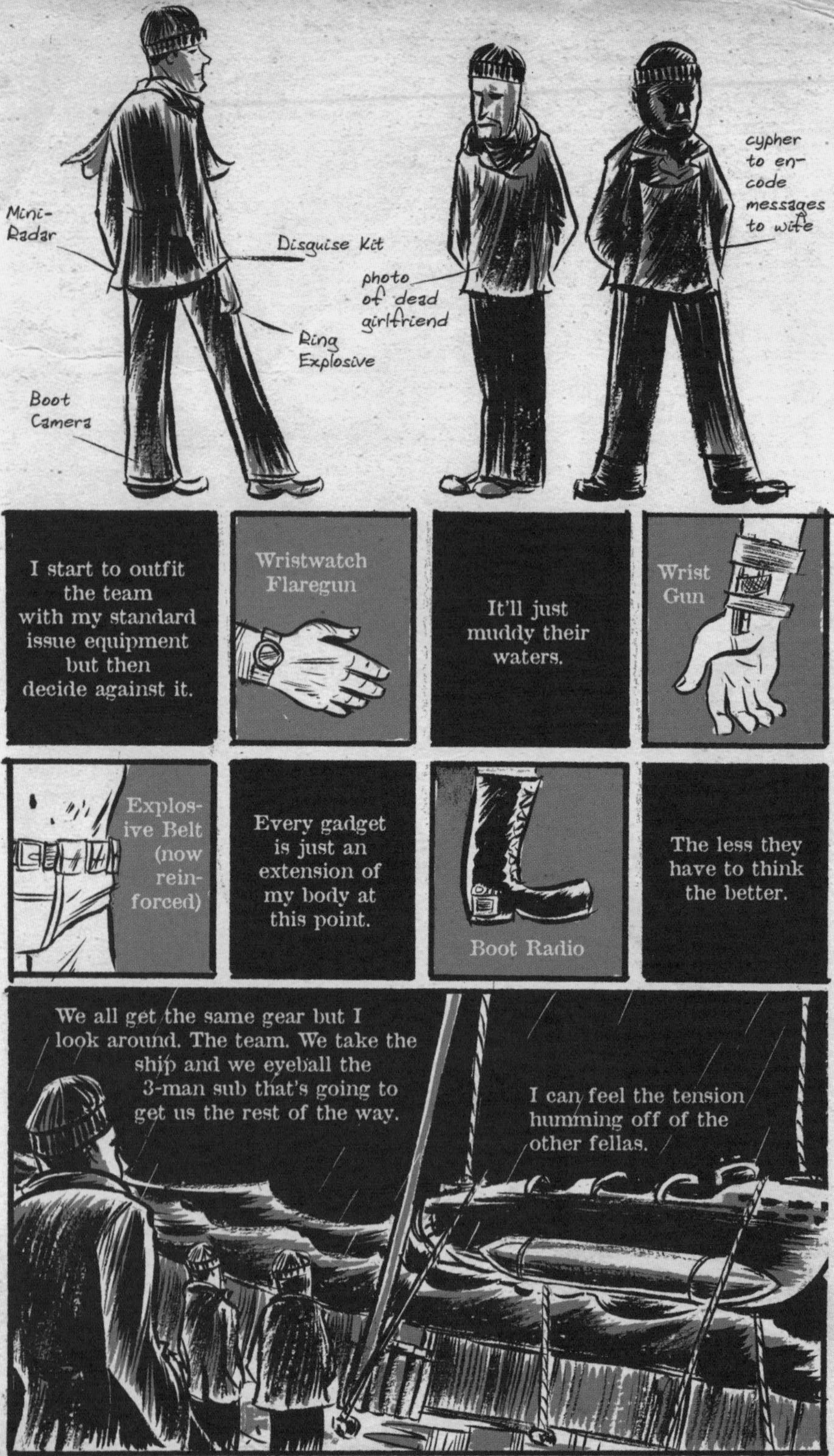

Mini-Radar
Disguise Kit
Ring Explosive
Boot Camera
photo of dead girlfriend
cypher to en-code messages to wife
I start to outfit the team with my standard issue equipment but then decide against it.
Wristwatch Flaregun
It'll just muddy their waters.
Wrist Gun
Explosive Belt (now reinforced)
Every gadget is just an extension of my body at this point.
Boot Radio
The less they have to think the better.
We all get the same gear but I look around. The team. We take the ship and we eyeball the 3-man sub that's going to get us the rest of the way.
I can feel the tension humming off of the other fellas.

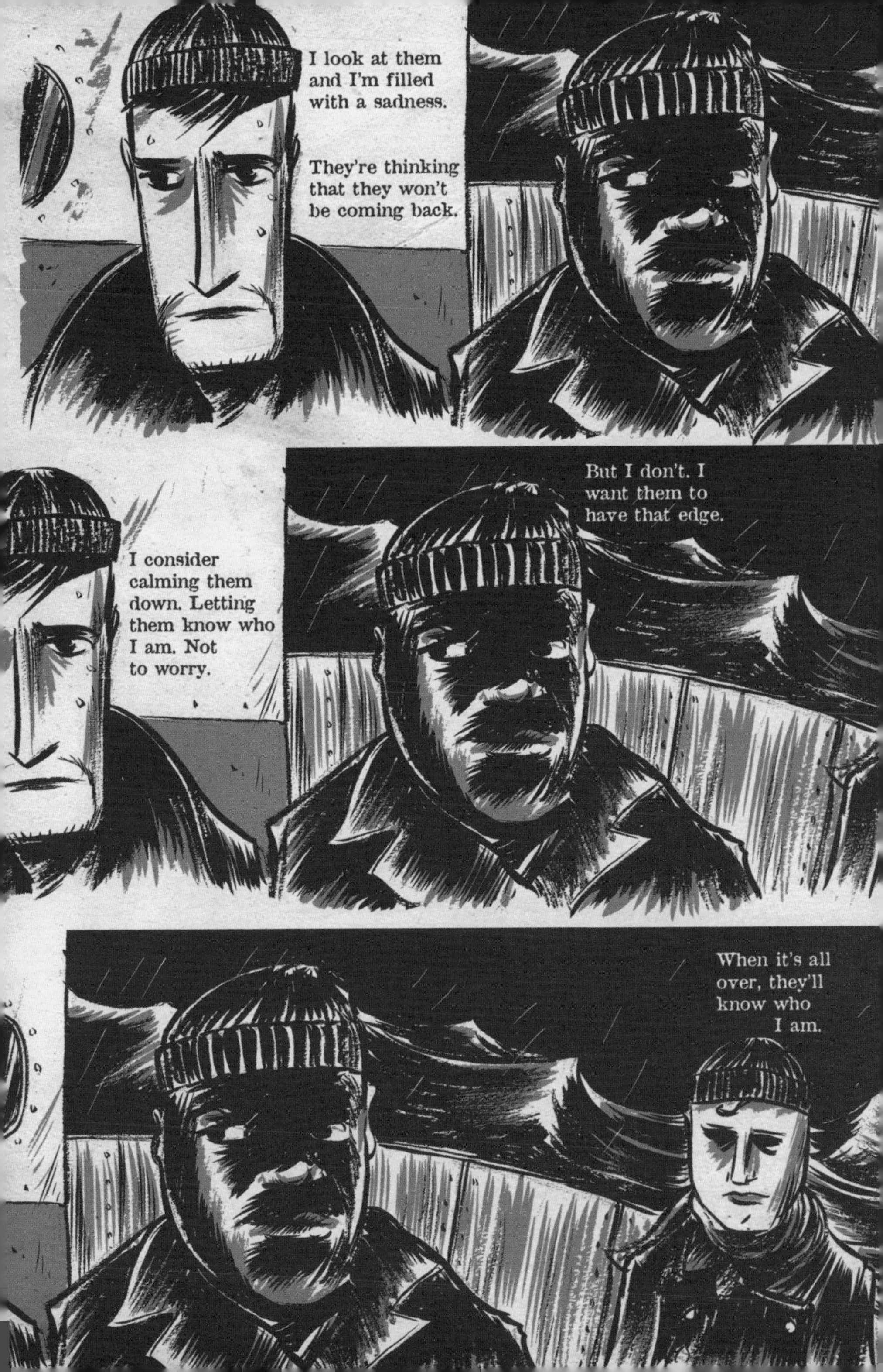
I look at them and I'm filled with a sadness.
They're thinking that they won't be coming back.
I consider calming them down. Letting them know who I am. Not to worry.
But I don't. I want them to have that edge.
When it's all over, they'll know who I am.

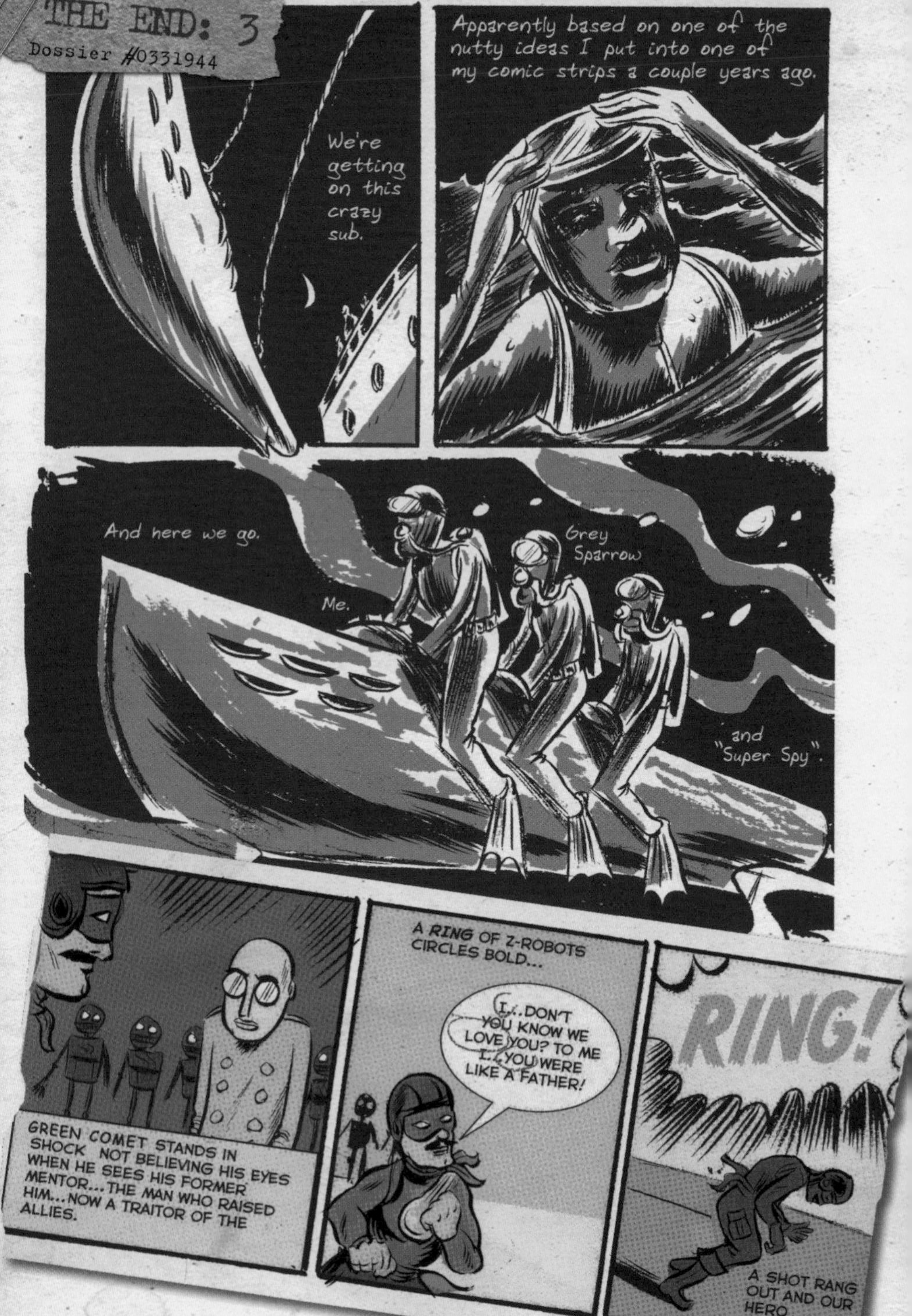
We're getting on this crazy sub.
Apparently based on one of the nutty ideas I put into one of my comic strips a couple years ago.
And here we go.
Me.
Grey Sparrow
and "Super Spy".
GREEN COMET STANDS IN SHOCK NOT BELIEVING HIS EYES WHEN HE SEES HIS FORMER MENTOR...THE MAN WHO RAISED HIM...NOW A TRAITOR OF THE ALLIES.
A RING OF Z-ROBOTS CIRCLES BOLD...
I...DON'T YOU KNOW WE LOVE YOU? TO ME I...YOU WERE LIKE A FATHER!
RING!
A SHOT RANG OUT AND OUR HERO COLLAPSES...

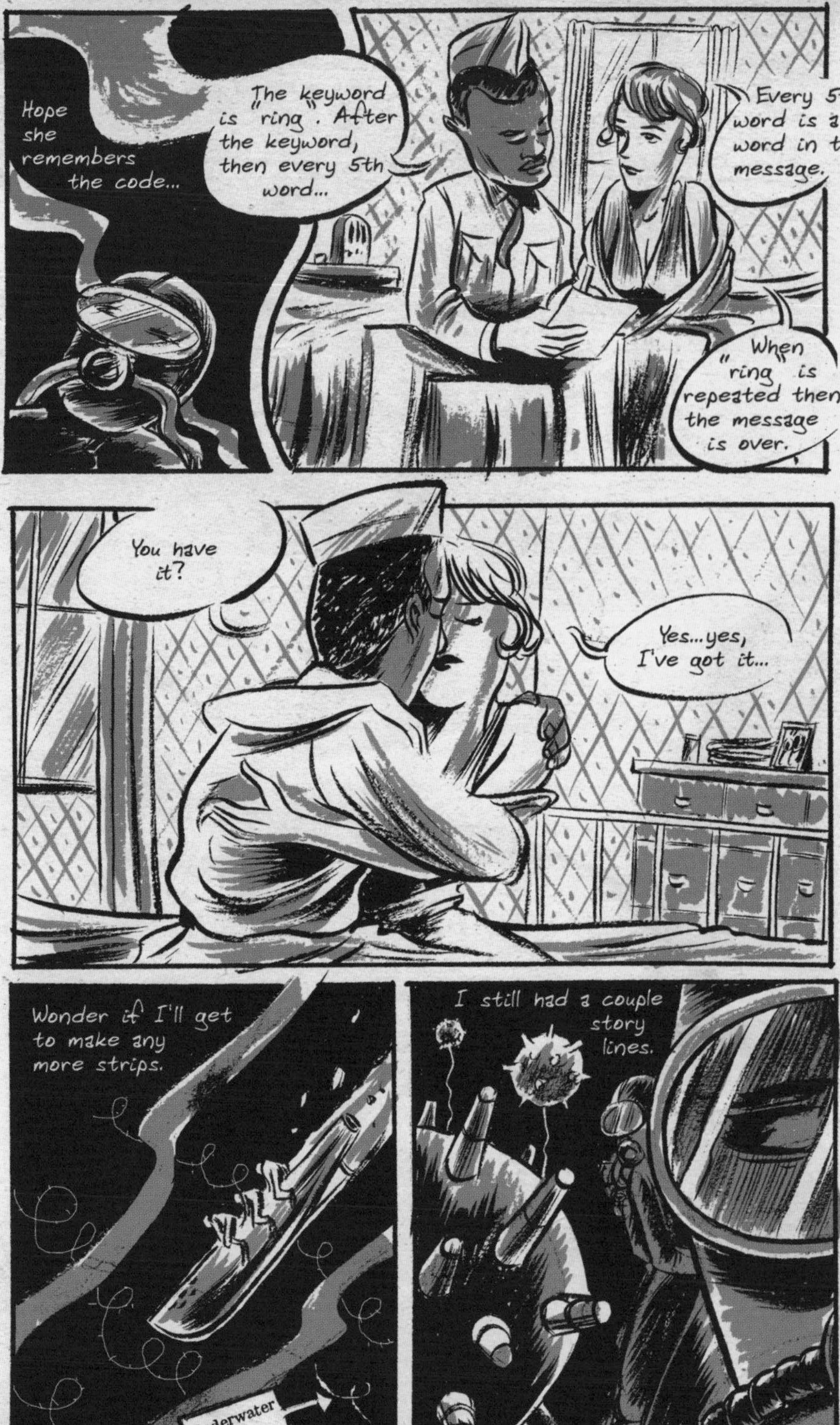
Hope she remembers the code...
The keyword is "ring". After the keyword, then every 5th word...
Every 5th word is a word in the message.
When "ring" is repeated then the message is over.
You have it?
Yes...yes, I've got it...
Wonder if I'll get to make any more strips.
Underwater barbed wire.
I still had a couple story lines.

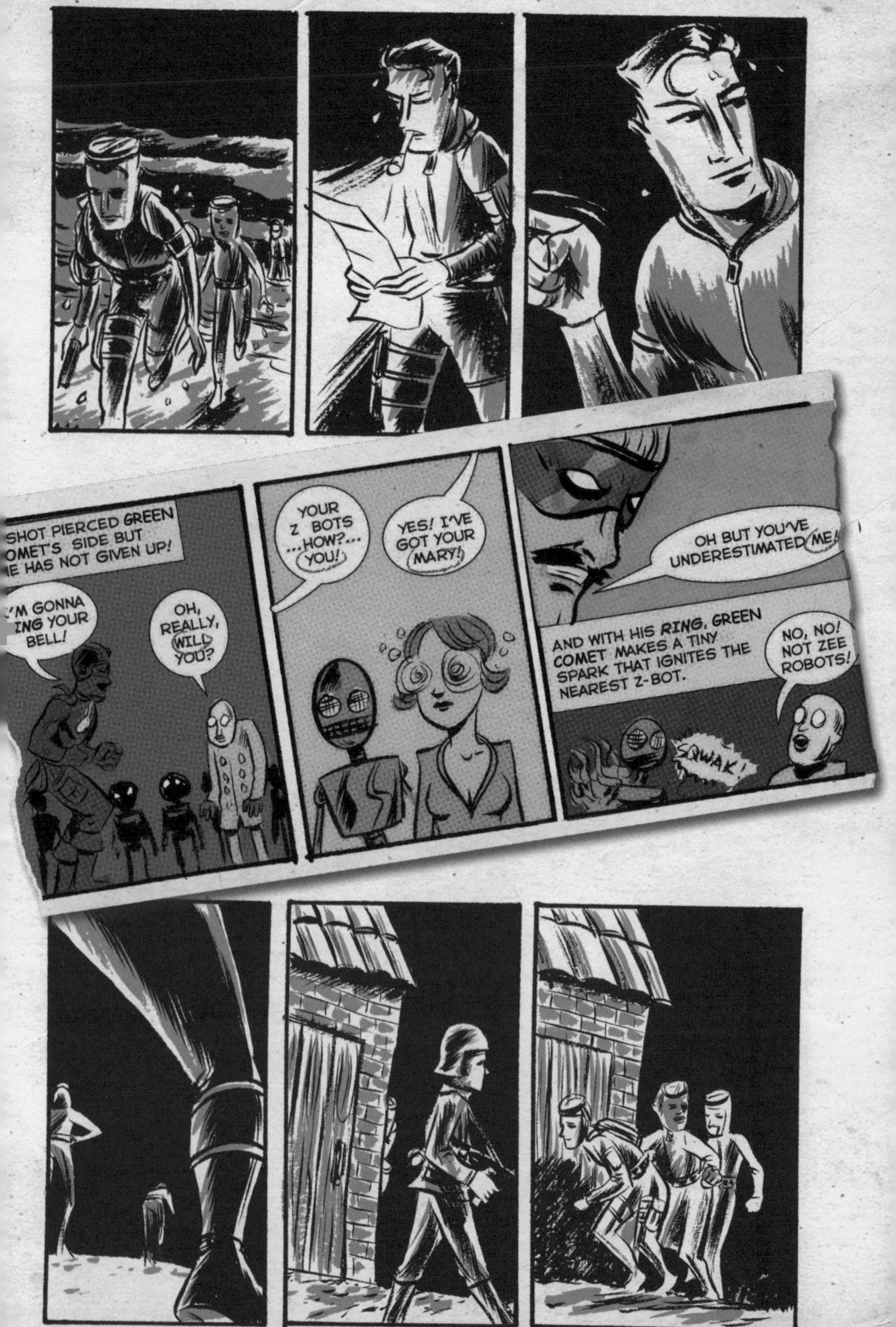
SHOT PIERCED GREEN
OMET'S SIDE BUT
E HAS NOT GIVEN UP!
'M GONNA
ING YOUR
BELL!
OH, REALLY, WILL YOU?
YOUR Z BOTS ...HOW?... YOU!
YES! I'VE GOT YOUR MARY!
OH BUT YOU'VE UNDERESTIMATED ME!
AND WITH HIS RING, GREEN COMET MAKES A TINY SPARK THAT IGNITES THE NEAREST Z-BOT.
NO, NO! NOT ZEE ROBOTS!
SQWAK!

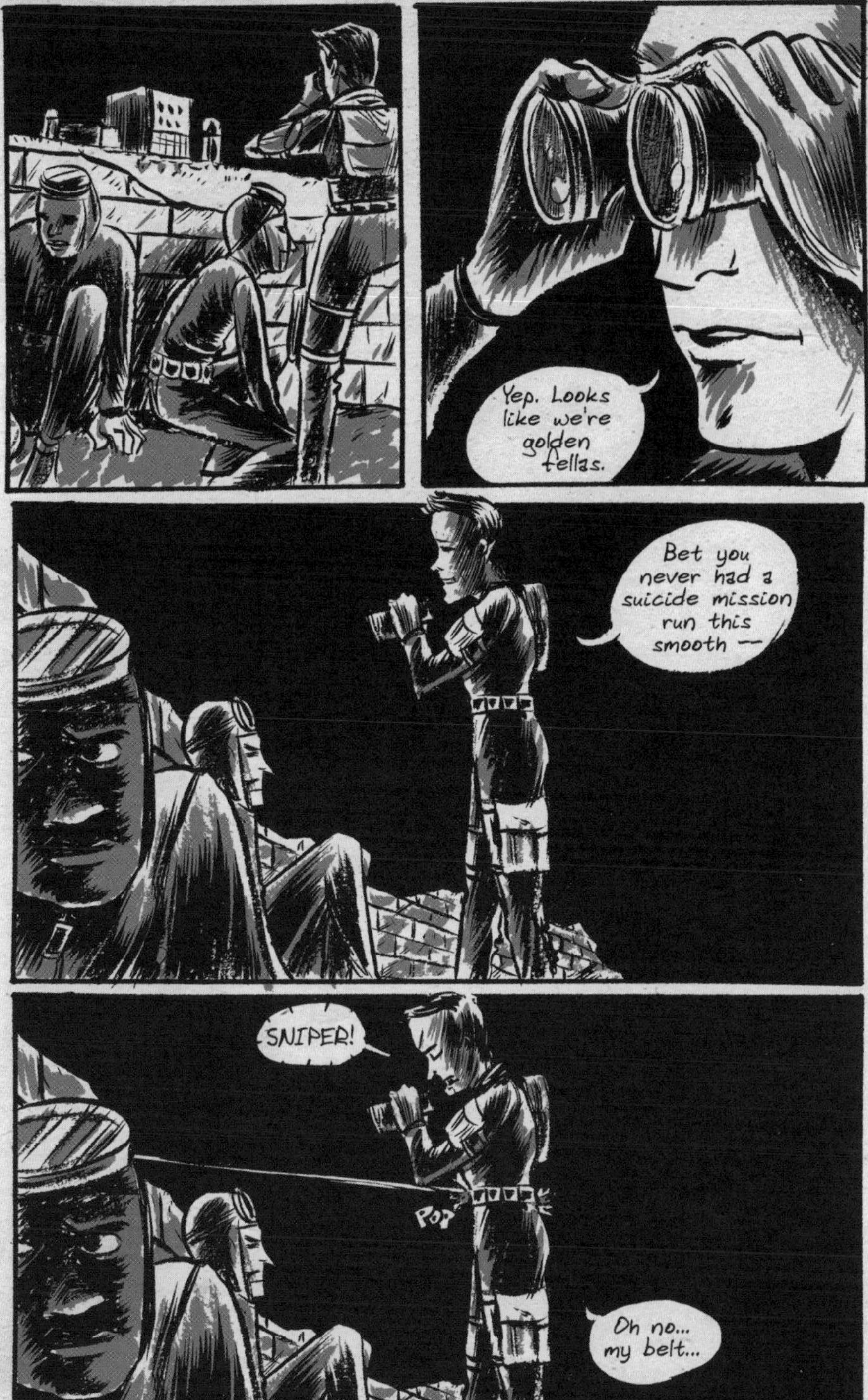
Yep. Looks like we're golden fellas.
Bet you never had a suicide mission run this smooth --
SNIPER!
POP
Oh no... my belt...

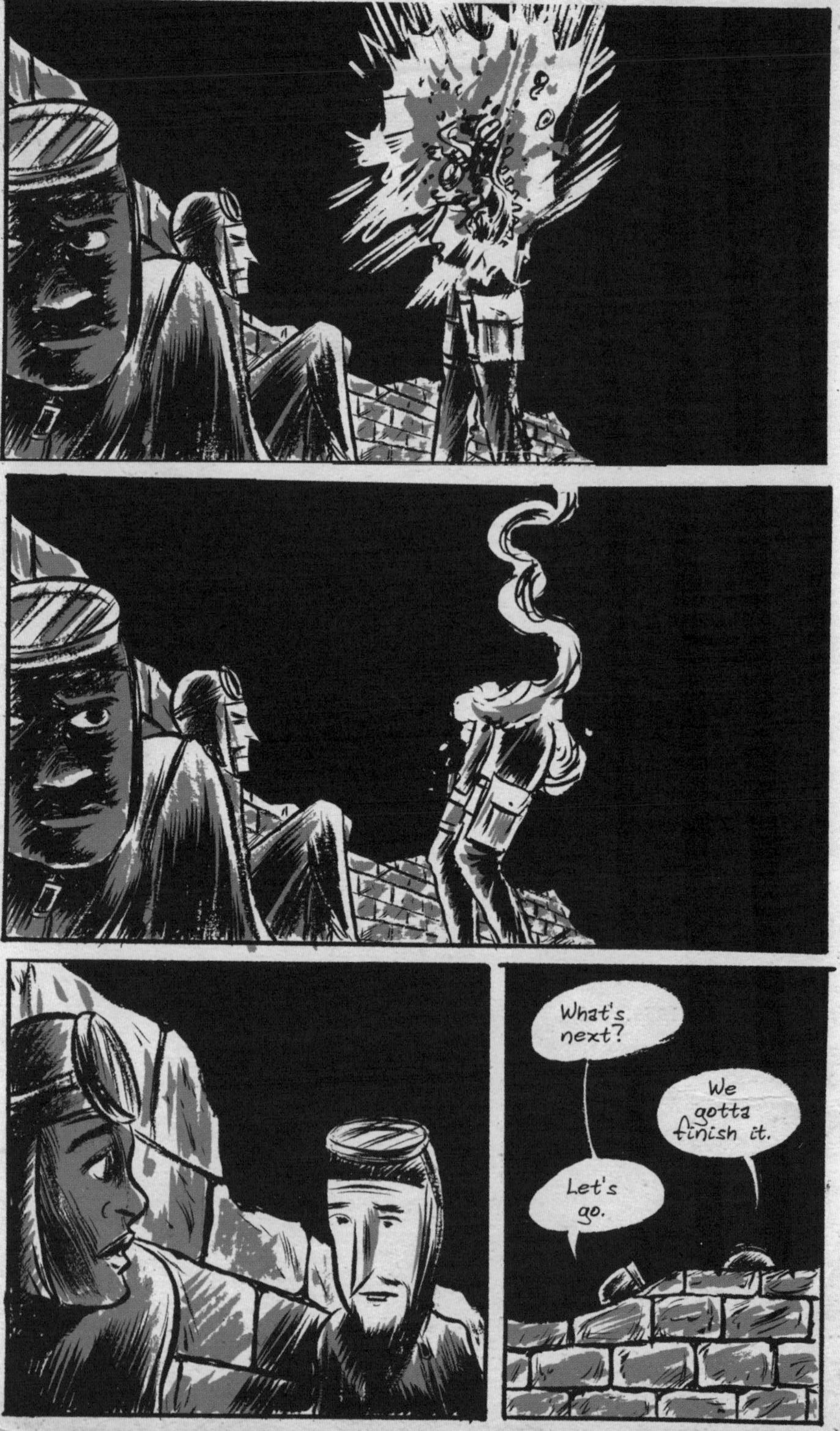
What's next?
We gotta finish it.
Let's go.

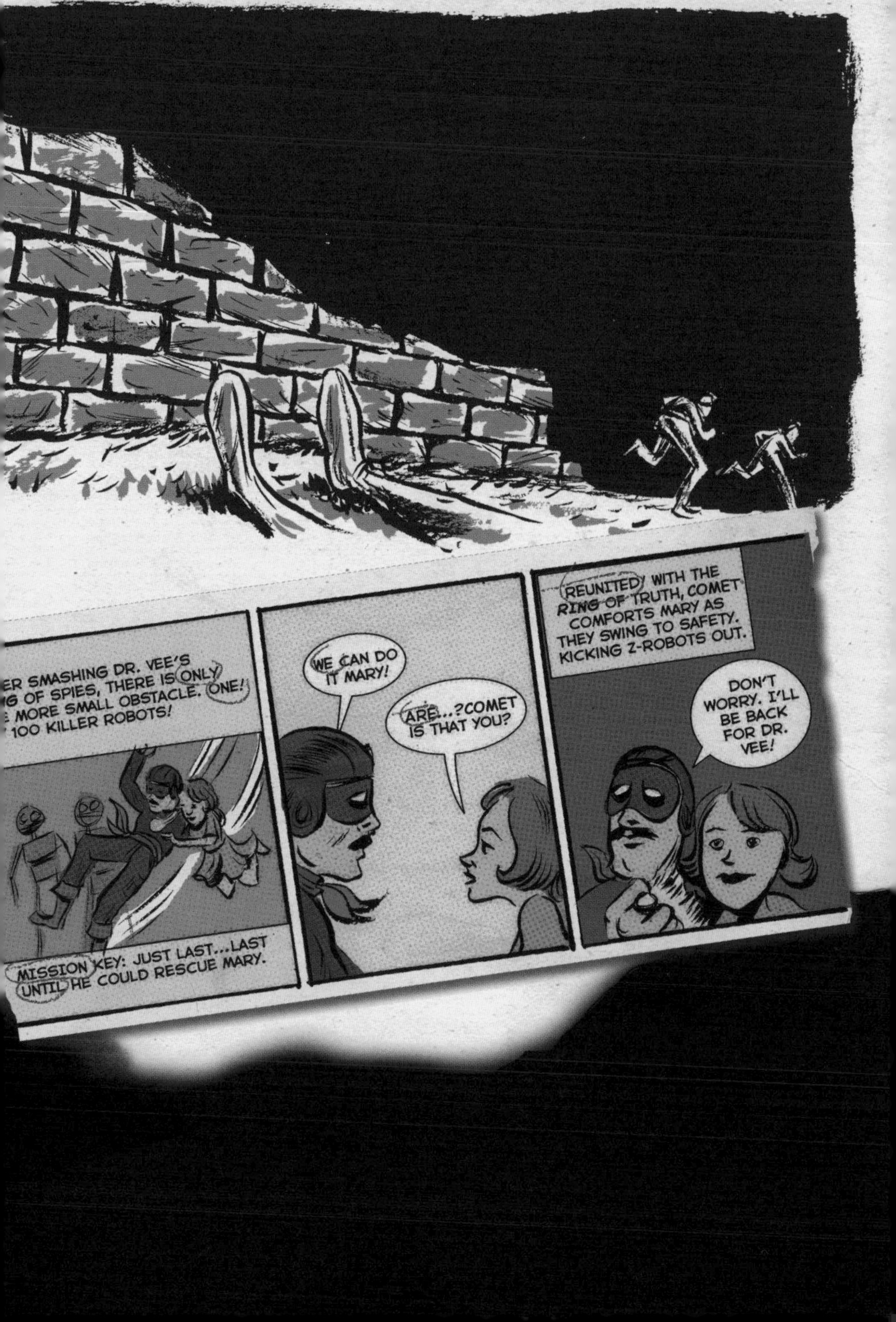

ER SMASHING DR. VEE'S
G OF SPIES, THERE IS ONLY
E MORE SMALL OBSTACLE. ONE!
100 KILLER ROBOTS!
MISSION KEY: JUST LAST...LAST
UNTIL HE COULD RESCUE MARY.
WE CAN DO IT MARY!
ARE...?COMET IS THAT YOU?
REUNITED WITH THE RING OF TRUTH, COMET COMFORTS MARY AS THEY SWING TO SAFETY. KICKING Z-ROBOTS OUT.
DON'T WORRY. I'LL BE BACK FOR DR. VEE!

THE END: 4

Dossier #0311944

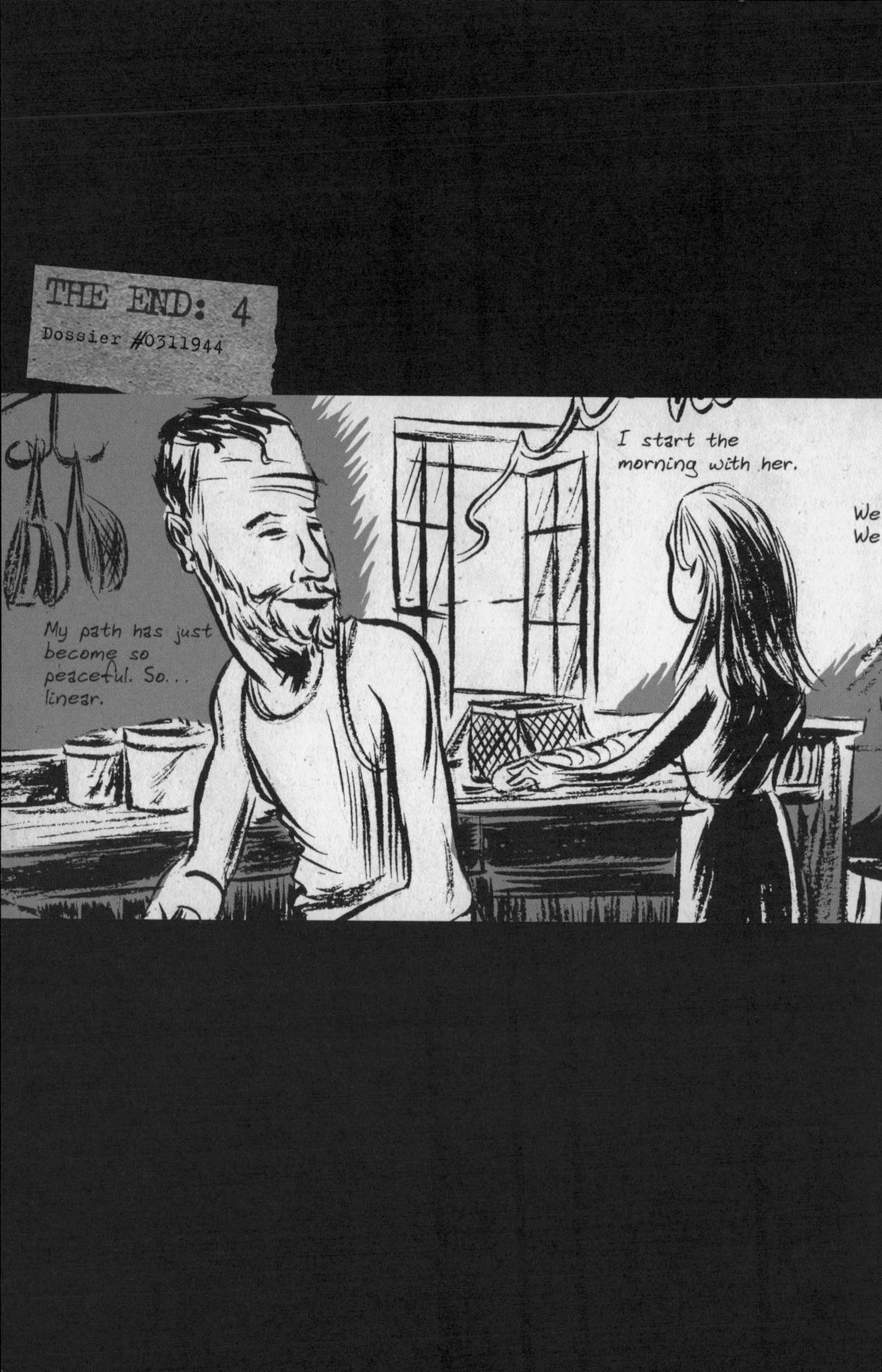
My path has just become so peaceful. So... linear.
I start the morning with her.
We
We

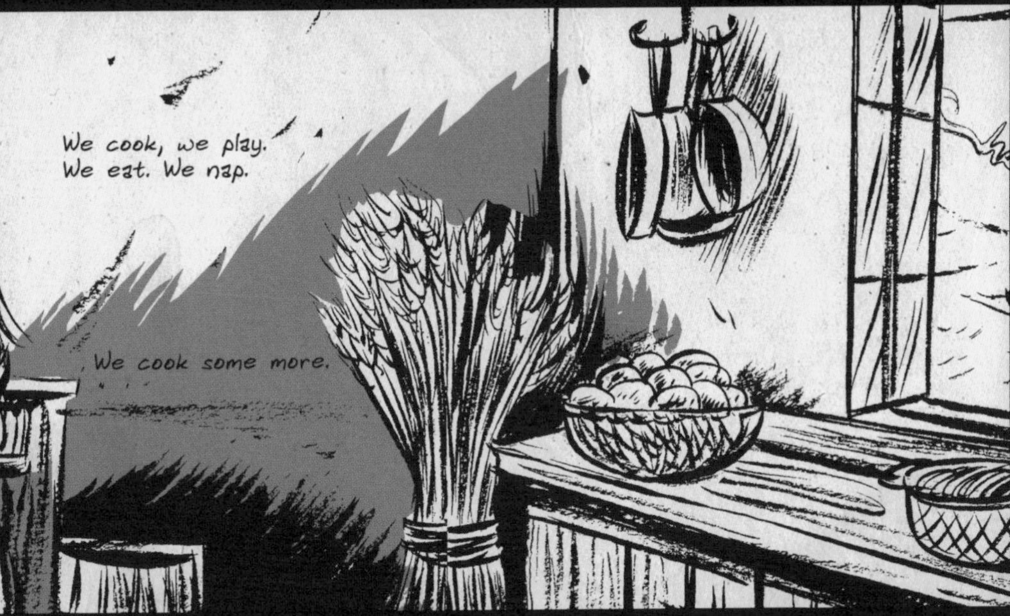
We cook, we play.
We eat. We nap.
We cook some more.

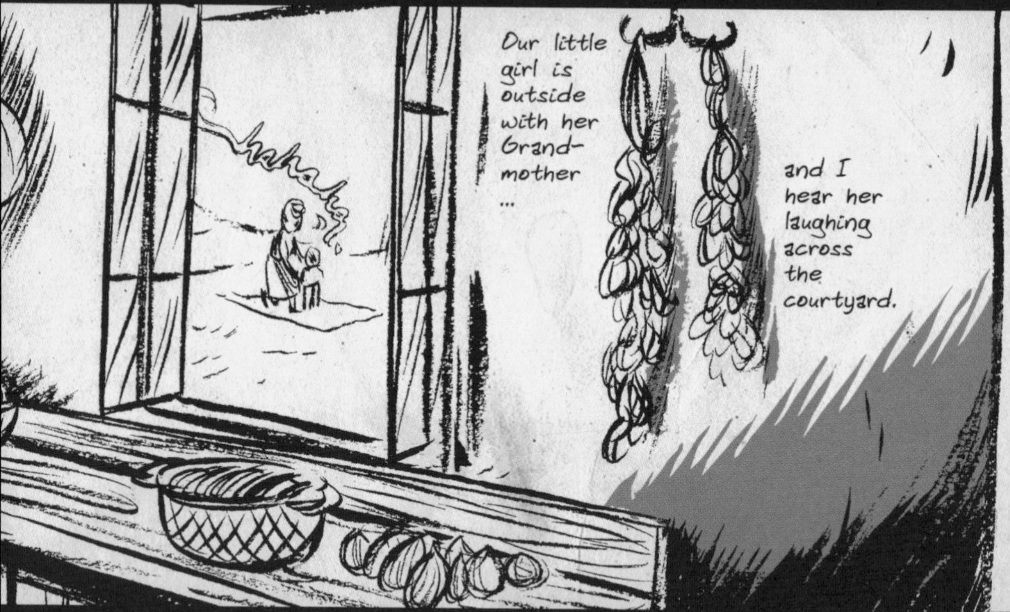
hahaha
Our little girl is outside with her Grand-mother ...
and I hear her laughing across the courtyard.

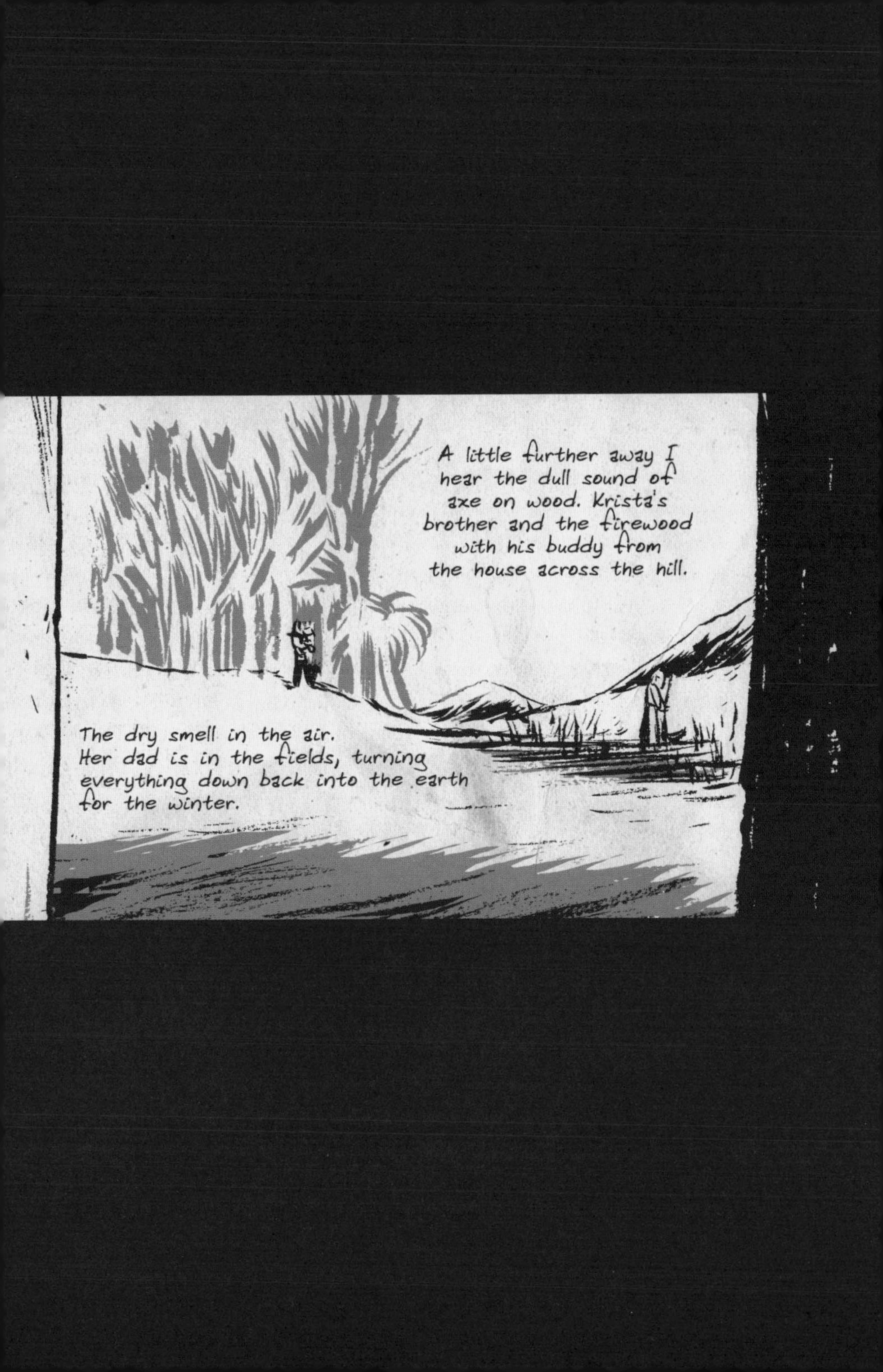
A little further away I hear the dull sound of axe on wood. Krista's brother and the firewood with his buddy from the house across the hill.
The dry smell in the air. Her dad is in the fields, turning everything down back into the earth for the winter.

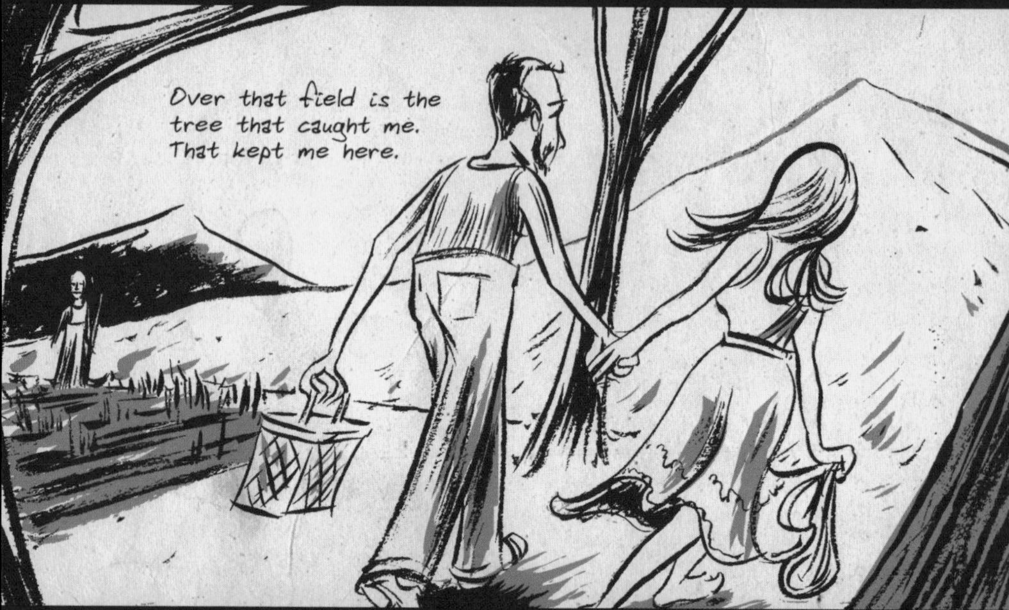
Over that field is the
tree that caught me.
That kept me here.

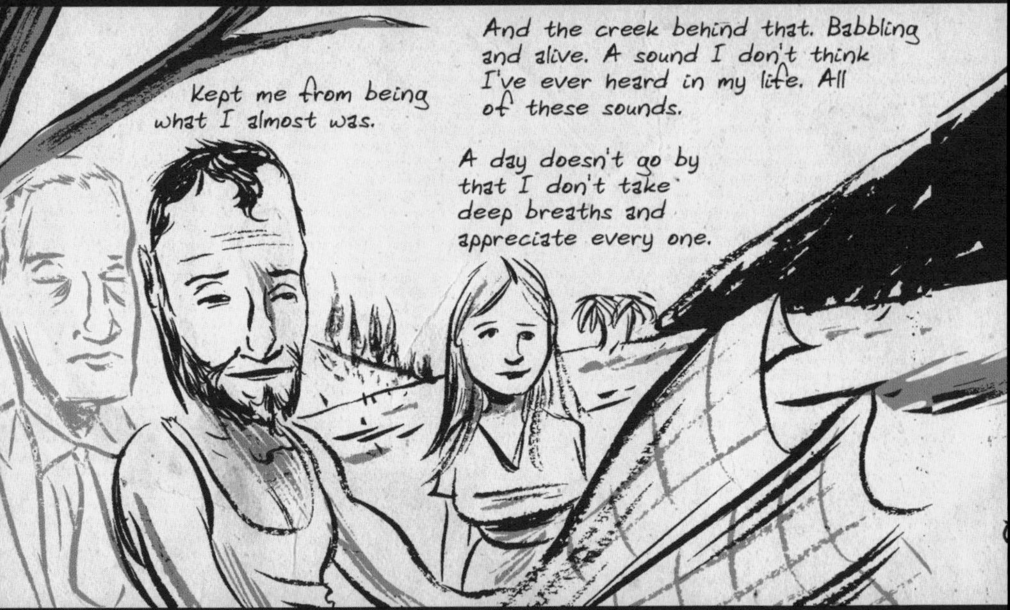
Kept me from being what I almost was.
And the creek behind that. Babbling and alive. A sound I don't think I've ever heard in my life. All of these sounds.
A day doesn't go by that I don't take deep breaths and appreciate every one.

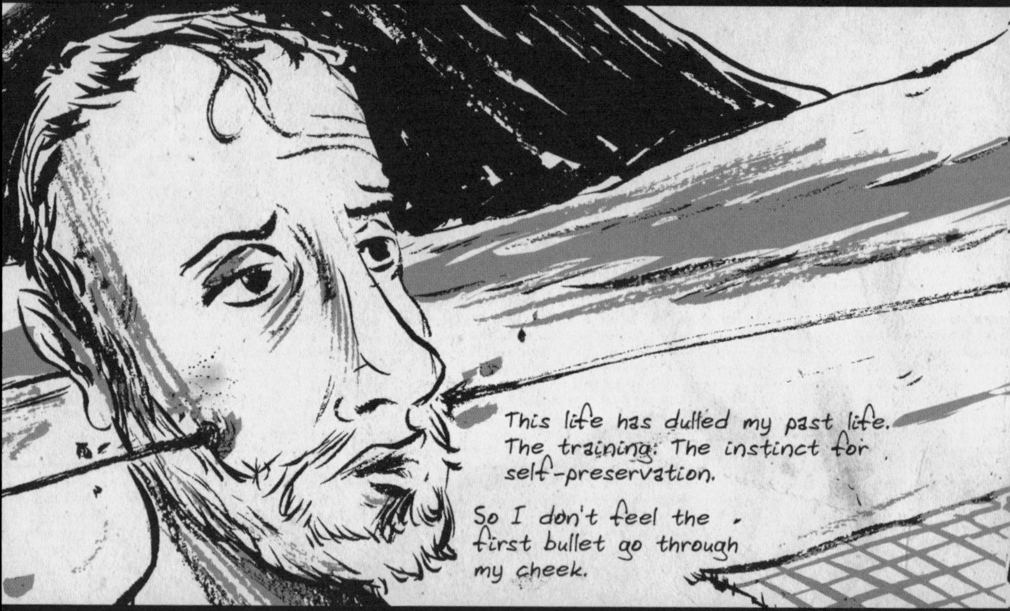
This life has dulled my past life. The training. The instinct for self-preservation.
So I don't feel the first bullet go through my cheek.

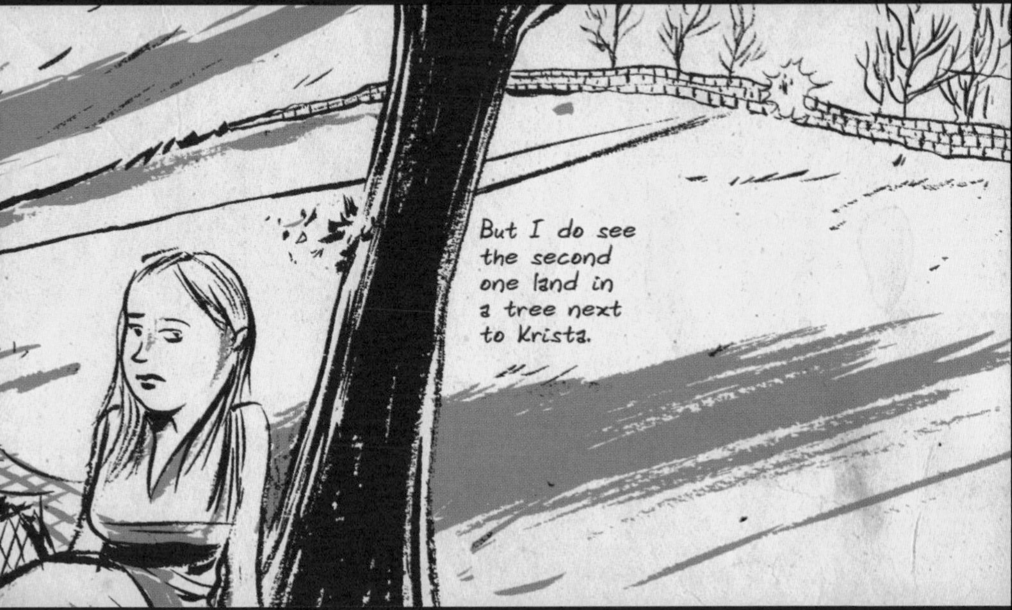
But I do see the second one land in a tree next to Krista.

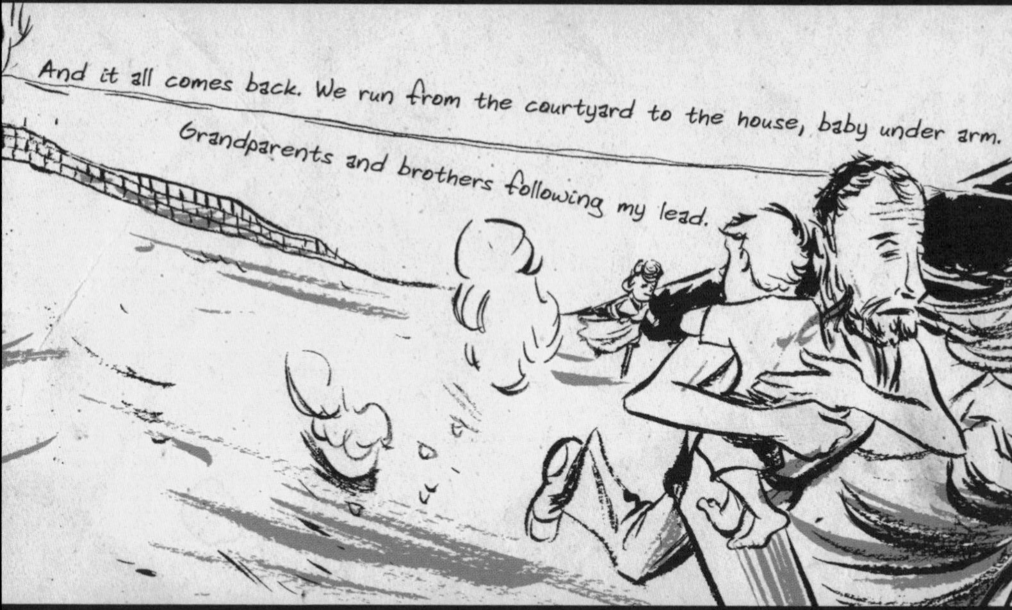
And it all comes back. We run from the courtyard to the house, baby under arm.
Grandparents and brothers following my lead.

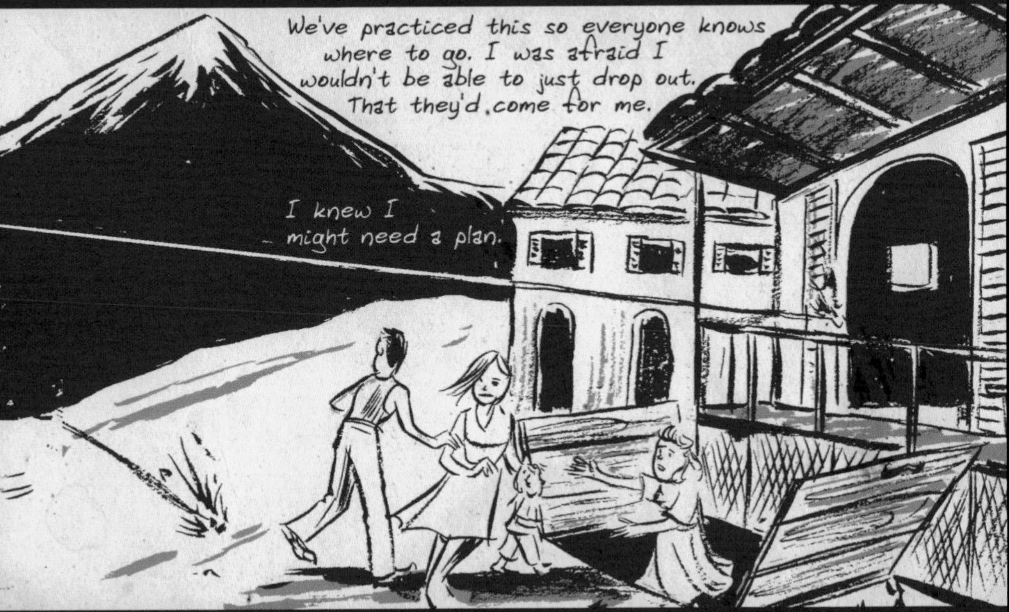
We've practiced this so everyone knows where to go. I was afraid I wouldn't be able to just drop out. That they'd come for me.
I knew I might need a plan.

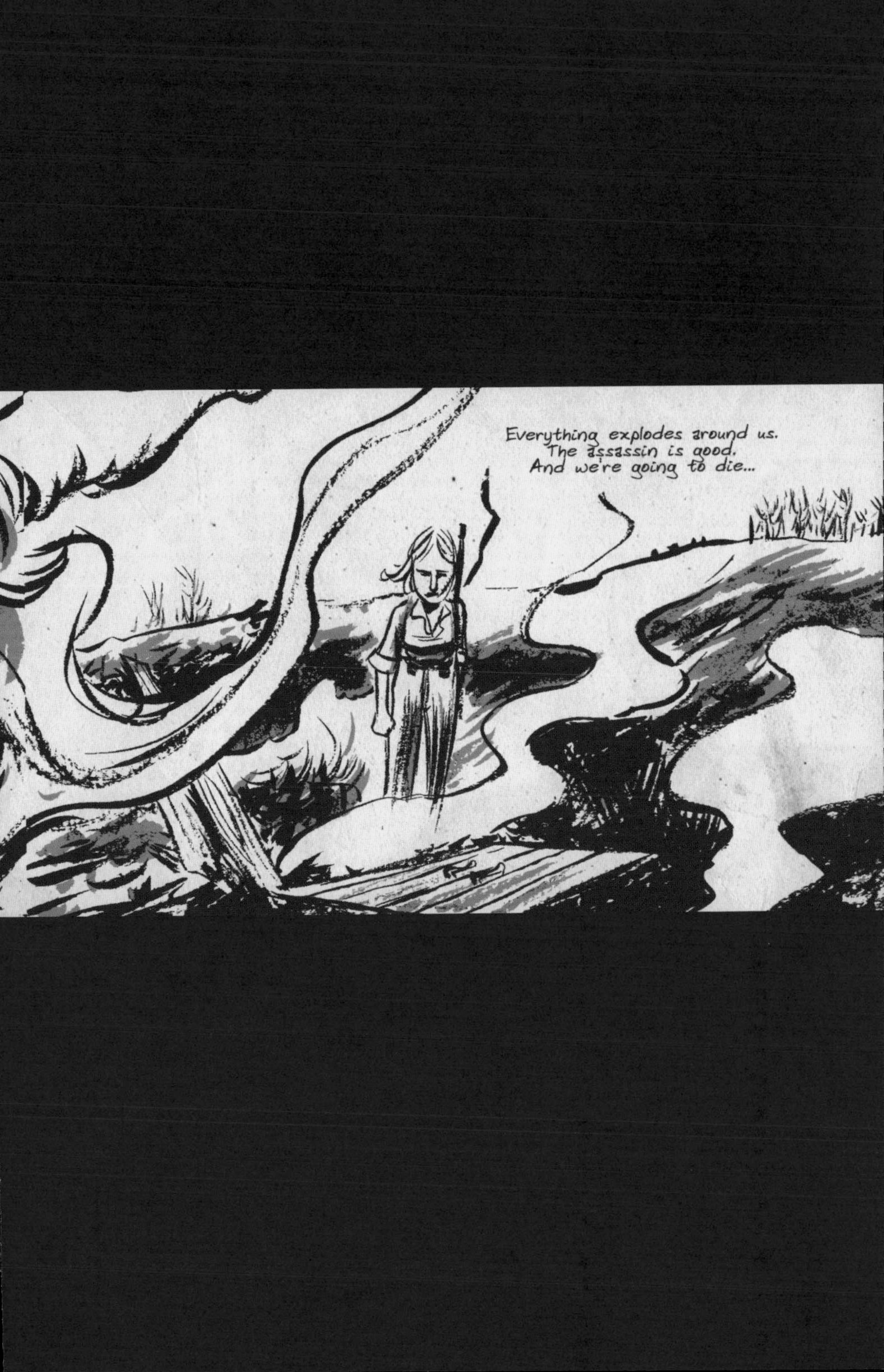
Everything explodes around us.
The assassin is good.
And we're going to die...

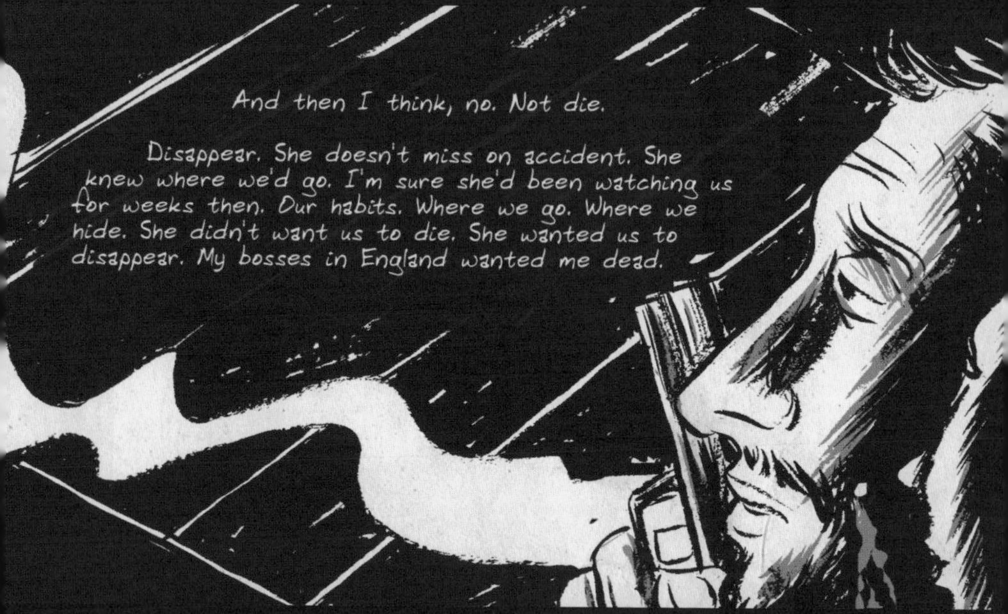
And then I think, no. Not die.
Disappear. She doesn't miss on accident. She knew where we'd go. I'm sure she'd been watching us for weeks then. Our habits. Where we go. Where we hide. She didn't want us to die. She wanted us to disappear. My bosses in England wanted me dead.

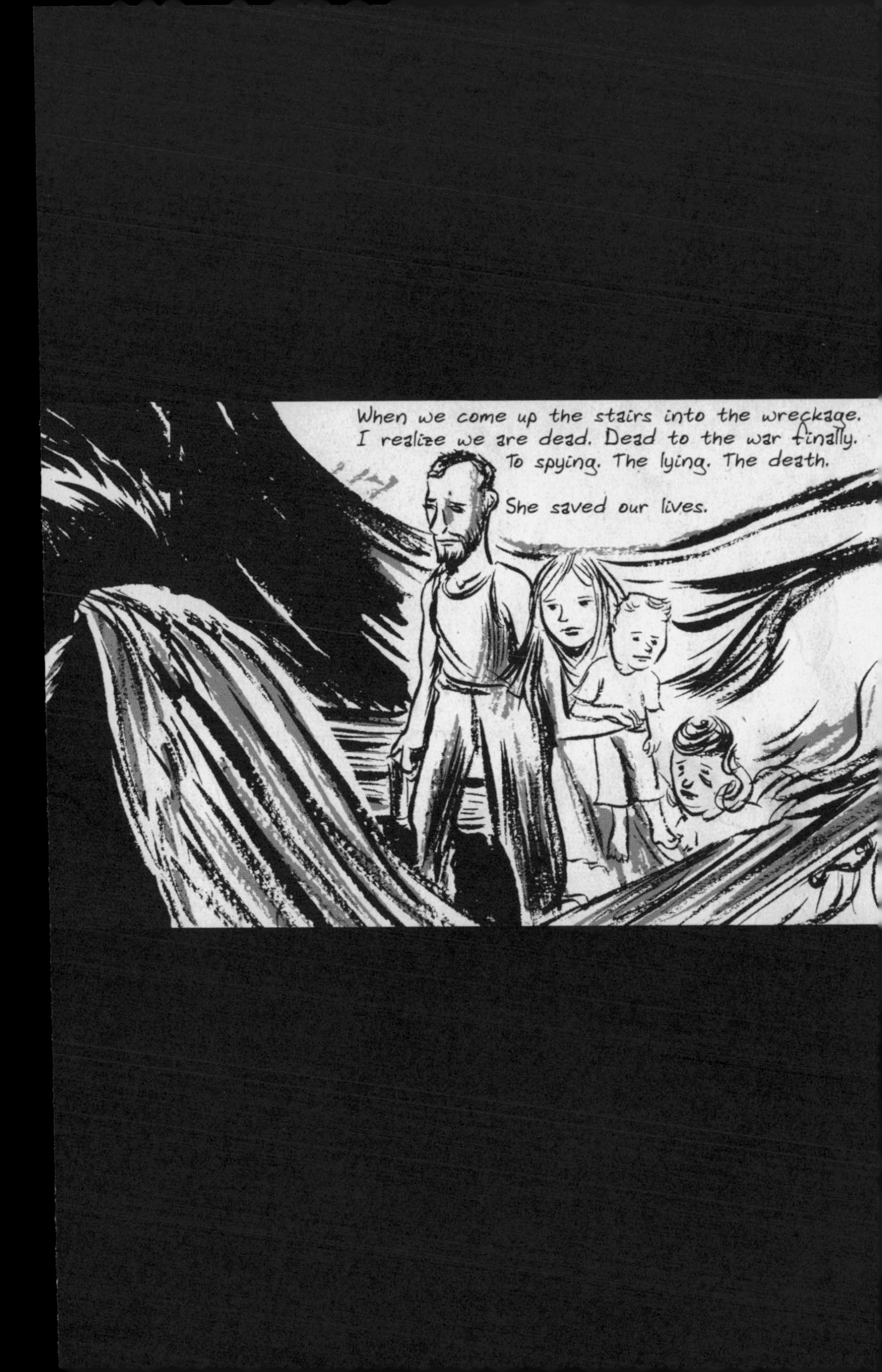
When we come up the stairs into the wreckage.
I realize we are dead. Dead to the war finally.
To spying. The lying. The death.
She saved our lives.

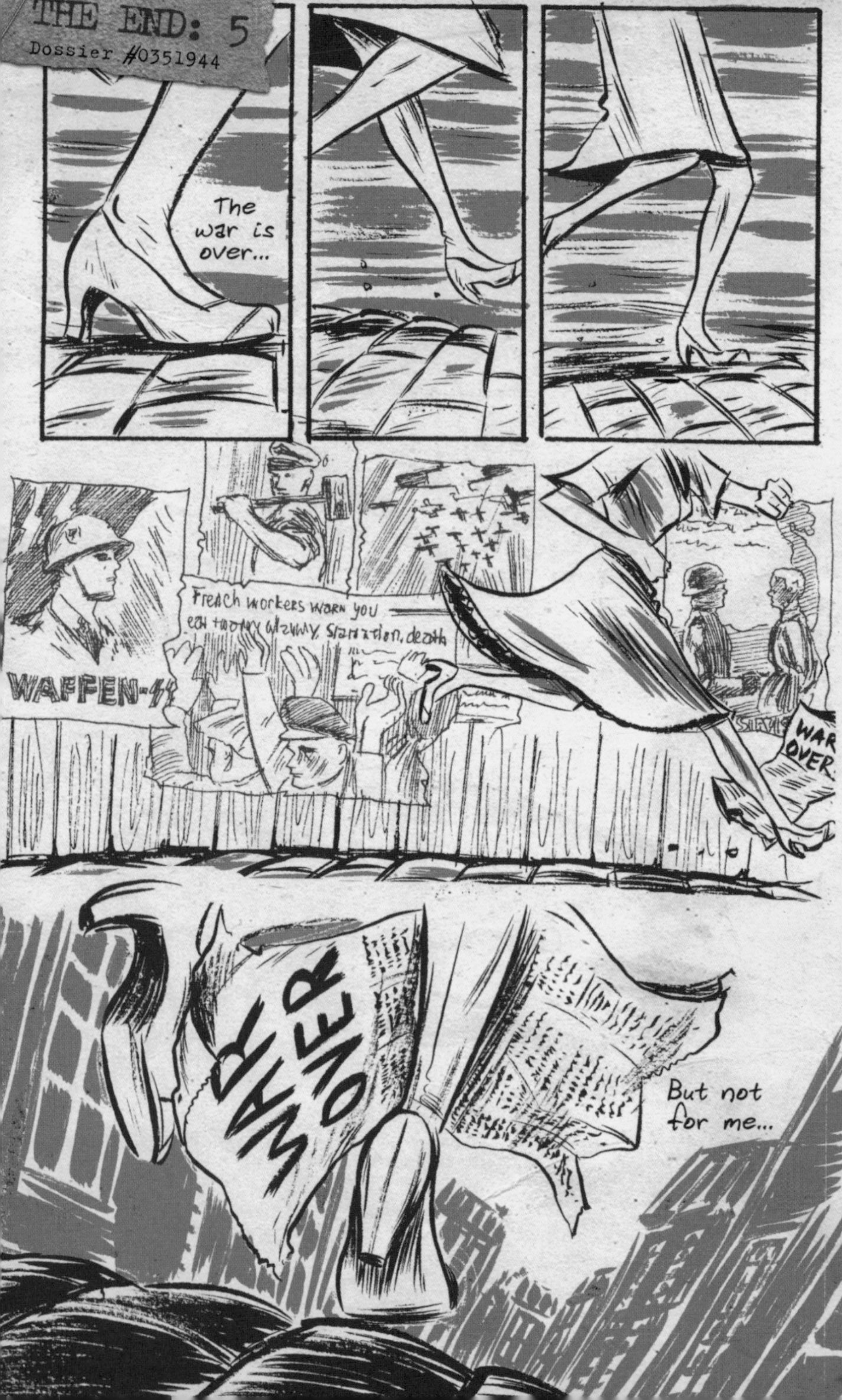
The war is over...
French workers warn you
WAFFEN-SS
WAR OVER
WAR OVER
But not for me...

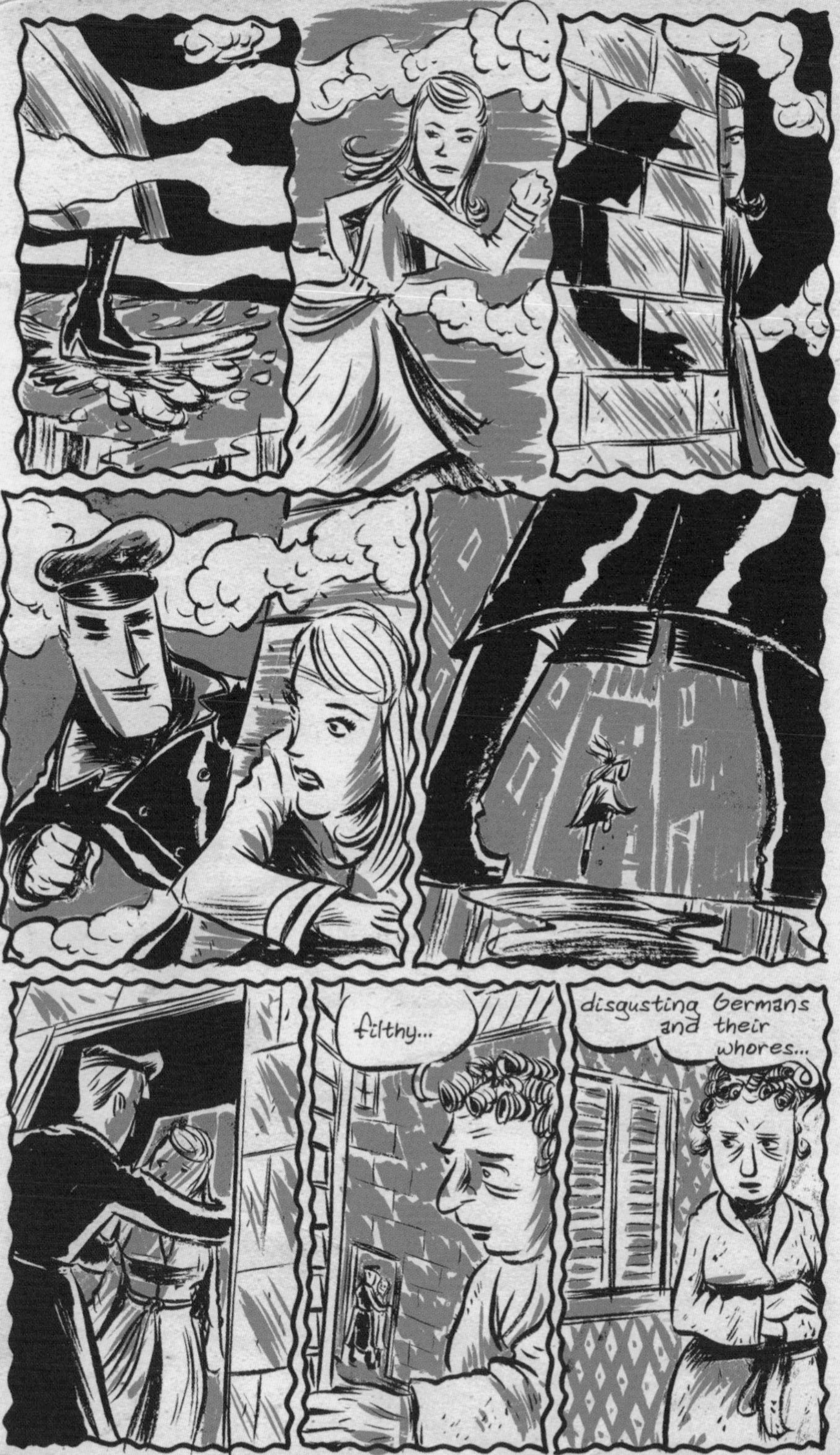
filthy...
disgusting Germans and their whores...

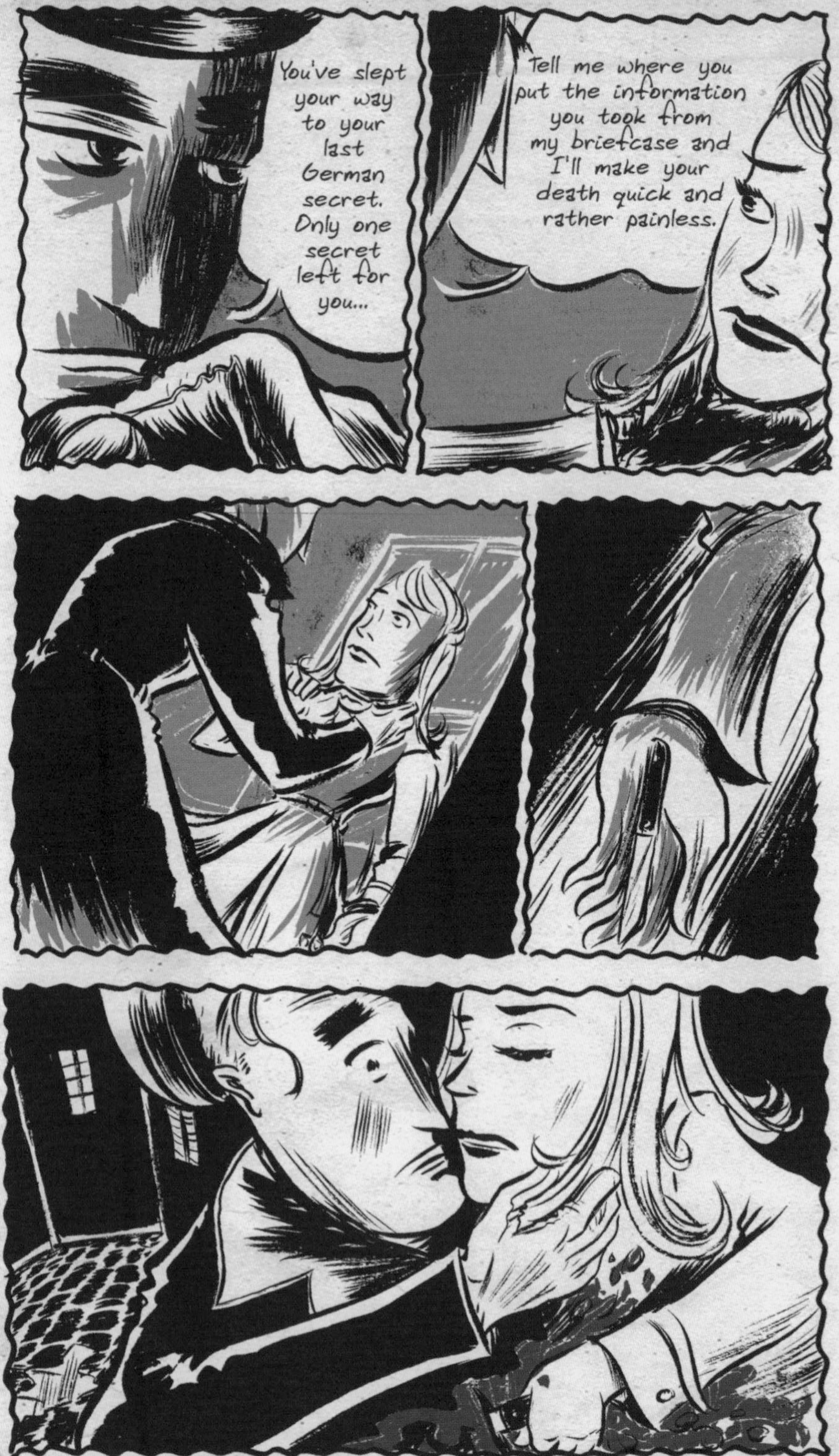
You've slept your way to your last German secret. Only one secret left for you...
Tell me where you put the information you took from my briefcase and I'll make your death quick and rather painless.

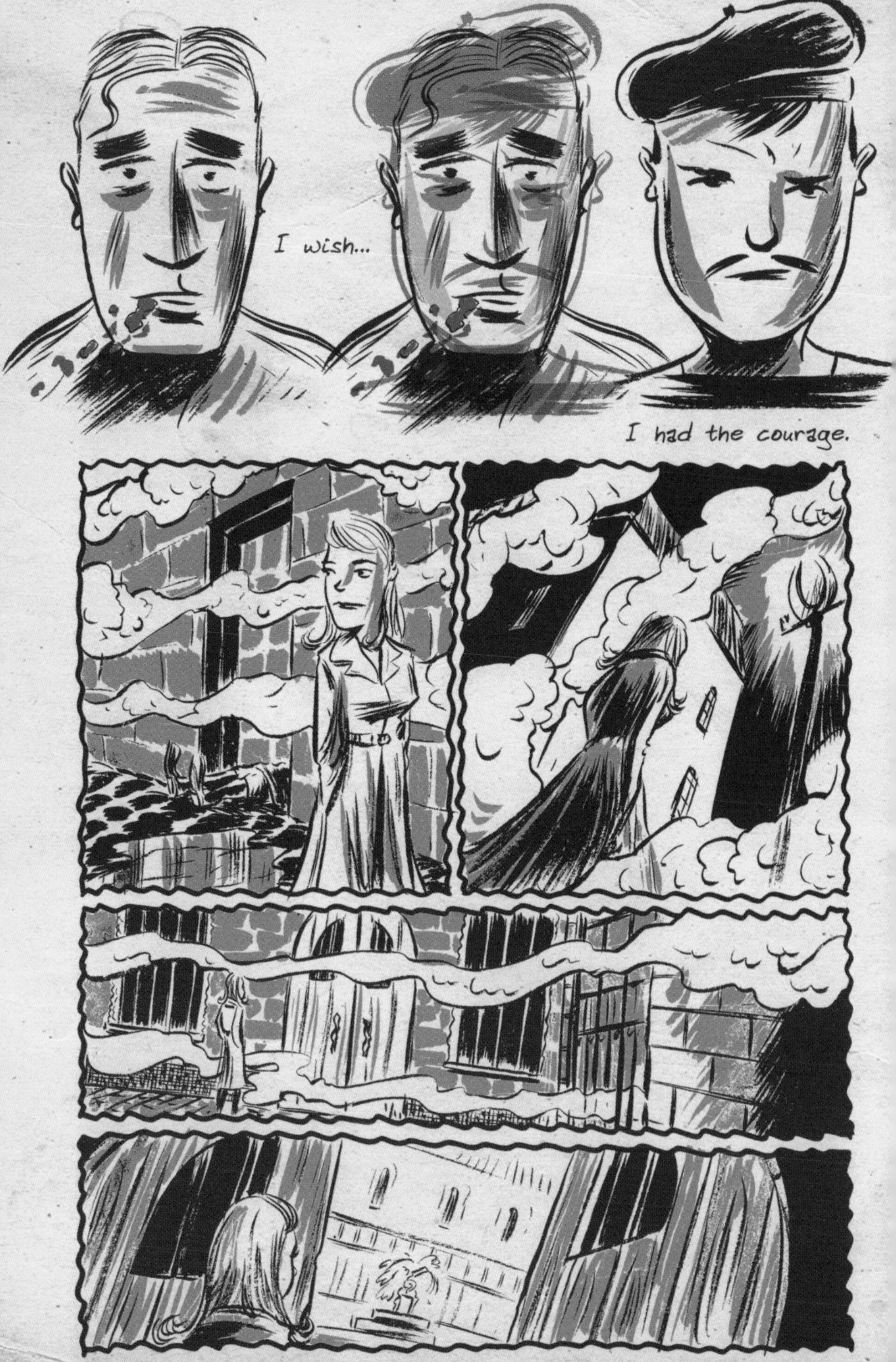
I wish...
I had the courage.

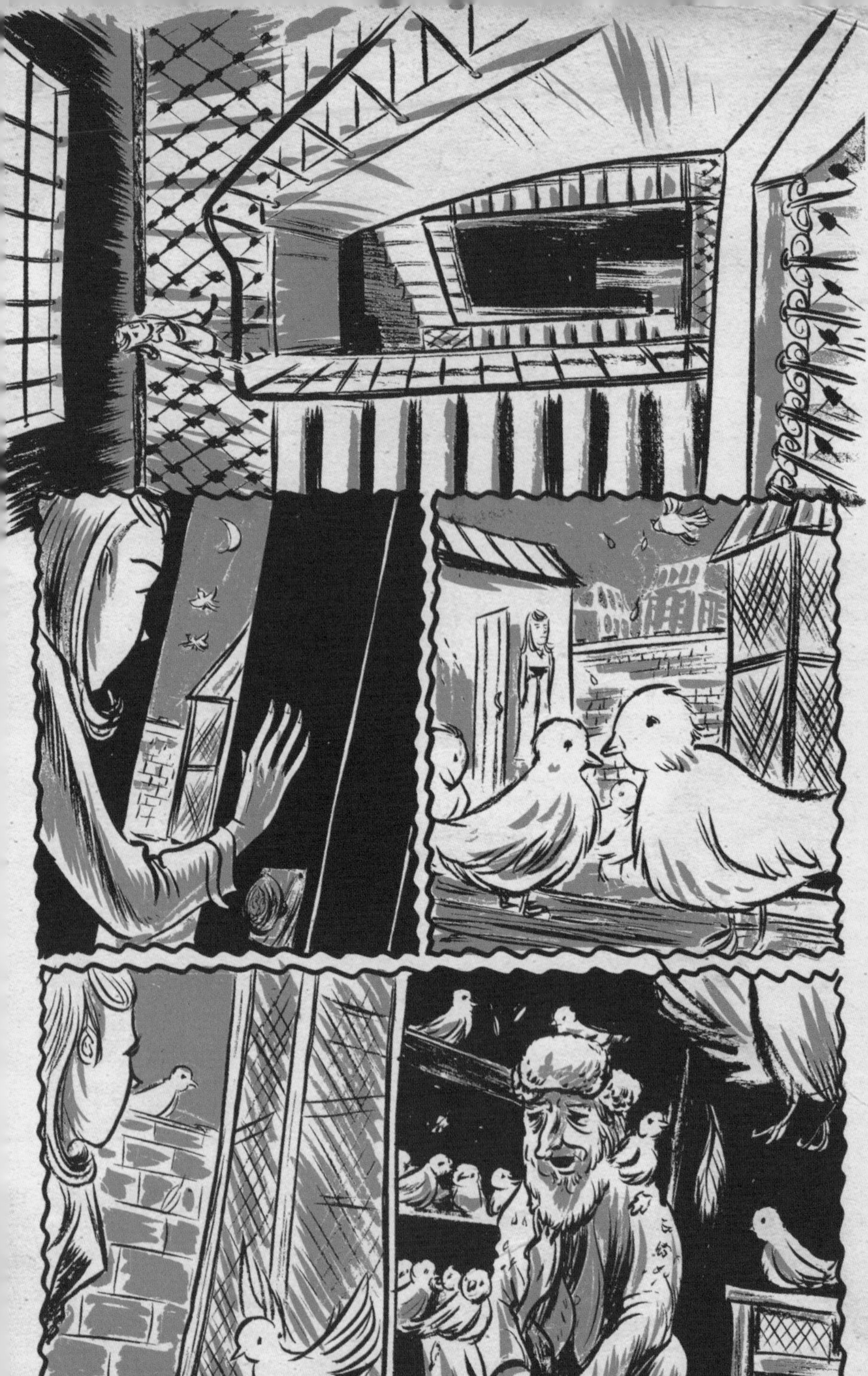

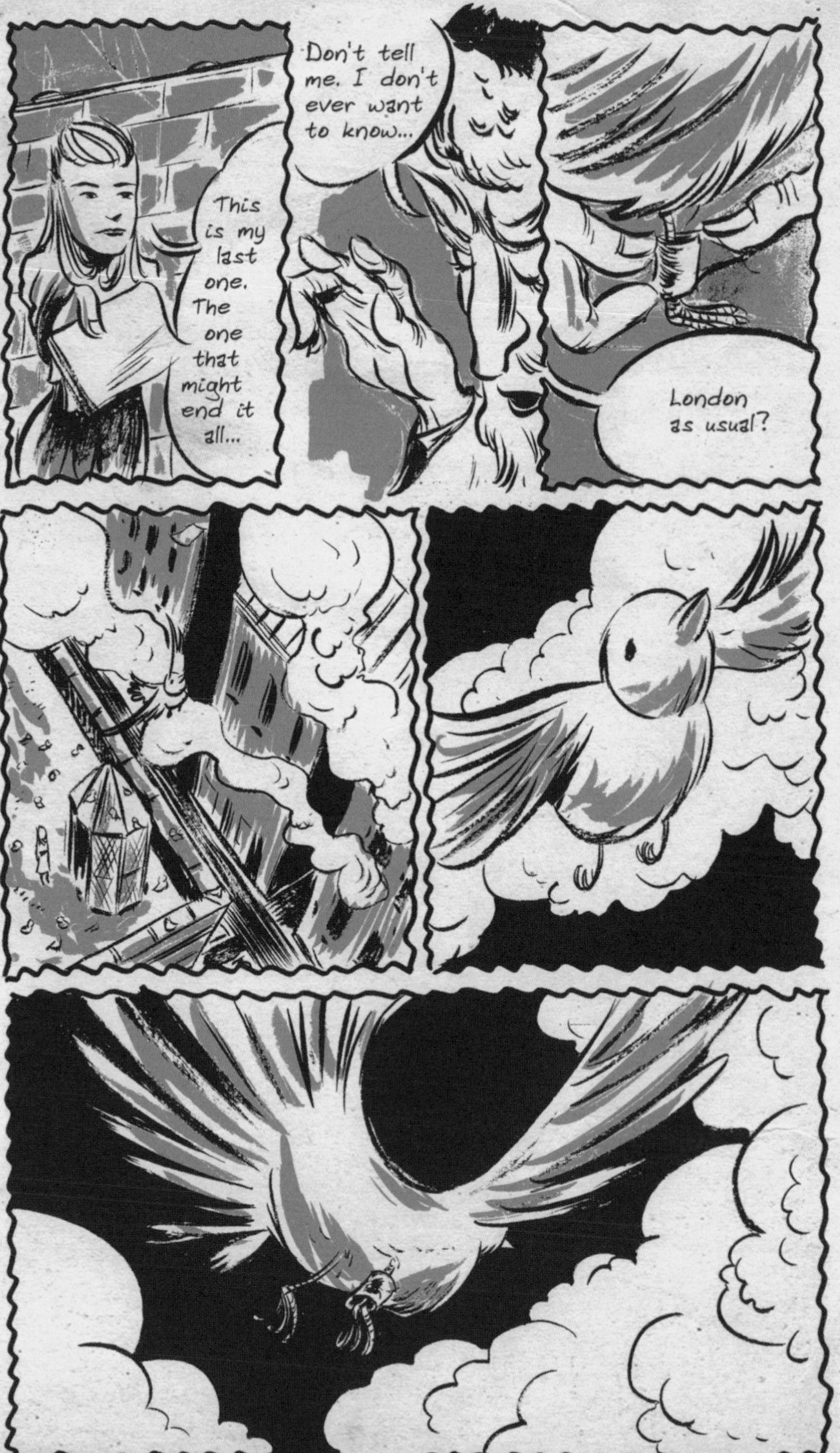
This is my last one. The one that might end it all...
Don't tell me. I don't ever want to know...
London as usual?

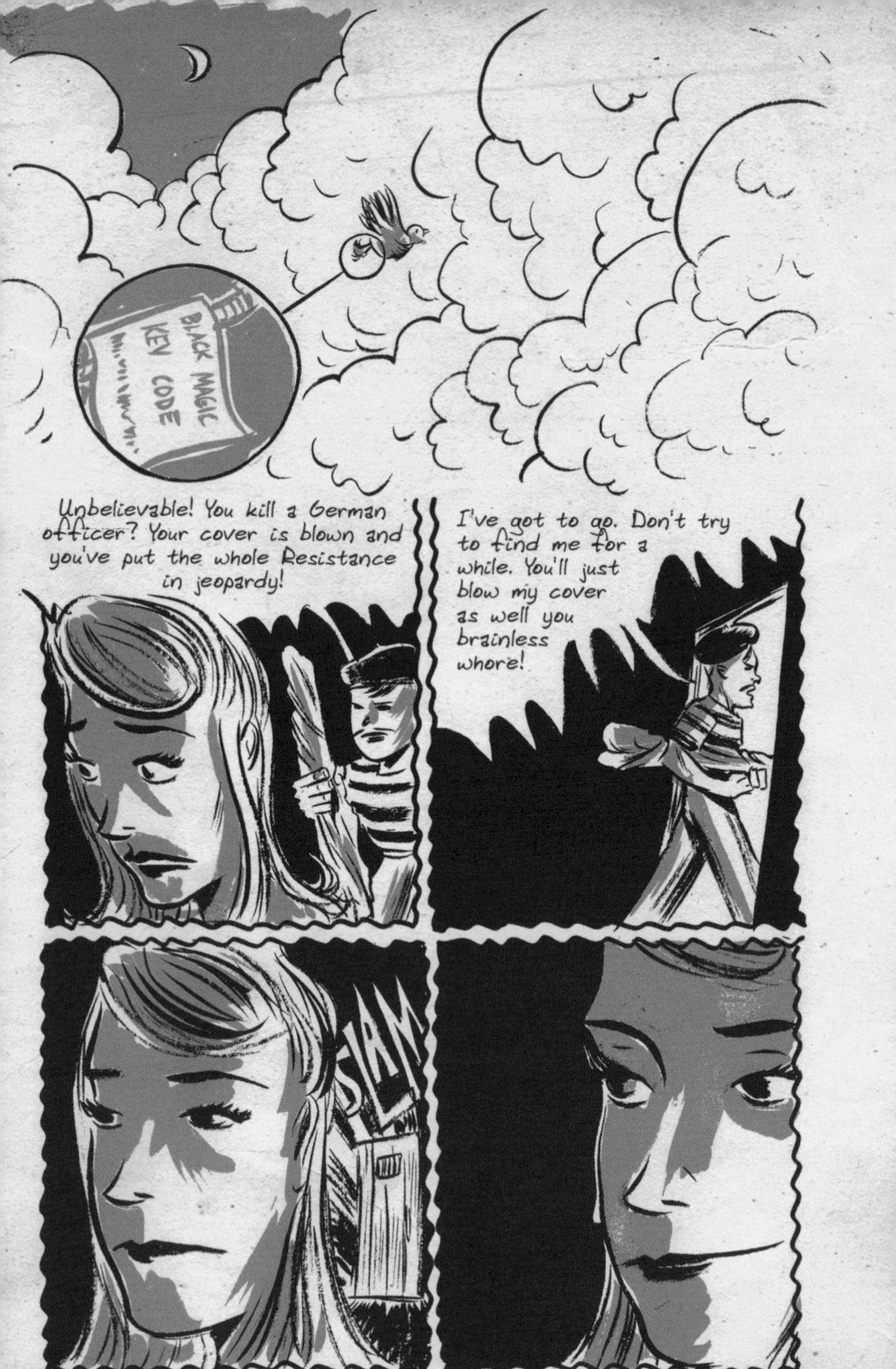
BLACK MAGIC KEY CODE
Unbelievable! You kill a German officer? Your cover is blown and you've put the whole Resistance in jeopardy!
I've got to go. Don't try to find me for a while. You'll just blow my cover as well you brainless whore!
SLAM

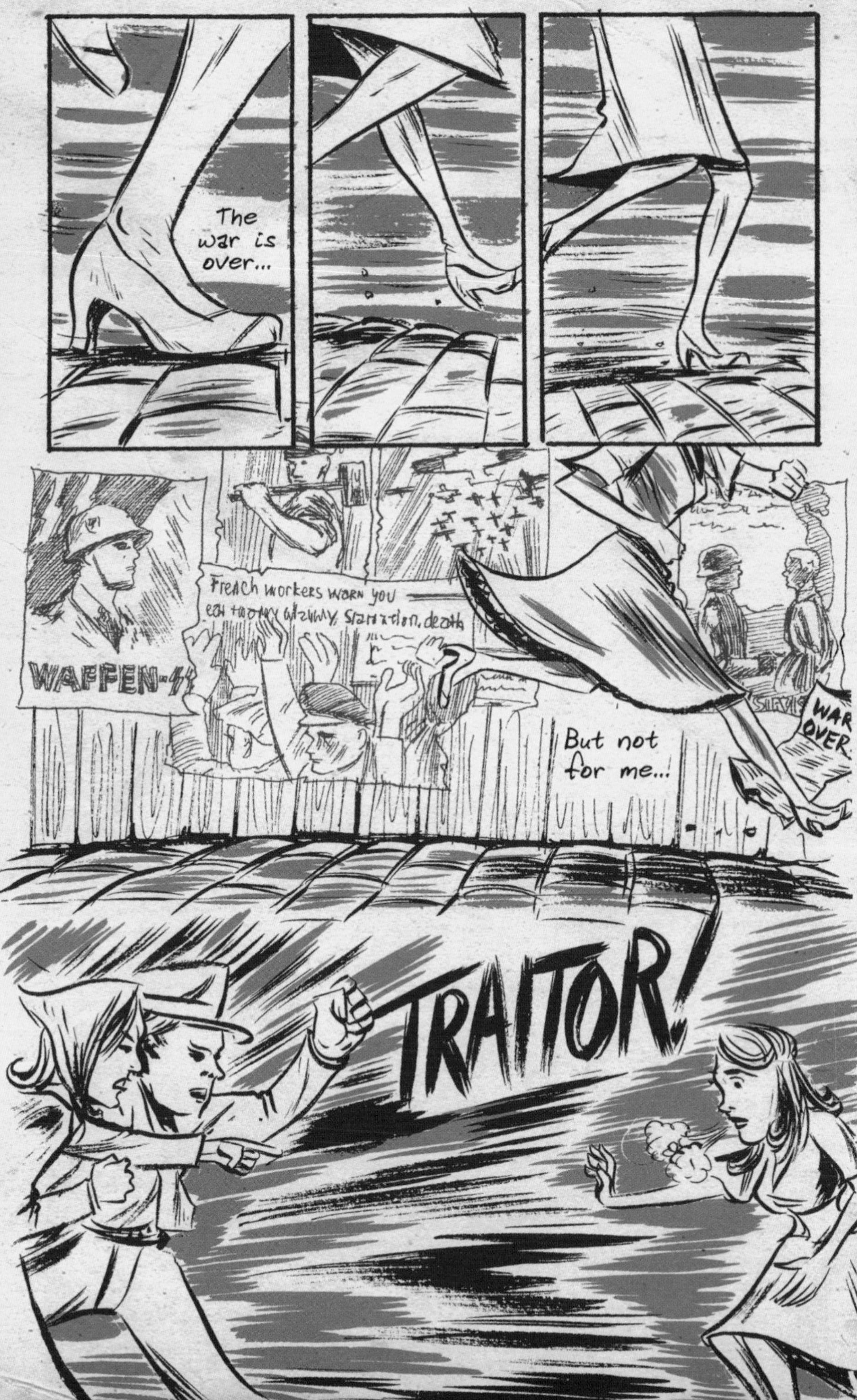
The war is over...
WAFFEN-
French workers warn you
WAR OVER
But not for me...
TRAITOR!

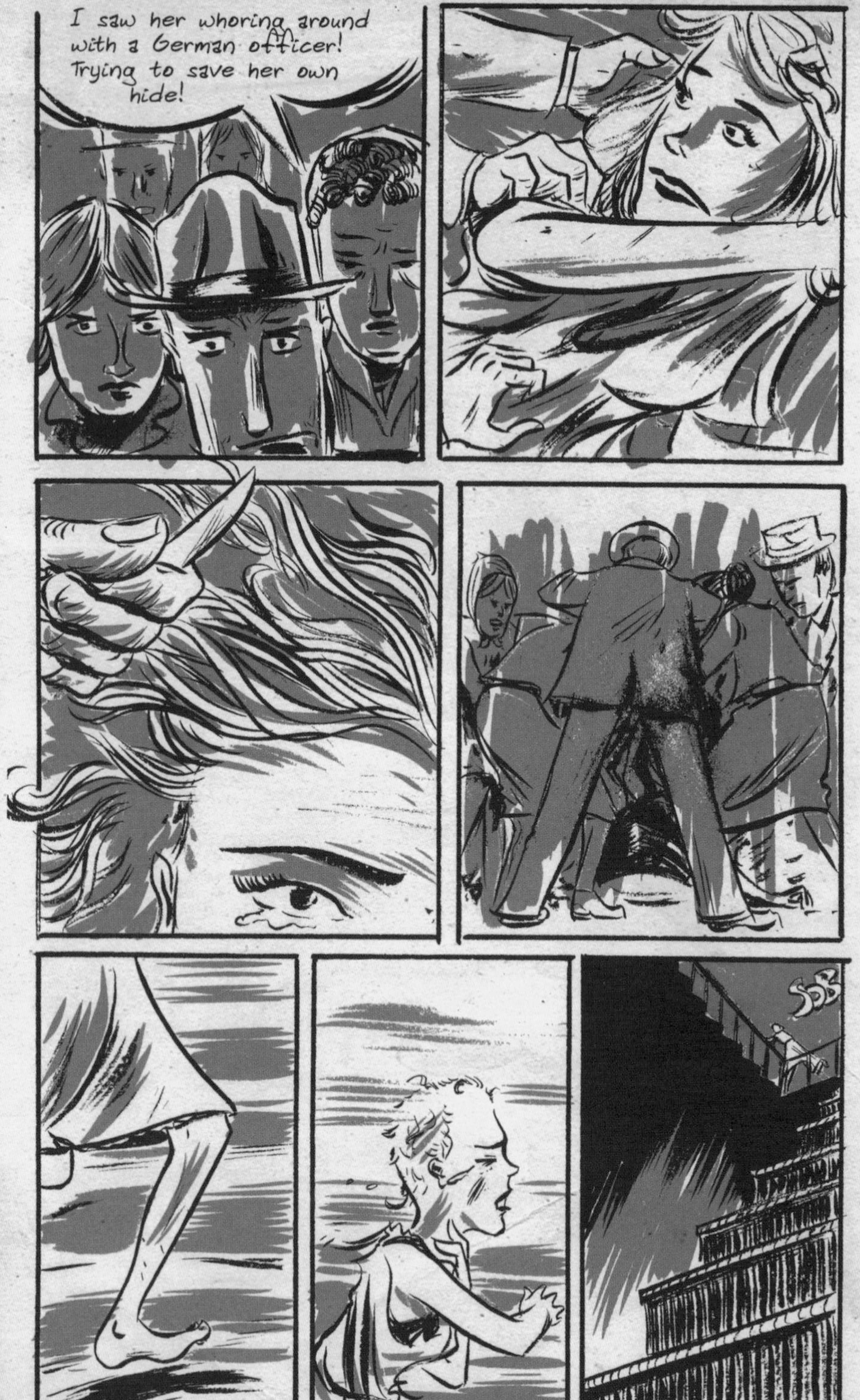
I saw her whoring around with a German officer! Trying to save her own hide!
SOB

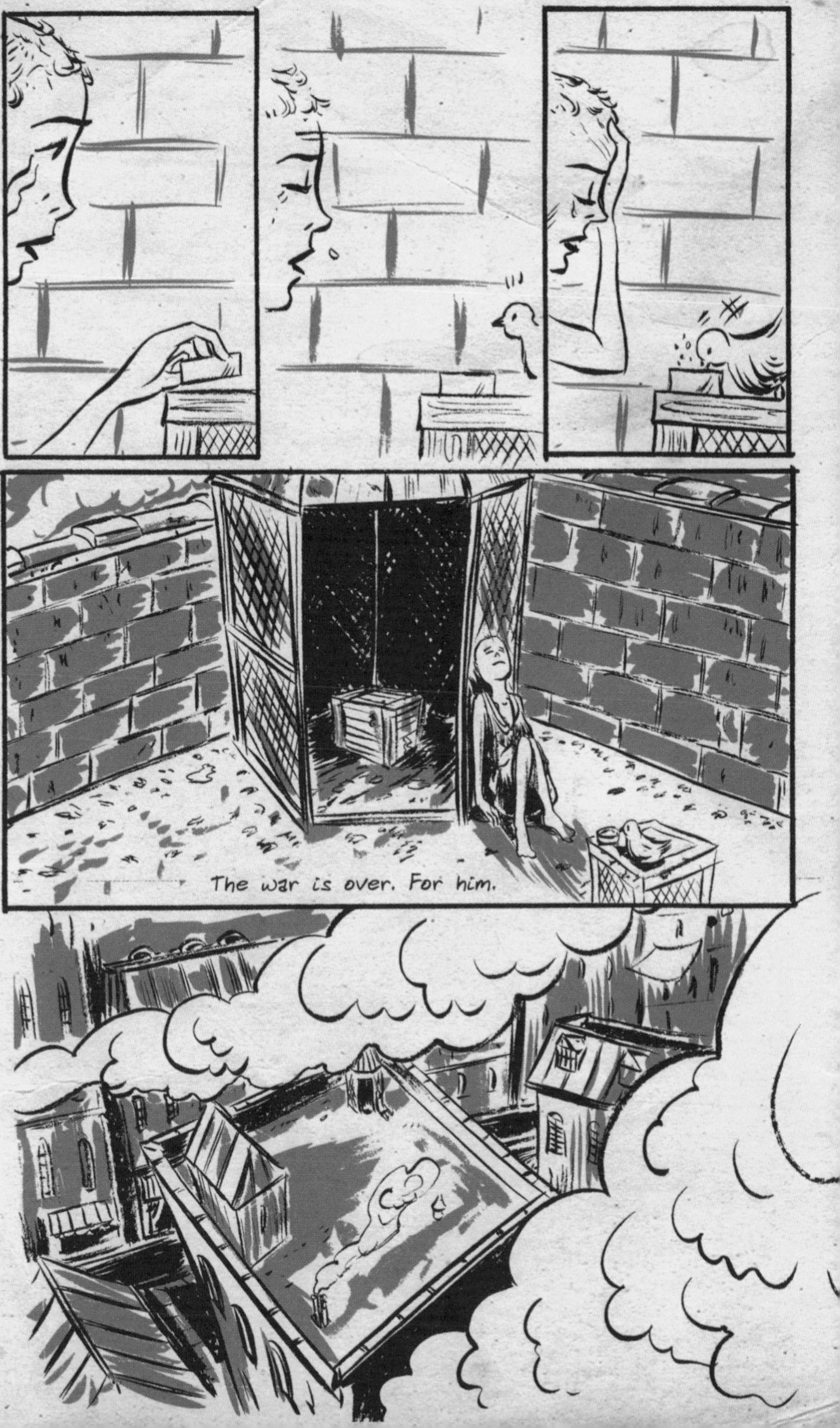
The war is over. For him.

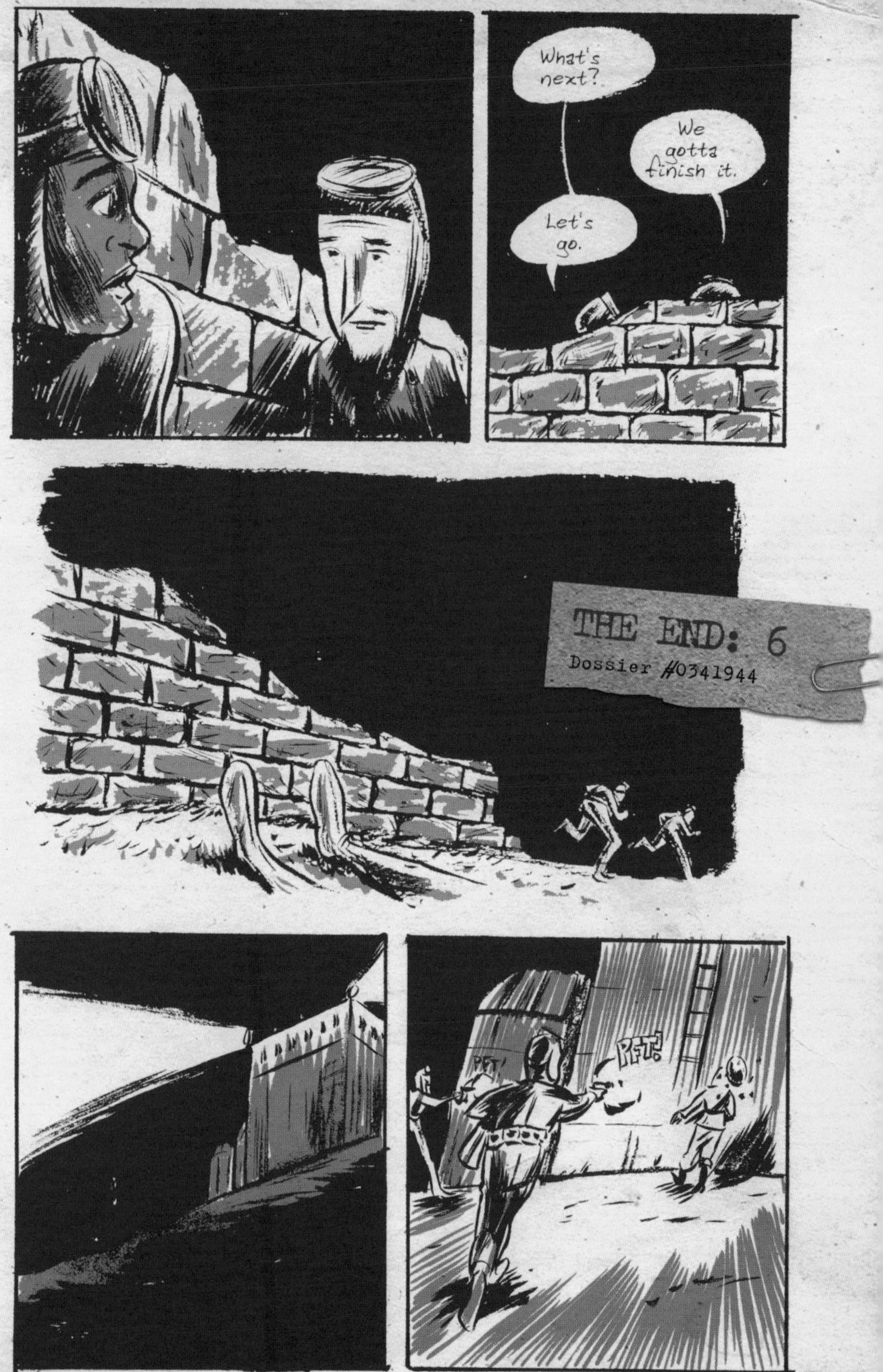
What's next?
We gotta finish it.
Let's go.
THE END: 6
Dossier #0341944
PFT!
PFT!

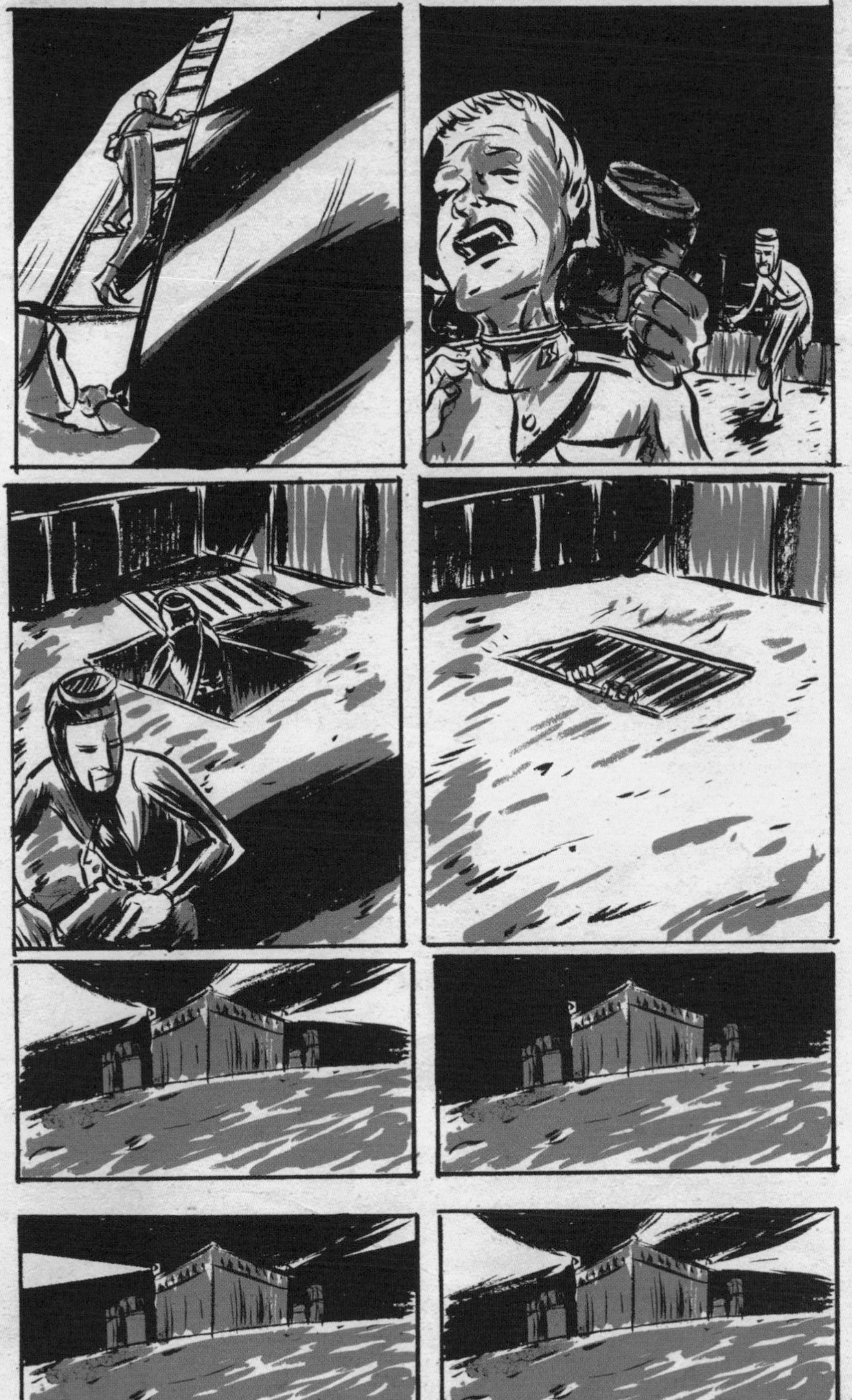

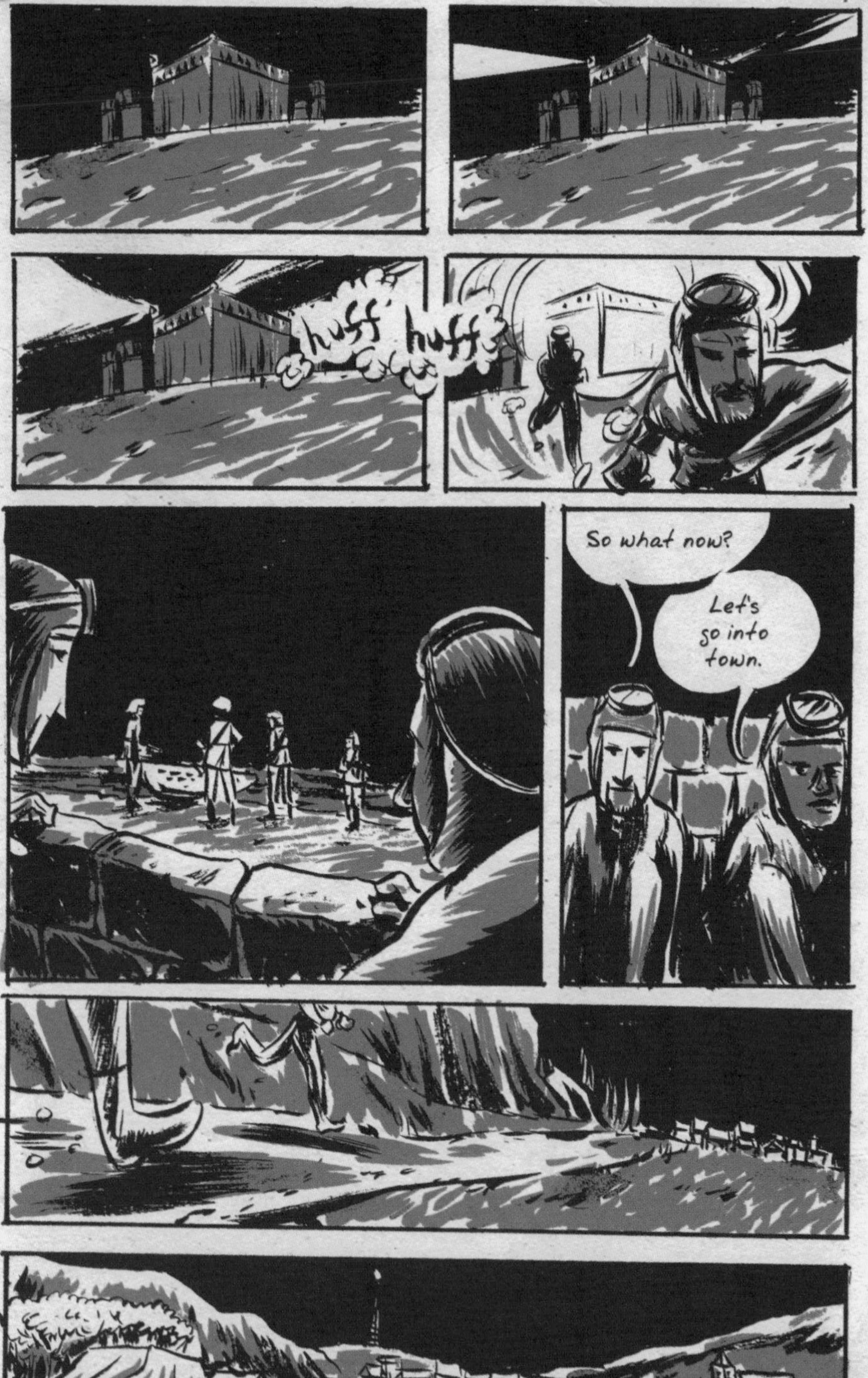
huff huff
So what now?
Let's go into town.

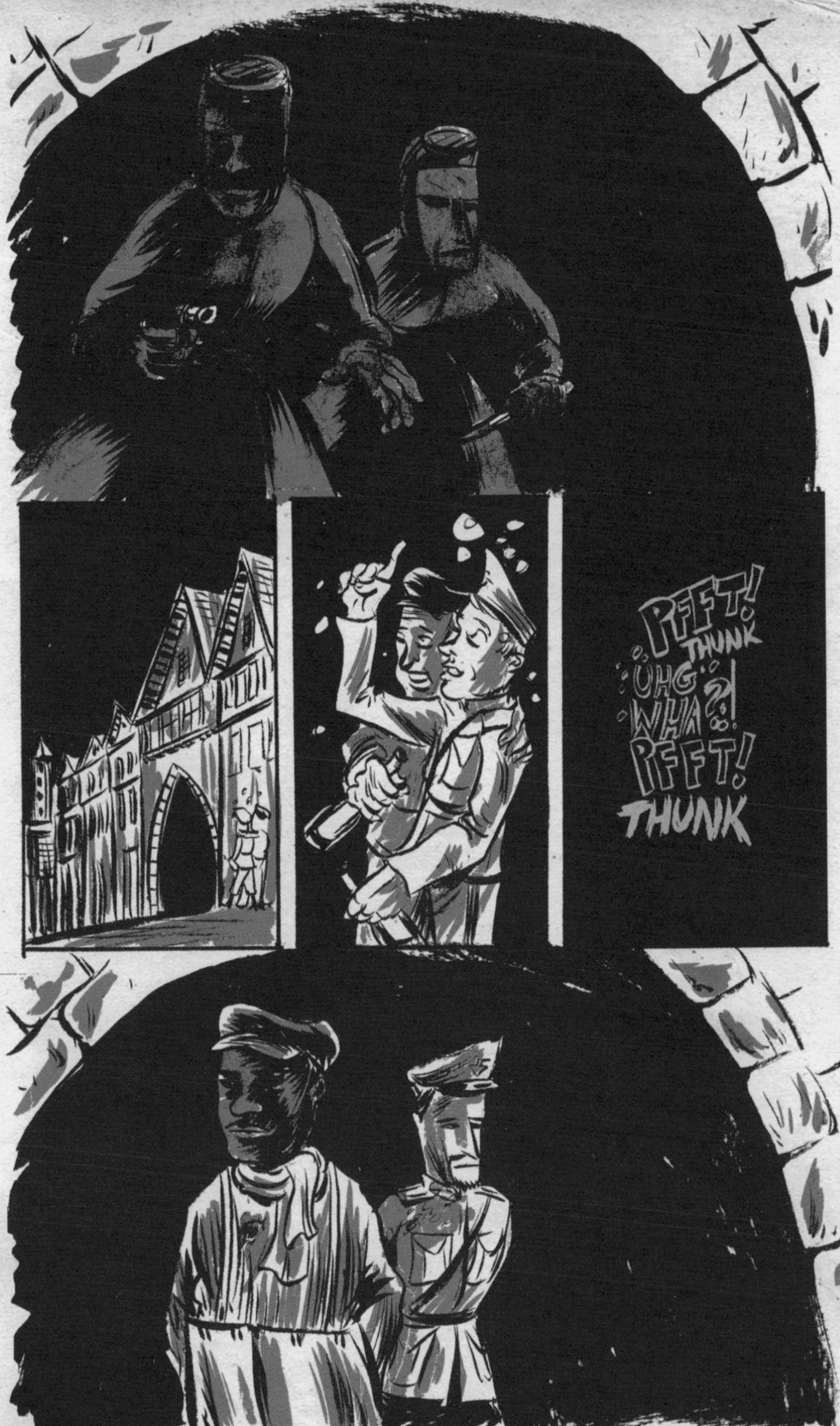
PFFT!
THUNK
UHG
WHA?!
PFFT!
THUNK

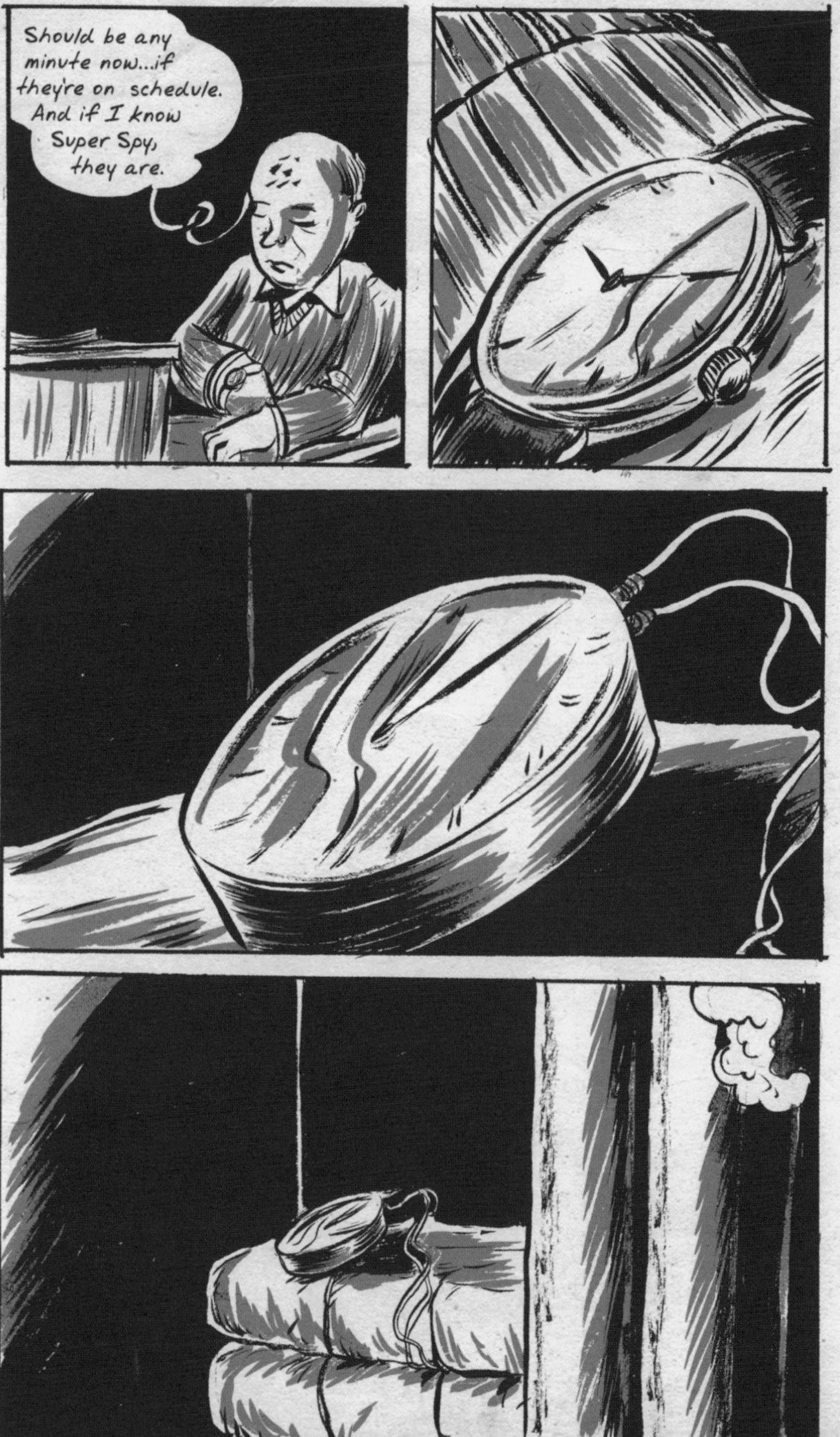
Should be any minute now...if they're on schedule. And if I know Super Spy, they are.

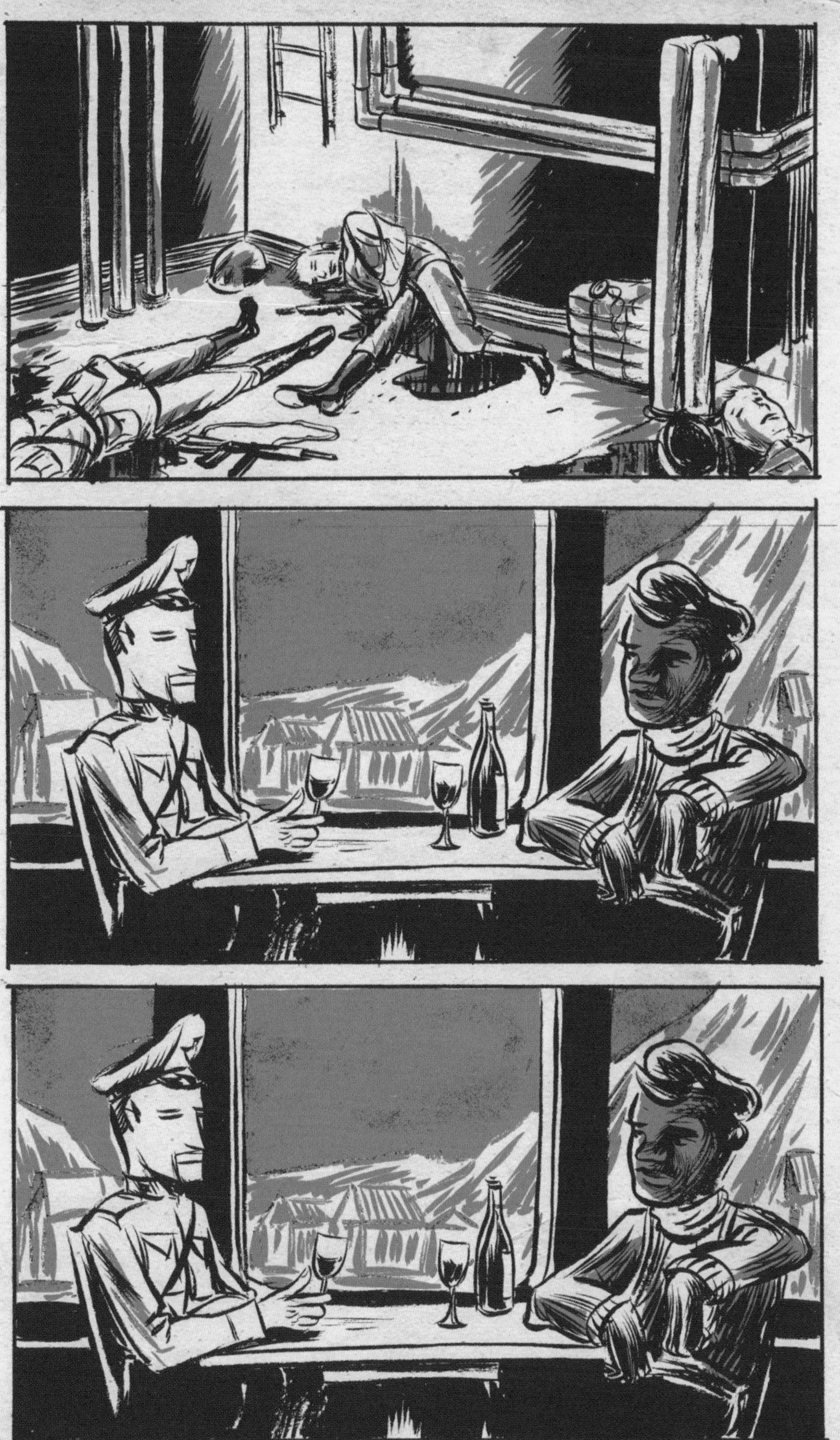

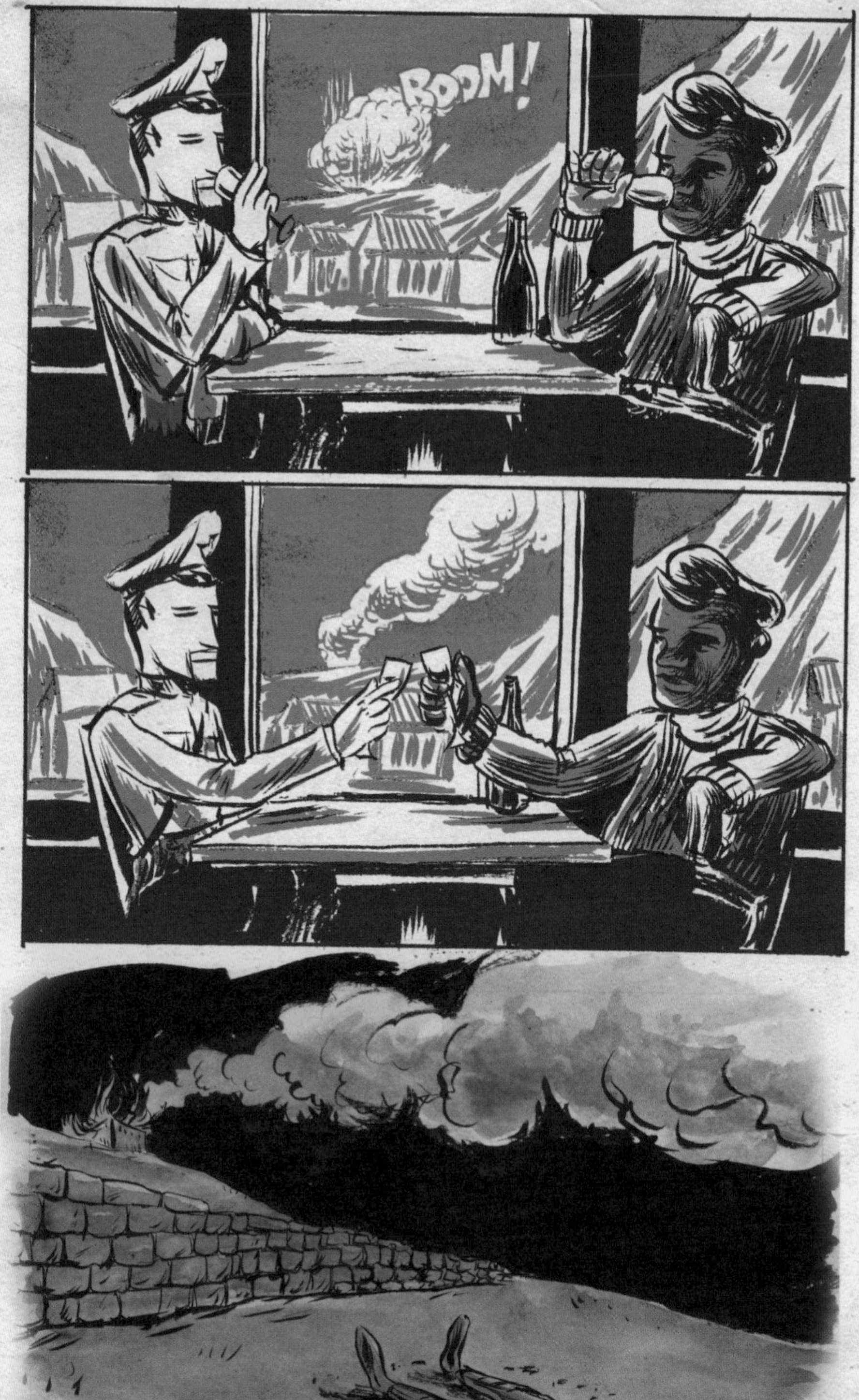
BOOM!

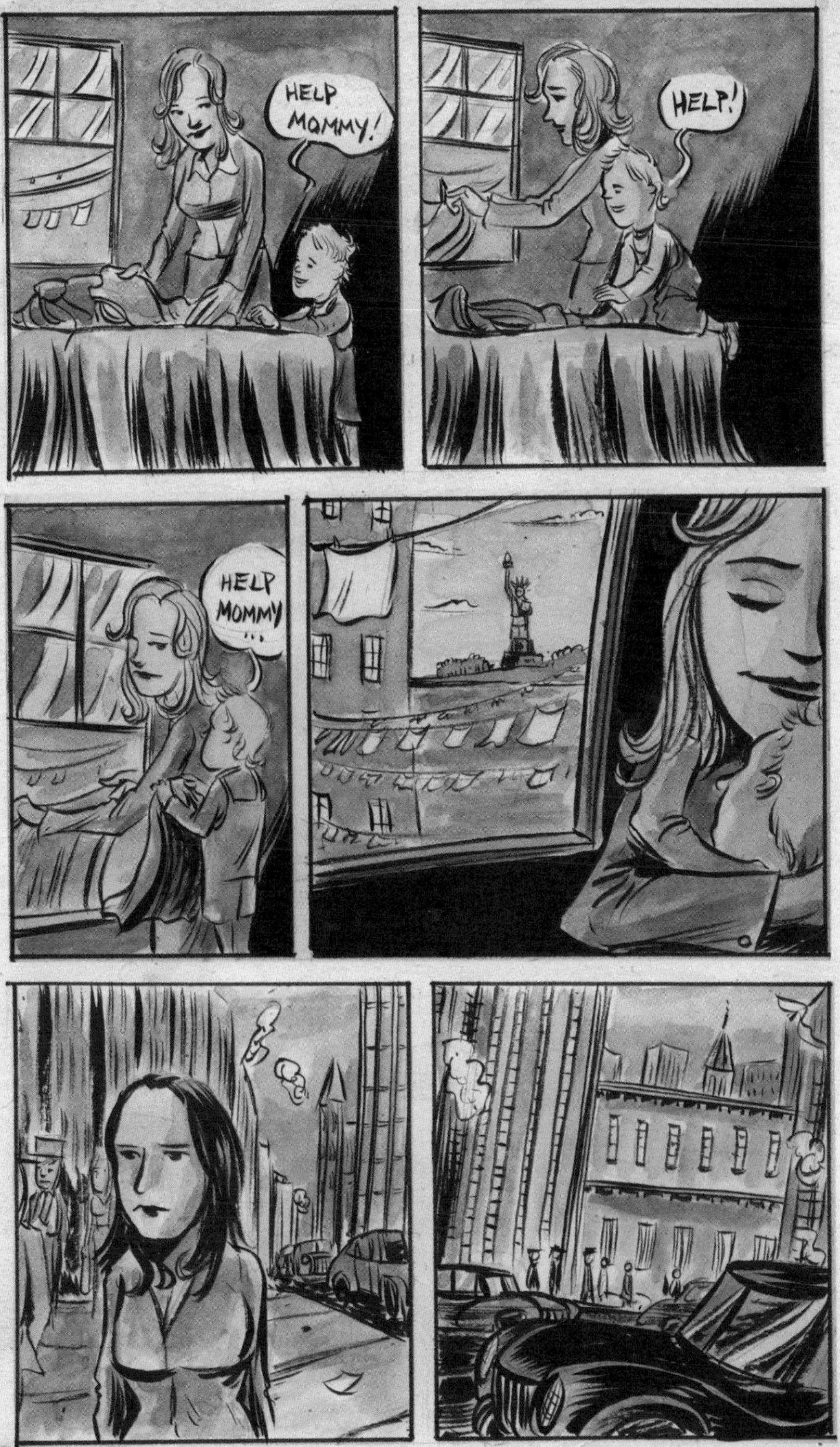
HELP MOMMY!
HELP!
HELP MOMMY ...

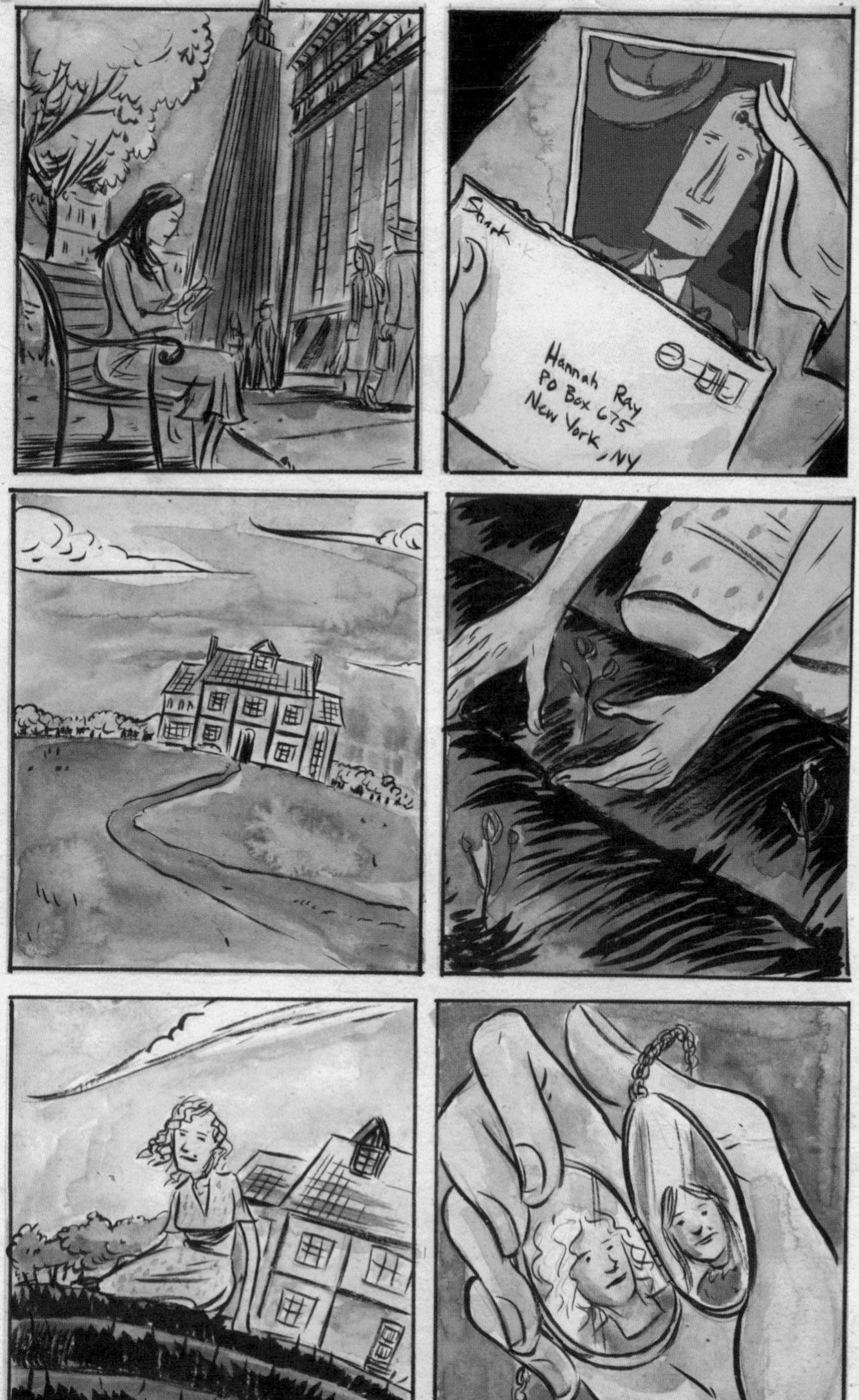
Shark
Hannah Ray
PO Box 675
New York, NY

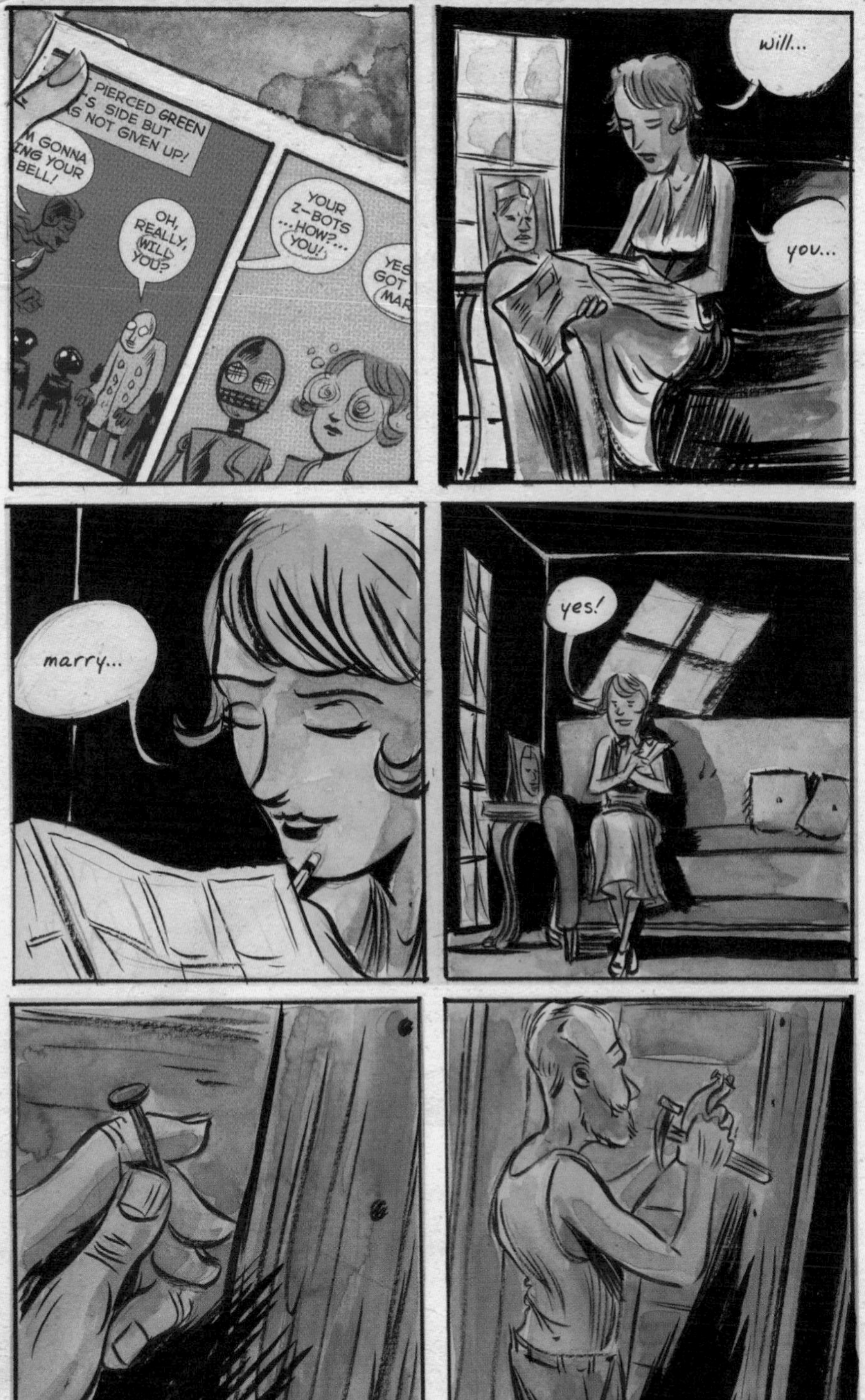
PIERCED GREEN
'S SIDE BUT
S NOT GIVEN UP!
M GONNA
NG YOUR
BELL!
OH, REALLY, WILL YOU?
YOUR Z-BOTS ...HOW?... YOU!
will...
you...
marry...
yes!

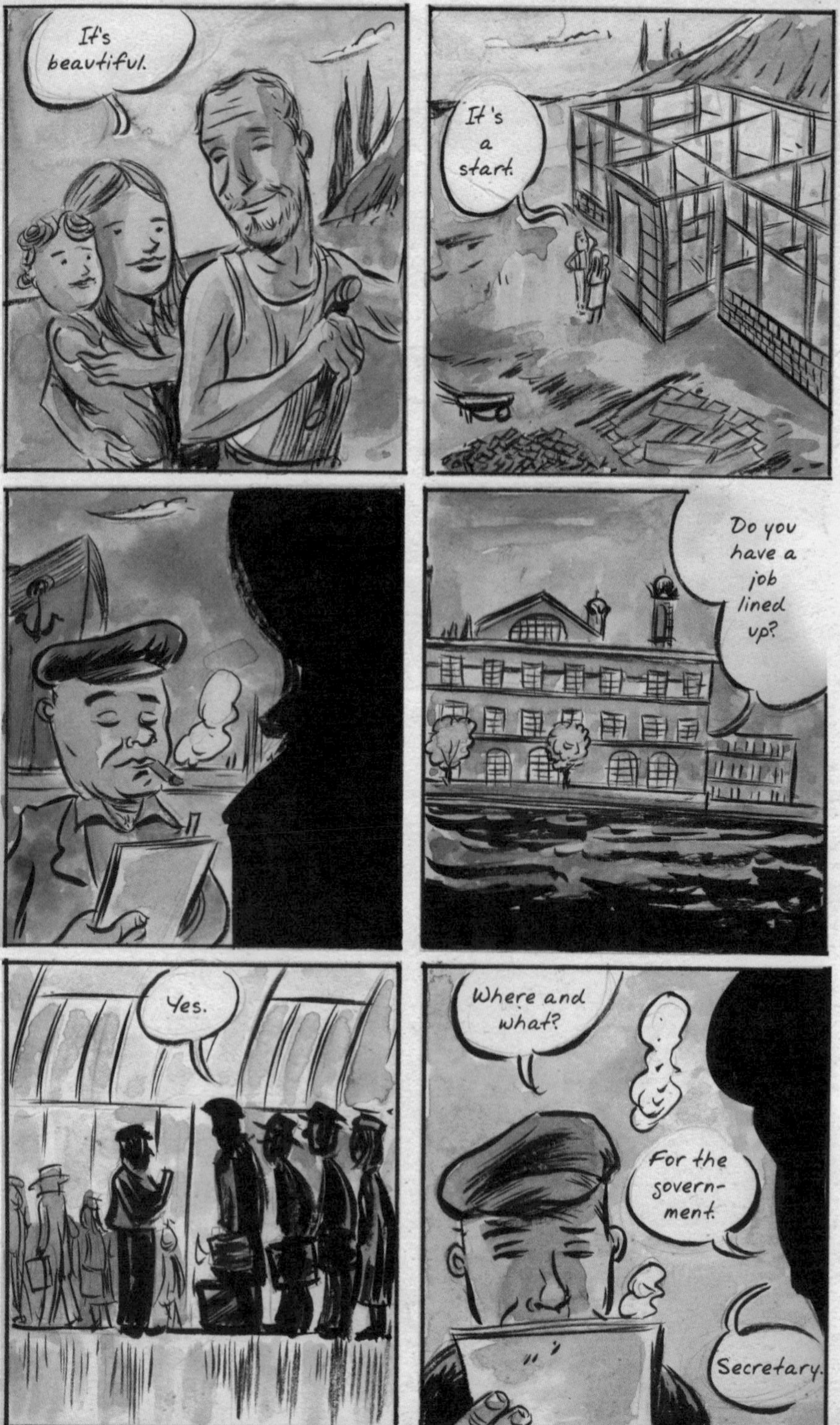
It's beautiful.
It's a start.
Do you have a job lined up?
Yes.
Where and what?
For the govern-ment.
Secretary.

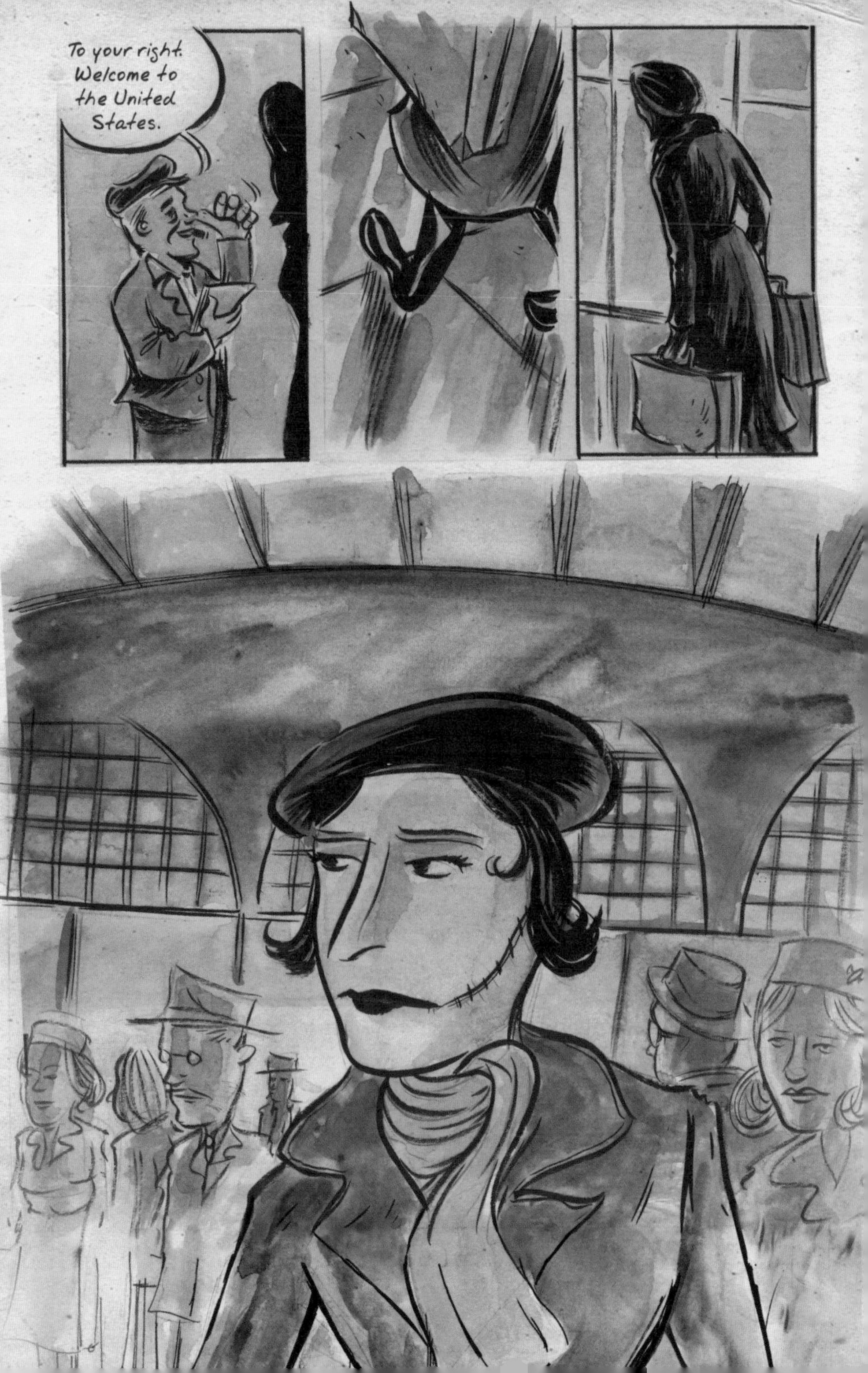
To your right. Welcome to the United States.

...every human creature is
constituted to be that profound secret
and mystery to every other.

— Charles Dickens